ROMAN CIVILIZATION

VOLUME II

ROMAN CIVILIZATION

SOURCEBOOK II:
THE EMPIRE

EDITED WITH AN INTRODUCTION

AND NOTES BY

NAPHTALI LEWIS & MEYER REINHOLD

HARPER TORCHBOOKS
Harper & Row, Publishers
New York, Hagerstown, San Francisco, London

ROMAN CIVILIZATION: THE EMPIRE

First HARPER TORCHBOOK *edition published 1966 by*
Harper & Row, Publishers, Inc.
10 East 53rd Street
New York, N.Y. 10022.

Library of Congress catalog card number: 51–14589

87 88 89 90   30 29 28 27 26 25 24 23

CONTENTS

PREFACE

"THE LIMITLESS MAJESTY OF ROME" under the Caesars, from the age of Augustus to Constantine and the triumph of Christianity, is the subject of the present volume. In these three and a half centuries Rome's ecumenical sway, extending across three continents from the Atlantic Ocean to the Caspian and Red seas, embraced many peoples of diverse cultural origins and different stages of social development. The source materials from this far-flung, many-faceted Roman world are rich and extensive, ranging from the activities of the highest levels of government to the lives of the humblest peasants and slaves. Besides a multitude of archaeological remains, there are extant an abundant literature in Latin and Greek and many tens of thousands of inscribed and written documents. Except for the works of the principal authors, however, the written records of the Roman Empire are for the most part accessible only to specialists. Of the six hundred or so selections from the literary, epigraphical, and papyrological sources included in this volume, more than two hundred are now for the first time made available in English translation.

As in Volume I, translations not otherwise identified are our own; those borrowed by us with little or no change are preceded by the notation *From* . . . ; those borrowed but considerably revised by us are indicated by the phrase *Adapted from.* . . . Copyright material is reproduced or adapted by us from the following works with the permission of their respective publishers: Cambridge University Press—W. D. Lowe, *Petronii Cena Trimalchionis;* Clarendon Press, Oxford—E. G. Hardy, *Three Spanish Charters and Other Documents,* and F. de Zulueta, *The Institutes of Gaius;* Egypt Exploration Society—A. S. Hunt, *The Oxyrhynchus Papyri,* Part XVII; Free Press—S. Levin, *Aelius Aristides: To Rome;* Harvard University Press—the translations of the Loeb Classical Library, and M. H. Morgan, *Vitruvius, The Ten Books on Architecture;* Johns Hopkins Press—A. C. Johnson, *Roman Egypt to the Reign of Diocletian,* and T. Frank, *Rome and Italy of the Empire* (Vols. II and V, respectively, of *An Economic Survey of Ancient Rome*); McGraw-Hill Book Co.—M. R. Cohen and I. E. Drabkin, *A Source Book of Greek Science;* National Council of the Churches of Christ in the U.S.A.—*American Standard Version Bible; Philological Quarterly*—M. Hadas's translation from the Babylonian Talmud in Vol. VIII (1929); Princeton University Press—C. Pharr, *The Theo-*

dosian Code; Bernard Quaritch Ltd.—B. P. Grenfell and A. S. Hunt, *The Amherst Papyri,* Vol. II; University of California Press—B. P. Grenfell, A. S. Hunt, and E. J. Goodspeed, *The Tebtunis Papyri,* Part II; University of Chicago Press—E. J. Goodspeed, *The New Testament, An American Translation;* University of Michigan Press—H. C. Youtie and O. M. Pearl, *Michigan Papyri,* Vol. VI; Yale University Press— E. R. Goodenough's translations of Diotogenes and Ecphantes in *Yale Classical Studies,* Vol. I (1928).

The complexities and similarities of the official imperial nomenclature frequently make it difficult for the reader to recognize which of several emperors is meant in a given text. In such cases we have adopted the typographical device of setting in capitals the name by which the emperor in question is commonly known today—e.g., Tiberius CLAUDIUS Caesar Augustus Germanicus; Emperor Caesar Marcus Aurelius Antoninus [CARACALLA] Augustus.

In the preparation of the Bibliography, which is intended to assist the reader interested in exploring further the topics treated in this volume, it seemed to us impractical to prepare a vademecum to the vast international bibliography on Roman civilization. We recognize indeed that many contributions of fundamental and decisive importance are thus omitted. But our decision to restrict the Bibliography to selected books and articles in English was dictated not only by considerations of space but even more by the needs of the students in our colleges, for whom this work is primarily intended. The realities of the American educational scene—in which this collection of source materials in English translation finds its very *raison d'être*—are that only a most exiguous number of our students have any acquaintance with either Latin or Greek, and very few possess facility in the use of any foreign language.

This book has profited at every turn from the efforts of our editor, Mr. J. Christopher Herold, and we would record here our deep gratitude to him for his devoted care. Our thanks are due to the emeritus general editor of the Records of Civilization, Professor Austin P. Evans, for his careful examination of our manuscript, and to the other members of the staff of the Columbia University Press who participated in the publication of this volume. Finally, it is our pleasure to record our thanks to the libraries of Dartmouth College and the University of Wisconsin for their traditional hospitality.

N.L.
M.R.

September, 1954

ROMAN CIVILIZATION

ABBREVIATIONS USED IN
CITING SOURCES

Abbott-Johnson = F. F. Abbott and A. C. Johnson, *Municipal Administration in the Roman Empire* (Princeton, 1926)

ADA = Regia Academia Italica, *Acta Divi Augusti*, Pars Prior (Rome, 1945)

AE = *L'Année Epigraphique* (Paris, 1888–)

CIL = *Corpus Inscriptionum Latinarum* (16 vols., Berlin, 1862–)

Dessau = H. Dessau, *Inscriptiones Latinae Selectae* (3 vols., Berlin, 1892–1916)

Dittenberger = W. Dittenberger, *Sylloge Inscriptionum Graecarum* (3d ed., 4 vols., Leipzig, 1915–1924)

Ehrenberg-Jones = V. Ehrenberg and A. H. M. Jones, *Documents Illustrating the Reigns of Augustus and Tiberius* (Oxford, 1949)

ESAR = T. Frank, ed., *An Economic Survey of Ancient Rome* (5 vols., Baltimore, 1933–1940)

Evelyn White-Oliver = H. G. Evelyn White and J. H. Oliver, *The Temple of Hibis in El Khargeh Oasis, Part II: Greek Inscriptions* (New York, 1938)

FIRA = *Fontes Iuris Romani Antejustiniani* (2d ed., 3 vols., Florence, 1940–1943)

IG = *Inscriptiones Graecae* (14 vols., Berlin, 1873–)

IGRR = *Inscriptiones Graecae ad Res Romanas Pertinentes* (3 vols., Paris, 1906–1927)

LCL = Loeb Classical Library

Mitteis = "Juristischer Teil, Zweite Hälfte: Chrestomathie," in L. Mitteis and U. Wilcken, *Grundzüge und Chrestomathie der Papyruskunde* (Leipzig and Berlin, 1912)

OGIS = W. Dittenberger, *Orientis Graeci Inscriptiones Selectae* (2 vols., Leipzig, 1903–1905)

SB = *Sammelbuch Griechischer Urkunden aus Ägypten* (5 vols. to date, Strasbourg and elsewhere, 1915–)

SEG = *Supplementum Epigraphicum Graecum* (11 vols. to date, Leiden, 1923–)

Select Papyri = A. S. Hunt and C. C. Edgar, *Select Papyri* (2 vols., London, 1932–1934; Loeb Classical Library)

Wilcken = "Historischer Teil, Zweite Hälfte: Chrestomathie," in L. Mitteis and U. Wilcken, *Grundzüge und Chrestomathie der Papyruskunde* (Leipzig and Berlin, 1912)

CHAPTER I

THE AUGUSTAN AGE

1. *"The Republic Restored": Establishment of the Principate*

In January of 27 B.C. a major reorganization of the Roman government took place. Octavian laid down his *de facto* military dictatorship, and constitutional government was reestablished. In an historic, carefully staged meeting of the senate—"having first briefed his most intimate friends among the senators," as Dio Cassius puts it (LIII. ii. 7)—he proclaimed the "restoration of the Republic" and offered to retire to private life. His renunciation was, of course, not accepted; instead, a series of powers was voted him which firmly established him as ruler of the Roman Empire. He consented to accept the proconsular power (a special extended military command) for ten years, and the consulship annually together with the tribunician power (which gave him effective control of the civil government). He was also awarded the honorary title of *Augustus*, which, together with the designation *Imperator*, subsequently became a fixed part of the official nomenclature of the emperors. Avoiding all official appellations suggestive of autocracy, Augustus preferred the informal title of *princeps* for himself in his new position. With its strong republican overtones—the leading senator under the Republic had been known as *princeps senatus*—this title had the effect of designating Augustus as "first citizen," *primus inter pares,* rather than a ruler over subjects. The senate, moreover, in theory retained its traditional functions, and was to be the "partner in government" of the *princeps;* and the popular assemblies were to continue to meet as in the past. Thus, officially, the Principate, as the new régime is called, was the Republic restored. In reality, however, the trappings of republican government formed a politically expedient constitutional façade for a new imperial administration under the sovereignty of a monarch in all but name.

Four years later a new constitutional settlement made the position of the *princeps* permanent: Augustus resigned the consulship and derived his principal authority thereafter from the tribunician power, granted for life, and the proconsular power, periodically renewed. Thus Augustus united under one authority both the powers wielded by the redoubtable republican tribunes such as the Gracchi (see Vol. I, §§ 97–100) and those exercised by the powerful generals of the civil-war period. These were henceforth the dual bases of the emperors' authority.

TRANSITION FROM REPUBLIC TO PRINCIPATE

Tacitus *Annals* i. ii, iii. 7–iv. 2

After the death of Brutus and Cassius, there was no longer any army loyal to the Republic; Pompey [1] had been crushed at Sicily; and, with Lepidus deposed and Antony dead, not even the Julian faction had any leader left except Caesar. Then, laying aside the title of triumvir and parading as a consul, and professing himself satisfied with the tribunician power for the protection of the plebs, Augustus enticed the soldiers with gifts, the people with grain, and all men with the allurement of peace, and gradually grew in power, concentrating in his own hands the functions of the senate, the magistrates, and the laws. No one opposed him, for the most courageous had fallen in battle or in the proscription. As for the remaining nobles, the readier they were for slavery, the higher were they raised in wealth and offices, so that, aggrandized by the revolution, they preferred the safety of the present to the perils of the past. Nor did the provinces view with disfavor this state of affairs, for they distrusted the government of the senate and the people on account of the struggles of the powerful and the rapacity of the officials, while the protection afforded them by the laws was inoperative, as the laws were repeatedly thrown into confusion by violence, intrigue, and finally bribery. . . .

At home all was peaceful; the officials bore the same titles as before. The younger generation was born after the victory of Actium, and even many of the older generation had been born during the civil wars. How few were left who had seen the Republic!

Thus the constitution had been transformed, and there was nothing at all left of the good old way of life. Stripped of equality, all looked to the directives of a *princeps* with no apprehension for the present, while Augustus in the vigorous years of his life maintained his power, that of his family, and peace.

POWERS AND TITLES OF THE EMPEROR

Dio Cassius *Roman History* LIII. xvii. 1–xviii. 3, xxi. 3–7
Adapted from LCL

In this way the power of both people and senate passed entirely into the hands of Augustus, and from this time [2] there was, strictly speaking,

[1] Sextus Pompey, son and political heir of Pompey the Great, is meant. See further Notes 21, 28, 29, 75, below.
[2] January, 27 B.C. Dio's account of the prerogatives of Augustus as emperor, written

a monarchy; for monarchy would be the truest name for it, even if two or three men later held the power jointly.[3] Now, the Romans so detested the title "monarch" that they called their emperors neither dictators nor kings nor anything of this sort. Yet, since the final authority for the government devolves upon them, they needs must be kings. The offices established by the laws, it is true, are maintained even now, except that of censor; but the entire direction and administration is absolutely in accordance with the wishes of the one in power at the time. And yet, in order to preserve the appearance of having this authority not through their power but by virtue of the laws, the emperors have taken to themselves all the offices (including the titles) which under the Republic possessed great power with the consent of the people—with the exception of the dictatorship. Thus, they very often become consuls, and they are always styled proconsuls [4] whenever they are outside the *pomerium*.[5] The title *imperator* is held by them for life, not only by those who have won victories in battle but also by all the rest, to indicate their absolute power,[6] instead of the title "king" or "dictator." These latter titles they have never assumed since they fell out of use in the constitution, but the actuality of those offices is secured to them by the appellation *imperator*.[7] By virtue of the titles named, they secure the right to make levies, collect funds, declare war, make peace, and rule foreigners and citizens alike everywhere and always—even to the extent of being able to put to death both *equites* and senators inside the *pomerium* [8]—and all the other powers once granted to the consuls and other officials possessing independent authority; and by virtue

---

early in the third century A.D., contains a number of anachronisms retrojected from his own day when the emperors exercised more autocratic powers. For instances see the following footnotes to this selection.

[3] Dio refers to the joint rule of Marcus Aurelius and Lucius Verus, and that of Severus, Caracalla, and Geta.

[4] It was not until Trajan's reign that the title proconsul became part of the official nomenclature of the emperors.

[5] For the *pomerium* of the city of Rome see Vol. I, § 6.

[6] Actually, the title *imperator*, while peculiar to Augustus' nomenclature, was officially disdained by Tiberius, Caligula, and Claudius. Though in common use unofficially, it did not become the standard title of the emperor until Vespasian's reign.

[7] In addition to the title of *imperator*, the official nomenclature of the emperors contains the number of times they were acclaimed *imperator* for military victories won under their auspices. Cf. Dio Cassius *Roman History* XLIII. xliv. 4: "For those who are *imperatores* in the special sense employ this title once, as they do their other titles, and place it first. But those of them who also achieve in war some deed worthy of it acquire also the title handed down by ancient custom, and accordingly an individual is termed *imperator* a second or a third time, or as many more times as the occasion may arise."

[8] Such arbitrary power was not acquired by the emperors until two centuries after Augustus.

of holding the censorship [9] they investigate our lives and morals as well
as take the census, enrolling some in the equestrian and senatorial orders
and removing others from these orders according to their will. By virtue of being consecrated in all the priesthoods and, in addition, from
their right to bestow most of them upon others, as well as from the
fact that, even if two or three persons rule jointly, one of them is *pontifex
maximus*, they hold in their own hands supreme authority over all matters both profane and sacred. The tribunician power, as it is called,
which once the most influential men used to hold, gives them the right
to nullify the effects of the measures taken by any other official, in case
they do not approve, and makes their persons inviolable; and if they
appear to be wronged in even the slightest degree, not merely by deed
but even by word, they may destroy the guilty party as one accursed,
without a trial.[10] The emperors, it should be explained, do not think
it lawful to be tribunes, inasmuch as they all belong to the patrician class,
but they assume the power of the tribunes in its entirety, as it was
at its height; and the number of the years of their rule is counted from
the assumption of this power, the theory being that they receive it
annually along with those who actually hold the office of tribune. These,
then, are the institutions they have taken over from the Republic, each
essentially in its traditional form and with the same title, so as to give
the impression of possessing no power that has not been granted
them. . . .[11]

Thus by virtue of these Republican titles they have clothed themselves with all the powers of the government, so that they actually possess all the prerogatives of kings without the usual title. For the appellation "Caesar" or "Augustus" confers upon them no actual power
but merely shows in the one case that they are the successors of their
family line, and in the other the splendor of their rank. The name
"Father" [12] perhaps gives them a certain authority over us all—the authority which fathers once had over their children; yet it did not signify
this at first, but betokened honor and served as an admonition both to
them to love their subjects as they would their children, and to their
subjects to revere them as they would their fathers. . . .

Augustus did not enact all laws on his sole responsibility, but some
of them he brought before the popular assembly in advance, in order
that, if any features caused displeasure, he might learn it in time and
correct them; for he encouraged everybody whatsoever to give him ad-

[9] Cf. Note 105.
[10] Another of Dio's anachronisms (cf. Note 2).
[11] For the statute granting imperial powers to Vespasian, see § 21.
[12] For the appellation "father of his country," see the selection from Suetonius below
and § 2, paragraph 35.

vice, in case anyone could think of any improvement in them, and he accorded them great freedom of speech; and he actually changed some provisions. Most important of all, he took as advisers for periods of six months the consuls (or the other consul, when he himself also held the office), one of each of the other kinds of officials, and fifteen men chosen by lot from the remainder of the senatorial body,[13] so that it was his custom to communicate proposed legislation after a fashion through these to all the other senators. For although he brought some matters before the whole senate, he generally followed this course, considering it better to take under preliminary advisement in a leisurely fashion most matters, and especially the most important ones, in consultation with a few; and sometimes he even sat with these men in trials. The senate as a body, it is true, continued to sit in judgment as before, and in certain cases transacted business with embassies and envoys from both peoples and kings; and the people and the plebs, moreover, continued to come together for the elections; but nothing was actually done that did not please Caesar. At any rate, in the case of those who were to hold office, he himself selected and nominated some;[14] and though he left the election of others in the hands of the people and the plebs, in accordance with the ancient practice, yet he took care that no persons should hold office who were unfit or elected as the result of factious combinations or bribery.

Dio Cassius *Roman History* LIII. xvi
Adapted from LCL

Such were the arrangements made, generally speaking, at that time; for in reality Caesar himself was destined to have absolute power in all matters for life, because he was not only in control of money matters (nominally, to be sure, he had separated the public funds from his own, but as a matter of fact he spent the former also as he saw fit) but also in control of the army. At all events, when his ten-year period[15] came to an end, there was voted him another five years, then five more, after that ten, and again another ten, and then ten for the fifth time, so

[13] This standing committee of the senate, established by Augustus in 27 B.C. and reorganized on a new basis in A.D. 13, served as a privy council and ultimately developed into the institution of an imperial cabinet. For the Republican antecedents of such advisory councils see, for example, Vol. I, pp. 266, 345-46.
[14] For the power of the emperors to nominate and commend candidates for office——recommendations which were tantamount to election—see also §§ 21, 30. For Julius Caesar's practice in this regard see Vol. I, p. 287.
[15] That is, of his proconsular power. From 23 B.C. on Augustus possessed *imperium maius* (superior power), that is proconsular power over all the provinces of the Empire, including the authority to supersede the acts of governors of senatorial provinces.

that by the succession of ten-year periods he continued to be sole ruler for life. And it is for this reason that the subsequent monarchs, though no longer appointed for a specified period but for their whole life once for all,[16] nevertheless always held a celebration every ten years, as if then renewing their sovereignty once more; and this is done even at the present day.

Now, Caesar had received many privileges previously, when the question of declining the sovereignty and that of apportioning the provinces were under discussion. For the right to fasten laurels to the front of the imperial residence and to hang the civic crown above the doors was then voted him to symbolize the fact that he was always victorious over enemies and savior of the citizens. The imperial palace is called Palatium, not because it was ever decreed that this should be its name but because Caesar dwelt on the Palatine and had his military headquarters there. . . . Hence, even if the emperor resides somewhere else, his dwelling retains the name of Palatium.

And when he had actually completed the reorganization, the name Augustus was at length bestowed upon him by the senate and by the people. . . . He took the title of Augustus, signifying that he was more than human; for all most precious and sacred objects are termed *augusta*. For which reason they called him also in Greek *sebastos* . . . meaning an august person.

Suetonius *Life of Augustus* lviii
From LCL

The whole body of citizens with a sudden unanimous impulse proffered him the title of "father of his country"—first the plebs, by a deputation sent to Antium, and then, because he declined it, again at Rome as he entered the theater, which they attended in throngs, all wearing laurel wreaths; the senate afterwards in the senate house, not by a decree or by acclamation, but through Valerius Messala. He, speaking for the whole body, said: "Good fortune and divine favor attend thee and thy house, Caesar Augustus; for thus we feel that we are praying for lasting prosperity for our country and happiness for our city. The senate in accord with the Roman people hails thee 'Father of thy Country.'" Then Augustus with tears in his eyes replied as follows (and I have given his exact words, as I did those of Messala): "Having attained my highest hopes, members of the senate, what more have I to ask of the immortal gods than that I may retain this same unanimous approval of yours to the very end of my life?" [17]

---

[16] The permanent grant of proconsular power began with the Emperor Tiberius.
[17] The title of "father of his country" (*pater patriae*) was bestowed on Augustus in
2 B.C.

2. The Accomplishments of Augustus
(Res Gestae Divi Augusti)

The following document, from the hand of Augustus, is perhaps the most famous ancient inscription—"the queen of Latin inscriptions" Mommsen called it. A vast literature has grown up around it—numerous editions, commentaries, and discussions of its nature and purpose.[18] Shortly before he died, Augustus deposited with the Vestal Virgins a number of state papers (see § 16, last selection) in one of which he set forth "an account of his accomplishments, which he desired to be inscribed on two bronze pillars to be set up before his mausoleum" (Suetonius *Life of Augustus* ci. 4). The *Res Gestae* is preserved in an almost complete copy, together with a Greek translation, inscribed on the walls of the temple of Rome and Augustus at Ancyra (modern Ankara), in the province of Galatia (hence it is commonly called the *Monumentum Ancyranum*); portions of the Greek and Latin texts have also been found in Apollonia and Antioch in Pisidia. Intended primarily for the people of the city of Rome, Augustus' account of his stewardship summarizes his career under three headings: the offices and honors conferred upon him (paragraphs 1–14); his expenditures out of his own funds for public purposes (paragraphs 15–24); his deeds in war and peace (paragraphs 25–35). Though largely factual, it is not an historical chronicle but a subjective political document. It is in the tradition of the inscriptions commemorating the achievements of distinguished Romans of the Republic and is similar in content to the well-known inscriptions set up by Oriental kings. Despite Augustus' profession of "restoring the Republic," a monarchical tone pervades the *Res Gestae*.

CIL, Vol. III, pp. 769–99 (= Ehrenburg-Jones, pp. 1–31 = *ADA*, pp. 20–63)

Below is a copy of the accomplishments of the deified Augustus by which he brought the whole world under the empire of the Roman people, and of the moneys expended by him on the state and the Roman people, as inscribed on two bronze pillars set up in Rome.[19]

1.[20] At the age of nineteen, on my own initiative and at my own expense, I raised an army by means of which I liberated the Republic, which was oppressed by the tyranny of a faction.[21] For which reason

[18] Discussions of and commentaries on this text may be found in W. Fairley, *Monumentum Ancyranum, The Deeds of Augustus* (Philadelphia, 1898); E. G. Hardy, *The Monumentum Ancyranum* (Oxford, 1923); F. W. Shipley, *Res Gestae Divi Augusti* (LCL, 1924); R. Rogers, K. Scott, and M. Ward, *Caesaris Augusti res gestae et fragmenta* (Boston, 1935).
[19] No trace of the original bronze inscription, set up before the mausoleum of Augustus in Rome, has been found.
[20] The inscription is divided into paragraphs which, for convenience in citing, are numbered in this translation.
[21] Antony and his adherents are meant. The period referred to is late 44 to early 43

the senate, with honorific decrees, made me a member of its order in the consulship of Gaius Pansa and Aulus Hirtius,[22] giving me at the same time consular rank in voting, and granted me the *imperium*. It ordered me as propraetor, together with the consuls, to see to it that the state suffered no harm.[23] Moreover, in the same year, when both consuls had fallen in the war, the people elected me consul and a triumvir for the settlement of the commonwealth.[24]

2. Those who assassinated my father [25] I drove into exile, avenging their crime by due process of law; and afterwards when they waged war against the state, I conquered them twice on the battlefield.[26]

3. I waged many wars throughout the whole world by land and by sea, both civil and foreign, and when victorious I spared all citizens who sought pardon. Foreign peoples who could safely be pardoned I preferred to spare rather than to extirpate. About 500,000 Roman citizens were under military oath to me. Of these, when their terms of service were ended, I settled in colonies or sent back to their own municipalities a little more than 300,000,[27] and to all of these I allotted lands or granted money as rewards for military service. I captured 600 ships, exclusive of those which were of smaller class than triremes.[28]

4. Twice I celebrated ovations, three times curule triumphs,[29] and I was acclaimed *imperator* twenty-one times.[30] When the senate decreed additional triumphs to me, I declined them on four occasions. I deposited in the Capitol laurel wreaths adorning my *fasces*, after fulfilling the vows which I had made in each war.[31] For successes achieved on land and on sea by me or through my legates under my auspices the

B.C., when Octavian (as Augustus was then known) was in coalition with the senate against Antony (cf. Vol. I, § 114). Noteworthy is the studied avoidance by Augustus in this document of the names of his opponents—such as Antony, Lepidus, Sextus Pompey, Brutus, Cassius—and the fact that the only Romans whom he names, other than consuls used to date events, are members of the imperial family.

[22] 43 B.C.

[23] The formula for the "ultimate decree of the senate" (see Vol. I, § 157). Augustus refers here to the war against Antony, which culminated in the two battles at Mutina (April, 43 B.C.).

[24] Cf. Vol. I, § 115.   [25] Julius Caesar, his adoptive father.

[26] The two battles of Philippi (42 B.C.).

[27] Tiberius inherited from Augustus an army of twenty-five legions (Tacitus *Annals* IV. v), or about 125,000 men; cf. § 6.

[28] The naval victories over Sextus Pompey (at Mylae and Naulochus), and over Antony and Cleopatra (at Actium) are meant.

[29] The two ovations occurred in 40 B.C. and 36 B.C., the first after the Peace of Brundisium concluded with Antony, the second after the defeat of Sextus Pompey. Augustus celebrated a triple triumph in 29 B.C. for victories in Dalmatia, at Actium, and in Egypt.

[30] In many cases the acclamation *imperator* was accorded to Augustus for victories gained by his legates; cf. Note 7, above.

[31] This is the well-known Republican custom, followed by victorious generals who

senate decreed fifty-five times that thanksgiving be offered to the immortal gods. Moreover, the number of days on which, by decree of the senate, such thanksgiving was offered, was 890. In my triumphs there were led before my chariot nine kings or children of kings. At the time I wrote this document, I had been consul thirteen times, and I was in the thirty-seventh year of my tribunician power.[32]

5. The dictatorship offered to me in the consulship of Marcus Marcellus and Lucius Arruntius [33] by the people and by the senate, both in my absence and in my presence, I refused to accept. In the midst of a critical scarcity of grain I did not decline the supervision of the grain supply, which I so administered that within a few days I freed the whole people from imminent panic and danger by my expenditures and efforts.[34] The consulship, too, which was offered to me at that time as an annual office for life, I refused to accept.

6. In the consulship of Marcus Vinicius and Quintus Lucretius, and again in that of Publius Lentulus and Gnaeus Lentulus, and a third time in that of Paullus Fabius Maximus and Quintus Tubero,[35] though the Roman senate and people unitedly agreed that I should be elected sole guardian of the laws and morals with supreme authority, I refused to accept any office offered me which was contrary to the traditions of our ancestors.[36] The measures which the senate desired at that time to be taken by me I carried out by virtue of the tribunician power.[37] In this power I five times voluntarily requested and was given a colleague by the senate.[38]

7. I was a member of the triumvirate for the settlement of the commonwealth for ten consecutive years.[39] I have been ranking senator for forty years, up to the day on which I wrote this document. I have been *pontifex maximus*, augur, member of the college of fifteen for performing sacrifices, member of the college of seven for conducting religious banquets, member of the Arval Brotherhood, one of the Titii sodales, and a fetial.[40]

---

were acclaimed *imperator*, of depositing laureled *fasces* in the Capitol in accordance with vows taken there before they set out for their provinces.

[32] A.D. 14.   [33] 22 B.C.

[34] This marks the beginning of the assumption by the Roman emperors of the *cura annonae* (administration of the grain supply) of Rome as a permanent function of the imperial administration.

[35] In 19, 18, and 11 B.C.

[36] In effect Augustus was thus offered permanent dictatorship in a new guise.

[37] Augustus refers to his moral and social legislation, the first installments of which were issued in 18 B.C. (see §§ 11–12).

[38] Marcus Agrippa, twice; Tiberius, three times.

[39] Actually more than ten years, for the triumvirate lasted from 43 to 32 B.C. The controversial question of the powers of Antony and Octavian in 32 B.C. has evoked heated scholarly discussion.

[40] On these traditional priestly offices under the Republic, see Vol. I, §§ 11, 47, 48,

8. In my fifth consulship I increased the number of patricians, by order of the people and the senate. Three times I revised the roll of senators. And in my sixth consulship,[41] with Marcus Agrippa as my colleague, I conducted a census of the people. I performed the *lustrum* [42] after an interval of forty-two years. At this *lustrum* 4,063,000 Roman citizens were recorded. Then a second time, acting alone, by virtue of the consular power, I completed the taking of the census in the consulship of Gaius Censorinus and Gaius Asinius.[43] At this *lustrum* 4,233,000 Roman citizens were recorded. And a third time I completed the taking of the census in the consulship of Sextus Pompeius and Sextus Appuleius,[44] by virtue of the consular power and with my son Tiberius Caesar as my colleague. At this *lustrum* 4,937,000 Roman citizens were recorded. By new legislation which I sponsored I restored many traditions of our ancestors which were falling into desuetude in our generation; and I myself handed down precedents in many spheres for posterity to imitate.

9. The senate decreed that vows for my health should be offered up every fifth year by the consuls and priests. In fulfillment of these vows, games were often celebrated during my lifetime, sometimes by the four most distinguished colleges of priests, sometimes by the consuls. Moreover, the whole citizen body, with one accord, both individually and as members of municipalities, prayed continuously for my health at all the shrines.

10. My name was inserted, by decree of the senate, in the hymn of the Salian priests. And it was enacted by law that I should be sacrosanct in perpetuity and that I should possess the tribunician power as long as I live.[45] I declined to become *pontifex maximus* in place of a colleague [46] while he was still alive, when the people offered me that priesthood, which my father had held. A few years later, in the consulship of Publius Sulpicius and Gaius Valgius, I accepted this priesthood, when death removed the man who had taken possession of it at a time of civil disturbance; and from all Italy a multitude flocked to my election such as had never previously been recorded at Rome.

11. To commemorate my return from Syria, the senate conse-

51, 52. All Roman emperors after Augustus held the first four of these priesthoods, the most important sacerdotal offices in the national religion.

[41] 28 B.C. The last census had been taken in 70/69 B.C.

[42] For this religious closing of the census, see Vol. I, § 56.

[43] 8 B.C.   [44] A.D. 14.

[45] Augustus was accorded the *sacrosanctitas* (inviolability) of a tribune in 36 B.C. The tribunician power was conferred upon him in 30 B.C., but it was only after the constitutional settlement of 23 B.C. that he began to date his regnal years by the number of years he had held this power. Cf. paragraph 4, above, and § 1, second selection.

[46] Lepidus was deposed from the Second Triumvirate in 36 B.C. but was permitted

crated an altar to Fortune the Home-bringer before the temple of Honor and Virtue at the Porta Capena, on which altar it decreed that the pontiffs and Vestal Virgins should make a yearly sacrifice on the anniversary of the day in the consulship of Quintus Lucretius and Marcus Vinicius [47] on which I returned to the city from Syria, and it designated that day *Augustalia* from my name.

12. On this occasion, by decree of the senate, a portion of the praetors and tribunes of the plebs, together with the consul Quintus Lucretius and the leading men, was sent to Campania to meet me, an honor which up to this time has been decreed to no one but myself. When I returned to Rome from Spain and Gaul in the consulship of Tiberius Nero and Publius Quintilius,[48] after successfully settling the affairs of those provinces, the senate, to commemorate my return, ordered an altar of the Augustan Peace [49] to be consecrated in the Campus Martius, on which it decreed that the magistrates, priests, and Vestal Virgins should make an annual sacrifice.

13. The temple of Janus Quirinus,[50] which our ancestors desired to be closed whenever peace with victory was secured by sea and by land throughout the entire empire of the Roman people, and which before I was born is recorded to have been closed only twice since the founding of the city, was during my principate three times ordered by the senate to be closed.

14. My sons Gaius and Lucius Caesar,[51] whom fortune took from me in their youth, were, in my honor, made consuls designate by the Roman senate and people when they were fifteen years old, with permission to enter that magistracy after a period of five years. The senate further decreed that from the day on which they were introduced into the Forum [52] they should attend its debates. Moreover, the whole body of Roman *equites* presented each of them with silver shields and spears and saluted each as *princeps iuventutis*.[53]

---

to retain the office of *pontifex maximus*. Upon his death in 13 B.C., Augustus was elected chief pontiff the following year. All subsequent emperors held this office.

[47] 19 B.C.   [48] 13 B.C.

[49] Extensive parts of the famous Altar of Peace, dedicated in 9 B.C., are extant. The whole monument has been reconstructed *in situ*.

[50] A small bronze shrine, with double doors on both ends, on the north side of the Forum. Cf. § 3, second selection.

[51] Grandsons of Augustus, the sons of Agrippa and Julia, adopted by him in 17 B.C. and marked out as his successors. Gaius died in A.D. 4, Lucius in A.D. 2. For honorary decrees to Gaius and Lucius, see § 16.

[52] That is, introduced to public life. This traditional Roman ceremony, which occurred at puberty, involved among other things the assumption of the *toga virilis* (toga of manhood); cf. § 16, second selection.

[53] That is, "leader of the youth." This title designated them as honorary heads of the young men of equestrian families who were organized in a kind of aristocratic Boy Scout movement.

15. To the Roman plebs I paid 300 sesterces apiece in accordance with the will of my father;[54] and in my fifth consulship[55] I gave each 400 sesterces in my own name out of the spoils of war; and a second time in my tenth consulship[56] I paid out of my own patrimony a largess of 400 sesterces to every individual; in my eleventh consulship[57] I made twelve distributions of food out of grain purchased at my own expense; and in the twelfth year of my tribunician power[58] for the third time I gave 400 sesterces to every individual. These largesses of mine reached never less than 250,000 persons. In the eighteenth year of my tribunician power and my twelfth consulship[59] I gave sixty *denarii* to each of 320,000 persons of the urban plebs. And in my fifth consulship[60] I gave out of the spoils of war 1,000 sesterces apiece to my soldiers settled in colonies. This largess on the occasion of my triumph was received by about 120,000 persons in the colonies. In my thirteenth consulship[61] I gave sixty *denarii* apiece to those of the plebs who at that time were receiving public grain; the number involved was a little more than 200,000 persons.

16. I reimbursed municipalities for the lands which I assigned to my soldiers in my fourth consulship, and afterwards in the consulship of Marcus Crassus and Gnaeus Lentulus the augur.[62] The sums involved were about 600,000,000 sesterces which I paid for Italian estates, and about 260,000,000 sesterces which I paid for provincial lands. I was the first and only one to take such action of all those who up to my time established colonies of soldiers in Italy or in the provinces. And afterwards, in the consulship of Tiberius Nero and Gnaeus Piso, and likewise of Gaius Antistius and Decimus Laelius, and of Gaius Calvisius and Lucius Passienus, and of Lucius Lentulus and Marcus Messalla, and of Lucius Caninius and Quintus Fabricius,[63] I granted bonuses in cash to the soldiers whom after the completion of their terms of service I sent back to their municipalities; and for this purpose I expended about 400,000,000 sesterces.

17. Four times I came to the assistance of the treasury with my own money, transferring to those in charge of the treasury 150,000,000 sesterces. And in the consulship of Marcus Lepidus and Lucius Arruntius[64] I transferred out of my own patrimony 170,000,000 sesterces to the soldiers' bonus fund, which was established on my advice for the purpose of providing bonuses for soldiers who had completed twenty or more years of service.

18. From the year in which Gnaeus Lentulus and Publius

---

[54] That is, Julius Caesar.   [55] 29 B.C.   [56] 24 B.C.   [57] 23 B.C.
[58] 12 B.C.   [59] 5 B.C.   [60] 29 B.C.   [61] 2 B.C.
[62] 30 and 14 B.C.   [63] In 7, 6, 4, 3, and 2 B.C.   [64] A.D. 6; cf. § 6.

Lentulus [65] were consuls, whenever the provincial taxes fell short, in the case sometimes of 100,000 persons and sometimes of many more, I made up their tribute in grain and in money from my own grain stores and my own patrimony.

19. I built the following structures: [66] the senate house and the Chalcidicum adjoining it; the temple of Apollo on the Palatine with its porticoes; the temple of the deified Julius; the Lupercal; the portico at the Circus Flaminius, which I allowed to be called Octavia after the name of the man who had built an earlier portico on the same site; the state box at the Circus Maximus; the temples of Jupiter the Smiter and Jupiter the Thunderer on the Capitoline; the temple of Quirinus; the temples of Minerva and Queen Juno and of Jupiter Freedom on the Aventine; the temple of the Lares at the head of the Sacred Way; the temple of the Penates on the Velia; the temple of Youth and the temple of the Great Mother on the Palatine.

20. I repaired the Capitol and the theater of Pompey with enormous expenditures on both works, without having my name inscribed on them. I repaired the conduits of the aqueducts which were falling into ruin in many places because of age, and I doubled the capacity of the aqueduct called Marcia by admitting a new spring into its conduit. I completed the Julian Forum and the basilica which was between the temple of Castor and the temple of Saturn, works begun and far advanced by my father, and when the same basilica was destroyed by fire, I enlarged its site and began rebuilding the structure, which is to be inscribed with the names of my sons; and in case it should not be completed while I am still alive, I left instructions that the work be completed by my heirs. In my sixth consulship [67] I repaired eighty-two temples of the gods in the city, in accordance with a resolution of the senate, neglecting none which at that time required repair. In my seventh consulship [68] I reconstructed the Flaminian Way from the city as far as Ariminum, and also all the bridges except the Mulvian and the Minucian.

21. On my own private land I built the temple of Mars Ultor and the Augustan Forum from spoils of war. On ground bought for the most part from private owners I built the theater adjoining the temple of Apollo which was to be inscribed with the name of my son-in-law Marcus Marcellus. In the Capitol, in the temple of the deified Julius,

---

[65] 18 B.C.
[66] To identify for the reader each of the public works listed in this and the two following paragraphs would require a series of footnotes longer than the text. A convenient source of information on the various structures is S. B. Platner, *A Topographical Dictionary of Ancient Rome*, rev. by T. Ashby (Oxford, 1929).
[67] 28 B.C.   [68] 27 B.C.

in the temple of Apollo, in the temple of Vesta, and in the temple of
Mars Ultor I consecrated gifts from spoils of war which cost me about
100,000,000 sesterces. In my fifth consulship [69] I remitted to the municipalities and colonies of Italy 35,000 pounds of crown gold [70] which they
were collecting in honor of my triumphs; and afterwards, whenever I
was acclaimed *imperator*, I did not accept the crown gold, though the
municipalities and colonies decreed it with the same enthusiasm as before.

22. I gave a gladiatorial show three times in my own name, and
five times in the names of my sons or grandsons; at these shows about
10,000 fought. Twice I presented to the people in my own name an exhibition of athletes invited from all parts of the world, and a third time
in the name of my grandson. I presented games in my own name four
times, and in addition twenty-three times in the place of other magistrates.[71] On behalf of the college of fifteen, as master of that college,
with Marcus Agrippa as my colleague, I celebrated the Secular Games [72]
in the consulship of Gaius Furnius and Gaius Silanus. In my thirteenth
consulship [73] I was the first to celebrate the Games of Mars, which subsequently the consuls, in accordance with a decree of the senate and a
law, have regularly celebrated in the succeeding years. Twenty-six
times I provided for the people, in my own name or in the names of my
sons or grandsons, hunting spectacles of African wild beasts in the
circus or in the Forum or in the amphitheaters; in these exhibitions about
3,500 animals were killed.

23. I presented to the people an exhibition of a naval battle across
the Tiber where the grove of the Caesars now is, having had the site
excavated 1,800 feet in length and 1,200 feet in width. In this exhibition thirty beaked ships, triremes or biremes, and in addition a great
number of smaller vessels engaged in combat. On board these fleets,
exclusive of rowers, there were about 3,000 combatants.

24. When I was victorious I replaced in the temples of all the communities of the province of Asia the ornaments which my opponent [74]
in the war had seized for his private use after despoiling the temples.
About eighty silver statues of myself, represented on foot, on horseback, or in a chariot, stood in the city; these I myself removed, and out
of the money therefrom I set up golden offerings in the temple
of Apollo in my own name and in the names of those who had honored
me with the statues.

[69] 29 B.C.
[70] For the significance of "crown gold," see § 119, second selection.
[71] These were games in the theatrical and circus shows.
[72] For the Secular Games celebrated in 17 B.C., see § 13.
[73] 2 B.C.
[74] Mark Antony.

25. I brought peace to the sea by suppressing the pirates.[75] In that war I turned over to their masters for punishment nearly 30,000 slaves who had run away from their owners and taken up arms against the state. The whole of Italy voluntarily took an oath of allegiance to me and demanded me as its leader in the war in which I was victorious at Actium.[76] The same oath was taken by the provinces of the Gauls, the Spains, Africa, Sicily, and Sardinia.[77] More than 700 senators served at that time under my standards; of that number eighty-three attained the consulship and about 170 obtained priesthoods, either before that date or subsequently, up to the day on which this document was written.

26. I extended the frontiers of all the provinces of the Roman people on whose boundaries were peoples not subject to our empire.[78] I restored peace to the Gallic and Spanish provinces and likewise to Germany, that is to the entire region bounded by the Ocean from Gades to the mouth of the Elbe river. I caused peace to be restored in the Alps, from the region nearest to the Adriatic Sea as far as the Tuscan Sea, without undeservedly making war against any people.[79] My fleet sailed the Ocean from the mouth of the Rhine eastward as far as the territory of the Cimbrians, to which no Roman previously had penetrated either by land or by sea. The Cimbrians, the Charydes, the Semnones, and other German peoples of the same region through their envoys sought my friendship and that of the Roman people.[80] At my command and under my auspices two armies were led almost at the same time into Ethiopia and into Arabia which is called Felix; and very large forces of the enemy belonging to both peoples were killed in battle, and many towns were captured. In Ethiopia a penetration was made as far as the town of Napata, which is next to Meroe; in Arabia the army advanced into the territory of the Sabaeans to the town of Mariba.[81]

27. I added Egypt to the empire of the Roman people.[82] Although I might have made Greater Armenia into a province when its king Artaxes was assassinated, I preferred, following the precedent of our

[75] The naval war with Sextus Pompey (cf. Note 1), which ended in 36 B.C.
[76] The war against Antony and Cleopatra, who were defeated at Actium in 31 B.C.
[77] On the form of the oath of allegiance to Augustus, see § 8, second selection.
[78] The emphasis is on the frontier policy in the West. The eastern provinces were hardly as well stabilized under Augustus. On the general frontier policy of Augustus, see § 10.
[79] On these campaigns see further § 10.
[80] The reference is to the campaign of A.D. 5, when Tiberius penetrated Germany as far as the Elbe river.
[81] This is the disastrous expedition of Aelius Gallus in 25/24 B.C. against Arabia Felix (Yemen); the punitive Ethiopian expedition under Gaius Petronius in 24-22 B.C. achieved greater success; see further § 10.
[82] On the death of Cleopatra in 30 B.C. On the special status of the province of Egypt, see Note 106.

ancestors, to hand over this kingdom, acting through Tiberius Nero, who was then my stepson, to Tigranes, son of King Artavasdes and grandson of King Tigranes. And afterwards, when this same people revolted and rebelled, after I subdued it through my son Gaius, I handed it over to the rule of King Ariobarzanes, son of Artabazus, king of the Medes, and after his death to his son Artavasdes. When the latter was killed, I dispatched to that kingdom Tigranes, a scion of the royal family of Armenia.[83] I recovered all the provinces extending beyond the Adriatic Sea eastward, and also Cyrenae, which were for the most part already in the possession of kings, as I had previously recovered Sicily and Sardinia, which had been seized in the slave war.[84]

28. I established colonies of soldiers in Africa, Sicily, Macedonia, in both Spanish provinces, in Achaea, Asia, Syria, Narbonese Gaul, and Pisidia. Italy, moreover, has twenty-eight colonies established by me, which in my lifetime have grown to be famous and populous.

29. A number of military standards lost by other generals I recovered, after conquering the enemy, from Spain, Gaul, and the Dalmatians. The Parthians I compelled to restore to me the spoils and standards of three Roman armies and to seek the friendship of the Roman people as suppliants.[85] The standards, moreover, I deposited in the inner shrine of the temple of Mars Ultor.

30. Through Tiberius Nero, who was then my stepson and legate, I conquered and subjected to the empire of the Roman people the Pannonian tribes, to which before my principate no army of the Roman people had ever penetrated; and I extended the frontier of Illyricum to the bank of the Danube River. An army of the Dacians which had crossed to our side of the river was conquered and destroyed under my auspices, and later on, my army crossed the Danube and compelled the Dacian tribes to submit to the orders of the Roman people.

31. Royal embassies from India, never previously seen before any Roman general, were often sent to me. Our friendship was sought through ambassadors by the Bastarnians and Scythians and by the kings of the Sarmatians, who live on both sides of the Don River, and by the kings of the Albanians and of the Iberians and of the Medes.[86]

32. The following kings fled to me as suppliants: Tiridates and

---

[83] On the Roman client states under Augustus, see further § 10.

[84] Provinces held by Antony and Sextus Pompey. Cf. paragraph 25, above.

[85] These were the standards lost by Crassus at the battle of Carrhae in 53 B.C. and in Mark Antony's disastrous operations against the Parthians in 40 and 36 B.C. They were restored as the result of diplomatic negotiations; Augustus' version is calculated to salve Roman pride.

[86] The peoples named in this sentence inhabited the fringes of the Roman Empire from the Carpathians to the Caucasus.

afterwards Phraates son of King Phraates, kings of the Parthians; Artavasdes, king of the Medes; Artaxares, king of the Adiabenians; Dumnobellaunus and Tincommius, kings of the Britons; Maelo, king of the Sugumbrians, and Segimerus[?], king of the Marcomannian Suebians.[87] Phraates son of Orodes, king of the Parthians, sent to me in Italy all his sons and grandsons, not because he was conquered in war, but seeking our friendship through pledge of his children. Under my principate numerous other peoples, with whom previously there had existed no exchange of embassies and friendship, experienced the good faith of the Roman people.

33. The peoples of the Parthians and of the Medes, through ambassadors who were the leading men of these peoples, received from me the kings for whom they asked: the Parthians, Vonones son of King Phraates, grandson of King Orodes; the Medes, Ariobarzanes son of King Artavasdes, grandson of King Ariobarzanes.

34. In my sixth and seventh consulships,[88] after I had put an end to the civil wars, having attained supreme power by universal consent, I transferred the state from my own power to the control of the Roman senate and people. For this service of mine I received the title of Augustus by decree of the senate, and the doorposts of my house were publicly decked with laurels, the civic crown was affixed over my doorway, and a golden shield was set up in the Julian senate house, which, as the inscription on this shield testifies, the Roman senate and people gave me in recognition of my valor, clemency, justice, and devotion. After that time I excelled all in authority, but I possessed no more power than the others who were my colleagues in each magistracy.

35. When I held my thirteenth consulship,[89] the senate, the equestrian order, and the entire Roman people gave me the title of "father of the country" and decreed that this title should be inscribed in the vestibule of my house, in the Julian senate house, and in the Augustan Forum on the pedestal of the chariot which was set up in my honor by decree of the senate. At the time I wrote this document I was in my seventy-sixth year.[90]

[87] Adiabenia was a district of Assyria; the Sugumbrians and Marcomannian Suebians were Germanic tribes.
[88] 28 and 27 B.C. The reorganization of 28–27 B.C. (see § 1) put an end to the unlimited powers exercised by Augustus without legal title from the expiration of the triumvirate in 32 B.C. to that date. Augustus justifies his extralegal position by affirming that he held it "by universal consent."
[89] 2 B.C.; cf. § 1, fourth selection.
[90] Four appendices (not part of the original document of Augustus), which summarize the expenditures and public works of Augustus, are here omitted.

3. *The Prince of Peace and the New Order*

The task of disseminating the official program of the new age among the
educated portion of the population was undertaken by Maecenas, who, next
to Agrippa (cf. §§ 15, 16), was the principal helper of Augustus in the first
half of his reign. The literary coterie which Maecenas gathered about him
rang the changes on the professed ideals of the new regime—peace and empire,
rededication to the ancestral virtues, the traditions and religion of the idealized past, and the benevolent administration of the *princeps*.

Anonymous *Panegyric on Piso* [91] 230–43

From LCL

The very bard [92] who makes his poem on Aeneas resound among
the Italian people, the bard who in his mighty renown treads Olympus
and in Roman accents challenges venerable Homer, perchance his poem
might have lurked obscure in the shadow of the grove, and he might
have but sung on a fruitless reed unknown to the peoples if he had
lacked a Maecenas. Yet it was not to one bard only that he opened his
doors, nor did he entrust his destinies to Vergil alone. Maecenas raised
to fame Varius,[93] who shook the stage with tragic mien; Maecenas
drew out the grand style of the thundering poet and revealed famous
names to the people of Greece. Likewise he made known to fame
songs resonant on Roman strings and the Italian lyre of graceful Horace.
Hail! ornament of the age, worshipful deservedly for all time, protection of the Pierian choir, beneath whose guardianship never did poet
fear for an old age of beggary.

Horace *Odes* IV. xv

When I wished to tell in lyric song of battles and the conquest
of cities, Apollo rebuked me and forbade my spreading tiny sails
upon the Tyrrhenian Sea. Thine age, O Caesar, has brought back fertile crops to the fields and has restored to our own Jupiter the military
standards stripped from the proud columns of the Parthians; [94] has closed
Janus' temple [95] freed of wars; has put reins on license overstepping
righteous bounds; has wiped away our sins and revived the ancient virtues through which the Latin name and the might of Italy waxed great,
and the fame and majesty of our empire were spread from the sun's bed

[91] Composed in the early part of the first century A.D.
[92] Vergil.
[93] Lucius Varius Rufus, eminent epic poet and dramatist of the Augustan Age,
friend and literary executor of Vergil.
[94] Cf. § 2, paragraph 29. This ode of Horace was written c.13 B.C.
[95] Cf. § 2, paragraph 13.

in the west to the east. As long as Caesar is the guardian of the state, neither civil dissension nor violence shall banish peace, nor wrath that forges swords and brings discord and misery to cities. Not those who drink the deep Danube shall violate the orders of Caesar, nor the Getae, nor the Seres,[96] nor the perfidious Parthians, nor those born by the Don River. And we, both on profane and sacred days, amidst the gifts of merry Bacchus, together with our wives and children, will first duly pray to the gods; then, after the tradition of our ancestors, in songs to the accompaniment of Lydian flutes we will hymn leaders whose duty is done, and Troy and Anchises and benign Venus' offspring.[97]

Not as uncritical in his praise as were some of his contemporaries, Vergil in his poems reflects a cautious optimism, mingling enthusiastic hopes with brooding doubts. Augustus while yet a triumvir initiated his policy of restoring Italian agriculture after the ravages of the civil wars, and Vergil was invited to lend his support with a work glorifying the agricultural life. He responded by producing the *Georgics,* a masterpiece of poetic art imbued with a nostalgic idealization of the simple agrarian life, in which, he hoped, the ancestral virtues might flourish again.

Vergil *Georgics* II. 458–74, 490–540

O happy beyond measure the tillers of the soil, if they but knew their blessings, on whom, far from the clash of arms, the earth most justly showers an easy livelihood from her soil! Even if no high mansion with proud portals pours forth from every room a mighty wave of men coming to pay their respects in the morning; even if men do not gape at pillars inlaid with lovely tortoise-shell, or at tapestries embroidered with gold, or at Corinthian bronzes; even if white wool is not dyed with oriental purple; even if the pure olive oil they use is not spoiled with perfume, yet they enjoy sleep without worry, and a life that cannot bring disillusionment but rather one that is rich in varied treasures, and peace in their broad farms, and grottoes, natural lakes, cool valleys, the lowing of cattle, and gentle slumber beneath a tree. Pastures are there and the haunts of wild game, and youth is hardy in toil and accustomed to simple fare; there the rites of the gods are observed and reverence for age survives; Justice took her last steps among these as she left the earth. . . .

Blessed was he who could discover the causes of things,[98] and tram-

---

[96] The Getae occupied the northern bank of the lower Danube; Seres is a generic name for peoples of central and east Asia—Chinese and Tibetans.

[97] Horace refers to the Trojan prince Aeneas (see Vol. 1, § 4), legendary ancestor of the Romans, from whom Julius Caesar and Augustus claimed direct descent.

[98] Vergil here exalts peace of mind attainable through the natural philosophy of Epicurus and Lucretius.

ple upon all fears and inexorable death and the roar of greedy Hades'
waters. Yet happy he too who has come to know the rustic gods, Pan,
aged Sylvanus, and the sister nymphs. He is moved neither by the *fasces*
which the people grant, nor by royal purple, nor by the conspiring
Dacians swooping down from the Danube, nor by the affairs of Rome
and the death throes of kingdoms. He has not had to grieve in pity for
the poor nor to envy those who have. He plucks the fruits of the trees
and reaps what the willing fields of their own accord produce and
knows nothing of the rigor of the law, the frenzied Forum, and the
public archives. Some ply unknown seas in their ships, rush to arms,
make their way into the royal palaces of kings; another attacks and
destroys cities and their hapless homes, to drink from jewelled cups and
sleep on Tyrian purple; another hoards his wealth and broods over
buried gold; another gapes with astonishment at the *Rostra;* another
stands open-mouthed and is carried away by the applause that rings
again and again through the theater from both plebs and senators; some
rejoice when drenched in the blood of brothers, and go into exile, abandoning their dear hearths and homes and seeking another country underneath another sun.

But the farmer upturns the earth with his curved plow; this is his
year-long toil, and thus he feeds his country and little grandchildren, his
herds of cattle and bullocks that have served him well. Nor is there
any halt throughout the year to the abundance of fruits or offspring of
flocks or sheaves of grain, and his furrows are ever piled high with
harvest and his granaries are filled to overflowing. When winter comes,
the Sicyan olives are pressed by the mills, the pigs return well fed
on acorns, the woods produce wild strawberries, and autumn drops
her varied fruits, and high up on sunny rocks mellow grapes are ripened.
Meanwhile, sweet children hang about his lips, his chaste household
preserves its purity, the cows' udders hang full of milk, and the fat kids
in the luxuriant meadow butt against each other locking horn with
horn. The master himself celebrates the festal days; stretched on the
grass, while about a fire in their midst his comrades wreath the bowl,
he pours libation and invokes thee, O Bacchus, and for the shepherds
of his flock he holds a contest of throwing the swift javelin at a mark
on an elm tree, and they bare their hardened bodies for the rustic
wrestling match.

This is the life the ancient Sabines once cherished; so, too, Remus
and his brother; [99] thus, surely, brave Etruria waxed strong, and Rome
became the fairest thing on earth, and encircled together her seven hills
with a wall. Yea, before the power of the Cretan kings and before

[99] That is, Romulus, mythical ancestor of the Romans.

impious mankind fed on slaughtered oxen, this was the life that was led on earth in the Golden Age of Saturn. Yea, not yet had they heard the blast of trumpet, not yet the ring of swords placed on hard anvils.

Vergil *Aeneid* vi. 756-853 (abridged)

Now then, I [100] shall describe the future glory that is to attend the Trojan people, the descendants from the Italian people that await you, illustrious souls destined to succeed to our name, and I shall unfold to you your fate. . . . Romulus, son of Mars . . . do you see how a double plume stands on his helmet, and how his father marks him out even now by his distinctive badge as one of the gods? Yes, my son, it is under his auspices that glorious Rome will extend her empire to the ends of the earth and her heroism to the sky, and will encircle together her seven hills with a wall, fortunate in her brood of heroes. . . . Now turn your eyes here, behold this stock, your Romans. Here is Caesar and the whole progeny of Iulus,[101] destined to come under the great vault of the sky. This, this is he, the man you have heard promised to you so often, Augustus Caesar, son of a god, who will once again establish the Golden Age in Latium, in the region once ruled by Saturn, and will extend the empire beyond the Garamantes [102] and the Indians. . . .

Those souls, now, which you see equally agleam in armor, harmonious now and as long as they are confined in darkness, alas! how great a war will they wage against each other if they reach the light of day, what battles, what carnage will ensue, the father-in-law descending from the ramparts of the Alps . . . the son-in-law arrayed against him with the forces of the east! [103] Do not, do not, my children, cherish such wars in your hearts, do not turn your country's mighty power against the vitals of your country; and do you first, you who derive your descent from the gods, do you forbear, cast the weapons from your hand, my descendant. . . .

Others, doubtless, will mould lifelike bronze with greater delicacy, will win from marble the look of life, will plead cases better, chart the motions of the sky with the rod and foretell the risings of the stars.[104] You, O Roman, remember to rule the nations with might. This will be

[100] The spirit of Anchises here foretells to his son Aeneas, who has come to visit him in Hades, the future glories of the Roman people.
[101] Son of Aeneas, also named Ascanius and Ilus (from Ilium), to whom the Julian family sought to trace its origin.
[102] A remote North African tribe dwelling in the region now known as Fezzan.
[103] The allusion is to the civil war between Julius Caesar and Pompey the Great, who married Caesar's daughter.
[104] Vergil here concedes to the Greek people superior achievements in the arts and sciences.

your genius—to impose the way of peace, to spare the conquered and crush the proud.

4. *Reorganization of the Senate*

The senatorial order, which had ruled the Roman Republic for hundreds of years, was absorbed into the Principate as a semi-hereditary aristocracy from which the emperors drew the highest imperial administrative and military officers. Together with the equestrian order, from which came the functionaries of the imperial civil service, the senatorial nobility formed the principal social base of the Principate. In three purgings of the rolls of the senate (29/28, 18, 13 B.C.), Augustus reorganized its personnel, weeding out unacceptable and politically unreliable members, reducing the membership to about 600, and establishing a property qualification of 1,000,000 sesterces. The reorganized senate, in addition to carrying out important administrative duties, became the principal legislative body of the state and a high court of justice (cf. §§ 29–30).

Dio Cassius *Roman History* LII. xlii. 1–7
Adapted from LCL

After this he held the office of censor,[105] with Agrippa as his colleague, and in addition to other reforms which he instituted he purged the senate. For as a result of the civil wars a large number of *equites* and even of men of lower rank were in the senate unjustifiably, so that the membership of that body had swollen to a thousand. Now, though it was his wish to remove these men, he did not erase any of their names himself but urged them rather to become their own judges on the basis of their knowledge of their families and their lives; he thus first persuaded some fifty to withdraw from the senate voluntarily, and then compelled 140 others to imitate their example. He disfranchised none of them, but posted the names of the second group, sparing the members of the first group the reproach of the publication of their names, because they had not delayed but had straightway obeyed him. So these men returned to private life . . . and he made some other men senators. . . . And at the same time, ostensibly at the senate's bidding, he increased the number of patrician families, because the greater part of the patricians had perished (indeed no class is so wasted in civil wars as the nobility) and because the patricians are regarded as

---

[105] Dio is in error. Neither in 29 B.C., to which year Dio refers, nor at any other time did Augustus hold the office of censor. This high Republican magistracy had become virtually defunct in the last decades of the Republic. Augustus assumed the functions of the censors by virtue of his consular power. See further Note 109.

indispensable for the performance of our traditional institutions. In addition to these measures, he forbade all members of the senate to go outside Italy unless he himself commanded or permitted them to do so. This restriction is still observed down to the present day: no senator is allowed to go abroad to any place except Sicily and Narbonese Gaul. Since these regions are close at hand and the inhabitants are unarmed and peaceful, those who have any possessions there have been given the right to go there as often as they like without asking permission. . . .[106]

Suetonius *Life of Augustus* xxxv. 1–3, xxxvii. 1–2
From LCL

Since the number of senators was swelled by a low-born and ill-assorted rabble (in fact, the senate numbered more than a thousand, some of whom . . . were wholly unworthy and had been admitted after Caesar's death through favor or bribery), he restored it to its former limits and distinction by two purges, one according to the choice of the members themselves, each man naming one other, and a second made by Agrippa and himself. (On the latter occasion it is thought that he wore a coat of mail under his tunic as he presided, and a sword by his side, while ten of the most robust of his friends among the senators stood about his chair. Cremutius Cordus [107] writes that even then the senators were not allowed to approach except one by one, and after the folds of their robes had been carefully searched.) Some he shamed into resigning, but he allowed even these to retain their distinctive dress, as well as the privileges of viewing the games from the orchestra and partaking in the public banquets of the order. Furthermore, that those who were chosen and approved might perform their duties more conscientiously and with less inconvenience, he provided that before taking his seat each member should offer incense and wine at the altar of the god in whose temple the meeting was held; that regular meetings of the senate should be held not oftener than twice a month, on the Kalends and the Ides; and that in the months of September and October none should be obliged to attend except a quorum drawn by lot, sufficient to pass decrees. He also adopted the plan of having privy councils [108] chosen by lot for terms of six months, with which to discuss in advance matters which were to come before the entire body. . . .

[106] Senators were explicitly excluded from Egypt. According to Tacitus (*Annals* II. lix. 4), "Augustus . . . set Egypt apart and forbade senators and high-ranking Roman *equites* from entering it without permission, for fear that whoever occupied that province, whose keys by land and sea [Pelusium and Alexandria] could be held with a very light garrison against mighty armies, would be able to distress Italy with famine."

[107] See § 23, fourth selection.   [108] See Note 13.

To enable more men to take part in the administration of the state, he devised new offices: the supervision of public buildings, of the roads, of the aqueducts, of the channel of the Tiber, of the distribution of the grain dole to the people, as well as the prefecture of the city, a board of three for choosing senators, and another for reviewing the companies of *equites* whenever it should be necessary. He appointed censors, an office which had long been discontinued.[109] He increased the number of praetors.

5. *The New Prefectures*

The administration of the imperial capital was placed on an efficient basis by Augustus and was gradually drawn under imperial control. Special administrative officials and permanent commissioners (cf. § 4) were developed by the first *princeps* to head bureaus which increasingly encroached upon the powers of the traditional Republican magistrates. The most important of these new departments were four prefectures established to take charge of various aspects of the security of Rome: the prefecture of the city, whose head was the chief constable of Rome and commanded the three urban cohorts of security police; the prefecture of the night patrol; the prefecture of the grain supply; and the prefecture of the Praetorian Guard (the emperor's bodyguard, nine cohorts of élite troops). The first of these great prefectures was held by senators of consular rank, the others by high-ranking *equites*. The duties of the first two are described in the following passages, which, being excerpted from the writings of the third-century jurists, Ulpian and Paulus, include some powers acquired by these prefects after the time of Augustus.

Justinian *Digest* I. xii. 1 (abridged), xv. 3

The prefect of the city has jurisdiction over all offenses whatsoever, not only those committed inside the city but also those outside the city in Italy, according to a rescript of the deified Emperor Severus addressed to Fabius Cilo, prefect of the city. He shall hear complaints against masters by slaves who have sought asylum at sacred images or have been purchased with their own money for the purpose of being manumitted. He shall also hear the complaints of needy patrons concerning their freedmen, especially if they declare that they are ill and wish to be supported by their freedmen. The authority to relegate and deport persons to an island designated by the emperor is vested in him. The same rescript begins as follows: "Inasmuch as we have entrusted

[109] Actually there were censors only once during the reign of Augustus, in 22 B.C. This date marks the end of the censorship as an independent office. Thereafter, though it was revived as an imperial prerogative by Claudius and the Flavians, the functions of this magistracy were absorbed into the imperial powers.

our city to your care;" therefore any offense committed within the city is held to be under the jurisdiction of the prefect of the city; and likewise any offense committed within a hundred miles is under the jurisdiction of the prefect of the city; an offense committed beyond the hundredth milestone is outside the purview of the prefect of the city. . . .

Maintenance of the public peace and of order at the spectacles is also held to be under the jurisdiction of the prefect of the city; and indeed he should also have soldiers stationed at various points for the purpose of maintaining the public peace and to report to him whatever occurs anywhere. The prefect of the city can debar anyone from the city, as well as from any one of the official districts [of Rome] and can debar him from a business or profession or from the practice of law or from the Forum, either temporarily or permanently. He can also debar him from the spectacles. . . .

The deified Severus declared in a rescript that those who are accused of having held unlawful assemblies [110] must be prosecuted before the prefect of the city. . . .

Augustus held that the protection of the public security belonged to no one more than to the emperor, and that no one else was equal to the task; accordingly, he stationed seven cohorts in suitable places, so that each cohort protected two districts of the city; [111] in command of the cohorts were tribunes, and at the head of all was an official . . . called the prefect of the night patrol.

The prefect of the night patrol tries incendiaries, housebreakers, thieves, robbers, and harborers of criminals, unless the individual is so vicious and notorious that he is turned over to the prefect of the city. And since fires are generally caused by the negligence of occupants, he either punishes with beating those who have been unduly careless in the use of fire, or he suspends the sentence of beating and issues a severe reprimand.

Housebreaking is generally committed in apartment houses and in warehouses where men deposit the most valuable part of their property, when either a storeroom or a closet or a money box is broken into; in which case the guards are generally punished. The deified Antoninus stated this in a rescript to Erucius Clarus, saying that if warehouses are broken into he can examine by torture the slaves guarding them, even if some of them may belong to the emperor himself.

It should be noted that the prefect of the night patrol must be on

[110] Cf. § 69.
[111] Established in A.D. 6, the corps of 7,000 *vigiles*, all freedmen, was distributed equally among the fourteen districts into which Augustus had divided Rome (cf. § 15, second selection).

duty the entire night, and should make his rounds appropriately shod
and equipped with water buckets and axes. He must notify all residents
to exercise care that no fire occur through any negligence; moreover,
he is directed to give notice that each resident should keep water on his
upper floor. He has also been assigned jurisdiction over those who take
care of clothing in baths for a fee; and if while taking care of clothing
they commit any fraud, he must try the case himself.

6. Military Reorganization

By 13 B.C. the demobilization of the huge civil-war armies was completed,
and Augustus undertook a definitive reorganization of the armed forces.
"The system which existed at his death was modified only in detail by his
successors during the first two centuries of our era, and traces of it remained
till the last days of the Western Empire" (*Cambridge Ancient History,* X,
220). To some 300,000 men—c.150,000 legionaries organized in twenty-
eight legions (cf. Note 114) and about the same number of provincial recruits
in the auxiliary units—was entrusted the task of defending the 4,000-mile-
long frontier (cf. § 10) and of policing the provinces. In and about Rome
were stationed several thousand troops comprising the emperor's bodyguard
(called the Praetorian Guard) and the city guard. The whole was a professional, long-service standing army, the control of which was lodged firmly
in the hands of the *princeps* (cf. § 8).

The expense of maintaining the military establishment was the largest
single item in the imperial budget. It was a constant and increasingly difficult
problem for Augustus and his successors to meet this expense without over-
straining the civilian economy. In addition, the veterans had to be provided
for after discharge. Until A.D. 6 a grant of land in a military colony continued
to be the veteran's principal reward for service. In that year Augustus established the Soldiers' Bonus Fund (*aerarium militare*), financed by an initial
grant of 170,000,000 sesterces from his own funds and by the income from a
one-percent tax on sales and a five-percent inheritance tax. Thereafter, military colonies were still established on occasion, but normally the veteran received his discharge bonus in cash.

On all these matters, see further Chapter VII.

Suetonius *Life of Augustus* xlix. 1–2

Of the military forces he distributed legions and auxiliaries among
the various provinces, stationed a fleet at Misenum and another at
Ravenna to guard the Upper and Lower Seas,[112] and selected the remaining number for the protection partly of the city and partly of his own
person. . . . However, he never allowed more than three [Praetorian]

[112] The Adriatic and Tyrrhenian Seas, respectively.

cohorts to remain in the city, and even those were without a permanent camp; the rest he regularly sent to winter or summer quarters in the neighboring towns. Furthermore, he placed all the soldiery everywhere on a specified scale of pay and bonuses and fixed the duration of military service and the rewards upon discharge according to each man's classification, in order to keep them from being tempted to revolution by age or by poverty after discharge. To have funds ready at all times without difficulty for their support and benefit he established the Soldiers' Bonus Fund, financed by new taxes.

Dio Cassius *Roman History* LV. xxiii. 1–xxiv. 8 (abridged)
Adapted from LCL

The soldiers were sorely displeased at the paltry character of the rewards given them for the wars which had been waged at this time, and none of them was willing to bear arms for longer than the stated period of his service. It was therefore voted that 20,000 sesterces should be given to members of the Praetorian Guard [upon discharge] after they had served sixteen years, and 12,000 to the other legionaries after they had served twenty years.[113] Twenty-three or, as others say, twenty-five legions of citizen soldiers were being supported at this time. . . .[114] In the days of Augustus . . . there were also allied forces of infantry, cavalry, and sailors, whatever their number may have been (for I cannot state the exact figures). Then there were the [emperor's] bodyguards . . . and the city guards . . . and also picked foreign horsemen called Batavians (because the men from the island of Batavia in the Rhine are excellent horsemen). I cannot, however, give their exact number any more than I can give that of the *evocati.*[115] These last-named Augustus began to make a practice of employing from the time when he called again into service against Antony the troops who had served with his father, and he maintained them afterwards; they constitute even now a special corps and carry switches, like the centurions.

7. *The Julian Law on Treason*

With the advent of the Principate, revision of the statutes dealing with injury to the majesty of the Roman people and its representatives became necessary because of the emperor's status as the chief authority of the state. Augustus'

[113] The time is A.D. 5. The periods of service were raised from twelve and sixteen years respectively; see further introduction to § 155.
[114] The figure twenty-five is the number of legions in existence at Augustus' death, after the annihilation of three legions in Germany (cf. § 10).
[115] Literally, "recalled"—that is, veterans who constituted a reserve.

Julian Law on Treason, the basic statute on the subject throughout the
Empire, adapted Republican legislation to the new constitutional situation.
The comprehensiveness and vagueness of the Roman concept of lese majesty
rapidly led to an enormous extension of its application through interpretation,
especially as it affected the majesty of the emperor; thus profession of Christianity, for example, was later treated as treasonable (cf. §§ 172–177). In the
reign of Augustus the special treason court of the Republic soon fell into
disuse, since treason cases were heard either by the emperor himself or by
the senate (of which the emperor was the leading member). The penalty remained under Augustus the same as it had been from the time of Sulla—
permanent banishment from Italy. Graver penalties were introduced in the
reign of Tiberius—confiscation of property, deportation, loss of civic rights,
and even death (see § 23).

Justinian *Digest* XLVIII. iv

The charge of treason . . . is lodged against a person through
whose agency, with malice aforethought, a plot is formed whereby,
without the order of the emperor, hostages perish, or whereby men
armed with weapons or stones are present in the city or assemble against
the state or occupy public places or temples, or whereby meetings or
assemblies take place or men are gathered together for seditious purposes; or a person through whose agency, with malice aforethought, a
plot is formed whereby any magistrate of the Roman people or a person possessing *imperium* or authority is slain or whereby anyone bears
arms against the state; or a person who sends a messenger or letter or
gives a signal to enemies of the Roman people, or who, with malice
aforethought, causes the enemies of the Roman people to be aided with
advice against the state; or a person who arouses or incites soldiers so as
to cause sedition or an uprising against the state; or a person who does
not depart from a province when he has been replaced by a successor;
or [a soldier] who deserts from the army; or a civilian who goes over
to the enemy; or a person who knowingly makes or cites a false entry
in the public records. . . .

Moreover, the Julian Law on Treason directs that a person who
injures the majesty of the state is liable to prosecution, such as one who
abandons his post in time of war or fails to [?] hold a stronghold or
gives up a military camp. Under the same law a person is also liable who,
without the order of the emperor, wages war or levies soldiers or mobi-
lizes an army; or who, when he has been superseded in his province,
does not turn over his troops to his successor; or who deserts his command or an army of the Roman people; or a person not holding public
office who knowingly and with malice aforethought exercises any
function belonging to an authority or magistrate; or who causes any of

the aforementioned acts to be done; or by whom with malice afore-thought anyone is bound by oath to act against the state; or by whom, with malice aforethought, an army of the Roman people is led into ambush or betrayed to the enemy; or by whom, with malice afore-thought, information is given whereby an enemy is prevented from coming into the power of the Roman people; or through whose agency, with malice aforethought, enemies of the Roman people are assisted with provisions, arms, weapons, horses, money, or anything else, or friends are turned into enemies of the Roman people; or who with malice aforethought so acts as to weaken the allegiance of a king of a foreign country to the Roman people; or whose action with malice aforethought results in facilitating the giving of hostages, money, or pack animals to enemies of the Roman people against the interests of the state; likewise, one who releases a defendant who has been impris-oned as a result of his confession of guilt before a court. . . .

A charge is extinguished by the death [of the accused], except in the case of a person accused of treason; for unless he is cleared of this charge by his heirs, the estate is confiscated by the privy purse. Clearly, not everyone accused of treason under the Julian Law is in this position, but only a person who is accused of high treason, that is, one motivated by hostile intent against the state or the emperor; but if a person is ac-cused of treason under any other section of the Julian Law, his death extinguishes the charge.

8. *Reorganization of Provincial Administration*

The historic division of the Empire in 27 B.C. into imperial and senatorial provinces was a political safeguard against the menace to Augustus and the new régime of the reemergence of the rival proconsuls and war lords whose ambitions had convulsed the Roman world in the last century of the Republic. In acquiring the proconsular power (cf. § 1) Augustus assumed the titular pronconsulship over the Spanish and Gallic provinces, Egypt, and Syria (to-gether with a small section of Asia Minor), and thus concentrated in the hands of the *princeps* the bulk of the military forces of the Empire, which were stationed in these strategic and generally less pacified provinces. Thus, with one stroke, Augustus placed under his control not only the standing armies but also the foreign policy of the Empire. It is true that some legions continued to be commanded by the proconsuls of the senatorial provinces of Africa, Macedonia, and Illyricum, but the *princeps* through his *maius im-perium* exercised effective control in these areas also (cf. Note 15 and § 9). Within the provinces Augustus continued the traditional Roman policy of supporting the propertied classes and of fostering local self-government in the variously constituted urban communities of the Empire. An important aspect of Augustus' provincial reorganization was his suppression of the flagrant abuses and the ruthless exploitation which had characterized the provincial administration of the Republic (cf. Vol. I, Chapter VI).

Dio Cassius *Roman History* LIII. xii–xv (abridged)
Adapted from LCL

Augustus declared that he would not personally govern all the provinces, and that in the case of such provinces as he should govern he would not do so indefinitely. And he did, in fact, restore to the senate the weaker provinces, on the ground that they were peaceful and free from war, while he retained the more powerful ones, alleging that they were insecure and precarious and either had enemies on their borders or were able on their own account to begin a serious revolt. His professed motive in this was that the senate might enjoy without fears the finest portion of the empire, while he himself had the hardships and the dangers; but his real purpose was that by this arrangement the senators should be unarmed and peaceful, while he alone had arms and maintained soldiers. Accordingly, Africa, Numidia, Asia, Greece with Epirus, the Dalmatian and Macedonian districts, Sicily, Crete, and the Cyrenaic portion of Libya, Bithynia with the adjoining Pontus, Sardinia, and Baetica [116] were held to belong to the people and the senate; while to Caesar belonged the remainder of Spain—that is, the districts of Tarraco and Lusitania—and all the Gauls—that is Gallia Narbonensis, Gallia Lugdunensis, Aquitania, and Belgica. . . . These provinces, then, together with Coele-Syria, as it is called, Phoenicia, Cilicia, Cyprus, and Egypt, fell at that time to Caesar's share; [117] for afterwards he gave Cyprus and Gallia Narbonensis back to the people, and for himself took Dalmatia instead. . . . All of those which came into the Roman Empire after this were added to the provinces of the one who was emperor at the time.

Such, then, was the division of the provinces. And wishing even so to divert the Romans far away from the idea that he was at all monarchical in his purposes, Caesar undertook for only ten years the government of the provinces assigned him; for he promised to reduce them to order within this period, and boastfully added that, if they should be pacified sooner, he would the sooner restore them, too, to the senate. Thereupon he first appointed the senators themselves to govern both classes of prov-

[116] There are anachronisms in Dio's list. In 27 B.C. there were only eight senatorial provinces. Greece was still attached to Macedonia; Numidia, then a client kingdom, was annexed to the province of Africa in 25 B.C.; Baetica did not become senatorial until later in Augustus' reign.
[117] This list, too, contains anachronisms (cf. Note 116) in the divisions and names of provinces.

inces, except Egypt. This province alone he assigned to an *eques*. . . .[118]
Next he ordained that the governors of senatorial provinces should be
annual magistrates, chosen by lot, except when a senator enjoyed privileges because of the large number of his children or because of his marital status.[119] These governors were to be sent out by action of the senate
in public meeting; they were to carry no sword at their belt nor to
wear military uniform; the name of proconsul was to belong not only
to the two ex-consuls but also to the others who had merely served as
praetors or who held the rank of ex-praetors. . . . The other governors, on the other hand, were to be chosen by the emperor himself and
were to be called his legates with the rank of praetor, even if they were
ex-consuls. Thus, of these two titles which had been in vogue so long
under the Republic, he gave that of praetor to the men chosen by him,
on the ground that from very early times it had been associated with
warfare, calling them propraetors; and he gave the name of consul to
the others, on the ground that their duties were more peaceful, styling
them proconsuls. For he reserved the actual titles of consul and praetor
for Italy, and designated all the governors outside of Italy as acting in
their stead. So, then, he caused the appointed governors to be known
as propraetors and to hold office for as long beyond one year as he
wished; [120] he made them wear the military uniform and a sword, which
gives them the power of inflicting punishment even on soldiers. . . .

It was thus and under these circumstances that the custom was established of sending out ex-praetors and ex-consuls as governors of the
two classes of provinces. In the one case, the emperor would commission
a governor to any province he wished and whenever he wished. . . . In
the case of the senatorial provinces, he assigned Asia and Africa on his
own responsibility to the ex-consuls, and all the other provinces to the
ex-praetors; but by public decree, applicable to all the senatorial governors, he forbade the allotment of any senator to a governorship before
the expiration of five years from the time he had held office in the
city. . . .[121]

This is the system followed in the case of the provinces of the
people. To the others, which are called the imperial provinces and have
more than one citizen-legion, are sent officials who are to govern them

---

[118] Cf. § 10, third selection. Later in Augustus' reign several smaller imperial provinces, garrisoned only by auxiliary troops, were assigned equestrian procurators or
prefects as governors.
[119] Cf. § 11.
[120] An extreme case is known of a man who held a series of such governorships for
twenty-four years under Augustus and Tiberius.
[121] This was a reenactment of a measure passed by the senate and Pompey in 53/52
B.C. Ex-consuls probably were required to wait ten years.

as legates; these are appointed by the emperor himself, generally from the ex-praetors. . . .

These, then, are the positions which belong to the senators. Passing now to the *equites*, the emperor himself selects *equites* to be sent out as military tribunes (both those who are prospective senators and others . . .), despatching some of them to take command of purely citizen troops, and others of the auxiliary troops as well. . . .[122] The procurators (for this is the name we give to the men who collect the public revenues and make disbursements according to the instructions given them) he sends out to all the provinces alike, to those of the people as well as to his own, and to this office *equites* are sometimes appointed and sometimes even freedmen, except where the proconsuls exact the tribute from the people they govern. The emperor gives instructions to the procurators, the proconsuls, and the propraetors, in order that they may go out to their provinces under definite orders. For both this practice and the giving of salaries to them and to the other officials was established at this time. In former times, of course, certain persons had contracted with the state to furnish the officials with all they needed for the conduct of their office; but under Caesar these officials for the first time began to receive a fixed salary. . . . The following regulations were laid down for them all alike: they were not to raise levies of soldiers or to exact money beyond the amount assessed, unless either the senate should so vote or the emperor so order; and when their successors arrived, they were to leave the province at once, and not to delay on the return journey, but to return within three months.

OATH OF ALLEGIANCE TO AUGUSTUS

When the client-king Deiotarus of Paphlagonia died in 6 B.C., his domain was annexed to the Empire and assigned to the province of Galatia. Three years later this oath of allegiance to Augustus was taken, first at Gangra, the administrative seat, by delegates from all the cities of the region, and subsequently by all the Paphlagonians in their local communities. Introduced by Augustus in the days of his death struggle with Antony, this personal oath of allegiance to the chieftain from the civilian population as well as the military became a standard ritual of the Principate (cf. § 20).

Dittenberger, *OGIS*, No. 532 (= Dessau, No. 8,781 = Abbott-Johnson, No. 37)

In the third year from the twelfth consulship of the Emperor Caesar Augustus, son of a god, March 6, in the . . . [123] at Gangra, the fol-

---

[122] Prospective senators were required to serve in the army at least one year as tribunes of legionary or auxiliary cohorts or as prefects of auxiliary cavalry.
[123] "Camp" and "civic center" have been proposed for the word lost in this lacuna.

lowing oath was taken by the inhabitants of Paphlagonia and the Roman businessmen dwelling among them:

"I swear by Jupiter, Earth, Sun, by all the gods and goddesses, and by Augustus himself, that I will be loyal to Caesar Augustus and to his children and descendants all my life in word, in deed, and in thought, regarding as friends whomever they so regard, and considering as enemies whomever they so adjudge; that in defense of their interests I will spare neither body, soul, life, nor children, but will in every way undergo every danger in defense of their interests; that whenever I perceive or hear anything being said or planned or done against them I will lodge information about this and will be an enemy to whoever says or plans or does any such thing; and that whomever they adjudge to be enemies I will by land and sea, with weapons and sword, pursue and punish. But if I do anything contrary to this oath or not in conformity with what I swore, I myself call down upon myself, my body, my soul, my life, my children, and all my family and property, utter ruin and utter destruction unto all my issue and all my descendants, and may neither earth nor sea receive the bodies of my family or my descendants, or yield fruits to them."

The same oath was sworn also by all the people in the land at the altars of Augustus in the temples of Augustus in the various districts. In this manner did the people of Phazimon, who inhabit the city now called Neapolis,[124] all together swear the oath in the temple of Augustus at the altar of Augustus.

VIOLATION OF SEPULTURE

The publication of this Greek inscription in 1930 caused a sensation because it was reported as "sent from Nazareth in 1878." Efforts were immediately made to connect the text with Jesus, but these have been futile; indeed, it is not even certain that the stone was found at Nazareth. The text, an undated copy of an imperial order, is assigned by most scholars to the reign of Augustus, though some still place it as late as A.D. 50/100. In it the desecration of graves is declared a capital crime. In Roman law this remained a civil offense until the end of the second century (cf. § 164); in the ancient Orient and the Hellenistic world it was a crime punishable by fine. Clearly, then, no alteration or imposition of Roman law is here involved. The emperors of the first two centuries continued the Republican practice of allowing the eastern provinces to operate as far as possible under their traditional institutions. Thus in the present instance the emperor deals with a specific local situation—profanation of cemeteries is known to have been involved, for example, in the outbreak of violence between Samaritans and Jews in A.D. 8— not by discarding the existing local law but merely by increasing its rigor.

[124] Modern Mersivan in Turkey, where this inscription was found.

SEG, Vol. VIII, No. 13 (= FIRA, Vol. I, No. 69)

Ordinance of Caesar. It is my pleasure that graves and tombs prepared for the cult of ancestors or children or kinsmen shall remain undisturbed in perpetuity. And if anyone brings information that someone has caused destruction, or has in any other manner cast out the
buried dead, or has with malice aforethought removed them to other
places to the detriment of the interred, or has removed tombstones or
other stones, I order that such a person be brought to trial for [violat-
ing] the cult of [dead] persons, just as is done in the case of gods. The
buried dead must in the future be accorded much more respect. Absolutely no one shall be allowed to disturb them. If anyone does, I desire
him to be sentenced to capital punishment for violation of sepulture.

9. *The Cyrene Edicts*

This long Greek inscription from Cyrene, first published in 1927 and widely
discussed since, constitutes the most important epigraphical find for the reign
of Augustus since the famous *Res Gestae*. It contains four imperial edicts
of 7/6 B.C. and a fifth, appending a decree of the senate, of 4 B.C. The first
edict revises the judiciary system of the province, patterned after the criminal
courts of Rome, by providing for mixed juries of Greeks and Romans in capital
cases. The second concerns a case which apparently established the precedent
for the prosecution (attested under subsequent emperors) of affronts to imperial statues under the law of *maiestas* (lese majesty: cf. §§ 7, 23). The
third edict, which limits the privileges of newly created Roman citizens, is
an important document on the subjects of multiple citizenship and compulsory
public services in the provinces. The fourth edict, dealing with the jury system
in Cyrene, supplements the first. The decree of the senate appended to the
fifth edict established a new, accelerated procedure by judicial commissions
of Roman senators in extortion cases limited to a claim for recovery and involving no concomitant capital charges against the accused public official.
Altogether these edicts shed invaluable light on the fusion of Hellenistic and
Roman law in the eastern provinces; since Crete-Cyrene was a senatorial
province, they also constitute important evidences of the emperor's *maius
imperium* (cf. Note 15).

SEG, Vol. IX, No. 8 (= FIRA, Vol. I, No. 68)

i

The Emperor Caesar Augustus, *pontifex maximus*, holding the tribunician power for the seventeenth year, acclaimed *imperator* fourteen
times, declares:

Since I find that there are all told in the provincial territory of Cyrene 215 Romans of all ages with a census rating of 2,500 *denarii* or more, from whom the jurors are chosen; [125] and since embassies from the cities of the province have complained bitterly that among these same Romans there exist certain conspiracies to oppress the Greeks in trials on capital charges, the same individuals acting in turn as accusers and as witnesses for one another; and since I myself have ascertained that some innocent people have in this way been oppressed and carried off to the supreme penalty, it is my view that, until the senate makes a decision on this matter or I myself find some better solution,[126] it will be the right and proper procedure for those governing the province of Crete and Cyrene to impanel in the provincial territory of Cyrene the same number of Greek jurors from the highest census rating as of Romans—no Greek or Roman to be less than twenty-five years of age, and none to have a census rating and property of less than 7,500 *denarii*, if there is a sufficient number of such persons, or, if the full number of jurors who need to be impaneled cannot be made up on this basis, they shall impanel men possessing half this census rating, but not less, as jurors in trials of Greeks on capital charges.

A Greek under indictment shall be given the right to decide, the day before the prosecution opens its case, whether he wants his jurors to be all Romans or half Greeks; and if he chooses half Greeks, then the balls shall be checked for equal weight [127] and the names shall be written on them, and from one urn the names of the Romans and from the other those of the Greeks shall be drawn until a total of twenty-five is obtained in each group. Of these the prosecutor may, if he wishes, dismiss one from each group, and the accused three out of the total, provided he does not dismiss either all Romans or all Greeks. Then all the others [after hearing the case] shall separate for the balloting, the Romans casting their votes separately in one box, the Greeks separately in a second; then a separate count shall be made of the votes on either side, and the governor shall pronounce in open court the verdict of the majority of all the jurors.

Furthermore, since the kinsmen of murdered persons generally do not leave unjustifiable deaths unavenged and it can be expected that those responsible will not lack Greek prosecutors to demand justice on

[125] This low census rating for jury service is indicative of the low level of wealth prevailing among Roman citizens in the province of Crete-Cyrene. At Rome the minimum property rating for jury duty was 100,000 *denarii*.
[126] This clause reflects the principle of collaboration between senate and *princeps* inherent in the constitution of the Principate (cf. above, p. 3).
[127] The lots ("balls") were checked for equal weight to equalize the chance of selection.

behalf of their slain relatives or fellow citizens, it is my view that all
who in the future govern Crete and Cyrene will act rightly and fittingly
if in the provincial territory of Cyrene they do not permit a Roman to
act as prosecutor of a Greek for the murder of a Greek man or woman,
except where someone who has been honored with Roman citizenship
takes action concerning the death of one of his relatives or fellow citizens.

ii

The Emperor Caesar Augustus, *pontifex maximus*, holding the
tribunician power for the seventeenth year, declares:

Publius Sextius Scaeva does not merit reproach or censure for ordering Aulus Stlaccius Maximus son of Lucius, Lucius Stlaccius Macedo
son of Lucius, and Publius Lacutanius Phileros, freedman of Publius, to
be sent on to me from the province of Cyrene under guard because
they had said that they had knowledge concerning my security and the
commonwealth and wished to declare it.[128] In so doing Sextius performed his duty conscientiously. However, since they have no information that concerns me or the commonwealth but have declared and
convinced me that they had misrepresented and lied about this in the
province, I have set them free and am releasing them from custody.[129]
But as for Aulus Stlaccius Maximus, whom the envoys of the Cyre-
naeans accuse of having removed statues from public places, among
them even the one on the base of which the city inscribed my name, I
forbid him to depart without my order until I have investigated this
matter.

iii

The Emperor Caesar Augustus, *pontifex maximus*, holding the tribunician power for the seventeenth year, declares:

Persons from the province of Cyrene who have been honored with
[Roman] citizenship I order nonetheless to perform in their turn the
personal compulsory public services of the Greeks. Excepted are those
to whom, by decree of my father or myself in accordance with a law
or a decree of the senate, exemption was granted together with citizenship. And even for those to whom such exemption was granted, it is my
pleasure that they shall be exempt only as to the property they possessed

---

[128] Cf. in § 8 the oath of allegiance in which the inhabitants of the Roman provinces
promised to report any such information that might come to their attention.

[129] It seems strange, at first sight, that Augustus should release these Romans without
punishment when they have confessed that they had lied, presumably to implicate
Greeks in Cyrene in charges of lese majesty. Augustus' action is to be explained as
one of his conciliatory measures intended to calm the seething animosity between
Greeks and Romans in the province. His concessions to the Greeks in the other
edicts were directed toward the same end.

at the time, but for all subsequent acquisitions they shall be subject to the usual charges.[130]

iv

The Emperor Caesar Augustus, *pontifex maximus*, holding the tribunician power for the seventeenth year, declares:

Regarding disputes which occur henceforth between Greeks within the province of Cyrene, excluding indictments for capital crimes, where the governor of the province must himself conduct the inquiry and render a decision or else set up a panel of jurors [131]—for all other cases it is my pleasure that Greek jurors shall be assigned unless some defendant or accused desires to have Roman citizens as jurors; and for those to whom in accordance with this decree of mine Greek jurors are assigned, it is my pleasure that no juror shall be assigned from the city from which either the plaintiff or the accuser or the defendant or the accused comes.

v

The Emperor Caesar Augustus, *pontifex maximus*, holding the tribunician power for the nineteenth year, declares:

A decree of the senate was passed in the consulship of Gaius Calvisius and Lucius Passienus, with me as one of those present at the writing.[132] Since it affects the welfare of the allies of the Roman people, I have decided to send it into the provinces, appended to this my prefatory edict, so that it may be known to all who are under our care. From this it will be evident to all the inhabitants of the provinces how much both I and the senate are concerned that none of our subjects should suffer any improper treatment or any extortion.

---

[130] Compulsory public services in the Roman Empire were of two kinds: those based on personal status (*munera personalia* or *corporalia*) and those based on property holdings (*munera patrimonialia*): cf. §§ 85, 97, 121, 134. In this edict Augustus enunciates the important principle, maintained by his successors, that a provincial's acquisition of Roman citizenship was compatible with retention of his original citizenship (cf. Vol. I, p. 389) and did not exempt him from the performance of *munera* in his local community unless the grant of citizenship was specifically accompanied by such exemption. Roman citizens of Italian origin residing abroad did at first enjoy exemption from such community obligations, but with the deterioration of municipal finances in the first and second centuries (see § 88), this privilege was progressively reduced by the emperors, until finally the universal-citizenship edict of Caracalla in A.D. 212 (see § 113) placed all Roman citizens on the same plane.
[131] As detailed in the first edict.
[132] Augustus' being recorded in the preamble as one of "those present at the writing" of the decree means that he was one of the sponsors of the decree in the senate; cf. the first paragraph of the decree, below. This is the only extant example of an emperor's participation in this formality.

Decree of the Senate

Whereas the consuls Gaius Calvisius Sabinus and Lucius Passienus Rufus spoke "Concerning matters affecting the security of the allies of the Roman people which the Emperor Caesar Augustus, our *princeps*, following the recommendation of the council which he had drawn by lot from among the senate,[133] desired to be brought before the senate by us," the senate passed the following decree:

Whereas our ancestors established legal process for extortion [134] so that the allies might more easily be able to take action for any wrongs done them and recover moneys extorted from them, and whereas this type of process is sometimes very expensive and troublesome for those in whose interest the law was enacted, because poor people or persons weak with illness or age are dragged from far-distant provinces as witnesses, the senate decrees as follows:

If after the passage of this decree of the senate any of the allies, desiring to recover extorted moneys, public or private, appear and so depose before one of the magistrates who is authorized to convene the senate, the magistrate—except where the extorter faces a capital charge —shall bring them before the senate as soon as possible and shall assign them any advocate they themselves request to speak in their behalf before the senate; but no one who has in accordance with the laws been excused from this duty shall be required to serve as advocate against his will.

In order that the cases of those bringing such charges in the senate may be heard, the magistrate who grants them access to the senate shall the same day in the presence of the senate, with not less than two hundred [members] on hand,[135] choose by lot four from all those of consular rank who are in Rome itself or within twenty miles of the city; likewise three from all those of praetorian rank who are in Rome itself or within twenty miles of the city; likewise two from all the other senators and those possessing the right to voice opinion in the senate who are then either in Rome or less than twenty miles from the city.[136] But he shall not choose anyone who is seventy years of age or over, or is the incumbent of a magistracy or an authority, or presiding officer of

[133] On the emperor's *consilium* see Note 13.
[134] See Vol. I, §§ 100, 146, 158.
[135] That is, about one third of the membership; cf. introduction to § 4.
[136] *Recuperatores* was the Latin term for the judges of such *ad hoc* tribunals. The three-category system by which their names were drawn was that used in appointing senatorial commissions. The twenty-mile radius from Rome was meant to correspond to a day's journey.

a law court, or commissioner of grain distribution; [137] or anyone prevented by illness from performing this duty, who excuses himself on oath before the senate and presents three members of the senate to attest this on oath; or anyone who is so closely related by family or marriage to the accused that he may not, in accordance with the Julian Judiciary Law,[138] be compelled to give evidence in a public action against his will; or anyone who the accused swears before the senate is hostile to him (but he shall not by such oath eliminate more than three). From the nine selected in this manner, the magistrate who does the drawing shall see to it that within two days those claiming the money and the one from whom they claim it make rejections in turn until five are left. If any of these judges dies before the case is decided, or some other cause prevents him from rendering his decision and his excuse is approved by the sworn statement of five members of the senate, then the magistrate, in the presence of the judges and of those claiming the money and the man from whom they claim it, shall again choose by lot from those members who are of the same rank or have held the same magistracies as the man who is being replaced, provided he does not thus choose a member who may not by this decree of the senate be chosen to try the accused.

The judges chosen shall hear and inquire into only those cases in which a man is accused of having appropriated money from a community or from private parties; and, rendering their decision within thirty days, they shall order him to restore such sum of money, public or private, as the accusers prove was taken from them. Those whose duty it is to inquire into and pronounce judgment in these cases shall, until they complete the inquiry and pronounce their judgment, be exempted from all public duties except public worship.

The senate decrees also that the magistrate who does the drawing of the judges—or, if he cannot, the ranking consul—shall preside over the proceedings and shall grant permission to summon those witnesses who are in Italy, with the proviso that he shall allow a man making a private claim to summon not more than five, and those pressing public claims not more than ten.[139]

---

[137] On the exemption of such officials from legal process during tenure of office cf. below, p. 70.
[138] This law of 17 B.C. regulated the procedures of the criminal courts.
[139] This and the two preceding paragraphs reduce drastically the delays and expenses in which the procedures of the extortion courts of the Republic involved the provincials. The republican practice allowed sixty days for constituting the jury; here the senatorial tribunal is constituted in final form within two days from the presentation of the complaint in the senate. The republican practice gave the parties the right to subpoena large numbers of witnesses from any part of the Empire (up

The senate likewise decrees that the judges who are selected in accordance with this decree of the senate shall pronounce in open court each his several finding, and what the majority pronounces shall be the verdict.

10. *Frontier and Foreign Policy*

Augustus, the "prince of peace," annexed more territory to the Roman Empire than did any of the famous conquering generals of the Republic. But his conquests were based on the essentially defensive strategic plan—to which his successors adhered with few exceptions (cf. §§ 25–28)—of protecting the Empire by means of strong, easily defensible natural barriers. In the West the Roman conquest of Spain, begun nearly two centuries earlier, was completed when the last vestiges of resistance surviving in remote mountain fastnesses were suppressed. In the East diplomatic negotiations with the Parthians led to the fixing of the Euphrates river as the frontier between the two empires and to recognition of the Roman protectorate over Armenia. To the South, an expedition aimed at acquiring the fabled riches and lucrative trade of Arabia Felix (modern Yemen) was a dismal failure; in Ethiopia, however, after a number of years of frontier warfare, Roman garrisons were established in a buffer zone south of the Egyptian border. In the North the frontier was advanced to the Danube, and in A.D. 5 Roman armies stood on the Elbe. But the great rebellion in Pannonia (A.D. 6–9) and the annihilation of three Roman legions in the Teutoburg Forest of Germany in A.D. 9 caused Augustus to pull in his horns. The conquest of Germany was abandoned, and the northern frontier of the Empire thereafter remained based on the Rhine and Danube rivers.

Suetonius *Life of Augustus* xxi, xxiii

Adapted from LCL

He subdued Cantabria, Aquitania, Pannonia, Dalmatia, and all Illyricum, as well as Raetia and the Vindelici and Salassi (Alpine tribes), some under his personal leadership, some by generals acting in his name. He also put a stop to the inroads of the Dacians, slaying great numbers of them together with three of their leaders, and forced the Germans back beyond the river Elbe, with the exception of the Suebi and the Sigambri, who submitted to him and were taken into Gaul and settled on lands near the Rhine. Other peoples, too, that were not entirely

---

to 120 witnesses under the Julian Law of 59 B.C.) and allowed them generous amounts of time—Cicero in his prosecution of Verres, for example, was given 110 days to collect witnesses. Here the number of witnesses is reduced to a maximum of five or ten; only persons within the borders of Italy can be subpoenaed as witnesses (*voluntary* witnesses from the provinces are of course not excluded); and the whole hearing is to be over and the verdict rendered within thirty days from the constitution of the tribunal.

peaceful he reduced to submission. But he never made war on any people without just and due cause, and he was so far from the desire of increasing his dominion or his military glory at any cost that he forced the chiefs of some of the barbarians to swear in the temple of Mars the Avenger that they would faithfully keep the peace for which they asked. In some cases, indeed, he tried exacting a new kind of hostages, namely women, because he realized that they disregarded pledges secured by males; but he always allowed them to take back their hostages as many times as they wished. On those who rebelled often or with unusual treachery he never vindictively visited any severer punishment than that of selling the prisoners on the conditions that they should not live while slaves in a country near their own nor be set free within thirty years. The reputation for prowess and moderation which he thus gained led even the Indians and the Scythians, nations known to us only by report, to send envoys voluntarily to sue for his friendship and that of the Roman people. The Parthians, too, readily yielded to his claim to Armenia, and at his demand surrendered the military standards which they had taken from Marcus Crassus and Mark Antony; they offered him hostages besides, and once when there were several claimants of their throne they accepted only the one chosen by him.[140]

. . . .

He suffered but two severe and ignominious defeats, both in Germany—those of Lollius and of Varus. The former was more humiliating than serious,[141] but the latter was almost fatal, since three legions were slaughtered with their general, his lieutenants, and all the auxiliaries.[142] When the news of this arrived, Augustus posted night watches throughout the city to prevent any disturbance, and he prolonged the terms of the governors of the provinces so that the allies might be held to their allegiance by experienced men with whom they were acquainted. Also, as had been done in the Cimbric and Marsic wars,[143] he vowed great games to Jupiter Best and Greatest if the condition of the commonwealth should improve. In fact, they say he was so overcome that for months on end he refused to cut his beard or hair and would from time

---

[140] Cf. Note 85.

[141] In 17 B.C. three German tribes launched a raid across the Rhine and defeated Marcus Lollius, governor of Gaul.

[142] According to Velleius Paterculus (*Compendium of Roman History* II. cxvii) the auxiliaries numbered six cohorts of infantry and three companies of cavalry.

[143] The Cimbrians, a Germanic people, in the course of their migrations toward the end of the second century B.C. inflicted several defeats on Roman armies in the Alpine regions and threatened to invade Italy until crushed by Marius near Vercellae (101 B.C.; cf. Vol. I, p. 206). The Marsic War was another, probably the earliest, name by which the Romans designated the Italic War (Vol. I, § 103).

to time dash his head against the door, crying: "Quintilius Varus, give me back my legions!" And he observed the day of the disaster each year as one of sorrow and mourning.

THE DISASTER IN GERMANY

Dio Cassius *Roman History* LVI. xviii–xix
Adapted from LCL

The following are the events that took place in Germany during this period. The Romans were holding portions of it . . . and soldiers of theirs were wintering there and cities were being founded. The barbarians were adapting themselves to Roman ways, were becoming accustomed to hold markets, and were meeting in peaceful assemblages. They had not, however, forgotten their ancestral habits, their native manners, their old life of independence, or the power derived from arms. Hence, so long as they were unlearning these old ways gradually and progressively under the eyes of the Roman garrisons, they were not disturbed by the change in their manner of life and were becoming different without noticing it. But when Quintilius Varus became governor of the province of Germany and was administering the affairs of these peoples as part of his duties, he strove to change them more rapidly. He issued orders to them as if they were enslaved, and exacted money as he would from subjects. To this they were in no mood to submit. The leaders longed for their former ascendancy, and the masses preferred their accustomed conditions to foreign domination. But they did not openly revolt, since they saw that there were many Roman troops near the Rhine and many within their own borders; instead, they received Varus as if prepared to do everything demanded of them, and thus they drew him far away from the Rhine into the land of the Cherusci, toward the Weser, and there by behaving in a most peaceful and friendly manner led him to believe that they would live submissively even without soldiers present.

Consequently he did not keep his legions together, as was proper in hostile country, but distributed many of the soldiers to helpless communities, which asked for them for the alleged purpose of guarding various points, arresting robbers, or escorting provision trains. . . . Then there came an uprising, first, by design, on the part of those who lived far off from him, so that Varus should march against them and so be more easily overpowered by them while proceeding through what was supposed to be friendly country, instead of putting himself on his guard as he would do if all became hostile to him at once. And so it came to pass. They escorted him as he set out, and then begged to be excused on the pretense that they would mobilize their allied contingents and quickly come to his aid. Then they took charge of their forces, which were held in readiness somewhere, and, after the men in each community had put to death the [Roman] soldiers in their midst for whom they had previously asked, they came upon Varus who was by now in almost inextricable forests. And there, at the very moment of revealing themselves as enemies instead of subjects, they wrought great and dire havoc.

THE SOUTHERN FRONTIER

The following is a vainglorious inscription in Latin and Greek, erected in 29 B.C. on the island of Philae, near the first cataract of the Nile, by Cornelius Gallus, the first Roman prefect of Egypt (he was also a poet, and a friend of Vergil). In it he celebrates his suppression of the Thebaid's revolt against the introduction of the Roman taxation system and his establishment of a Roman protectorate over a buffer zone south of the cataract (see further Note 147). In addition to the present inscription, Gallus "set up statues of himself practically everywhere in Egypt, and inscribed the list of his achievements on the pyramids" (Dio Cassius LIII. xxiii. 5). As a result he was recalled in disgrace, and he committed suicide (26 B.C.).

CIL, Vol. III, No. 14,147 (5) (= Dessau, No. 8,995)

Gaius Cornelius Gallus son of Gnaeus, Roman *eques*, first prefect of Alexandria and Egypt after the overthrow of the kings by Caesar, son of a god—having been victorious in two pitched battles in the fifteen days within which he suppressed the revolt of the Thebaid, capturing five cities—Boresis, Coptus, Ceramice, Diospolis Magna, and Ophiëum [144]—and seizing the leaders of these revolts; having led his army beyond the Nile cataract, a region into which arms had not previously been carried either by the Roman people or by the kings of Egypt; [145] having subjugated the Thebaid, the common terror of all the kings; [146] and having given audience at Philae to envoys of the king of the Ethiopians, received that king under [Roman] protection, and installed a prince over the Triacontaschoenus,[147] a district of Ethiopia—dedicated this thank offering to his ancestral gods and to the Nile his helpmate.

[144] Diospolis Magna was the name of the city of Thebes; Ceramice and Ophiëum were two of its districts.
[145] Here Gallus' boastfulness degenerates into sheer untruth. Both Pharaohs and Ptolemies had extended their rule south of the cataract at times.
[146] The powerful priesthood of Amon, centered in Thebes, had been a constant thorn in the side of the Egyptian kings from earliest times.
[147] "Thirty-schoenium Land," the region from the first to the second cataract (c.165 miles), which thus became a Roman protectorate under an Ethiopian client-king. This arrangement was impermanent, however. Nine years later, after an

CLIENT STATES

As the above inscription indicates, Augustus continued the policy, begun under the Republic, of buttressing some frontiers with buffer zones under Roman protectorate (see § 2, paragraphs 27, 32–33). The Romans preferred to control these remote and economically backward frontier regions indirectly through native princes because it would have been much more expensive to install and maintain the administrative machinery of Roman rule. But their very weakness made them in the long run unreliable bases of Roman power, and in the course of the first century most of these vassal states—by this time considerably Romanized in their ways—were annexed to the Empire.

Suetonius *Life of Augustus* xlviii
From LCL

Except in a few instances he either restored the kingdoms of which he gained possession by right of conquest to those from whom he had taken them, or joined them to other foreign nations. He also united with mutual ties the kings with whom he was in alliance and was very ready to propose and favor marriages or friendships among them. He never failed to treat them with all consideration as integral parts of the empire, regularly appointing guardians for such as were too young to rule or feeble-minded until they grew up or recovered, and he brought up the children of many, educating them together with his own.

Strabo *Geography* xiv. v. 6
Adapted from LCL

The region [of Cilicia Trachea] was naturally well adapted to the business of piracy both by land and by sea [148]—by land because of the height of the mountains and the populous tribes living beyond them on plains and farm lands that are large and easily overrun; and by sea because of the wealth of ship-building timber, harbors, fortresses, and secret recesses. With all this in view, the Romans deemed it better for the region to be ruled by kings than to be under Roman prefects sent to administer justice, who were not likely always to be present or to have armed forces with them.

Ethiopian raid on the Egyptian frontier and the consequent Roman invasion of Ethiopia in force, this buffer zone was reduced by Augustus to twelve *schoenia* (c.66 miles); in this the Romans maintained a string of military posts which successfully prevented any further violation of the southern frontier until the middle of the third century.

[148] Cf. Vol. I, § 131.

CIL, Vol. V, No. 7,231 (= Dessau, No. 94); 9/8 B.C.

This inscription is found on an arch at Segusio (Susa) in the Cottian Alps.

[Dedicated] to the Emperor Caesar Augustus, son of a god, *pontifex maximus*, holding the tribunician power for the fifteenth year, acclaimed *imperator* thirteen times, by Marcus Julius Cottius, son of King Donnus, prefect [149] of the following tribes—the Segovii, Segusini, Belacori, Caturiges, Medulli, Tebavii, Adanates, Savincates, Ecdinii, Veaminii, Venisami, Iemerii, Vesubianii, and Quadiates—and by the tribes which are under his command.

11. *Social Legislation: Fostering the Family*

In 18 B.C. Augustus launched his program of social and moral regeneration. Its goals were to restore public morality and to encourage marriage and family life, especially in the upper classes, and to assure the domination of the Italian stock in the Empire by increasing the birth rate. To these ends he enacted three laws. In the Julian Law on Curbing Adultery he took the unprecedented step of making adultery a criminal offense punishable by exile and loss of property and even sanctioned the killing of an adulterer caught in the act. The Julian Law on Classes Permitted to Marry, supplemented in A.D. 9 by the Papian-Poppaean Law, with which its provisions are frequently fused in the sources, eliminated some (but not all) class barriers to marriage, penalized celibacy, granted privileges to married people, and rewarded childbearing (see § 64). Though these laws remained on the books down to the time of Justinian and were included in his codification, their efficacy was at best limited—Juvenal (*Satires* ii. 37) called them "dormant"; Tertullian (*Apology* iv) called them "most futile." The essence of their futility lay in the fact that the moral symptoms which they attempted to abate by legislative fiat were produced by underlying socioeconomic conditions that remained unaltered. (The situation is neatly epitomized by the fact that the consuls from whom the Papian-Poppaean Law took its name were both bachelors.) The result was widespread evasion and opposition, to which the emperors responded with occasional palliatives and numerous individual dispensations.

THE SLACKENING OF THE MARRIAGE BOND

In this ode, published in 23 B.C., Horace comments on the prevalance of marital infidelity as part of the general decline of religion and morality in Roman society.

[149] Apparently Cottius had been placed in charge of these tribes with the rank of a Roman prefect. In A.D. 44 he was allowed to assume the title of king, which his father had borne.

Horace *Odes* III. vi (abridged)

Adapted from LCL

Thy father's sins, O Roman, thou though guiltless shalt expiate, till thou dost restore the crumbling temples and shrines of the gods and their statues soiled with grimy smoke. 'Tis by holding thyself the servant of the gods that thou dost rule; with them all things begin; to them ascribe the outcome! Outraged by neglect, they have visited unnumbered woes on sorrowful Italy. . . . Teeming with sin, our times have sullied first the marriage bed, our offspring, and our homes; sprung from this source, disaster's stream has overflowed the people and the fatherland. . . . The young maiden even now trains herself in coquetry and, impassioned to her finger tips, plans unholy amours. Anon she seeks young paramours at her husband's board, nor stops to choose on whom she will swiftly bestow illicit joys when lights are banished, but openly when bidden, and not without her husband's knowledge, she rises, be it some peddler summons her, or the captain of some Spanish ship, lavish purchaser of shame. . . . What do the ravages of time not injure! Our parents' age, worse than our grandsires', bore us still less worthy and destined soon to produce an offspring still more wicked.

THE JULIAN LAW ON CURBING ADULTERY

Various legal sources, collected in *ADA*, pp. 112–28 (abridged)

"No one shall hereafter commit debauchery or adultery knowingly and with malice aforethought." These words of the law apply to him who abets as well as to him who commits debauchery or adultery.

The Julian Law on Curbing Adultery punishes not only defilers of the marriages of others . . . but also the crime of debauchery when anyone without the use of force violates either a virgin or a widow of respectable character.

By the second section [of the law] a father, if he catches an adulterer of his daughter . . . in his own home or that of his son-in-law, or if the latter summons him in such an affair, is permitted to kill that adulterer with impunity, just as he may forthwith kill his daughter.

A husband also is permitted to kill an adulterer of his wife, but not anyone at all as is the father's right. For this law provides that a husband is permitted to kill [a procurer, actor, gladiator, convicted criminal, freedman, or slave] caught in the act of adultery with his wife in his own home (but not in that of his father-in-law). And it directs a husband who has killed any one of these to divorce his wife without delay. Moreover, he must make a report to the official who has jurisdiction in the place where the killing has occurred and he must divorce his wife; if he does not do this, he does not slay with impunity.

The law punishes as a procurer a husband who retains his wife after she has been caught in adultery and lets the adulterer go (for he ought to be enraged at his wife, who violated his marriage). In such a case the husband should be punished since he cannot claim the excuse of ignorance or feign patience on the pretext of not believing it.

He by whose aid or advice with malice aforethought it is made possible for a man or woman caught in adultery to evade punishment through bribe or any other collusion is condemned to the same penalty as is fixed for those who are convicted of the crime of procuring.

He who makes a profit from the adultery of his wife is scourged. . . . If a wife receives any profit from the adultery of her husband she is liable under the Julian Law as if she were an adultress. . . . Anyone who marries a woman convicted of adultery is liable under this law.

The law prescribes that when notice of divorce has been sent on suspicion of the crime of adultery, the emancipation of slaves who belong to the wife or husband or their parents is to be delayed for a space of two months, reckoned from the date of the divorce, to allow for employing examination under torture if the need arises.

It was enacted that women convicted of adultery be punished by confiscation of half of their dowry and a third of their property and by relegation to an island, and that the male adulterers be punished by like relegation to an island and by confiscation of half of their property, with the proviso that they be relegated to different islands.

THE JULIAN LAW ON CLASSES PERMITTED TO MARRY AND THE PAPIAN-POPPAEAN LAW

Suetonius *Life of Augustus* xxxiv

Among the laws which he revised or enacted were a sumptuary law and laws on adultery and chastity, on bribery, and on classes permitted to marry. The last of these he amended somewhat more severely than the others, but in the face of the clamor of opposition he was unable to push it through until he had withdrawn or mitigated some of the penalties and increased the rewards. . . . And when he saw that the intent of the law was being evaded by betrothal with immature girls and by frequent changes of wives, he shortened the duration of betrothals [150] and set a limit on divorces.

[150] He ordered that girls might not be betrothed before the age of ten, and he limited the duration of engagements to a maximum of two years. Tacitus adds (*Annals* III.

Dio Cassius *Roman History* LIV. xvi. 1–2
From LCL

He laid heavier assessments upon the unmarried men and women
and on the other hand offered prizes for marriage and the begetting of
children. And since among the nobility there were far more males than
females, he allowed all [free men] who wished, except senators, to
marry freedwomen, and ordered that their offspring should be held
legitimate.

Tacitus *Annals* III. xxv

Augustus in his old age supplemented the Julian Laws with the
Papian-Poppaean Law in order to increase the penalties on celibacy
and enrich the treasury. But people were not driven thereby to marriage and the rearing of children in any great numbers, so powerful
were the attractions of the childless state. Instead the number of persons
courting danger grew steadily greater, for every household was under-
mined by the denunciations of informers; and now the country suffered
from its laws, as it had previously suffered from its vices.

Various legal sources, collected in *ADA*, pp. 166–98 (abridged)

The Julian Law provides as follows: No one who is or shall be a
senator, or a son, grandson born of a son, or great-grandson born of a
son's son of any one of these, shall knowingly and with malice aforethought have as betrothed or wife a freedwoman or any woman who
herself or whose father or mother is or has been an actor. And no daughter of a senator or granddaughter born of a son or great-granddaughter
born of a grandson (a son's son) shall knowingly and with malice aforethought be betrothed or married to a freedman or to a man who himself
or whose father or mother is or has been an actor, and no such man shall
knowingly and with malice aforethought have her as betrothed or wife.

Freeborn men are forbidden to marry a prostitute, a procuress, a
woman manumitted by a procurer or procuress, one caught in adultery,
one convicted in a public action, or one who has been an actress.

Conditions added contrary to laws and imperial decrees or to morality—such as, "if you do not marry," or "if you have no children"—
carry no weight.

In the seventh section of the Julian Law priority in assuming the
fasces is given not to the consul who is older but to the one who has

xxviii) that the rewards offered for successful prosecution of evaders of these laws
stimulated the rise of professional spies and informers (cf. § 23).

more children than his colleague either in his power [151] or lost in war. . . . But if both are married and the fathers of the same number of children, then the time-honored practice is restored and the one who is older assumes the *fasces* first.

Persons are exempted from serving as guardians or trustees for various reasons, but generally because of their childern, whether they are in the father's power or free from his power. For anyone who has three living children in Rome, or four in Italy, or five in the provinces, can, after the example of the other compulsory public services, be exempted from serving as guardian or trustee.

No freedman who has two or more sons or daughters of his own in his power (excepting one who has been an actor or who has hired out his services to fight with animals) shall be obliged to give, do, or perform for his patron or patroness or their children services as gift or duty, or anything else which he may have sworn, promised, or bound himself to in return for his freedom.

A freedwoman who is married to her patron shall not have the right of divorce . . . as long as the patron wants her to be his wife.

A man or wife can, by virtue of marriage, inherit a tenth of the other's estate. But if they have living children from a previous marriage, in addition to the tenth which they take by virtue of marriage they receive as many tenths as the number of children. Likewise a common son or daughter lost after the day of naming adds one tenth, and two lost after the ninth day add two tenths. Besides the tenth they can receive also the usufruct of a third part of the estate, and whenever they have children the ownership of the same part.

Sometimes a man or wife can inherit the other's entire estate, for example, if both or either are not yet of the age at which the law requires children—that is, if the husband is under twenty-five and the wife under twenty; or if both have while married passed the age prescribed by the Papian Law—that is, the man sixty, the woman fifty. . . . They enjoy testamentary freedom in each other's favor if they have obtained the "right of children" from the emperor,[152] if they have a common son or daughter, or if they have lost a fourteen-year-old son or twelve-year-old daughter or two three-year-olds or three after the day of naming. . . .[153] Likewise if the wife has a child by her husband within ten months after his death she takes the whole of his estate.

Sometimes they inherit nothing from each other, that is, if they contract a marriage contrary to the Julian and Papian-Poppaean Law

[151] That is, minors or unmarried females.
[152] Cf. §§ 64, 163.   [153] Cf. § 83, second selection.

(for example if anyone marries a woman of ill repute or a senator marries a freedwoman).

Bachelors also are forbidden by the Julian Law to receive inheritances or legacies. . . . Likewise by the Papian Law childless persons, precisely because they have no children, lose one half of inheritances and legacies.

The Julian Law exempted women from marriage for one year after the death of a husband and six months after a divorce; the Papian Law [raised these to] two years after the death of a husband and a year and six months after a divorce.

In keeping with the thirty-fifth section of the Julian Law, those who without just cause prevent any children in their power from marrying or refuse to give a dowry . . . are compelled to give them in marriage and bestow dowry.

Since the [passage of the] Papian Law the portion of one who is ineligible lapses and belongs to those named in the will who have children.

If there is no one entitled to the possession of an estate, or if there is someone but he has failed to exercise his right, the estate passes to the public treasury.

12. *Social Legislation: Restrictions on Manumission and Citizenship*

In keeping with his policy of preserving and invigorating the Italian stock as a core of imperial administrators and soldiers (cf. §§ 6, 11), Augustus placed brakes on the traditional practice of granting Roman citizenship to manumitted slaves, establishing at the same time a hierarchy of status in the freedman class. For a variety of reasons there had been an extraordinarily high rate of manumissions, especially of Greeks and Orientals, in the last decades of the Republic and in the early years of the Principate. A large class of freedmen, enjoying actual but not statutory freedom, had come into being through the widespread practice of informal manumission (see § 67). By the Junian Law (probably of 17 B.C.) the status of these freedmen was regularized, but they were assigned to a new social category, that of the Junian Latins, who possessed limited civic rights with the opportunity for advancement to full citizenship. Augustus' most important measures for limiting the admission of ex-slaves into the Roman body politic were the Fufian-Caninian Law of 2 B.C., which restricted testamentary manumissions (the commonest of the formal methods of emancipating slaves), and the Aelian-Sentian Law of A.D. 4, which placed checks on the freeing of slaves during the lifetime of their masters and on the acquisition of full citizenship by freedmen. The latter statute also created a new category for freedmen of questionable character, assimilated to the *dediticii peregrini* (surrendered foreigners), who were permanently debarred from Roman citizenship and forbidden to live within one hundred miles of Rome.

THE FREEDMAN PROBLEM: A CONTEMPORARY VIEW

Dionysius of Halicarnassus *Roman Antiquities* IV. xxiv. 4–8
Adapted from LCL

Things have come to such a state of confusion and the noble traditions of the Roman commonwealth have become so debased and sullied that some who have made a fortune by robbery, housebreaking, prostitution, and every other base means, purchase their freedom with the money so acquired and straightway are Romans. Others, who have been confidants and accomplices of their masters in poisonings, murders, and crimes against the gods or the state, receive from them this reward. Some are freed so that they can receive the monthly allowance of grain given at the public expense, or any other largess distributed by the leading men to the poor among the citizens, and bring it to those who have granted them their freedom. And others owe their freedom to the levity of their masters and to their vain thirst for popularity. I, at any rate, know of some men who have allowed all their slaves to be freed after their death, so that when dead they might be called good men and their funerals might be attended by a throng of mourners wearing liberty caps [154] on their heads. . . .

Such great reproaches and disgraces hard to wipe out should not be allowed into the body politic. I should like to see the censors, preferably—or, if not they, then the consuls, for it requires some important magistracy—take this matter in hand, inquiring into those freed each year, who they are and why and how they were freed, just as they inquire into the lives of the *equites* and the senators; after which they should enroll in the tribes such of them as they find worthy of citizenship and allow them to remain in the city, but should expel from the city the foul and corrupt herd.

THE FUFIAN-CANINIAN LAW

Various legal sources, collected in *ADA*, pp. 202–5

By the Fufian-Caninian Law a limitation on manumitting slaves by will was established. A person who has more than two but not more than ten slaves is permitted to manumit up to one half of this number.

---

[154] The *pilleus*, a cap worn by emancipated slaves as a symbol of their freedom.

And a person who has more than ten but not more than thirty slaves is permitted to manumit up to one third of this number. And a person who has more than thirty but not more than one hundred is given the power of manumitting up to one fourth. Finally, a person who has more than one hundred but not more than five hundred is permitted to manumit not more than one fifth. The law takes no account of a person who has more than five hundred nor does it establish a ratio therefor, but it prescribes that no one is permitted to manumit more than one hundred. On the other hand, if anyone has only one or two slaves, he is not affected by this law, and therefore has unrestricted power of manumission.

If anyone desires to manumit by will more than the above-indicated number entails, the order [in which they are listed] shall be followed, freedom being effective only for those who were named first, up to the number entailed in the explanation outlined above. Similarly, if the names of slaves granted freedom by a will have been written in a circle, none shall be free, since no order of manumission is to be found; for the Fufian-Caninian Law nullifies what has been done to evade the law.

THE AELIAN-SENTIAN LAW

Various legal sources, collected in *ADA*, pp. 205–19 (abridged)

Under the [Aelian-Sentian] Law a master under twenty years of age is not permitted to manumit a slave in any other manner except by the rod [155] after proof of adequate cause for manumission before a council.[156]

When the emperor manumits a slave he does not apply the rod, but at his pleasure a person becomes free who is manumitted in accordance with the law of Augustus.

Moreover, the age requirement for [the manumission] of a slave was introduced by the Aelian-Sentian Law. For this law did not allow slaves under thirty to become manumitted Roman citizens in any other way except through emancipation by the rod, after proof of adequate cause for manumission before a council.

The same law provides that a slave under thirty years who has been manumitted by the rod shall not become a Roman citizen unless cause has been proved before a council . . . but it stipulates that a person manumitted by will is in the same status as if he were free with the consent of the master, and therefore he becomes a Latin.

[155] A formal method of manumission before a praetor or other competent official; cf. further introduction to § 67.
[156] The manumission councils set up by this law consisted of five senators and five *equites* in Rome and of twenty Roman citizens in the provinces, chosen by the magistrate who presided at the hearings.

In accordance with the Aelian-Sentian Law, anyone under thirty who has been manumitted and has become a Latin, if he marries either a Roman citizen or a Latin colonist or a woman of the same status as himself, and so attests with not less than seven adult Roman citizens as witnesses, and begets a child, when this child reaches the age of one the right is granted him by this law to come before a praetor, or in the provinces before the provincial governor, and prove that, in accordance with the Aelian-Sentian Law, he has married and has a one-year-old child from this marriage; and if the one before whom the case is proved finds that this is so, then the Latin himself and his wife, if she also is of the same status, and the child, if it also is of the same status, are ordained to be Roman citizens.[157]

13. *Restoration of the State Religion*

The essence of Augustus' religious policy was an "alliance of the throne and the altar." Characteristically, he restored the façade of the decaying state religion (cf. Vol. I, § 178), imposing new content upon the old forms, deftly fusing the ancestral state cult and its Hellenic incrustations with the rapidly growing ruler cult (see § 14). Oriental cults were banished from Rome; obsolete priesthoods, religious traditions, and rituals were revived; many temples were restored and new ones built (cf. § 15). Of particular significance was Augustus' elevation of the temple of Apollo on the Palatine Hill (where the imperial palace stood) to a position of importance rivaling that of Jupiter on the Capitoline. The most spectacular manifestation of Augustus' religious policy—and perhaps the most spectacular event in the entire religious history of Rome—was the epochal celebration of the *Ludi Saeculares* (Secular Games) in 17 B.C.[158] This solemn pageant, traditionally a centennial expiatory rite commemorating the end of an era, was transformed by Augustus into a thanksgiving ceremonial ushering in a new golden age, to coincide with the completion of his basic reforms.

Suetonius *Life of Augustus* xxxi. 1–4

Adapted from LCL

After he had finally assumed the office of *pontifex maximus* . . . he collected whatever prophetic writings of Greek or Latin origin were in circulation anonymously or under the names of irresponsible authors

[157] The Aelian-Sentian Law also required birth declarations; for examples see §154, third and fourth selections.
[158] The Secular Games, last celebrated in 146 B.C., were not held in 46 because of the civil war. By the convenient discovery of an oracle certifying that the last games had occurred in 126 B.C., coupled with the learned advice of Ateius Capito, an eminent jurist and expert on religious law, that the ancient Etruscan *saeculum* (century) was 110 years, the year 17 B.C. was more or less harmonized with the tradition of a centennial celebration.

and burned more than 2,000 of them, retaining only the Sibylline Books and making a selection even among these; and he deposited them in two gilded cases under the pedestal of the Palatine Apollo. . . .[159] He increased the number and prestige of the priests and also their privileges, in particular those of the Vestal Virgins. Moreover, when there was occasion to choose another Vestal in place of one who had died, and when many used all their influence to avoid submitting their daughters to the hazard of the lot, he solemnly swore that if anyone of his granddaughters were of eligible age he would have proposed her name. He also revived some of the ancient rites which had gradually fallen into disuse, such as the augury of safety,[160] the office of the *flamen Dialis*,[161] the ceremonies of the Lupercalia, the Secular Games, and the festival of the crossroads.[162] At the Lupercalia he forbade beardless youths to join in the running, and at the Secular Games he would not allow young people of either sex to attend any entertainment by night except in the company of some adult relative. He ordained that the protecting deities of the crossroads should be decorated with flowers twice a year, in spring and summer.[163]

THE SECULAR GAMES

This huge marble inscription contains the official records of the board of fifteen for performing sacrifices, headed by Augustus and Agrippa, which conducted the Secular Games of 17 B.C. The beginning of the inscription is lost. Of the extant portion, lines 1–49, too fragmentary to warrant translation, contain a letter of Augustus to the board of fifteen informing it of the dates and the arrangements to be made for the celebration, and a series of edicts by the board to the populace announcing the celebration and informing it of arrangements for the distribution of purificatory materials, the offering of first-fruits, and the games, festivals, and sacred banquets to be presented. Next are recorded the two following decrees of the senate.

[159] Augustus thus transferred the sacred oracular books from the temple of Jupiter on the Capitol, where they had been stored during the Republic (cf. Vol. I, § 52), to the shrine of the "imperial" god.
[160] An ancient augural ceremony conducted annually in times of peace to determine whether it was proper to pray for the safety of the Roman people.
[161] Because of the numerous taboos imposed upon this priest of Jupiter (see Vol. I, § 49) no one could be found to fill this office between 87 and 11 B.C.
[162] This festival (*Compitalia*) of the lower classes of Rome, held at street corner shrines (cf. § 54, first selection), had been abolished by Caesar (cf. Vol. I, p. 288, Note 116). On the Lupercalia see Vol. I, p. 480.
[163] This revived cult (cf. Chapter IV, Note 2) was associated henceforth with the imperial cult.

CIL, Vol. VI, No. 32,323, lines 50–63, 90–168 (= FIRA, Vol. I, No. 40
= Dessau, No. 5,050)

May 23, in the Julian Voting Hall.[164]. . . Present at the writing
were . . . Aemilius Lepidus, Lucius Cestius, and Lucius Petronius
Rufus. . . .

Whereas the consul Gaius Silanus reported that after a lapse of
many years the Secular Games would be celebrated in the present year
under the direction of the Emperor Caesar Augustus and Marcus
Agrippa,[165] holders of the tribunician power, and that, because as many
as possible ought to view these games out of religious duty and also because no one will attend such a spectacle again,[166] it seemed proper to
permit . . . those who were not yet married to be present with impunity on the days of these games; and whereas he asked the senate what
it was pleased to do in the matter, concerning this matter the senate
decreed as follows: Since these games have been ordained for religious
purposes and since it is not granted to any mortal to view them more
than once . . . those who are liable under the Law on Classes Permitted
to Marry [167] shall be permitted to view with impunity the games which
the masters of the board of fifteen for performing sacrifices will present.

And on the same day in the same place, the same were present at
the writing, and the following decree of the senate was passed.

Whereas the consul Gaius Silanus declared that it was appropriate
for the preservation of the memory of this great benevolence of the
gods that a record of the Secular Games be inscribed on a bronze and
on a marble column, both to be erected for the future remembrance of
the event in the place where the games would be held, and asked the
senate what it was pleased to do in the matter, concerning this matter
the senate decreed as follows: The consuls, one or both, for the future
remembrance of the event shall erect in that place a column of bronze
and a second of marble on which a record of these games has been inscribed, and they shall likewise contract for this work and shall order
the praetors who are in charge of the treasury [168] to pay to the contractors the sum for which they have contracted.

[164] Planned by Julius Caesar, this enormous structure was completed by Augustus
and Agrippa in 26 B.C. With the obsolescence of the popular assemblies in the early
Empire, it was converted to other uses, such as meetings and shows.
[165] Cf. § 2, paragraph 22.   [166] That is, during the lifetime of that generation.
[167] See § 11. Unmarried men and women were forbidden by this law to attend public
spectacles.
[168] In 23 B.C. Augustus transferred the management of the public treasury from the
quaestors, who were usually relatively young men near the beginning of their public
careers, to two of the annual praetors, who would be men of greater experience in
public office.

[Lines 64–75 record another edict of the board, dated May 25, clarifying details of the participation of the populace in the celebration; lines 76–89 describe the distribution of purificatory materials and the offering of first-fruits on May 26–31.]

On the following night [169] in the Campus Martius near the Tiber the Emperor Caesar Augustus sacrificed to the Fates according to the Greek rite [170] nine ewes as whole burnt offerings, and by the same rite nine female goats, and he uttered the following prayer:

"O Fates! As it has been prescribed for ye in those books [171]—and by virtue of this may every good fortune come to the Roman people, the Quirites—let sacrifice be made to ye with nine ewes and nine female goats. I beseech and pray ye, just as ye have increased the empire and majesty of the Roman people, the Quirites, in war and in peace, so may the Latins ever be obedient; grant everlasting safety, victory, and health to the Roman people, the Quirites; protect the Roman people, the Quirites, and the legions of the Roman people, the Quirites, and keep safe and sound the state of the Roman people, the Quirites; be favorable and propitious to the Roman people, the Quirites, to the board of fifteen, to me, to my house and my household; and deign to accept this sacrifice of nine ewes and nine female goats, perfect for sacrificing. To these ends be ye honored by the sacrifice of this ewe,[172] become ye favorable and propitious to the Roman people, the Quirites, to the board of fifteen, to me, to my house and my household." [173]

After the sacrifice was completed, the presentation of plays was begun at night on a stage without the addition of a theater and without setting up seats; [174] and 110 matrons,[175] who had been designated by the board of fifteen, held *sellisternia*,[176] setting up two seats for Juno and Diana.

On June 1 in the Capitol the Emperor Caesar Augustus sacrificed a perfect bull to Jupiter Best and Greatest, and in the same place Marcus

---

[169] May 31. Our translation of the remainder of this inscription incorporates restorations based on the similar text in § 167.

[170] So conducted since the ceremony was ordained by a Sibylline oracle (cf. Vol. I, §§ 52–53), which has been preserved (see Zosimus *New History* II. vi). In the inscription the Fates are called by their Greek name.

[171] The Sibylline Books.

[172] Roman formalism would require the repetition of the prayer for each animal sacrificed.

[173] For earlier examples of this archaic formula, see Vol. I, § 54 and p. 150.

[174] This was the ancient Roman custom before the erection of formal theaters under Greek influence.

[175] One for each year of the Etruscan *saeculum* (cf. Note 158).

[176] Sacred banquets for female divinities at which their images were seated on chairs. For the similar *lectisternium*, at which images of the gods were placed on couches, see Vol. I, p. 142.

Agrippa sacrificed another, and they uttered the following prayer:

"O Jupiter Best and Greatest! As it has been prescribed for thee in those books—and by virtue of this may every good fortune come to the Roman people, the Quirites—let sacrifice be made to thee with this splendid bull. I beseech and pray thee," the rest as above.

At the sacral vessel were Caesar, Agrippa, Scaevola, Sentius, Lollius, Asinius Gallus, Rebilus.[177]

Then the presentation of Latin plays was begun in a wooden theater, which had been erected in the Campus Martius along the Tiber; and the mothers of families held *sellisternia* in the same manner; and the theatrical performances which had been begun at night were not interrupted.

[Lines 110–14 contain an edict of the board ordering a suspension of mourning during the celebration.]

Further, at night near the Tiber the Emperor Caesar Augustus made a sacrifice to the *Ilithyiae* [178] of nine sacrificial cakes, nine *popana*, and nine *phthoes* [179] and uttered the following prayer:

"O *Ilithyia!* As it has been prescribed for thee in those books— and by virtue of this may every good fortune come to the Roman people, the Quirites—let sacrifice be made to thee with nine *popana*, nine sacrificial cakes, and nine *phthoes*. I beseech and pray thee," the rest as above.

On June 2 in the Capitol the Emperor Caesar Augustus sacrificed a cow to Queen Juno, and in the same place Marcus Agrippa sacrificed another, and he uttered the following prayer:

"O Queen Juno! As it has been prescribed for thee in those books —and by virtue of this may every good fortune come to the Roman people, the Quirites—let sacrifice be made to thee with a splendid cow. I beseech and pray thee," the rest as above.

Then Marcus Agrippa[?] led the 110 married mothers of families who had been designated by the board of fifteen [?] in the following prayer:

"O Queen Juno! If there be any better fortune that may come to the Roman people, the Quirites . . . we married mothers of families on bended knees beseech and pray [?] thee . . . just as thou hast increased the empire and majesty of the Roman people, the Quirites, in war and in peace, so may the Latins ever be obedient; grant everlasting

[177] Members of the board of fifteen, which had at least twenty-one members at this time. The college had been enlarged in keeping with Augustus' policy of increasing the number of priesthoods.
[178] Greek goddesses of childbirth.
[179] Both of these were special sacrificial cakes of Greek origin.

safety, victory, and health to the Roman people, the Quirites; protect the Roman people, the Quirites, and the legions of the Roman people, the Quirites, and keep safe and sound the state of the Roman people, the Quirites; be favorable and propitious to the Roman people, the Quirites, to the board of fifteen for performing sacrifices, to us. . . . This we 110 married mothers of families of the Roman people, the Quirites, on bended knees beseech and pray of thee. . . ."

Further, at night near the Tiber the Emperor Caesar Augustus sacrificed a pregnant sow . . . to Mother Earth and uttered the following prayer:

"O Mother Earth! As it has been prescribed for thee in those books —and by virtue of this may every good fortune come to the Roman people, the Quirites—let sacrifice be made to thee . . . with a perfect pregnant sow. I beseech and pray thee," the rest as above.

The matrons held *sellisternia* on this day in the same manner as on the previous day.

On June 3 on the Palatine the Emperor Caesar Augustus and Marcus Agrippa offered sacrifice to Apollo and Diana with nine sacrificial cakes, nine *popana*, and nine *phthoes*, and they uttered the following prayer:

"O Apollo! As it has been prescribed for thee in those books— and by virtue of this may every good fortune come to the Roman people, the Quirites—let sacrifice be made to thee with nine *popana*, nine sacrificial cakes, and nine *phthoes*. I beseech and pray thee," the rest as above. "O Apollo! Just as I have offered thee *popana* and have uttered the proper prayer, to this same end be thou honored by the offering of these sacrificial cakes and become favorable and propitious." Likewise with the *phthoes*. [Prayer] to Diana with the same words.

And when the sacrifice was completed, twenty-seven previously designated boys and the same number of girls, with both parents living, sang a hymn,[180] and in the same manner in the Capitol. The hymn was composed by Quintus Horatius Flaccus.[181]. . .

When the theatrical performances had ended at the . . . hour near the place where the sacrifice had been offered on the previous nights and where the theater and stage had been erected, turn posts were set up and chariot races were presented, and Potitus Messalla presented trick riders.

And an edict was issued as follows:

"The board of fifteen for performing sacrifices declares: We have supplemented the customary games with seven days of additional games,

---

180 On the Palatine Hill.
181 The famous Secular Hymn by Horace is extant.

commencing on June 5: Latin plays in the wooden theater which is near the Tiber, at the second hour; Greek informal shows in the theater of Pompey, at the third hour; Greek stage plays in the theater which is in the Circus Flaminius,[182] at the fourth hour. . . ."

On June 11 an edict was issued as follows: "The board of fifteen for performing sacrifices declares: On June 12 we shall present an animal hunt in . . . and circus games.[183]. . ."

All these celebrations were conducted by the board of fifteen for performing sacrifices: the Emperor Caesar Augustus, Marcus Agrippa . . . Gnaeus Pompey, Gaius Stolo, Gaius S. . . , Marcus Marcellus. . . . [The rest is lost.]

14. *Emperor Worship*

The Principate brought with it an important new element in Roman religion —emperor worship. This institution endured in the form in which Augustus organized it as long as the Principate itself (cf. § 168). In the eastern provinces Augustus was naturally regarded as the successor of the divine monarchs of the Oriental and Hellenistic dynasties. Alive to the centralizing and unifying force of this bond of devotion to the reigning house, Augustus sanctioned the continuance of the ruler cult in the East by a series of *ad hoc* directives and fostered its spread in the West in a modified form which would not clash with Roman religious tradition. When the passage of time had brought familiarity and acceptance, he was able, as *pontifex maximus* in 13/12 B.C., to organize the imperial cult as part of the state worship. In Italy and the West the imperial cult was fitted into Roman tradition by being devoted not to the living emperor, but to his *genius,* or tutelary spirit; the emperor himself, after the precedent of Julius Caesar, was deified after death (cf. § 17). In the Greek-speaking provinces, on the other hand, Augustus himself was worshipped as a god—commonly in association with the goddess Roma— from the very beginning of his sole rule. "The different forms which the worship of Augustus took in Rome, Italy and the provinces illustrate the different aspects of his rule—he is Princeps to the Senate, Imperator to army and people, King and God to the subject peoples of the Empire" (R. Syme, *The Roman Revolution* [Oxford, 1939], p. 475).

Dio Cassius *Roman History* LI. XX. 6–8
Adapted from LCL

Octavian meanwhile, besides attending to the general business, gave permission for sacred precincts to Rome and to his father Caesar, whom

[182] That is, the theater of Marcellus, which was, however, not fully completed until some years later.
[183] That is, chariot races.

he named the hero Julius,[184] to be dedicated in Ephesus and Nicaea. (These cities had at that time attained chief place in Asia and Bithynia, respectively.) And he ordered the Romans resident in these cities to pay honor to these divinities. But the aliens, whom he styled Hellenes, he allowed to consecrate certain precincts to himself—the Asians in Pergamum, the Bithynians in Nicomedia. This practice, beginning under him, has continued under other emperors not only among the Hellenic peoples but also among all the others subject to the Romans. For in the capital itself and in the rest of Italy no emperor, however worthy of renown, has dared to do this; still, even there various divine honors are bestowed after their death upon such emperors as have ruled uprightly, and in fact shrines are even built to them.

NARBO HONORS AUGUSTUS' BIRTHDAY

Altars were erected to the divine spirit (*numen, genius*) of Augustus in various places in Italy and the western provinces. The altar at Narbonne, in southern France, contains two inscriptions, the first celebrating the erection of the altar in A.D. 11, the second its formal dedication in 12/13. The altar is stated to have been erected in gratitude for Augustus' reconciliation of some local class dispute about which no details are given.

CIL, Vol. XII, No. 4,333 (= Dessau, No. 112)

i

In the consulship of Titus Statilius Taurus and Lucius Cassius Longinus, September 22. Vow taken to the divine spirit of Augustus by the populace of the Narbonensians in perpetuity: "May it be good, favorable, and auspicious to the Emperor Caesar Augustus, son of a god, father of his country, *pontifex maximus*, holding the tribunician power for the thirty-fourth year; to his wife, children, and house; to the Roman senate and people; and to the colonists and residents of the Colonia Julia Paterna of Narbo Martius, who have bound themselves to worship his divine spirit in perpetuity!"

The populace of the Narbonensians has erected in the forum at Narbo an altar at which every year on September 23—the day on which the good fortune of the age bore him to be ruler of the world—three Roman *equites* from the populace [185] and three freedmen shall sacrifice one animal each [186] and shall at their own expense on that day provide the colonists and residents with incense and wine for supplication to his

184 In Latin *Divus Julius* (the deified Julius). The time is 29 B.C.
185 That is, not members of the local senate.
186 The animals sacrificed to the *genius* of the emperor were bulls (the characteristic sacrifice to Jupiter, most solemn and most expensive of the sacrifices).

divine spirit. And on September 24 [187] they shall likewise provide incense and wine for the colonists and residents. Also on January 1 they shall provide incense and wine for the colonists and residents. Also on January 7, the day on which he first entered upon the command of the world,[188] they shall make supplication with incense and wine, and shall sacrifice one animal each, and shall provide incense and wine for the colonists and residents on that day. And on May 31, because on that day in the consulship of Titus Statilius Taurus and Manius Aemilius Lepidus [189] he reconciled the populace to the decurions, they shall sacrifice one animal each and shall provide the colonists and residents with incense and wine for supplication to his divine spirit. And of these three Roman *equites* and three freedmen one. . . . [The rest of this inscription is lost.]

ii

The populace of Narbo has dedicated the altar of the divine spirit of Augustus . . . under the regulations recorded below.

"O divine spirit of Caesar Augustus, father of his country! When this day I give and dedicate this altar to you, I shall give and dedicate it under such regulations and such rules as I shall here this day publicly declare to be the groundwork both of this altar and of its inscriptions: If anyone wishes to clean, decorate, or repair it as a voluntary service, it shall be lawful and permissible.[190] If anyone sacrifices an animal without making the customary additional offering, it shall nevertheless be accounted properly done. If anyone wishes to donate a gift to this altar or honor it, he shall be permitted, and the same regulation as applies to the altar shall apply to such gift. The other regulations for this altar and its inscriptions shall be the same as those for the altar of Diana on the Aventine Hill. Under these regulations and these rules, just as I have stated, on behalf of the Emperor Caesar Augustus, father of his country, *pontifex maximus*, holding the tribunician power for the thirty-fifth year; of his wife, children, and house; of the Roman senate and people;

---

[187] The birthday of Augustus was regularly celebrated for two days: cf. "Calendar of Holidays" below (pp. 65–66). The *genius* was associated with a Roman from birth and was especially honored on his birthday.

[188] Cf. *ibid*.

[189] A.D. 11. Lepidus, consul during the first part of the year, was replaced by Longinus, who is cited at the beginning of the inscription. Since the consulship was largely an honorary office under the Empire, the emperors frequently resorted to this practice of appointing several consuls, each to hold office for part of a year, as a means of (1) rewarding more men with this honor, and (2) providing the requisite number of men of consular rank to fill the high administrative posts.

[190] The Latin phrase *ius fas* means that something is in accordance with the laws of man and the dictates of religion, respectively.

and of the colonists and residents of the Colonia Julia Paterna of Narbo Martius, who have bound themselves to worship his divine spirit in perpetuity, I give and dedicate this altar to you that you may be favorably and kindly disposed."

ASIA HONORS AUGUSTUS' BIRTHDAY

Beginning in 29 B.C. in the eastern provinces and in 12 B.C. in the West, Augustus authorized the establishment of provincial assemblies. These bodies, organized on a representative basis, possessed no legislative, judicial, or administrative powers. Annual meetings were held at which the principal business was the maintenance of the imperial cult, review of the administration of the governor and procurators, and appeals to the emperor on behalf of the entire province. The following decree was passed (probably in 9 B.C.) by the league of the Greek cities in the province of Asia in response to a letter from the governor suggesting that it would be a suitable token of their gratitude for Augustus' many benefactions if they adopted his birthday as their New Year's Day. To accomplish this the cities had to realign their Macedonian lunar months in conformity with the Julian solar calendar.

OGIS, No. 458, lines 30–62 (= Ehrenberg-Jones, No. 98)

It was decreed by the Greeks in the province of Asia, on motion of the high priest Apollonius son of Menophilus, of Azanium: Whereas the providence which divinely ordered our lives created with zeal and munificence the most perfect good for our lives by producing Augustus and filling him with virtue for the benefaction of mankind, blessing us and those after us with a savior who put an end to war and established peace; and whereas Caesar when he appeared exceeded the hopes of all who had anticipated good tidings, not only surpassing the benefactors born before him but not even leaving those to come any hope of surpassing him; and whereas the birthday of the god marked for the world the beginning of the good tidings through his coming, and [the cities of] Asia decreed in Smyrna, when Lucius Volcacius Tullus was high priest and Papias was secretary, that a crown be awarded to the one suggesting the greatest honors for the god; and whereas Paullus Fabius Maximus, proconsul of the province sent for its preservation by that god's right hand and purpose,[191] benefited the province with his own suggestions—the extent of which benefactions no one could succeed in telling adequately—and suggested for the honor of Augustus a thing

[191] In his equally fulsome letter which evoked this decree, the governor speaks of Augustus' coming as, *inter al.*, marking "the end of men's regretting that they had been born." Similarly, the city of Myra in Lycia hailed him as "the god Augustus Caesar, son of a god, ruler of land and sea, benefactor and savior of the whole world" (*IGRR*, Vol. III, No. 719). Augustus' reorganization of provincial administration (§ 8) had eliminated, if not all, at least the grossest of the abuses of Republican times.

hitherto unknown by the Greeks, namely, beginning their calendar with the god's nativity;

Therefore—may Good Fortune and Safety attend!—it has been decreed by the Greeks in the province of Asia that the New Year shall begin in all the cities on September 23, which is the birthday of Augustus; that, to be sure that the day corresponds in every city, they use also the Greek date along wih the Roman date; that the first month—named Caesar, as previously decreed—be reckoned beginning with September 23, the birthday of Caesar; that the crown decreed for the one suggesting the greatest honors in behalf of Caesar be given to the proconsul Maximus, and that he also be proclaimed in these words at every celebration of the athletic games held at Pergamum in honor of Rome and Augustus: "Asia crowns Paullus Fabius Maximus for having most piously invented the honors for Caesar;" that he be proclaimed in like manner also at the games held in the city in honor of Caesar; that the communication of the proconsul and the decree of Asia be inscribed on a stele of white marble, which is to be set up in the sacred precinct of Rome and Augustus [in Pergamum]; and that the public advocates for the year shall see to it that in the leading cities of the assize districts the communication of Maximus and the decree of Asia are inscribed on steles of white marble, and that these steles are set up in the temples of Caesar.

THE MONTH AUGUST

This decree of the senate, changing the name of the month Sextilis to Augustus, was passed in 27 B.C., but the honor was not officially accepted by the emperor until 8 B.C., when he made some necessary adjustments in the calendar.

Macrobius *Saturnalia* I. xii. 35 (= *FIRA*, Vol. I, No. 42)

"Whereas in the month Sextilis the Emperor Caesar Augustus entered upon his first consulship and conducted three triumphs into the city, and the legions were brought down from the Janiculum and served under his aegis and oath, and also in this month Egypt was brought into the power of the Roman people, and in this month an end was put to the civil wars; and whereas for these reasons this month is and has been most fortunate for this Empire, the senate decreed that this month be named August." Likewise a plebiscite was passed on the same subject on motion of Sextus Pacuvius, tribune of the plebs.

CALENDAR OF HOLIDAYS

Fragments are extant from some twenty different calendars of Augustan festivals. The following calendar comes from Cumae in Italy and dates probably from some time after A.D. 4. Its list of holidays is representative, not comprehensive; many others are recorded in other *fasti*. Cities often honored Augustus by making the day of his visit their New Year, and this may be the reason why this calendar begins in August.

CIL, Vol. X, No. 8,375 (= Dessau, No. 108)

August 19. On this day [in 43 B.C.] Caesar entered upon his first consulship. Thanksgiving.

September . . .[192] On this day [in 36 B.C.] the army of Lepidus surrendered to Caesar. Thanksgiving.

September 23 and 24. Birthday of Caesar [63 B.C.]. Sacrifice of an animal to Caesar. Thanksgiving.

October 7. Birthday of Drusus Caesar [15/11 B.C.]. Thanksgiving to Vesta.

October 18.[193] On this day [in 48 B.C.?] Caesar assumed the toga of manhood. Thanksgiving to Hope and Youth.

November 16. Birthday of Tiberius Caesar [42 B.C.]. Thanksgiving to Vesta.

December 15. On this day [in 19 B.C.] the altar of Fortune the Homebringer, who brought Caesar back from the overseas provinces, was dedicated. Thanksgiving to Fortune the Home-bringer.

January 7. On this day [in 43 B.C.] Caesar first assumed the *fasces*. Thanksgiving to Jupiter the Eternal.

January 16. On this day [in 27 B.C.] Caesar was named Augustus. Thanksgiving to Augustus.

January 30. On this day [in 9 B.C.] the altar of the Augustan Peace was dedicated. Thanksgiving to the sovereignty of Caesar Augustus, guardian of the Roman citizens and of the world.

March 6. On this day [in 12 B.C.] Caesar was elected *pontifex maximus*. Thanksgiving to Vesta and to the public household gods of the Roman people, the Quirites.

April 14. On this day [in 43 B.C.] Caesar won his first military victory. Thanksgiving to Augustan Victory.

April 16. On this day [in 43 B.C.] Caesar was first acclaimed *imperator*. Thanksgiving to the Good Fortune of his rule.

May 12. On this day [in 19 B.C.] the temple of Mars was dedicated. Thanksgiving to the Labors of Mars.

May 24. Birthday of Germanicus Caesar [15 B.C.]. Thanksgiving to Vesta.

[192] Some day between the 4th and the 22d.
[193] Or 19th.

July 12. Birthday of the deified Julius [Caesar. 100 B.C.]. Thanksgiving
to Jupiter, to Mars the Avenger, and to Venus the Procreator.
[The rest of the inscription is too fragmentary for restoration.]

15. *Public Works*

On Augustus' public works see § 2, paragraphs 19–21. The construction of
public works at their own expense was a traditional practice of prominent
citizens under the Republic. Augustus, actively assisted by his associates
(notably Agrippa), carried on this tradition with unprecedented splendor
and munificence. He thereby established a precedent for future emperors, who
bestowed innumerable adornments and improvements—aqueducts, harbors,
temples, colonnades, streets, markets, arches, etc. (many of them still standing)—upon the city of Rome, Italy, and the provinces (cf. also § 39).

VITRUVIUS' DEDICATION TO AUGUSTUS

Vitruvius *Architecture* I. Preface 2–3
From LCL

I observed that you cared not only about the common life of men
and the constitution of the state but also about the provision of suitable
buildings; so that the state was not only made greater through you by
its new provinces, but the majesty of the empire also was expressed
through the eminent dignity of its public buildings. Hence I conceived
that the opportunity should be taken at once of bringing before you
my proposals about such things. . . .

Since, then, I was indebted to you for such benefits that to the end
of my life I had no fear of poverty, I set about the composition of this
work for you. For I perceived that you have built, and are now building, on a large scale. Furthermore, with respect to the future, you have
such regard to public and private buildings that they will correspond
to the grandeur of our history, and will be a memorial to future ages.

"A CITY OF MARBLE"

Suetonius *Life of Augustus* xxviii. 3–xxx. 2
Adapted from LCL

Since the city was not adorned as befitted the majesty of the empire
and was exposed to flood and fire, he so beautified it that he could justly
boast that he had found it a city of brick and left it a city of marble.[194]

[194] This is, of course, a rhetorical exaggeration.

and he certainly made it safe for the future, so far as human foresight could provide.

He erected many public works, foremost among them the following: his Forum, with the Temple of Mars the Avenger; the Sanctuary of Apollo on the Palatine; and the Temple of Jupiter the Thunderer on the Capitol. His reason for building the Forum was the increase in the number of people and lawsuits, which seemed to call for still a third Forum, since two [195] were no longer adequate. . . . He vowed the Temple of Mars when he undertook the war of Philippi to avenge his father; accordingly, he decreed that in it the senate should deliberate on wars and requests for triumphs, from it men on their way to the provinces with military commands should be escorted, and to it victors on their return should bring the tokens of their triumphs. He erected the Sanctuary of Apollo in that part of his abode on the Palatine for which the soothsayers declared that the god had shown his desire by striking it with lightning; and he joined to it colonnades with Latin and Greek libraries, and when he was getting to be an old man it was there that he often held meetings of the senate or certified the panels of jurors. He dedicated the temple to Jupiter the Thunderer because of a narrow escape; for on his Cantabrian expedition during a march by night a flash of lighting grazed his litter and struck dead the slave who was lighting the way. He constructed some works too in the name of others—his grandsons, his wife, and his sister—such as the colonnade and basilica of Gaius and Lucius, the colonnades of Livia and Octavia, and the theater of Marcellus. More than that, he often urged other prominent men to adorn the city with new monuments or to restore and embellish old ones, each according to his means. And many works were erected at that time by many men: for example, the Temple of Hercules and the Muses by Marcius Philippus, the Temple of Diana by Lucius Cornificius, the Hall of Liberty by Asinius Pollio, the Temple of Saturn by Munatius Plancus, a theater by Cornelius Balbus, an amphitheater by Statilius Taurus, and by Marcus Agrippa in particular many magnificent structures.

He divided the area of the city into districts and neighborhoods and arranged that the former should be under the charge of annual magistrates selected by lot and the latter under captains elected by the people of the respective neighborhoods. To guard against fires he devised a system of stations of night watchmen,[196] and to control the floods he widened and cleared out the bed of the Tiber, which had for some time been filled with rubbish and narrowed by jutting buildings. Further, to make the approach to the city easier from every direction, he per-

[195] That is, the original Roman Forum and the adjacent Forum of Julius Caesar.
[196] See § 5.

sonally undertook to rebuild the Flaminian Road as far as Ariminum and assigned the rest of the highways to men who had been honored with triumphs to pave out of their spoils money.

He restored sacred edifices which had gone to ruin through lapse of time or had been destroyed by fire and adorned both these and the other temples with most lavish gifts; for example, in a single donation he deposited in the shrine of Jupiter Capitolinus 16,000 pounds of gold and precious stones and pearls worth 50,000,000 sesterces.

THE ADMINISTRATION OF THE AQUEDUCTS

Frontinus *The Water Supply of Rome* II. xcviii–cxxix (abridged)

First Marcus Agrippa, after his aedileship (which he held after his consulship), served as a sort of permanent commissioner of works and services which he himself had created.[197] Inasmuch as the available supply now warranted it, he determined how much water should be allotted to the public structures, how much to the collection basins, and how much to private consumers. He also kept his own private gang of slaves for the maintenance of the aqueducts, reservoirs, and collection basins. This gang was given to the state as its property by Augustus, who had inherited it from Agrippa.

After him, in the consulship of Quintus Aelius Tubero and Paullus Fabius Maximus,[198] decrees of the senate were passed and a law was promulgated on this subject. . . . Augustus also subsumed in an edict the rights to be enjoyed by those drawing water according to Agrippa's records, thus making the whole matter subject to his own grants. . . . For the maintenance and operation of the whole system he named Messala Corvinus commissioner, and gave him as assistants Postumius Sulpicius, an ex-praetor, and Lucius Cominius, a junior senator. They were allowed to wear regalia as though magistrates, and concerning their duties the following decree of the senate was passed:

"Whereas the consuls, Quintus Aelius Tubero and Paullus Fabius Maximus, spoke concerning the duties and privileges of the water commissioners appointed with the approval of the senate by Augustus Caesar, and asked the senate what it was pleased to do in the matter;

"Concerning this matter the senate decreed as follows: that it is

---

[197] In 33 B.C. Agrippa undertook the aedileship in order to help win over the Roman populace to the side of Octavian against Antony. Among his vast expenditures of that year (cf. Vol. I, § 172), he repaired and enlarged the water supply of Rome. Thereafter, Agrippa maintained unofficial supervision of the Roman aqueducts until his death in 12 B.C. The office of commissioner of water supply was created the following year (cf. the next paragraph); some of the pertinent legislation of that year is cited below.

[198] 11 B.C.

the pleasure of this body that those who are in charge of the public water supply, when they go outside the city in discharge of their duties, shall have each of them two lictors, three public slaves, and an architect, and the same number of secretaries, clerks, assistants, and criers as those who direct the distribution of grain to the people; that when they have business inside the city on the same duties they shall make use of all the same attendants except the lictors; that the water commissioners shall submit to the treasury the list of attendants granted them by this decree of the senate within ten days of its passage, and to those whose names are thus submitted the praetors of the treasury [199] shall grant and assign, as compensation, as much food per year as the commissioners of the grain distribution customarily give and allot, and they shall be authorized to draw money for that purpose without prejudice to themselves; that the consuls, Quintus Aelius and Paullus Fabius, both or either as they deem best, shall with the assistance of the praetors in charge of the treasury contract for the furnishing to the commissioners of tablets, paper, and everything else necessary for the exercise of their office; and further that, inasmuch as the commissioners of thoroughfares and of grain distribution discharge their public duties for a fourth of the year, the water commissioners shall be exempted [for a like period] from legal proceedings, private or public." . . .

I shall now indicate what the water commissioner must attend to, and the law and decrees of the senate which serve to establish his procedures. With regard to the right of drawing water in private establishments he must see that no one draws water without a written authorization from Caesar—that is, that no one draws public water which he has not been authorized to and that no one draws more than he has been authorized to. . . . He must exercise great vigilance against manifold forms of fraud. The channels outside the city must be frequently inspected with great care to check on the granted quantities. The same must be done in the case of the reservoirs and the public fountains, so that the water may flow day and night without interruption. . . .

The right to granted water does not pass [automatically] to an heir, a buyer, or any new owner of the property. But public baths long ago received the privilege that water once granted them should remain theirs in perpetuity. . . .

No one doubts, I am sure, that the aqueducts nearest the city—that is, the last seven miles, which are built of squared-stone masonry—must be especially protected, both because they are structures of the greatest magnitude and because each one carries several water courses. If it is ever necessary to interrupt these, they will deprive the city of the

[199] Cf. Note 168.

greater part of its water supply. But there are remedies even for this difficulty: a temporary structure is built up to the level of the inoperative aqueduct and a channel made of lead troughs is connected to bypass the interrupted section. . . .

Very often, moreover, damages arise from illegal acts of property owners who injure the channels in numerous ways. In the first place, they obstruct the space around the aqueducts, which by decree of the senate is to be kept clear, with buildings or trees (the trees do the greater damage, because their roots break apart the vaultings and the sides). Again, they run local and country roads right over the aqueducts themselves. Finally, they shut off access for maintenance and repairs. All such acts have been provided against in the following decree of the senate:

"Whereas the consuls, Quintus Aelius Tubero and Paullus Fabius Maximus, observed that the routes of the aqueducts coming into the city were being obstructed with tombs and buildings and planted with trees, and asked the senate what it was pleased to do;

"Concerning this matter the senate decreed as follows: That, since encumbrances damage the public aqueducts and obstruct the repair of channels and conduits,[200] it is the pleasure of the senate that about the springings, arches, and walls a space of fifteen feet shall be left clear on both sides, and about the underground channels and conduits inside the limits of the city and the buildings adjoining the city a space of five feet on both sides; that hereafter no tomb or building may be erected in these places, and no trees planted; and that if there are now any trees within this space they shall be cut down, excepting any immediately adjacent to a country house or enclosed inside buildings. If anyone acts contrary to these provisions the fine for each infraction shall be 10,000 sesterces, of which one half shall be given as a reward to the accuser whose efforts are chiefly responsible for obtaining the conviction of the person acting contrary to this decree of the senate, and the other half shall be paid into the public treasury; and the water commissioners shall hold court and render judgment in such cases." . . .

[The six decrees of the senate of 11 B.C. were supplemented two years later by the Quinctian Law, which provided in part:] "Whoever after the passage of this law intentionally and maliciously pierces or breaks or is responsible for piercing or breaking the channels, conduits, arches, pipes, tubes, reservoirs, or collection basins of the public waters which are brought into the city, or who does other damage so as

---

[200] The text is corrupt here; our translation renders the apparent general sense. Another decree of the senate of the same year (quoted by Frontinus II. cxxv) mentions that Augustus, following Agrippa's example, undertook to defray the cost of aqueduct repairs from his privy purse (cf. § 2, paragraph 20).

to prevent the said waters or any portion thereof from going, falling, flowing, reaching, or being brought into the city of Rome or so as to prevent their free flow, distribution, allotment, or discharge into reservoirs or collection basins in the city of Rome or in places or buildings which are or may in the future be adjacent to the city or in gardens, estates, or grounds to whose owners or possessors water has been or shall be given or granted, shall be condemned to pay a fine of 100,000 sesterces to the Roman people. In addition, anyone who maliciously does any of these things shall be condemned to repair, restore, reestablish, build, erect, or promptly remove it all [as the case may be] in good faith and all in such manner as the water commissioner orders.[201] Whoever is or shall be water commissioner, or if there is no water commissioner then the praetor who handles disputes between citizens and aliens, shall compel or constrain [the offender] by fine or bond, and the said commissioner, or in the event that there is no commissioner then the said praetor, shall have the right and power of compelling, constraining, fixing fine, or accepting bond. If a slave does any of these things, his master shall be condemned to pay 100,000 sesterces to the Roman people."

[The remainder of the law is concerned with preventing the obstruction of the aqueduct rights of way and subjects violators to the same fine (100,000 sesterces) as those guilty of wilful damage.]

16. *Provision for the Succession*

Augustus' carefully laid plans to hand on the Principate in a direct line of descent were frustrated by a series of premature deaths which in the end left his wife's son, Tiberius Claudius Nero, as the nearest reliable person to whom he could turn for a successor. A further irony is the fact that, whereas Augustus' successor was not a descendant of his, less than thirty years after his death a grandson of Mark Antony ascended the throne as the Emperor Claudius.

AUGUSTUS' DYNASTIC POLICY

Tacitus *Annals* i. iii. 1–5

To consolidate his control Augustus raised his sister's son Claudius Marcellus, who was still a mere stripling, to the pontificate and curule aedileship, and Marcus Agrippa, not a noble by birth but a good soldier

---

[201] This sentence is incomplete in the MSS; the last four words, supplied by us, complete the apparent sense.

and his partner in victory, to two consecutive consulships. On Marcellus' death soon afterward [202] he took Agrippa as his son-in-law. His stepsons, Tiberius Nero and Claudius Drusus, he honored with imperial titles, even though his own family was still intact—for he had admitted Agrippa's children, Gaius and Lucius, into the house of the Caesars, and even before they had laid aside the purple-bordered toga of boyhood he had had a consuming desire, beneath a pretense of reluctance, to have them named leaders of the youth and consuls designate.[203] After Agrippa departed this life and premature death (or their stepmother Livia's treachery) [204] cut off Lucius and Gaius Caesar—the former while on his way to our armies in Spain, the latter while returning, weakened by a wound, from Armenia—since Drusus had long since perished, Nero alone remained of the stepsons, and everything centered on him.[205] He was adopted as a son, as colleague in *imperium*, as associate in the tribunician power, and was paraded before all the armies. . . . But in addition, mind you, in order to provide himself with additional safeguards, Augustus placed Drusus' son Germanicus in command of the eight legions on the Rhine and ordered Tiberius to adopt him, even though there was a grown son in Tiberius' house.

RESOLUTION ON THE COMING OF AGE OF
GAIUS CAESAR

When Gaius and Lucius Caesar, the grandsons whom Augustus adopted as his sons and heirs apparent, reached the age of fifteen and assumed the toga

[202] In 23 B.C. He had been married to Augustus' only child, Julia, but the marriage produced no children. Two years after Marcellus' death Julia was married to Agrippa, who, to further Augustus' dynastic purpose, divorced his second wife— Augustus' niece Marcella—whom he had married some eight years before and who had already borne him children. At the time of their marriage Julia was about eighteen years old, Agrippa slightly older than her father. This marriage produced five children.

[203] Gaius and Lucius Caesar, the two eldest sons of Julia and Agrippa, were born in 20 and 17 B.C., respectively, and were formally adopted by Augustus in the latter year. The honors mentioned here were accorded them when they came of age in 5 and 2 B.C., respectively. A letter is extant (in Aulus Gellius *Attic Nights* xv. vii. 3) in which Augustus, writing to Gaius in A.D. 1 remarks, "I pray the gods that I may be permitted to pass whatever time is left me with us all in good health and the state flourishing, while you learn to play the part of upright men and prepare to succeed to my position."

[204] An allegation, for which there is no evidence, of the type that proliferated in the atmosphere of dynastic aspiration and intrigue characteristic of the Empire.

[205] Agrippa died in 12 B.C., Drusus in 9 B.C., Lucius Caesar in A.D. 2, and Gaius Caesar in A.D. 4. Tiberius was adopted by Augustus in A.D. 4, four months after the last of these deaths. The clause of his will (recorded in Suetonius *Life of Tiberius* xxiii) in which he named Tiberius as his heir reveals the bitter frustration of Augustus' dynastic hopes: "Since a cruel fortune has snatched from me my sons Gaius and Lucius, Tiberius Caesar is to be my heir to two thirds of my estate."

of manhood, the cities of the Roman Empire resounded with ringing resolutions of public joy. The following inscription was erected at Sardis in 5 B.C.

IGRR, Vol. IV, No. 1,756, lines 6–27 (= Ehrenberg-Jones, No. 99)

On motion of the *strategi* Metrodorus son of Conon, Clinius, Musaeus, and Dionysius—

Whereas Gaius Julius Caesar, the eldest of the sons of Augustus has —as has been fervently prayed for—assumed in all its splendor the pure-white toga [of manhood] in place of the purple-bordered toga [of youth], and all men rejoice to see the prayers for his sons rising together to Augustus;

And whereas our city in view of so happy an event has decided to keep the day which raised him from a boy to a man as a holy day, on which annually all shall wear wreaths and festal garb, and the annual *strategi* shall offer sacrifices to the gods and render prayers through the sacred heralds for his preservation; to unite in consecrating an image of him set up in his father's temple; also on the day on which the city received the good news and the decree was ratified, to wear wreaths and perform most sumptuous sacrifices to the gods; and to send an embassy concerning these matters to go to Rome to congratulate him and Augustus;

Therefore it was resolved by the council and the people to dispatch envoys chosen from the most distinguished men for the purpose of bringing greetings from the city, of delivering to him the copy of this decree sealed with the public seal, and of discussing with Augustus the common interests of the province of Asia and of the city. . . .

The Emperor Caesar Augustus, son of a god, *pontifex maximus*, holding the tribunician power for the nineteenth year, to the chief magistrates and council of Sardis, greeting. Your envoys, Iollas son of Metrodorus and Menogenes son of Isidorus, grandson of Menogenes, had an audience with me in Rome and presented me with the decree sent by you in which you make known your resolutions concerning yourselves and express your joy on the coming to manhood of the elder of my sons. I commend you, therefore, for your earnest endeavor to demonstrate your gratitude to me and all my house for the benefits you receive from me. Farewell.

RESOLUTION ON THE DEATH OF GAIUS CAESAR

The untimely deaths of Augustus' adopted sons evoked extravagant manifestations of patriotic grief throughout the Empire. The following is the resolution passed by the town council of Pisa on the death of Gaius Caesar in A.D. 4 (the parallel resolution adopted two years earlier for Lucius Caesar is also extant: *CIL*, Vol. XI, No. 1,420 = Dessau, No. 139). We omit the introduction of the resolution, which follows the form used by the senate at Rome for its decrees.

CIL, Vol. XI, No. 1,421 (= Dessau, No. 140)

Whereas observations were made that the actions recorded below were taken when there were no magistrates in our colony on account of the election campaign—

Since on April 2 the news reached us that Gaius Caesar, son of Augustus (father of his country, *pontifex maximus*, guardian of the Roman Empire and protector of the whole world), grandson of a god— after the consulship which he had auspiciously completed by waging war beyond the farthest dominions of the Roman people and after he had administered the state well and had conquered or received under our protection most warlike and mighty peoples—had been wounded defending the state and had as a result of this mischance been snatched by cruel fates from the Roman people when he had already been designated *princeps* most just and most like his father in virtues, and sole protector of our colony; and since this event, coming when the mourning had not yet subsided which the entire colony had undertaken as a result of the death of his brother Lucius Caesar, consul designate, augur, our patron, leader of the youth, has renewed and increased the grief of all, individually and collectively;

For these reasons, all the decurions and colonists (since at the time of this misfortune there were in the colony no duovirs or prefects or anyone in charge of the administration of justice) agreed, in consideration of the magnitude of so great and unexpected a calamity, that from the day on which his death was announced to the day on which his bones are brought back and buried and the due rites are performed to his departed spirit all should wear mourning, keep the temples of the immortal gods, the public baths, and all shops closed, and abstain from festivity, and the matrons in our colony should make public lamentation; that the day on which Gaius Caesar died, viz., February 21, should go down in history and be observed at the present time by order and wish of all as a day of mourning like that of the Allia,[206] and that it should be expressly forbidden to hold, plan, or announce for or on that day, viz., February 21, any public sacrifice, thanksgivings, weddings, or public banquets or to hold or view on that day any theatrical performances or circus games; that every year on that day solemn public sacrifice

[206] Cf. Vol. I, p. 74.

shall be offered to his departed spirit by the magistrates or by those who are in charge of the administration of justice at Pisa in the same place and in the same manner as the solemn sacrifice established in honor of Lucius Caesar; that an arch adorned with the spoils of the peoples conquered or received under our protection by him shall be erected in a much-frequented place in our colony, and that upon it shall be placed a statue of him standing in his triumphal attire and, flanking this, two gilded equestrian statues of Gaius and Lucius Caesar; that, as soon as we can lawfully elect and have duovirs for the colony, the first duovirs elected shall submit this decision of the decurions and all the colonists to the [body of] decurions so that it may be legally enacted by the exercise of their public authority and entered by their authorization in the public records; and that meanwhile Titus Statulenus Juncus, flamen of Augustus, *pontifex minor* of the public worship of the Roman people, shall be requested to go with envoys, explain the present unavoidable circumstances of the colony, and report this proper public action and disposition of all by delivering a notification to the Emperor Caesar Augustus, father of his country, *pontifex maximus*, holding the tribunician power for the twenty-sixth year (and this Titus Statulenus Juncus, leader of our colony, flamen of Augustus, *pontifex minor* of the public worship of the Roman people, has done, delivering the notification, as stated above, to the Emperor Caesar Augustus, *pontifex maximus*, holding the tribunician power for the twenty-sixth year, father of his country).

It is hereby decreed by the decurions that all that was done, enacted, and decided by the unanimous agreement of all classes on April 2 in the consulship of Sextus Aelius Catus and Gaius Sentius Saturninus, shall be so done, carried out, conducted, and observed by Lucius Titius son of Aulus and by Titus Allius Rufus son of Titus, the duovirs, and by whoever hereafter shall be duovirs, prefect, or any other magistrates in our colony, and that all these things shall be done, carried out, conducted, and observed in perpetuity; and that Lucius Titius son of Aulus and Titus Allius Rufus son of Titus, the duovirs, shall see to it that everything recorded above shall in accordance with our decree be in the presence of the proquaestors entered by the town clerk in the public records at the earliest opportunity. Adopted.

THE WILL AND LAST DOCUMENTS OF AUGUSTUS

Dio Cassius *Roman History* LVI. xxx. 5–xxxiii. 5 (abridged)

On the 19th of August, the day on which he had first become consul, he passed away. He lived 75 years, 10 months, and 26 days (he had been born on the 23d of September) and was sole ruler, from the time of his victory at Actium, 44 years less 13 days. . . . The body of Augustus was borne from Nola by the leading men of each city in succession, and when it reached the outskirts of Rome the *equites* received it and conveyed it by night into the city.

The next day there was a meeting of the senate. . . . Drusus took his will from the Vestal Virgins, with whom it had been deposited, and brought it into the senate. Those who had witnessed the document examined their seals, and then it was read in the hearing of the senate. . . . Polybius, an imperial freedman, read the will, as it was not proper for a senator to perform any such function. In it, according to some, two thirds of the inheritance was left to Tiberius and the remainder to Livia; for, in order that she too might have some enjoyment of his estate, he had asked the senate for permission to leave her so much, which was more than the amount allowed by law.[207] These two, then, were named as heirs. He also directed that many articles and sums of money should be given to many persons related and unrelated to him, not only to senators and *equites* but also to kings; to the people he left 40,000,000 sesterces,[208] and to the soldiers 1,000 sesterces apiece to the Praetorians, half that amount to the city guard, and 300 each to the rest of the citizen soldiery.[209] Moreover, he ordered that to the children whose patrimony he had inherited while they were still small the whole amount should be paid back with accumulated interest when they reached manhood. (This, in fact, had been his practice even in his lifetime; for whenever he succeeded to the estate of anyone who had offspring he would restore it all to the man's children, immediately if they were already grown up, otherwise later.) Nevertheless, though such was his attitude toward the children of others, he did not restore his own daughter from exile,[210] although he did hold her worthy of bequests, and he instructed that she should not be buried in his own mausoleum. So much was made clear by the will.

Four more documents were then brought in, and Drusus read them. In the first were written detailed instructions for his funeral. In the second, which moreover he ordered to be inscribed on bronze tablets to be set up in front of his mausoleum, were recorded all the acts which

[207] The Voconian Law of 169 B.C. allowed a woman to inherit a maximum of 100,000 sesterces. In addition Livia was by the will admitted into the Julian family with the name of Augusta (Suetonius *Life of Augustus* ci).
[208] Suetonius (*ibid.*) mentions in addition a bequest to the tribes of 3,500,000 sesterces. The individual legacies, he reports, ran as high as 20,000 sesterces.
[209] That is, the legionaries: cf. introduction to § 155.
[210] In 2 B.C., in keeping with his social legislation (cf. § 11), Augustus banished his notorious daughter Julia for adultery. Political as well as moral considerations may have been involved.

he had performed.[211] The third contained an account of military matters, of the public revenues and expenditures, the amount of money in the treasuries,[212] and all other such matters relating to the Empire. The fourth contained commands and injunctions for Tiberius and for the public, such as not to free many slaves, lest they fill the city with a promiscuous rabble, and not to naturalize large numbers of citizens, so that there should be a marked difference between themselves and their subjects.[213] He exhorted them to entrust the public business to all men of intellectual and practical ability and not to let it depend on any one person; in this way no one would set his mind on absolutism, nor would the state, on the other hand, go to ruin if one man fell. He advised them to be satisfied with the *status quo* and to suppress completely any desire to increase the Empire to greater size; for then, he said, it would be difficult to guard, and as a result they would run the risk of losing what they already had.[214]

17. *The Deification of Augustus*

Dio Cassius *Roman History* LVI, xlvi
Adapted from LCL

[The senate [215]] declared Augustus immortal, assigned to him a college of priests and sacred rites, and made Livia, who was already called Julia and Augusta,[216] his priestess; they also permitted her to employ a lictor when she exercised her sacred office. On her part, she bestowed a million sesterces upon a certain Numerius Atticus, a senator and ex-praetor, because he swore that he had seen Augustus ascending to heaven in the manner of the traditions concerning Proculus and Romulus.[217] A shrine voted by the senate and built by Livia and Tiberius was erected to him in Rome, and others in many different places, some of the communities building them voluntarily and others unwillingly. Also the house at Nola where he passed away was made a precinct sacred to him. While his shrine in Rome was being erected, they placed a golden image of him on a couch in the temple of Mars and to this they paid all the honors that they were afterwards to give to his statue. Other

---

[211] This document, the only one of the four that has been preserved, is the famous "Accomplishments of Augustus" (§ 2).
[212] That is, the state treasury (*aerarium*) and the emperor's privy purse (*fiscus*).
[213] Cf. § 12.   [214] Cf. § 10.
[215] Meeting on September 17, five or six days after the funeral.
[216] Cf. Note 207.
[217] The legend was that Julius Proculus, a Roman senator, declared that Romulus had appeared to him shortly after his death as the god Quirinus.

honors voted him were that his image should not be borne in anybody's funeral procession, that the consuls should celebrate his birthday with games like those in honor of Mars, and that the tribunes of the plebs, since they were sacrosanct, should manage these Augustan Games. These officials conducted everything in the customary manner. . . . Besides this Livia had a private festival in his honor for three days in the palace, and this ceremony is still continued down to the present day by whoever is emperor.

CHAPTER II

THE ROMAN PEACE (A.D. 14–192):
IMPERIAL POLICY AND ADMINISTRATION

The century and a half from the accession of Tiberius to the renewal of bar-barian incursions during the reign of Marcus Aurelius is known traditionally as the era of the *Pax Romana* (Roman Peace). This designation is the prod-uct of imperial propaganda, contemporary laudations (cf. § 110), and mod-ern idealization of the ecumenical character of the Roman Empire and the orderliness of civilized life within its frontiers. "You see," says Epictetus (A.D. c.50–120) in one of his *Discourses* (III. xiii. 9), "that the emperor appears to provide us with profound peace, that there are no longer wars nor battles nor extensive brigandage nor piracy, but at any hour we may travel the roads or sail from the rising of the sun to its setting." In modern times Gibbon, for example, was moved to proclaim, "If a man were called to fix the period in the history of the world, during which the condition of the human race was most happy and prosperous, he would, without hesitation, name that which elapsed from the death of Domitian to the accession of Commodus."

But more recent scholarship has sought to strike a more realistic balance by emphasizing that the "limitless majesty of the Roman Peace" rested upon the might of Roman arms and the collaboration of the propertied classes in all parts of the Empire; that the masses of the laboring people remained in the main an apolitical multitude only lightly touched by Roman culture, rigidly controlled, and systematically exploited; and that the economy of the Empire even at its height was highly unstable and generative of growing socioeco-nomic maladjustments which were to erupt in the massive crisis of the third century (Chapter VI).

18. *Augustus' Successor*

With Tiberius firmly established in the last years of Augustus' life as co-regent and designated successor (§ 16), the transfer of power on Augustus' death proceeded without incident. Any stirrings of wishful hope for a return to republican government that might have been entertained by unrealistic members of the nobility were promptly dissipated. On the other hand Tiberius, himself of noble family, continued the Principate essentially on the pattern laid down by his predecessor, going out of his way particularly, at least in the first part of his reign, to encourage the senate to exercise its "partnership" in the government (cf. § 29).

Dio Cassius *Roman History* LVII. vii–ix (abridged)

As long as Germanicus lived [1] Tiberius exercised the imperial of-

---

[1] Germanicus, Tiberius' nephew and adopted son (cf. § 16), died A.D. 19.

fice in the following general manner. He did little or nothing on his own responsibility but brought all matters, even the slightest, before the senate and consulted that body as a partner. In the Forum had been erected a tribunal, on which he sat and administered justice in public; and he always acted with advisers,[2] after the manner of Augustus—in fact, he would take no important step without first consulting the others. After setting forth his own opinion he would not only grant everyone complete freedom to express disagreement but even tolerated it when some occasionally voted in opposition to him. . . .

In all other matters, too, he acted in this same manner. He would not allow freemen to call him master, nor any but the soldiers to call him *imperator*. The title of "father of his country" he rejected absolutely. That of Augustus he did not assume—in fact, he never permitted it even to be voted him—but he did not object to hearing it spoken or to reading it in writing, and whenever he sent messages to kings he would regularly include it in his letters. Generally he was called Caesar, sometimes Germanicus (from the exploits of Germanicus) or, in accordance with ancient usage, *princeps senatus* [3] (which he himself used, too). He often used to say, "I am master of the slaves, *imperator* of the soldiers, and *princeps* of the rest." He would pray, whenever some such occasion arose, to live and rule as long as it might be advantageous to the state. And he was likewise so democratic in all matters that he would permit no unusual celebration on his birthday [4] and would not allow people to swear by his Fortune,[5] and if anyone after swearing by it was accused of perjury he would not prosecute. . . . No sacred precinct was set apart for him in those days either by his own choice or otherwise; and no one was allowed to set up an image of him, for he promptly and expressly forbade any city or private citizen to do so. To this prohibition, it is true, he attached the proviso "unless I grant permission," but he added, "I will not grant it." [6] He would have no truck with charges that he had been insulted or accorded insufficient respect by someone (they were already calling even such things lese majesty and were bringing many cases to trial on that charge), and he accepted no such indictment as to himself, although he upheld the majesty of Augustus in this respect, too. At first he did not even punish any of those accused in regard to the latter, and he even released some who had been accused of perjuring themselves when swearing by the Fortune of Augustus; but as time went on he put very many to death.[7]

[2] Cf. Chapter I, Note 13.   [3] See above, p. 3.   [4] In contrast to Augustus: cf. § 14.
[5] On such oaths cf. Chapter V, Note 168.
[6] On Tiberius' attitude to emperor worship, see § 168, first and second selections.
[7] Cf. § 23.

19. *The Problem of the Succession*

For half a century after the death of Augustus, while there existed members of the Julio-Claudian (i.e., Augustan-Tiberian) house, the succession to the Principate remained within that family, though not without dynastic intrigue and murders. The decisive power of the armed forces was apparent from the start, when the prefect of the Praetorian Guard was the first after the consuls to swear allegiance to Tiberius, and it was not long before the military intervened openly in emperor making. The Praetorian prefects were the leaders in the assassination of Caligula, and, though Claudius was next in the line of succession, it was the Praetorians who placed him on the throne (A.D. 41). In A.D. 68 Nero's doom was sealed by the disaffection of legions and Guard. With Nero's death the Julio-Claudian line was extinct, and in the ensuing year four generals in different parts of the Empire were proclaimed emperor by their respective forces. Thus, in Tacitus' classic remark (*Histories* I. iv), "was revealed a secret of the imperial power, that the emperor could be created elsewhere than at Rome." Vespasian, who emerged the victor at the end of the "Year of the Four Emperors," was succeeded by his two sons, Titus and Domitian, in turn; this dynasty, the Flavian, ended with Domitian's assassination in A.D. 96. Thereafter a series of emperors without sons of their own put into practice the policy, hastily but futilely extemporized by Galba in 69, whereby the emperor adopted the ablest man available as his son, chief aide, and successor. Marcus Aurelius, the last of these so-called Good Emperors, whose reigns covered nearly a century (A.D. 96–180), reverted to the dynastic principle, designating his son Commodus as his successor despite his awareness of the young man's many shortcomings. In 192 Commodus, too, was slain, and the throne became once again the plaything of the armies (see Chapter VI).

THE LEGIONS PROCLAIM VESPASIAN EMPEROR

Tacitus *Histories* II. lxxix–lxxxi (abridged)

The first step in transferring the imperial power to Vespasian was taken at Alexandria by Tiberius Alexander, who promptly on July 1 administered to his legions the oath of allegiance to him.[8] That day was thereafter celebrated as the first day of Vespasian's principate, even though the army of Judaea took the oath before him in person on July 3. . . . All was done by the impulsive action of the soldiers, without a formal meeting, without a massing of the legions. . . . One day, as Vespasian emerged from his bedchamber, a few soldiers standing by

[8] Tiberius Julius Alexander, a Jewish apostate, was prefect of Egypt. The year is A.D. 69.

in the usual formation for saluting a legate, saluted him as emperor; then others ran up, calling him Caesar and Augustus and heaping on him all the titles of the Principate. Their minds had passed from apprehension to confidence in fortune's favor. Vespasian showed no elation, arrogance, or change at the turn of events. As soon as he dispelled the mist which such exaltation had spread before his eyes, he spoke as befitted a soldier and listened to the joyful intelligence pouring in from every quarter. For Mucianus,[9] who was waiting for precisely this, now administered to his eager soldiers the oath of allegiance to Vespasian. . . . Before July 15 all Syria had sworn the same allegiance. . . . All the provinces washed by the sea as far as Asia and Achaea, and all the territory extending inland to Pontus and Armenia, took the oath.

THE PRINCIPLE OF ADOPTION

Tacitus *Histories* I. xv–xvi

Adapted from the translation of A. J. Church and W. J. Brodribb
(Cambridge and London, 1864)

We are told that Galba, taking hold of Piso's hand, spoke to this effect: "If I were a private man, and were now adopting you under the curiate law before the pontiffs, as our custom is, it would be a high honor to me to introduce into my house a descendant of Gnaeus Pompey and Marcus Crassus; and it would be a distinction to you to add to the nobility of your lineage the honors of the Sulpician and Lutatian houses. As it is, I who have been called to the imperial power by the unanimous agreement of gods and men am moved by your splendid endowments and patriotism to offer to you, a man of peace, the Principate over which our ancestors fought, and which I myself obtained by war. I am following the example of the deified Augustus, who placed on an eminence next to his own first his nephew Marcellus, then his son-in-law Agrippa, afterwards his grandsons, and finally his stepson Tiberius Nero. But Augustus looked for a successor in his own family. I look for one in the state, and not because I have no relatives or companions of my campaigns. But it was not by campaigning for office that I myself received the imperial power, and the proof of my decision may be found in the connections—not only mine but yours as well—that I have passed over for you. You have a brother, as noble as yourself and older, who would be well worthy of this fortune, were you not worthier. . . .

[9] Governor of the province of Syria, and henceforth the spearhead of Vespasian's successful bid for the throne.

"Could the vast frame of this Empire have stood and preserved its balance without a directing spirit, I was not unworthy of inaugurating a republic. As it is, matters have long since come to the pass where my age can confer no greater boon on the Roman people than a good successor, your youth no greater than a good emperor. Under Tiberius, Gaius, and Claudius, we were the inheritance, so to speak, of a single family. The exercise of choice which begins with us will be a substitute for freedom.[10] Now that the house of the Julians and the Claudians has come to an end, adoption will discover the worthiest successor in each case. To be begotten and born of princes is a mere accident, and is reckoned as no more. In adoption there is nothing that need bias the judgment, and if you wish to make a choice, a unanimous opinion points out the man.[11] Let Nero be ever before your eyes, swollen with the pride of a long line of Caesars. . . . I have no need to advise you further at this time; all my purpose is fulfilled if I have made a good choice in you. The most practical and the shortest method of distinguishing between good measures and bad is to think what you yourself would or would not like under another emperor. Here, unlike nations ruled by kings, we do not have one particular family of masters and the rest slaves. You will have to rule over men who can bear neither complete slavery nor complete freedom."

Dio Cassius Roman History LXVIII. iii. 4–iv. 2

Nerva, therefore, finding himself held in such contempt [by the Praetorians] because of his old age, ascended the Capitol and proclaimed aloud, "May it be auspicious to the Roman senate and people and to myself: I adopt Marcus Ulpius Nerva Trajanus." . . . Thus Trajan became Caesar[12] and later emperor, even though there were relatives of Nerva living. But Nerva did not esteem family relationship above the welfare of the state, and though Trajan was a Spaniard and not an Italian or an Italiote, he adopted him nonetheless despite that. No foreigner had previously held the Roman sovereignty; but Nerva believed in judging a man by his ability and not by his nationality.

Dio Cassius Roman History LXIX. xx. 1–xxi. 1
Adapted from LCL

Hadrian convened at his house the most prominent and most respected of the senators and . . . spoke to them as follows: "I, my

---

[10] By "freedom" Tacitus means a republican constitution.

[11] Tacitus wrote this in the reign of Trajan, one of the "Good Emperors," brought to the throne by the adoption principle (cf. introduction to this section). The flattery in these words is obvious.

[12] The official title of the emperor designate. The reigning emperor used this title along with that of Augustus.

friends, have not been permitted by nature to have a son, but you have made it possible by legal enactment. Now there is this difference between the two methods—that a begotten son turns out to be whatever sort of person heaven pleases, whereas one that is adopted a man takes to himself by his own choice. Thus by the process of nature a maimed and witless child is often given to a parent, but by deliberate selection one of sound body and sound mind is certain to be chosen. For this reason I formerly selected Lucius Commodus before all others—I could not even have prayed to have such a child myself. But since heaven has bereft us of him, I have found an emperor for you in his place, whom I now give you. He is noble, mild, tractable, prudent, neither so young as to do anything reckless nor so old as to neglect aught. He has been brought up according to the laws and has held commands in accordance with our ancestral customs, so that he is not ignorant of any matters pertaining to the imperial office but can handle them all effectively. I refer to Aurelius Antoninus here. Although I know him to be the least inclined of men to become involved in public affairs and far from any such desire, still I feel sure he will not deliberately disregard either me or you but will accept the office even against his will."

So it was that Antoninus became emperor. And since he had no male offspring, Hadrian adopted for him Commodus' son Commodus, and in addition to him Marcus Annius Verus; for he wished to designate as far ahead as possible even those who were afterward to be emperors.

THE BREAK WITH THE PRINCIPLE OF ADOPTION

Dio Cassius *Roman History* LXXII. i
From LCL

Commodus was not naturally wicked but, on the contrary, as guileless as any man that ever lived. His great simplicity, however, together with his cowardice, made him the slave of his companions, and it was through them that he at first, out of ignorance, missed the better life and then was led on into lustful and cruel habits, which soon became second nature. And this, I think, Marcus [Aurelius] clearly perceived beforehand. Commodus was nineteen years old when his father died, leaving him many guardians, among them the best of the senators; but Commodus rejected their suggestions and counsels.

20. *Expressions of Allegiance to the Emperor*

Upon the accession of a new *princeps* appropriate celebrations were proclaimed throughout the Empire. In addition, following the precedent established by Augustus (cf. § 8), the military forces and the entire civilian population took an oath of allegiance to the new emperor and renewed this oath on each anniversary of his accession. And every year on January 3 prayers were offered in the Capitol in Rome and in the military camps and the provinces throughout the Empire for the health and safety of the emperor during the year ahead. It is worth noting how the language of these declarations grows in fulsomeness with the increasing autocracy of the régime (cf. § 24).

Tacitus *Annals* i. vii. 3

The oath of allegiance to Tiberius Caesar was sworn first by the consuls, Sextus Pompeius and Sextus Appuleius, then in their presence by Seius Strabo and Gaius Turranius, prefects of the Praetorian cohorts and of the grain supply, respectively, and then by the senate, the soldiers, and the people.

CIL, Vol. II, No. 172 (= Dessau, No. 190 = Abbott-Johnson, No. 47); A.D. 37

To Gaius Ummidius Durmius Quadratus, legate of the Emperor Gaius Caesar Germanicus with rank of praetor.

Oath of the Aritensians

I solemnly swear that I will be an enemy to those who I learn are enemies to Gaius Caesar Germanicus. If anyone brings or shall bring danger to him and his welfare, I will not cease to pursue him with arms and deadly war on land and on sea till he has paid the penalty to him; I will hold neither myself nor my children dearer than his welfare; and I will regard as enemies of mine those who have hostile intentions against him. If I knowingly swear or shall swear falsely, then may Jupiter Best and Greatest and the deified Augustus and all the other immortal gods cause me and my children to be deprived of fatherland, safety, and all good fortune.

May 11 [13] in Old Aritium,[14] in the consulship of Gnaeus Acerronius Proculus and Gaius Petronius Pontius Nigrinus, in the magistracy of Vegetus son of Tallicus and . . . ibius son of . . . arionus.

[13] This oath was taken fifty-two days after the death of Tiberius. The time it took for the news of an emperor's accession to be brought from Rome to the governors of the different provinces, and then to be disseminated by them throughout their provinces, varied considerably with all sorts of circumstances. The two papyrus texts given below in this section show that Nero's accession was made known in Middle Egypt thirty-five days after it took place in Rome, while in the case of Pertinax it was sixty-four days before the governor of the province (who was in Lower Egypt) knew of the event. Other papyri reveal that in Middle and Upper Egypt Trajan was thought to be still alive some four months after his death.

[14] In Lusitania in Spain.

Dittenberger, No. 797 (= Abbott-Johnson, No. 48); A.D. 37

In the consulship of Gnaeus Acerronius Proculus and Gaius Pontius Petronius Nigrinus.

Decree of the Assians on motion of the people [15]

Whereas the rule of Gaius Caesar Germanicus Augustus, hoped and prayed for by all men, has been proclaimed and the world has found unbounded joy and every city and every people has been eager for the sight of the god since the happiest age for mankind has now begun, it was decreed by the council and the Roman businessmen among us and the people of Assus [16] to appoint an embassy chosen from the foremost and most distinguished Romans and Greeks [17] to seek an audience and congratulate him, and beg him to remember the city with solicitude, as he personally promised when together with his father Germanicus he first set foot in our city's province.[18]

Oath of the Assians

We swear by Zeus the Savior and by the deified Caesar Augustus and by the ancestral Holy Maiden [19] to be loyal to Gaius Caesar Augustus and all his house and to regard as friends whomever he chooses and as enemies whomever he censures. If we remain faithful to our oath may it go well with us; if we swear falsely, the opposite.

Oxyrhynchus Papyrus No. 1,021 (= *Select Papyri*, No. 235); A.D. 54
From LCL

The Caesar who was owed to his ancestors, god manifest, has gone to join them, and the emperor whom the world expected and hoped for has been proclaimed; the good genius of the world and source of all blessings, Nero Caesar, has been proclaimed. Therefore ought we all wear garlands and with sacrifices of oxen give thanks to all the gods. Year 1 of Nero Claudius Caesar Germanicus, the 21st of the month New Augustus.[20]

[15] There was not, as in the case of most municipal decrees, merely an individual mover (as, for example, in § 14, third selection).
[16] A city in the province of Asia.
[17] The envoys' names, appended in the document but omitted here, show that one Roman and four Greeks were chosen.
[18] The distortion of the facts in this adulation is striking. Germanicus' visit to Asia occurred in A.D. 18. At that time Caligula was only six years old and was not even in line for the succession, since his elder brothers Nero and Drusus were still living.
[19] Athena Polias. Tiberius is not named here along with Augustus because he was not deified. On Tiberius' attitude toward emperor worship see § 18 and § 168, first and second selections.
[20] November 17; cf. Note 13, above. The Egyptian month Hathyr was renamed New Augustus in honor of Tiberius, who was born in November (cf. § 14, last

Pliny *Letters* Book x, Nos. 52–53

[Pliny to the Emperor Trajan] [21]

The day, my lord, on which you preserved the Empire by taking up the imperial power, we celebrated with all the joy you deserve, praying the gods to keep you safe and prosperous for the human race, whose protection and security rest upon your welfare. We administered the oath of allegiance both to our fellow soldiers, who rendered it in the customary manner, and to the people of the province, who emulated them with the same devotion.

[The Emperor Trajan to Pliny]

I was pleased to learn from your letter, my dear Pliny, with what dutifulness and joy my fellow soldiers and the provincials celebrated under your leadership the day of my accession.

Berlin Papyrus No. 646 (= *Select Papyri*, No. 222); A.D. 193

Mantennius Sabinus to the *strategi* of the Heptanomia [22] and of the Arsinoite Nome, greeting. I have ordered a copy of the edict sent by me to the most illustrious Alexandria to be appended hereto, so that you may all be informed and may hold festival for the like number of days. I wish you good health. Year 1 of the Emperor Caesar Publius Helvius Pertinax Augustus, Phamenoth 10.[23]

Copy of edict: It is meet, people of Alexandria, that you should hold festival for the most fortunate accession of our lord the Emperor Publius Helvius Pertinax Augustus, *princeps* of the sacred senate, father of his country, and of Publius Helvius Pertinax his son, and of Flavia Titiana Augusta [his wife], offering public sacrifice and prayer en masse on behalf of his enduring rule and of all his house, and wearing garlands for fifteen days beginning from today.

21. *The Powers of the Emperor*

Each emperor was constitutionally invested with his powers by the formality of a decree passed in the senate, followed by a comprehensive law

---

selection). The text of this document is not an official proclamation received from Rome or from the prefect of Egypt but a local proclamation issued upon receipt of the news in the village of Oxyrhynchus; cf. the prefect's edict in the last selection of this section.

[21] The date of these letters is A.D. 111/13; cf. Vol. I, p. 26.

[22] The "Seven Nomes" region of Middle Egypt. Mantennius Sabinus was the prefect of Egypt.

[23] March 6; cf. Note 13, above. Pertinax, for whose "enduring rule" the prefect orders fifteen days of celebration, was slain by a band of Praetorians on March 28.

enacted in the popular assembly. This bronze tablet—the sole extant document of its kind—contains the end of the law of investiture which conferred the imperial powers upon Vespasian, enumerating the various rights which had in one way or another accrued to the emperor during the first century of the Principate. The formulas of this enactment, however, are mainly those of a decree of the senate rather than of a law. The explanation lies in the fact that the senate first decreed the *imperium* to Vespasian, about December 20, A.D. 69, and the assembly subsequently incorporated this decree of the senate in its own statute, enacted early in January, A.D. 70. Vespasian, however, dated the beginning of his reign from July 1, A.D. 69, when he was acclaimed emperor by the legions in Egypt (cf. § 19, first selection).

CIL, Vol. VI, No. 930 (= FIRA, Vol. I, No. 15)

. . . that he shall have the right, just as the deified Augustus and Tiberius Julius Caesar Augustus and Tiberius Claudius Caesar Augustus Germanicus had,[24] to conclude treaties with whomever he wishes;

And that he shall have the right, just as the deified Augustus and Tiberius Julius Caesar Augustus and Tiberius Claudius Caesar Augustus Germanicus had, to convene the senate, to put and refer [25] proposals to it, and to cause decrees of the senate to be enacted by proposal and division of the house;

And that when the senate is convened [in special session] pursuant to his wish, authorization, order, or command, or in his presence, all matters transacted shall be considered and observed as fully binding as if the meeting of the senate had been regularly convoked and held;

And that at all elections especial consideration shall be given to those candidates for a magistracy, authority, *imperium,* or any post whom he has recommended to the Roman senate and people or to whom he has given and promised his vote; [26]

And that he shall have the right, just as Tiberius Claudius Caesar Augustus Germanicus had, to extend and advance the boundaries of the *pomerium* [27] whenever he deems it to be in the interest of the state;

And that he shall have the right and power, just as the deified Augustus and Tiberius Julius Caesar Augustus and Tiberius Claudius Caesar Augustus Germanicus had, to transact and do whatever things

[24] Only these three predecessors of Vespasian are named because Nero had been officially declared "of damned memory," and Caligula was practically so regarded, while the brief reigns of Galba, Otho, and Vitellius were considered ephemeral.
[25] Other interpretations, less satisfactory, of the Latin *remittere* are "withdraw from consideration," "return for further consideration."
[26] The earlier emperors possessed the right of *commendatio* (cf. p. 7), but more restricted than that here granted to Vespasian. Such candidates of the emperor appear in § 30.
[27] See Vol. I, § 6.

divine, human, public and private he deems to serve the advantage and the overriding interest of the state;

And that the Emperor Caesar Vespasian shall not be bound by those laws and plebiscites which were declared not binding upon the deified Augustus or Tiberius Julius Caesar Augustus or Tiberius Claudius Caesar Augustus Germanicus, and the Emperor Caesar Vespasian Augustus shall have the right to do whatsoever it was proper for the deified Augustus or Tiberius Julius Caesar Augustus or Tiberius Claudius Caesar Augustus Germanicus to do by virtue of any law or enactment;

And that whatever was done, executed, decreed, or ordered before the enactment of this law by the Emperor Caesar Vespasian Augustus, or by anyone at his order or command, shall be as fully binding and valid as if they had been done by order of the people or plebs.[28]

Sanction

If anyone in consequence of this law has or shall have acted contrary to laws, enactments, plebiscites, or decrees of the senate, or if he shall have failed to do in consequence of this law anything that it is incumbent on him to do in accordance with a law, enactment, plebiscite, or decree of the senate, it shall be with impunity, nor shall he on that account have to pay any penalty to the people, nor shall anyone have the right to institute suit or judicial inquiry concerning such matter, nor shall any [authority] permit proceedings before him on such matter.

22. *An Imperial Triumph*

One of the most coveted honors of the Republic, the celebration of a triumph by victorious generals (cf. Vol. I, § 90), came to an end in the reign of Augustus. The precedent for this was set by Augustus' ablest general, Marcus Agrippa, who refused all triumphs voted him. The last triumph recorded in the Calendar of Triumphs (Vol. I, p. 3) occurred in 19 B.C. Thereafter this honor was reserved for the emperors and the imperial family. As a substitute, conquering generals were awarded *ornamenta triumphalia* (triumphal decorations). One of the most spectacular triumphs of the imperial period was celebrated jointly by Vespasian and Titus in A.D. 71 after the Jewish War.

[28] This omnibus clause was especially necessary in Vespasian's case because of the interval of six months between his elevation by the eastern legions and his formal accession (cf. introduction to this section).

Josephus *Jewish War* VII. v. 122–156 (abridged)
Adapted from LCL

Previous notice having been given of the day on which the triumphal procession would take place, not a soul among the countless multitude in the city remained at home; all issued forth and occupied every position where it was at all possible to stand, leaving only room for the necessary passage of those upon whom they were to gaze.

The troops, while it was still night, had all marched out in centuries and cohorts under their commanders. . . . About the time dawn was breaking Vespasian and Titus issued forth, crowned with laurel and clad in the traditional purple robes, and proceeded to the porticoes of Octavia; for here the senate and the chief magistrates and those of equestrian rank were awaiting their coming. A platform had been erected in front of the porticoes, with chairs of ivory placed for them upon it; to these they mounted and took their seats. Instantly, acclamations rose from the troops, all bearing ample testimony to their valor. The princes were unarmed, in silk robes, and crowned with laurel. Vespasian, having acknowledged their acclamations, which they wished to prolong, gave the signal for silence. Then, amidst profound and universal stillness, he rose and, covering most of his head with his mantle, recited the customary prayers, Titus also praying in like manner. . . . The princes . . . having donned their triumphal robes and sacrificed to the gods . . . sent the procession on its way, driving off through the theaters, in order to give the crowds a better view.

It is impossible adequately to describe the multitude of those spectacles and their magnificence . . . for the collective exhibition on that day of almost everything that men who have ever been blessed by fortune have one by one acquired . . . displayed the majesty of the Roman Empire. . . .

The war was shown in numerous representations, in separate sections, affording a very vivid picture of its episodes. Here was to be seen a prosperous country being devastated, there whole battalions of the enemy slaughtered; here a party in flight, there others being led into captivity; walls of surpassing size demolished by engines, mighty fortresses overpowered; cities with well-manned defenses completely mastered and an army pouring within the ramparts, an area all deluged with blood, the hands of those incapable of resistance raised in supplication; temples being set on fire, houses pulled down over their owners' heads; and, after general desolation and woe, rivers flowing, not over a cultivated land, nor supplying drink to man and beast, but across a country still on every side in flames. . . .

The spoils in general were borne in promiscuous heaps; but conspicuous above all stood out those captured in the temple at Jerusalem. These consisted of a golden table, many talents in weight, and a candelabrum, likewise made of gold. . . .[29] After these, and last of all the spoils, was carried a copy of the Law of the Jews. Then followed a large party carrying images of victory, all made of ivory and gold. Behind them drove first Vespasian, followed by Titus; while Domitian rode alongside them, in magnificent apparel and mounted on a horse that was a remarkable sight.

The triumphal procession ended at the temple of Jupiter Capitolinus, on reaching which they halted, for it was a time-honored custom to wait there until the execution of the enemy's general was announced. This was Simon bar Giora, who had just figured in the procession among the prisoners,[30] and then, with a noose around him and scourged meanwhile by his escorts, had been dragged to the spot abutting on the Forum, where Roman law requires that malefactors condemned to death should be executed.[31] After the announcement that Simon was no more and the shouts of universal applause which greeted it, the princes began the sacrifices and, having duly offered these with the customary prayers, withdrew to the palace.

CIL, Vol. VI, No. 944 (= Dessau, No. 264) [32]

The Roman senate and people [dedicated this] to the Emperor Titus Caesar Vespasian Augustus, son of the deified Vespasian, *pontifex maximus*, holding the tribunician power for the tenth year, acclaimed *imperator* seventeen times, consul eight times, father of his country, their *princeps*, because with the guidance and plans of his father, and under his auspices, he subdued the Jewish people and destroyed the city of Jerusalem, which all generals, kings, and peoples before him had either attacked without success or left entirely unassailed.

23. Lese Majesty

The law on treason was revised under Augustus to embrace affronts to the majesty of the emperor (cf. §§ 7, 9). But lack of specificity as to what constituted "impairment" of his majesty made the law—as administered by

[29] The table of the shewbread and the seven-branched menorah. These, together with other spoils from the temple, appear on the reliefs depicting this triumphal procession on the inner walls of the extant Arch of Titus, erected at the edge of the Forum shortly after Titus' death.
[30] Seven hundred Jewish prisoners were paraded in the triumph, together with the two Zealot leaders, Simon bar Giora (son of the proselyte) and John of Gischala. The latter was imprisoned for life.
[31] The Roman state prison at the foot of the Capitoline Hill.
[32] From an arch in Rome, no longer extant, erected in A.D. 80/81.

some emperors, at least—an insidious instrument of terror; and the high rewards offered for convictions (usually one fourth of the property of the condemned) brought into being a host of spies, professional informers (*delatores*), and agents provocateurs. Tacitus dwells on the pernicious extension of the law's scope and the unrestrained encouragement of informers as leading characteristics of the reign of Tiberius. But recent scholarship has shown that Augustus' successor was in the main correct and moderate in his application of the law (cf. § 18). It seems clear that Tacitus retrojected to the times of Tiberius the reign of terror through which he lived under Domitian.

NEW APPLICATIONS OF THE LAW OF TREASON

Tacitus *Annals* I. lxxii–lxxiii

Tiberius gave new impetus to the law of treason. This law had the same name in olden times, but other matters came under its jurisdiction —betrayal of an army, or inciting the plebs to sedition, in short, any public malfeasance which diminished the majesty of the Roman people.[33] Deeds alone were subject to accusation then, words went unpunished. Augustus was the first to conduct trials for libel within the scope of this law, provoked to it by Cassius Severus' wanton defamation of respectable men and women in his impudent writings. Next Tiberius, when consulted by the praetor Pompeius Macer as to whether such trials for treason should be placed on the calendar, replied that the laws must be enforced. He too had been exasperated by verses, which were circulated anonymously, attacking his cruelty, his arrogance, and his estrangement from his mother.

It will not be without value to relate the first experiments in such charges, made in the cases of two unpretentious Roman *equites*, Falanius and Rubrius. . . . Against Falanius the accuser alleged that he had admitted among the votaries of Augustus . . . a certain Cassius, a mime of unnatural vice, and that when selling some gardens he had included a statue of Augustus in the sale. Against Rubrius it was charged that he had violated the divinity of Augustus by perjury. When these charges came to Tiberius' attention he wrote to the consuls that a place in heaven had not been decreed to his father in order that the honor might be turned to the destruction of the citizens. Cassius the actor had, along with others of the same occupation, taken part in the games which his own mother had consecrated to the memory of Augustus; nor was it sacrilegious to let statues of Augustus, like the effigies of other divinities, go with the property in sales of gardens and houses. As to [Rubrius'] oath, it should be treated exactly as if he had deceived Jupiter; the gods' injuries were the gods' concern.[34]

---

[33] On this phrase cf. Vol. I, pp. 83, 178.
[34] In other words, in these first "trial balloon" cases of A.D. 15 Tiberius rejected the

A ROMAN HOLIDAY FOR INFORMERS

Tacitus *Annals* I. lxxiv. 1–2

Caepio took up a way of life which the miseries of the age and the impudence of men soon rendered popular. Indigent, unknown, and restless, he first wormed his way, by means of his private reports, into the confidence of his pitiless sovereign. It was not long before he had become a terror to the entire nobility. He acquired the favor of one man [35] and the hatred of all, and those who followed the example that he set rose from beggary to riches, from objects of contempt to objects of fear, till at last they crowned the ruin of others by their own.

Tacitus *Annals* IV. xxx. 3–5

It was proposed that informers should receive no rewards when a person accused of treason took his life by his own hand before the completion of the trial. The motion was on the point of being carried when Tiberius, with considerable asperity and unusual frankness, spoke up for the informers, complaining that the laws would be ineffective and the state brought to the brink of disaster. "Better," he said, "subvert the constitution than remove its guardians." Thus the informers, a breed invented for the public ruin and never adequately curbed even by penalties, were lured on by rewards.

AN INFORMER FOILED

Seneca *On Benefits* III. xxvi

Under Tiberius Caesar there was such a common and almost universal frenzy for bringing charges of treason that it decimated the Roman citizenry more severely than did the whole civil war. It seized upon the talk of drunks, upon innocent words spoken in jest. Nothing was safe. Anything served as an excuse for venting this rage, and the fate of the accused was never in doubt, for there was but one outcome.

Paulus, a man of praetorian rank, was dining with company once, wearing a ring with a conspicuous stone engraved with a likeness of Tiberius Caesar. It would be very silly for me to try at this point to find a polite way of saying—he took a chamberpot in his hands. This action was noticed simultaneously by Maro, one of the notorious spies

---

idea that the actions alleged constituted lese majesty. The last clause, incidentally, was a maxim of Roman law; cf. the constitution of Alexander Severus of A.D. 223, cited in Justinian *Code* IV. i. 2: "Scorn for the sanctity of an oath has its own sufficient avenger in the god."

[35] The Emperor Tiberius. This passage is from Tacitus' narrative for A.D. 15; the passage which follows refers to A.D. 23.

of that time, and by a slave of Paulus. While the trap was being set, the slave drew off the ring from the finger of his drunken master. And when Maro called the company to witness that the emperor's image had been brought into contact with filth and began to affix his signature to the accusation, the slave showed the ring on his own hand.[36]

AGENTS PROVOCATEURS

Epictetus [37] *Discourses* IV. xiii. 5
From LCL

In this fashion the rash are ensnared by the soldiers in Rome. A soldier, dressed like a civilian, sits down by your side and begins to speak ill of Caesar, and then you, too, just as though you had received from him some guarantee of good faith in the fact that he began the abuse, tell likewise everything you think, and the next thing is—you are led off to prison in chains.

SUBVERSIVE HISTORY

Tacitus *Annals* IV. xxxiv–xxxv

Adapted from the translation of A. J. Church and W. J. Brodribb
(London, 1876)

In the consulship of Cornelius Cossus and Asinius Agrippa, Cremutius Cordus was arraigned on a new and hitherto unheard-of charge—that he had published a history in which he praised Marcus Brutus and called Gaius Cassius the last of the Romans.[38] His accusers were Satrius Secundus and Pinarius Natta, creatures of Sejanus.[39] That

[36] A similar story occurs in a fragment of Dio Cassius' fifty-eighth book: "Tiberius put to death a man of consular rank on the charge of having carried in his bosom a coin bearing the emperor's likeness when he retired to a latrine."

[37] A teacher of Stoic philosophy (A.D. c.50–120), who taught at Nicopolis in Epirus after Domitian's expulsion of philosophers from Rome. He is the author of the famous *Enchiridion*, or *Manual*.

[38] Cremutius Cordus was an historian of note, whose works are lost. His trial, which took place in A.D. 25 before the senate with the emperor present, has become through Tacitus' brilliant rhetoric a *cause célèbre*. Actually, since Brutus and Cassius had been legally proclaimed traitors and outlaws, it is doubtful whether Cordus' trial appeared to his contemporaries as a particularly radical extension of the types of trials for libel mentioned in the first selection of this section. Similarly, drinking to the memory of Brutus and Cassius on their birthdays and writing a laudatory biography of Cato the Younger were among the crimes that brought death in Nero's reign to Publius Clodius Thrasea Paetus. Domitian put to death the author of a biography praising Paetus, and his books, like Cordus', were publicly burned. On the burning of books under Augustus, see Vol. I, p. 373; Vol. II, pp. 55–56.

[39] Lucius Aelius Sejanus was prefect of the Praetorian Guard, and a veritable viceroy in this period of Tiberius' reign. He plotted to secure the succession for himself,

was enough to ruin the accused; in addition, the emperor listened with angry mien to his defense, which Cremutius, resolved to give up his life, began thus:

"It is my words, Conscript Fathers, which are here impeached, so innocent am I of any guilty act. And even these words are not against the emperor or the emperor's mother, who are alone comprehended under the law of treason. I am said to have lauded Brutus and Cassius, whose careers so many have described and no one mentioned without praise. Titus Livius, whose reputation for eloquence and truthfulness is second to none, extolled Gnaeus Pompey in such laudatory terms that Augustus called him "the Pompeian," yet this was no obstacle to their friendship. Scipio, Afranius,[40] this very Cassius, this same Brutus, he nowhere describes as brigands and traitors—the terms now applied to them—but repeatedly as illustrious men. Asinius Pollio's writings hand down a glorious account of them, and Messalla Corvinus used to speak with pride of Cassius as his general; yet both these men prospered to the end with wealth and preferment.[41] To that book of Marcus Cicero's in which he praised Cato to the skies, what other answer did Caesar the dictator make but an oration written in reply, as if he were pleading before a jury? The letters of Antony, the harangues of Brutus contain invectives against Augustus, false to be sure, but extremely violent; the poems of Bibaculus and Catullus,[42] crammed with abuse of the Caesars, are still read—and the deified Julius and the deified Augustus themselves bore all this and let it pass. . . . To every man posterity gives his due honor, and if a fatal sentence hangs over me there will be no lack of people to remember me as well as Cassius and Brutus."

He then left the senate and ended his life by starvation. The senators decreed that his books should be burned by the aediles; but they survived in concealment and were afterwards republished—which disposes one all the more to laugh at the folly of men who suppose that tyranny in the present can actually cause the succeeding age to forget. On the contrary, the persecution of genius fosters its influence; foreign despots, and all who have imitated their barbarity, have merely begotten infamy for themselves and glory for their victims.

---

and before his dramatic fall in A.D. 31 he was able to put even members of the imperial household, including the heir apparent, out of the way on charges of treason.

[40] Scipio and Afranius were Pompey's father-in-law and lieutenant, respectively.

[41] Asinius Pollio and Messalla Corvinus were both prominent men of letters and affairs of the Augustan period.

[42] The famous poet Gaius Valerius Catullus, c.84 B.C.–54 B.C. Bibaculus was his contemporary.

24. Evolution of the Principate: From "First Citizen" to Benevolent Despot

The "partnership in government" with the senate which was inherent in the Augustan conception of the Principate quickly proved to be unworkable. The senate receded into impotence (cf. § 29), and the emperor's domination became more and more complete. From all quarters of the Empire we hear a chorus of praise for the ruler of the Roman world, swelling in volume and adulation as we pass from the Julio-Claudians and Flavians of the first century to the "Good Emperors" of the second. We find it in poetry, history, philosophy, and other writings, as well as in the language of officialdom (cf., for example, § 20). The dominant theme in this constant paeaning is the enjoyment of peace and prosperity under the protection of an all-wise, all-powerful, all-virtuous, divinely ordained ruler. Opposition of subject peoples to Roman rule was not completely dead, however. It manifested itself in sporadic revolts and in the continued production of popular anti-Roman literature (cf. Vol. I, § 147; Vol. II, § 110).

Strabo *Geography* vi. iv. 2 (at end)
From LCL

Italy—though it has often been torn by faction, at least since it has been under the Romans—and Rome itself have been prevented by the excellence of their form of government and of their rulers from proceeding too far in the ways of error and corruption. But it would be a difficult thing to administer so great a dominion otherwise than by turning it over to one man, as to a father. At all events, never have the Romans and their allies thrived in such peace and plenty as that which was afforded them by Augustus Caesar from the time he assumed the absolute authority and is now being afforded them by his son and successor, Tiberius, who is making Augustus the model of his administration and decrees.

Velleius Paterculus *Compendium of Roman History* ii. cxxvi. 2–5
From LCL

Credit has been restored in the Forum, strife has been banished from the Forum, canvassing for office from the Campus Martius,[43] discord from the senate house; justice, equity, and industry, long buried in oblivion, have been restored to the state; the magistrates have regained their authority, the senate its honor, the courts their dignity; rioting

[43] In A.D. 14 Tiberius discontinued the election of magistrates by the Centuriate Assembly in the Field of Mars (Vol. I, § 27), and transferred this prerogative to the senate, which was thereafter the sole electoral organ of the state.

in the theater has been suppressed; all have either been imbued with the wish to do right or have been forced to do so. Right is now honored, evil is punished; the humble man looks up to the great but does not fear him, the great has precedence over the lowly but does not despise him. When was the price of grain more reasonable, the blessings of peace greater? The Augustan peace, which has spread to the regions of the east and of the west and to the bounds of the north and of the south, preserves every corner of the world safe from the fear of brigandage. The munificence of the Emperor [Tiberius] takes upon itself the accidental losses not merely of individual citizens but of whole cities. The cities of Asia have been restored,[44] the provinces have been freed from the oppression of their magistrates. Honor ever awaits the worthy; for the wicked punishment is slow but sure; fair play now has the upper hand over influence, and merit over campaigning for office, for the best of emperors teaches his citizens to do right by doing it himself, and though he is the greatest among us in power, he is still greater by his example.

PLINY'S ENCOMIUM ON TRAJAN

Under the Principate the consulship (now mainly an honorary distinction) and other high offices were attained upon nomination by the emperor. It was customary for the consul on entering office to deliver a speech thanking the emperor for this preferment and mark of favor. An extant example of these fulsome panegyrics is that delivered by Pliny the Younger in A.D. 100, when he held the consulship for two months (cf. Chapter I, Note 189). In the reworked and expanded form in which he published this panegyric it runs to some 18,000 words. In it Pliny celebrates the career, acts, and virtues of the Emperor Trajan.

Pliny *Panegyric Addressed to the Emperor Trajan* lxv–lxxx (abridged)

You [45] have spontaneously subjected yourself to the laws, to the laws which, Caesar, no one ever drafted to be binding upon the *princeps*.[46] But you desire to have no more rights than we; and the result is that we

---

[44] A series of earthquakes in A.D. 17 caused great damage in Asia Minor. Tiberius sent Sardis a gift of 10,000,000 sesterces, and at his bidding the senate granted that city a five-year remission of taxes (cf. § 37). Similar assistance was given to the other stricken cities. In A.D. 23 two earthquake-stricken cities (one in Asia, one in Greece) were accorded a three-year remission of taxes. Similar cases are recorded under other emperors.

[45] Trajan. Pliny shifts back and forth in his panegyric, addressing now the emperor, now the senate.

[46] Cf. Justinian *Digest* I. iii. 31 (quoting Ulpian): "The emperor is not bound by the laws."

would like you to have more. What I now hear for the first time, now learn for the first time, is not, "The *princeps* is above the laws," but "The laws are above the *princeps*, and the same restrictions apply to Caesar when consul as to others." He swears fidelity to the laws in the presence of attentive gods—for to whom should they be more attentive than to Caesar? . . .

Hardly had the first day of your consulship dawned when you entered the senate house and exhorted us, now individually, now all together, to resume our liberty, to take up the duties of imperial administration shared, so to speak, between yourself and us, to watch over the public interests, to rouse ourselves. All emperors before you said about the same, but none before you was believed. People had before their eyes the shipwrecks of many men who sailed along in a deceptive calm and foundered in an unexpected storm. . . . But you we follow fearlessly and happily, wherever you call us. You order us to be free: we will be. You order us to express our opinions openly: we will pronounce them. It is neither through any cowardice nor through any natural sluggishness that we have remained silent until now; terror and fear and that wretched prudence born of danger warned us to turn our eyes, our ears, our minds, away from the state—in fact, there was no state altogether. But today, relying and leaning upon your right hand and your promises, we unseal our lips closed in long servitude and we loose our tongues paralyzed by so many ills. . . .

Here is the picture of the father of our state as I for my part seem to have discerned it both from his speech and from the very manner of its presentation. What weight in his ideas, what unaffected genuineness in his words, what earnestness in his voice, what confirmation in his face, what sincerity in his eyes, bearing, gestures, in short in his whole body! He will always remember his advice to us, and he will know that we are obeying him whenever we make use of the liberty he has given us. And there is no fear that he will judge us reckless if we take advantage unhesitatingly of the security of the times, for he remembers that we lived otherwise under an evil *princeps*.[47]

It is our custom to offer public prayers [48] for the eternity of the Empire and the preservation of the emperor . . . "if [he] has ruled the state well and in the interest of all." . . . You reap, Caesar, the most glorious fruit of your preservation from the consent of the gods. For when you stipulate that the gods should preserve you only "if you

[47] Domitian, whose reign of terror Pliny is here contrasting with the enlightened rule of Trajan.
[48] Annually on January 3; cf. introduction to § 20.

have ruled the state well and in the interest of all," you are assured that you do rule the state well since they preserve you.[49] And so you pass in security and joy the day which tortured other emperors with worry and fear when in suspense, thunderstruck, uncertain how far they could rely on our patience, they awaited from here and there the messages of public servitude. . . .

In judicial inquiries, what soft severity [you display], what clemency without weakness! You do not sit as judge intent on enriching your privy purse,[50] and you want no reward for your decision other than to have judged rightly. Litigants stand before you concerned not for their fortunes, but for your good opinion, and they fear not so much what you may think of their case as what you may think of their character. O care truly that of a *princeps*, and even of a god, to reconcile rival cities, to calm peoples in ferment, less by imperial command than by reason, to impede the injustices of magistrates, to annul everything that ought not have been done, in fine, in the manner of the swiftest star to see all, hear all, and like a divinity be present and be helpful forthwith wherever invoked! Such, I imagine, are the things that the father of the world [51] regulates with a nod when he lets his glance fall upon the earth and deigns to count human destinies among his divine occupations. Henceforth free and released in this area he can attend to the sky alone, since he has sent you to fill his role toward the human race. You fulfill that function, and you are worthy of him who entrusted it to you, since each of your days is devoted to our greatest good, to your greatest glory.

THE BLESSINGS OF IMPERIAL RULE

Plutarch *Precepts of Statecraft* xxxii

The greatest blessings that cities can enjoy are peace, prosperity, populousness, and concord. As far as peace is concerned the people have no need of political activity, for all war, both Greek and foreign, has been banished and has disappeared from among us. Of liberty the

---

[49] This recalls a prayer of Augustus reported by Suetonius (*Life of Augustus* xxviii. 2): "May I be permitted to set the state on a safe and sound base and to reap from that act the fruit I seek, so that I may be called the creator of the best of governments and bear with me when I die the hope that the foundation of the state which I have laid will remain unshaken."

[50] Nero, Vespasian, and Titus carried out large-scale confiscations of private estates (cf. § 42), many of them belonging to persons convicted of treason (cf. § 7). In one famous case, Nero is said to have put out of the way six wealthy landowners who together possessed half the area of the province of Africa, so that he could acquire their properties; see below, pp. 166–67.

[51] Jupiter.

people enjoy as much as our rulers allot them, and perhaps more would not be better. A bounteous productiveness of soil; a mild, temperate climate; wives bearing "children like to their sires," [52] and security for the offspring—these are the things that the wise man will ask for his fellow citizens in his prayers to the gods.

Aelius Aristides [53] *To Rome* xxix–xxxiii, lx (abridged)
From the translation of S. Levin (*Glencoe, Illinois, 1950*)

Extensive and sizable as the Empire is, perfect policing does much more than territorial boundaries to make it great. . . . Like a well-swept and fenced-in front yard . . . the whole world speaks in unison, more distinctly than a chorus; and so well does it harmonize under this director-in-chief that it joins in praying this Empire may last for all time. All everywhere are ruled equally. The mountain people are lowlier in their submissiveness than the inhabitants of the most exposed plains. The owners and occupants of rich plains are your peasants. Continent and island are no longer separate. Like one continuous country and one people, all the world quietly obeys. Everything is carried out by command or nod, and it is simpler than touching a string. If a need arises, the thing has only to be decided on, and it is done. The governors assigned to cities and provinces govern their various subjects; but among themselves and in relation to one another, all of them alike are governed . . . [by] the supreme governor, the chief executive. They are convinced that he knows what they are doing better than they know it themselves. They fear and respect him more than any slave could fear his master standing over him personally and giving orders. None of them are so proud that they can sit still if they so much as hear his name. They leap up, praise him, bow, and utter a double prayer—to the gods on behalf of him, and to him on their own behalf. If they feel the slightest doubt about their subjects' lawsuits, public or private, or whether petitions should be granted, they immediately send to him and ask what to do, and they wait for a signal from him, as a chorus from its director.[54] No need for him to wear himself out making the rounds of the whole Empire, or to be in one place after another adjusting the affairs

[52] A quotation from Hesiod *Works and Days* 233.
[53] Publius Aelius Aristides (A.D. 117–c.185) was one of the celebrated Greek rhetoricians of his day. A native of Mysia, he traveled and lectured in many places. Two of his treatises and over fifty of his speeches are extant. This panegyric idealizing the Roman emperor and Empire was delivered by him in Rome about the year 150. A comprehensive study of the oration, with translation and detailed commentary, has recently been published by J. H. Oliver in *Transactions of the American Philosophical Society*, Vol. XLIII (1953), Part 4.
[54] Pliny's letters to the Emperor Trajan, a number of which appear in this volume, afford a vivid illustration of this statement.

of each people whenever he sets foot in their country. Instead, he can very easily sit and manage the whole world by letters, which are practically no sooner written than delivered, as if flown by birds. . . . The constitution is a universal democracy under the one man that can rule and govern best.

THE QUALITY OF MERCY

"Historia Augusta" Life of Avidius Cassius [55] viii–xi (abridged)
From LCL

When someone said that Antoninus [56] deserved blame because he was so indulgent toward his enemy and his enemy's children and loved ones, and indeed toward everyone whom he had found involved in the revolt . . . he pointed out that in the case of all the emperors who had been slain there had been reasons why they deserved to die, and that no emperor generally recognized as good had been conquered by a pretender or slain. . . . No rebels had succeeded in overcoming either Augustus, or Trajan, or Hadrian, or his own father, and, although there had been many of them, they had been killed either against the wishes or without the knowledge of those emperors. Antoninus himself, moreover, asked the senate to refrain from inflicting severe punishment on those who were implicated in the rebellion; he made this request at the very same time in which he requested that during his reign no senator be subjected to capital punishment [57]—an act which won him great affection. . . .

There is extant a letter of Faustina's to her husband, in which she urges Marcus to punish Cassius severely. . . . The following letter will show what Antoninus wrote to her in reply: [58] "Truly, my Faustina, you are over-anxious about your husband and our children. While I was at the villa in Formiae I reread the letter wherein you urge me to take vengeance on Avidius' accomplices. However, I shall spare his children, son-in-law, and wife, and I will write to the senate to forestall any immoderate confiscation or cruel punishment. For there is nothing which endears a Roman emperor to mankind as much as the quality of mercy. This quality caused Caesar to be deified and made Augustus a

---

[55] Governor of Syria, who revolted in A.D. 175 and proclaimed himself emperor. The revolt was quickly suppressed, and Cassius slain.
[56] That is, Marcus Aurelius.
[57] This was, apparently, a policy instituted by Nerva and continued by the succeeding "Good Emperors."
[58] Like many of the documents included in these biographies (see Vol. I, p. 31), these "letters" are generally agreed to be pure forgeries.

god; it was this characteristic, more than any other, that gained your father the honor of the name Pius. . . ."

THE BENEVOLENT DESPOT

The following excerpts [59] from the works of two Pythagoreans, apparently of the second century, present philosophical rationales of the intermediate stage that the position of the Roman emperor had then reached in its evolution from *primus inter pares* (cf. p. 3) to absolute monarch by divine right. Though both treatises are strongly imbued with Stoic doctrine, they reveal an interesting difference in concept. "Diotogenes admits the divinization of the king rather than his divinity. It is the majesty of his function and the resemblance of terrestrial royalty to divine royalty that give him a divine aspect: he is the lieutenant of God on earth, and his imitator. . . . The ideal of Diotogenes is human rather than divine." But for the more mystical Ecphantes the king was created by the supreme god in his own image, to govern mankind as the god governs the universe (cf. the selection from Pliny's *Panegyric,* above). His king is divine by nature, and his function stems from his divinity, while Diotogenes' king derives divinity from his function. Under either concept, however, "the king or emperor, presented in the guise of a mediator and savior . . . promises the human community to bring about an order of things which, by reproducing the [perfect] organization of the universe, corresponds to the will of God and assures the salvation of humanity." (The quotations are translated from L. Delatte, *Les Traités de la royauté d'Ecphante, Diotogène et Sthénidas* [Liége, 1942], pp. 289–90.)

Diotogenes *On Kingship* (fragment)

Adapted from the translation of E. R. Goodenough, Yale Classical Studies, *1 (1928), 66–68*

The duties of a king are threefold: military leadership, the dispensing of justice, and the cult of the gods. . . . Accordingly, the perfect king must be a good commander, judge, and priest, for these are fitting and proper to a king's supremacy and virtue alike. For the task of a pilot is to save the ship, of a charioteer to save the chariot, of a physician to save those who are ill, while the task of a king and captain is to save those who are in danger in war. . . . In dispensing and distributing justice, whether as a whole in public law or to individuals in private law, it is right for a king to act as does God in his reign and command over the universe—in public matters by harmonizing the whole with his single rule and reign, and in individual matters by bring-

[59] Preserved by John of Stobi (Joannes Stobaeus; fifth[?] century) in his *Anthology* IV. vii. 61, 64.

ing details into accord with this same harmony and reign. The king is also occupied in being good and beneficent to his subjects, and that according to justice and law. The third duty, that is the worship of the gods, is no less fitting for a king. For the Best should be honored by the best man, and the Reigning Principle by the man who reigns. Now God is the best of the things most honored by inherent nature, and the king is best in the earthly and human realm. And king bears the same relation to state as God to universe; and state is to universe as king is to God. For the state, made up as it is by the harmonizing of many different elements, is an imitation of the order and harmony of the universe, while the king, who has absolute rule and is himself Animate Law, has been transfigured into a god among men.

Ecphantes *On Kingship* (fragment)

Adapted from the translation of E. R. Goodenough, Yale Classical Studies, *1 (1928),* 76–78

The king is like the rest [of mankind] in his earthly tabernacle, inasmuch as he is formed out of the same material; but he is fashioned by the supreme artificer, who in making the king used himself as archetype. Accordingly the king, as a copy of the higher king, is a single and unique creation, for he is on the one hand always intimate with the one who made him, while to his subjects he appears in the light of royalty. . . . And the very fact that a divine being rules well causes the king's subjects to be ruled well by him. So then I suppose that the earthly king can in no particular fall short of the virtue of the heavenly king; but just as the king is an alien and foreign thing which has come down from heaven to mankind, so one would suppose his virtues also were the work of divinity and his through divinity.

25. *Foreign and Frontier Policy*

The foreign policy of the Roman Empire in the first two centuries A.D. was substantially that bequeathed to it by Augustus—nonaggressive imperialism, defense and security of the borders, with prime attention to the watch on the Rhine-Danube frontier against the restless Germanic tribes, and on the desert-river-mountain frontier in Syria and Asia Minor against the Parthian Empire. To achieve this policy with an economy of means, imposed by the limited financial and military resources of the Empire, succeeding emperors adhered, with rare exceptions (see § 27), to Tiberius' "policy of conducting foreign affairs by astute diplomacy and of keeping war at a distance" (Tacitus *Annals* VI. xxxii. 1), though occasional campaigns were initiated to consolidate and shorten frontier lines. In addition to buffer zones of client states, the emperors relied on the traditional Roman policy of "divide and rule," fostering internal conflicts and discord among the peoples beyond the borders and winning over some of their leaders to a pro-Roman orientation. "May the tribes," prayed Tacitus, writing in A.D. 98, "ever retain if not love for us, at least hatred for each other; for while the fate that overtakes empires is at our heels, fortune can grant no greater boon than discord among our foes" (*Germany* xxxiii).[60] From the end of the first century on, further protection was provided along the land frontiers of the Empire by the construction of *limites,* continuous massive barriers guarded by forts and observation towers, the most impressive remains of which is "Hadrian's Wall" in northern Britain.

Appian *Roman History* Preface. vii
Adapted from LCL

Possessing the best part of the earth and sea, they have, on the whole, aimed to preserve their Empire by diplomacy rather than to extend their sway indefinitely over poor and profitless tribes of barbarians, some of whom I have seen at Rome negotiating and offering themselves as subjects; but the emperor would not accept them because they would be of no use to him. They give kings to a great many other peoples whom they do not need to have under their rule. To some of these subject peoples they make disbursements in addition, deeming it dishonorable to give them up even though they are costly. They surround the Empire with great armies and they garrison the whole stretch of land and sea like a single stronghold.

THE PEOPLES ON THE FRONTIERS

The *Germany* of Tacitus is the most extensive ancient account of a people with whom the Romans were in contact on the frontiers of their Empire. Only a few excerpts from this monograph are given here. A brief glimpse of the lower Danube frontier a century earlier is contained in one of the works written by the poet Ovid during his exile at Tomis (modern Constanta in Rumania) on the Black Sea.

Tacitus *Germany* vii, xi, xiii–xiv, xvi, xxvi
Adapted from LCL

They obtain their kings on the basis of birth, their generals on the basis of courage. The authority of their kings is not unlimited or arbi-

---

[60] Cf. Tacitus *Agricola* xii: "Our most effective weapon against the most powerful tribes [in Britain] is that they have no common policy. Seldom do two or three peoples come to an agreement to repel a common danger; thus, they fight singly, and all are conquered."

trary. Their generals control them by example rather than command, and by means of the admiration which attends upon energy and a conspicuous place in the front line. But capital punishment, imprisonment, even flogging are permitted only to the priests, and then not as a penalty or under the general's orders but as an inspiration from the god whom they suppose to accompany them on campaign. Certain totems, in fact, and emblems are fetched from groves and carried into battle. The strongest incentive to courage lies in this, that neither chance nor casual grouping makes the squadron or wedge, but family and kinship. . . .

On small matters the chiefs consult, on larger questions the community, but with this limitation, that even the matters whose decision rests with the people are first handled by the chiefs. They meet, unless there is some unforeseen and sudden emergency, on specified days—when the moon, that is, is new or at the full. They regard this as the most auspicious herald for the transaction of business. They count not by days as we do, but by nights. . . . It is a failing of their freedom that they do not meet at once, when commanded, but waste a second and a third day by dilatoriness in assembling. When the throng is pleased to begin, they take their seats carrying arms. Silence is called for by the priests, who thenceforward have power also to coerce. Then kings or chiefs are listened to, in order of age, birth, glory in war, or eloquence, with the prestige that belongs to their counsel rather than with any prescriptive right to command. If the advice tendered is displeasing, they reject it by shouting; if it pleases them, they clash their spears. . . .

They transact no business, public or private, without arms in their hands. Yet the custom is that no one takes arms until the state has endorsed his competence. Then, in the assembly itself, one of the chiefs or his father or his relatives equip the young man with shield and spear. This corresponds with them to assuming the toga [of manhood] and is a youth's first public distinction. Before this he was regarded as a member of his household, but now as a member of the state. Conspicuously high birth or signal services on the part of ancestors confer the rank of chief, even in the case of very young men; they mingle with others of maturer strength and long-tested valor, who are not ashamed to be seen among their retinue. In the retinue itself degrees are observed, depending on the judgment of him whom they follow. There is great rivalry among the retainers to decide who shall have the first place with his chief, and among the chieftains as to who shall have the largest and most spirited retinue. To be surrounded always by a large band of chosen youths means rank, strength, glory in peace, protection in war. . . .[61]

[61] Medieval feudalism grew, in part, from the institution here described by Tacitus.

Should it happen that the community where they are born is in-active with long years of peace and quiet, many of the high-born youths voluntarily seek those tribes which are at the time engaged in some war. For peace is unwelcome to this people, and they distinguish themselves more readily in the midst of dangers. Besides, a great retinue cannot be maintained except by war and violence, for it is to the generosity of their chief that they look for the war horse and the murderous and masterful spear. Banqueting and a certain rude but lavish munificence take the place of pay. . . .

It is well known that none of the German tribes lives in cities and that they do not even allow houses to touch one another. They live separately and scattered, according as spring, meadow, or grove ap-peals to each man. They lay out their villages not, after our fashion, with buildings contiguous and connected; everyone keeps a clear space round his house. . . .

Land is taken up by a village as a whole, in quantity according to the number of the cultivators. They then distribute it among them-selves on the basis of rank, such distribution being made easy by the extent of the domain occupied.

Ovid *Laments* v. vii. 11–20, 39–56
From LCL

Though upon this coast there is a mixture of Greeks and Getans, it derives more from the scarce-pacified Getans. Great hordes of Sarma-tians and Getans go and come upon their horses along the roads. Among them is not one who does not bear quiver and bow, and darts yellow with viper's gall. Harsh voices, grim countenances, veritable pictures of Mars, neither hair nor beard trimmed by any hand, right hands not slow to stab and wound with the knife which every barbarian wears fastened at his side. . . .

I busy my mind with studies beguiling my grief, trying to cheat my cares. What else am I to do, all alone on this forsaken shore, what other resources for my sorrows should I try to seek? If I look upon the country, 'tis devoid of charm, nothing in the whole world can be more cheerless; if I look upon the men, they are scarce men worthy of the name; they have more of cruel savagery than wolves. They fear not laws; right gives way to force, and justice lies conquered beneath the aggressive sword. With skins and loose breeches they keep off the evils of the cold; their shaggy faces are protected with long locks. A few retain traces of the Greek tongue, but even this is rendered barbarous by a Getic twang. . . . I, the Roman bard . . . am forced to utter most things in the Sarmatian tongue.

Ovid *Laments* v. x. 15–39
From LCL

Countless tribes round about threaten cruel war, thinking it base to live if not by plunder. Without, nothing is secure; the citadel itself is defended by meager walls and by its strategic site. When least expected, the foe swarms upon us like birds, and when scarce well seen is already driving off the booty. Often within the walls, when the gates are closed, we gather deadly missiles right in the streets. Rare then is he who ventures to till the fields, for the wretch must plow with one hand, and hold arms in the other. The shepherd wears a helmet while he plays upon his pitch-cemented reeds, and instead of a wolf the timorous ewes dread war. Scarce with the fortress's aid are we defended; and even within that the barbarous mob mingled with the Greeks inspires fear. For without distinction among us dwell the barbarians, occupying more than half of the dwellings. Even should you not fear them, you may loathe the sight of their chests covered with hides and with their long hair. Even those who are believed to derive their descent from the Greek city wear Persian trousers instead of the dress of their fathers. They communicate in the tongue they share; I must make myself understood by gestures. Here it is that I am a barbarian, understood by nobody; the Getans laugh stupidly at Latin words, and in my presence they often talk maliciously about me in perfect security.

A PRO-ROMAN GERMAN CHIEFTAIN

Tacitus *Annals* i. lvii. 6–lix. 8

Segestes himself was also present,[62] a stately sight, unafraid, secure in the knowledge that he had been a good ally. His speech was to this effect: "This is not the first day of my steadfast loyalty toward the Roman people. From the time I was granted citizenship [63] by the deified Augustus, I have chosen my friends and enemies in accordance with your interests, not from hatred of my fatherland . . . but because it was my conviction that the Romans and Germans have the same interests and that peace is better than war. Therefore I accused Arminius, the ravisher of my daughter, the violater of your treaty, before Varus,[64] who was then in command of the army. . . . I threw Arminius into chains and I endured the same at the hands of his followers. And now at

[62] The time is A.D. 15, during Germanicus' unauthorized invasion of Germany. Segestes, leader of the pro-Roman party in Germany, is here addressing Germanicus, who had just rescued him from Arminius (that is, Hermann), chief of the Cheruscans, who was married to Segestes' daughter, Thusnelda.
[63] The granting of Roman citizenship both to client kings and to prominent native leaders was established policy in the late Republic and during the Empire.
[64] Cf. § 10, second selection.

last that I have access to you, I declare my preference for the old over the new, for peace over disorder, not for a reward, but to absolve myself of the charge of bad faith and at the same time to be a suitable mediator for a German tribe, if they show preference for repentence rather than destruction. . . ."

When news of Segestes' surrender and of his favorable reception was spread, it was received with hope or grief, according as each was against or desirous of war. . . . Arminius rushed about among the Cheruscans demanding war against Segestes, war against Caesar. And he did not restrain his taunts: "Let Segestes dwell on the conquered bank; let him restore to his sons his priesthood for the worship of men; [65] the Germans will never quite excuse the fact that they saw the *fasces* and toga between the Elbe and the Rhine. . . . If you prefer your fatherland, your ancestors, and your ancient traditions to masters and new colonies, follow Arminius as your leader to glory and freedom rather than Segestes to disgraceful servitude." [66]

26. *Client States*

The borders of the Empire were cushioned at various points by vassal states ruled by client princes invested with their power by the emperor (cf. § 10). These client kings contributed to the security of the frontiers by restraining their own peoples (cf. Tacitus *Agricola* xiv: "the old, long-established policy of the Roman people of employing kings too as instruments of enslavement") and by repelling attacks from beyond their own borders. Gradually most of the client kingdoms in North Africa, Syria, Asia Minor, and Thrace were absorbed into the provincial system during the first century of the Principate. From the time of the Flavian emperors it was principally on the Rhine-Danube frontiers and along the Euphrates that such buffer states were retained. Early in the Principate occasional subsidies were granted to client states, but in time such payments came to be expected, and by the second century they were made annually. Later, such subsidies were paid to border peoples to buy off their threatened attacks against the Empire (see §§ 28, 116).

Dio Cassius *Roman History* LX. viii. 1–3
From LCL

Next Claudius restored Commagene to Antiochus, since Caligula, though he had himself given him the district, had taken it away again;

---

[65] That is, of the emperors.
[66] In recording the assassination of Arminius in A.D. 19 by his own kinsmen, Tacitus (*Annals* II. lxxxviii. 3–4) calls Arminius "assuredly the liberator of Germany, who challenged the Roman people not in the early stage, as other kings and leaders, but at the height of their Empire. . . . He is still a theme of song among the barbarian tribes."

and Mithridates the Iberian, whom Caligula had summoned and imprisoned, was sent home again to resume his throne. To another Mithridates, a descendant of Mithridates the Great, he granted the kingdom of Bosporus, giving to Polemo some land in Cilicia in place of it. He enlarged the domain of Agrippa of Palestine, who, happening to be in Rome, had helped him to become emperor, and he bestowed on him the rank of consul; and to his brother Herod he gave the rank of praetor and a principality. And he permitted them to enter the senate and to express thanks to him in Greek.

Tacitus *Germany* xli–xlii

Closer to us—to follow the course of the Danube now, as I previously followed that of the Rhine—lies the state of the Hermundurians, which is loyal to the Romans. Accordingly, they are the sole Germans with whom trade is carried on not on the river bank but far within our territory, and even in the most flourishing colony [67] of the province of Raetia. They cross over everywhere unguarded; and while to other tribes we display only our arms and camps, to these we have thrown open our houses and villas, for they do not covet them. . . .

Next to the Hermundurians dwell the Naristians, and then the Marcomannians [68] and the Quadians. The Marcomannians are especially famous and powerful. . . . Nor are the Naristians and Quadians inferior to them. This area is, as it were, the van of Germany, as far as it is bounded by the Danube. The Marcomannians and the Quadians down to our time still had native kings, of the noble line of Maroboduus and Tudrus; now they accept even foreign kings, but the power and sovereignty of the kings stem from Roman authority. On occasions they are aided by our armed forces, more often by subsidies, but their domestic power is not thereby reduced.[69]

THE CORONATION OF TIRIDATES

In the reign of Nero, Roman suzerainty over the vassal state of Armenia, long a bone of contention between Rome and Parthia, was challenged by Vologeses, ruler of the Parthian empire, who placed his brother Tiridates on the throne of Armenia. By a major stroke of diplomacy Tiridates was permitted to retain the kingdom, provided he acknowledged Roman overlordship and received his crown from Nero. This compromise between the two great powers, symbolized by the coronation of Tiridates in Rome in A.D. 66, assured

[67] Augusta Vindelicorum (modern Augsburg).
[68] Their name signifies "men of the mark," that is, "border people."
[69] For the invasions of the Empire by these Germanic peoples during the reign of Marcus Aurelius, see § 28, second selection.

a half century of stability and peace on the eastern frontier. The name of a Roman centurion recently discovered carved on a mountain face in Azerbaijan —farther east than any previously known Roman inscription—attests the presence of Roman soldiery by the western shore of the Caspian Sea in A.D. 89/96.

Dio Cassius *Roman History* LXIII. i. 2–v. 4 (abridged)
Adapted from LCL

Tiridates set out for Rome, bringing with him not only his own sons but also those of Vologeses, Pacorus, and Monobazus.[70] Their progress all the way from the Euphrates was like a triumphal procession. . . . The prince covered the whole distance as far as Italy on horseback, and beside him rode his wife, wearing a golden helmet in place of a veil, so as not to go counter to her native customs by letting her face be seen. In Italy he was conveyed in a chariot sent by Nero and met the emperor at Naples. . . . He refused, however, to obey the order to lay aside his sword when he approached the emperor, but fastened it to the scabbard with nails. Yet he knelt upon the ground, and with arms crossed called him master, and did obeisance. . . .

After this Nero conducted him to Rome and set the diadem upon his head. The entire city had been decorated with torches and garlands, and great crowds of people were to be seen everywhere, the Forum being especially full. . . . Everything had been prepared during the night; and at daybreak Nero, wearing the triumphal garb and accompanied by the senate and the Praetorian Guards, entered the Forum. He ascended the *Rostra* and seated himself upon a chair of state. Next Tiridates and his retinue passed between lines of armed troops drawn up on either side, took their stand before the *Rostra*, and did obeisance to the emperor as they had done before. At this a great roar went up, which so alarmed Tiridates that for some moments he stood speechless, in terror of his life. Then, silence having been proclaimed, he recovered courage and quelling his pride made himself subservient to the necessities of the occasion, caring little how humbly he spoke, in view of the prize he hoped to obtain. These were his words: "Master, I am the descendant of Arsaces, brother of the kings Vologeses and Pacorus, and thy slave. And I have come to thee, my god, to worship thee as I do Mithras.[71] Whatever destiny thou spinnest for me shall be mine; for thou art my fate and my fortune." Nero replied to him as follows: "Well hast thou done to come hither in person, that meeting me face to face thou mayest enjoy my grace. For what neither thy father left thee

[70] Pacorus was a brother of Tiridates; Monobazus was king of Adiabene, a client state of Parthia.
[71] For the worship of Mithras in the Roman Empire, see introduction to § 171.

nor thy brothers gave and preserved for thee, this do I grant thee. King of Armenia I now declare thee, that both thou and they may understand that I have the power to take away kingdoms and to bestow them." At the close of these words he bade him ascend by the approach which had been built in front of the *Rostra* expressly for this occasion, and when Tiridates had been made to sit beneath his feet, he placed the diadem upon his head.

27. *Territorial Expansion*

Only two significant departures from the nonaggressive foreign policy of the Empire occurred in the first two centuries. The conquest of Britain was undertaken in the reign of Claudius primarily to protect the security of Gaul by removing a formidable focus of Celtic national independence across the Channel; southern Britain was rapidly overrun and organized into a province (A.D. 43–47), though prolonged military operations, lasting about a century, were required to end native resistance. At the beginning of the second century a radical extension of the long-established borders was projected by the soldier-emperor Trajan, who launched successive wars across the two most critical points of the frontiers and carved out the new provinces of Dacia, north of the Danube, and of Armenia, Mesopotamia, and Assyria, east of the Euphrates. At his death in A.D. 117 the Empire stood at its greatest territorial extent. But Trajan's aggressive policy had overtaxed the manpower and financial resources of the Empire; Hadrian upon his accession promptly returned to the traditional defensive policy, abandoning Trajan's annexations beyond the Euphrates but retaining Dacia because of its economic advantages.

THE CONQUEST OF BRITAIN

Dio Cassius *Roman History* LX. xix. 1–xxii. 1 (abridged)
Adapted from LCL

Aulus Plautius, a senator of great renown, made a campaign against Britain; for a certain Bericus,[72] who had been driven out of the island as the result of an uprising, had persuaded Claudius to send a force there. . . . [The Roman forces] put in to the island and found none to oppose them. For the Britons as a result of their inquiries had not expected that they would come and had therefore not assembled beforehand. And even when they did assemble, they would not come to close quarters with the Romans but took refuge in the marshes and the forests, hoping to wear them out in fruitless effort, so that, just as in the days of Julius Caesar,[73] they should sail back with nothing accomplished.

---

[72] A British chieftain.   [73] See Vol. I, § 87.

Plautius, accordingly, had a great deal of trouble in searching them out; but when at last he did find them, he first defeated Caratacus and then Togodumnus, the sons of Cunobellinus,[74] who was dead. (The Britons were not self-governing, but were divided into groups under various kings.) After the flight of these kings he gained by capitulation a part of the Bodunnians, who were ruled by the Catuvellanians; and leaving a garrison there, he advanced farther. . . .

Though Togodumnus perished, the Britons were far from yielding, but united all the more firmly to avenge his death. Plautius became afraid, and instead of advancing farther, proceeded to guard what he had already won, and sent for Claudius. For he had been instructed to do this in case he met with any stubborn resistance. And, in fact, extensive equipment, including elephants, had already been assembled for the expedition.

When the message reached him, Claudius . . . set out for the front. He sailed down the river to Ostia, and from there he was conveyed to Marseilles; thence, advancing partly by land and partly along the rivers, he came to the ocean and crossed over to Britain, where he joined the legions that were waiting for him near the Thames. Taking over the command of these, he crossed the stream, and engaging the barbarians, who had gathered at his approach, he defeated them in battle and captured Camulodunum,[75] the capital of Cunobellinus. Thereupon he brought over to his side numerous tribes, some by treaty, others by force, and was acclaimed *imperator* several times, contrary to precedent (for no one man may receive this appellation more than once for one and the same war). He deprived the conquered of their arms and handed them over to Plautius, bidding him also subjugate the remaining districts. Claudius himself now hastened back to Rome,[76] sending ahead the news of his victory. . . . The senate on learning of his achievement gave him the title Britannicus and granted him the celebration of a triumph.

CIL, Vol. VI, No. 920 (= Dessau, No. 216) [77]

To Tiberius Claudius Caesar, son of Drusus, Augustus Germanicus, *pontifex maximus*, holding the tribunician power for the eleventh year, consul five times, acclaimed *imperator* . . . times, father of his country, the Roman senate and people [dedicated this] because he received the surrender of eleven kings of Britain conquered without any reverse

---

[74] Cunobellinus (Cymbeline) had built up a powerful Belgic empire in Britain. His death in A.D. 42 led to internal disorders which facilitated Roman intervention.
[75] The site of modern Colchester.
[76] Claudius spent only sixteen days in Britain.
[77] From an arch in Rome erected A.D. 51/52.

and because he was the first to subject to the sovereignty of the Roman
people barbarian tribes across the ocean.

TRAJAN'S ANNEXATION OF DACIA

Dio Cassius *Roman History* LXVIII. vi. 1, xiii. 1–xiv. 3
From LCL

After spending some time in Rome, Trajan made a campaign against
the Dacians; for he took into account their past deeds and was grieved at
the amount of money they were receiving annually, and he also observed
that their power and their arrogance were increasing. . . .

Trajan constructed over the Danube a stone bridge for which I
cannot sufficiently admire him.[78] Brilliant, indeed, as are his other
achievements, this surpasses them. For it has twenty piers of squared
stone 150 feet in height above the foundations and sixty in width, and
these, standing at a distance of 170 feet from one another, are connected
by arches. How, then, could one fail to be astonished at the expenditure
made upon them, or at the way in which each of them was placed in a
river so deep, in water so full of eddies, and on a bottom so muddy? . . .
The very fact that the river in its descent is here contracted from a great
flood to such a narrow channel, after which it again expands into a
greater flood, makes it all the more violent and deep, and this feature
must be considered in estimating the difficulty of constructing the
bridge. This, too, then, reveals the magnitude of Trajan's designs, though
the bridge is of no use to us; for merely the piers are standing, affording no means of crossing. . . . Trajan built the bridge because he
feared that some time when the Danube was frozen over war might be
made upon the Romans on the farther side, and he wished to facilitate
access to them by this means. Hadrian, on the contrary, was afraid that
it might also make it easy for the barbarians, once they had overpowered
the guards at the bridge, to cross into Moesia, and so he removed the
superstructure.

Trajan, having crossed the Danube by means of this bridge, conducted the war with safe prudence rather than with haste; and eventually, after a hard struggle, vanquished the Dacians. . . . Decebalus,[79]
when his capital and all his territory had been occupied and he was him-

[78] Trajan's famous bridge at Drobetae (Turnu-Severin, Rumania), erected in A.D.
106, was the work of the Syrian architect Apollodorus. Some of the piers are still
in situ.
[79] King of the Dacians, who had unified the region during the reign of Domitian.
His inroads into the province of Moesia led to a campaign by Domitian against
Dacia, but the threat of attacks by other trans-Danubian tribes induced Domitian to
grant Decebalus a favorable peace (A.D. 89), including huge subsidies.

self in danger of being captured, committed suicide; and his head was brought to Rome. In this way Dacia became subject to the Romans,[80] and Trajan founded cities there.

HADRIAN RETURNS TO A DEFENSIVE POLICY

"Historia Augusta" Life of Hadrian v. 1–3
From LCL

On taking possession of the imperial power Hadrian at once resumed the policy of the early emperors and devoted his attention to maintaining peace throughout the world. For the nations which Trajan had conquered began to revolt; the Moors, moreover, began to make attacks, and the Sarmatians to wage war, the Britons could not be kept under Roman sway, Egypt was thrown into disorder by riots, and finally Libya and Palestine showed the spirit of rebellion. Whereupon he relinquished all the conquests east of the Euphrates and the Tigris, following, as he used to say, the example of Cato, who urged that the Macedonians, because they could not be held as subjects, should be declared free and independent.

28. *The Danube Frontier*

The weakest part of the northern frontiers remained the Danube. Continued payment of subsidies to peoples beyond the borders for help in guarding the frontiers and Trajan's effort to drive a wedge between Rome's enemies by occupying Dacia failed to stabilize the area. Early in the Principate a drastic policy was introduced—the settlement of barbarian tribes on the Roman side of the frontier in exchange for border military service. From the middle of the second century the pressures on the Empire's frontiers grew in intensity, and the "philosopher-king," Marcus Aurelius, was compelled to spend nearly his entire reign at war. New impetus was given by Marcus Aurelius to the assignment to barbarians of lands in border provinces, and this policy was continued by succeeding emperors, notably Pertinax and the Severi (see § 116). This practice introduced increasing numbers of Germans into the Roman provinces and armed forces, with far-reaching consequences for the future.

CIL, Vol. XIV, No. 3,608 (= Dessau, No. 986) [81]

To Tiberius Plautius Silvanus Aelianus son of Marcus, of the Aniensian tribe, pontiff, priest of Augustus, member of the board of three

---

[80] The dates of Trajan's Dacian Wars are A.D. 101–2, 105–6. Scenes from his campaigns in Dacia are depicted on the reliefs of the famous Column of Trajan in Rome.
[81] From the mausoleum of the Plautian family at Tibur (modern Tivoli), Italy.

for minting bronze, silver, and gold, quaestor of Tiberius Caesar, legate of the Fifth Legion in Germany, urban praetor, legate and member of the staff of Claudius Caesar in Britain,[82] consul,[83] proconsul of Asia, legate with the rank of praetor in Moesia.[84] To this province he transplanted—and forced to pay tribute—more than 100,000 Transdanubians with their wives and children, chiefs and kings. He suppressed an incipient disturbance of the Sarmatians, although he had sent a great part of his army to the expedition against Armenia. Kings hitherto unknown or hostile to the Roman people he brought to the bank which he guarded, to honor the Roman standards. He restored to the kings of the Bastarnians and the Rhoxolanians their sons, and to the king of the Dacians his brothers, who had been captured or rescued from the enemy. From other kings he received hostages. By these measures he both strengthened and advanced the peace of the province. He also dislodged the king of the Scythians from the siege of Chersonesus,[85] which is beyond the Dnieper river. He was the first to add to the grain supply of the Roman people a great quantity of wheat from that province [Moesia]. While he was legate in Spain he was recalled to assume the prefecture of the city, and during his prefecture the senate honored him with triumphal decorations on motion of the Emperor Caesar Augustus Vespasian, whose address contained the words recorded below:

"He governed Moesia so ably that the bestowing of triumphal decorations on him should not have been delayed to my time, save only that in the course of the delay he obtained a more distinguished honor, namely the prefecture of the city."

The Emperor Caesar Augustus Vespasian made him consul for a second time [86] while he held the said prefecture of the city.

Dio Cassius *Roman History* LXXI. iii. 1–2, xi. 1–xii. 2

From LCL

Marcus Aurelius himself fought for a long time, in fact almost his entire life, one might say, with the barbarians in the region of the Danube, with both the Iazyges and the Marcomannians, one after the other, using Pannonia as his base. . . .

Many of the Germans, too, from across the Rhine advanced as far as Italy and inflicted many injuries upon the Romans. They were in turn attacked by Marcus Aurelius, who opposed to them his lieutenants Pompeianus and Pertinax; and Pertinax (who later became emperor)

---

[82] Cf. § 27, first selection.   [83] A.D. 45.   [84] Probably early in Nero's reign.
[85] This flourishing city was near modern Sevastopol in the Crimea.
[86] A.D. 74.

greatly distinguished himself. Among the corpses of the barbarians there were found even women's bodies in armor. . . .

Marcus Aurelius remained in Pannonia in order to give audience to the embassies of the barbarians; for many came to him at this time also.[87] Some of them, under the leadership of Battarius, a boy twelve years old, promised an alliance; these received money and succeeded in restraining Tarbus, a neighboring chieftain, who had come into Dacia and was demanding money and threatening to make war if he should fail to get it. Others, like the Quadians, asked for peace, which was granted them, both in the hope that they might be detached from the Marcomannians, and also because they gave him many horses and cattle and besides promised to surrender all the deserters and captives— 13,000 at first, and later all the others as well. The right to attend the markets,[88] however, was not granted them, for fear that the Marcomannians and the Iazyges, whom they had sworn not to receive and not to let pass through their territory, should mingle with them and, passing themselves off for Quadians, should reconnoiter the Roman positions and purchase provisions. Besides these that came to Marcus many other envoys were sent, some by tribes and some by peoples, offering surrender. Some of them were sent on campaigns elsewhere, as were also the captives and deserters who were fit for service; others received land in Dacia, Pannonia, Moesia, the province of Germany, and in Italy itself. Those who were settled at Ravenna made an uprising and even went so far as to seize possession of the city; for this reason Marcus did not again bring any of the barbarians into Italy but even banished those who had previously come there. . . .

The Astingians, led by their chieftains Raüs and Raptus, came into Dacia with their entire households, hoping to secure both money and land in return for their alliance. . . . In response to urgent supplications addressed to Marcus Aurelius they received from him both money and the privilege of asking for land in case they should inflict some injury upon those who were fighting against him.

Dio Cassius *Roman History* LXXII. ii. 2–iii. 3

From LCL

Although he might easily have destroyed them, Commodus made terms with the Marcomannians,[89] for he hated all exertion and was eager

---

[87] The campaign of A.D. 169–70 is the subject of this passage. The Column of Marcus Aurelius, still standing in Rome, commemorates victories won in the campaigns against various tribes in 172–75.

[88] That is, in the towns (usually fortress towns) on the Roman side of the Danube.

[89] Renewed incursions in 178–80 by Quadians and Marcomannians had determined

for the comforts of the city. In addition to the conditions which his father had imposed upon them he also demanded that they restore to him the deserters and the captives that they had taken in the meantime and that they furnish annually a stipulated amount of grain—a demand from which he subsequently released them. Moreover, he obtained some arms from them and soldiers as well, 13,000 from the Quadians and a smaller number from the Marcomannians; and in return for these he relieved them of the requirement of an annual [military] levy. However, he further commanded that they should not assemble often nor in many parts of the country, but only once each month and in one place, and in the presence of a Roman centurion; and, furthermore, that they should not make war upon the Iazyges, the Burians, or the Vandilians. On these terms, then, he made peace, and abandoned all the outposts in their country beyond the strip along the frontier that was neutralized. . . . He compelled the others to take an oath that they would never dwell in nor use for pasturage a five-mile strip of their territory next to Dacia.[90] When 12,000 of the neighboring Dacians had been driven out of their own country and were on the point of aiding the others, they were dissuaded . . . from their purpose, with the promise that some land in our Dacia would be given them.

29. *The Role of the Senate*

The senate was maintained by the emperors of the first two centuries as a major governmental organ alongside the imperial administration. It elected the magistrates (cf. above, Note 43), enacted legislation, and served as a trial bench for major offenses (cf. §§ 7, 23). But the elections became increasingly a routine formality as the candidates were more and more designated by the emperors; and the senate's legislative function rapidly degenerated into voicing perfunctory assent to motions submitted by the emperor either in person or through the consuls. Thus, though the emperors in general were careful to maintain and even increase the visible prestige and dignity of the order, the senate was no longer an independent, policy-making body but only a legislative and administrative instrument of the *princeps*. Indeed, it waited upon the emperor's initiative and performed his will with such sedulous servility that it even evoked his open scorn. "What men—ready for slavery!" is said to have been Tiberius' comment on senate meetings (Tacitus

Marcus Aurelius to seek a permanent solution by annexing additional provinces across the Danube—a design cut short by his sudden death at Vienna in 180. Commodus' return to diplomatic settlements was short-lived.
[90] These provisions are essentially the same as the terms imposed some years earlier by Marcus Aurelius (Dio Cassius *Roman History* LXXI. xv–xvi).

Annals III. lxv). The history of the senate under the Principate is one of increasing subservience and decreasing importance proceeding *pari passu* with the increasing autocracy of the emperor (cf. § 24).

Berlin Papyrus No. 611, col. 3, lines 10–22 (= *FIRA*, Vol. I, No. 44);
A.D. 42/51

The following is an excerpt from an address on trial procedures delivered in the senate by the Emperor Claudius.

If these proposals meet with your approval, Conscript Fathers, say so at once, frankly and honestly. If, however, you disapprove, find another solution, but do it here in this temple. Or if you want to take more time to consider the matter at greater leisure, take it, so long as you remember that, in whatever order you are called, you must state your own view. For, Conscript Fathers, it is altogether unbecoming to the majesty of this body to have one man alone, the consul designate, state his view here, copying it word for word from the motion of the consuls; and the rest of you utter but one word, "I agree," and leave saying, "Well, we spoke."

Pliny *Letters* Book VIII, No. 6. 1–11 (abridged)

Gaius Plinius to his dear Montanus, greeting.

I recently noticed the monument of Pallas [91] with this inscription: "For his fidelity and loyalty toward his patrons the senate decreed to him the insignia of praetorian rank together with 15,000,000 sesterces, of which he accepted the honor alone." Afterwards it seemed to me worth while to look up the actual decree of the senate. I found it so copious and effusive that that most arrogant inscription seemed modest and even humble by comparison. . . . I pass by their offering to a slave the insignia of praetorian rank (for they were slaves themselves who did it), I pass by their voting that Pallas should not merely be exhorted but even compelled to wear the gold ring.[92] . . . Truly memorable is . . . the senate's thanking Caesar in the name of Pallas for bestowing the highest honor upon him at their suggestion and for affording the senate an opportunity of demonstrating their good will toward him. . . . The decree goes on: "Since no more agreeable occasion of liberality could be afforded the Roman senate and people than the opportunity of

[91] The Emperor Claudius entrusted the operation of his most important administrative departments to a number of freedmen of the imperial household, who, as a result, became veritable powers behind the throne and amassed tremendous fortunes, including landed estates in Egypt (cf. § 42, fifth selection). Pallas was the financial secretary and second in importance only to Narcissus, who was a kind of secretary general (cf. introduction to § 31).
[92] A mark of equestrian rank.

increasing the wealth of the most thrifty and most trustworthy guardian of the emperor's property, the senate would have wished to decree that he be given 15,000,000 sesterces out of the public treasury and, because his is a spirit far removed from desires of this kind, all the more earnestly to beg the father of the state to constrain him to yield to the senate's wish. But since the best of emperors and father of the state has, at Pallas' request, desired the part of the resolution concerned with giving him 15,000,000 sesterces out of the public treasury to be withdrawn, the senate hereby affirms that, although it would gladly and justly have set about decreeing that sum among other honors to Pallas on account of his fidelity and diligence, yet in this matter too it is yielding to the desire of its *princeps*, whom, in its judgment, it is not right to oppose in any matter." [93]

Pliny *Letters* Book II, No. 11. 1–19 (abridged)

Gaius Plinius to his dear Arrianus, greeting.[94]

It is always a source of pleasure to you when something is done in the senate that is worthy of that order. . . . Learn then what took place in the last few days—something memorable in view of the prominence of the person involved, salutary in the severity of the example, everlasting because of the importance of the affair.

Marius Priscus [95] was accused by the people of Africa, which he had governed as proconsul. Without making any defense he asked that the case be referred to a senatorial trial commission. Cornelius Tacitus and I, assigned as counsel for the provincials, felt obliged in good conscience to inform the senate that because of Priscus' barbarity and fiendishness the charges against him were beyond the competence of such a commission, since he had accepted bribes to condemn and even execute innocent persons. . . .[96]

The case was adjourned to the next meeting of the senate, which presented a most awesome spectacle. The emperor himself presided, since he was consul. In addition it was the month of January, when the senate, like everything else [in Rome], is at its most crowded. . . . Picture to

[93] Tacitus too tells of this incident of A.D. 52 (*Annals* XII. liii): "Soranus Barea, consul designate, proposed that the senate decree the insignia of praetorian rank and 15,000,000 sesterces to Pallas, and Cornelius Scipio added that public thanks should be rendered because a scion of the kings of Arcadia was subordinating his ancient nobility to the public interest and allowing himself to be ranked among the emperor's assistants. Claudius declared that Pallas was content to have the honor and remain in his former poverty. And so a decree of the senate was publicly posted in which a freedman possessing 300,000,000 sesterces was overwhelmed with praises for his old-fashioned frugality."

[94] This letter was written in A.D. 100.

[95] This is the Marius of the classic remark of Juvenal quoted in Vol. I, pp. 370–71.

[96] Capital crimes were excluded from the purview of this special senatorial trial commission; cf. § 9, v.

yourself our concern and anxiety at having to speak on so important a matter before such a gathering, and in the presence of the emperor. I have spoken in the senate on more than one occasion, you know— nowhere, indeed, do I have a friendlier audience. Yet this time I was perturbed by a novel anxiety, as if everything were new to me. Besides the considerations already mentioned, I was aware of the difficult nature of the case. There stood before me a man until lately of consular rank, until lately a member of the board of seven for conducting religious banquets, and now neither of these. It was an exceedingly onerous task to prosecute a convicted man. . . .[97]

However, I collected my spirits and wits as best I could and launched into my speech, and the approval of the listeners was as great as my own concern had been. I spoke for almost five hours, and four water-clocks were added to the twelve of largest size which had been allowed me. Indeed the very factors that had appeared as difficulties and impediments when I was waiting to speak proved advantageous when I was actually speaking. The emperor showed such solicitude, such care (it would be too much to say concern) for me, that he frequently urged a freedman of mine standing behind me to have me spare my voice and breath, thinking I was exerting myself beyond what my slight frame could bear.

Claudius Marcellinus replied in behalf of Marcianus.[98] The senate then adjourned to the following day, for the next speech could not have been begun without being interrupted by nightfall. . . .[99] It was a fine thing, like olden times, to see the senate interrupted by the night, called together three days in a row, held in session three days in a row. Cornutus Tertullus, consul designate, an excellent man ever firm in the cause of truth, moved that Marius pay into the public treasury the 700,000 sesterces he had accepted, and that Marius be banished from Rome and Italy and Marcianus from Africa in addition. He concluded with the further motion that, whereas Tacitus and I had faithfully and vigorously discharged the role of advocate assigned to us, the senate judged that we had acted in a manner worthy of the duty entrusted to us.

30. Senatorial Careers

The senatorial order remained under the Principate the highest social and political class of the Roman state. But the noble families of the Republic, deci-

[97] Before this trial on the bribery charge Priscus had already been convicted of practicing extortion in his province and stripped of his honors.
[98] One of the men accused of bribing Priscus.
[99] The senate could not legally act after nightfall; cf. Vol. I, p. 400.

mated by the civil wars and by persecution under the Julio-Claudian emperors, provided a steadily declining portion of the membership. To make up the full complement the emperors adopted the policy of bringing in new members from other classes, especially *equites* and upper-class provincials. The minimum property qualification for belonging to this nobility was 1,000,000 sesterces. The senatorial order provided the men of praetorian and consular rank, who held the higher magistracies at Rome and most of the top posts in the army and in the administration of the provinces, imperial as well as senatorial. Tombstones and statue bases with inscriptions recording the careers of men of senatorial rank are extant in great numbers. A small but representative selection is given below, in chronological order ranging from the time of Augustus to the middle of the second century (cf. also the first selection in § 28). In these inscriptions, offices and honors are usually listed in chronological sequence—either in the order in which they were obtained, following an ascending order of importance, or in descending order, beginning with the last and highest.

CIL, Vol. IX, No. 2,845 (= Dessau, No. 915)

[Histonium, Samnium]

Publius Paquius Scaeva son of Scaeva and Flavia, grandson of Consus and Didia, great-grandson of Barbus and Dirutia; quaestor; member—after his quaestorship, in accordance with a decree of the senate —of the board of ten for judging lawsuits; member—after his quaestorship and membership on the board of ten for judging lawsuits, in accordance with a decree of the senate—of the board of four for capital cases; tribune of the plebs; curule aedile; criminal-court judge; praetor of the treasury; as proconsul governed the province of Cyprus; commissioner of the roads outside the city of Rome for five years in accordance with a decree of the senate; proconsul extraordinary a second time by authority of Augustus Caesar, and by decree of the senate sent to restore order in the remainder of the province of Cyprus; fetial; cousin and also husband of Flavia daughter of Consus, grand-daughter of Scapula, great-granddaughter of Barbus, laid to rest [here] together with her.

CIL, Vol. X, No. 5,182 (= Dessau, No. 972)

[Casinum, Latium]

To Gaius Ummidius Durmius Quadratus [100] son of Gaius, of the Teretine tribe; consul; member of the board of fifteen for performing public sacrifices; legate of Tiberius Caesar Augustus in the province of Lusitania; legate of the deified Claudius in Illyricum, and of the same and

[100] This is the same man who appears as governor of Lusitania in § 20, second selection.

of Nero Caesar Augustus in Syria; proconsul of the province of Cyprus; quaestor of the deified Augustus and of Tiberius Caesar Augustus; curule aedile; praetor of the treasury; member of the board of ten for judging lawsuits; curator of the public archives; prefect for distributing grain in accordance with a decree of the senate.

CIL, Vol. III, No. 4,013 (= Dessau, No. 1,005)

[Andautonia, Pannonia Superior]

Dedicated in gratitude to our patron, Lucius Funisulanus Vettonianus son of Lucius, of the Aniensian tribe; military tribune of the Legion VI Victrix; quaestor of the province of Sicily; tribune of the plebs; praetor; legate of the Legion IV Scythica; prefect of the public treasury; commissioner of the Aemilian Way; consul; member of the board of seven for conducting religious banquets; legate with rank of praetor in the province of Dalmatia, likewise in the province of Pannonia, likewise in Moesia Superior; decorated by the Emperor Domitian Augustus Germanicus [101] in the Dacian War with four crowns (the mural, the rampart-storming, the naval, and the golden), four parade spears, and four detachment banners.[102]

CIL, Vol. XI, No. 5,211 (= Dessau, No. 991)

[Fulginiae, Umbria]

Dedicated in gratitude to our excellent patron Gnaeus Domitius . . . Curvius Tullus son of Sextus; consul; proconsul of the province of Africa; fetial; prefect of all auxiliary forces against the Germans; who, when he was praetor designate as candidate of the emperor,[103] was detailed by the Emperor Vespasian Augustus as legate with rank of praetor to the army stationed in Africa and was raised to praetorian rank *in absentia;* decorated by the Emperor Vespasian Augustus and by

[101] The name of Domitian is effaced. This was the regular practice with the names of emperors declared "of damned memory" after death; cf. below, Note 110.
[102] Vettonianus was apparently cited four times for bravery, receiving as decorations on each occasion a military crown, an untipped spear, and the "company colors." These military crowns are described in Aulus Gellius *Attic Nights* v. vi. 16–19: "The mural crown is that which is awarded by a commander to the man who is first to mount the wall and force his way into an enemy's town; therefore it is ornamented with representations of the battlements of a wall. A camp [rampart-storming] crown is presented by a commander to the soldier who is first to fight his way into an enemy's camp; that crown has a palisade as its insigne. The naval crown is commonly awarded to the armed man who is first to board an enemy ship in a sea fight; it is decorated with representations of the beaks of ships. The mural, camp, and naval crowns are regularly made of gold." (Adapted from the Loeb Classical Library.)
[103] Cf. above, Note 26.

Titus Caesar, son of the emperor, with the mural, rampart-storming, and golden crowns, with three parade spears, and three detachment banners; enrolled among the patricians; tribune of the plebs; quaestor of Caesar Augustus; military tribune of the Legion V Alauda; member of the board of ten for judging lawsuits.

CIL, Vol. XIV, No. 3,610 (= Dessau, No. 1,071)

[Tibur, Latium]

To Gaius Popilius Carus Pedo son of Gaius, of the Quirine tribe; consul; member of the board of seven for conducting religious banquets; member of the priesthood of [the deified] Hadrian; legate of the Emperor Caesar Antoninus Augustus Pius with rank of praetor in Upper Germany and of the army encamped therein; commissioner of public works; prefect of the public treasury; commissioner of the Aurelian (old and new), Cornelian, and Triumphal Ways; legate of the Legion X Fretensis, from which position he resigned; praetor; tribune of the plebs; quaestor of the deified Hadrian Augustus; candidate of the emperor in all his offices; tribune (broad stripe [104]) of the Legion III Cyrenaica; honored with military decorations by the deified Hadrian for [bravery in] the Jewish campaign; member of the board of ten for judging lawsuits. The senate and people of Tibur [dedicated this to him], the patron of the municipality, protector of the highest type, for his excellent services to the community.

31. *Equestrian Careers*

Certain key posts, such as the great prefectures (see introduction to § 5), and most of the middle-grade administrative and military offices were assigned to men of the equestrian class, which, unlike the senate with its nostalgic memory of republican rule, was wholehearted in its support of the imperial régime. Thus there developed a public career for *equites* paralleling the senatorial career, and eventually encroaching upon it.

A major segment of the equestrian career was the civil service. The basis of the civil service organization was laid by the Emperor Claudius, who divided the record-keeping and related routine operations of his administration into five or more departments and placed one of his most trusted freedmen in charge of each (cf. above, Note 91). One department handled the voluminous correspondence in Latin and Greek which passed between the emperor and all parts of the Empire in the form of letters, reports, resolutions, memo-

---

[104] The distinctive emblem of tribunes on military service prior to entering upon a senatorial career; those preparing for equesterian careers wore a narrow stripe.

randa, etc. The functionary in charge of this office (*ab epistulis*) was thus a kind of secretary general to the emperor. The accounting office (*a rationibus*) handled the finances of the fisc, or privy purse, into which flowed the revenues from the emperors' many estates all over the Empire, from the imperial provinces, and—increasingly as financial control was progressively centralized in the hands of the emperor—even from the senatorial provinces. Requests and petitions to the emperor were the concern of the secretary *a libellis*, while the secretary *a cognitionibus* prepared all papers bearing on judicial cases coming before the emperor for decision. The secretary *a studiis* probably took care of the emperor's private library and provided him with references and material for speeches and edicts. The Flavian emperors and their successors retained and expanded this organizational structure, but, leaving the menial and clerical jobs to slaves and freedmen, they appointed with increasing frequency *equites* to the administrative posts, including the important and influential departmental secretaryships, which ranked just under the equestrian prefectures. Under the Emperor Hadrian the civil service was given its definitive organization, with fixed salaries for each rank and a fixed course of promotion. Moreover, completely separate careers were henceforth available in the civil and the military services. This separation, a departure from the age-old tradition of Roman public life, while it doubtless made for efficiency through specialization, was like Hadrian's military reorganization (§§ 148–150) fraught with long-term consequences for the future.[105]

The financial qualification for the equestrian order was a minimum worth of 400,000 sesterces. Admission was by birth or through promotion by the emperor. Except in individual cases this promotion was withheld from freedmen but readily granted to their sons. The following is a sampling from the numerous extant inscriptions recording equestrian careers of the first two centuries; as in the senatorial careers, the offices are generally arranged in ascending or descending order. It is noteworthy that the last of these inscriptions is a completely civilian career.

CIL, Vol. VI, No. 31,856 (= Dessau, No. 1,327)

[Rome]

Lucius Julius Vehilius Gratus Julianus; prefect of the Praetorian Guard; prefect of the grain supply; financial secretary to the emperor; prefect of the praetorian fleet of Misenum; prefect of the praetorian

---

[105] "The separation of the civilian from the military career was dangerous, not because it deprived men engaged in administration of some slight acquaintance with the army, but because . . . a bureaucracy of civilians was likely to be confronted before long with a more formidable body of men whose occupation was wholly military. And so it befell. In the conflict which began before the end of the second century the civilians were helpless before the army, power passed to men whose distinction in war was their only fame." (Quoted from *Cambridge Ancient History*, XI, 432.)

fleet of Ravenna; imperial procurator placed in command of a detachment at the time of the war in Britain; imperial procurator of the province of Lusitania and Vettonia; imperial procurator placed in command of a detachment in . . . ; imperial procurator and prefect of the Black Sea fleet; imperial procurator placed in command of a detachment in Achaea and Macedonia and [sent] into Spain against the rebellious Castabocans and Moors; commander of detachments at the time of the German and Sarmatian wars; prefect of the Tampian Company; prefect of the Herculean Company; tribune of the First Ulpian Cohort of the Pannonians; prefect of the Third Augustan Cohort of the Thracians; honored with military decorations by the Emperors Antoninus and Verus for the victory in the Parthian War, likewise by Antoninus and Commodus for the victory in the German and Sarmatian wars. . . . [The rest is lost.]

CIL, Vol. VI, No. 798 (= Dessau, No. 1,448)

[Rome]

Gnaeus Octavius Titinius Capito; [106] prefect of a cohort; military tribune; honored with the parade spear and the rampart-storming crown; secretary general to the emperor [107] and procurator of the imperial estate bureau; again secretary general of the deified Nerva, and on his motion awarded the insignia of praetorian rank by decree of the senate; a third time secretary general of the Emperor Caesar Trajan Augustus Germanicus; prefect of the night patrol; dedicated this thank offering to Vulcan.

CIL, Vol. VI, No. 1,625*b* (= Dessau, No. 1,340)

[Rome]

To Marcus Petronius Honoratus son of Marcus, of the Quirine tribe; prefect of the First Cohort of the Raetians; military tribune of the dutiful and faithful Legion I Minervia; prefect of the dutiful and faithful Augustan Company of the Thracians; procurator of the mint; procurator of the five-percent tax on inheritances; procurator of the provinces of Belgium and the two Germanies; financial secretary to the emperor; prefect of the grain supply; prefect of Egypt; minor pontiff. The oil merchants from Baetica [dedicated this to him], their patron.

[106] He is mentioned by Pliny in his *Letters* as a gentleman and man of letters of the period.
[107] Domitian, whose name is deliberately omitted; cf. Note. 101.

CIL, Vol. V, No. 867 (= Dessau, No. 1,339)

[Aquileia, Venetia]

To Tiberius Claudius Secundinus son of Tiberius, of the Palatine tribe, Lucius Statius Macedo; [108] chief centurion [109] of the Legion IV Flavia Felix; tribune of the first cohort of the night patrol; tribune of the eleventh cohort of the city guard; tribune of the eighth cohort of the Praetorian Guard; chief centurion a second time; prefect of the Legion II Trajana Fortis; procurator of the five-percent tax on inheritances; procurator of the provinces of Lugdunensis and Aquitania; financial secretary to the emperor; prefect of the grain supply. Lucius Saufeius Julianus [dedicated this to him], the best of friends.

CIL, Vol. X, No. 7,584 (= Dessau, No. 1,359)

[Carales, Sardinia]

To Marcus Cosconius Fronto son of Marcus, of the Pollian tribe; chosen aide-de-camp by the consul; prefect of the first cohort . . . ; military tribune of the Legion I Italica; imperial procurator for Pontus, Bithynia, Interior Pontus, and Paphlagonia for the revenue of the five-percent tax on inheritances; imperial procurator for Asia, Lycia, Phrygia, Galatia, and the Cyclades islands, likewise for the revenue of the five-percent tax on inheritances; subprefect of the grain supply of the city [of Rome]; imperial procurator for the revenue of the iron mines of Gaul; imperial procurator and prefect of the province of Sardinia. Lucretius, imperial freedman, keeper of records of the province of Sardinia, [dedicated this to him], his excellent and most just chief.

Dessau, No. 9,200

[Baalbek, Syria]

To Gaius Velius Rufus son of Salvius; first centurion of Legion XII Fulminata; prefect of detachments of Legions IX . . . , I Adjutrix, II Adjutrix, II Augusta, VIII Augusta, IX Hispana, XIV Gemina, XX Victrix, and XXI Rapax; tribune of the thirteenth urban cohort; general of the African and Mauretanian army [sent] to subdue the peoples which are in Mauretania; decorated in the Jewish War by the Emperor Vespasian and the Emperor Titus with the rampart-storming crown, collars, breastplates, and armlets, likewise decorated

[108] These two sets of names belong to one person, not two. Beginning in the second century it became customary to add to one's own (father-derived) names those of such persons as maternal grandfathers, great-grandfathers, and adoptive fathers.
[109] The *primipilus*, or centurion of the first maniple of the *triarii* (cf. Vol. I, p. 434).

with the mural crown, two parade spears, and two detachment banners, and in the war of the Marcomannians, Quadians, and Sarmatians, against whom he made an expedition through the kingdom of King Decebalus of the Dacians, with the mural crown, two parade spears, and two detachment banners; procurator of the Emperor Caesar Augustus [Domitian] Germanicus in the province of Pannonia and Dalmatia; likewise procurator of the province of Raetia, with power of life and death. He was sent into Parthia and brought back to the Emperor Vespasian Epiphanes and Callinicus, the sons of King Antiochus [of Commagene], together with a large number of tribute-paying persons. Marcus Alfius Olympiacus son of Marcus, of the Fabian tribe, standard bearer, veteran of Legion XV Apollinaris [erected this].

CIL, Vol. XIV, No. 2,922 (= Dessau, No. 1,420)

[Praeneste, Latium]

To Titus Flavius Germanus son of Titus; superintendent of the most fortunate second German triumph of the Emperor Caesar Lucius Aurelius Commodus Augustus; [110] honored by the same with the most illustrious priesthood of minor pontiff; procurator of the five-percent tax on inheritances; procurator of the imperial estate bureau; procurator of the Great Games; procurator of the Morning Games; [111] procurator of the districts of the city with the added charge of paving streets in two parts of the city; procurator of the five-percent tax on inheritances for Umbria, Etruria, Picenum, and the district of Campania; procurator for child assistance [112] in Lucania, Bruttium, Calabria, and Apulia; commissioner of public works and religious edifices in good repair; aedile; *duovir;* flamen of the deified Augustus; *duovir quinquennalis;* [113] patron of the colony. Cerdo, his freedman, [dedicated this to him], patron incomparable, together with his sons, Flavius Maximinus, Germanus, and Rufinus, honored with equestrian rank.

[110] Commodus, like Nero and Domitian, was upon his death declared "of damned memory"; hence his name, as well as the following words "by the same," were chiseled out on this inscription: cf. Note 101. Such effacement of imperial names from subsequent inscriptions in this volume will not be indicated.
[111] The Great, or Roman, Games were annual votive games to Jupiter Capitolinus, instituted, according to Roman tradition, by the ancient king Tarquinius Priscus (Vol. I, p. 55). At the height of their popularity, in the early Empire, these games were celebrated for fifteen days (September 4–19). The occasion of the Morning Games is not known; it is known from references in literature, however, that when circus games were being held, the combats with wild animals were customarily held in the mornings (cf. § 57, second selection).
[112] Cf. § 89.
[113] Cf. Vol. I, p. 419, Note 63.

APPOINTMENT OF A PRAETORIAN PREFECT

The following much-mutilated papyrus contains a fragment from an official letter from the Emperor Domitian to Lucius Laberius Maximus, the prefect of Egypt, appointing him to succeed one of the two prefects of the Praetorian Guard who had just been promoted to senatorial rank. In the second half of the first century the equestrian career appears to have culminated in this sequence of offices, whereas in the first half of the century advancement was generally from the praetorian to the Egyptian prefecture.

Comptes-rendus de l'Académie des Inscriptions et Belles-Lettres, 1947, p. 376; A.D. 84

. . . by reason of your character and devotion, my dear Maximus . . . and you have always received rewards from me. Still, I have not been content that appointment to the prefecture of Egypt should mark the pinnacle of your career, but when I transferred Julius Ursus,[114] who . . . was long desirous of it, to the most honorable order, I immediately took cognizance of your most devoted loyalty and industry and have made you the colleague . . . of Cornelius Fuscus,[115] with whom I hope you will not only discharge the duties of office most diligently but will also be most cordially in equal fellowship. I desire you to fly here, my dear Maximus, with favorable sea at the earliest opportunity. . . . I doubt not you will be most desirous of remaining[?] by my side. . . . [The rest is lost.]

32. *Extension of Roman Citizenship*

Under the Principate, Roman citizenship spread gradually to the provinces, progressively leading the Empire in the direction of cultural unity. Augustus' conservative policy with regard to the extension of Roman citizenship to non-Italians (see § 12) was, in part, a reaction to the unpopularity in Italy of Julius Caesar's granting of citizenship to a number of wealthy and influential men among the various Gallic tribes and his enrollment of some of these new citizens in the Roman senate. With the advent of the Emperor Claudius a more liberal policy of extending citizenship to urban communities in the Romanized provinces was initiated. Claudius thus laid the basis of the systematic process, widely extended by the Flavian emperors, which, with

[114] Probably Lucius Julius Ursus, who was appointed consul by Domitian in A.D. 83. Maximus succeeded him in turn as prefect of the grain supply, prefect of Egypt, and prefect of the Praetorian Guard.
[115] The other Praetorian prefect.

Trajan and Hadrian, brought to the Principate emperors born of Roman families in Spain, and which by the beginning of the third century led to almost universal enfranchisement (see § 113). In this process Roman citizenship was conferred by the emperors upon entire communities in the provinces by the grant of colonial or municipal status, and upon meritorious individuals (cf. the similar grants under the Republic: Vol. I, §§ 103, 135, 152). In a special class was the grant of Roman citizenship to individuals as a reward for military service (see § 155). Newly enfranchised citizens customarily adopted the family name of the emperor who authorized the grant; hence the large number of persons named Claudius, Flavius, and Aelius in the first two centuries A.D. The inscriptions reveal many persons of provincial origin who attained the senatorial and equestrian careers. In the process of expansion "the value and meaning of the franchise change; it becomes a *passive* citizenship, in Mommsen's phrase, and is no longer sought for its political significance but as an honour, or out of sentiment; the old privileges and duties of *civis Romanus* are effaced, and the extension of the citizenship becomes the sign of the unification of the Empire within one abiding system of law" (A. N. Sherwin-White, *The Roman Citizenship,* p. 168).

ENFRANCHISEMENT OF ALPINE TRIBES

The Anaunians, Tulliassians, and Sindunians were peoples living under the jurisdiction of the municipality of Tridentum (modern Trento) in the Italian Alps. In the reign of Claudius it was discovered that, though they had for some time been conducting their affairs as Roman citizens, they had never been granted such status *de jure.* To avoid the confusion that would result from the invalidation of property titles, marriages, and other such economic and social relationships contracted in good faith, the emperor in A.D. 46 issued an edict formally granting Roman citizenship to these peoples. The edict is preserved on a bronze tablet found at Val di Non near Trento.

CIL, Vol. V, No. 5,050 (= Abbott-Johnson, No. 49 = *FIRA,* Vol. I, No. 71)

The edict of Tiberius Claudius Caesar Augustus Germanicus which is recorded below was issued in the consulship of Marcus Junius Silanus and Quintus Sulpicius Camerinus, on March 15, in the imperial villa at Baiae.

Tiberius Claudius Caesar Augustus Germanicus, *pontifex maximus,* holding the tribunician power for the sixth year, acclaimed *imperator* eleven times, father of his country, designated consul for the fourth time, declares:

Whereas, owing to ancient unsettled disputes which were of long standing even in the times of my uncle Tiberius Caesar—disputes which concerned only the people of Como and the Bergaleians, as far as my memory serves—Tiberius sent Pinarius Apollinaris for the settlement of the same; and whereas the latter at first because of the obstinate retirement of my uncle, and then because in the Principate of Gaius he was not requested by him to make a report, not unwisely neglected to do so; and whereas subsequently Camurius Statutus reported to me that a good many fields and woodlands are subject to my jurisdiction; [116]

I have for the matter under consideration sent Julius Planta, my friend and adviser. And since he has investigated and examined the matter with the utmost care, in consultation with my procurators, both those who were in the vicinity and those in other parts of the region, with regard to all other matters I grant him permission to make decision and render judgment in accordance with the facts laid before me in the memorandum prepared by him.

But with regard to the status of the Anaunians, the Tulliassians, and the Sindunians, some of whom, as the informer is said to have proved, are merely attributed [117] to the Tridentines, while some do not even have such connection, although I am aware that persons of this category do not have too strong a basis for Roman citizenship; nevertheless, since they are said to have been in possession thereof by long usage and are so amalgamated with the Tridentines that they cannot be separated from them without serious harm to the flourishing municipality, I permit them by my indulgence to retain the legal status which they believed was theirs. And I am all the more inclined to do this because a number of this group are said to be actually serving in my Praetorian Guard, several indeed to have held officer rank, and some are said to be judging cases enrolled as members of jury panels at Rome.

And in granting them this benefaction, I order that all acts performed or done by them acting as if Roman citizens, whether among themselves or in relations with the Tridentines or others, shall be valid, and I allow them to keep the names which, when acting as if Roman citizens, they previously used.

ADMISSION OF PROVINCIALS TO THE SENATE

In A.D. 48 Claudius, acting as censor, proposed to fill some of the vacancies in the Roman senate with prominent citizens from the Gallic provinces. Despite the opposition of various senators, Claudius persevered, and thereby provided the impetus which led gradually to the transformation of the senate into a body whose members were recruited from the entire Empire. The following account of Tacitus is a paraphrase of the address delivered by Claudius in the senate. Part of the actual address is preserved in a bronze inscription

[116] That is, these lands belonged to the imperial estates.
[117] That is, these peoples were subject to the jurisdiction of the municipality but did not enjoy full civic rights in the community.

found at Lyons. This inscription begins in the middle of a lengthy historical disquisition, here omitted, to show that innovations were characteristic of Roman history and that earlier Romans were liberal in their policy toward foreigners. A detailed comparison of the Lyons inscription with Tacitus' text is made by K. Wellesley in *Greece and Rome,* I (1954), 13–33.

Tacitus *Annals* XI. xxiii. 1–xxv. 1

In the consulship of Aulus Vitellius and Lucius Vipstanus, when the question of filling up the membership of the senate was debated, the leading men of Gallia Comata, as it is called,[118] who had long before attained the rights of allies and Roman citizenship, sought the privilege of obtaining public offices at Rome. There was much talk of every kind on this issue, and a variety of arguments in opposition was expressed before the emperor. "Italy," some asserted, "is not so feeble that it is unable to furnish its capital with a senate. . . . Let [the Gauls] by all means enjoy the title of citizens, but let them not cheapen the distinctions of the senators and the honors of the magistracies."

The emperor was not impressed by these and similar arguments. He at once spoke out in opposition, and, convening the senate, he addressed them as follows: "[The experience of] my ancestors . . . induces me to employ the same policy in governing the state, namely that of transferring to this city all outstanding persons, wherever found. I am fully aware that the Julian family came from Alba, the Coruncanian from Camerium, the Porcian from Tusculum, and, not to search into the past, that members have been brought into the senate from Etruria, Lucania, and the whole of Italy, that Italy itself finally was extended to the Alps,[119] so that not only individuals but even regions and tribes were amalgamated into our state. We had stable peace at home, and our foreign relations were in an excellent state in the days when the people beyond the Po were admitted to citizenship, and when, under the pretext of settling our legions throughout the world, we reinforced our exhausted Empire by joining to ourselves the most vigorous of the provincials. Do we regret that the Balbian family came over from Spain, and others not less illustrious from Narbonese Gaul? Their descendants are still here, and are not second to us in patriotism. . . .

"If you review all our wars, none was ended in a shorter time than that with the Gauls. Thenceforth there has been an unbroken and loyal peace. Mingled with us as they are now, in their way of life, in their culture, and by intermarriage, let them bring us their gold and wealth

---

[118] Literally, "long-haired Gaul," a name derived from a custom of the natives in the three Gauls conquered by Julius Caesar (see Vol. I, p. 204).

[119] By Caesar, who granted citizenship to the inhabitants of the Po Valley (Cisalpine Gaul) at the beginning of the Civil War, in 49 B.C.

rather than keep it in isolation. Everything, members of the senate, which is now considered to be of the highest antiquity was once new. Plebeian magistrates came after patrician, Latin magistrates after the plebeian, magistrates of other peoples of Italy after the Latin. This practice, too, will establish itself, and what we are this day defending by precedents will itself be a precedent."

The emperor's address was followed by a decree of the senate, and the Aeduans were the first to obtain the right of becoming senators at Rome.

CIL, Vol. XIII, No. 1,668, col. 2 (= Abbott-Johnson, No. 50 = FIRA, Vol. I, No. 43)

. . . Surely both my great-uncle, the deified Augustus, and my uncle, Tiberius Caesar, were following a new practice when they desired that all the flower of the colonies and the municipalities everywhere —that is, the better class and the wealthy men—should sit in this senate house. You ask me: Is not an Italian senator preferable to a provincial? I shall reveal to you in detail my views on this matter when I come to obtain approval for this part of my censorship. But I think that not even provincials ought to be excluded, provided that they can add distinction to this senate house.

Look at that most distinguished and most flourishing colony of Vienna,[120] how long a time already it is that it has furnished senators to this house! From that colony comes that ornament of the equestrian order—and there are few to equal him—Lucius Vestinus, whom I cherish most intimately and whom at this very time I employ in my affairs. And it is my desire that his children may enjoy the first step in the priesthoods, so as to advance afterwards, as they grow older, to further honors in their rank. . . . I can say the same of his brother, who because of this wretched and most shameful circumstance cannot be a useful senator for you.

The time has now come, Tiberius Caesar Germanicus,[121] now that you have reached the farthest boundaries of Narbonese Gaul, for you to unveil to the members of the senate the import of your address. All these distinguished youths whom I gaze upon will no more give us cause for regret if they become senators than does my friend Persicus, a man of most noble ancestry, have cause for regret when he reads among the portraits of his ancestors the name Allobrogicus.[122] But if you agree that these things are so, what more do you want, when I point out to

[120] Modern Vienne, Dauphiné, France. [121] Claudius here addresses himself.
[122] An honorary name derived from the Allobroges, a Gallic tribe over whom one of Persicus' ancestors probably won a military victory.

you this single fact, that the territory beyond the boundaries of Narbonese Gaul already sends you senators, since we have men of our order from Lyons and have no cause for regret. It is indeed with hesitation, members of the senate, that I have gone outside the borders of the provinces with which you are accustomed and familiar, but I must now plead openly the cause of Gallia Comata. And if anyone, in this connection, has in mind that these people engaged the deified Julius in war for ten years, let him set against that the unshakable loyalty and obedience of a hundred years, tested to the full in many of our crises. When my father Drusus was subduing Germany, it was they who by their tranquillity afforded him a safe and securely peaceful rear, even at a time when he had been summoned away to the war from the task of organizing the census which was still new and unaccustomed to the Gauls. How difficult such an operation is for us at this precise moment we are learning all too well from experience, even though the survey is aimed at nothing more than an official record of our resources. [The rest is lost.]

GRANT OF CITIZENSHIP TO AN EGYPTIAN

Pliny *Letters* Book x, Nos. 5-7

[Pliny to the Emperor Trajan]

Last year, my lord, when I was attacked by a very serious illness and in danger of my life, I called in a therapist, whose solicitude and devotion I can adequately reward only by your gracious benevolence. I therefore beg you to grant him Roman citizenship; for he is of alien status, the freedman of an alien woman. His name is Harpocras, and his patroness, now long since dead, was Thermuthis, daughter of Theo.

I beg you also to grant full citizen rights [123] to Hedia and Harmeris, freedwomen of Antonia Maximilla, a lady of the highest rank, at whose instance I make this request of you.

[Pliny to the Emperor Trajan]

I thank you, my lord, for your ready compliance in bestowing full citizen rights on the freedwomen of the lady related to me, and Roman citizenship on Harpocras, my therapist. But as I was preparing a declaration, as you had directed, of his age and census rating, I was advised by persons more informed than myself that, since he is an Egyptian, I should have obtained for him first Alexandrine citizenship, then Roman. Not realizing that there was any difference between Egyptians and other aliens,[124] I had contented myself with writing you only that

---

[123] Slaves manumitted by a woman, even though she possessed Roman citizenship, acquired only the lesser Latin status; cf. § 12 and introduction to § 83.
[124] On the special disabilities of Egyptians, see § 99. They were rigidly excluded

he had been manumitted by an alien woman and that his patroness had long since died. Still, I do not regret this ignorance of mine, since it has resulted in my being further obligated to you on behalf of the same man.

And so, that I may enjoy your benefaction in proper form, I beg you to confer upon him both Alexandrine and Roman citizenship. That your kindness may encounter no further delay, I have already sent his age and census rating to your freedmen,[125] as you had directed.

[Trajan to Pliny]

Following the precedent set by the emperors it is my policy not to grant Alexandrine citizenship indiscriminately. But, since you have already obtained Roman citizenship for Harpocras, your therapist, I cannot deny you this further request. You will have to let me know from what nome he comes, so that I may send a letter for you to my friend Pompeius Planta, the prefect of Egypt.

33. Social Policy and Urbanization

Through the evolution of inherent socioeconomic forces and the conscious policy of the emperors (especially Augustus, Claudius, Vespasian, and Trajan) the Roman Empire at its height assumed the appearance of a vast aggregate of cities. The policy of extending Roman citizenship to meritorious individuals and groups in Romanized areas and of converting advanced rural areas into urban communities was calculated to achieve two fundamental aims: to develop an Empire-wide base of privileged supporters of the regime, and to spread the burdens of administration and tax collection among the numerous self-governing municipalities (cf. §§ 82–88). A further result, however, was the eventual polarization of society into two strata, *honestiores* (a propertied, educated, office-holding upper class) and *humiliores*.

Most of the evidence on these imperial policies is to be found in archaeological and epigraphical remains. The following is an idealized, rhetorical evaluation of the Empire in the middle of the second century. (For Aelius Aristides, see above, Note 53.)

Aelius Aristides *To Rome* lix–lx, lxiii–lxxi, xciii–civ

Adapted from the translation of S. Levin
(Glencoe, Illinois, 1950)

Most noteworthy by far and most marvelous of all is the grandeur of your concept of citizenship[?]. There is nothing on earth like it.

___

from both Roman and Alexandrine status, being forbidden to marry even a freedman of an Alexandrian.
[125] That is, secretaries (see above, Note 91).

For you have divided all the people of the Empire—when I say that, I mean the whole world—in two classes: the more cultured, better born, and more influential everywhere you have declared Roman citizens and even of the same stock; the rest vassals and subjects. Neither sea nor any intervening distance on land excludes one from citizenship. No distinction is made between Asia and Europe in this respect. Everything lies open to everybody; and no one fit for office or a position of trust is an alien. There exists a universal democracy under one man, the best *princeps* and administrator. . . .

You have not made Rome a world's conceit, by letting nobody else share in it. No, you have sought out the complement of citizens it deserves. You have made the word "Roman" apply not to a city but to a universal people—and, at that, not just one of all the peoples there are, but equivalent to all the rest. You no longer classify peoples as Greek or barbarian. . . . You have redivided mankind into Romans and non-Romans. So far have you extended the name of your city. Under this classification there are many in each city who are no less fellow citizens of yours than of those of their own stock, though some of them have never seen this city. You have no need to garrison their citadels; the biggest and most influential men everywhere keep watch over their own native places for you. You have a double hold upon those cities—from right here and through the Roman citizens in each.

No envy sets foot in your Empire. You have set an example in being free from envy yourselves, by throwing open all doors and offering to qualified men the opportunity to play in turn a ruler's part no less than a subject's. No hatred creeps in either from those who fail to qualify. Since the state is universal and like one city, magistrates naturally treat the governed not as aliens but as their own. Besides, the state imparts to all peoples security from the men in power among them. If these men presume to do anything irregular, your wrath and punishment will promptly catch up with them.

So, of course, things as they are satisfy and benefit both poor and rich. No other way of life remains. There is one pattern of government, embracing all. Under you, what was formerly thought incapable of conjunction has been united, rule of an Empire at once strong and humane, mild rule without oppression[?]. Thus towns are free of garrisons, whole provinces are adequately guarded by battalions and cavalry companies, which are not stationed in force in the various cities of each people but scattered through the countryside among a multitude of the population, so that many provinces do not know where their garrison is.[126]

But if a city anywhere, through excessive bigness, has outgrown its

[126] On the garrison army of the second century, see §§ 148–150.

capacity to use self-restraint, you do not withhold from such the men needed to take charge of and watch over it.[127]

Moreover, all people are happier to send in their tribute to you than anyone would be to collect it for himself from others. . . .

Instead of quarreling over empire and primacy, through which all wars formerly broke out, some of your subjects . . . relax in utmost delight, content to be released from troubles and miseries, and aware that they were formerly engaged in aimless shadow-boxing. Others do not know or remember what territory they once ruled. . . . But they accepted your leadership fully, and in a flash revived. How they came to this they cannot say; they know nothing, except to look with awe upon the present state of affairs. . . . Whether there ever were wars is now doubted; most people hear of them in the category of empty legends. Whenever they occurred somewhere along the frontiers, as is natural in a vast, measureless empire . . . then just like legends the wars passed by quickly and so did talk of them. Such profound peace has come to you, although war is your ancestral way of life. . . .

Were there ever so many cities, inland and maritime? Were they ever so thoroughly modernized? Could a person in the past travel thus, counting up the cities by the number of days on the road, sometimes even going past two or three of them . . . ?

The upshot is that not only were former empires so inferior at the top, but also the peoples whom they ruled were none of them on a par, in numbers or in caliber, with those same peoples under you. You may contrast the tribe of the past with the city there today. Indeed, it may be said that they were virtually kings of wilderness and fortresses, while you alone govern cities.

Now under you all the Greek cities emerge. All the monuments, works of art and adornments in them mean glory for you, the same as an adornment in your suburbs. Seashore and interior are filled with cities, some founded and others enlarged under you and by you. Ionia, the great prize, is rid of garrisons and satraps, and stands out as a model of elegance to the world. She now outstrips her old self by as much as she was formerly reputed to be ahead of other peoples in taste and refinement.

And in Egypt, Alexander's august and immense city has become an ornament of your supremacy. . . . You continue to care for the Greeks as for foster parents. You protect them; you raise them up as though prostrate. The best of them, even those who were once rulers, you leave free and independent. . . .

The whole world, as on a holiday, has doffed its old costume—of

---

[127] For the agents of the central administration who served as curators of municipalities in the second century, see § 88.

iron—and turned to finery and all festivities without restraint. All other competition between cities has ceased, but a single rivalry obsesses every one of them—to appear as beautiful and attractive as possible. Every place is full of gymnasia, fountains, gateways, temples, shops, and schools. . . . Gifts never stop flowing from you to the cities; and because of your impartial generosity to all, the leading beneficiaries cannot be determined. Cities shine in radiance and beauty, and the entire countryside is decked out like a pleasure ground. . . . Festivity, like a holy, unquenchable fire, never fails, but goes around from one place to the next and is always somewhere, for it fits in with the universal prosperity. And so, only those outside your Empire, if there are any, are fit to be pitied for losing such blessings. . . . Greek and barbarian can now readily go wherever they please with their property or without it. It is just like going from their own to their own country. Neither the Cilician Gates nor the narrow, sandy approaches through Arabia to Egypt present any danger. Nor do impassable mountains, vast stretches of river, or inhospitable barbarian tribes. For safety, it is enough to be a Roman, or rather, one of your subjects. . . .

You have surveyed the whole world, built bridges of all sorts across rivers, cut down mountains to make paths for chariots, filled the deserts with hostels, and civilized it all with system and order. . . .

One might thus appraise and evaluate the state of things before your rule and under you: before it, they were all mixed up topsy-turvy, drifting at random. But with you in charge, turmoil and strife ceased, universal order and the bright light of life and government came in, laws were proclaimed, and the gods' altars acquired sanctity. . . . Now, universal and manifest freedom from fear has been granted to all—the earth itself and its inhabitants. It appears to me that they are wholly rid of oppression, while getting many opportunities for good guidance, and that the gods, looking benevolently on your empire, helped in ordering it and have vouchsafed you secure possession of it.

34. *Taxation: The Grain Supply of Rome (Annona)*

Famine was an ever-present threat in antiquity, especially in the large urban centers, and bread riots were a common phenomenon (cf. § 87). In Rome the food problem became especially acute with the decline of Italian cereal production in the second century B.C. (cf. Vol. I, p. 441). Thereafter, one of the chief tasks of the government was the *cura annonae*—keeping the capital city supplied with grain from overseas provinces and maintaining normal market prices. Under the Republic this was one of the duties of the aediles, but it was found necessary on several critical occasions to appoint special grain commissioners. Augustus made the *cura annonae* one of the emperor's permanent responsibilities, and it remained a department of the imperial administrative structure for over five hundred years. At its head was the prefect of the grain supply. In addition to its headquarters and central storehouses in Rome the department had substations at the Italian harbors of Puteoli and Ostia, where the new harbor of Portus was built in A.D. 42 especially to provide improved facilities for handling the grain supply. There were also agents, offices, and storehouses in other important ports of the Empire, and in the prime grain-producing provinces, Egypt and Africa. Altogether this far-flung organization conducted the largest single shipping operation in the Empire, and the emperors enacted special measures to assure a sufficiency of bottoms for the transportation of the *annona*. While no comprehensive statistics are available, one ancient source records that under Augustus Rome received 20,000,000 *modii* a year from Egypt, and another states that in the first century the Egyptian grain tribute fed the city for four months. On the grain fleet, see further §§ 45–46.

Tacitus *Annals* iii. liv. 6–8

The following is a part of Tacitus' paraphrase of a letter from the Emperor Tiberius to the senate, A.D. 22.

But no one makes any proposal about the fact that Italy is dependent on supplies from abroad, that the life of the Roman people is tossed every day at the mercy of wave and wind. And if the harvests of the provinces ever fail to come to the aid of our masters, slaves, and fields, then our parks and villas [in Italy] will support us forsooth. This, Conscript Fathers, is one of the services that the emperor assures; if neglected, this will drag the state down in utter ruin.

"A HUNGRY PEOPLE DOES NOT LISTEN TO REASON"

Tacitus *Annals* vi. xiii. 1–2, xii. xliii [128]

The excessive price of grain led practically to insurrection, and for several days the theater was the scene of many demands shouted with greater boldness than was customary toward the emperor. Aroused by this, Tiberius upbraided the magistrates and the senators for failing to restrain the populace by the authority of the state, and reminded them

[128] These selections refer to the years 32 and 51, respectively. The quotation in the caption is from Seneca *On the Shortness of Life* xviii. 5. The same thought is also given pithy expression by Seneca's nephew, the poet Lucan, in his *Pharsalia* iii. 55–58: "The grain supply provides the mainsprings of hatred and popularity. Hunger alone sets cities free, and reverence is purchased when rulers feed the lazy mob: a hungry populace knows no fear." For other food riots see § 87. In addition to supplying food, the emperors relied also on spectacles and circus games to keep the Roman populace quiet; cf. § 57.

of the provinces from which he imported the supply of grain and of
how much greater a supply it was than Augustus had provided.

.   .   .   .

Many prodigies occurred in that year. . . . A shortage of grain
again and the resulting famine were regarded as a portent. And people
did not merely grumble in private, but they surrounded Claudius with
mutinous clamor as he sat in judgment, drove him to the edge of the
Forum, and kept jostling him about until the arrival of a band of soldiers
made it possible for him to force his way through the hostile throng.
It was ascertained that the city had provisions for fifteen days, no more,
and the desperate situation was relieved only by the great mercy of
the gods and the mildness of the winter. And yet, by heaven, in former
times Italy used to export supplies for the legions into far-distant provinces, and even now it does not suffer from infertility, but it is we who
prefer to cultivate Africa and Egypt and commit the life of the Roman
people to ships and all their risks.

Suetonius *Life of Claudius* xviii–xix
Adapted from LCL

Claudius always gave scrupulous attention to the care of the city and
the supply of grain. . . . When there was a scarcity of grain because
of long-continued droughts, he was once stopped in the middle of the
Forum by a mob and so pelted with abuse and at the same time with
pieces of bread that he was barely able to make his escape to the palace
by a back door. After this experience he resorted to every possible means
to bring supplies to Rome, even in the winter season. To the importers
he held out the certainty of profit by assuming the expense of any loss
that they might suffer from storms.[129] To those who built merchant
ships he accorded great benefits adapted to the conditions of each,
namely, to a citizen, exemption from the Papian-Poppaean Law; to one
of Latin rights, full citizenship; to women, the privileges of mothers of
four children.[130] And all these provisions are in force today.

[129] Cf. the similar arrangement during the Second Punic War, in Vol. I, §§ 92–93.
Tiberius, besides fixing grain prices, granted a subsidy of two sesterces per *modius*
to grain merchants (Tacitus *Annals* ii. lxxxvii). For special privileges accorded to
shipowners engaged in the grain trade, see §§ 46, 122.
[130] For the significance of these different privileges, see §§ 11, 12, 64, 163.

THE NEW HARBOR AT PORTUS
Dio Cassius *Roman History* LX. xi. 1-4
From LCL

On the occasion of a severe famine he considered the problem of providing an abundant food supply, not only for that particular crisis but for all future time. For practically all the grain used by the Romans was imported, and yet the region near the mouth of the Tiber had no safe landing places or suitable harbors, so that their mastery of the sea was rendered useless to them. Except for the cargoes brought in during the summer season and stored in the warehouses, they had no supplies for the winter; for if anyone ever risked a voyage at that season, he came to grief. In view of this situation Claudius undertook to construct a harbor, and would not be deterred even when the architects, upon his enquiring how great the cost would be, answered, "You don't want to do it!"—so confident were they that the huge expenditures necessary would shake him from his purpose if he should learn the cost beforehand. He, however, conceived an undertaking worthy of the dignity and greatness of Rome, and he brought it to accomplishment. In the first place, he excavated a very considerable area of shore, built retaining walls on every side of the excavation, and then let the sea into it; secondly, in the sea itself he constructed huge moles on both sides of the entrance and thus enclosed a large body of water, in the midst of which he reared an island and placed on it a tower with a beacon light.

TRANSPORTING THE GRAIN TO ROME

Seneca speaks of the workaday cares of the functionaries who "see to it that the grain pours into the storehouses unadulterated through fraud or negligence on the part of those who transport it, that it does not collect moisture and become heated and spoiled, that it tallies in measure and weight" (*On the Shortness of Life* xix. 1). An example of the precautions taken in the collection of the *annona* is afforded by the following text, written on a small pottery jar which contained a sealed sample of a shipment of grain loaded on two river boats in Middle Egypt for transportation to Alexandria. There the sample would be opened and compared with the cargoes to make sure the latter had not suffered adulteration or spoilage en route; if they had, the loss would have to be made good by the region of origin. The soldiers who accompanied the shipment guarded both the sealed sample and the cargoes against tampering and theft; in the second century this duty was transferred, in Egypt at least, to civilians as a compulsory public service. From Alexandria the *annona*—except for a small part retained for feeding the administration

and the soldiers stationed in the province—was transshipped to Rome, doubtless under similar precautions. The second text below is a letter from a man
who made the trip from Egypt to Italy on a grain ship as a member of the
crew or possibly as one of the soldiers of the guard.

Journal of Juristic Papyrology, IV (1950), 106–15; 2 B.C.

From the Oxyrhynchite nome

Ammonius son of Ammonius, pilot of a government boat with the
emblem . . . attached to him as escort being Lucius Oclatius, soldier
of Legion XXII, second cohort, century of Maximus Stoltius; and
Hermias son of Petalus, pilot of a second boat with the emblem *Egypt*,
attached to him as escort being Lucius Castricius, soldier of Legion XXII,
fourth cohort, century of Titus Pompeius. This is a sample of the cargo
we have loaded from the harvest of the 28th year of Augustus—
Ammonius, 433¼ artabs of wheat, loaded to the rail; Hermias, likewise
433¼ artabs of wheat—a total of 866½ artabs of wheat consigned by
Leonidas and Apollonius, *sitologoi* of the Lower Toparchy, Eastern
Division, plus the supplement of one half artab of wheat per hundred.
We loaded from the 2d of Hathyr to the 4th of the same month, and
we have sealed [this jar] with both our seals, Ammonius' with a figure
of Ammon, Hermias' with a figure of Harpocrates. Year 29 of Augustus,
Hathyr 4.

Berlin Papyrus No. 27 (= *Select Papyri*, No. 113); second or third
century A.D.

Irenaeus to Apollinarius, his dearest brother, many greetings. I pray
continually for your health, and I myself am well. I want you to know
that I reached land [131] on the 6th day of the month Epeiph [June 30],
and we finished unloading on the 18th of the same month [July 12]. I
went up to Rome on the 25th of the same month [July 19], and the place
received us as the god willed.[132] We are daily expecting our discharge,
so that up to today nobody in the grain fleet has been able to leave. I
salute your wife warmly, and Serenus, and all who love you, each by
name. Farewell. Mesore 9 [August 2].

35. *Taxation: Customs Duties and Transit Tolls*

In addition to direct taxes on land (*tributum*) and other personal property,
the central government imposed a variety of indirect taxes (*vectigalia*) upon

---

[131] At Ostia-Portus, in all probability.
[132] This noncommittal phrase suggests that the visit was not an unmitigated success.

the inhabitants of the Empire. According to Tacitus (*Annals* XIII. 1–li), when Nero, in A.D. 58, considered abolishing all indirect taxes, he was dissuaded by senators who pointed out that "the dissolution of the Empire [would result] if the revenues by which the state was supported were diminished," and that "every care had been taken to maintain an exact balance between the amount of income and necessary expenditures." The most important of the indirect taxes were the customs dues (*portorium*) exacted at harbors and at certain points along the road system. For the collection of this impost the Roman Empire was divided, probably under Tiberius, into about ten large customs districts. At the land and sea frontiers of these districts customs dues were exacted on goods entering or leaving, and at certain points within these districts (for example, at bridges or ferries) transit tolls were collected. The *portorium* was not a protective tariff, since it was payable on exports and imports alike; its purpose was simply to provide another source of revenue for the imperial fisc. Except on the eastern frontier of the Empire, where the rich oriental luxury trade was taxed at the rate of 25 percent, the rate at the district borders was generally 2 or 2½ (in some cases 5) percent *ad valorem;* the tolls collected inside customs districts were generally at a much lower rate. In addition to this imperial duty, many towns had the right to collect local *octrois* and transit tolls for their municipal treasuries (see § 86, first selection).

The system of collection of the imperial customs underwent a threefold evolution: the practice, begun under the Republic, of farming the collection by regions to companies of publicans, continued during the early imperial period, under the close surveillance of the imperial administration; at the end of the first century, probably under Trajan, these associations were replaced by individual collectors general (*conductores*) for each customs district, who received a fixed percentage of the revenues; and this system continued until the time of Marcus Aurelius and Commodus, who progressively eliminated the *conductores* in favor of direct collection under imperial procurators. In Egypt, Syria, and Judaea, however, the Hellenistic system of leasing the collection to tax farmers at each customs station separately continued throughout the period of the Principate. Under the Dominate this system was extended, probably by Constantine, to the entire Empire.

THE PRIVILEGES OF HISTRIA

A cluster of five Greek cities on the Black Sea coast of Thrace was placed under Roman rule by Augustus but granted local autonomy. One of these cities was the trading center of Histria (modern Istria, in Rumania), located near the southernmost, or Peuce, mouth of the Danube river delta. In A.D. 46, when Thrace, till then a client kingdom, became a Roman province and a customs barrier was established along the south bank of the lower Danube, the farmers of the customs dues of Thrace attempted to tax Histria's hitherto exempt products. This resulted in a recurring battle between the customs collectors and the city, as shown by this bilingual inscription which records repeated confirmations of Histria's traditional privileges in A.D. c.49 to 100 by the governors of Moesia, under whose jurisdiction the Greek cities of the Thracian coast had been placed.

SEG, Vol. I, No. 329 (= *AE*, 1919, No. 10)

Boundary Determination of Laberius Maximus [133] ...

I have determined the Histrian boundaries to be the following: ... Peuce Island, Lake Halmyris from ... of the Argamensians, thence from the top of the ridge ... to the confluence of the Picusculus and Gabranus rivers, thence from the mouth of the Gabranus to its source, thence ... to the Sampaeus river, thence to the Turgiculus river ... from the Calabaeus river, about 516[?] miles. ...

Letter of Sabinus

Flavius Sabinus [134] to the magistrates, council, and people of Histria, greeting. It will be the care of the prefect Aruntius Flamma [135] to preserve your rights around Peuce unimpaired. I have given him instructions to this effect, and I will talk also to Aemilianus, my successor, and will give you complete support.

Another letter of the same Sabinus. Flavius Sabinus, governor, to the magistrates, council, and people of Histria, greeting. Even if the tax along the bank of the Danube extends as far as the sea and [your] city is at some distance from the river mouths, nevertheless, since your envoys have assured me and the prefect Asiaticus stated that practically the only revenue of the city was that from pickling fish, I judged it proper for you to retain, in accordance with your custom, the same right of fishing in the Peuce mouth and of bringing in pine wood for personal needs free from tax; for in the matter of your requirements of the wood you have undisputed boundaries and complete use thereof not subject to tax.

[The next part of the inscription contains three letters from the governors of Moesia of A.D. 51–54 confirming the privileges of the city.]

Copy of the letter of Marius Laberius Maximus, legate of the emperor with rank of praetor, in the third consulship of the Emperor Caesar Trajan Augustus Germanicus and of Julius Frontinus, October 25. Certified copy taken from the official records of Marius Laberius

---

[133] Governor of Moesia in A.D. 100.
[134] Brother of the later Emperor Vespasian. The date of this letter is A.D. 49; the letter which follows this appears to be slightly earlier.
[135] He was probably the local commander of the nearest frontier garrison.

Maximus, legate of the emperor with rank of praetor. Permission . . .
to Fabius Pompeianus . . . when Charagonius Philopalaestrus, farmer
of the customs dues of the river bank in Thrace, was demanding that he
be given the dues of Lake Halmyris and Peuce in accordance with . . .
the right of collecting the customs dues . . . of Dimum . . . up to
. . . . [The rest is lost.]

RIGHT OF SEARCH

Pseudo-Quintilian *Declamations* ccclix [136]

The following is part of the regulations of a customs bureau.

Except for means of transportation, all articles shall be subject to
a tax of 2½ percent, payable to the tax farmer. The tax farmer has the
right of search. Undeclared articles shall be confiscated. The person
of a matron may not be searched.

Oxyrhynchus Papyrus No. 36 (= Wilcken, No. 273); second or early third century

The following is a fragment of the regulations governing the collection of
duties payable at the customs barrier either at Memphis (for Nile-borne
traffic) or at one of the Red Sea ports of Egypt.

. . . if the customs collector requires the boat to be unloaded, the
merchant shall unload. If anything other than what he declared is found,
it shall be liable to confiscation; but if nothing is found, the customs collector shall reimburse the merchant for the expense of unloading . . .
and they shall receive from the tax farmers a written certification, so
that they may be unmolested thereafter. . . . [The rest is lost.]

Princeton Papyrus No. 20 (= SB, No. 8,072); second century

Malpractices on the part of customs collectors in connection with clearance
of cargoes are revealed in this fragment from an edict of the prefect of Egypt.

. . . prefect of Egypt declares: I am informed that the tax farmers
have employed exceedingly clever devices against those passing through
the country and, in addition, are fraudulently demanding charges not
due them and are laying hold of those who are in haste, so that some
may buy from them a speedier departure. I therefore order them to
desist from such greed. . . . [The rest is fragmentary.]

[136] From one of two collections of *declamationes* (cf. introduction to § 73), transmitted under Quintilian's name but of uncertain authorship; cf. Vol. I, p. 23.

THE TARIFF OF ZARAI

This inscription, found at Zaraï, contains the customs regulations of an interior station of the province of Africa. The tariff was posted in A.D. 202. As at other interior barriers, these duties were not calculated *ad valorem* and were smaller than those exacted at the frontier stations of the customs districts.

CIL, Vol. VIII, No. 4,508

In the consulship of the Emperor Caesar Lucius Septimius Severus Augustus Pius for the third time and of the Emperor Caesar Marcus Aurelius Antoninus Augustus Pius. Customs regulation instituted after the departure of the cohort.[137]

Regulation for tax per head

Slaves, each	1½	*denarii*
Horse; mare	1½	"
Mule; she-mule	1½	"
Ass; cow [138]	½	*denarius*
Pig	1	sesterce
Suckling pig	½	"
Sheep; goat	1	"
Kid; lamb	½	"
Cattle for market,[139] duty-free		

Regulation for imported clothing

Dinner mantle	1½	*denarii*
Tunic costing 300 sesterces[?]	1½	"
Blanket [140]	½	*denarius*
Purple cloak	1	"
Other African clothing, per garment	½	"[?]

Regulation on hides

Hide, dressed	½	*denarius*
Hide, with hair	½	sesterce
Sheepskin; goatskin	½	"
Supple saddle hides, per 100 lbs.	...	
Coarse hides, per 100 lbs.	½	*denarius*
Glue, per 10 lbs.	½	sesterce
Sponges, per 10 lbs.	½	"

[137] The reason for the posting of a new tariff after the removal of the garrison from this post is not clear. There is no evidence that the customs were ever collected by the military. Because of the special needs of the soldiers—who were, moreover, exempt from customs dues on articles purchased for their personal needs—their departure probably rendered the previous tariff schedule obsolete.
[138] Or bull.   [139] That is, at Zaraï.   [140] Or counterpane.

Miscellaneous[?] customs regulations

Cattle: beasts of burden, duty-free; other items as above		
Wine, per amphora; *garum*,[141] per amphora	1	sesterce
Dates, per 100 lbs.	½	*denarius*
Figs, per 100 lbs.	...	
Green peas in the pod[?], per 10 *modii*	...	
Nuts, per 10 *modii*	...	
Resin, pitch, alum, per 100 lbs.	...	
Iron. . . .		

[The rest is lost.]

THE TARIFF OF COPTUS

This inscription, dating from A.D. 90, contains a schedule, not of customs dues (as formerly thought), but of toll fees charged various categories of persons and goods for permits to use one of the roads connecting the caravan terminal of Coptus on the Nile with Red Sea ports. These roads were provided by the government with water stops, caravanserais, and protective garrisons, and the charges were doubtless intended to defray the expense of maintaining these services.

IGRR, Vol. I, No. 1,183 (= *OGIS*, No. 674)

By order of Mettius Rufus[?], prefect of Egypt. Lucius Antistius Asiaticus, prefect of Mt. Berenice, has had engraved on this stone the sums which must be exacted in accordance with the regulations by the tax farmers of the toll fees subject to the jurisdiction of the customs controller in Coptus.

For a captain in the Red Sea trade	8	drachmas
For . . .	6	"
For a lookout officer	10	"
For a guard	10	"
For a sailor	5	"
For a shipwright's helper	5	"
For an artisan	8	"
For courtesans	108 [142]	"
For sailors'[?] women	20	"
For soldiers' women	20	"
For a permit for a camel	1	obol
For seal on permit	2	obols

[141] A fish sauce very popular among the Romans.
[142] This high fee represents not (as used to be thought) an attempt to discourage prostitution, but rather a form of tax upon that occupation.

For each permit for a man outbound up country [143]	1 drachma
For [permits for] all women, at the rate of	4 drachmas
For a donkey	2 obols
For a covered wagon	4 drachmas
For a mast	20 "
For a yardarm	4 "
For a funeral (going and return)	1 drachma 4 obols

The ninth year of the Emperor Caesar Domitian Augustus Germanicus, Pachon 15.

36. *The Imperial Post*

One of the enduring innovations of Augustus was the establishment of an imperial post (*cursus publicus*) for official dispatches and personages. The burden of maintaining and financing the relays of horses and carriages, the posting stations, and the hostels for official travelers was imposed upon the cities and towns on the trunk roads in all parts of the Empire through which the service ran. Protests by communities against the heavy costs and against irregularities in the requisitioning of the services led to various relief measures by the emperors. In the second century a separate imperial bureau was established to administer the imperial post. Though under Hadrian and Septimius Severus the entire costs were temporarily assumed by the fisc, by the end of the third century responsibility for the maintenance of the post became one of the compulsory duties of local officials.

Suetonius *Life of Augustus* xlix. 3

To enable what was going on in every province to be reported and known more speedily and promptly, Augustus stationed at short intervals along the military roads first young men, and later conveyances. The latter arrangement appeared the more convenient, since the same man brings a dispatch all the way from its source and can, if occasion demands, be questioned as well.

CIL, Vol. III, No. 7,251 (= Dessau, No. 214)

[Tegea, Greece, A.D. 49/50]

Tiberius Claudius Caesar Augustus Germanicus, *pontifex maximus*, holding the tribunician power for the ninth year, acclaimed *imperator* sixteen times, father of his country, declares:

[143] In addition to toll fees, an extra charge was made for the requisite official permit.

Whereas I have often tried to lighten for the colonies and municipalities not only of Italy but also of the provinces, and likewise for the communities of every province, the burdens of providing conveyances; and whereas it seems to me that I have devised many and sufficient remedies, still . . . men's negligence. . . . [The rest is lost.]

Pliny *Letters* Book X, Nos. 45–46, 120

[Pliny to the Emperor Trajan]

I beg, my lord, that you write and free me from uncertainty about permits to use the imperial post which have expired—whether you wish them to be honored at all and for how long. For I fear that I may err through ignorance in one of two directions—either approving illegal permits or blocking necessary ones.

[Trajan to Pliny]

Travel permits which have expired must not be in use. I therefore make it an especial rule to send out new permits to all the provinces before there can be any need of them.

[Pliny to the Emperor Trajan]

Up to this time, my lord, I have granted permits to use the imperial post to no one and for no purpose except in your service. This fixed rule of mine has been broken by an emergency. My wife, hearing of her grandfather's death, wanted to rush to her aunt, and I thought it hard to refuse her a permit, as the amenities of such an obligation depend on speed, and I knew that you would approve the reason for a journey dictated by filial devotion. I write you this because it seemed to me I should be ungrateful not to confess that along with other benefits I owe this too to your kind favor that, in reliance upon it, I did not hesitate to act as if I had consulted you, when I should have acted too late had I waited to consult you.

[Trajan's reply consists of one sentence approving Pliny's action.]

37. *Remission of Taxes*

Among the forms of help granted by the emperors to distressed areas was a remission of, or moratorium on, the payment of taxes. In the second century, as the Roman Empire proved unable to produce year in and year out the revenues demanded by the imperial regime, the emperors began to resort on occasion to wholesale cancellation of tax arrears. By this palliative they attempted to achieve a kind of economic "pump priming" and thereby strengthen the allegiance of the peoples of the Empire. Thus, in addition to the erection of the following inscription at Rome, Hadrian's tax remission was celebrated also by the issuance of coins bearing the legend: "Nine hundred million sesterces in old arrears canceled."

CIL, Vol. VI, No. 967 (= Dessau, No. 309); A.D. 118

[Dedicated by] the Roman senate and people to the Emperor Caesar Trajan Hadrian Augustus, son of the deified Trajan Parthicus, grandson of the deified Nerva, *pontifex maximus*, holder of the tribunician power for the second year, twice consul, the first and only one of all the emperors to cancel 900,100,000 sesterces owed to the fisc and by this liberality to render not only the citizens now living but also their descendants free from worry.

"Historia Augusta" *Life of Hadrian* vii. 6

Hadrian canceled a countless sum of money owed to the fisc by private debtors in Rome and Italy, and also vast sums of arrears in the provinces, and he burned the records of indebtedness in the Forum of the deified Trajan in order to strengthen the general sense of security.

Dio Cassius *Roman History* LXXI. xxxii. 2

Marcus Aurelius remitted all debts incurred by anyone to the imperial fisc or to the state treasury over a period of forty-five years in addition to the fifteen years of Hadrian,[144] and he ordered all the records relating to these debts to be burned in the Forum.

38. *Imperial Largess*

From the time of Augustus, the distribution of largess to the soldiery and the populace of Rome was reserved for the emperors. This policy of keeping the army and people contented and loyal through repeated donatives to the soldiers and through *frumentationes* (grain doles) and *congiaria* (gifts of money) to the Roman populace was maintained for centuries and constituted a heavy drain on the imperial fisc. It has been estimated that in the 250 years between the dictatorship of Caesar and the accession of Septimius Severus about 1,500,000,000 *denarii* were expended by the emperors on *congiaria* alone. In time the soldiers came to consider such donatives a regular emolument, and quickly became disaffected from an emperor who neglected to distribute donatives they considered due them. In A.D. 68–69, and again in 193, when

---

[144] That is, Hadrian's remissions extended to A.D. 133, and Marcus Aurelius forgave arrears from 178 back to 133.

the Principate was disputed by several claimants, the Praetorian Guard readily transferred their support to the highest bidder (see §§ 111–112).

Dio Cassius *Roman History* LIX. ii. 1–4

By paying to the others all the bequests made by Tiberius as if they were his own, Caligula gained among the masses some reputation for generosity. And together with the senate he immediately inspected the Praetorian Guards when they were drilling, and distributed to them the 1,000 sesterces apiece which had been bequeathed to them, and he added an equal amount to this on his own account. And to the people he paid the 45,000,000 sesterces which had been bequeathed to them, and in addition the 240 sesterces apiece which they had not received on the occasion of his assuming the toga of manhood, together with an additional 60 sesterces in interest. He also honored the bequests to the urban cohorts, to the night patrol, to those on the army rolls who were outside Italy, and to any other group of citizen troops who were in the smaller garrisons, the urban cohorts receiving 500 sesterces apiece, and all the rest 300. . . . In some instances it was through fear of the people and the soldiers that he did this, but for the most part on principle.[145]

39. *Public Works*

An enormous number of public works in Rome, Italy, and the provinces was erected out of the funds of the imperial fisc. The remains of many of these are still to be seen in all parts of the Empire. Characteristically utilitarian, the public monuments of the imperial builders, both religious and civic, were executed on a grandiose scale. An important purpose of the extensive public works programs of the emperors was to provide employment for surplus labor. An anecdote relates that when a mechanical engineer offered to transport heavy columns inexpensively, Vespasian refused to permit the labor-saving device to be used, declaring, "You must allow me to feed my poor commons" (Suetonius *Life of Vespasian* xviii). On the public works of the Principate, cf. also § 2, paragraphs 19–21; and §§ 15, 54, 141.

Suetonius *Life of Claudius* xx
Adapted from LCL

The public works which Claudius completed were great and essential rather than numerous; they were in particular the following: an

[145] Cf. Suetonius *Life of Claudius* x. 4: "[When he was acclaimed emperor by the Praetorian Guard], Claudius permitted the armed assembly to swear allegiance to him, and promised 15,000 sesterces to each man, the first of the Caesars to secure the fidelity of the soldiery by bribery"; Dio Cassius *Roman History* LX. xii. 4: "On the first anniversary of the day he had been declared emperor, Claudius did nothing

aqueduct begun by Caligula; also the drainage channel of Lake Fucinus [146] and the harbor at Ostia, although in the case of the last two he knew that Augustus had refused the former to the Marsians in spite of their frequent requests, and that the latter had often been considered by the deified Julius but given up because of its difficulty. He brought to the city on stone arches the cool and abundant springs of the Claudian aqueduct . . . and at the same time the channel of the New Anio, distributing them into many beautifully ornamented fountains. He made the attempt on the Fucine Lake as much in the hope of gain as of glory, inasmuch as there were some who offered to drain it at their own cost provided the land that was drained be given them. He finished the drainage canal, which was three miles in length, partly by leveling and partly by tunneling a mountain, a work of great difficulty requiring eleven years, although he had 30,000 men at work all the time without interruption. He constructed the harbor at Ostia [147] by building curving breakwaters on the right and left, while before the entrance he placed a mole in deep water. To give this mole a firmer foundation he first sank the ship in which the great obelisk had been brought from Egypt,[148] and then securing it by piles built upon it a very lofty tower after the model of the Pharus at Alexandria, to be lighted at night and guide the course of the ships.

"Historia Augusta" *Life of Hadrian* xix. 9–13

From LCL

He built public works in all places and without number, but he inscribed his own name on none of them except the temple of his father Trajan. At Rome he restored the Pantheon, the voting enclosure, the Basilica of Neptune, many temples, the Forum of Augustus, the Baths of Agrippa, and dedicated all of them in the names of their original builders.[149] Also he constructed the bridge named after himself, a tomb

---

out of the ordinary except to give the Praetorians one hundred sesterces, a thing he did every year thereafter."

[146] In Central Italy, in the Marsian region. The engineering work, not completed until A.D. 52, was only partially successful. The complete drainage of the lake was not achieved until the nineteenth century.

[147] Cf. § 34.

[148] From Heliopolis, in the reign of Caligula. This is the obelisk which now stands before St. Peter's, in the Vatican. The ship in which it was transported to Rome is decribed in Pliny *Natural History* xvi. cci–ccii.

[149] All of the structures mentioned by name in this sentence were built in the principate of Augustus, all but the Forum by Agrippa. The restored Pantheon bears the inscription "Marcus Agrippa son of Lucius, consul three times, built this" (*CIL*, Vol. VI, No. 896).

on the bank of the Tiber,[150] and the temple of the Bona Dea. With the aid of the architect Decrianus he lifted the Colossus [151] and, keeping it in an upright position, moved it away from the place in which the Temple of Rome now stands, though its weight was so vast that he had to furnish for the work as many as twenty-four elephants. This statue he then consecrated to the Sun after removing the features of Nero,[152] to whom it had previously been dedicated, and he also planned with the assistance of the architect Apollodorus [153] to make a similar one for the Moon.

ROAD BUILDING

The construction and maintenance of the highway network which spanned the Empire, serving military, administrative, and commercial needs, was a perennial task. The manual labor was usually performed by common laborers recruited locally, but in addition the soldiers stationed in the provinces were frequently detailed to road building and repair. The emperor in whose reign construction or repair took place was honored by appropriate commemorative inscriptions; his name appeared also on the milestones placed along the roads. A few representative specimens of the hundreds of these inscribed stones, which have been found throughout the Mediterranean world, follow below.

CIL, Vol. III, No. 7,203

[Asia Minor, near Smyrna, A.D. 75]

The Emperor Caesar VESPASIAN Augustus, *pontifex maximus*, holding the tribunician power for the sixth year, acclaimed *imperator* thirteen times, father of his country, consul six times, designated consul for a seventh time, censor, saw to the repair of the roads.

CIL, Vol. III, No. 8,267

[Right bank of Danube, A.D. 100 [154]]

The Emperor Caesar Nerva TRAJAN Augustus Germanicus, son of the deified Nerva, *pontifex maximus*, holding the tribunician power for the fourth year, father of his country, consul three times, built this road by cutting through mountains and eliminating the curves.

[150] The famous Mausoleum of Hadrian, now called Castel Sant' Angelo, still stands as one of the familiar landmarks of modern Rome.
[151] A colossal bronze statue of Nero, over 100 feet high.
[152] This is an error. The rededication of the statue to the Sun had taken place during the reign of Vespasian.
[153] Cf. Note 78.
[154] Inscribed on a cliff between Viminacium and Retiaria (in modern Serbia), about 20 miles west of Trajan's bridge across the Danube into Dacia (cf. § 27, third selection).

CIL, Vol. III, No. 14,149 (21–22) (= Dessau, No. 5,834)

[Road to Petra, A.D. 111]

The Emperor Caesar Nerva Trajan Augustus Germanicus Dacicus, son of the deified Nerva, *pontifex maximus*, holding the tribunician power for the fifteenth year, acclaimed *imperator* six times, consul five times, father of his country, after reducing Arabia to the status of a province, through the agency of Gaius Claudius Severus, imperial legate with rank of praetor, opened and paved a new road from the border of Syria to the Red Sea.

54 [miles]

CIL, Vol. IX, No. 6,075 (= Dessau, No. 5,875)

[Appian Way, A.D. 123]

The Emperor Caesar Trajanus Hadrian Augustus, son of the deified Trajan Parthicus, grandson of the deified Nerva, *pontifex maximus*, holding the tribunician power for the seventh year, consul three times, rebuilt the Appian Way for 15¾ miles where it had become unusable through age, adding 1,147,000 sesterces to the 569,100 sesterces which the landowners contributed.[155]

IGRR, Vol. I, No. 1,142

[Antinoöpolis, Egypt, A.D. 137]

The Emperor Caesar Trajanus Hadrian Augustus, son of the deified Trajan Parthicus and grandson of the deified Nerva, *pontifex maximus*, holding the tribunician power for the twenty-first year, twice acclaimed *imperator*, three times consul, father of his country, built from Berenice to Antinoöpolis through secure and level country the New Hadrian Way, with copious cisterns, resting stations, and garrisons at intervals along the route. Year 21, Phamenoth 1.

[155] *On the Conditions of Fields,* a work on surveying by Siculus Flaccus, who lived in the second half of the first century A.D., has an instructive passage in this connection (C. Thulin, *Opuscula agrimensorum veterum* [Leipzig, 1923], p. 110): "There are, first, public roads, which are built at state expense and named after their originators. These roads are under the supervision of commissioners, who let the construction to contractors. For certain of these roads, however, a certain sum of money is levied periodically on the landowners of the region." Actually, the major expense of road building under the Empire was borne not by the impoverished state treasury but by the imperial fisc.

AE, 1904, No. 21

[North Africa, A.D. 152]

The Emperor Caesar Titus Aelius Hadrianus Augustus [Antoninus] Pius, *pontifex maximus*, holding the tribunician power for the fifteenth year, consul four times, restored the road through the Numidian Alps, when it had broken down because of age, by rebuilding the bridges, draining swamps, and strengthening the sections which had sunk. [The work was carried out] under the direction of Marcus Valerius Etruscus, his legate with rank of praetor.

CIL, Vol. II, No. 4,712

[Córdoba, Spain, A.D. 35/36]

Tiberius Caesar Augustus, son of the deified Augustus, grandson of the deified Julius, *pontifex maximus*, consul five times, acclaimed *imperator*, holding the tribunician power for the thirty-seventh year. [Road] from Janus Augustus at the Baetis [Guadalquivir] river to the [Atlantic] Ocean.

64 [miles]

CIL, Vol. VIII, No. 10,048

[North Africa, A.D. 123]

The Emperor Trajanus Hadrian Augustus, grandson of the deified Nerva, son of the deified Trajan Parthicus, *pontifex maximus*, holding the tribunician power for the seventh year, consul three times, had the road from Carthage to Theveste paved by the Legion III Augusta under the command of Publius Metilius Secundus, imperial legate with rank of praetor.

85 [miles]

CIL, Vol. II, No. 4,906

[Road from Spain to Aquitaine, A.D. 134]

The Emperor Caesar Hadrian Augustus, son of the deified Trajan Parthicus, grandson of the deified Nerva, *pontifex maximus*, holding the tribunician power for the eighteenth year, acclaimed *imperator*, consul three times, father of his country.

From Cara: 3 miles

CHAPTER III

THE ROMAN PEACE (A.D. 14–192): ECONOMIC LIFE

40. *Economic Resources of the Empire*

Evidence on the natural resources, products, and trade of the different parts of the Empire is abundant, but it consists in large part of isolated data scattered throughout the sources. The following selections contain a number of representative examples on which good texts are available. Particularly important sectors of the economy—such as agriculture, mining, and trade—and various types of business activity are treated separately in this chapter. For a more extensive treatment of the sources on the economic life of the Roman Empire the reader is referred to T. Frank, ed., *An Economic Survey of Ancient Rome*, Vols. II–V.

SPAIN

The chief importance of Spain in the economy of the Empire lay in her rich mineral deposits. "Almost all Spain," says Pliny (*Natural History* III. iii. 30), abounds in mines of lead, iron, tin, silver, and gold." For the imperial administration of the mines of the Iberian Peninsula, see § 43.

Strabo *Geography* III. ii. 6, 8 (abridged)
From LCL

There are exported from Turdetania [1] large quantities of grain and wine, and also olive oil, not only in large quantities but also of best quality. And further, wax, honey, and pitch are exported from there, and large quantities of kermes,[2] and ruddle [3] which is not inferior to the Sinopean earth. And they build their ships there out of native timber; and they have salt quarries in their country, and not a few streams of salt water. Not unimportant, either, is the fish-salting industry that is carried on, not only from this region but also from the rest of the seaboard outside the Pillars [Strait of Gibraltar], and the product is not inferior to that of the Pontus [Black Sea]. Formerly much cloth came from Turdetania, but now wool, especially of the raven-black sort, which is surpassingly beautiful; at all events, the rams are bought for breeding purposes at a talent apiece. Surpassing, too, are the delicate

---

[1] A region in the southwestern part of the Iberian Peninsula.
[2] A crimson dyestuff obtained from the dead bodies of the female of the scale insect *coccus ilicis*, very common in the Mediterranean area.
[3] Spanish cinnabar is meant.

fabrics which are woven by the people of Salacia.[4] Turdetania also has a great abundance of cattle of all kinds, and of game. . . . The abundance of the exports of Turdetania is indicated by the size and the number of the ships, for merchantmen of the greatest size sail from this region to Puteoli and to Ostia, the seaport of Rome. . . .[5]

The whole country of the Iberians is full of metals, although not all of it is so rich in fruit, or so fertile either, in particular that part of it which is well supplied with metals. It is rare for a country to be fortunate in both respects, and it is also rare for the same country to have within a small area an abundance of all kinds of metals. But as for Turdetania and the territory adjoining it, there is no worthy word of praise left to him who wishes to praise their excellence in this respect. Up to the present moment, in fact, neither gold, nor silver, nor yet copper, nor iron, has been found anywhere in the world, in a natural state, either in such quantity or of such good quality. And gold is not only mined but is also washed down; that is, the gold-bearing sand is carried down by the rivers and torrents, although it is often found in the waterless districts also; but in these districts it cannot be seen, whereas in the watered districts the gold dust glitters. Besides, they flood the waterless districts by conducting water thither, and thus they make the gold dust glitter; and they also get the gold out by digging pits and by inventing other means for washing the sand; and the so-called "gold washeries" are now more numerous than the gold mines.

Diodorus of Sicily *Historical Library* v. xxxv–xxxviii (abridged)
From LCL

Since we have set forth the facts concerning the Iberians, we think that it will not be foreign to our purpose to discuss the silver mines of the land; for this land possesses, we may venture to say, the most abundant and most excellent known sources of silver, and to the workers of this silver it returns great revenues. . . . The Iberians, having come to know the peculiar qualities possessed by silver, sank notable mines, and as a consequence, by working the most excellent and, we may say, the most abundant silver to be found, they received great revenues. The manner, then, in which the Iberians mine and work the silver is as follows. The mines being marvelous in their deposits of copper and gold and silver, the workers of the copper mines recover from the earth they dig out a fourth part of pure copper, and among the unskilled workers in silver there are some who will take out a Euboeic talent [6] in three days; for all

[4] Modern Alcácer do Sal, Portugal.
[5] Cf. Strabo *Geography* III. ii. 5: "All their foreign trade is carried on with Italy and Rome."
[6] About 57 lbs. avoirdupois.

the ore is full of solid silver dust which gleams forth from it. Consequently, a man may well be filled with wonder both at the nature of the region and at the diligence displayed by the men who labor there. Now at first unskilled laborers, whoever might come, carried on the working of the mines, and these men took great wealth away with them, since the silver-bearing earth was convenient at hand and abundant; but at a later time, since the Romans made themselves masters of Iberia, a multitude of Italians have swarmed to the mines and taken away great wealth with them, such was their greed.[7] For they purchase a multitude of slaves whom they turn over to the overseers of the working of the mines; and these men, opening shafts in a number of places and digging deep into the ground, seek out the seams of earth which are rich in silver and gold; and not only do they go into the ground a great distance, but they also push their diggings many stades in depth and run galleries off at every angle, turning this way and that, in this manner bringing up from the depths the ore which gives them the profit they are seeking. . . .

The slaves who are engaged in the working of the mines produce for their masters revenues in sums defying belief, but they themselves wear out their bodies both by day and by night in the diggings under the earth, dying in large numbers because of the exceptional hardships they endure. For no respite or pause is granted them in their labors, but compelled beneath blows of the overseers to endure the severity of their plight, they lose their lives in this wretched manner, although certain of them who can endure it, by virtue of their bodily strength and their persevering souls, suffer such hardships over a long period; indeed death in their eyes is more to be desired than life, because of the magnitude of the hardships they must bear. . . .

Tin also occurs in many regions of Iberia, not found, however, on the surface of the earth as certain writers continually repeat in their histories, but dug out of the ground and smelted in the same manner as silver and gold. For there are many mines of tin in the country above Lusitania and on the islets which lie off Iberia out in the Ocean and are called because of that fact Cassiterides.[8] And tin is brought in large quantities also from the island of Britain to the opposite Gaul, whence

[7] Diodorus describes here conditions prevailing during the last decades of the Roman Republic. At first state property, the mines in the Iberian Peninsula had by the first century B.C. passed into private ownership. During the first century of the Empire all mines were gradually brought under the imperial fisc and administration (see § 43).

[8] That is, "Tin Islands," the location of which is much debated; the name probably applies to all the North Atlantic tin lands, especially Cornwall in Britain and the nearby Scilly Islands. The importance of Cornish tin in the economy of the Mediterranean fell off during the Empire because of the competition of the Spanish tin deposits.

merchants transport it on horses through the interior of Celtica both to Marseilles and to the city of Narbonne.

GAUL

The Gallic provinces were famous for their foodstuffs, yielded large quantities of building stones, and possessed vigorous mining, pottery, and textile industries.

Strabo *Geography* IV. i. 2, ii. 1–2 (abridged)
From LCL

The whole of this country is watered by rivers: some of them flow down from the Alps, the others from the Cemmenus [Cévennes] and the Pyrenees; and some of them are discharged into the Ocean, the others into Our Sea. Further, the districts through which they flow are plains, for the most part, and hilly lands with navigable watercourses. The river beds are by nature so well situated with reference to one another that they afford transportation from either sea into the other; for the cargoes are transported only a short distance by land, with an easy transit through plains, but most of the way they are carried on the rivers —on some into the interior, on the others to the sea. The Rhone offers an advantage in this regard; for not only is it a stream of many tributaries . . . but it also connects with Our Sea, which is better than the Outer Sea [Ocean], and traverses a country which is the most favored of all in that part of the world. For example, the same fruits are produced by the whole of the province of Narbonese Gaul as by Italy. As you proceed toward the north and the Cemmenus [Cévennes] mountains, the olive-planted and fig-bearing land indeed ceases, but the other things still grow. Also the vine, as you thus proceed, does not easily bring its fruit to maturity. All the rest of the country produces grain in large quantities, and millet, and nuts, and all kinds of livestock. And none of the country is untilled except parts where tilling is precluded by swamps and woods. . . .

Most of the Ocean coast of the Aquitanians is sandy and thin-soiled, thus growing millet, but it is rather unproductive of other products. Here, too, is the gulf [Bay of Biscay] which, along with the Galatic Gulf [Golfe du Lion], which is within the coastline of Narbonese Gaul, forms the isthmus. . . . The gulf is held by the Tarbellians, in whose land the gold mines are most important of all; for in pits dug only to a slight depth they find slabs of gold as big as the hand can hold, which at times require but little refining; but the rest is gold dust and nuggets, the nuggets, too, requiring no great amount of working. . . . Among the

Petrocorians there are fine iron works, and also among the Bituriges Cubi; among the Cadurcians, linen works; among the Rutenians, silver mines; and the Gabalians also have silver mines. The Romans have given the "Latin right" [9] to certain of the Aquitanians, such as the Auscians and the Convenians.

ITALY

Though Italy was primarily an importer and consumer, especially of basic foodstuffs and luxury products (see §§ 34, 44–48), it continued during the Empire to be a heavy producer of wine, olive oil, and livestock and, in addition, maintained flourishing pottery, glass, metal-ware, and textile industries.

Liguria

Strabo *Geography* IV. vi. 2
Adapted from LCL

Speaking generally, this whole coastline from the port of Monaco as far as Etruria [10] is not only exposed to the wind but harborless as well, except for shallow mooring places and anchorages. And lying above it are the enormous beetling cliffs of the mountains, which leave only a narrow pass next to the sea. This country is occupied by the Ligurians, who live on sheep, for the most part, and milk, and a drink made of barley; they pasture their flocks in the districts next to the sea, but mainly in the mountains. They have there in very great quantities timber that is suitable for shipbuilding, with trees so large that their diameter is sometimes found to be eight feet. And many of these trees, even in the variegation of the grain, are not inferior to the thyine wood for the purposes of table making. These, accordingly, the people bring down to the emporium of Genoa, as well as flocks, hides, and honey, and take back with them in exchange olive oil and Italian wine (the little wine they have in their country is mixed with pitch [11] and harsh). And this is the country from which come not only the stunted horses and mules called *ginni*, but also the Ligurian tunics and coarse cloaks. And they also have in their country enormous quantities of red amber, which by some is called *electrum*.

Cisalpine Gaul

Strabo *Geography* v. i. 12
From LCL

As for the excellence of the regions, it is evidenced by their goodly store of men, the size of their cities, and their wealth, in all of which

[9] See § 12 and introduction to § 83.   [10] That is, the present-day Italian Riviera.
[11] Resinated wine remains a staple product in Greece to the present.

respects the Romans there have surpassed the rest of Italy. For not only does the tilled land bring forth fruits in large quantities and of all sorts, but the forests have acorns in such quantities that Rome is fed mainly on the herds of swine that come from there. And the yield of millet is also exceptional, since the soil is well watered; and millet is the greatest preventive of famine, since it withstands every unfavorable weather and can never fail, even though there be scarcity of every other grain. The country has wonderful pitch works, also; and as for the wine, the quantity is indicated by the jars, for the wooden ones are larger than houses; and the good supply of pitch helps much toward the excellent smearing the jars receive. As for wool, the soft kind is produced by the regions round Mutina [Modena] and the river Scoltenna (the finest wool of all); the coarse, by Liguria and the country of the Symbrians, from which the greater part of the households of the Italians is clothed; and the medium, by the regions around Patavium [Padua], from which are made the expensive carpets and covers and everything of this kind that is woolly either on both sides or only on one. But as for the mines, at the present time they are not being worked here as seriously as before— perhaps on account of the fact that those in the country of the Transalpine Gauls and in Spain are more profitable.

The Iron Mines at Elba

Diodorus of Sicily *Historical Library* v. xiii. 1–2
Adapted from LCL

Off the city of Etruria known as Populonia there is an island which men call Aethalia.[12] It is about 100 stades distant from the coast and received the name it bears from the smoke (*aethalus*) which lies so thick about it. For the island possesses a great amount of iron ore, which they quarry in order to melt and cast and thus secure the iron, and they possess a great abundance of this ore. Now those who are engaged in the working of the ore crush the rock and burn the lumps which they have thus broken in certain igneous furnaces; and in these they smelt the lumps by means of a great fire and form them into pieces of moderate size which are in their appearance like large sponges. These are bought up by traders in exchange [for money or goods] and are then transported to Puteoli [13] or the other trading stations, where there are men who purchase such cargoes and who, with the aid of a multitude of artisans in metal whom they have collected, work it further and manufacture iron objects of every description. Some of these are worked into

---

[12] The Greek name of Elba.
[13] In Campania, where the iron fabricating industry of Italy was concentrated; the modern Pozzuoli.

the shape of armor, and others are ingeniously fabricated into shapes well suited for two-pronged forks and sickles and other such tools; and these are then transported by traders to every region, and thus many parts of the inhabited world have a share in the usefulness which accrues from these products.

GREECE

Strabo *Geography* IX. i. 23
From LCL

Of the mountains [of Attica], those which are most famous are Hymettus, Brilessus, and Lycabettus; and also Parnes and Corydallus. Near the city are most excellent quarries of marble, the Hymettian and Pentelic. Hymettus also produces the best honey. The silver mines in Attica were originally valuable, but now they have failed. Those who worked them, when the mining yielded only meager returns, melted again the old refuse, or dross, and were still able to extract from it pure silver, since the workmen of earlier times had been unskillful in heating the ore in furnaces. But though the Attic honey is the best in the world, that from the district of the silver mines is said to be much the best of all.

BITHYNIA AND PONTUS

Strabo *Geography* XII. iii. 12–13, 40
Adapted from LCL

Both Sinopitis and all the mountainous country extending as far as Bithynia and lying above the aforesaid seaboard have shipbuilding timber that is excellent and easy to transport. Sinopitis produces also the maple and the mountain nut, the trees from which they cut the wood used for tables. And the whole of the tilled country situated a little above the sea is planted with olive trees.

After the mouth of the Halys comes Gazelonitis, which extends to Saramene; it is a fertile country and is everywhere level and productive of everything. It has also a sheep industry, that of raising flocks covered with skins and yielding soft wool,[14] of which there is a very great scarcity throughout the whole of Cappadocia and Pontus. The country also produces gazelles, of which there is a scarcity elsewhere. . . .

Mount Sandaracurgium,[15] not far away from Pimolisa . . . is

[14] This ancient custom of protecting fine wool by tying hides around the sheep is still practiced in Asia Minor.
[15] The name means "realgar mine" (realgar is red sulphide of arsenic).

hollowed out in consequence of the mining done there, since the workmen have excavated great cavities beneath it. The mine used to be worked
by publicans, who used as miners the slaves sold in the market because of
their crimes; for, in addition to the painfulness of the work, they say
that the air in the mines is both deadly and hard to endure on account
of the grievous odor of the ore, so that the workmen are doomed to a
quick death. What is more, the mine is often left idle because of the
unprofitableness of it, since the workmen [required] number more than
two hundred and are continually spent by disease and death.

ASIA

Strabo *Geography* XII. viii. 14, 16 (abridged)
From LCL

Synnada is not a large city; but there lies in front of it a plain planted
with olives, about sixty stadia in circuit[?]. And beyond it is Docimaea,
a village, and also the quarry of "Synnadic" marble (so the Romans call
it, though the natives call it "Docimite" or "Docimaean"). At first this
quarry yielded only stones of small size, but on account of the present
extravagance of the Romans great monolithic pillars are taken from it,
which in their variety of colors are so nearly like the alabastrite marble;
so that, although the transportation of such heavy burdens to the sea is
difficult, still, both pillars and slabs, remarkable for their size and beauty,
are conveyed to Rome. . . .

The country round Laodicea produces sheep that are excellent not
only for the softness of their wool, in which they surpass even the
Milesian wool, but also for its raven-black color, so that the Laodiceans
derive rich revenue from it, as do also the neighboring Colossians from
the color which bears the same name.[16]

SYRIA AND JUDAEA

Strabo *Geography* XVI. ii. 9, 23, 42 (abridged)
From LCL

Then one comes to Laodicea, situated on the sea. It is a city most
beautifully built, has a good harbor, and has territory which, besides its
other good crops, abounds in wine. Now this city furnishes most of the
wine to the Alexandrians, since the whole of the mountain which lies
above the city and is possessed by it is covered with vines almost as far
as the summits. . . .

[16] "Colossian" wool was dyed purple or madder-red.

The Tyrian purple has proven itself by far the most beautiful of all; the shellfish are caught near the coast, and the other things requisite for dyeing are easily got; and although the great number of dye works makes the city unpleasant to live in, yet it makes the city rich through the superior skill of its inhabitants. . . .

Lake Sirbonis [17] is large; in fact, some state that it is 1,000 stadia in circuit; however, it extends parallel to the coast to a length of slightly more than 200 stadia, is deep to the very shore, and has water so heavy that there is no use for divers, and any person who walks into it and proceeds no farther than up to his navel is immediately raised afloat. It is full of asphalt. The asphalt is blown to the surface at irregular intervals from the midst of the deep. . . . They reach the asphalt on rafts and chop it and carry off as much as they each can.

EGYPT

Besides being one of the principal grain producing regions of the Empire, Egypt was—as it had been from Pharaonic times—the center of the cultivation of the papyrus plant and of the manufacture therefrom of the paper of antiquity.

Pliny Natural History XIII. xxii–xxiii. 71–77

Papyrus grows in the marshes of Egypt, or in the sluggish waters of the Nile, where they have overflowed and lie stagnant in pools that do not exceed about three feet in depth. The root, which lies obliquely, has the thickness of a man's arm; the stalk is triangular and tapers gracefully upward to a height of not more than about fifteen feet. . . . The natives employ the roots as wood—not only for firewood but also for making various utensils and vessels. From the plant itself, by plaiting it, they also construct boats, and from the inner bark they make sails and mats, and also cloth, as well as coverlets and ropes; they chew it also, both raw and boiled, though they swallow only the juice. . . .

Paper is prepared from papyrus by splitting it with a needle into very thin strips, made as broad as possible. That of the first quality comes from the center of the plant, and other grades in the order of the splitting. The first quality used to be called "hieratic," from its being in early times entirely reserved for religious books. But through adulation it received the name of "Augustan," just as that of second quality was called "Livian" after his wife; thus the name "hieratic" came to designate that of third grade. The next quality was called "amphitheatric," from

---

[17] The name used by Strabo is erroneous, for he proceeds to describe the Dead Sea (Lake Asphaltites).

the place of its manufacture.[18] The skillful workshop of Fannius at Rome took this grade and by a very careful process of alteration rendered it much finer, so that out of a common grade he made it a paper of first quality, and gave his own name to it, while that which did not receive this additional processing retained its original name of "amphitheatric." Next to this is the "Saitic" paper, named after the town where it is produced in very large quantities, being made of cuttings of inferior quality. The "Taeneotic" paper, from a place in the vicinity, is manufactured from the materials that are still nearer the outside rind; this is so coarse that it is sold by weight, not by quality. As for the type known as "commercial," it is useless for writing and serves for covering other paper and as wrappers for merchandise—whence its name, from the word for merchants. After this comes the papyrus [rind], the outer part of which resembles the bulrush; it is useless even for making ropes, with the exception of those used in water.

The various kinds of paper are processed upon a board moistened with Nile water, the muddy liquid of which has the effect of glue.[19] First, an upright layer is spread upon the board, the full length of the papyrus available being used after the strips have been trimmed off at either end; after which cross strips are used, producing a lattice work effect. Next, the sheets are pressed with presses, and then dried in the sun; after which they are joined together. The quality of each succeeding sheet is progressively inferior down to the poorest. There are never more than twenty sheets to a roll.[20]

NORTH AFRICA

Pliny *Natural History* XVIII. xxi

Nothing is more prolific than wheat. Nature has given it this attribute since she nourishes man chiefly on it. A single *modius* of wheat, if the soil is suitable, like that of the Byzacium plain in Africa, yields 150 *modii*. From that region the deified Augustus received from his procurator—incredible as it seems—a shipment of almost 400 shoots grown

---

[18] That is, near the amphitheater of Alexandria. Manufacture took place near the source of the raw material (cf. Vol. I, p. 42), in the Delta region of the Nile, where were located also the town of Saïs and the Taenea district (near Alexandria) mentioned below.
[19] Actually, any water has the same effect. Two layers of raw papyrus strips, if pressed together when moist, will adhere to each other upon drying.
[20] This refers, of course, to the standard rolls of blank paper as prepared in the workshops for shipment and sale. The user would then cut from these rolls as much paper as he required for specific purposes, or, if the roll were not long enough, as for a book, he would glue on additional sheets from another roll.

from a single grain (the correspondence on this matter is still extant).[21]
Nero, similarly, received 360 stalks grown from one grain. The plains
of Leontini and elsewhere in Sicily, the whole of Baetic Spain, and
especially Egypt, yield wheat a good hundredfold.[22]

41. *Agriculture: the Large Estate; Rise of Tenancy*

The agricultural economy of the Roman world had been persistently evolving
since late republican times (see Vol. I, § 166) in the direction of large estates.
During the first two centuries of the Principate, both in Italy and in the provinces, latifundia, the most important of which were the imperial domains
(see § 42), were the basic form of agricultural organization, though small-
scale husbandry persisted in many areas. Despite contemporary moralizing
denunciations of the mushrooming of the latifundia, Italian agriculture,
which continued to concentrate on olive and wine production, does not appear to have been in a state of economic decay. Throughout most parts of the
Empire, absentee landowners, through the development of more efficient and
intensive exploitation of land and labor force, derived comfortable profits
from their estates. But in the first century there began a momentous transformation in the agricultural labor force, which was to have far-reaching consequences. Powerful economic and social forces converged to render slave
labor in this area of the economy relatively unprofitable. To insure a cheap
and stable labor supply, latifundists increasingly leased their estates in
smaller parcels to the growing class of free tenant farmers (*coloni*), often
ex-slaves. By the second century, slave-operated latifundia were becoming
obsolete and tenancy was becoming prevalent. Gradually formalized by imperial legislation, this institution, called the colonate, contained the seeds
of manorial serfdom and was one of the most significant heritages of the
Roman world to feudal times (cf. § 136).

"THE LATIFUNDIA HAVE RUINED ITALY"

Pliny *Natural History* XVIII. vii. 35

The men of olden times believed that above all moderation should
be observed in landholding, for indeed it was their judgment that it was
better to sow less and plow more intensively. Vergil, too, I see agreed
with this view. To confess the truth, the latifundia have ruined Italy,
and soon will ruin the provinces as well. Six owners were in possession

---

[21] Josephus (*Jewish War* II. xvi. 383) informs us that Africa supplied the city of
Rome annually with grain sufficient for eight months, a quantity estimated at
40,000,000 *modii*; see further introduction to § 34.
[22] The yields mentioned in this passage, if accurate, must be taken as exceptional
occurrences.

of one half of the province of Africa at the time when the Emperor Nero had them put to death.

MANAGEMENT OF A LARGE ESTATE

It is instructive to compare these directions with those of Cato and Varro (Vol. I, § 166). It is apparent that Columella, writing in the first century, had in view much larger estates even than these writers of the two preceding centuries.

Columella *On Agriculture* I. vi–ix (abridged)
Adapted from LCL

The size of the villa and the number of its parts should be proportioned to the whole enclosure, and it should be divided into three groups: the *villa urbana* (manor house), the *villa rustica* (farmhouse), and the *villa fructuaria* (storehouse). The manor house should be divided in turn into winter apartments and summer apartments, in such a way that the winter bedrooms face the southeast, and the winter dining room faces the west. The summer bedrooms, on the other hand, should look toward the south, but the dining rooms of that season should look toward the southeast. The baths should face the northwest, that they may be lighted from midday up to evening. The promenades should have a southern exposure, so as to receive both the maximum of sun in winter and the minimum in summer. But in the part devoted to farm uses there will be placed a spacious and high kitchen, that the rafters may be free from the danger of fire, and that it may offer a convenient place for the slave household to stop in at every season of the year. It will be best that cubicles for unfettered slaves be built facing the south; for those who are in chains there should be an underground prison, as wholesome as possible, receiving light through a number of narrow windows built so high from the ground that they cannot be reached with the hand.

For cattle there should be stables which will not be troubled by either heat or cold; for animals broken to work, two sets of stalls—one for winter, another for summer; and for the other animals which it is proper to keep within the farmstead there should be places partly covered, partly open to the sky, and surrounded with high walls so that the animals may rest in the one place in winter, in the other in summer, secure against attacks by wild animals. But stables should be roomy and so arranged that no moisture can flow in and that whatever is made there may run off quickly, to prevent the rotting of either the bases of the walls or the hoofs of the cattle. Ox stalls should be ten feet wide, or nine at least—a size which will allow room for the animal to lie down and for the oxherd to move around in it when performing his duties. The feedracks should not be too high for the ox or pack animal to feed from without inconvenience while standing. Quarters should be provided for the overseer alongside the entrance, so that he may have oversight of all who come in and go out; and for the steward over the entrance for the same reason, and also so that he may keep close watch on the overseer; and near both of these there should be a storehouse in which all farm gear may be collected, and within it a closet for the storing of the iron implements.

Cells for the herdsmen and shepherds should be adjacent to their animals, so that they may conveniently run out to care for them. And yet all should be quartered as close as possible to one another, so that the diligence of the overseer may not be overtaxed in making the rounds of the several places, and also that they may be witnesses of one another's industry and diligence.

The storehouse part is divided into rooms for oil, for presses, for wine, for the boiling down of must; lofts for hay and chaff; and storerooms and grain bins—in such a manner that those on the ground floor take care of liquid products, such as oil and wine for marketing, while dry products, such as grain, hay, leaves, chaff, and other fodder, should be stored in lofts. But the grain lofts, as I have said, should be reached by ladders and should receive ventilation through small openings on the north side; for that exposure is the coolest and the least humid, and both these factors contribute to the preservation of stored grain. The same reason holds true in the placing of the wine room on the ground floor; and it should be far removed from the baths, oven, dunghill, and other filthy places which give off a foul odor, and no less so from cisterns and running water, from which is derived a moisture that spoils the wine. . . .

The press rooms especially and the storerooms for oil should be warm, because every liquid is more readily thinned with heat and thickened by great cold; and if oil freezes, which seldom happens, it becomes rancid. But as it is natural heat that is wanted, arising from the climate and the exposure, there is no need of fire or flame, as the taste of oil is spoiled by smoke and soot. For this reason the pressing room should be lighted from the southern side, so that we may not find it necessary to employ fires and lamps when the olives are being pressed.

The cauldron room, in which boiled wine is made, should be neither narrow nor dark, so that the attendant who is boiling down the must may move around without inconvenience. The smoke room, too, in which timber not long cut may be seasoned quickly, can be built in a section of the farmhouse adjoining the farmhouse baths (it is important also that there be such places in which the household may bathe—but only on holidays; for the frequent use of baths is not conducive to physical vigor). Storerooms for wine will be situated to advantage over these places from which smoke is usually rising, for wines age more rapidly when they are brought to an early maturity by a certain kind of smoke. For this reason there should be another loft to which they may be removed, to keep them from becoming tainted, on the other hand, by too much smoking.

As for the situation of the farmhouse and the arrangement of its several parts, enough has been said. It will be necessary, next, that the farmhouse have the following near it: an oven and a mill, of such size as may be required by the number of tenant farmers; at least two ponds, one to serve for geese and cattle, the other in which we may soak lupines, elm withes, twigs, and other things suitable for our needs. There should also be two manure pits, one to receive the fresh dung and keep it for a year, and a second from which the old is hauled; but both of them should be built shelving with a gentle slope, in the manner of fish ponds, and built up and packed hard with earth, so as not to let the moisture drain away. . . .

The threshing floor is to be placed, if possible, in such manner that it can be viewed from above by the master, or at least by the farm manager. Such a floor is best when paved with hard stone, because the grain is thus threshed out quickly, since the ground does not give way under the beating of the hoofs and threshing sledges, and the winnowed grain is cleaner and is free from small stones and clods, which a dirt floor nearly always casts up during the threshing. . . .

The orchards, too, and the gardens should be fenced all around and should lie close by, in a place to which there may flow all manure-laden seepage from barnyard and baths, and the watery lees squeezed from olives; for both vegetables and trees thrive on nutriment of this sort, too.

After all these things have been obtained or constructed, the master must give special attention, among other things, to laborers; and these are either tenant farmers or slaves (unfettered or in chains). He should be civil in dealing with his tenant farmers, should show himself affable, and should be more exacting in the matter of work than of payments, as this gives less offense yet is, generally speaking, more profitable. For when land is carefully tilled, it usually brings a profit, and never a loss except when it is assailed by unusually severe weather or robbers; and therefore the tenant does not venture to ask for reduction of his rent. But the master should not be insistent on his rights in every particular to which he has bound his tenant, such as the exact day for payment of

money, or the matter of demanding firewood and other trifling contributions; attention to such matters causes country folk more trouble
than expense. . . . I myself remember having heard Publius Volusius,
an old man who had been consul and was very wealthy, declare that
estate to be most fortunate which had natives of the place as tenant
farmers and which held them by reason of long association, even from
the cradle, as if born on their own father's property. So I am decidedly
of the opinion that repeated re-letting of a farm is a bad thing, but that
a worse thing is the tenant farmer who lives in town and prefers to till
the land through his slaves rather than by his own hand. Saserna [23] used
to say that from a man of this sort the return was usually a lawsuit instead
of income, and that for this reason we should take pains to keep with us
tenants who are country-bred and at the same time diligent farmers,
when we are not able to till the land ourselves or when it is not feasible
to cultivate it with our own household; though this does not happen
except in districts which are desolated by the severity of the climate and
the barrenness of the soil. But when the climate is moderately healthful
and the soil moderately good, a man's personal attention never fails to
yield a larger return from his land than does that of a tenant. Even reliance on an overseer yields a larger return, except in the event of extreme
carelessness or greed on the part of that slave. There is no doubt that
in general both these offenses are either committed or fostered through
the fault of the master, inasmuch as he has the authority to prevent such
a person from being placed in charge of his affairs or to see to it that he
is removed if so placed. On far-distant estates, however, which it is not
easy for the owner to visit, it is better for every kind of land to be under
free farmers than under slave overseers, but this is particularly true
of grain land. To such land a tenant farmer can do no great harm, as he
can to vineyards and trees, while slaves do it tremendous damage: they
let out oxen for hire, and they keep them and other animals poorly fed;
they do not plow the ground carefully, and they charge the account
with far more seed than they have actually sown; what they have committed to the earth they do not foster so that it will make the proper
growth; and when they have brought it to the threshing floor, every day
during the threshing they lessen the quantity either by trickery or by
carelessness. For they themselves steal it and do not guard against the
thieving of others, and even when it is stored away, they do not enter it
honestly in their accounts. The result is that both manager and hands
are offenders, and the land pretty often gets a bad name. Therefore my
opinion is that an estate of this sort should be leased if, as I have said, it
cannot have the presence of the owner.

[23] Hostilius Saserna, a writer on agriculture of the late republican period.

The next point is with regard to slaves—over what duty it is proper to place each, and to what sort of tasks to assign them. So my advice at the start is not to appoint an overseer from the sort of slaves who are physically attractive, and certainly not from that class which has been engaged in the voluptuous occupations of the city. This lazy and sleepy-headed class of slaves, accustomed to idling, to the Field of Mars, the circus and the theaters, to gambling, to taverns, to bawdy houses, never ceases to dream of these follies; and when they carry them over into their farming, the master suffers not so much loss in the slave himself as in his whole estate. A man should be chosen who has been hardened by farm work from his infancy, one who has been tested by experience. . . . He should be of middle age and of strong physique, skilled in farm operations or at least very painstaking, so that he may learn the more readily; for it is not in keeping with this business of ours for one man to give orders and another to give instruction, nor can a man properly exact work when he is being tutored by an underling as to what is to be done and in what way. Even an illiterate person, if only he have a retentive mind, can manage affairs well enough. Cornelius Celsus [24] says that an overseer of this sort brings money to his master oftener than he does his book, because, being illiterate, he is either less able to falsify accounts or is afraid to do so through a second party, because that would make another aware of the deception.

But be the overseer what he may, he should be given a woman companion to keep him within bounds and moreover in certain matters to be a help to him. . . . He must be urged to take care of the equipment and the iron tools, and to keep in repair and stored away twice as many as the number of slaves requires, so that there will be no need of borrowing from a neighbor; for the loss in slave labor exceeds the cost of articles of this sort. In the care and clothing of the slave household he should have an eye to usefulness rather than appearance, taking care to keep them fortified against wind, cold, and rain, all of which are warded off with long-sleeved leather tunics, garments of patchwork, or hooded cloaks. If this be done, no weather is so unbearable but that some work may be done in the open. He should be not only skilled in the tasks of husbandry but should also be endowed, as far as the servile disposition allows, with such qualities of mind that he may exercise authority without laxness and without cruelty, and always humor some of the better hands, at the same time being forbearing even with those of lesser worth, so that they may rather fear his sternness than detest his cruelty. . . .

In the case of the other slaves, the following are, in general, the

[24] See Chapter IV, Note 179.

precepts to be observed, and I do not regret having held to them myself: to talk rather familiarly with the country slaves, provided only that they have not conducted themselves unbecomingly, more frequently than I would with town slaves; and when I perceived that their unending toil was lightened by such friendliness on the part of the master, I would even jest with them at times and allow them also to jest more freely. Nowadays I make it a practice to call them into consultation on any new work, as if they were more experienced, and to discover by this means what sort of ability is possessed by each of them and how intelligent he is. Furthermore, I observe that they are more willing to set about a piece of work on which they think that their opinions have been asked and their advice followed. Again, it is the established custom of all men of caution to inspect the slaves in the prison, to find out whether they are carefully chained, whether the places of confinement are quite safe and properly guarded, whether the overseer has put anyone in fetters or removed his shackles without the master's knowledge. . . . And the investigation of the householder should be the more painstaking in the interest of slaves of this sort, that they may not be treated unjustly in the matter of clothing or other allowances, inasmuch as, being subject to a greater number of people, such as overseers, taskmasters, and jailers, they are the more liable to unjust punishment, and again, when smarting under cruelty and greed, they are more to be feared. Accordingly, a careful master inquires not only of them, but also of those who are not in bonds, as being more worthy of belief, whether they are receiving what is due them under his instructions. He also tests the quality of their food and drink by tasting it himself and examines their clothing, mittens, and foot covering. In addition, he should give them frequent opportunities for making complaints against those persons who treat them cruelly or dishonestly. In fact, I now and then avenge those who have just cause for grievance, as well as punish those who incite the slaves to revolt or who slander their taskmasters; and, on the other hand, I reward those who conduct themselves with energy and diligence. Also, to women who are unusually prolific, and who ought to be rewarded for the bearing of a certain number of offspring, I have granted exemption from work and sometimes even freedom after they have reared many children: a mother of three children received exemption from work,[25] a mother of more, her freedom as well. Such justice

---

[25] Cf. in § 11 the similar privileges for the free and freedman classes enacted by Augustus. During the Pax Romana slave owners turned more and more to breeding and rearing slaves in their homes and on their estates—practices they scorned in the heyday of their conquests, when huge supplies of war captives were dumped into the slave markets. Cf. the exaggerated but realistic evidence in Petronius' *Satyricon* liii. 1–2: "His bookkeeper read aloud . . . 'July 26, born on the Cumaean estate belonging to Trimalchio, slave boys 30, girls 40.'"

and consideration on the part of the master contributes greatly to the increase of his estate. . . .

This, too, I believe: that the duties of the slaves should not be confused to the point where all take a hand in every task. For this is by no means to the advantage of the husbandman, either because no one regards any particular task as his own or because, when he does make an effort, he is performing a service that is not his own but common to all, and therefore shirks his work to a great extent; and yet fault cannot be fastened upon any one man because many have a hand in it. For this reason plowmen must be distinguished from vine dressers, and vine dressers from plowmen, and both of these from men of all work. Furthermore, squads should be formed, not to exceed ten men each, which the ancients called *decuriae* and approved of highly, because that limited number was most conveniently guarded while at work and the size was not disconcerting to the person in charge as he led the way. Therefore, if the field is of considerable extent, such squads should be distributed over sections of it and the work should be so apportioned that men will not be by ones or twos, because they are not easily watched when scattered; and yet they should not number more than ten, lest, on the other hand, when the band is too large, each individual may think that the work does not concern him. This arrangement not only stimulates rivalry, but also discloses the slothful; for, when a task is enlivened by competition, punishment inflicted on the laggards appears just and free from censure.

THE PROFITABLENESS OF AGRICULTURE

Columella *On Agriculture* III. iii (abridged)
Adapted from LCL

Now, before discoursing on the planting of vines, I think it not out of place to lay down, as a sort of foundation for the coming discussion, the principle that we should carefully weigh and investigate in advance whether viticulture will enrich the proprietor. . . . And most people would be doubtful on this point, to such an extent that many would avoid and dread such an ordering of their land and would consider it preferable to own meadows and pastures, or woodland for cutting. . . .

Those devoted to the study of agriculture must be informed of one thing first of all—that the return from vineyards is a very rich one. . . . We can hardly recall a time when grain crops, throughout at least the greater part of Italy, returned a yield of four to one.[26] Why, then,

---

[26] A very low rate indeed, reflecting the continuing decline of cereal culture in Italy. The yield in the provinces, and even in parts of Italy in the preceding century, was many times higher (cf. § 40, last selection).

is viticulture in disrepute? Not, indeed, through its own fault, but because of human failings. . . . Most people, in fact, strive for the richest possible yield at the earliest moment; they make no provision for the time to come, but, as if living merely from day to day, they put such demands upon their vines and load them so heavily with young shoots as to show no regard for succeeding generations. After committing all these acts, or at any rate most of them, they would rather do anything at all than admit their own guilt; and they complain that their vineyards do not yield them a return—vineyards which they themselves have ruined through greed, or ignorance, or neglect. But if any who combine painstaking care with scientific knowledge receive not forty or at least thirty amphoras per *iugerum* according to my reckoning but, using a minimum estimate as Graecinus [27] does, twenty, they will easily outdo in the increase of their ancestral estates all those who hold fast to their hay and vegetables. And he is not mistaken in this, for, like a careful accountant, he sees, when his calculations are made, that this kind of husbandry is of the greatest advantage to his estate. For, admitting that vineyards demand a very generous outlay, still seven *iugera* require the labor of not more than one vine dresser, upon whom people in general set a low value, thinking that even some malefactor may be acquired from the auction block; but I, disagreeing with the opinion of the majority, consider a high-priced vine dresser of first importance. And supposing his purchase price to be 6,000—or better, 8,000—sesterces, when I estimate the seven *iugera* of ground as acquired for just as many thousand sesterces,[28] and that vineyards . . . with their stakes and withes are set out for 2,000 sesterces per *iugerum*, still the total cost, reckoned to the last penny, amounts to 29,000 sesterces. Added to this is interest at six percent per annum, amounting to 3,480 sesterces for the two-year period when the vineyards, in their infancy as it were, are delayed in bearing. The sum total of principal and interest thus comes to 32,480 sesterces. And if the husbandman will enter this amount as a debit against his vineyards just as a moneylender does with a debtor, in order that the owner may realize the aforementioned six-percent interest on that total as a perpetual annuity, he must take in 1,950 sesterces every year. By this reckoning the return from seven *iugera*, even according to the [minimum] estimate of Graecinus, exceeds the interest on 32,480 sesterces. For, assuming that the vineyards are of the very worst sort, still, if taken care of, they will yield certainly one *culleus* [29] of wine to

[27] Julius Graecinus, a senator, who wrote a work on viticulture in the early first century.
[28] That is, 7,000 sesterces. The price of the slave is deliberately set very high; cf. introduction to § 52.
[29] A bulk liquid measure, equivalent to twenty amphoras.

the *iugerum;* and even though every forty urns are sold for 300 sesterces, which is the lowest market price, still seven *cullei* bring a total of 2,100 sesterces—a sum far in excess of the interest at six percent. And these figures, as we have given them, are based on the calculations of Graecinus. But our own opinion is that vineyards which yield less than three *cullei* to the *iugerum* should be rooted out. And, even so, we have made our calculations up to this point as if there were no quicksets to be taken from the trenched ground; though this item alone, at a favorable price, would clear the entire cost of the land, if only the land belongs not to the provinces but to Italy.[30]

THE GROWTH OF TENANCY

Pliny *Letters* Book III, No. 19

Gaius Plinius to his dear Calvisius Rufus, greeting.

As usual, I call on you to advise me about my property. Lands adjoining my property, and even jutting into it, are for sale. Many things in them tempt me, but there are some factors—hardly minor ones—which deter me. First, I am tempted by just the attractiveness of rounding out my estate; second, because it would be at once convenient and pleasurable. For the same work could go on in both places, they could be visited at the same traveling expense, and they could be kept under the same overseer and practically the same agents, and while one villa is cared for and kept fully equipped, the other can be merely looked after. One should add in the reckoning the cost of the furnishings, the cost of the stewards, the gardeners, the artisans, and even the equipment for hunting. It makes the greatest difference whether one assembles these in one place or disperses them in several. On the other hand, I am afraid that it is risky to expose so much property to the same storms, the same contingencies; it seems safer to make trial of the uncertainties of fortune by distributing one's investments. Also, much pleasure is afforded by the change in climate and by the actual travel between one's estates.

Now the chief reason for my deliberation is the following: while the

[30] Examples of exceptionally profitable viticulture through intensive cultivation are cited in Pliny *Natural History* XIV. v. Here, as in olive culture, Italy in the first century was already feeling the competition of the provinces. Cf. Pliny *Natural History* XIV. viii. 71: "In the Spanish provinces the vineyards of Laeetanum are renowned for their abundant yield, while for quality those of Tarragona, Lauron, and the Balearic Islands bear comparison with the choice vintages of Italy"; Columella *On Agriculture* Preface 20: "And so, in 'this Latium and this Saturnian land,' where the gods had taught their progeny the fruits of the fields, we now auction off contracts for the importation of grain from the overseas provinces, so as not to suffer from hunger, and we store away wines from the Cyclades Islands and from the Baetic and Gallic regions."

property is fertile, rich, and well supplied with water, and consists of meadows, vineyards, and woods that produce an income from timber which though modest is steady, this fertility of the soil is plagued by the cultivators' lack of means. For the previous owner a number of times sold the securities [for their leases], and while he thus reduced the arrears of the tenant farmers for the time being, he drained their resources for the future, the lack of which caused the arrears to mount again. A number of them, therefore, have to be supplied with industrious slaves; for I myself have none in chains anywhere, nor does anyone in those parts.

Finally, you should know at what price the property can, apparently, be bought—3,000,000 sesterces, though at one time the price was 5,000,000. But on account of the impoverishment of the tenant farmers and the general distress of the times, the returns from landed property as well as prices have dropped You ask whether I can easily get together this 3,000,000 sesterces. Indeed, practically all my investments are in real estate, though I do have some money out at interest, and it will not be difficult for me to borrow. I can get the money from my mother-in-law, whose purse I use as if it were my own. Do not therefore be concerned about this, if there are no hindrances on the other counts, to which I want you please to give your most careful consideration. For in the planning of investments, as in everything else, you have an abundance of experience and foresight. Farewell.

Pliny *Letters* Book x, No. 8. 5–6

[Pliny to the Emperor Trajan]

I beg . . . that you grant me a leave of absence. . . .[31] For the leasing of the lands which I possess in the same region [32] cannot possibly be postponed, particularly since the rent is over 400,000 sesterces,[33] and the new tenant should attend to the pruning, which is close at hand. Moreover, repeated bad seasons oblige me to think of reductions in rents, the accounting of which I cannot undertake except in person. I shall therefore be indebted to your indulgence, my lord . . . for the opportunity of settling my private affairs, if you grant me . . . a leave of absence for thirty days. For I cannot specify a shorter time, since both the municipality and the lands to which I refer are over 150 miles away.

[31] Pliny held a minor office at Rome at this time, probably A.D. 99.
[32] Probably Tifernum-on-Tiber, in Italy: cf. § 90, last selection.
[33] It is not clear whether this amount is the annual rent or covers a period of years.

Pliny *Letters* Book IX, No. 37 (abridged)

Gaius Plinius to his dear Paulinus, greeting.

. . . I am detained by the necessity of leasing my estates so as to set them in order for several years. In which connection I am obliged to adopt new arrangements. For in the last five-year period, despite large reductions [of rent], the arrears mounted. Hence several tenants no longer have any concern to reduce a debt which they despair of being able to pay off; they even seize and consume whatever is produced, acting like people who think they no longer have to be thrifty since it is not their own property. The growing evils, therefore, have to be faced and relieved. There is one method of remedying them—to lease not for a rent in money but on shares, and then to place some of my men to superintend the work and guard the produce. . . . It is true that this requires great integrity, keen eyes, and many hands. However, I must try the experiment and, as in a chronic disease, try and see what help a change may bring.

LEASES OF LAND

The following two documents illustrating tenancy arrangements are representative of a large number of such leases and rent receipts extant among the papyri from Egypt.

Amherst Papyrus No. 91; A.D. 159

Adapted from the translation of B. P. Grenfell and A. S. Hunt
(London, 1901)

To Hero son of Sarapio, a minor, with his guardian Ischyrio son of Herodes, and with the concurrence of the minor's mother, Heroïs, from Aphrodisius son of Acusilaus, of the metropolis [Arsinoë]. I wish to lease the eleven arouras or thereabouts of vineland belonging to Hero in one parcel near the village of Euhemeria for two years from the current twenty-third year of the lord Antoninus Caesar, at a total yearly rent for all the arouras, not including seed, of forty artabs of wheat by the four-*choinix-dromus* measure, subject to no charge or risk. I will perform the annual operations: [maintaining] the embankments, irrigation, plowing, hoeing, dredging of irrigation canals, sowing, weeding, and all else that is fitting, at my own expense and at the proper seasons, doing nothing injurious. I will sow the arouras in the first year with any crops I choose except *cnecus*,[34] and in the second year one half with

[34] The safflower, an oleaginous plant still grown in Egypt.

wheat and the other half with light crops.[35] The annual expense of transporting [produce delivered] to the state shall be borne by me, Aphrodisius, but all the other state charges by Hero. I will pay the yearly rent in the month of Payni,[36] new, pure, unadulterated, and unmixed with barley, at the village of Theadelphia; and at the end of the period I will deliver the arouras with the produce, after being sown as aforesaid, duly harvested, and free from rushes, coarse grass, and refuse of all sorts, if you consent to the lease. Aphrodisius, aged forty years, with a scar in the middle of his forehead. Year 23 of the lord Antoninus Caesar, Hathyr 12.

Amherst Papyrus No. 105; A.D. 127
Adapted from the translation of Grenfell and Hunt

Chaeremo son of Polydeuces to Anubio son of Sarapio, greeting.

I have received from you all the rent from the produce of the current eleventh year of the lord Hadrian Caesar from my land which you cultivated in the Lower Suburb near Magdola Mirê in the holding of Attinus, and I have no claim against you, the state charges being payable by me. The eleventh year of the Emperor Caesar Trajanus HADRIAN Augustus, Mesore 25.

42. *Imperial Estates and Agrarian Policy*

By far the biggest landowner in the Roman Empire was the emperor. As *princeps* he possessed estates all over the Empire, some inherited from various local dynasties on their extinction, others bequeathed by or confiscated from private owners. Each estate was operated under the supervision of a resident imperial procurator, who carried out the general policies laid down by the emperors within the framework of local conditions and traditions. While specific details might thus vary from place to place even within a single province, certain general features do stand out. We are best informed about the estates in Africa and Egypt, the two major sources of Rome's food supply. The general procedure in both these provinces was to lease parcels of the estate to tenant farmers (*coloni*) for varying periods; a significant difference is seen in the fact that in Africa the tenant's obligations under the lease were to deliver a certain share of the crops and furnish a number of days' labor to the lessor, while in Egypt the leases were for a stipulated rental payable in kind. In some places the procurators leased large tracts to lessees-in-chief (*conductores*), who cultivated part themselves and sublet the rest to

---

[35] Such rotation of crops is frequently specified in ancient leases of land.
[36] That is, May/June (cf. introduction to § 51), the height of the harvest season in Egypt.

coloni. While slaves were undoubtedly used to some extent as agricultural laborers, they appear more often as household or administrative assistants (bailiffs, secretaries, etc.) of the chief lessees or procurators, who were themselves often imperial freedmen.

Like other large estates, those of the emperor were affected in the first two centuries by the growing shortage of agricultural manpower. In Egypt (and doubtless elsewhere as well), when not enough voluntary tenants appeared, the remaining land was assigned to neighboring individuals or villages for compulsory cultivation. In addition, the emperors began to offer the tenant farmers special inducements to stimulate and assure production. The Mancian Law, dating probably from the late first century and confirmed and liberalized by Hadrian, offered two major concessions to *coloni* who took possession of waste or abandoned land on imperial or private estates and established domiciles thereon: (1) quasi ownership of any such land as long as they kept it under cultivation, limited only by inability to sell, and (2) rent-free occupation for the first five or ten years, depending on the crops grown. Thus, like the Gracchi and their followers in republican times (cf. Vol. I, §§ 96–99), but with considerably greater success,[37] the Roman emperors attempted to create a solid and stable class of tenant farmers on the latifundia. As time passed and the *coloni* handed on their holdings to their heirs, both the holding and the "owner's" status came to be regarded as hereditary; thus the *coloni* became the forerunners of the praedial serfs of the Middle Ages (cf. §§ 123, 136).

IMPERIAL ESTATES IN AFRICA

The following three inscriptions come from the Bagradas (modern Medjerda) valley in North Africa. They are open to varying interpretations on a number of points of detail, owing to the physical mutilation of the stones, the barbarity of the stonecutters' Latin, and the uncertainty of the specific connotation of some terms. Where different possibilities exist, our translation gives, usually without further comment, what we regard as the sense most congruent with the known facts.

CIL, Vol. VIII, No. 25,902 (= Abbott-Johnson, No. 74 = *FIRA*, Vol. I, No. 100)

[The inscription of Henchir Mettich, A.D. 116/17]

For the preservation of our Augustus, the Emperor Caesar TRAJAN Germanicus Parthicus, excellent *princeps*[?], and all his sacred house. Issued by the procurators Licinius Maximus and Felicior, imperial freedman, on the basis of the Mancian Law.

Anyone living within the estate of Villa Magna Variana—that is,

[37] Recently published texts have shown that in the late fifth century, under Vandal rule, there were still "Mancian fields" in North Africa.

in Siga village—is permitted to bring those fields which are unsurveyed [38] under cultivation under the terms of the Mancian Law, whereby anyone who brings such land under cultivation acquires a personal usufruct.[39] Of the crops produced on such land they must in accordance with the Mancian Law deliver shares to the owners, or to the chief lessees or bailiffs, of this estate as follows: The tenant farmers shall render to the chief lessees or bailiffs of this estate their own estimate of the total yield of every kind of crop which they will have to bring to the threshing floor and thresh; and if the chief lessees or bailiffs of this estate in return send notice of precisely what shares will be due from the tenant farmers, the tenant farmers shall without personal liability [40] guarantee in writing the shares of the said crop which they must deliver, and they shall be obligated to deliver the said shares to the chief lessees or bailiffs of this estate.

Those who have or shall have farmsteads in the estate of Villa Magna Variana, or Siga village, must deliver in full to the owners of this estate, or to their chief lessees or bailiffs, the shares of produce and wine of every kind customary under the Mancian Law, namely: one third of the wheat from the threshing floor, one third of the barley from the threshing floor, one fourth of the beans from the threshing floor, one third of the wine from the vat, one third of the oil extracted, one *sextarius* of honey per hive. Anyone having more than five hives must give the entire amount to the owners, chief lessees, or bailiffs of this estate at the time when the honey is collected. If anyone transfers hives, swarms, bees, or honey jars from the estate of Villa Magna, or Siga village, to land where the share is one-eighth with intent to defraud the owners or their [?] chief lessees or bailiffs, the hives, swarms, bees, honey jars, and honey in them[?] shall belong in their entirety to the chief lessees or bailiffs of this estate.

[Two brief clauses, omitted here, deal with the harvests from existing olive and fig orchards.]

If any fig orchard is started hereafter, the one who plants it is allowed to retain full possession of the crop of such fig orchard for five successive harvests; after the fifth harvest he must deliver to the chief lessees or bailiffs of this estate the customary share under the same regulation mentioned above.[41]

[38] Usually uncleared scrub or marginal land; cf. the second paragraph of the following inscription.

[39] *Usus proprius* implies the right to acquire prescriptive title against eviction.

[40] The Latin here is *sine fraude,* which usually has the legal sense of "without personal risk," or "with impunity," but perhaps it should be taken here literally to mean "without deceit," or "in good faith."

[41] The amount of the "customary share" is not specified either here or in the preceding clause.

New vineyards may be planted and cultivated in place of old ones on the following terms: The person who does so shall retain full possession of the product of such vineyard for the next five harvests after such planting, but, similarly, after the fifth harvest after such planting takes place they must give to the chief lessees or bailiffs of this estate, in accordance with the Mancian Law, one third of the crop.

An olive orchard may be planted and cultivated in such place where a person brings uncultivated land under cultivation on the following terms: He shall be entitled to retain full possession of the crops of the olive orchard thus planted for the next ten harvests after such planting, but, similarly, after these harvests he must likewise give one third of the oil extracted to the chief lessees or bailiffs of this estate. Anyone who grafts wild olives must give one third after five years.[42]

If any fields have been or are planted to grass in the estate of Villa Magna Variana, or Siga village, excepting those fields which have vetches,[43] the crops of such fields shall be given[?] to the chief lessees or bailiffs; the overseers must claim[?] it.

For cattle which are pastured within the estate of Villa Magna, or Siga village, four *asses* must be paid for each head to the chief lessees or bailiffs of the owners of this estate.

If anyone cuts down, destroys, carries away, carries off, burns, or cuts off from the estate of Villa Magna, or Siga village, a standing or hanging crop, ripe or unripe, the loss of the following two years . . . shall be borne by the tenant farmer, who must deliver the fixed share to the chief lessees or bailiffs of this estate.[44]

[The next clause, which is badly mutilated, probably assured the right to bequeath and mortgage land brought under cultivation under the provisions of the Mancian Law.]

If anyone has brought or brings a plot of uncultivated land under cultivation and has erected or erects . . . a building thereon and afterwards ceases or gives up cultivation, at the time when such plot has ceased or ceases to be cultivated the right of cultivation which existed or exists is and will continue in force for a period of exactly two years after the day on which he ceases to cultivate; after the two-year period the chief lessees or bailiffs shall have the right to cultivate such

---

[42] In other words, the ten-year exemption is given to those who set out young new olive shoots and nurse them along to full growth; the exemption period is halved where grafts are made on grown stock, since such trees reach the bearing stage much sooner.

[43] For soil improvement.

[44] The presumption of this clause that any damage to the crop is the *colonus'* fault may of course have been qualified in the lacuna by some such statement as, "if due to negligence on his part."

plots.[45] If such a plot was cultivated the year before and ceases to be cultivated, the chief lessee or bailiff of this estate shall notify the person to whom such plot is said to belong that it must be cultivated; if, after he gives such notice, the villager, according to sworn testimony, does not resume cultivation and persists likewise in the following year, the chief lessee or bailiff of this estate shall have the right after the two-year period to cultivate such plot without redress [to the previous cultivator].

[There follows one brief clause too mutilated for restoration.]

Tenant farmers living within the estate of Villa Magna, or Siga village, must perform per man each year in full for the owners, or for their chief lessees or bailiffs, two days' labor at plowing, two[?] days' labor at harvesting, and one day's labor at each kind of cultivating, making two days' labor per man.

Landless laborers[?] [46] of this estate must within . . . of a year submit their names to the chief lessees or bailiffs of this estate and arrange for[?] the one day's work as overseers which they must each perform in the fields. . . . [The rest is lost.]

CIL, Vol. VIII, No. 25,943, cols. 1–3, supplemented by No. 26,416
(= Abbott-Johnson, No. 93 = FIRA, Vol. I, No. 101, supplemented
by No. 102)

[The inscriptions of Ain-el-Jemala and Ain Wassel, A.D. 117/38]

[Petition of tenant farmers to the procurators of the estate:] . . . we ask, procurators, that through the foresight which you exercise in the name of Caesar, you be minded to have regard for us and for his advantage, and grant us the land which is swampy and wooded to plant with olive orchards and vineyards on the terms in force on the neighboring Neronian estate in accordance with the Mancian Law. . . .

Statement of the procurators of the Emperor Caesar HADRIAN Augustus: Since it is the order of our Caesar, in the untiring care with which he assiduously watches over mankind's interests, that all parts of the land suitable for olives and vines as well as for grains be brought under cultivation, therefore by the grace[?] of his foresight the right is granted to all to take possession even of those parts among the leased-

---

[45] The last eight words have been supplied by us to render the apparent sense; instead of "right" many scholars understand "obligation." Similar restorations are made in the next sentence.

[46] The term is *coloni inquilini;* there is no agreement among scholars as to how, if at all, they differed from other *coloni*. This clause is followed by another, even more mutilated, providing similar guard duty for *stipendiarii* living on the estate; the meaning of *stipendiarii* is also uncertain.

out surveyed parcels of the Blandian and Udensian estates and of those parts of the Lamian and Domitian estate adjoining [47] the Tuzritan estate which are not being exploited by the chief lessees. Those who so take possession are granted the right—comprehended in the law of Hadrian on waste lands and fields which have lain uncultivated for ten successive years—of possessing and enjoying the usufruct of the land, and of leaving it to their heirs. No greater shares of produce shall be exacted from the Blandian and Udensian estate than tenant farmers pay by virtue of Caesar's supreme beneficence: anyone who takes possession of places neglected by the chief lessees shall give one third of the crops, which is the share customarily given; also from those sections of the Lamian and Domitian estate adjoining the Tuzritan he shall give the same. From olive trees which anyone sets out or grafts onto wild olives trees, no share of the crops obtained shall be exacted for the next ten years; of fruits no share shall be exacted for the next seven years, and no fruits shall ever be subject to division other than those sold by the possessors. Whatever shares of the dry produce anyone must give he shall give for the next five years to the person in whose leasehold he occupies a field, and after that time to the account of the fisc.

CIL, Vol. VIII, Nos. 10,570 and 14,464, col. 2, line 1–col. 4, line 8
(= Abbott-Johnson, No. 111 = *FIRA*, Vol. I, No. 103)

[The inscription of Sûk-el-Khmis, A.D. 180/83]

[Petition to the emperor from Lurius Lucullus on behalf of estate tenants:] . . . that you may know of the collusion[?] which your procurator has practiced without limit not only with Allius Maximus, our adversary, but with practically all the chief lessees, in violation of right and to the detriment of your fisc. As a result he has not only re-frained for so many years past from investigating when we petitioned and pleaded and cited your divine order, but he has even yielded to the wiles of the said Allius Maximus, the chief lessee, who stands so high in his favor, to the point of sending soldiers into the said Burunitan estate and ordering some of us to be seized and tortured, others fettered, and some, including even Roman citizens, beaten with rods and cudgels; and the only thing we did to deserve this was that, in the face of injury so palpable and so oppressive in relation to the measure of our insignif-icance, we had resorted to sending a letter of complaint beseeching your majesty's aid. The evidence of our injury, Caesar, can be judged from the fact that . . . perform work. . . . This has driven us, most

---

[47] Or "attached to." The name that follows is spelled Thusdritan in *CIL*, Vol. VIII, No. 26,416. The same phrase appears a few lines below.

wretched of men, now again to implore your divine providence, and
we therefore ask you, most sacred Emperor, to come to our aid. Let
the procurators also, not to mention the chief lessee, be deprived of the
right, as they are deprived by the section of the law of Hadrian cited
above, of increasing to the tenant farmers' detriment the shares of crops
or the labor or teams to be furnished, and, as provided in the records of
the procurators deposited in your archives of the Carthaginian district,
let us owe annually per man not more than two days' work at plowing,
two at cultivating, and two at harvesting, and let there be no dispute
about this, inasmuch as it has been inscribed in bronze and observed as
the established practice down to the present day by absolutely all our
neighbors on every side and confirmed to be such by the abovemen-
tioned records of the procurators. Succor us, and—since we are poor
peasants sustaining life by the toil of our hands and no match, in our
relations with your procurators, for the chief lessee, who stands very
high in their favor because of his lavish gifts and is well known to each
of them in succession by virtue of the lease—have pity on us, and deign
to instruct by your sacred rescript that we are to perform no more
service than we are obligated to in accordance with the law of Hadrian
and with the records of your procurators, that is, three periods of two
days' work per man, so that through the benefaction of your majesty
we, your own peasants, born and raised on your estates, may be harassed
no further by the chief lessees of lands belonging to the fisc.

The Emperor Caesar Marcus Aurelius COMMODUS Antoninus Augustus Sarmaticus Germanicus Maximus to Lurius Lucullus and the
others represented by him: In view of established tradition and my
order, procurators will see to it that nothing more than three periods
of two days' work per man [48] is unjustly exacted from you in violation
of established practice.

IMPERIAL ESTATES IN EGYPT

Information about the imperial estates in Egypt is provided by a considerable
body of papyri. The two documents given below illustrate their economic
operations and the history of their ownership. The first emperors distributed
large numbers of these estates to members of the imperial family and to favored associates; but in the era of confiscations initiated by Nero and intensified by Vespasian and Titus (cf. Chapter II, Note 50) these estates were
practically all repossessed by the emperor.

[48] The words "more than . . . per man" were probably not in the emperor's rescript, but were inserted by the *coloni* who set up the inscription.

Milan Papyrus No. 6; A.D. 25

To Aphrodisius son of Zoilus, lessee of the estate of Julia Augusta [49] and the children of Germanicus Caesar, from Harthotes son of Marres. If I am granted the right to gather papyrus and rush from the marsh [in an area extending] from the limits of Theoxenis to the boundaries of Philoteris, and to weave mats therefrom and sell them in any villages of the nome I choose during the twelfth year of Tiberius Caesar Augustus, I engage to pay four drachmas of silver and fifteen obols together with the appropriate supplemental and receipt fees, which I will remit in three installments in Epeiph, Mesore, and the month of Augustus [50] next year if you see fit to grant me this on the aforesaid terms. Farewell. Year 12 of Tiberius Caesar Augustus, Payni 24.

Rylands Papyrus No. 171; A.D. 56/57

To Euschemo, agent of the estate of Tiberius Claudius Doryphorus, formerly owned by Narcissus,[51] in the Arsinoite nome, from Papus son of Trypho, of Heraclia in the Themistes division, living in the farmstead of Antonia wife of Drusus. . . .[52] I desire to lease for four years from the coming third year of the Emperor Nero Claudius Caesar Augustus Germanicus twenty-seven arouras . . . in the vicinity of the said village . . . in two parcels . . . bounded as follows: on the south, crown land;[53] on the north, crown land on the lake shore; on the west, grounds of Pa. . . ; on the east, grounds of the estate of Maecenas. . . . I will pay a total yearly rental of . . . artabs per aroura, including the one artab of wheat per aroura which I receive for seed. . . . [The rest is lost.]

AN IMPERIAL CATTLE RANCH IN ITALY

The following inscription concerns a cattle-raising imperial estate in the mountains of central Italy. It contains orders protecting the lessees of the

[49] The name of Livia, Augustus' wife, after his death; cf. Chapter I, Note 207.
[50] Not our month August, but the first month of the Egyptian calendar, Thoth (August 29–September 27), which was renamed in honor of Augustus, who was born in September; cf. Chapter II, Note 20.
[51] Narcissus was the freedman and secretary general of the Emperor Claudius (cf. Chapter II, Note 91). Nero had deprived him of the estate and granted it to his own freedman and notorious favorite, Doryphorus.
[52] Nero Claudius Drusus, brother of the Emperor Tiberius, married the younger Antonia, daughter of Mark Antony. Germanicus and the Emperor Claudius were born of this marriage.
[53] Land belonging to the emperor's privy purse, so called because inherited by him from the Ptolemaic dynasty of Egypt.

estate against molestation by the local authorities and provides incidentally one of the earliest evidences for the exercise of the police power in Italy by the Praetorian Prefect.

CIL, Vol. IX, No. 2,438 (= Abbott-Johnson, No. 109 = FIRA, Vol. I, No. 61); A.D. 169/72

Bassaeus Rufus and Macrinius Vindex to the magistrates of Saepinum, greeting. We have appended a copy of a letter written to us by Cosmus, freedman of the emperor and financial secretary,[54] together with that which was subjoined to his, and we warn you to refrain from abusing the lessees of the flocks of sheep to the serious detriment of the fisc, lest it be necessary to investigate the matter and punish the act, if the facts are as reported.

Letter of Cosmus, freedman of the emperor and financial secretary, written to Bassaeus Rufus and Macrinius Vindex, prefects of the Praetorian Guard, eminentissimi viri: I have appended a copy of a letter written to me by Septimianus, my fellow freedman and assistant, and I beg that you be good enough to write to the magistrates of Saepinum and Bovianum to refrain from abusing the lessees of the flocks of sheep, who are under my supervision, so that by your kindness the account of the fisc may be secured against loss.

Letter written by Septimianus to Cosmus: Since the lessees of the flocks of sheep, who are under your supervision, are now repeatedly complaining to me that they frequently suffer injury along the paths of the mountain pasturages at the hands of the imperial police[55] and magistrates at Saepinum and Bovianum, inasmuch as they detain in transit draught animals and shepherds that they have hired, saying that they are runaway slaves and have stolen draught animals—and under this pretext even sheep belonging to the emperor are lost to them in such disturbances—we considered it necessary to write them again and again to act more temperately, so that the imperial property might suffer no loss. And since they persist in the same insolence, saying that they will pay no attention to my letters and that it will do no good even if you write to them, I request, my lord, that, if you deem fit, you notify Bassaeus Rufus and Macrinius Vindex, prefects of the Praetorian Guard, eminentissimi viri, to issue letters to the said magistrates and police. . . . [The rest of this concluding sentence is fragmentary.]

[54] Cf. introduction to § 31.
[55] Stationarii. These were soldiers stationed at guard posts, which were placed along the roads throughout the Empire to serve as local gendarmeries.

RECLAMATION OF MUNICIPAL LAND

Inducements to tenant farmers similar to those in effect on the imperial estates are attested by the following inscription from Thisbae, in Greece. The fact that these rules were issued to the town by the governor of the province is another of the many evidences of the direct intervention of the central government in municipal affairs (cf. Vol. I, p. 469, Vol. II, § 88).

Dittenberger, No. 884, lines 1–54 (= Abbott-Johnson, No. 129);
late second or early third century

Marcus Ulpius . . . proconsul, declares: Anyone of the Thisbaeans desiring to plant [with vines or olives] a parcel of the public or temple[?] lands being cultivated in the territory under my jurisdiction shall transmit to the magistrates of the city a petition indicating the plot he desires to occupy and the annual rental he will pay for each *plethrum* [56] . . . in accordance with the decree of the council or assembly. . . . The occupier shall receive for each parcel a remission of the rental of the first five years. Thereafter he shall pay each year the annual rental of the occupied parcel on the fifteenth of the month of Alalcomenius.[57] Magistrates failing to collect the revenue shall be liable for what they did not collect. If any occupier does not plant within the five-year period, the magistrates shall seize and resell the parcel and shall collect from him the rental which he had engaged to pay for the five-year period. If he plants only a portion in order to qualify for [remission of] the five years' rental, the magistrate shall not collect the rental but shall sell the parcel, both the idle and the planted parts, to a citizen on the following terms, namely, that the value of the planted part be delivered to the city and the rental of the whole be paid each year in the full amount which the former holder had agreed to pay, with the rental of the five-year period being conceded to the purchaser for the idle part alone. Each citizen may occupy not more than . . . *plethra*. If, however, anyone is found to have planted more than this, the magistrates shall sell [the excess?] on the following terms to any of the citizens desiring it, namely, that the city obtain from him the rental in the full amount which the former holder had agreed to pay for each *plethrum;* if no one is willing to buy it, they shall collect from the first occupier the existing rental in the full amount which he had undertaken to pay for each *plethrum*. . . .

If anyone should with fraudulent intent mortgage any of the public parcels to an alien and should be convicted thereof, the city shall con-

[56] A land measure, 10,000 square feet.
[57] This month, the last of the year in the Boeotian calendar, corresponded approximately to November.

fiscate the mortgaged parcel and the alien creditor shall exact payment of the debt from the other property of the mortgagor. If anyone should bequeath any of the parcels to an alien relative or friend, his gift shall be invalid, and the parcel shall belong to the city. If anyone should die intestate and without lawful heirs, the city shall be heir to its own property on both accounts.[58]

43. Operation and Administration of Mines

Most mines were government property. Under the Republic their exploitation had been leased by the censors, like other public contracts, to companies of publicans (cf. Vol. I, p. 385). Under the Empire the publican system was progressively replaced, in mining as in other activities, by more direct governmental operation. Like the imperial estates, the mining districts were placed under the control of resident procurators, each of whom issued his own local rules to implement general imperial policies. The mining villages were usually not organized along municipal lines; instead, the procurator, like his counterpart on a landed estate, personally exercised the administrative and judicial authority in the village and district. Gangs of slaves and convicts (cf. § 165) constituted the traditional labor force of mines in antiquity. Here, too, however, the emperors (notably Hadrian) encouraged small entrepreneurs by offering those who put unopened or abandoned mines into operation much the same conditions and privileges as were extended to estate tenants who expanded the cultivated area: the mine holding, too, was contingent upon uninterrupted operation; the fisc received a one-half share of the output; the operator was even called *colonus* (as well as "proprietor," or "occupier"); in addition, these operators even had the right to sell their holdings under certain conditions.

The two inscriptions that follow come from the copper- and silver-mining district of Vipasca (near modern Aljustrel, Portugal). The first details the conditions of mine tenure and operation; the second contains some of the procurator's regulations governing a variety of other economic activities in the mining district.

FIRA, Vol. I, No. 104 and *Iura*, II (1951), 127–33; A.D. 117/38

. . . to his dear Ulpius Aelianus,[59] greeting.
. . . he shall make immediate payment. If anyone does not do so

---

[58] That is, first because the private property of heirless persons fell to the state, and secondly because the city, in all the concessions offered, never actually relinquished title to these lands.

[59] The procurator of the Vipasca mines, an imperial freedman as shown by his bearing the family names of Trajan and Hadrian; cf. introduction to § 66. The sender, whose identity is lost in the preceding lacuna, was some higher official, perhaps the provincial procurator.

and is convicted of having smelted ore before paying the price as specified above, his share as occupier shall be confiscated and the entire diggings shall be sold by the procurator of the mines. Anyone who proves that the tenant has smelted ore before paying the price of the half share belonging to the fisc shall receive one fourth.

Silver [60] diggings must be worked in accordance with the details contained in these regulations. Their prices will be kept in accordance with the liberality of the most sacred Emperor Hadrian Augustus, whereby the ownership of the share belonging to the fisc belongs to the first person to offer the price for the diggings and pay down to the fisc the sum of 4,000 sesterces.

If anyone strikes ore in one out of five diggings, he shall, as stated above, carry out the work in the others without interruption. If he does not do so, another shall have a legal right to take possession. If anyone after the twenty-five days granted for raising working capital actually begins regular operations but then stops operations for ten consecutive days, another shall have the right to take possession. If a diggings sold by the fisc is idle for six consecutive months, another shall have a legal right to take possession on condition that when the ore is extracted therefrom one half shall be, according to customary practice, reserved to the fisc.

The occupier of diggings shall have the right to have any partners he wishes on condition that each partner contribute his proportionate share of the expenses. If anyone does not do so, then the one who covers the expenses shall have an account of the expenses covered by himself posted on three consecutive days in a most frequented place in the forum, and shall demand of his partners through the public crier that each contribute his proportionate share of the expenses. If anyone does not thus contribute or does anything with malice aforethought to avoid contributing or to deceive one or more of his partners, he shall not have his share of such diggings, and that share shall belong to the partner or partners who cover the expenses. Alternatively, tenants who cover expenses in such diggings in which there are many partners shall have a legal right to recover from their partners anything that is shown to have been expended in good faith. Tenants shall have the right to sell among themselves, at as high a price as they can, even shares of diggings purchased from the fisc and paid for. Anyone who wishes to sell his share or buy shall submit a declaration to the procurator who is in charge of the mines; otherwise he shall not be allowed to buy or sell. Anyone who is a debtor of the fisc shall not be allowed to give away his share.

[60] The preceding paragraph presumably refers to copper mines; cf. the arrangement in the last two paragraphs.

Ore extracted and lying at the diggings must be conveyed to the smelters by those to whom it belongs between sunrise and sunset; anyone convicted of having removed ore from the diggings after sunset in the night shall have to pay to the fisc the sum of 1,000 sesterces. A stealer of ore, if he is a slave, shall be whipped by the procurator and sold on this condition, that he shall be kept perpetually in chains and not tarry in any mine or mining district; the price of the slave shall belong to the owner. If the thief is a free man, the procurator shall confiscate his property and debar him forever from the mining district.

All diggings shall be carefully propped and reinforced, and the tenant of each diggings shall provide new and suitable replacements for rotten material. It shall be forbidden to touch or damage pillars or props left for reinforcement, or to do anything with malice aforethought to render the said pillars or props unsafe or. . . . If anyone is convicted of having injured, weakened, or damaged[?] a diggings, or of having done anything with malice aforethought to render such diggings unsafe, if he is a slave he shall be whipped at the discretion of the procurator and sold by his master on this condition, that he shall not tarry in any mine [or mining district]; if he is a free man, the procurator shall appropriate his property to the fisc and debar him forever from the mining district.

Anyone who operates copper diggings shall avoid the ditch that drains the water from the mines and leave a space of not less than fifteen feet on either side. It shall be forbidden to damage the ditch. The procurator shall permit the driving of a drift from the ditch for the purpose of discovering new mines, on condition that the drift be not more than four feet in width and depth. It shall be forbidden to look for or chop out ore within fifteen feet on either side of the ditch.[61] If anyone is convicted of having done anything different in the drifts, if he is a slave he shall be whipped at the discretion of the procurator and sold by his master on this condition, that he shall not tarry in any mine [or mining district]; if he is a free man, the procurator shall appropriate his property to the fisc and debar him forever from the mining district.

[61] Diodorus, in his account of mining in Spain (see § 40, second selection), gives the following description of mine drainage (*Historical Library* v. xxxvii. 3): "Now and then down deep they come upon rivers flowing underground, the force of which they overcome by diverting their inundating streams through transverse channels. For, driven as they are by fully justified expectations of profits, they push their several enterprises to the very limit and, most surprising of all, they draw off the streams of water by means of Egyptian screws, as they are called, which Archimedes of Syracuse invented when he visited Egypt. By means of these they carry the water in successive lifts to the mouth and dry up the bottom of the mine." Several of these ancient Archimedean pumps have actually been found in the mining region of southern Spain. The standard screw was a wooden cylinder twenty inches in diameter and fourteen feet long, but since it was worked on an incline it achieved a net vertical lift of only five feet.

Anyone who operates silver diggings shall avoid the ditch that drains the water from the mines and shall leave a space of not less than sixty feet on either side. He shall work the diggings occupied by him or allotted to him within the boundaries prescribed, and shall not advance beyond nor collect leavings nor drive drifts outside the limits of the diggings allotted. . . . [The rest is lost.]

CIL, Vol. II, No. 5,181 (= Dessau, No. 6,891 = FIRA, Vol. I,
No. 105); second century

OF THE ONE-PERCENT TAX ON AUCTION TRANSACTIONS. The farmer of the tax on sales held at auction within the district of the Vipasca mines shall receive one percent from the seller except on sales which the procurator of the mines holds at the emperor's order. The tax farmer may not collect [62] one percent on the price of diggings which the procurator of the mines sells. If, after the auction has begun, everything is knocked down in one lot, [63] the seller shall nonetheless be required to pay one percent to the tax farmer, or to his partner or agent. The tax farmer, or his partner or agent, if he wishes. . . . The tax farmer, or his partner or agent, shall collect one percent also of any amount that is withdrawn from auction. If anyone has property for sale through the auctioneer and he does not sell it at auction but sells it himself by contract within ten days of placing it with the auctioneer, he shall nonetheless be required to give one percent to the tax farmer, or to his partner or agent. If anything owed the tax farmer, or his partner or agent, in accordance with this section of the regulations, is not given, paid, or secured within the next three days after the debt is incurred, he shall have to pay double.

OF THE AUCTIONEERING FEE. Whoever leases the auctioneering concession shall provide an auctioneer within the district. On a sale of 100 *denarii* or less he shall collect a fee of two percent from the seller, on a sale of over 100 *denarii*, one percent. Anyone who sells slaves through the auctioneer shall be required to pay the concessionaire, or his partner or agent . . . *denarii* per head if he sells five or a smaller number, three *denarii* per head if he sells a larger number. If the procurator of the mines sells or leases any property for the account of the fisc, the concessionaire, or his partner or agent, shall be required to furnish an auctioneer for such property. Anyone who posts a list with a view to selling any property whatever shall be required to pay one *denarius* to the concessionaire, or to his partner or agent. The purchaser of diggings

[62] Instead of "may not collect," some scholars restore the inscription at this point to read "shall collect from the purchaser," citing the similar provision in the next paragraph.
[63] That is, the transaction becomes in effect a straight sale rather than an auction.

sold by the procurator of the mines shall be required to pay one percent; if he does not pay it within three days, he shall have to pay double, and the concessionaire, or his partner or agent, shall have the right to obtain security. Anyone who sells mules, asses, or horses, male or female, through the auctioneer shall be required to pay three *denarii* per head. Anyone who places slaves or any other property for sale through the auctioneer and sells it himself by contract within thirty days shall nonetheless be required to pay the fee[?] to the concessionaire, or to his partner or agent.

OF THE MANAGEMENT OF THE BATHS. The lessee of the baths or his partner shall, in accordance with the terms of his lease running to June 30 next, be required to heat the baths and keep them open for use entirely at his own expense every day from daybreak to the seventh hour for women, and from the eighth hour to the second hour in the evening for men, at the discretion of the procurator in charge of the mines. He shall be required to provide a proper supply of running water for the heated rooms, to the bath tub up to the highest level and to the basin, for women as well as for men. The lessee shall charge men one half *as* each and women one *as* each. Imperial freedmen or slaves in the service of the procurator or on his payroll are admitted free; likewise minors and soldiers. At the expiration of the lease the lessee, or his partner or agent, shall be required to return in good condition all the bath equipment consigned to him, excepting any rendered unusable through age. He shall be duly required to wash, dry, and coat with fresh grease every thirty days the bronze implements which he uses. If any needed repair prevents the proper operation of the baths, the lessee shall be entitled to prorate the rental for that period; beyond this, whatever else he may do for the purpose of operating the said baths, he shall be entitled to no reduction of rental. The lessee shall not be allowed to sell wood except for branch trimmings unsuited for fuel; [64] if he does anything in violation of this, he shall have to pay to the fisc 100 sesterces for each sale. If these baths are not properly kept open for use, then the procurator of the mines shall have the right to fine the lessee up to 200 sesterces every time they are not kept open properly. The lessee shall at all times have on hand a supply of wood sufficient for . . . days.

OF THE SHOEMAKING TRADE. Anyone who makes any of the shoes or thongs which shoemakers customarily handle, or who drives or sells

[64] Either because the bath fuel was supplied by the government or—more likely—to prevent the lessee of the baths from infringing the monopoly of the firewood concessionaire.

shoemaker's nails, or who is convicted of selling within the district anything else which shoemakers are entitled to sell, shall have to pay double to the concessionaire, or to his partner or agent. The concessionaire shall sell nails in accordance with the regulations of the iron mines. The concessionaire, or his partner or agent, shall have the right to obtain security. No one will be allowed to repair shoes, except to mend or repair his own or his master's[?]. The concessionaire shall be required to offer all types of shoes for sale; if he does not, everyone shall have a legal right to purchase wherever he wishes.

OF THE BARBERING TRADE. The concessionaire shall be entitled to operate with the assurance that no one else in the village of the Vipasca mines or within the district thereof shall practice barbering for profit. Anyone who so practices barbering shall have to pay the concessionaire, or his partner or agent . . . *denarii* for each use of the razors, and the said razors shall be forfeited to the concessionaire. Slaves attending to their masters or their fellow slaves are excepted. Itinerant barbers not sent by the concessionaire shall not have the right to practice barbering. The concessionaire, or his partner or agent, shall have the right of obtaining security; anyone who hinders his receiving security shall have to pay five *denarii* for each such act. The concessionaire shall engage one or more skilled workers in proportion [to the need].

OF THE FULLERS' SHOPS. No one to whom the concessionaire, or his partner or agent, has not leased or granted the right shall be allowed to do work on new or used clothing for pay. Anyone convicted of any violation of this shall have to pay the concessionaire, or his partner or agent, three *denarii* for each garment. The concessionaire, or his partner or agent, shall have the right to obtain security.

OF THE FEE FOR EXPLOITING SLAG DUMPS AND ROCK DEPOSITS. Anyone who wishes in the district of the Vipasca mines . . . to clean, crush, smelt, process, break up, sift, or wash silver or copper slag or slag dust scooped out by measure or weight, or who undertakes to execute work of any kind in the quarries, shall within the next three days declare what slaves and hired laborers he will send to do this, and shall pay the concessionaire . . . each month on or before the last day of the month; if he does not do so, he shall have to pay double. Anyone who brings into the mining district scoopings of copper or silver from ore dumps in other places shall have to pay one *denarius* per 100 pounds to the concessionaire, or to his partner or agent. If anything is owed the concessionaire, or his partner or agent, in accordance with this section of the regulations, and is not paid or secured on the day on which the obligation is incurred, he shall have to pay double. The concessionaire, or his partner or agent, shall have the right to obtain security, and any of the said slag that is cleaned, crushed, smelted, processed, broken up, sifted, or washed, and any stone slabs that are dressed in the quarries, shall be forfeited to the concessionaire, or his partner or agent, if whatever is owed him is not paid. Slaves and freedmen of silver or copper smelters working in the smelteries of their masters or patrons are excepted.

SCHOOLTEACHERS. It is decreed that schoolteachers are exempt from taxation at the hands of the procurator of the mines.[65]

CLAIMS TO DIGGINGS, OR PERMIT FEE[?]. Anyone who, in accordance with the regulations issued for the mines,[66] stakes a claim to or occupies a diggings or a diggings site within the district of the Vipasca mines with a view to maintaining a legal right shall within the next two days after such claim or occupancy declare to the farmer of this revenue, or his partner or agent. . . . [The rest is lost.]

A LABOR CONTRACT

The following contract, written on a waxed tablet found in the gold-mining district of Dacia, illustrates the use of free labor in mining operations.

CIL, Vol. III, p. 948, No. X (= FIRA, Vol. III, No. 150a); A.D. 164

In the consulship of Macrinus and Celsus, May 20. I, Flavius Secundinus,[67] at the request of Memmius son of Asclepius (because he declared that he was illiterate) [68] have here recorded the fact that he declared that he had let, and he did in fact let, his labor in the gold mine to Aurelius Adjutor from this day to November 13 next for seventy *denarii* and board. He shall be entitled to receive his wages in installments. He shall be required to render healthy and vigorous labor to the above-mentioned employer. If he wants to quit or stop working against the employer's wishes, he shall have to pay five sesterces for each day, deducted from his total wages. If a flood hinders operations, he shall be required to prorate accordingly.[69] If the employer delays payment of the wages when the time is up, he shall be subject to the same penalty after three days of grace.

[65] On the tax exemption of teachers in the Roman Empire, cf. § 74.
[66] The reference is presumably to the regulations preserved in part in the preceding inscription.
[67] Probably a clerk in the mine office.
[68] But he could sign his name, which is affixed at the end of the contract.
[69] This prorated reduction probably did not apply to board but only to wages.

Done at Immenosum Maius.

[Signed] Titus son of Beusans, also known as Bradua; Socratio son of Socratio; Memmius son of Asclepius.[70]

44. *Internal Trade*

The unity of the Empire during the Roman Peace, and its excellent harbor facilities and road system, produced an expansion of commercial activity unequaled until modern times. Internal trade, far more important than foreign commerce (see § 47), was predominantly in products of prime necessity—grain, and raw materials, especially for military purposes. In the first century, Italy was the great consuming center, and the capital city of Rome the principal market. Later, with the growing economic development of the provinces, Italy lost this dominant commercial position as an intense interprovincial and intraprovincial trade sprang up. Most of the traffic of the Roman Empire was water-borne, since overland transportation was cumbersome and costly. Shipping was in the hands mostly of the peoples of the Eastern Mediterranean, the most active of whom in this sphere were the Syrians. The common carrier was a ship (or river boat) owner who sailed his own vessel, carrying cargoes on his own account or on consignment for others. Shippers often joined in partnerships or associations (cf. § 46), and some of these established importing and distribution agencies, often with their own docks and warehouses, at Rome, the ports serving Rome, and in other important harbors of the Empire.

Pliny *Letters* Book x, No. 41

[Pliny to the Emperor Trajan]

. . . In the territory of the city of Nicomedia [71] there is a very extensive lake,[72] over which marbles, produce, firewood, and timber are transported by ship to the trunk road at modest cost and effort. Thence they are conveyed in wagons to the sea with great labor and greater expense. The Nicomedians therefore desire to connect the lake with the sea.[73] This project requires many hands; but these, on the other hand, are available, for the countryside, and particularly the city, is exceedingly populous. And one may definitely hope that everybody will very gladly engage in a project which will be profitable to all.

[70] Since the last signature is that of the laborer being hired in this contract, the first two signatories were presumably agents or partners acting for the employer rather than witnesses.

[71] The capital of the province of Bithynia, situated on the trunk road connecting the Danube provinces with the eastern frontier. The city carried on a large export trade with Rome.

[72] Modern Sabandja Göl.

[73] This sentence gives the sense of an obvious lacuna in the text.

It only remains for you to send, if you deem proper, a civil engineer or an architect to examine carefully whether the lake lies above sea level; the experts of this region maintain that it is about sixty feet higher. I find there is in the same vicinity a trench which was cut by one of the kings. But as it is unfinished, it is uncertain whether it was for the purpose of draining the adjacent lands or of connecting the lake with the river; [74] it is equally doubtful whether it is unfinished because of the intervening death of the king or abandonment of the hope of completing the project. But—you will forgive my being ambitious for your glory —I am urged on by this very fact and ardently desire that what kings merely began should be brought to completion by you.

Dittenberger, No. 1,229 (= *IGRR*, Vol. IV, No. 841)

[Hierapolis, Phrygia, second century?]

Flavius Zeuxis, merchant, who sailed seventy-two trips around Cape Malea [75] to Italy, built this tomb for himself and his children, Flavius Theodorus and Flavius Theudas, and for any to whom they grant permission.

A TYRIAN AGENCY AT PUTEOLI

The financial straits of this agency of Tyrian merchants at Puteoli, the chief port of Italy in republican times, reflects the sharp drop in business at this Campanian port not only because of the successful competition of the harbor at Ostia, nearer Rome, but because of the general decline of Italian commerce in the second century.

IG, Vol. XIV, No. 830, lines 1–19 (= *OGIS*, No. 595 = *IGRR*, Vol. I, No. 421);
A.D. 174

Letter written to the city of Tyre, the sacred, inviolable and autonomous metropolis of Phoenicia and of other cities, and mistress of a fleet. To the chief magistrates, council, and people of their sovereign native city, from the [Tyrians] resident in Puteoli, greeting.

By the grace of the gods and the good fortune of our lord the emperor [76] there is many a commercial agency in Puteoli, as most of you know, and ours excels the others both in adornment and in size. In the past this was cared for by the Tyrians resident in Puteoli, who were numerous and wealthy; but now this care has devolved on us, who are few in number, and since we pay the expenses for the sacrifices and services to our ancestral gods consecrated here in temples, we do not have the means to pay the agency's annual rent of 250 *denarii*, especially

[74] The ancient Sangarius [modern Sakriya], which flows into the Black Sea.
[75] See Note 86.   [76] Marcus Aurelius.

as the expenses of the Puteoli Ox-Sacrifice Games [77] have in addition been imposed on us. We therefore beg you to provide for the agency's continued existence. And it will continue if you make the 250 *denarii* paid annually for rent your concern; for the remaining expenses, including those incurred to refurbish the agency for the birthday festival of our lord the emperor, we set down to our own account, so as not to burden the city.[78] And we remind you that the agency here—unlike the one in the capital, Rome—derives no income either from shipowners or from merchants. We therefore appeal to you and beg you to make provision for this unfortunate circumstance.

Written in Puteoli, July 23, in the consulship of Gallus and Flaccus Cornelianus.

[The letter is followed by an extract from the minutes of the meeting of the council of Tyre held on December 8, A.D. 174, at which, after it was pointed out that the agency at Rome had always paid the Puteoli agency's rent from its receipts, the council voted that this practice be continued.]

AGENCIES AT OSTIA

The excavations at Ostia have uncovered a large piazza flanked on three sides by porticoes containing over sixty offices of shipping agencies and other organizations connected with the port's commerce. In front of each office was a mosaic pavement executed in a design appropriate to the business of the house. A number of mosaic floors contained also inscribed legends; those sufficiently well preserved are given here (the arabic numerals are editorial additions to indicate the position of each office in sequence around the piazza). Most of the mosaics date from the time of Commodus.

CIL, Vol. XIV, No. 4,549

1. Clodius Primigenius, Claudius Crescens, *quinquennales*. Caulkers, ropemakers.
2. Association of pelt-dealers of Ostia and Portus here.
3. Ships' carpenters association.
10. Shipowners of Misua [79] here.
12. Shipowners from Hippo Diarrhytus.
14. Agency of Sabrata.
15, 16. Shipowners and merchants, at their own expense.[80]

[77] Nothing further is known about these games.
[78] That is, Tyre.
[79] The towns named in Nos. 10–18, 23, and 34 were in North Africa; those in Nos. 19 and 21 in Sardinia; Narbo in No. 32 was the capital and commercial center of Southern Gaul (*Gallia Narbonensis*).
[80] Since the office space in the portico was provided by the imperial government, "at their own expense" here and below probably refers to the cost of laying the mosaic pavement.

17. Shipowners of Gummi, at their own expense.
18. Shipowners of Carthage, at their own expense.
19. Shipowners of Turris.
21. Shipowners and merchants of Carales.
23. Shipowners of Syllecthum.
32. Shipowners of Narbo.
34. Shipowners of Curubis, at their own expense. Agency of the grain merchants of the colony of Curubis.
43. Tiber boatmen, at their own expense.

SPEED OF TRAVEL

The speeds in the voyages mentioned here average better than one hundred miles a day, or five knots, slightly better than half the normal speed of tramp steamers used in the grain trade today. The average speed of Roman cargo vessels was about three knots with a favoring wind. Comparative figures for overland transport may be found in § 47, second selection, according to which an Arabian caravan averaged twenty-three Roman miles a day; and in Pliny's statement (*Natural History* VII. xx. 84) that the Emperor Tiberius "completed by carriage the longest twenty-four hours' journey on record when hastening to Germany to his brother Drusus, who was ill: this covered two hundred [Roman] miles."

Pliny *Natural History* XIX. i. 3-4

Two prefects of Egypt, Galerius and Balbillus, made the passage from the Straits of Sicily to Alexandria in under seven and six days, respectively. Fifteen years later Valerius Marianus, a senator of praetorian rank, made Alexandria from Puteoli in less than nine days, in summertime, on a very light breeze. To think that [commerce] brings Cádiz, by the Strait of Gibraltar, within seven days of Ostia, Hither Spain within four days, the province of Narbonese Gaul within three, and Africa, even on a very gentle breeze, within two (as happened to Gaius Flavius, legate of the proconsul Vibius Crispus)!

45. *How the Grain of Egypt Was Transported to Rome*

The two selections given here are our most detailed ancient descriptions of the size of the vessels of the Alexandrian grain fleet and of the routes by which they reached Italy. The usual route was to follow the prevailing winds north to Asia Minor, thence west via Crete to Malta, and thence north to Puteoli or Ostia, the ports of Rome. The burden of the ship described by Lucian has been variously estimated; the most recent study puts it at 1,200 to 1,300 tons. The average merchantman had a draught of fifty tons.

Lucian [81] *The Ship* i–ix (abridged)

Lycinus. Timolaus . . . [you're a] tireless sightseer.

Timolaus. Well, Lycinus, what do you expect of a person who has nothing to do and hears that such an unusually large ship has put into Piraeus,[82] one of the grain ships from Egypt to Italy? What is more, I believe that you and Samippus there came down from the city for no other reason but to see the ship.

Lycinus. So we did, and Adimantus . . . came along with us; only I don't know where he is—he got lost in the crowd of spectators. We came together to the ship and went on board. . . .

Timolaus. I remember now, Samippus, where it was we lost Adimantus. It was when we were standing all that time looking up at the mast, counting the layers of hides, and watching in amazement the sailor going up the reefs, then running up there on the yardarm, perfectly safe, supporting himself by the yardarm tackling. . . .

Samippus. Incidentally, what a big ship! About 180 feet long, a shipbuilder would say, and something over a quarter of that in beam; and the maximum depth from deck to keel, through the hold, about 44 feet. And then the height of the mast; what a huge yardarm it has; and what a forestay it requires to secure it! And how the stern rises with its gentle curve, with its gilded beak, balanced at the opposite end by the long rising extension of the prow, with [a figure of] the name-goddess of the ship, Isis, on either side! Now, as to the other ornamental details, the paintings and the fiery bright topsail, I was more astonished by the anchors, and the capstans and windlasses, and the stern cabins. The size of the crew could be compared to that of an army. And they were saying she carried enough grain to feed everybody in Attica for a year. . . .

Timolaus. They set sail with a moderate wind from the Pharus,[83] and sighted Acamas [84] on the seventh day. Then a west wind blew up, and they were carried off their course as far as Sidon. On their way thence they fell in with a heavy gale, and on the tenth day came through

[81] Lucian of Samosata on the Euphrates was born A.D. c.120 and died after 180. He was a traveling lecturer and wrote about eighty pieces in Greek, mostly satirical dialogues. *The Ship* was written c.165.

[82] The point is that vessels of the Alexandrian grain fleet were not often seen in Piraeus. This ship (the "Isis") had encountered foul winds on its course westward from Asia Minor, and the skipper decided to lay over in the harbor of Athens. When the "Isis" arrived there, the Athenians streamed down to the harbor to see the unusual sight.

[83] The lighthouse of Alexandria, Egypt.

[84] The northwestern promontory of Cyprus, modern Hagios Epiphanios.

the straits to the Chelidon Isles; [85] and there they all nearly went to the bottom . . . on a pitch dark night. However, the gods were responsive to their lamentation and showed them a fire from Lycia, which enabled them to identify that place, and a bright star—either Castor or Pollux—appeared at the masthead and guided the ship into the open sea on their left, just as she was making straight for the cliff. Thence, having once fallen off their proper course, they sailed through the Aegean beating up against adverse Etesian winds until they came to anchor in Piraeus yesterday, the seventieth day out from Egypt, so far off their course were they carried. Whereas if they had properly taken Crete on their right, they would have sailed beyond Malea [86] and been in Italy by this time.

SAINT PAUL'S VOYAGE TO ITALY

Acts of the Apostles 27. 1–28. 13 (abridged)
Adapted from The New Testament, An American Translation

When it was decided that we were to sail for Italy, Paul and some other prisoners were turned over to a centurion of the Augustan Cohort, named Julius.[87] We went on board an Adramyttian ship bound for the ports of Asia, and put to sea. We had a Macedonian from Thessalonica, named Aristarchus, with us. The next day we put in at Sidon, and Julius kindly entrusted Paul to his friends, to whom he went to be taken care of. Putting to sea from there, we sailed under the lee of Cyprus, as the wind was against us, and after traversing the Cilician and Pamphylian waters, we reached Myra in Lycia. There the centurion found an Alexandrian [grain] ship bound for Italy, and put us on board her. For a number of days we made slow progress and had some difficulty in arriving off Cnidus. Then, as the wind kept us from going on, we sailed under the lee of Crete, off Cape Salmone, and with difficulty coasted along it and reached a place called Fair Havens, near the town of Lasea.

As a great deal of time had now passed, and navigation had become dangerous,[88] for the Day of Atonement was already over, Paul began to warn them. . . . But the centurion was more influenced by the pilot and the shipowner than by what Paul had to say, and as the harbor was not fit to winter in, the majority favored putting to sea again, in the hope

[85] Off the southern coast of Asia Minor, between Cyprus and Rhodes.
[86] The southern promontory of the Peloponnese, famous for its treacherous weather and seas. To reach Italy from Piraeus the "Isis" would have to double Cape Malea, a danger to which ships keeping the usual course south of Crete were not exposed.
[87] The place is Caesarea in Judaea, the time A.D. 60.
[88] Shipment of grain from Egypt to Italy (cf. § 34) was suspended during the winter because of the danger.

of being able to reach and winter in Phoenix, a harbor in Crete facing west-south-west and west-north-west. When a moderate south wind sprang up, thinking their object was within reach, they weighed anchor and ran close along the coast of Crete. But soon a very violent wind—the Euroclydo [Northeaster], as it is called—rushed down upon it. The ship was caught by it and could not face the wind, so we gave way and let her run before it. As we passed under the lee of a small island called Cauda, we managed with great difficulty to secure the ship's boat. After hoisting it on board, they used ropes to brace the boat, and as they were afraid of being cast on the Syrtis banks,[89] they lowered the gear and let the ship drift. The next day, as the storm continued to be violent, they began to throw the cargo overboard, and on the next they threw the ship's tackle overboard with their own hands. For a number of days neither the sun nor the stars were visible, and the storm continued to rage, until at last we gave up all hope of being saved. . . .

It was the fourteenth night of the storm, and we were drifting through the Adriatic, when about midnight the sailors began to suspect that there was land ahead. On taking soundings they found a depth of twenty fathoms, and a little later, taking soundings again, they found a depth of fifteen. Then, as they were afraid we might go on the rocks, they dropped four anchors from the stern and waited anxiously for daylight. The sailors wanted to escape from the ship, and actually lowered the boat into the sea, pretending that they were going to run out anchors from the bow, but Paul said to the centurion and the soldiers, "You cannot be saved unless these men stay on board." Then the soldiers cut the ropes that held the boat and let it drift away. Until daybreak Paul kept urging them all to take something to eat. . . . We were about seventy-six souls on board.[90] When they had had enough to eat, they threw the wheat into the sea, in order to lighten the ship.

When daylight came they could not recognize the coast, but they saw a bay with a beach and determined to run the ship ashore there if possible. So they cast off the anchors and left them in the sea; at the same time they undid the lashings of the rudders, and hoisting the foresail to the wind they made for the beach. But they struck a shoal and ran the ship aground. The bow stuck and could not be moved, while the stern began to break up under the strain. The soldiers proposed to kill the prisoners, for fear some of them might swim ashore and escape, but the centurion wanted to save Paul, so he prevented them from doing this, and ordered all who could swim to jump overboard first and get to land,

[89] Of North Africa.
[90] A variant reading gives the number on board as 276. The lower figure is probably to be preferred.

and the rest to follow on planks or other pieces of the wreckage of the boat. So they all got safely to land.

After our escape we learned that the island was called Malta. The natives showed us remarkable kindness, for they made a fire and welcomed us all, because of the rain that had come on and the cold. . . . Three months later we sailed on an Alexandrian ship with Castor and Pollux as its figurehead which had wintered at the island. We put in at Syracuse and stayed there three days; then we weighed anchor and reached Regium. A day later a south wind sprang up, and the following day we arrived at Puteoli.[91]

46. Privileges for Shipowners

"Those are called *navicularii* (shipowners)," says a scholiast on Cicero's oration *In Favor of the Manilian Law,* "who transport grain to the city or wherever the emperor is." Because the imperial government relied on private shippers to transport supplies to Rome and the military forces, *collegia* of shipowners were the first trade associations to be granted official recognition and privileges, chiefly exemption from compulsory municipal services. These associations, with which it was more convenient for the government to contract than with individual shipowners, are first known in great numbers from about the time of Hadrian; they remained free agents until the third century, when, with increasing encroachment of the state in all areas, they were absorbed into the imperial service (see §§ 122, 135).

Gaius *Institutes* I. xxxiic

Likewise, by an edict of Claudius, Latins [92] acquire Roman citizenship if they build a seagoing vessel of a capacity of not less than 10,000 *modii* of grain, and if that ship, or another in its place, carries grain to Rome for six years.[93]

Justinian *Digest* L. vi. 6

Merchants who assist in provisioning the city with grain, and also shipowners who service the grain supply of the city, obtain exemption from compulsory public services as long as they are engaged in activity of this sort. For it has been properly decided that their risks should be compensated, or rather encouraged, by rewards, in order that those who perform services abroad that are both of a public nature and accom-

---

[91] For a description of the arrival of an Alexandrian grain fleet at Puteoli and the attendant bustle, see Seneca *Letters* LXXVII. 1–3.
[92] That is, Junian Latins (cf. § 12).
[93] For other privileges enacted by Claudius to encourage shipowners to enter the grain trade, see § 34, third selection.

panied by danger and effort may be free from annoyances and expenses at home. For it is not even too much to say that they are absent on public business while they serve the grain supply of the city.

A fixed pattern has been given to the exemption granted to shipowners—this exemption only they themselves possess; it does not extend either to their children or to their freedmen. This is set forth in imperial enactments. The deified Hadrian stated in a rescript that only shipowners of maritime vessels who serve the grain supply of the city possess exemption.

Although anyone may belong to the association of shipowners, nevertheless a person who does not own one or more ships and does not meet all the requirements provided by the imperial enactments cannot avail himself of the privileges granted to shipowners. And the deified brothers [94] stated the following in a rescript: "There are some persons who claim to be shipowners engaged in transporting grain and olive oil to the markets of the Roman people and therefore exempt, and who demand release from compulsory services, but who neither actually sail nor have the greater part of their property invested in shipowning and commercial activities. Such persons shall be deprived of exemption." . . .

The deified [Antoninus] Pius also stated in a rescript that whenever a question arose as to any shipowner, an investigation should be made as to whether he is assuming the role of a shipowner for the purpose of avoiding compulsory services.

47. *Foreign Trade*

In its trade with regions beyond its borders, especially the Far East, from which it imported large quantities of luxury goods, the Roman Empire showed an adverse trade balance which resulted in a sizable and steady drain of specie (cf. introduction to § 60). From the northern and eastern shores of the Black Sea came slaves, hides, salt fish, shipbuilding timber, linen, hemp, wax, and pitch. With the Baltic region there was a lively commerce in amber. The oriental trade brought aromatics from Arabia (which the inhabitants of the Roman Empire consumed in enormous quantities for ceremonial and personal use), spices, cotton, Chinese silk, and numerous other luxuries from India. Several important caravan routes led overland from Central Asia to the Syrian ports of the Mediterranean, but as these passed through the Parthian Empire and were subject to its tolls, the bulk of the Empire's Indian and Arabian wares was carried by water to the Red Sea ports of Egypt, and thence down the Nile to Alexandria, the central clearing house of this eastern trade. The fourth selection below is from a kind of "Trader's Guide to the

[94] The Emperors Marcus Aurelius and Lucius Verus.

Red Sea and Indian Ocean," written in the middle of the first century A.D. by a Greek merchant of Egypt actively engaged in the India trade. Striking recent discoveries are an ivory statuette of the Indian goddess Lakhshmi at Pompeii, and Italian pottery and other evidences of settlements of Roman merchants in Indian ports.

THE AMBER TRADE

Pliny *Natural History* xxxvii. xi

It is certain that amber is a product of the islands of the Northern Ocean, and that it is the substance called by the Germans *glaesum.* . . . Amber is imported by the Germans into Pannonia especially, and thence the Veneti . . . a people very close to Pannonia and dwelling on the shores of the Adriatic, first made it famous. . . .[95] At the present day the peasant women of the region beyond the Po wear necklaces of amber, primarily as ornaments but also for its medical value; for amber, indeed, is believed to be good for tonsils and throat ailments. . . .

From Carnuntum [96] in Pannonia to the coast of Germany from which the amber is imported is a distance of about 600 miles—a fact which has only recently been ascertained. And there is still alive a Roman *eques* who was sent there by Julianus, the manager of the gladiatorial exhibitions for the Emperor Nero, to procure this product. Journeying along the coasts and through markets there, he brought back such great quantities of amber that the nets which are used for holding back the wild beasts and for protecting the podium [97] were studded with amber. The arms, too, the litters,[98] and all the equipment of one particular day [of spectacles] were decorated with amber, to vary the display of each separate day. The largest piece of amber that this personage brought to Rome weighed thirteen pounds.

INCENSE FROM ARABIA

Pliny *Natural History* xii. xxxii. 63–65
From LCL

Frankincense after being collected is conveyed to Sabbatha [99] on camels, one of the gates of the city being opened for its admission; the kings have made it a capital offense to turn aside [camels so laden] from

[95] Archaeological discoveries have shown that amber had been transported along this route from the Baltic to the Mediterranean since very ancient, perhaps prehistoric times. During the Principate, Aquileia in Northern Italy was the principal manufacturing and distributing center for amber goods.
[96] A key Roman frontier fortress on the Danube, between Vienna and Bratislava.
[97] Where the emperor and nobles sat in the amphitheater.
[98] On which slain gladiators were removed.
[99] The capital of the kingdom of Saba—the Sheba of the Bible—in the southwestern part of the Arabian peninsula (Arabia Felix).

the high road. At Sabbatha a tithe estimated by measure and not by weight is taken by the priests for the god they call Sabis, and the incense is not allowed to be put on the market until this has been done; this tithe is drawn upon to defray what is a public expenditure, for actually on a fixed number of days the god graciously entertains guests at a banquet. It can only be exported through the country of the Gebbanites,[100] and accordingly a tax is paid on it to the king of that people as well. Their capital is Thomna, which is 1,487½ [Roman] miles distant from the town of Gaza in Judaea on the Mediterranean coast; the journey is divided into sixty-five stages with halts for camels. Fixed portions of the frankincense are given to the priests and the king's secretaries, but beside these the guards and their attendants and the gate keepers and servants also have their pickings. Indeed all along the route they keep on paying, at one place for water, at another for fodder, or the charges for lodging at the halts, and the various *octrois;* so that expenses mount up to 688 *denarii* per camel before the Mediterranean coast is reached; and then again payment is made to the tax farmers of our Empire.[101] Consequently the price of the best frankincense is six, of the second best five, and the third best three *denarii* a pound.

THE INDIA TRADE

Pliny *Natural History* VI. xxvi. 100–106
From LCL

Such was the route followed by the fleet of Alexander the Great; but subsequently it was thought that the safest line was to start from Syagrus,[102] a promontory of Arabia, with a west wind (the name for which in those parts is Hippalus [103]) and make for Patale,[104] the distance

[100] That is, by camel caravan. Much of the traffic also went by sea to Egypt, as Strabo (*Geography* XVI. iv. 24) tells: "Now the cargoes [of aromatics] are conveyed from Leuce Come to Petra, and thence to Rhinocolura, which is in Phoenicia near Egypt, and thence to the other peoples; but at the present time they are for the most part transported on the Nile to Alexandria; and they are brought from Arabia and India to Myus Hormus, and they are conveyed by camels over to Coptus in the Thebaid, which is situated on a canal of the Nile, and then to Alexandria."
[101] Cf. § 35.
[102] Ras Fartak, on the south coast of Arabia, at the entrance to the Gulf of Aden.
[103] The Indian Ocean monsoon, called Hippalus by the Greeks and Romans after the mariner who discovered that these seasonal winds could be used for direct passage between the mouth of the Red Sea and India. The date of Hippalus' discovery is generally placed c.100 B.C. or A.D. c.50. The earlier date, preferred by the most recent scholarship, would explain the great increase in Alexandrian shipping to India in the reign of Augustus, when, according to Strabo (*Geography* II. v. 12), "as many as 120 vessels were sailing from Myus Hormus [on the Red Sea] to India, whereas formerly, under the Ptolemies, only a very few ventured to undertake the voyage and to carry on traffic in Indian merchandise."
[104] The Indian ports and market towns mentioned in this and the following selection

being reckoned as 1,332 [Roman] miles. The following period considered it a shorter and safer route to start from the same cape and steer for the Indian harbor of Sigerus, and for a long time this was the course followed, until a merchant discovered a shorter route, and the desire for gain brought India nearer; indeed, the voyage is made every year, with companies of archers on board, because the seas used to be very greatly infested by pirates. And it will not be amiss to set forth the whole of the voyage from Egypt, now that reliable knowledge of it is for the first time accessible. It is an important subject, in view of the fact that in no year does India absorb less than 50,000,000 sesterces of our Empire's wealth, sending back merchandise to be sold with us at a hundred times its original cost.

Two miles from Alexandria is the town of Juliopolis. The voyage up the Nile from there to Coptus is 309 miles, and takes twelve days when the midsummer trade winds are blowing. From Coptus the journey is made with camels, stations being placed at intervals for the purpose of watering; the first, a stage of 22 miles, is called Hydreuma; [105] the second is in the mountains, a day's journey on; the third at a second place named Hydreuma, 85 miles from Coptus; the next is in the mountains; next we come to Apollo's Hydreuma, 184 miles from Coptus; again a station in the mountains; then we get to New Hydreuma, 230 miles from Coptus. There is also an Old Hydreuma, known by the name of Trogodyticum, where a garrison is stationed on outpost duty [106] at a caravanserai accommodating two thousand travelers; it is 7 miles from New Hydreuma. Then comes the town of Berenice, where there is a harbor on the Red Sea, 257 miles from Coptus. [107] But as the greater part of the journey is done by night because of the heat, and the days are spent at the stations, the whole journey from Coptus to Berenice takes twelve days.

Traveling by sea begins at midsummer before the Dog Star rises or immediately after its rising, [108] and it takes about thirty days to reach Ocelis in Arabia or Cane in the frankincense-producing district; there is also a third port named Muza, which is not called at on the voyage to India, and is used only by merchants trading in frankincense and Arabian perfumes. [109] . . . The most advantageous way of sailing to India is to

---

were located along the west coast of the Indian subcontinent.
[105] That is, "Watering Place."
[106] For such a garrison, see § 149, second selection.
[107] Still another road led from Coptus to the Red Sea port of Myus Hormus. Later, a third led to Berenice from Antinoöpolis on the Nile (see § 39). For the toll fees charged for the use of these roads, see § 35.
[108] That is, in July.
[109] Of the three Arabian ports mentioned in this sentence, Muza corresponds

set out from Ocelis; from that port it is forty days' voyage, if the Hippalus is blowing, to the first trading station in India, Muziris—not a desirable port of call, on account of the neighboring pirates, who occupy a place called Nitriae, nor is it specially rich in articles of merchandise; and furthermore the roadstead for shipping is a long way from the land, and cargoes have to be brought in and carried out in boats. . . . There is another more serviceable port, belonging to the Nelcyndian tribe, called Becare. . . .

Travelers set sail from India on the return voyage at the beginning of the Egyptian month of Tybi, which is our December, or at all events before the sixth day of the Egyptian Mechir, which equals January 13 in our calendar—so making it possible to return home within a year. They set sail from India with a southeast wind [110] and after entering the Red Sea continue the voyage with a southwest or south wind.

Anonymous *Navigation of the Erythraean Sea* xlix, lvi

Adapted from W. H. Schoff, The Periplus of the Erythraean Sea

Into this market town [of Barygaza] are imported wine, Italian preferred, also Laodicean and Arabian; copper, tin, and lead; coral and topaz; thin clothing and imitations of all kinds; bright-colored girdles a cubit wide; storax, sweet clover, crude glass, realgar, antimony; gold and silver coin, on which there is a profit when exchanged for the money of the country; and ointment, but not very costly and not much. And for the king there are brought into those places very costly vessels of silver, singing boys, beautiful maidens for the harem, fine wines, thin clothing of the finest weaves, and the choicest ointments. There are exported from these places spikenard, costus, bdellium-myrrh, ivory, agate and carnelian, buckthorn, cotton cloth of all kinds, silk cloth, mallow-colored cloth, yarn, long pepper, and such other things as are transported here from the market towns [of the interior]. . . .

To these market towns [Becare and Nelcynda] they send large ships on account of the great quantity and bulk of pepper and *malabathrum*.[111] There are imported here principally a great quantity of coin; topaz; thin clothing (not much); figured linens; antimony, coral, crude glass, copper, tin, lead; wine (not much, but as much as at Barygaza); realgar and orpiment; and wheat enough for the sailors, for this is not

---

to modern Mocha, on the Red Sea coast; Ocelis was located c.50 miles to the south, near Pirim Island; and Cane was on the south coast, c.200 miles east of Aden.
[110] In reality, the northeast monsoon.
[111] A famous cinnamon aromatic of antiquity (Indian *tamala patram*).

dealt in by the merchants there. There is exported pepper, which is produced in quantity in only one region near these markets. . . . Besides this there are exported great quantities of fine pearls, ivory, silk cloth, spikenard from the Ganges, *malabathrum* from the places in the interior, transparent stones of all kinds, diamonds and sapphires, and tortoise shell.

ALEXANDRIA, THE CROSSROADS OF THE WORLD

Dio Chrysostom *Discourses* xxxii. 36, 40
From LCL

Your city is vastly superior in point of size and situation, and it is admittedly ranked second among all cities beneath the sun. For not only does the mighty land of Egypt constitute the framework of your city— or, more accurately, its appanage—but the peculiar nature of the river [Nile], when compared with all others, defies description with regard to both its marvelous habits and its usefulness; [112] and furthermore, not only have you a monopoly of the shipping of the entire Mediterranean by reason of the beauty of your harbors, the magnitude of your fleet, and the abundance and the marketing of the products of every land, but also the outer waters that lie beyond are in your grasp, both the Red Sea and the Indian Ocean, whose name was rarely heard in former days. The result is that the trade, not merely of islands, ports, a few straits and isthmuses, but of practically the whole world is yours. For Alexandria is situated, as it were, at the crossroads of the whole world, of even the most remote nations thereof, as if it were a market serving a single city, a market which brings together into one place all manner of men, displaying them to one another and, as far as possible, making them a kindred people. . . . For I behold among you, not merely Greeks and Italians and people from neighboring Syria, Libya, Cilicia, not merely Ethiopians and Arabs from more distant regions, but even Bactrians and Scythians and Persians and a few Indians.

48. *Rome the Emporium of the World*

Aelius Aristides [113] *To Rome* xi–xiii

Around [the Mediterranean] lie the continents far and wide, pouring an endless flow of goods to you. There is brought from every land

[112] Cf. § 100.   [113] See Chapter II, Note 53.

and sea whatever is brought forth by the seasons and is produced by all countries, rivers, lakes, and the skills of Greeks and foreigners. So that anyone who wants to behold all these products must either journey through the whole world to see them or else come to this city. For whatever is raised or manufactured by each people is assuredly always here to overflowing. So many merchantmen arrive here with cargoes from all over, at every season, and with each return of the harvest, that the city seems like a common warehouse of the world. One can see so many cargoes from India, or, if you wish, from Arabia Felix, that one may surmise that the trees there have been left permanently bare, and that those people must come here to beg for their own goods whenever they need anything. Clothing from Babylonia and the luxuries from the barbarian lands beyond arrive in much greater volume and more easily than if one had to sail from Naxos or Cythnos to Athens, transporting any of their products. Egypt, Sicily, and the civilized part of Africa are your farms. The arrival and departure of ships never ceases, so that it is astounding that the sea—not to mention the harbor—suffices for the merchantmen. . . . And all things converge here, trade, seafaring, agriculture, metallurgy, all the skills which exist and have existed, anything that is begotten and grows. Whatever cannot be seen here belongs completely to the category of nonexistent things.

49. *The Financial Panic of A.D. 33*

Julius Caesar, when dictator, in order to check the hoarding of currency and the decline in real estate values caused by the unsettled conditions of the Civil War, had passed a law which apparently required owners of capital to invest a certain portion or amount in the purchase of Italian land. Thereafter the law fell into desuetude until the Emperor Tiberius revived it in A.D. 33, with the apparent double purpose of supporting sagging real estate prices and of reducing luxury spending (cf. § 60). This sudden enforcement of the law caused a wholesale calling in of loans, and the immediate result was a wave of forced sales, a precipitous collapse of property values, and widespread financial ruin. Land could be picked up cheaply by those with ready cash, and this undoubtedly contributed further to the growth of latifundia in Italy (§ 41). To restore credit and enable debtors to discharge their debts without losing their land, Tiberius then created a temporary "land bank" authorized to make interest-free loans in amounts up to one half the value of the land offered as security. Tacitus' account of the episode, given below, is characteristically dramatic and moralizing. It is interesting to note that succeeding emperors, or at least some of them, continued the general policy of protecting the value of Italian land: Trajan, for example, decreed that candidates for office must have one third of their capital invested in such land.

Tacitus Annals VI. xvi–xvii

Informers in great numbers pounced upon those who kept increasing their liquid assets through loans at interest in violation of the law of the dictator Caesar which sets up regulations for moneylending and landholding within Italy—a law which had long since become a dead letter because the public welfare is subordinated to private profit. The curse of moneylending has, to be sure, been an inveterate one in the city, and a very frequent cause of civil discord and dissension. . . . On this occasion Gracchus, the praetor to whom the investigation of this matter had fallen, was impelled by the great number of persons endangered to lay the matter before the senate. The senators, in alarm (for no one was free from guilt in the matter), begged the emperor for indulgence; and with his consent everyone was allowed the next year and six months in which to arrange his finances in accordance with the requirements of the law.

The result was a scarcity of money, since all debts were called in at the same time and because, with so many persons condemned and their property sold off, specie was accumulating in the fisc or the state treasury.[114] To obviate this the senate had directed everyone to invest two thirds of his loan principal in lands anywhere in Italy.[115] But creditors were calling for payment in full, and it did not suit those called upon to impair their credit [by defaulting]. So at first there was a mad scramble and pleading [for loans], then the praetor's tribunal was in an uproar. The buying and selling that had been devised as a remedy had the contrary effect, for the moneylenders had stored up all the money needed for the purchase of land. The abundance of land offered for sale caused a drop in prices; the more heavily burdened with debt a man was, the harder he found it to sell off, and many a fortune toppled; financial ruin dashed rank and reputation headlong. At length the emperor came to the rescue by distributing 100,000,000 sesterces among the banks and affording an opportunity of borrowing for three years without interest if the debtor offered the state twice the amount in land as security. Thus credit was restored, and little by little private lenders too reappeared on the scene.

---

[114] Tacitus cannot resist adding this second causal clause, one of his favorite themes (cf. § 23), even though it is alien to the immediate subject.

[115] According to Suetonius (<i>Life of Tiberius</i> xlviii. 1) the senate had also provided that debtors need pay only two thirds of their debts when due.

50. *Real Estate Transactions*

RESTRICTIONS ON SPECULATION

This bronze tablet from Herculaneum records two decrees of the Roman senate from the reigns of Claudius and Nero, respectively. The first forbids the deliberate, profit-motivated destruction of buildings in Rome and Italy. (Similar provisions were applied in provincial municipalities: cf. Vol. I, pp. 416, 423, Vol. II, § 83, second selection.) Strabo, writing a few decades earlier, describes the prevalence of such activity (*Geography* v. iii. 7): "They build incessantly because of the collapses and fires and repeated sales, which go on incessantly, too. Indeed, the repeated sales are intentional collapses, so to speak, since they tear down some and build others in their place to their heart's desire." The second decree of the senate, ruling that the first does not apply in a given case, specifically reaffirms the first, so as to leave no possibility of interpreting this *ad hoc* ruling as a precedent opening the door to exceptions from the general prohibition.

CIL, Vol. X, No. 1,401 (= Dessau, No. 6,043 = FIRA, Vol. I, No. 45); A.D. 45/6 and 56

i

In the consulship of Gnaeus Hosidius Geta and Lucius Vagellius, September 22. Decree of the senate.

Since the foresight of our excellent emperor has made provision also for the permanence of the buildings of our city and of all Italy, which he has himself benefited not only by his most august precept but also by his own example, and since protection to public and private structures alike is fitting and appropriate to the happiness of the approaching age,[116] and since all ought to refrain from a most vicious kind of speculation and not bring about an appearance most incompatible with peace by the demolition of homes and villas; the senate decrees that if anyone purchases any building as a speculation, in order by tearing it down to obtain more than the price at which he purchased it, then he shall pay to the state treasury double the sum at which he bought the said property and the matter shall nonetheless be laid before the senate. And since a sale involving such evil precedent is no more admissible than such purchase, in order that sellers who knowingly and with malice aforethought sell contrary to this expressed will of the senate may also be restrained, the

[116] This refers to the imminent celebration by Claudius of the Secular Games, signalizing the advent of a new era (cf. § 167, last selection).

senate decrees that such sales shall be invalid. The senate affirms, however, that [this decree] shall in no wise affect owners who with the intention of remaining in possession of their properties transfer parts from
one to another of the said properties, provided this is not done for the
purpose of speculation.

Adopted. Present in the senate: 383.[117]

ii

In the consulship of Quintus Volusius and Publius Cornelius,
March 2. Decree of the senate.

Whereas Quintus Volusius and Publius Cornelius spoke on the appeal of Alliatoria Celsilla and asked the senate what it was pleased to see
done in this matter, concerning this matter the senate decreed as follows:

Since the decree of the senate which was passed on motion of the
deified Claudius on September 22 in the consulship of Hosidius Geta
and Lucius Vagellius, *clarissimi viri*, provided that no one should tear
down a home or villa in order to make himself a profit and no one purchase or sell any such property for purposes of speculation; established a
penalty for the purchaser who acted contrary to that decree of the
senate, whereby anyone who purchased any such property would be
compelled to pay to the state treasury double the price at which he
purchased it, and the sale of the one who sold it would be invalid; but
made no change in the case of those who with the intention of remaining
in possession of their properties transferred parts from one to another
of the said properties, provided they did not make the changes for purposes of speculation;

And since the relatives of Alliatoria Celsilla, the wife of Atilius
Lupercus, *vir ornatissimus*, set forth to this body that her father, Allia-
torius Celsus, had purchased in the region of Mutina landed property,
including buildings, known as Macer's Fields, in which place a market
used to be operated in former times but had now for some years ceased
to be held, and the said buildings were becoming dilapidated through
age and were not going to be repaired for use because no one lived in
them and no one wanted to move into deserted ruins;

Celsilla should suffer no damage, fine, or penalty if the said buildings discussed in this body were either demolished or sold, either by
themselves or together with the land, on terms allowing the purchaser to
pull down or remove them with impunity to himself. Others, however,
were to be warned to refrain from such a shameful kind of speculation
in the future, especially in this age, in which it would be more appropriate for new buildings to be raised and for all to be adorned, as a shining

[117] The total membership of the senate at this time was about 600; cf. § 4.

reflection of the happiness of the world, rather than for any part of Italy to be disfigured by the ruins of buildings and for the indifference[?] of former times to continue to the present . . . so that it might be said that the Roman state was already exhausted with old age.[118]

Adopted. Present in the senate: . . . .

RENTAL ADVERTISEMENTS

These are among the numerous notices found painted on house walls at Pompeii; other texts from Pompeii's walls will be found in Vol. I, p. 430, Vol. II, §§ 84, 93.

CIL, Vol. IV, Nos. 138 and 1,136 (= Dessau, Nos. 6,035, 5,723 =
FIRA, Vol. III, No. 143) [119]

i

In the Arrius Pollio block owned by Gnaeus Alleius Nigidius Maius, to let from the fifteenth of next July, shops with their stalls, high-class second-story apartments, and a house. Prospective lessees may apply to Primus, slave of Gnaeus Alleius Nigidius Maius.

ii

On the property owned by Julia Felix, daughter of Spurius, to let from the thirteenth of next August to the thirteenth of the sixth August hence, or five consecutive years, the élite Venus Baths, shops, stalls, and second-story apartments. Interested parties may apply to the lessor in the matter.[120]

CIL, Vol. VI, No. 33,860 (= Dessau, No. 5,913 = *FIRA*, Vol. III, No. 145*b*)

This inscription, found at Rome and dating from the second century, must have been affixed to the wall of a warehouse.

In this private warehouse [121] of Quintus Tineius Sacerdos Clemens [122] . . . for rent from this day or from July 1 [123] storerooms,

[118] The inscription is broken near the end, and about half of this last clause is lost. Our translation gives the sense, which seems fairly clear.
[119] These inscriptions date, at the latest, from A.D. 79, the year in which Pompeii was buried in the famous eruption of Vesuvius.
[120] The last sentence is conjectural. In familiar or formulaic expressions like this the Romans commonly abbreviated by writing only the initial letter of each word. While the meaning of many such abbreviations is known with certainty, many others still remain riddles for which scholars have proposed various solutions.
[121] There were also in Rome imperial granaries and warehouses in which storage space could be rented by private individuals.
[122] Perhaps the consul of A.D. 158.
[123] Annual leases in Rome commonly ran from July 1 to June 30.

magazines, passageways, chests, floor sections, and storage space for chests.

SALE OF PART OF A HOUSE

Michigan Papyrus No. 257; A.D. 30

I, Didyme daughter of Petesuchus son of Chambuchis, with my husband Harpuonsis son of Orseus as guardian, acknowledge that I have sold to Marres son of Dionysius son of Cambuchis the one-third share that I own in one fourth of a three-story house and courtyard and all their appurtenances,[124] common and undivided, in Talei.[125] The boundaries of the entire house and courtyard are: on the south of the house, the house of Petermuthis son of Orseus, the smith; on the south of the court-yard, the courtyard of Zeno son of Ptolemaeus; on the north, the house of Anubio and his brother, the fuller; on the west, the courtyard of Zeno son of Ptolemaeus; on the east, the royal road. And I have received from Marres the entire agreed-upon contract price of the sold share in full, by hand, out of the house,[126] and I will guarantee the sale as aforesaid with every guarantee against all public and private encumbrances and every kind of tax. Herodes son of Herodes wrote for them because they are illiterate.

[Signature] Marres son of Dionysius son of Cambuthis [sic]. The sale has been made to me as aforesaid. Diodorus son of Ptolemaeus wrote for him because he is illiterate.

LOAN ON MORTGAGE

Oxyrhynchus Papyrus No. 2,134, lines 8–35; A.D. 170
Adapted from the translation of A. S. Hunt (London, 1927)

Helene, minor, daughter of Psosnaus and Eudaemonis, with her son Diodorus, also known as Longinus son of Amois son of Diodorus, inhabitant of Chusis, as her guardian [127] and surety for the payment of all that is secured under this mortgage, to Spartas son of Pausanias (son of Sarapio) and Didyme, inhabitant of the city of Oxyrhynchus, greeting. I acknowledge that I have received from you the sum of 1,800 silver drachmas of the imperial coinage, to which nothing has been added, with

---

[124] That is, the right of ingress and egress, and possibly other privileges as well.
[125] A village in the Arsinoite nome of (Lower) Egypt.
[126] The phrase, "out of the house," does not refer to the object of the sale; it is part of the Graeco-Egyptian formula for immediate cash payment.
[127] Here is an extreme example of the kind of situation which could arise from the early marriage of Egyptian girls: Helene, though still a minor (that is, under twenty-five) has a son old enough to serve as her legal representative and sign on her behalf.

interest at the rate of 3 obols per mina per month [128] from the present
month of Mecheir to the month of . . . in the coming twelfth year,
or 189 drachmas altogether, making a total of principal and interest of
1,989 silver drachmas, on the security of four arouras in full, of rectangular shape, of catoecic [129] grain-bearing, arable land out of the five
arouras . . . belonging to me near the said Chusis in the Hermopolite
nome and forming part of a total of twenty arouras, joint and undivided, held with Chesphibis son of Petosiris and others. [The description
of the boundaries is here omitted.] And I will repay the total sum of
1,989 silver drachmas to you or your agents with no delay on Phaophi
30 in the coming twelfth year of the lord [MARCUS AURELIUS] Antoninus Caesar Armeniacus Medicus Parthicus Maximus, and if I do not
repay as stated, you shall in place thereof have the ownership of the
aforesaid arouras, and it shall be lawful for you to make use of and dispose of them in whatever way you choose, and I will perforce guarantee
them completely against all claims with every guarantee, free from
liability to cultivate royal or domain land and every other obligation
henceforth, and whenever you please it is lawful for you to make your
claim to the mortgage and to the said arouras through the property
record office of the Hermopolite nome without requiring my presence or
concurrence. If I violate any of these provisions, it shall be invalid, and
I will furthermore forfeit in respect of any kind of violation the damage
and, in addition thereto, a penalty of six hundred silver drachmas
and an equal sum to the public treasury, with no disturbance to their
validity, and the mortgage, which is done in duplicate in identical terms
without erasure or insertion by the hand of me, Diodorus also known
as Longinus, shall nonetheless remain valid. Year 10 of the Emperor
Caesar MARCUS AURELIUS Antoninus Augustus Armeniacus Medicus
Parthicus Maximus, Mecheir 24.

[Signatures] I, Helene, minor, have received from you, Spartas, the
1,800 drachmas with interest at the rate of 3 obols amounting to 189
drachmas on the security of the four arouras, and I will repay the principal with the total interest on Phaophi 30 in the coming year or else you
shall have the ownership of the said arouras, and I will guarantee them
as aforesaid. I, Diodorus, also known as Longinus son of Amois, have
been appointed my mother's guardian, and wrote for her because she is
illiterate, and I am surety for the payment of what is secured under the
mortgage, the same date.

[128] This comes to 0.5 percent per month, or 6 percent per annum; cf. introduction
to § 51.
[129] Land originally granted by the Ptolemies to Greek and Macedonian military
settlers (catoeci). See also Chapter V, Note 167.

FORECLOSURE OF A MORTGAGE

Oxyrhynchus Papyrus No. 485, lines 8–35 (= Mitteis, No. 246); A.D. 178

To Antoninus also known as Pudens, priest, chief justice, and officer in charge of the circuit and other courts, from Serenus, freedman of Apollonianus son of Sarapio, inhabitant of Oxyrhynchus. On Augustus [130] 11 in the eighteenth year just past I loaned, in accordance with a public contract drawn in the record office of the said Oxyrhynchus, to Sarapias daughter of Podo son of Horus, her mother being Thaësis, inhabitant of Psobthis, the metropolis of the Little Oasis, the sum of 900 silver drachmas at interest of 1 drachma per mina per month,[131] the principal [to be repaid] on Caesaraeus [132] 30 in the said eighteenth year just past, with the proviso that if she did not repay on the due date there would remain with me and my heirs and assigns, in place of the principal and any interest she did not repay, the possession and ownership of the slave Sarapias belonging to her and then about twenty-five years old, on the various terms included in the loan and in the provisions written into it for my protection concerning flight or death of the slave.[133] Now since the due date has passed and repayment has not been made to me, I request that you instruct [your clerk] to write to the *strategus* of the Oxyrhynchite nome to transmit a copy of this to Sarapias if she is alive, and if not to her heirs of age or, if they are minors, to their legal guardians, whose names will be ascertained on the spot, so that they may be informed and make repayment to me or know that I shall have recourse to the appropriate legal proceedings for assuming possession, as is fitting. Year 19 of the lords [MARCUS] AURELIUS Antoninus and Aurelius COMMODUS Augusti, Phaophi. . . .

51. *Loans*

Credit operations, large and small, formed an important part of the private and business life of the Roman world. Numerous extant documents, especially among the papyri, illustrate the different types of contracts in use—loans in money or in kind, secured or unsecured, running for a fixed term or payable on demand. The standard interest rate on money loans was 1 percent

[130] See Note 50.
[131] This equals 12 percent per annum; cf. introduction to § 51.
[132] The Egyptian month Mesore (July 25–August 23), so renamed in honor of one of the emperors, probably Augustus; cf. Chapter II, Note 20.
[133] While mortgages were usually taken on real estate, other forms of property could serve, as this text shows.

per month (but often half that rate for real-estate mortgages); that on loans in kind, which were usually repayable after the next harvest, was (in Egypt, at least) 50 percent. For mortgage loans, see the two selections immediately preceding.

A LOAN COMPANY

The following text, inscribed on waxed tablets found in the Dacian gold-mining district,[134] records the formation of a lending partnership. One of the partners appears as an individual lender in the text following this.

CIL, Vol. III, pp. 950, 2,215, No. XIII (= *FIRA*, Vol. III, No. 157); A.D. 167

Between Cassius Frontinus and Julius Alexander a moneylending partnership from last December 23 in the consulship of Pudens and Pollio to April 12 next coming was agreed to on the following terms, namely, that they would be obligated to assume in equal shares whatever accrued from the capital in this partnership, whether profit or loss occurred.

To this partnership Julius Alexander contributed 500 *denarii* in cash and on loan, and Secundus, slave and agent of Cassius Palumbus, contributed 267 *denarii* for Frontinus. . . .

In this partnership, if either one is found to have perpetrated a fraud with malice aforethought, he shall have to pay the other 1 *denarius* for each *as* . . . and 20 *denarii* for each *denarius*. . . . And when the contract period is completed, they shall each recover the aforesaid sums less loans outstanding, and shall divide any surplus. Cassius Frontinus demanded the formal acknowledgment that this would be given, done, and warranted, and Julius Alexander formally promised.[135]

Of this agreement two sets of tablets have been signed and sealed.[136] Likewise, 50 *denarii* are due to Cossa, which he shall be entitled to receive from the above-named partners.[137]

Done at Deusara on March 28 in the consulship of Verus (for the third time) and Quadratus. [Signatures illegible.]

[134] These documents were normally written on a triptych, or unit of three tablets, in duplicate "inner" and "outer" texts separated by the signatures.
[135] This was the Roman formula of oral contractual agreement known as *stipulatio*. In the presence of witnesses one contracting party (the lender, lessor, buyer, etc., as the case might be) *stipulated*, and the other party gave his *promise* or *assent* thereto. Cf. the similar language in the three texts following this.
[136] That is, two copies, one to be retained by each party.
[137] There is no indication of the nature of this obligation.

A DEMAND LOAN

CIL, Vol. III, p. 934, No. V (= *FIRA*, Vol. III, No. 122); A.D. 162

Julius Alexander demanded the formal acknowledgment that 60 *denarii* of good coin [138] would be duly paid on any day he demanded it, and Alexander son of Cariccus formally promised that it would be paid. And he declared that he had received the aforementioned 60 *denarii* in cash as a loan, and that he owed this sum. And Julius Alexander demanded the formal acknowledgment that the interest thereon at the rate of 1 percent per thirty days from this day would be paid to Julius Alexander, or to whomever the right thereto might in the future belong, and Alexander son of Cariccus formally promised that it would be paid. Titius Primitius stood surety for the due and proper payment of the aforementioned principal together with the interest.[139]

Done at Alburnus Major on October 20 in the consulship of Rusticus (for the second time) and Aquilinus.

[Signatures] of Lucius Vasidius Victor. . . ; Bato son of. . . ; Titius Primitius; Alexander son of Cariccus, the debtor himself.

52. *Slave Sales*

The prices of ordinary slaves attested in the first and second centuries range roughly from 200 to 1,000 *denarii*. Talented or specially desirable slaves of course fetched much higher prices. The first contract below is, like those in § 51, a waxed triptych from the Dacian goldmining district; the second is a papyrus found in the Arsinoite nome of Egypt but executed in Syria.

CIL, Vol. III, pp. 940, 2,215, No. VII (= *FIRA*, Vol. III, No. 88); A.D. 142

Dasius, a Breucian,[140] purchased and received by legal transfer for 600 *denarii* from Bellicus son of Alexander, with Marcus Vibius Longus acting as surety, the boy Apalaustus, or whatever other name he may have, of Greek origin. . . .

It is warranted that this boy has been handed over in good health, that he is guiltless of theft or other delict, and that he is not a vagrant, a runaway, or an epileptic.[141] And if anyone evicts from his possession the

---

[138] Or perhaps, as below, "properly" is meant—that is, "be properly and duly paid."
[139] See Note 120.
[140] The Breucians were an Illyrian people settled by the Save river in Lower Pannonia.
[141] Such warranties are provided for in the edict of the curule aediles of Rome, which reads: "Any persons who sell slaves shall inform the purchasers of what

said boy in question or any part [142] of him, thereby preventing the afore-mentioned purchaser or anyone to whom the said property may in the future belong from duly using, enjoying, having, and possessing it, Dasius the Breucian demanded the formal acknowledgment that in that case he would be duly paid in good coin [143] double any amount thus evicted from his possession, and Bellicus son of Alexander formally promised that it would be paid, and Vibius Longus likewise stood surety for the same. [144]

And Bellicus son of Alexander declared that he had received and had from Dasius the Breucian 600 *denarii* as the price for the said afore-mentioned boy.

Done in the camp town of Legion XIII Gemina on May 16 in the consulship of Rufinus and Quadratus.

[Signatures] of Appius Proclus, veteran of Legion XIII Gemina; Antonius Celer; Julius Viator; Ulpius Severinus; Lucius Firmius Primitivus; Marcus Vibius Longus, surety; Bellicus son of Alexander, seller.

Archaeologia, LIV (1895), 433-38 (= *FIRA*, Vol. III, No. 132); A.D. 166

Gaius Fabullius Macer, subaltern of the trireme "Tigris" of the praetorian fleet of Misenum, purchased from Quintus Julius Priscus, soldier of the same trireme in the same fleet, a boy of trans-Euphrates origin named Abbas, also known as Eutyches or by whatever other name he is called, about seven years old, at a price of 200 *denarii* and the customs duty per head. [145] Fabullius Macer demanded the formal acknowledgment in accordance with the edict that the boy was in good health, and that if anyone evicted from his possession the said boy or any part of him the whole sum would be duly repaid without the formality of notification, and Quintus Julius Priscus formally promised. Gaius Julius Antiochus, private of the trireme "Virtue," stood surety and warranty for the same.

And the seller, Quintus Julius Priscus, stated that he had received and had from Gaius Fabullius Macer, the purchaser, the said aforemen-

---

disease or fault each has, who is a runaway or a vagrant, or is under indictment for a delict; and all this they shall openly and duly declare when they sell such slaves. . . . Likewise, if any slave has committed a capital offense, or has made any attempt to commit suicide, or has been sent into the arena to fight with wild animals, they shall openly declare all this at the sale; for we will grant a trial for such causes. Furthermore, if anyone is said to have sold contrary to these provisions knowingly and with malice aforethought, we will grant a trial" (Justinian *Digest* XXI. i. 1. 1).

[142] Cf. § 67, last selection.   [143] Cf. Note 138.

[144] On this formulaic procedure, cf. Note 135.

[145] See § 35. The boy Abbas was obviously taken captive in Mesopotamia in the period of the Roman operations against Parthia under Lucius Verus, brought back by his captors to Greek-speaking Roman Syria, and given a Greek name, Eutyches ("Good Luck").

tioned 200 *denarii* in good coin duly paid in cash, and that he had transferred to him the aforementioned slave Eutyches on satisfactory terms.

Done at Seleucia Pieria in the winter camp of the detachment of the praetorian fleet of Misenum on May 24 in the consulship of Quintus Servilius Pudens and Aulus Fufidius Pollio.

[Signatures and a docket follow.]

53. *Apprenticeship Contracts*

Oxyrhynchus Papyrus No. 275; A.D. 66

Trypho son of Dionysius son of Trypho, his mother being Thamunis daughter of Onnophris, and Ptolemaeus son of Pausirio son of Ptolemaeus, weaver, his mother being Ophelous daughter of Theo, both parties being inhabitants of Oxyrhynchus, mutually agree that Trypho has apprenticed to Ptolemaeus his son Thoönis, whose mother is Saraëus daughter of Apio and who is not yet of age, for a period of one year from this day to serve him and perform all the duties given him by Ptolemaeus in connection with the weaving trade in all its branches as he himself knows it. The boy is to be fed and clothed during the whole period by his father Trypho, who is also to be responsible for all the taxes upon the boy, on condition that Ptolemaeus shall pay him 5 drachmas per month on account of victuals and 12 drachmas on account of clothing at the termination of the whole period.[146] Trypho shall not have the right to withdraw the boy from Ptolemaeus until the completion of the period, and if there are any days during it on which he fails to fulfill his obligation he shall produce him for an equal number of days after the period or shall pay a penalty of 1 silver drachma for each day; the penalty for withdrawing him within the period shall be 100 drachmas, and an equal sum to the public treasury. If Ptolemaeus on his part fails to instruct the boy thoroughly he shall be liable to the same penalties. This

---

[146] These specific arrangements varied, of course, from contract to contract. In Oxyrhynchus Papyrus No. 725 (A.D. 183), for example, the apprentice also lives at home, and the father undertakes to "produce him to attend the teacher for the stipulated period [five years] every day from sunrise to sunset"; in addition, the apprentice is allowed "twenty holidays a year on account of festivals without any deduction from his wages," and the contract also provides for no salary for the first two years and seven months, and for wages increasing from twelve to sixteen to twenty-four drachmas a month over the rest of the five-year period. As for the reference to taxes in the present contact, since the boy was a minor (under fourteen) he would not be subject to the poll tax but only to the tax on trades; early in the second century the prefect Vibius Maximus rescinded the trades tax on minors.

contract of apprenticeship is valid. Year 13 of Emperor Nero Claudius Caesar Augustus Germanicus, month of Augustus,[147] the 21st.

I, Ptolemaeus son of Pausirio son of Ptolemaeus, my mother being Ophelous daughter of Theo, will carry out all the provisions in the one year. I, Zoilus son of Horus son of Zoilus, my mother being Dieus daughter of Soceus, wrote for him because he is illiterate. Year thirteenth of the Emperor Nero Claudius Caesar Augustus Germanicus, month of Augustus, the 21st.

Oxyrhynchus Papyrus No. 724 (= *Select Papyri*, No. 15); A.D. 155
From LCL

Panechotes, also called Panares, ex-*cosmetes* of Oxyrhynchus, through his friend Gemellus, to Apollonius, writer of shorthand, greeting. I have placed with you my slave Chaerammon, to learn the signs which your son Dionysius knows, for a period of two years from the present month Phamenoth of the eighteenth year of the lord Antoninus Caesar, for the fee agreed upon between us of 120 silver drachmas, with exception of feast days; and of this sum you have had a first installment of 40 drachmas, and you will receive a second installment of 40 drachmas when the boy has learned the whole commentary [148] by heart, and the third installment, the remaining 40 drachmas, you will receive at the end of the period when the boy can write and read from prose of all kinds without fault. If you make him perfect within the period, I will not wait for the aforesaid terminal date, but I shall not have the right to remove the boy within the period, and he shall remain with you after the period for as many days or months as he may have been absent from work. Year 18 of the Emperor Caesar Titus Aelius Hadrianus Antoninus Augustus Pius, Phamenoth 5.

[147] See Note 50.   [148] A collection of shorthand symbols.

CHAPTER IV

THE ROMAN PEACE (A.D. 14–192): SOCIETY AND CULTURE

54. *The Grandeur of Rome*

With these descriptions should be compared § 141, which, though composed at a later date, lists monuments and landmarks most of which were already in existence in the first and second centuries.

Pliny *Natural History* III. v. 66–67

In the principate and censorship of Vespasian and Titus, in the 826th year after the city's foundation,[1] the walls of Rome, embracing the seven hills, measured 13.2 miles in circumference. The city itself is divided into fourteen districts, and has 265 intersections with guardian *Lares*.[2] A measurement running from the milestone set up at the head of the Roman Forum [3] to each of the city gates—which today number thirty-seven if the Twelve Gates are counted as one and the seven of the old gates that no longer exist are omitted—gives a total of 20.765 miles in a straight line. But the measurement of all the thoroughfares block by block, from the same milestone to the outermost edge of the buildings including the Praetorian Camp,[4] totals a little more than sixty miles. And if one should consider in addition the height of the buildings,[5] he would assuredly form a fitting appraisal and would admit that no city has existed in the whole world that could be compared with Rome in size. On the east it is enclosed by the Rampart of Tarquin the Proud, a work among the leading wonders of the world, for he raised it as high as the walls where the approach was level and the city most exposed. On the other sides it was protected by lofty walls or steep hills, but the increasing spread of buildings has added many suburbs.

[1] A.D. 73.
[2] There were little shrines of these household gods at the central crossroads of each neighborhood. The division of the city into fourteen districts was organized by Augustus; cf. § 15, second selection.
[3] See Chapter VI, Note 139.
[4] The Praetorian cohorts, stationed partly in Rome and partly in neighboring towns by Augustus (cf. § 6, first selection), were concentrated by Tiberius in a permanent camp just outside the Viminal Gate.
[5] "To reduce the number of collapses Augustus lowered the height of new buildings and forbade that they be raised higher than seventy feet on the public streets" (Strabo *Geography* v. iii. 7).

Strabo *Geography* v. iii. 8
Adapted from LCL

So much, then, for the blessings with which nature supplies the city; but the Romans have added still others, which are the result of their foresight. For if the Greeks had the repute of being most felicitous in the founding of cities, in that they aimed at beauty, strength of position, harbors, and productive soil, the Romans had the best foresight in those matters which the Greeks took but little account of, such as the construction of roads and aqueducts, and of sewers that could wash out the filth of the city into the Tiber. . . . The sewers, vaulted with close-fitting stones, have in some places left room enough for wagons loaded with hay to pass through them. And water is brought into the city through the aqueducts in such quantities that veritable rivers flow through the city and the sewers; and almost every house has cisterns and service pipes and copious fountains—with which Marcus Agrippa concerned himself most, though he also adorned the city with many other structures.[6] In a word, the early Romans took but little account of the beauty of Rome, because they were occupied with other—greater and more necessary—matters; whereas the later Romans, and particularly those of today and in my time, have not fallen short in this respect either but have filled the city with many beautiful structures. Pompey, the deified Caesar, Augustus, his sons and friends, and wife and sister, have outdone all others in their zeal for buildings and in the expense incurred.[7] The Campus Martius contains most of these, and thus, in addition to its natural beauty, it has received still further adornment as the result of foresight. The size of the Campus is awe-inspiring, since it affords space at the same time for chariot races and every other equestrian exercise unhindered by the great multitude of people exercising themselves by playing ball, trundling hoops, and wrestling; and the works of art

[6] Pliny tells us (*Natural History* XXXVI. xv. 121) that "Agrippa in his aedileship . . . created 700 cisterns, 500 fountains, and 130 reservoirs, many of them magnificently adorned. Upon these structures he erected 300 statues of bronze or marble and 400 marble columns." Like modern writers, almost every ancient writer who talks about Rome singles out the aqueducts and water supply for admiring praise. The most complete and detailed information on this subject is contained in *The Water Supply of Rome* by Sextus Julius Frontinus, who became water commissioner in A.D. 97. His book gives the name, date and type of construction, length, and purpose (drinking, washing, etc.) of each of the nine aqueducts; describes the maintenance of the system by slave gangs; tells of water rates, fraudulent diversion of public water to private uses, fines for unlawful use, damage, or pollution, and a host of other matters. Selections from this work are given in § 15.

[7] Cf. § 15. This passage was apparently written before the death of Augustus, since, unlike Caesar, he is not called "deified"; among subsequent emperors Hadrian was particularly noted for the number and sumptuousness of his public works (cf. § 39 and Note 9 below).

situated around the Campus Martius, and the ground covered with grass
throughout the year, and the crowns of the hills that rise above the river
and extend as far as its bed, presenting the appearance of a stage painting—all this affords a spectacle from which it is hard to tear one's self
away. And near this Campus is still another,[8] and colonnades around it
in very great numbers, and sacred precincts, and three theaters, and an
amphitheater, and very costly temples in close succession to one another. . . . Believing this place most sacred, they erected in it also the
tombs of their most illustrious men and women. The most noteworthy is
the one called the Mausoleum, a great mound near the river on a lofty
foundation of white marble, thickly covered with evergreen trees to
the very summit. On top is a bronze image of Augustus Caesar; beneath
the mound are the tombs of himself and his kinsmen and intimates;[9]
behind the mound is a large sacred precinct with wonderful promenades;
and in the center of the Campus around his crematorium is a wall, this
too of white marble, surrounded by a circular iron fence and planted
with black poplars inside. And again if, on passing to the Old Forum,
one should see forum after forum ranged alongside it, and basilicas, and
temples, and should see also the Capitol and the works of art there and
those on the Palatine and in Livia's Promenade, one would easily forget
the things outside. Such is Rome.

55. *The Great Fire at Rome*

In A.D. 64 Rome was gutted by a disastrous fire which raged for nine days
(July 18–26). Though there is no credible evidence for the familiar charges
that Nero was responsible for setting fire to the capital or that he "fiddled
while Rome burned," contemporary public opinion was receptive to such
rumors because of Nero's previous crimes and because in rebuilding the
city he appropriated a sizable area in the center of the city for a new imperial
palace, the *Domus Aurea* (Golden House). To silence the hostile talk, Nero
found a scapegoat in the adherents of the tiny Christian sect; thus began the
first persecution of Christians; cf. further §§ 172–177.

Tacitus *Annals* xv. xxxviii–xliv (abridged)

A disaster followed, whether the result of accident or of the emperor's guile is uncertain, as authors have given both versions, but graver

[8] Actually, this is a part of the Campus Martius.
[9] Imperial burials filled the Mausoleum of Augustus by the time of Hadrian, who
erected a new mausoleum on the opposite bank of the Tiber; cf. Chapter II, Note
150.

and more dreadful than any other which has befallen this city through the ravages of fire. It started first in that part of the Circus which adjoins the Palatine and Caelian Hills, where, amid the shops containing inflammable wares, the conflagration broke out, instantly gathered strength, and, driven by the wind, swept down the length of the Circus. There were no residences fenced with masonry, or temples surrounded by walls, or anything else to act as an obstacle. The blaze in its fury ran first through the level portions of the city, rose to the hills, then again devastated the lower places, outstripping all remedial measures, so rapid was the scourge and so completely was the city at its mercy owing to the narrow winding lanes and irregular streets which characterized old Rome. . . .

Nero at this time was at Antium and did not return to the city until the fire approached the house which he had built to connect the palace and the Gardens of Maecenas.[10] It could not, however, be stopped from consuming the palace, the house, and everything around. But, for the relief of the homeless and roving populace, he threw open the Campus Martius, the public structures of Agrippa, and even his own gardens, and put up temporary structures to receive the destitute multitude. The necessities of life were brought up from Ostia and neighboring towns, and the price of grain was reduced to three sesterces a *modius*. These acts, though popular, were of no effect, because a rumor had spread about that, at the very time when the city was in flames, the emperor had mounted his private stage and sung of the destruction of Troy, comparing present misfortunes with the calamities of the past.

At last, on the sixth day, the conflagration was brought to an end at the foot of the Esquiline Hill by the demolition of the buildings over a vast area, so that the uninterrupted violence of the fire encountered clear ground and open sky, as it were. But before people had laid aside their fears or regained hope, the fire attacked again, mostly in the less congested parts of the city; as a result, though there was less loss of life, the temples of the gods and the porticoes devoted to enjoyment were destroyed on a wider scale. . . .

Rome is divided into fourteen districts;[11] of these, four remained untouched, three were leveled to the ground, and in the other seven were left only a few shattered, half-burned relics of houses. . . . But Nero profited by his country's desolation, and erected a mansion in which the jewels and gold, objects long familiar and vulgarized by our extrava-

[10] These gardens were on the Esquiline Hill and were connected with the imperial palace (on the Palatine) by the *Domus Transitoria* (Passage House).
[11] Cf. above, Note 2.

gance, were not so much the marvels as were the fields and pools, the woods on one side and the open spaces and views on the other to provide a sense of isolation. . . .

The parts of the city unoccupied by the mansion were built up, not as was the case after the burning by the Gauls,[12] without any discrimination or order but with regular rows of streets and broad thoroughfares, with a restriction on the height of buildings,[13] with open spaces, and with porticoes added to shade the fronts of the tenement blocks. Nero promised to erect these porticoes at his own expense and to hand over the building sites to the owners cleared of debris. He also offered bounties in proportion to each person's rank and financial resources, and fixed a time within which they could obtain them if they completed their houses or tenement blocks. He gave orders for the rubbish to be dumped in the marshes of Ostia, and for the ships which had brought up grain by the Tiber to sail down loaded with rubbish. The buildings themselves were to be solidly constructed to a specified extent of stone from Gabii or Alba, without wooden beams, because that rock [14] is impervious to fire; and they were to be enclosed not by party walls but each by its own walls. Then, to make the water supply, which individuals had illegally tapped, more abundant and available for public use in more places, guards were appointed; and everyone was to keep aids for putting out fires in the open air. These changes, which were welcomed for their utility, also added beauty to the new city. There were, however, some who thought that its old appearance had been more conducive to health, since the narrow lanes and high roofs were not so much penetrated by the sun's rays, while now the open space, unprotected by any shade, burned with a more oppressive heat. . . .

But all human efforts, all the largesses of the emperor, all the propitiations of the gods, failed to dispel the sinister belief that the conflagration had been ordered. Consequently, to scotch the rumor, Nero fastened the guilt and inflicted the most exquisite tortures upon a group hated for their abominations,[15] whom the populace called Christians. Christus, from whom the name had its origin, had been condemned to death in the reign of Tiberius by the procurator Pontius Pilate, and the pernicious superstition, thus suppressed for the moment, was breaking out again not only in Judaea, the original source of this evil, but even in Rome, where all things horrible or shameful from all parts of the world collect and become popular. First, then, those who confessed membership were

---

[12] Vol. I, § 14.   [13] Cf. above, Note 5.
[14] The volcanic peperino, found in the hills near Rome.
[15] The early Christians were commonly believed by their contemporaries to practice infanticide, incest, and other horrors; cf. §§ 172–174.

arrested; then, on their information, great numbers were convicted, not so much of guilt for the conflagration as of hatred of the human race. And mockery was added to their deaths: they were covered with the skins of wild beasts and torn to death by dogs, or they were nailed to crosses and, when daylight failed, were set on fire and burned to provide light at night. Nero had offered his gardens for the spectacle, and was providing circus games, mingling with the populace in the dress of a charioteer or driving a chariot. Hence, though they were deserving of the most extreme punishment, a feeling of pity arose as people felt that they were being sacrificed not for the public good but because of the savagery of one man.

56. *Roman Baths*

The famous Roman baths (*thermae*), grandiosely and sumptuously executed, served as vast community, recreation, and social centers not only in Rome itself but in every municipality of the Empire. The utilitarian character of much of Roman architecture is summed up in the classic remark of Frontinus (*The Water Supply of Rome* I. vi): "With so many indispensable structures for so many aqueducts, compare, if you will, the idle pyramids or the useless, though famous, works of the Greeks."

Lucian [16] Hippias, or The Bath (abridged)
From LCL

The building suits the magnitude of the site, accords well with the accepted idea of such an establishment, and shows regard for the principles of lighting. The entrance is high, with a flight of broad steps of which the tread is greater than the pitch, to make them easy to ascend. On entering, one is received into a public hall of good size, with ample accommodations for servants and attendants. On the left are the lounging rooms, also of just the right sort for a bath, attractive, brightly lighted retreats. Then, besides them, a hall, larger than need be for the purposes of a bath, but necessary for the reception of richer persons. Next, capacious locker rooms to undress in, on each side, with a very high and brilliantly lighted hall between them, in which are three swimming pools of cold water; it is finished in Laconian marble, and has two statues of white marble in the ancient style, one of Hygeia, the other of Aesculapius.

On leaving this hall, you come into another which is slightly warmed instead of meeting you at once with fierce heat; it is oblong, and has

[16] See Chapter III, Note 81.

an apse on each side. Next to it, on the right, is a very bright hall, nicely fitted up for massage, which has on each side an entrance decorated with Phrygian marble, and receives those who come in from the exercising floor. Then near this is another hall, the most beautiful in the world, in which one can stand or sit with comfort, linger without danger, and stroll about with profit. It also is refulgent with Phrygian marble clear to the roof. Next comes the hot corridor, faced with Numidian marble. The hall beyond it is very beautiful, full of abundant light and aglow with color like that of purple hangings. It contains three hot tubs.

When you have bathed, you need not go back through the same rooms, but can go directly to the cold room through a slightly warmed chamber. Everywhere there is copious illumination and full indoor daylight. . . . Why should I go on to tell you of the exercising floor and of the cloak rooms? . . . Moreover, it is beautified with all other marks of thoughtfulness—with two toilets, many exits, and two devices for telling time, a water clock that makes a bellowing sound and a sundial.

Seneca *Moral Epistles* lvi. 1–2

I live over a bathing establishment. Picture to yourself now the assortment of voices, the sound of which is enough to sicken one. When the stronger fellows are exercising and swinging heavy leaden weights in their hands, when they are working hard or pretending to be working hard, I hear their groans; and whenever they release their pent-up breath, I hear their hissing and jarring breathing. When I have to do with a lazy fellow who is content with a cheap rubdown, I hear the slap of the hand pummeling his shoulders, changing its sound according as the hand is laid on flat or curved. If now a professional ball player comes along and begins to keep score, I am done for. Add to this the arrest of a brawler or a thief, and the fellow who always likes to hear his own voice in the bath, and those who jump into the pool with a mighty splash as they strike the water. In addition to those whose voices are, if nothing else, natural, imagine the hair plucker keeping up a constant chatter in his thin and strident voice, to attract more attention, and never silent except when he is plucking armpits and making the customer yell instead of yelling himself. It disgusts me to enumerate the varied cries of the sausage dealer and confectioner and of all the peddlers of the cook shops, hawking their wares, each with his own peculiar intonation.

57. *"Bread and Circus Games:" Gladiatorial Shows, Chariot Races, Prize Fights*

"The people which once bestowed *imperium, fasces,* legions, everything, now foregoes such activities and has but two passionate desires: bread and circus games"—Juvenal's classic sarcasm (x. 78–81) is merely the best-known and most trenchant of a host of witnesses in literature, inscriptions, and papyri, to the Roman populace's "enthusiasm for actors and passion for gladiators and horses . . . the talk at home . . . and in the schools" (Tacitus *Dialogue on Oratory* xxix). The most important features of the Roman games were chariot races, wild animal fights, and gladiatorial combats; in the last-named, slaves and condemned criminals were pitted, equipped with varying amounts of armor, against other gladiators or against wild beasts. The emperors provided these amusements with lavish hand, as a means of keeping the populace amused and out of mischief: under the Empire circus games were held at Rome on fifty days of the year. In addition, there was a revival, under imperial encouragement and patronage, of the Greek athletic meets, which had declined after the heyday of the Greek city-states. These were now introduced in Italy as well, while Roman spectacles spread to the cities of the Hellenistic East, as famous festivals of the past were restored to their old splendor and many new ones organized throughout the Empire. An Empire-wide athletes' guild, with Hercules as patron divinity, was organized with imperial sanction and favor. Its members, professional athletes mainly from the Hellenized eastern provinces, toured the Empire, competing at the various meets. Athletes enjoyed extraordinary honors and privileges at home and abroad, including the right of obtaining pensions from their native cities as rewards for important victories. Many of these professional athletes accumulated considerable wealth. Galen, however, in his *Exhortation on the Choice of a Profession* (ix–xi), gives us the other side of the picture, stressing their overindulgence in food and sleep, their battered and disfigured bodies, their tendency toward early obesity, and their resultantly shorter-than-average life expectancy. Some of the following texts date from the third century, but they are in most particulars equally applicable to the period of this chapter.

Fronto *Elements of History* xvii

It was the height of political wisdom for the emperor not to neglect even actors and the other performers of the stage, the circus, and the arena, since he knew that the Roman people is held fast by two things above all, the grain supply [17] and the shows, that the success of the government depends on amusements as much as on serious things. Neglect of serious matters entails the greater detriment, of amusements

[17] Cf. § 34.

the greater unpopularity. The money largesses [18] are less eagerly desired than the shows; the largesses appease only the grain-doled plebs singly and individually, while the shows keep the whole population happy.[19]

GLADIATORIAL SHOWS

Seneca *Moral Epistles* vii. 3–5

I chanced to stop in at a midday show, expecting fun, wit, and some relaxation, when men's eyes take respite from the slaughter of their fellow men. It was just the reverse. The preceding combats were merciful by comparison; now all trifling is put aside and it is pure murder. The men have no protective covering. Their entire bodies are exposed to the blows, and no blow is ever struck in vain. . . . In the morning men are thrown to the lions and the bears, at noon they are thrown to their spectators. The spectators call for the slayer to be thrown to those who in turn will slay him, and they detain the victor for another butchering. The outcome for the combatants is death; the fight is waged with sword and fire. This goes on while the arena is free.[20] "But one of them was a highway robber, he killed a man!" Because he killed he deserved to suffer this punishment, granted. . . . "Kill him! Lash him! Burn him! Why does he meet the sword so timidly? Why doesn't he kill boldly? Why doesn't he die game? Whip him to meet his wounds! Let them trade blow for blow, chests bare and within reach!" And when the show stops for intermission, "Let's have men killed meanwhile! Let's not have nothing going on!"

CAREER OF A FAMOUS CHARIOTEER

This monument to the charioteer Diocles was erected by admirers and stablemates, perhaps upon his retirement at the age of forty-two after twenty-four years of driving in races. Only the first part of this long inscription is given here.

CIL, Vol. VI, No. 10,048 (= Dessau, No. 5,287)

[Rome, A.D. 146]

Gaius Appuleius Diocles, charioteer of the Red Stable,[21] a Lusitanian Spaniard by birth, aged 42 years, 7 months, 23 days. He drove his first

---

[18] *Congiaria:* cf. § 38.
[19] The last two words are supplied to complete the apparent sense.
[20] That is, during an intermission in the scheduled program; cf. the end of this selection.
[21] There were four organized chariot-racing "stables" (*factiones*) at Rome (and later at Constantinople), known by their colors as the Blues, Greens, Reds, and Whites.

chariot in the White Stable, in the consulship of Acilius Aviola and Corellius Pansa. He won his first victory in the same stable, in the consulship of Manius Acilius Glabrio and Gaius Bellicius Torquatus. He drove for the first time in the Green Stable in the consulship of Torquatus Asprenas (for the second time) and Annius Libo. He won his first victory in the Red Stable in the consulship of Laenas Pontianus and Antonius Rufinus.[22]

Grand totals: He drove chariots for 24 years, ran 4,257 starts,[23] and won 1,462 victories, 110 in opening races.[24] In single-entry races[25] he won 1,064 victories, winning 92 major purses, 32 of them (including 3 with six-horse teams) at 30,000 sesterces, 28 (including 2 with six-horse teams[26]) at 40,000 sesterces, 29 (including 1 with a seven-horse team[27]) at 50,000 sesterces, and 3 at 60,000 sesterces; in two-entry races he won 347 victories, including 4 with three-horse teams at 15,000 sesterces; in three-entry races he won 51 victories.[28] He won or placed 2,900 times, taking 861 second places, 576 third places, and 1 fourth place at 1,000 sesterces;[29] he failed to place 1,351 times.[30] He tied a Blue for first place 10 times and a White 91 times, twice for 30,000 sesterces.[31] He won a total of 35,863,120 sesterces. In addition, in races with two-horse teams for 1,000 sesterces he won three times, and tied a White once and a Green twice.[32] He took the lead and won 815 times, came from behind to win 67 times, won under handicap 36 times, won in various styles 42 times,

[22] These consulships correspond to A.D. 122, 124, 128, and 131, respectively.

[23] This comes to an average of 177 races a year for the twenty-four years of Diocles' career, or an average of three to four races on each of the fifty circus days of the year.

[24] Literally, "from the procession." Before the races began there was a grand parade (*pompa*) through the streets to the circus; a special distinction apparently attached to the opening race after the parade.

[25] Races in which each of the four stables ran only one chariot. In these star events, which offered the biggest purses, the stables naturally entered only their topnotch drivers.

[26] Farther on the inscription tells that both these victories were won on the same day, an unprecedented record.

[27] "A number of horses never before this exhibited at the games," the inscription later informs us.

[28] This sentence gives a breakdown of Diocles' 1,462 victories by types of races. A breakdown according to his racing feats is given below.

[29] The sum is specified to make it clear that his one fourth place was a prize-winning finish. Fourth place did not win a prize when there were only four chariots in the race.

[30] These figures add up to 4,251 of the 4,257 total recorded above. The remaining six races are mentioned a few lines below.

[31] These ties are obviously included in the above tabulations of wins.

[32] These are the six races which complete Diocles' grand total of 4,257; cf. above, Note 30. It is noteworthy that while these six races are included in his total number of starts, they are not included in arriving at the total of 1,462 wins enumerated above and below.

and won in a final dash 502 times [33] (216 over the Greens, 205 over the Blues, 81 over the Whites). He made nine horses 100-time winners, and one a 200-time winner.

[The remainder of the inscription (about three fifths), under the heading "His Records," lists in great detail, naming record-holding drivers and horses, the various records which Diocles broke: "the champion of all charioteers . . . he excelled the charioteers of all the stables who ever participated in the races of the circus games."]

CERTIFICATE OF MEMBERSHIP IN THE ATHLETES' GUILD

The certificate proper, signed by various guild and meet officials, is preceded by the texts of three imperial rescripts, which are recited as evidence of the favor which earlier emperors accorded the guild.

British Museum Papyrus No. 1,178 (= Wilcken, No. 156), lines 8–83; A.D. 194

Tiberius CLAUDIUS Caesar Augustus Germanicus Sarmaticus, *pontifex maximus*, holding the tribunician power for the sixth year, designated consul for a fourth time, acclaimed *imperator* twelve times, father of his country, to the Traveling Athletes' Guild, greeting.[34] The gold crown sent me by you on the occasion of my victory over the Britons I received gladly as constituting a token of your loyalty to me. The envoys [bringing the crown] were Tiberius Claudius Hermas, Tiberius Claudius Cyrus, and Dio son of Miccalus, citizen of Antioch. Farewell.

Tiberius CLAUDIUS Caesar Augustus Germanicus Sarmaticus, *pontifex maximus*, holding the tribunician power for the seventh year, consul six times, acclaimed *imperator* eighteen times, father of his country, to the Traveling Athletes' Guild Dedicated to Hercules, greeting.[35] In two resolutions transmitted to me simultaneously you informed[?] me that Gaius Julius Antiochus, king of Commagene, and Julius Polemo, king of Pontus, my esteemed friends,[36] were treated by you with all zeal and regard when they were holding the games instituted by them in my name.[37] I was pleased with you for your service to them, and I

[33] The figures in this sentence up to this point give another breakdown of the total of 1,462 wins. The "final-sprint" victories were presumably the most highly regarded, since they are further broken down by opposing stables in the following parentheses.
[34] The emperor's appellatives fix the date of this letter as A.D. 46.
[35] The date of this rescript is A.D. 47.
[36] That is, client kings (cf. § 26). Their Romanized names should be noted; cf. Chapter I, Note 149.
[37] That is, the Athletes' Guild of the Roman Empire cooperated with Antiochus and Polemo by participating in games which they staged in Claudius' honor (probably in connection with his celebration of the Secular Games in A.D. 47; cf. Chapter III, Note 116).

was made cognizant of—though I was not surprised at—their good will toward myself and their consideration concerning you. Those inscribed in the resolutions were: Diogenes son of Miccalus, citizen of Antioch, who was just recently made high priest of the guild, and whom I also deemed worthy, together with his two daughters, of Roman citizenship; Sandogenes son of . . . ; and Dio[?] son of Miccalus, citizen of Antioch. Farewell.

The Emperor Caesar VESPASIAN Augustus to the Sacred Traveling Athletes' Guild Dedicated to Hercules, greeting.[38] Knowing the high repute and distinction of you athletes, I too propose to preserve all the privileges granted you by Claudius at your request. Farewell.

The Sacred Hadrianic Antoninian Septimian Traveling Athletes' Guild [39] Dedicated to Hercules and the presider-over-games [40] and the Emperor Caesar Lucius SEPTIMIUS SEVERUS Pertinax Augustus, to the members of the said guild, greeting. Know ye that Herminus, also known as Morus, from Hermopolis, boxer, about . . .[41] years old, is a fellow member of our guild and has paid the entire regulation initiation fee of 100 *denarii* in full. We have therefore written to you, so that you may be informed. Farewell.

Done at Naples, Italy, at the forty-ninth quadrennial performance of the great Augustan Italian Roman Games, in the consulship of Lucius SEPTIMIUS SEVERUS Pertinax Augustus (for the second time) and Claudius Septimius Albinus Caesar (for the second time), September 23,[42] the following being high priests of athletic meets everywhere, lifetime athletic-meet presidents, and overseers of imperial baths: Marcus Aurelius Demostratus Damas,[43] citizen of Sardis, Alexandria, Antinoöpolis, Athens, Ephesus, Smyrna, Pergamum, Nicomedia, Miletus, Lacedaemon, and Tralles,[44] pancratiast,[45] twice clean-sweep winner,[46]

---

[38] Though not here dated, this rescript would appear from its nature to belong to the early part of Vespasian's reign, or A.D. c.70.

[39] In *IG*, Vol. XIV, No. 956 (early fourth century) the name is given as "The Sacred World-Wide Traveling Athletes' Guild."

[40] In Classical Greece this epithet referred most commonly to Hermes, sometimes also to Zeus, Poseidon, and Apollo. Since there is no evidence connecting the Athletes' Guild with any of these gods, perhaps the preceding "and" in the Greek text was written by mistake and the epithet is intended for Hercules, the guild's patron god.

[41] This notice of membership was obviously a form letter, with the member's name, origin, athletic specialty, and age to be inserted in the appropriate place. In this case the space for the age was never filled in.

[42] This was the birthday of Augustus. Little seems to be known about these Augustan Games at Naples, which are mentioned here and in the document following this.

[43] His career is recorded in the next selection.

[44] On these multiple citizenships see Note 48 below.

[45] A competitor in the *pancratium*, a combined boxing-and-wrestling match.

[46] This term, which may be translated more literally as "complete-cycle winner,"

undefeated boxing champion, star performer, and Marcus Aurelius Demetrius, citizen of Alexandria, of Hermopolis, pancratiast, clean-sweep winner, wrestler, star performer, and Marcus Aurelius Chrysippus . . . citizen of Smyrna, of Alexandria, wrestler, clean-sweep winner, star performer; the lifetime president officiating at the meet being Marcus Aurelius Demetrius, high priest and overseer of imperial baths; the presidents of the guild being Alexander II son of Athenodorus, citizen of Myra and Ephesus, wrestler, pancratiast, star performer, and Prosdectus son of . . . citizen of Mytilene, runner, star performer; the treasurer being C . . . ctabenus son of Proclus, citizen of Ephesus, trainer, star performer; the secretary of the guild being Publius Aelius Euctemo, chief secretary of the meet.

[Signatures] I, Alexander II also known as Athenodorus, citizen of Myra and Ephesus, wrestler, pancratiast, victor in the Pythian, Augustan, and Halian [47] Games, star performer, president of the Sacred Athletes' Guild, hereby certify that Herminus, also known as Morus, from Hermopolis, boxer, was elected to membership in my presence in Naples, Italy, at the forty-ninth quadrennial celebration, [and that he paid] 100 *denarii*.

[The signature of Prosdectus is mutilated.]

I, C . . . ctabenus son of Proclus, citizen of . . . of Ephesus, trainer, clean-sweep winner, twice [proclaimed] best of the Greeks, treasurer of the sacred guild, hereby certify that Herminus, also known as Morus, from Hermopolis, boxer, was elected to membership in my presence in Naples, Italy, at the forty-ninth quadrennial celebration.

I, Marcus Aurelius Demetrius, high priest of athletic meets everywhere, lifetime athletic-meet president, overseer of imperial baths, pancratiast, clean-sweep winner, wrestler, star performer, hereby certify in Naples that Herminus, also known as Morus, from Hermopolis, boxer, was elected to membership in my presence at the forty-ninth quadrennial celebration.

I, Publius Aelius Euctemo, chief secretary of the meet, executed this document as secretary of the guild.

CAREER OF A FAMOUS ATHLETE

This inscription is cut on the base of a statue which was erected to a star athlete in the stadium of his native city of Sardis. Inscriptions in his honor have been found also at Delphi, Ephesus, and Rome.

---

designated an athlete who had been victorious in the four great Greek games—the Olympic, Pythian, Isthmian, and Nemean—in a row.

[47] The Doric Greek form of Helian, that is, games in honor of the sun god, Helius, held at Rhodes.

IGRR, Vol. IV, No. 1,519 (= W. H. Buckler and D. M. Robinson, *Sardis*,
Vol. VII, Part 1 [Leyden, 1932], No. 79); A.D. 212/17

Marcus Aurelius Demostratus Damas, citizen of Sardis, Alexandria,
Antinoöpolis, Nicomedia, Tralles, Ephesus, Smyrna, Miletus, Pergamum,
Corinth, Athens, Argus, Lacedaemon, Delphi, and Elis,[48] won a total
of 100[plus] events, including 68 at sacred iselastic [49] games, in Italy,
Greece, Asia, and Alexandria, to wit: in the Olympic Games at Pisa [in
Greece] . . . ; in the Pythian at Delphi, 3; in the Isthmian, 5; in the
Nemean . . . ; in the Shield at Argus, 3; in the Capitoline Games at
Rome, 2; at Puteoli, 2; at Naples . . . ; in the Actian Games, 2; at
Athens, 10 (Panathenaea . . . ; Panhellenia, 3; Olympea . . . ; Hadria-
nea, 1); at Rhodes in the Halian Games,[50] 3; at Sardis in the Chrysanthine, 4; at Ephesus, 9; at Smyrna, 6; at Pergamum in the Augustan
Games, 3; at Alexandria. . . . At Rome in the Victory Games of the
lords Emperors Antoninus and Commodus [51] he was crowned with a
golden crown and took a gold prize. He requested and obtained from
our lords the most divine Emperors Severus and Antoninus [52] the succession of his sons to his high-priesthood and athletic-meet presidencies.

The statue was erected by his sons, Aurelius Damas, high priest of
athletic meets everywhere, lifetime athletic-meet president, and overseer of imperial baths, many-time winner, star performer; Marcus
Demostratianus, many-time winner, star performer; Demostratus Hege-
monides, many-time winner, star performer; and Damianus, athletic-
meet president.

The purse-prize games in which he won victories. . . . [The list
follows, but is too fragmentary to warrant translation.]

He was the first and only one of men of all time to win 20 events
for juveniles at sacred games [53] and 48 events at sacred games after advancing from youth to manhood, including the boxing contest in the
Pythian Games at Delphi, in the Isthmian, in the Nemean, and in the
Hadrianic Philadelphan at Alexandria. He was honored by the deified

[48] In addition to his native citizenship Demostratus Damas had been granted all these
honorary citizenships, in much the same way as visiting notables today are granted
"the keys of the city." In A.D. 194, when the preceding document was written, he
had not yet received four of these honors.
[49] Games so designated entitled a victor to a triumphal entry into and a pension for
life from his native town.
[50] Cf. above, Note 47.
[51] These games were held toward the end of A.D. 176 in connection with the triumphs
of Marcus Aurelius and Commodus celebrating victories over the Germans (Marcomannians: cf. § 28) and the Sarmatians.
[52] Caracalla.
[53] The subject of this paragraph, as distinguished from the money-prize games of
the preceding paragraph. The prize in the sacred games was the traditional wreath
of victory.

Marcus and the deified Commodus with full-fledged Alexandrine citizenship and with the following athletic-meet presidencies: of the Capitoline Games at Rome, of the Chrysanthine at Sardis, of the League of Asia [54] at Sardis, of the Didyman at Miletus, of the Hadrianic Philadelphan at Alexandria, of the Augustan at Alexandria, of the Seleucan at Alexandria, of the games at Antinoöpolis and all games in Egypt, of the League of Asia at Tralles, of the League of Bithynia at Nicomedia, of the Euryclean at Lacedaemon; and he was honored by the deified Severus and our lord the most divine Emperor Antoninus with many other great honors and with the athletic-meet presidencies of the Pian Games [55] at Puteoli and of the Augustan Games at Naples.

AN ATHLETE CLAIMS HIS PENSION

Hermopolis Papyri Nos. 52–56, col. 4 (= *Select Papyri*, No. 306); A.D. 267

To the most excellent council of Hermopolis, the great, ancient, most august, and most illustrious city, from Aurelius Leucadius, Hermopolitan, victor in sacred games, pancratiast, through Aurelius Appianus, also known as Demetrius, Hermopolitan, appointed his executor. I request that an order be issued me for payment of the following sums from the municipal account toward my pension: For the victory and crown which I won at the sacred iselastic [56] games, for the period from Phamenoth [1] of the tenth year to Mecheir 30 of the fourteenth year, or forty-eight months at 180 drachmas per month: [57] 1 talent 2,640 drachmas. And for the victory and crown which I won at the sacred iselastic world-championship juvenile games, ranking with the Olympic Games, held in the colony of Sidon, for the period from Phamenoth 6 of the eleventh year to and including Mecheir of the fourteenth year, or thirty-five months and twenty-five days at 180 drachmas per month: 1 talent 450 drachmas. This makes a total claim of two talents three thousand ninety drachmas of silver (2 tal. 3,090 dr. silv.), without prejudice to any right of the city and the council in the matter.

Year 14 of the Emperor Caesar Publius Licinius GALLIENUS Germanicus Maximus Persicus Maximus Pius Felix Augustus, Phamenoth.

[54] Cf. § 14, introduction to third selection.
[55] In honor of Antoninus Pius.
[56] Cf. above, Note 49.
[57] For comparative purposes it may be noted that at this time skilled labor and legionary soldiers (even after the fifty-percent increase granted the latter by Caracalla) were paid at the rate of about sixty drachmas a month.

PRIVILEGES FOR THE GRANDSON OF AN ATHLETE

Hermopolis Papyrus No. 119 *verso*, col. 3, lines 8–16 (= Wilcken, No. 158, and
Aegyptus, XXXI [1951], 155–56); A.D. 266/67

The Emperor Caesar Publius Licinius GALLIENUS Pius Felix Augustus to Aurelius Plutio, greeting. You acted rightly and properly in taking care of the orphan child and in writing to me concerning him. The
dictates of justice as well as the considerations which you urge in your
request bid me grant the favor readily. For, since his grandfather was
Asclepiades and his father Nilus, men who were famous in the athletic
world, how could it fail to be in order for him to obtain everything[?]
readily? Accordingly, Aelius Asclepiades, also known as Nilus, is to be
exempted from all taxes[?], offices,[58] and compulsory public services,
so that he may enjoy the benefit of my grant because of the fame of his
ancestors.

58. *The Saturnalia at Rome*

This poem commemorates a celebration of the Saturnalia in the reign of
Domitian. This seven-day festival, which began annually on December 17,
was characterized by merriment, revelry, and exchange of gifts; in addition,
for one day slaves were released from their duties and regaled by their masters.

Statius [59] *Silvae* I. vi (abridged)
From LCL

Hence, father Phoebus and stern Pallas! Away, ye Muses, go, keep
holiday; we will call you back at the New Year. But Saturn, slip your
fetters and come hither, and December tipsy with much wine, and
laughing Mirth and wanton Wit, while I recount the glad festival of
our merry Caesar and the banquet's drunken revel.

Scarce was the new dawn stirring, when already sweetmeats were
raining from the line,[60] such was the dew the rising east wind was
scattering; the famous fruit of the Pontic nut groves, or of Idume's fertile slopes,[61] all that devout Damascus grows upon its boughs[62] or
thirsty Caunus ripens,[63] falls, gratis, in a generous profusion. Biscuits

[58] That is, office-holding liturgies.
[59] Publius Papinius Statius (A.D. c.40–c.95), born at Naples, was a prominent court
poet of the Flavian period. His most important works were occasional poems entitled *Silvae* and two epics, the *Thebaid* and the *Achilleid*.
[60] Dainties were scattered among the populace from a rope stretched across the
amphitheater.
[61] Palestinian dates.   [62] Damson (Damascene) plums.   [63] Figs.

and melting pastries, Amerian fruit [64] not overripe, must cakes, and bursting dates from invisible palms were showering down. . . . Let Jupiter send his tempests through the world and threaten the broad fields, while our own Jove sends us showers like these!

But lo! another multitude, handsome and well dressed, as numerous as that upon the benches, makes its way along all the rows Some carry baskets of bread and white napkins and more luxurious fare; others serve languorous wine in abundant measure. . . . Thou dost nourish alike the circle of the noble and austere and the folk that wear the toga, and since, O generous lord, thou dost feed so many multitudes, haughty Annona knoweth nought of this festival. . . .[65] One table serves every class alike, children, women, common people, knights, and senators: freedom has loosed the bonds of awe. Nay even thyself—what god could have such leisure, or vouchsafe as much?—thou didst come and share our banquet. And now everyone, be he rich or poor, boasts himself the emperor's guest.

Amid such excitements and strange luxuries the pleasure of the scene flies quickly by: women untrained to the sword take their stand, daring, how recklessly, men's battles! . . . Then comes a bold array of dwarfs. . . . They give and suffer wounds, and threaten death— with fists how tiny! . . .

Now as the shades of night draw on, what commotion attends the scattering of largess! Here enter maidens easily bought; here is recognized all that in theaters wins favor or applause for skill or beauty. Here a crowd of buxom Lydian girls are clapping hands, here tinkle the cymbals of Cádiz, there troops of Syrians are making uproar, there are theater folk, and they who barter common sulphur for broken glass. . . .[66] Countless voices are raised to heaven, acclaiming the emperor's Saturnalia festival; with loving enthusiasm they salute their lord. This liberty alone did Caesar forbid them. . . .[67]

For how many years shall this festival abide! Never shall age destroy so holy a day! While the hills of Latium remain and Father Tiber, while thy Rome stands and the Capitol thou hast restored to the world, it shall continue.

[64] Apples and pears.
[65] That is, there is such an abundance that the usual problems of the grain supply of Rome do not exist.
[66] That is, junk dealers.
[67] That is the liberty to address him as "lord" (*dominus*). Cf., however, introduction to § 168.

59. *The World Metropolis: Wealth and Misery*

Juvenal *Satires* iii (abridged)
Adapted from the translation of J. D. Lewis (London, 1873)

Although distressed at the departure of my old friend, yet I commend him for determining to fix his abode at unfrequented Cumae. . . .[68] It is the gateway to Baiae, and a pleasant seashore delightful to retire to. I prefer even Prochyta to the Suburra.[69] For what place have we seen so wretched, so lonely that you would not think it worse to be in dread of fires, the perpetual collapse of houses, the thousand dangers of the cruel city—and poets reciting in the month of August? . . .

"Let those remain," [said my friend], "who turn black into white, to whom it comes easy to contract for work on temples, rivers, harbors, cleaning sewers, carrying corpses to funeral pyres, and to put up slaves for sale at auction. These men, formerly hornblowers and constant attendants of the municipal amphitheaters, with their puffed-out cheeks well-known from town to town, now produce gladiatorial shows, and when the mob turns its thumbs up kill off anyone you like to please the people. . . . What should I do in Rome? I know not how to lie; if a book is bad, I cannot praise it and ask for a copy; I am ignorant of astrology; I neither will nor can promise the death of a father; I never inspected the entrails of frogs. Let others know how to carry to a married woman the presents and messages of her lover. . . .

"What people is now most in favor with our rich men, and what people I would particularly shun I will hasten to tell you, nor shall shame prevent me. I cannot bear, Romans, a Greek Rome; and yet, how small a portion of our dregs is from Greece! Long since Syrian Orontes [70] has flowed into the Tiber, and has brought with it its language and manners. . . . The coming of the Greek has brought us a Jack-of-all-trades—grammarian, rhetorician, geometrician, painter, wrestling manager, prophet, ropewalker, physician, magician; he knows everything. Bid the hungry Greekling go to heaven, he will go. . . . Shall I not shun the purple robes of these fellows? Shall such a one sign his name before me and recline at dinner propped up on a better couch,[71] though imported to Rome by the same wind as plums and figs! . . .

[68] On the coast of Campania.
[69] Prochyta (modern Procida) is a barren island off the west central coast of Italy; Suburra was a disreputable quarter in Rome.
[70] The largest river of Syria.
[71] This refers to the ancient custom of reclining on couches at dinner parties. Certain locations on the couches were considered places of honor.

"What, moreover—to speak plainly—are the services of the poor man, what are his good offices worth here, if he takes pains to hurry in his toga before daybreak, when a praetor is urging on his lictor and bidding him go with all speed, since the childless matrons have been long awake, for fear his colleague be beforehand in paying his morning respects to Albina and Modia? [72] Here the son of freeborn parents walks on the left of a rich man's slave; another gives to Calvina or Catiena, to enjoy her favors once and again, as much as tribunes in the legion receive; but you, [poor man], when the face of a dressed-up harlot pleases you, hesitate and are doubtful. . . . 'How many slaves does he keep? How many *iugera* of land does he possess? How numerous and how large are the dishes at his dinners?' The credence accorded a man is in proportion to the amount of money he keeps in his strongbox. . . . Why add that this same poor man furnishes everybody with material and occasions for jest, if his cloak is dirty and torn, if his toga is a trifle shabby and one of his shoes shows a break in the leather, or if more than one tear reveals the coarse, recently applied thread where the rent has been sewn together? There is nothing about unhappy poverty that is crueler than this, that it makes men ridiculous. . . . The poor among the Romans ought to have emigrated in a body long ago. Not easily do those emerge from obscurity whose noble qualities are cramped by domestic poverty. But at Rome the attempt is still harder for them; a great price must be paid for a wretched lodging, a great price for slaves' keep, a great price for a modest little dinner. A man is ashamed to dine off earthenware. . . . Here splendor of dress is carried beyond people's means; here something more than is enough is occasionally borrowed from another man's strongbox. This vice is common to all of us; here all of us live in a state of pretentious poverty. In a word, in Rome everything costs money. . . .

"Who fears or ever has feared the collapse of a house at cool Praeneste, or at Volsinii situated among the wooded hills, or at simple Gabii, or on the heights of sloping Tibur? [73] We inhabit a city supported to a great extent by slender props; for in this way the bailiff saves the houses from falling. And when he has plastered over the gaping hole of an old crack, he bids us sleep securely, with ruin overhanging us. The place to live in is where there are no fires, no noctural alarms. . . . Already your third story is smoking; you yourself know nothing about

[72] Legacy hunting is one of the most frequently mentioned vices of imperial Rome. The patron-client relationship of the early Republic (cf. Vol. I, § 8) had by this time been reduced to the formality of having the client attend the morning "greeting" (*salutatio*) in the reception room of his patron and receive a gift (*sportula*) of food or money.
[73] These are representative country towns in Latium and Etruria.

it; for if the alarm begins from the bottom of the stairs, the last man to know there is a fire will be the one who is protected from the rain only by the roof tiles, where the gentle doves lay their eggs. . . . A wretched man has lost the little he had; but the crowning point of his misery is this, that though he is naked and begging for scraps, no one will help him with food, no one with the shelter of a roof. If the great house of Asturicus has been destroyed, we have the matrons and nobles in mourning, the praetor adjourns his court; then we groan over the accidents of the city, then we detest fires. The fire is still burning, and already someone runs up to make a present of marble, to contribute to the expenses of rebuilding. One will contribute nude white statues, another some masterpieces of Euphranor or Polyclitus; some lady will give antique ornaments of Asiatic gods; another man, books and bookcases and a statue of Minerva to put among them; another, a bushel of silver plate. Persicus, most sumptuous of childless men, replaces what is lost by choicer and more numerous objects and is in fact with reason suspected of having himself set fire to his own house. If you are able to tear yourself away from the circus games, an excellent house can be bought at Sora, or Fabrateria, or Frusino, for the same price at which you now rent a dark hole for a year. . . .

"Many a sick man dies here from want of sleep, the sickness itself having been produced by undigested food clinging to the fevered stomach. For what rented lodgings allow of sleep? It takes great wealth to sleep in the city. Hence the origin of the disease. The passage of carriages in the narrow winding streets, and the abuse of the drivers of the blocked teams would rob even [the heaviest sleepers] of sleep.

"If a social duty calls him, the rich man will be carried through the yielding crowd and will speed over their heads on his huge Liburnian litter bearers; he will read on his way, or write, or even sleep inside, for a litter with closed windows induces sleep. Yet he will arrive before us. We in our hurry are impeded by the wave in front, while the multitude which follows us presses on our back in dense array; one strikes me with his elbow, another with a hard pole, one knocks a beam against my head, another a wine jar. My legs are sticky with mud; before long I am trodden on all sides by large feet, and the hobnails of a soldier stick into my toe. . . .

"Observe now the different and varied dangers of the night. What a height it is to the lofty roofs, from which a tile brains you, and how often cracked and broken utensils fall from windows—with what a weight they mark and damage the pavement when they strike it! You may well be accounted remiss and improvident about sudden accidents if you go out to supper without making a will. There are just so many fatal chances as there are wakeful windows open at night when you are passing by. Hope, then, and carry this pitiable prayer about with you, that they may be content merely to empty broad wash basins over you. The drunken and insolent fellow who has not chanced to fall on someone suffers tortures. . . . But though heated with wine, he keeps clear of the man whom the scarlet cloak, the very long train of attendants, the many torches, and the bronze lamp point out as one to be avoided. Me, whom the moon or the brief light of a candle whose wick I regulate and adjust is wont to escort home, he despises. Mark the preliminaries of the wretched brawl, if brawl it be, where you strike and I alone am beaten. He stands facing you, and orders you to stand; you must obey, for what are you to do when a madman forces you, and moreover one stronger than yourself? . . . It is all one whether you try to say anything or draw back in silence. They beat you in either case; then in anger they make you post bail. This is the liberty of a poor man: after being beaten, he prays, and after being thrashed with fisticuffs he entreats, to be allowed to retire from the scene with a few teeth left him. Nor yet are such things all you have to fear, for there will not be wanting one to plunder you after the houses are shut, and all the shops everywhere are quiet, their shutters closed fast with bolts. Sometimes, too, the swift footpad plies his business with a weapon, as often as the Pomptine marshes and the Gallinarian forest are kept safe by an armed guard, and all these fellows run from there to this place just as to a game preserve. . . .

"The greatest amount of iron is used in making chains, so that one may fear that there will not be enough to make plows, and that there will be a shortage of mattocks and hoes. Happy our remote ancestors! Happy one may call the ages which in days of yore, under kings and tribunes, saw Rome content with a single prison."

60. *The Spread of Luxury*

Luxurious living became a feature of Roman upper-class life in the last centuries of the Republic, as the wealth from conquest flowed in upon the capital (cf. Vol. I, §§ 170–172). But luxury attained unprecedented heights in the first two centuries of the Empire, spreading not only among the upper classes but also among the large class of *nouveau-riche* freedmen, whose vulgar taste in conspicuous consumption is a stock theme in contemporary literature (cf. also § 66). "At the lowest reckoning," says Pliny the Elder (*Natural History* XII. xli. 84) "India, China, and the Arabian peninsula drain our Empire of 100,000,000 sesterces every year—that is what our luxuries and womenfolk cost us." Latin literature continues, as before, to be full of moralizing strictures on the decline from the sturdy ancestral mores, but the few attempts by the government to curb such excesses, such as Tiberius' attempt to revive and enforce the sumptuary legislation of Augustus, were at best only partially and temporarily successful.

Tacitus Annals III. lii. 1–liv. 5

Gaius Sulpicius and Decimus Haterius were the next consuls.[74] It was a year free from disturbance in foreign affairs, but at home there was an uneasy anticipation of stern measures against the luxury which had broken all bounds in everything on which wealth is lavished. Some expenditures, though considerable, were kept secret, generally by concealing the true prices; but the costly preparations for gluttony and dissipation had become the subject of endless gossip and aroused concern lest an emperor of old-fashioned frugality react with too drastic reforms. In fact, when Gaius Bibulus raised the subject, the other aediles too had argued that the sumptuary law was disregarded,[75] that illegal prices for necessities were rising daily and could not be stopped by half-way measures; and the senate, when its counsel was sought, had referred the matter without discussion to the emperor.

Tiberius, after repeated deliberation as to whether such extravagant desires could be kept in check, whether such restraint might not cause yet greater harm to the state, and how ill-advised it would be to attempt something that he would not achieve or that, if enforced, would entail the degradation and disgrace of men of distinction, finally wrote the senate a letter to the following effect:

". . . What am I to start with prohibiting and cutting down to the standard of old? The vast size of the country manors? The number of slaves of every nationality? The weight of silver and gold? The marvels in bronze and painting? The indiscriminate dress of men and women,[76] or that luxury peculiar to the women alone which, for the sake of jewels, diverts our riches to foreign and even hostile peoples?

"I am not unaware that at dinner parties and social gatherings these excesses are condemned and a limit is demanded. But let anyone enact a law imposing penalties, and those very same persons will clamor that the state is being subverted, that this means ruin for every member of high society, that no one is guiltless. . . . The many laws devised by our ancestors, the many passed by the deified Augustus, are dead let-

---

[74] A.D. 22.
[75] Probably the most recent of the sumptuary laws is meant, that of Augustus of 22 B.C. (See Vol. I, p. 462).
[76] There is an echo here of Tiberius' legislation six years earlier when he "forbade men to wear silk clothing and also forbade anyone to use golden tableware except for religious purposes" (Dio Cassius *Roman History* LVII. xv. 1).

ters, the former buried in oblivion, the latter—to our greater shame—
in contempt. And this has made luxury bolder. For when you crave
something not yet forbidden, you are in fear that you may be forbidden it; but when you have once crossed forbidden ground with
impunity, neither fear nor shame is left. Why then did frugality prevail
in olden times? Because everyone practiced self-control, because we
were all citizens of one city. Even when we were masters of Italy alone,
we did not have the temptations of today. Victories in foreign wars
taught us to devour the substance of others, victories in civil wars, our
own. . . ."

Seneca Moral Epistles lxxxvi. 1–7 (abridged)

I am resting at the very country house that once belonged to
Scipio Africanus. . . . It was therefore a great pleasure to me to contrast Scipio's ways with our own. In this tiny recess the "terror of
Carthage," to whom Rome owes the fact that she was captured only
once,[77] used to wash clean his body wearied with work in the fields.
For he kept himself occupied and cultivated the soil with his own
hands, as was the practice among the Romans of old. Beneath this dingy
roof he stood, this cheap floor bore his weight.

But who nowadays could bear to bathe in such fashion? We think
ourselves poor and mean if our walls are not resplendent with large
and costly mirrors; if our marbles from Alexandria are not set off by
mosaics of Numidian stone, if they are not covered all over with an
elaborate coating variegated to look like painting;[78] if our vaulted
ceilings are not concealed in glass; if our swimming pools—into which
we lower our bodies after they have been drained weak by copious
sweating—are not lined with Thasian marble, once a rare sight in a
temple, or if the water does not flow from silver spigots. I have so far
been speaking of ordinary installations; what shall I say when I come
to the baths of freedmen? What a host of statues, of columns that support nothing but are set up as decorations merely for the sake of spending money! What masses of water that fall crashing in cascades! We have
become so luxurious that we will tread upon nothing but precious stones.

Pliny Natural History XIII. xxix. 92
From LCL

There still exists a table that belonged to Marcus Cicero for which
with his slender resources and, what is more surprising, at that date, he
paid half-a-million sesterces, and also one is recorded as belonging to

[77] That is, only by the Gauls in 390 B.C., and not also by Hannibal.
[78] Marble was tinted by being rubbed with a mixture of oil and wax.

Asinius Gallus that cost a million. Also two hanging tables were sold at auction by King Juba, of which one fetched 1,200,000 sesterces and the other a little less. A table that was lately destroyed in a fire came down from the Cethegi and had changed hands at 1,300,000 sesterces —the price of a large estate, supposing somebody preferred to devote so large a sum to the purchase of landed property.

Pliny Natural History ix. lviii. 117–18

I have seen Lollia Paulina [79] . . . at an ordinary betrothal banquet covered with emeralds and pearls interlaced with each other and shining all over her head, hair, ears, neck, and fingers, their total value amounting to 40,000,000 sesterces, and she herself ready at a moment's notice to show the bills of sale in proof of ownership: they were not presents from an extravagant emperor but heirlooms acquired actually with the spoils of provinces. This is the outcome of plunder, it was for this that Marcus Lollius disgraced himself by taking gifts from kings throughout the East [80] . . . that his granddaughter might glitter in the lamplight covered with 40,000,000 sesterces!

A SUMPTUOUS DINNER

The following selection is from the best-known part of the <i>Satyricon</i>—the long account of the banquet at the house of Trimalchio, a millionaire freedman pictured as living in riotous splendor in a town in Campania (cf. § 66, first selection). Though characterized by ironical and scornful exaggeration to emphasize the vulgarity of the man and his class, the description is instructive nonetheless.

Petronius Satyricon xxxi. 3–xxxiv. 4
Adapted from the translation of W. D. Lowe, Petronii Cena Trimalchionis
(Cambridge, 1905)

At length we took our places, and slaves from Alexandria poured iced water on our hands and other attendants for the feet came in and pared our toenails very carefully. And even during this unpleasant duty they were not silent, but continued to sing the whole time. I wanted to see whether the whole slave ménage could sing, so I asked for a drink. A slave supplied it at once, singing every bit as shrilly, as did anyone you asked to give you something; you would have thought it a theatrical

---

[79] The Emperor Caligula's third wife, whom he took from her husband in A.D. 38 and divorced the following year. Ten years later this millionairess was a strong but unsuccessful candidate for the hand of the Emperor Claudius.
[80] Marcus Lollius, an early senatorial supporter of Octavian, was the first legate sent by Augustus, in 25 B.C., to govern the newly-formed province of Galatia.

troupe rather than a dining room in a private gentleman's house. All the same, the appetizer course was very elegantly served; for all but Trimalchio had now taken their places, the chief seat being reserved for the host after the latest fashion. Well, on the tray of relishes stood an ass made of Corinthian bronze, with two panniers, which contained white and black olives. This figure was flanked by two dishes, which had Trimalchio's name and the weight of the silver engraved on their edge; and on them were mounted salvers in the shape of little bridges, laden with dormice sprinkled with honey and poppyseed.[81] There were also sausages smoking-hot on a silver gridiron, with damsons and pomegranates sliced up and placed beneath it.

We were engaged in discussing these delicacies, when Trimalchio himself was carried in to a flourish of music. His appearance, bolstered up as he was among tiny cushions, made those who weren't expecting it burst into laughter. For he had poked his close-shaven pate out of his scarlet mantle and had wrapped up his neck, already well-covered with clothes, in a napkin with a broad purple stripe and fringes all around. He was wearing as well a huge, lightly gilded [82] ring on the little finger of the left hand and actually had on the last joint of the next finger a smaller ring, which I thought was of solid gold but was as a matter of fact picked out with star-like designs in iron. And to show that he had other costly trinkets besides, he had drawn back his sleeve and bared his right arm, which was adorned with a gold band and an ivory circlet fastened by a plate of shining metal.

Then, picking his teeth with a silver toothpick, he vouchsafed the following remark: "My friends, I did not really want to come to dinner just yet, but I have sacrificed my own convenience so as not to keep you waiting any longer by my absence. Still, you will allow me to finish my game." A slave followed him carrying a draughtboard of juniper wood and draughts of crystal; and I noticed one most elegant refinement, namely the use of gold and silver coins instead of the usual black and white counters. Meanwhile, as he continued the game, using all manner of coarse expressions,[83] a tray was placed before us, as we were still busy with the appetizers, containing a basket in which there was a hen carved in wood with her wings spread out round her just as if she were sitting on eggs. Up stepped two slaves and, while the band played a loud fanfare, they began to rummage in the straw, dividing among the guests the peahen's eggs which they dug out one after the

[81] The sumptuary laws vainly forbade the use of dormice as food; cf. below p. 468. They are still a delicacy in modern Italy.
[82] To give the appearance of the gold ring which was the sign of equestrian rank.
[83] Literally, "weavers' expressions," emphasizing Trimalchio's lowly origins.

other. Trimalchio, turning to this exhibition, remarked: "My friends, I ordered peahens' eggs to be set under a hen, and by Jove I am afraid they are half-hatched already; but let us try whether we can still suck them." Spoons weighing at least half a pound each were handed to us and we broke the eggs, which were made of rich pastry. To tell the truth I nearly threw my share away, for I thought it had developed into a chick already. But I heard one of the other guests, who was an old hand at these tricks, say, "There ought to be something good here"; so I broke up the shell in my hand and found a fine, plump beccafico,[84] well seasoned with pepper, hidden inside the yolk.

Trimalchio had interrupted his game, and had already had all the same dishes served him; and he had in a loud voice invited anyone of us who wished to take a second glass of mead, when all of a sudden, at a signal given by the band, the appetizer trays were quickly removed, likewise by a singing troupe. But in the middle of the scurry an entrée dish was dropped, and when a slave picked it up from the ground Trimalchio abused him and ordered his ears boxed, and told him to throw the dish down again. In came one of the slaves in charge of dishes and with a broom began to sweep away the silver dish along with the rest of the litter. He was followed by two hairy Ethiopian slaves carrying little wineskins, like those used to sprinkle the sand in the amphitheater,[85] and they poured wine over our hands—for no one so much as offered water.

61. *A Rich Man's Country Residence*

In this letter Pliny gives a detailed description of his suburban seaside villa at Laurentum, where he lived in the winter. In other letters he describes a villa in Etruria, where he spent his summers, and two villas on Lake Como, near his native town. These sumptuous residential villas have little in common with the villas of agricultural estates, for which see § 41, second selection. For detailed studies of Pliny's villas, with plans, see H. Tanzer, *The Villas of Pliny the Younger* (New York, 1924).

Pliny *Letters* Book II, No. 17

Gaius Plinius to his dear Gallus, greeting.

You are surprised that I am so fond of my Laurentine villa . . . but you will cease to be when you come to know the charm of the villa, the convenience of its location, and the extent of the shoreline. It is

---

[84] The "figpecker," still an Italian delicacy; cf. below p. 468.
[85] Saffron was sprinkled in the amphitheaters to make the air sweeter.

only seventeen miles from the city; so that after getting through with business you can be here with the day's work safely done and disposed of. Two roads give access to it: the Laurentine and Ostian roads lead to it, but you must turn off the Laurentine road at the fourteenth milestone, off the Ostian road at the eleventh. Both of them are sandy part of the way, and somewhat heavy and tedious for a team, but short and easy on horseback. The scenery on all sides is varied: at times the path is hemmed in by woods, at others it extends and opens over broad meadows, where many flocks of sheep and many herds of horses and cattle, driven down from the mountains by the winter, fatten on the grass and vernal warmth.

The villa is spacious enough for my needs, and the upkeep is not expensive. In the first part of it the entrance room is plain but not mean. Next there are colonnades that come together in a form very much like the letter D, enclosing a small but pleasant area. This affords an excellent retreat in bad weather, as it is protected by windows, and much more by the overhanging roof. Beyond the middle of this there is an attractive inner court, and next a very handsome dining room which runs out towards the shore and is gently washed by the last lappings of the breakers whenever the sea is stirred up by the southwest wind. On every side this room has folding doors or equally large windows, and so it affords a view from the sides and the front over three different seascapes. From the rear you see the inner court, the portico, and the enclosed area, then another portico, then the entrance room, the woods, and the far-distant mountains.

To the left of this dining room, somewhat recessed, is a large salon, then a second smaller one, one of whose windows faces east, the other west, also affording a view of the sea but a more unstudied one. The angle formed by the projection of this room and the dining room retains and increases the warmth of the very clear sunlight. This serves as a winter retreat, and also as a gymnasium for my household; here there are no winds except those which bring unsettled weather, and it is not until the fair weather is gone that the place loses its usefulness. Attached to the angle is another chamber with a bay window, whose windows admit sun all day long. Set in the wall of this room is a closet like a bookcase containing books that should be reread, not merely read. Attached to this is a bedroom connected to a passageway with a hollow floor and walls fitted with pipes from which it receives hot air circulated in all directions at a healthful temperature. The rest of this side of the house is reserved for the use of the slaves and freedmen, most of the rooms being elegant enough to accommodate guests.

On the other side is a very charming bedroom. Then another room, which can serve as a large bedroom or a small dining room, gets a good deal of light from the sun and a good deal from the reflection of the sea. Beyond this is a bedroom with an antechamber, suitable for summer use because of its height and also for winter use because it is sheltered and protected from all winds. Another bedroom and anteroom are joined to this one by a common wall.

Next comes the spacious and expansive cold room of the baths, in the opposite walls of which are two bath tubs curving outward as if forced out of the wall; these are quite roomy, when you consider how near the sea is. Adjacent are the anointing room, the furnace room, and also the steam room; then come two small chambers, tasteful rather than sumptuous. Attached to these is a splendid warm pool, where one may swim and have a view of the sea. Close by is the ball court, which receives the very hot afternoon sun.

At this point there rises a tower which contains two apartments on the ground floor, the same number above, and in addition has a view far out to sea and commanding a long stretch of coast and very charming villas. There is also a second tower containing a bedroom with eastern and western exposure. Behind this is a wine closet and a grain storeroom, and on the floor below a dining room where one hears only a gentle and faint crashing sound when the sea is stormy; it overlooks the garden and the promenade which surrounds the garden.

The promenade is bordered with box trees and with rosemary where box trees are missing; for the box grows well in the part which is sheltered by the buildings but withers where it is exposed to the sky, the wind, and the spray of the sea, however far away it is. Adjacent to the inner side of the promenade is a soft shady path, soft and yielding even to bare feet. The garden is thickly planted with mulberry and fig trees, for which the soil here is especially favorable, though not so suitable for others. There is a dining room here which, though removed from the sea, enjoys a view not inferior to one over the sea. Round the rear of it run two apartments whose windows overlook the entrance of the villa and another garden, lush and in country style.

Next, a covered gallery extends, almost large enough for a public structure. It has windows on both sides, more on the side facing the sea, fewer on the garden side, there being one here for every two on the other side. When the day is fair and serene, these are all kept open; but if it is windy, those on the side where the wind is gentle are kept open without discomfort. Before the covered gallery is a terrace perfumed with violets. The warmth is intensified by the reflection of the sun beating on the gallery, which both absorbs the sun's heat and checks and keeps off the northeast wind; and it is as warm in front as it is cool in the rear. In the same manner it checks the southwest wind, and thus it breaks the force of and halts winds blowing from any direction. This is the charm of this spot in the winter; but it is greater in the summer. For in the morning the terrace, and in the afternoon the nearest part of the promenade and garden, are made comfortably shady by it, and as the days grow longer or shorter, the shade that is cast is now shorter, now longer in one place or the other. The covered gallery itself is then shadiest when the sun is hottest and falls directly on the roof. In addition, when the windows are open, westerly breezes come in and blow through, and it never becomes close with stale and stagnant air.

At the head of the terrace and the gallery is a garden apartment, my favorite, really my favorite, for I had it constructed myself. It contains a sun parlor, one side of which has a view of the terrace, the other of the sea, and both are exposed to the sun; and also a bedroom with a view of the covered gallery from its folding doors and of the sea from a window. Opposite the center wall is my retreat, very neatly recessed, which by its glazed windows and by opening or drawing the curtains can be joined to or shut off from the bedroom. It contains a couch and two chairs. Below is the sea, behind are villas, above are woods. These varied views can be seen from the windows either separately or in one panorama. Adjoining the retreat is a chamber for sleeping and napping. Neither the voices of the servants nor the murmur of the sea, nor even the fury of storms penetrate this, nor lightning, nor even daylight, unless the windows are open. The explanation of this deep and perfect solitude is an intervening passageway which separates the walls of the bedroom from the garden, and so every sound is absorbed by the empty space between. Attached to the bedroom is a very small heating apparatus, which through a tiny window lowers or raises the temperature as required. Next come a chamber and antechamber which reach out to the sun and catch the first rays of its rising and even retain it in the afternoon, though receiving it at an angle. When I retire to this apartment, I fancy myself far away even from my own villa, and I take particular pleasure in it especially at the Saturnalia, when the remaining parts of the house resound with the license and the festive shouting of those days,[86] for I don't hinder their festivities, and they don't disturb my studies.

Among these conveniences and pleasures there is one drawback— lack of running water, but there are wells, or rather springs, for they are on the surface. And the nature of this coast is quite remarkable, for wherever you dig, you at once encounter water, pure and not even

86 See § 58.

slightly spoiled by the nearness of the sea. The nearby forests afford an abundant supply of fuel; all other necessities are supplied by the town of Ostia. Indeed, a man living modestly would find the village adequate, which is separated from my villa by only one other villa. In this village there are three public bathing establishments, a great convenience if perchance a sudden arrival or a rather short stay makes it inadvisable to heat up the bath at home.

The coast is adorned by villas in pleasing diversity, some in groups, some isolated, so that you get the impression of many cities, whether you look at them from the sea or the shore. The beach is sometimes soft from long periods of calm, but more often it is made hard by the repeated pounding of the waves. It is true that the sea does not abound in expensive fish, though it yields soles and excellent prawns. But my villa supplies even inland products, particularly milk, for cattle gather there from the pastures whenever they seek water or shade.

Now don't you think I have good reason to dwell and live in and cherish my retreat? You are too citified if you do not have a yearning for it. And I wish you did. Then to the many great gifts of my little villa would be added the supreme recommendation of your companionship. Farewell.

62. A Roman Gentleman's Daily Round

Pliny *Letters* Book IX, No. 36

Gaius Plinius to his dear Fuscus, greeting.

You ask how I arrange my day in summertime at my Tuscan villa. I rise when I please, generally at the first hour, often earlier, but seldom later. The windows remain closed; for I am wonderfully removed by the silence and darkness from the things which distract one, and I am free and left to myself. . . . This is when I do my thinking, if I have any composing on hand; I think in finished phrases, like a person actually writing and correcting. This is the way I compose, now less, now more, depending on whether the subject is easy or difficult and how much my memory can retain. Then I call my amanuensis and, letting in the daylight, I dictate to him what I have composed; he leaves, is presently summoned once again, and is again dismissed. About the fourth or fifth hour (for I do not observe a definite, fixed hour), as the weather permits, I betake myself to the terrace or the covered portico, and there I meditate upon and dictate the rest. Then I enter my carriage, and there also I do the same as I did walking or lying down; by this change my attention is refreshed, and it lasts longer. I sleep a little again, and then I take a walk; and after that I read aloud and with vigor a Greek or Latin oration, not so much for the sake of my voice as of my digestion, though the voice is strengthened also. Then I walk again, am anointed, take my exercise, and bathe. When I sup with my wife or a few persons, a book is read; and after supper there is a dramatic reading from a comedy, or music. Then I walk with my domestics, among whom are some learned men. Thus the evening is lengthened by varied conversation, and however long the day, it is quickly spent.

Sometimes the order of some of the activities is changed. For instance, if I have lain abed longer or walked more than usual, after my siesta and the recitation exercise I take a ride on horseback instead of in a carriage, because it is quicker and takes less time. Friends from the neighboring towns visit and claim for themselves a part of the day; and sometimes, by an opportune interruption, they afford me relaxation when I am fatigued. Occasionally I hunt, but I always have my writing tablets with me, so that even though I should catch nothing I may not come home empty-handed. I do not devote enough time to my tenant farmers, at least so it seems to them; yet I find that their rustic complaints give a fillip to my writing and to these citified activities. Farewell.

63. *Marriage by Arrangement*

This letter gives us a vivid picture of how marriages were arranged in the upper classes, and reveals also some of the criteria used in these circles for judging the suitability of a match.

Pliny *Letters* Book 1, No. 14

Gaius Plinius to his dear Junius Mauricus, greeting.

You request me to look for a husband for your niece; and it is fitting for you to give me this commission rather than anyone else. For you know how much I esteemed and loved that great man, her father, and with what encouragement he helped me in my youth, and how he caused me to appear to deserve the praises he used to bestow upon me. You could not give me a more important or more pleasant commission, nor could I undertake a more honorable task than to choose a young man worthy of begetting the grandchildren of Rusticus Arulenus.

Such a person would take a long time to find, were not Minicius Acilianus ready to hand, almost as if by prearrangement. While he loves me very warmly with the affection usual between young men (for he is just a few years younger), he reveres me as he would an old man; for he is as desirous of modeling himself on me and of being instructed by me as I was by you and your brother.

He is a native of Brixia,[87] a city of that Italy of ours, the Italy which still retains and preserves much of the modesty, the frugality, and even the rustic simplicity of the olden days. His father is Minicius Macrinus, one of the leading men of the equestrian order, who desired no higher status; for though elevated to praetorian rank by the deified Vespasian, he very steadfastly preferred an honorable repose to this display—or shall I call it rank—of ours. His maternal grandmother is Serrana Procula, of the municipality of Padua. You are acquainted with the manners of the place; yet Serrana is even to the Paduans a model of strictness. He is fortunate in having also Publius Acilius as his uncle, a man of almost unequaled gravity, wisdom, and integrity. In short, there is nothing in his entire family which would not please you as if it were in your own. As for Acilius himself, he has great energy as well as great application, joined with a high degree of modesty. He has already passed with the greatest credit through the offices of quaestor, tribune, and praetor, so that he has already spared you the necessity of canvassing for him. He has the look of a gentleman, fresh-colored and blooming, and a natural handsomeness in his whole build together with a certain senatorial grace. I think that these factors should not be slighted in the least, for this is a kind of reward that should be given to the chastity of maidens.

I don't know whether to add that his father is very rich. For when I consider the kind of person you are, for whose niece I am seeking a husband, I feel it is unnecessary to mention wealth. But when I look at the public morality and even the laws of the state, according to which a person's wealth claims paramount attention, it certainly merits some notice. And, indeed, where children—in fact, a goodly number of them —are to be thought of, this consideration too is to be weighed in arranging matches. You may perhaps think that I have indulged my affection and exaggerated beyond the merits of the case. But I stake my integrity that you will find everything far greater than what I am telling you in advance. I do love the young man very warmly, as he deserves; but it is one of the characteristics of a lover not to overburden the object of one's affection with praises. Farewell.

64. The "Three-Children Privilege"

The legislation of Augustus which established privileges for parents of three children and legal disabilities for the unmarried and childless (see §§ 11,

[87] Modern Brescia, in northern Italy, the region where Pliny was born.

163) remained on the statute books till the sixth century. The emperors, however, frequently granted the "three-children privilege" to prominent individuals who lacked the requisite number of children. The first to receive the
grant in this honorary fashion was Augustus' own wife, Livia. Pliny, who
received such a grant himself from the Emperor Trajan, here requests it for
the well-known biographer Suetonius; in another letter he mentions having
obtained it for another old friend. Constantine exempted the Christian clergy
from the operation of these laws; see § 179, third selection.

Pliny Letters Book x, Nos. 94–95

[Pliny to the Emperor Trajan]

Suetonius Tranquillus, my lord, is a person of the highest honesty,
integrity, and learning; in consequence of his character and interests I
have long since made him one of my intimate friends, and my affection
for him has increased the more I have come to know him. Two reasons
make the "three-children privilege" necessary for him: that the bequests
of his friends may be fulfilled,[88] and because he has had an unfruitful
marriage. What the cruelty of fortune has denied him he hopes to obtain from your kindness through my intercession. I know, my lord, what
a great indulgence I am requesting; but I am making the request of one
whose kindness I obtain in all my requests. How eagerly I wish to obtain
this favor you can gather from the fact that I would not make such a
request in my absence [89] if I were only moderately interested.

[Trajan to Pliny]

You cannot fail to know, my dearest Pliny, how sparingly I grant
these benefits, since I am wont to declare even in the senate that I have
not exceeded the number which I assured that illustrious body I would be
content with. I have, however, granted your request and have directed
that there be entered in my records that I have given the "three-children
privilege" to Suetonius Tranquillus on my usual conditions.

65. The Stoic Creed and the Upper Classes

Greek Stoicism, adapted to Roman needs from the second century B.C. on,
was the only important philosophical system that attained widespread acceptance in the Roman ruling classes. It held a particular appeal for them
because of its cosmopolitanism and pantheism, its concept of the brotherhood
of all mankind, and its righteous justification of monarchy, Roman imperial-

---

[88] Being childless, Suetonius stood to lose half of every legacy, in accordance
with the Augustan legislation.
[89] Pliny is writing from Bithynia, where he was governor at that time.

ism, and *status quo*. They espoused Stoic doctrine as a kind of religious creed to help them face with equanimity and fortitude the upheavals to which their lives were frequently subject at the whim of capricious emperors. Some of its adherents even became a focus of philosophical opposition to such emperors, and the school suffered vigorous persecution at the hands of Nero, Vespasian, and Domitian. But Stoicism made its peace with the "Good Emperors," and in the person of Marcus Aurelius a Stoic philosopher mounted the throne. With the triumph of the mystery religions in the crisis of the third century, Stoicism was eclipsed after five hundred years of existence; Christianity, however, had by then absorbed and thereafter carried forward some of its teachings.

Seneca *Natural Questions* III. Preface. 10–17
Adapted from the translation of J. Clarke (London, 1910)

What is the principal thing in human life? . . . To raise the soul above the threats and promises of fortune; to consider nothing as worth hoping for. For what does fortune possess worth setting your heart upon? . . . What is the principal thing? To be able to endure adversity with a joyful heart; to bear whatever betide just as if it were the very thing you desired to have happen to you. For you would have felt it your duty to desire it, had you known that all things happen by divine decree. Tears, complaints, lamentations are rebellion [against divine order]. What is the principal thing? A heart in the face of calamity resolute and invincible, an adversary, yea a sworn foe to luxury;[90] neither anxious to meet nor anxious to shun peril; a heart that knows how to fashion fortune to its will without waiting for her; which can go forth to face ill or good dauntless and unembarrassed, paralyzed neither by the tumult of the one nor the glamor of the other. What is the principal thing? Not to admit evil counsel into the heart, and to lift up clean hands to heaven; to seek for no advantage that some one must give and some one lose in order that it may reach you; to pray—a prayer that no one will oppose—for purity of heart; as for other blessings that are highly esteemed by humanity, even should some chance bring them to your home, to regard them as sure to depart by the same door by which they entered. What is the principal thing? To lift one's courage high above all that depends on chance; to remember what man is, so that

[90] The wide divergence between Seneca's high-sounding Stoic principles and the facts of his public and private life cannot escape comment. Tacitus says of him (*Annals* XIII. xlii): "By what wisdom, by what principles of philosophy had he acquired 300,000,000 sesterces within four years of [Nero's] royal favor? At Rome the childless and their wills are snared in his nets, as it were; Italy and the provinces are drained by his enormous usury." Dio Cassius (*Roman History* LXII. ii) maintains that he helped to precipitate the rebellion of A.D. 61 in Britain by suddenly recalling 40,000,000 sesterces invested in loans in that province.

whether you may be fortunate, you may know that this will not be for long, or whether you may be unfortunate, you may be sure you are not so if you do not think yourself so.

What is the principal thing? To have life on the very lips, ready to issue when summoned.[91] This makes a man free, not by right of Roman citizenship but by right of nature. He is, moreover, the true freeman who has escaped from bondage to self; that slavery is constant and unavoidable—it presses us day and night alike, without pause, without respite. To be a slave to self is the most grievous kind of slavery; yet its fetters may easily be struck off, if you will cease to make large demands upon yourself, if you will cease to seek a personal reward for your services, and if you will set before your eyes your nature and your age, even though it be the bloom of youth; if you will say to yourself, "Why do I rave, and pant, and sweat? Why do I ply the earth? Why do I haunt the Forum? Man needs but little, and that not for long."

66. Freedmen

Freedmen constituted a numerous and important class in the life of the Roman Empire. It became almost customary for a master to free at least part of his slave household in his will, as a means either of flattering his own vanity or of showing his gratitude for faithful service. In addition, even during the master's lifetime slaves were frequently able to purchase their freedom with the savings (*peculium*) they were allowed to accumulate, and many were granted manumission as a free gift. Such slaves usually had domestically useful or commercially profitable skills or business experience. Freedmen were, accordingly, to be found in practically all occupations and enterprises large and small, and many amassed considerable fortunes. Indeed, the "wealth of freedmen" became proverbial.

The relation of the ex-slave to his ex-master, parts of whose name he now as a rule added to his former slave name, was that of client to patron (cf. Vol. I, p. 59). The patron was expected to look out for his freedman's welfare. The freedman in return was legally obligated to render to his patron *obsequium et officium*, "obedience and services" of various kinds, including support if the patron should fall into need (cf. § 5); freedmen who were delinquent in these duties were liable to severe punishment, including beating with rods, exile, forced labor in the mines, and even reduction to slavery again. A recently published inscription commemorating a young man "murdered by his freedman and avenged" (*Syria*, XXVII [1950], 238) is reminiscent of slaves rising against cruel masters. But generally the tie between

[91] Seneca alludes to the Stoic solution of personal crises by suicide. Seneca himself was compelled by imperial order to commit suicide for implication in a conspiracy against the life of Nero.

patron and freedman was close and friendly. Patrons commonly provided burial places for their freedmen's families in the same tomb with their own, and wealthy freedmen, too, often built such common tombs; and though patrons were legally entitled to share in the estates of their freedmen (excepting those who had three—freedwomen, four—children), they frequently did not exercise this right but, on the contrary, left legacies from their own estates to their freedmen.

The freedmen of Roman citizens normally entered into the Roman citizen body, but they were ineligible for equestrian or senatorial rank, for the highest Roman and municipal magistracies and priesthoods, and for the military echelons reserved for freeborn citizens; and at Rome they were in addition the objects of severe social discrimination, being treated as upstarts. These disabilities generally did not apply, however, to their sons, and their grandsons enjoyed complete equality with other freeborn Romans: the poet Horace and the Emperor Pertinax, for example, were sons of freedmen. While excluded from the top offices, freedmen staffed many of the innumerable menial and clerical posts in the municipal and imperial administrations, and the priesthood of the cult of Augustus (*seviri,* "board of six") was practically reserved to them. This office of *Augustalis,* the discharge of which involved considerable expense for its incumbents, was the pinnacle of a freedman's career, except for those of their own freedmen whom the emperors appointed to the important administrative procuratorships and the imperial secretaryships.

WEALTHY FREEDMEN

In the course of his famous banquet, the ex-slave Trimalchio tells the story of his rise from slavery to freedom and wealth. Though fictional and deliberately exaggerated for heightened effect—it is told, for instance, in appropriately plebeian language to emphasize the contrast between Trimalchio's vulgar ostentation and his pretense of upper-class refinement—the story is essentially realistic, affording a brief but precious glimpse into an important segment of Italian society (cf. § 60, last selection).

Petronius *Satyricon* lxxv. 8–lxxvii. 6
Adapted from the translation of W. D. Lowe, Petronii Cena Trimalchionis
(Cambridge, 1905)

Come, my friends, make yourselves at home. I too was once just like you, but by my ability I've reached my present position. What makes man is the heart, the rest is all trash. "I buy well, and I sell well;" others have different ideas. I am ready to burst with good luck. . . . My good management brought me to my present good fortune. I was only as big as the candlestick here when I came from Asia, in fact I used to measure myself by it every day and I smeared my lips with the lamp oil to get a hairy face quicker. Still for fourteen years I was my master's favorite.

And where's the disgrace in doing what one's master tells one? All the same I managed to get into my mistress' good graces, too (you know what I mean: I hold my tongue, as I am not one to boast).

But by heaven's help I became master in the house, and then I took in my fool of a lord. To be brief, he made me co-heir with the emperor to his property, and I got a senator's fortune.[92] But no one is ever satisfied, and I wanted to go into business. To cut it short, I built five ships, I loaded them with a cargo of wine—it was worth its weight in gold at that time— and I sent it to Rome. You would have thought I had ordered my bad luck: every ship was wrecked; it's a fact, no story. In one day Neptune swallowed up 30,000,000 sesterces. Do you think I failed? No, I swear the loss only whetted my appetite as if nothing had happened. I built more ships, larger, better, and luckier ones, and everybody called me a courageous man—you know, a great ship shows great strength. I loaded them with wine again, bacon fat, beans, perfume, and slaves. At this point Fortunata [93] did the loyal thing: she sold all her jewelry, all her dresses, and put in my hand 100 gold pieces.[94] This was the leaven which made my fortunes rise. The gods' wishes are soon fulfilled. On one voyage I cleared a round 10,000,000 sesterces. I immediately bought back all the estates that had belonged to my patron. I built a mansion, I bought up young slaves to sell, and beasts of burden: everything I touched grew like a honeycomb.

Once I was worth more than my whole native town put together, I quit the game: I retired from business and started lending money, financing freedmen. I must admit, just when I was wanting to give up my business, I was urged to do so by an astrologer who had just chanced to come to our town, some kind of Greek named Serapas, a man in the counsels of the gods. This man actually mentioned events that I had forgotten; he told me everything as pat as needle and thread; he seemed to be able to see my very insides, and told me everything but what I'd had for dinner the day before. You'd have thought he'd lived with me always. Habinnas, you were there with us, I believe, when he said: "You used your wealth to get your wife. You are unlucky in your friends. No one is ever as grateful to you as he ought to be. You own vast estates. You are nourishing a snake in your bosom." [95] And, well, I really don't

[92] In the first century many wealthy testators resorted to naming the emperor their co-heir as a device for insuring their estates against confiscation (cf. Chapter II, Note 50). Millionaires of lowly origin often left this kind of will also as a means of raising their family's social standing. Some of the emperors refused on principle to accept such legacies except from close friends or in other special cases. A senator's fortune was at least a million sesterces.

[93] Trimalchio's wife.   [94] 10,000 sesterces.

[95] A reference to his wife, Fortunata, with whom Trimalchio has a spat at the banquet shortly before this narrative begins. A few sentences below he again refers to her as a "viper."

see why I shouldn't tell you, I've still got thirty years, four months, and two days to live. What's more, I shall soon receive a legacy. That's what my fortune tells me. But if I am allowed to extend my estates to Apulia, [96] I'll have done well enough in my lifetime. Meantime, with Mercury watching over me,[97] I built this residence. As you know, it was a cottage; now it's fit for a god. It's got four dining rooms, twenty bedrooms, two marble colonnades, and the upstairs apartments, my own bedroom where I sleep, this viper's [98] boudoir, an excellent porter's lodge, and enough guest rooms for all my guests—in fact, when Scaurus [99] came here he didn't want to put up anywhere else, even though he can stay at his father's friend's by the sea. And there are lots of other things, which I'll show you presently. Believe me, have a penny, you're worth a penny; have something, you'll be treated like something. And so your friend, once a mere worm, is now a king.

CIL, Vol. XI, No. 5,400 (= Dessau, No. 7,812)
[Assisi]

Publius Decimius Eros Merula, freedman of Publius, clinical doctor, surgeon, oculist, member of the board of six. For his freedom he paid 50,000 sesterces. For his membership on the board of six he contributed to the community 2,000 sesterces. For the erection of statues in the temple of Hercules he gave 30,000 sesterces. For paving streets he contributed to the municipal treasury 37,000 sesterces. On the day before he died he left an estate of . . . sesterces.

GRATEFUL FREEDMEN AND PATRONS

A large marble plaque, found in Rome, has the following inscriptions below the heads of a man and a woman in high relief.

CIL, Vol. VI, No. 2,170 (= Dessau, No. 5,010)

[Under the man's bust:] Lucius Antistius Sarculo son of Gnaeus, of the Horatian tribe, Salian priest of Alba, and also master of the [college of] Salians.

[Under the woman's bust:] Antistia Plutia, freedwoman of Lucius.[100]

[Under both:] Rufus, freedman, and Anthus, freedman, made

---

[96] Earlier in the story Trimalchio was said to have estates near Tarracina (in Latium) and Tarentum (in Calabria).
[97] Mercury was the patron god of businessmen.
[98] Cf. above, Note 95.
[99] The cognomen of three of Rome's old noble families.
[100] As his wife's name shows, Lucius Antistius Sarculo, like many middle-class Romans, freed and married one of his female slaves.

[these] busts at their own expense for their patron and patroness in return for their kindnesses.

The following are a few of the hundreds of dedicatory inscriptions on tombs which throw light on patron-freedman relations; another example appears in § 31. Cf. also § 72 and introduction.

CIL, Vol. XII, No. 4,490; Vol. XI, No. 108; Vol. VI, No. 11,027; Vol. VI, No. 22,915 (= Dessau, Nos. 8,221–22); Vol. X, No. 4,142; Vol. VI, No. 9,222 (= Dessau, No. 7,695); Vol. X, No. 8,192

i
[Narbonne, France]
To the spirits of the departed. To Marcus Ulpius Eutyches, imperial freedman, surveyor[?], his freedmen to their patron most well-deserving.

ii
[Ravenna, Italy]
To the spirits of the departed. Titus Veturius Florus, veteran . . . lived fifty-five years. Erected by Titus Veturius Pothinus, freedman, to his well-deserving patron. Frontage 10 feet, depth 8 feet.

iii
[Rome]
Marcus Aemilius Artema built this for Marcus Licinius Successus, his well-deserving brother, and for Caecilia Modesta, his wife, and for himself and his freedmen and freedwomen and their descendants, with the exception of the freedman Hermes, whom, because of his offenses, I forbid access, approach, or any admittance to this tomb.

iv
[Rome]
Sextus Nerianus Romulus built this for himself and Cordia Helpis, his wife most dear, and for their freedmen and freedwomen and their descendants of either sex stemming from us. If anyone alters this inscription in an attempt to bring into this tomb the body, bones, or ashes of another family, he shall not have access and shall have to pay to the treasury of the Roman people the sum of 50,000 sesterces. Let no malice aforethought attend this tomb!

v
[Capua, Italy]
[Ashes of] Flavia Nicê, freedwoman, most sweet in her affection and services and attentions, she loved her patron. Titus Flavius Celadus, imperial freedman, erected this.

vi
[Rome]

To the spirits of the departed. [Remains of] Marcus Canuleius Zosimus; he lived twenty-eight years; his patron erected this to a well-deserving freedman. In his lifetime he spoke ill of no one; he did nothing without his patron's consent; there was always a great weight of gold and silver in his possession, and he never coveted any of it; in his craft, Clodian engraving,[101] he excelled everybody.

vii
[Puteoli (Pozzuoli), Italy]

To Grania Clara, freedwoman of Aulus, a worthy freedwoman; she lived twenty-three years and never caused me any vexation, save by her death.

67. *Manumission*

Most common of the forms of manumission was the grant of freedom by the master's last will and testament. However, the master could also in his own lifetime (or after his death through his heir) liberate a slave by the ancient *vindicta* (rod) ceremony, a mock lawsuit before one of the higher magistrates, who affirmed the slave's freedom; the master thereupon gave him a slap, symbolizing, it is thought, his last indignity as a slave and emphasizing his future immunity from such treatment (this ritual is analogous to, and perhaps the source of, the accolade of medieval knighthood). There were also the informal methods of manumission, which were popular because of their simplicity: a master could write a letter granting his slave freedom; or he could have the slave sit at table with him; or he could announce the slave's emancipation in the presence of a few friends (*inter amicos*) as witnesses. These different forms of Roman manumission are described by our legal sources; only the testamentary manumission (for which see § 71) and the *inter amicos* type (given below) have thus far appeared in actual documents. The Greek-speaking eastern provinces, where most of the extant manumission documents come from, continued even after Caracalla's general grant of Roman citizenship (see § 113) to use Greek forms and formulas.

Among the indirect imposts of the Roman Empire was a tax of 5 percent of the value of all liberated slaves (for examples see § 71, second and third selections). With the great increase in manumission under the Empire, this tax became an important source of revenue for the fisc.

---

[101] Pliny (*Natural History* XXXIII. xi. 139) mentions this as one of "the varying fashions in silver plate," without giving any details.

MANUMISSION "INTER AMICOS"

This deed of manumission is recorded on a wooden diptych found in Egypt. The text of the deed is in Latin, the signatures in Greek. Though it dates from the third century, it illustrates a practice prevailing during the entire Principate.

Mitteis, No. 362 (= *FIRA*, Vol. III, No. 11); A.D. 221

Marcus Aurelius Ammonio son of Lupercus (son of Sarapio) and Terheuta, of the ancient and illustrious [city of] Hermopolis Major, manumitted in the presence of friends his house-born female slave Helene, about thirty-four years old, and ordered her to be free, and received for her freedom from Aurelius Ales son of Inarous, of the village of Tisichis in the Hermopolite nome, 2,200 imperial drachmas,[102] which the said Ales son of Inarous made a present of to the aforementioned freedwoman Helene.[103]

Done at Hermopolis Major ancient and illustrious, July 25, in the consulship of Gratus and Seleucus, year 4 of the Emperor Caesar Marcus Aurelius Antoninus [ELAGABALUS] Pius Felix Augustus, month of Mesore, 1st day.

[Signatures] I, Marcus Aurelius Ammonio son of Lupercus son of Sarapio, freed in the presence of friends my house-born female slave Helene, about thirty-four years old, and I received for her ransom 2,200 imperial drachmas from Aurelius Ales son of Inarous, as stated above.

I, Aurelius Ales son of Inarous, paid in full the 2,200 drachmas, and I will make no claim on the aforementioned freedwoman Helene. I, Aurelius Ammonius son of Herminus, wrote for him because he is illiterate.

GREEK MANUMISSIONS

The *agoranomi* (market supervisors), officials who regulated buying and selling and kept the records of business transactions, are here instructed to issue a certificate of emancipation to a slave who has purchased his freedom. The writers of this authorization were probably the collectors of taxes and fees on transfers of property. The manumission under the aegis of Zeus, Ge, and Helius, the gods of heaven, earth, and sun, is a survival from the Greek form of emancipation through sale or dedication of the slave to a god.

[102] Though in most of the eastern half of the Empire the Greek drachma was equated with the Roman *denarius*, in Egypt the equivalent of the *denarius* was the tetradrachm, so that an Egyptian drachma equaled a Roman sesterce. On prices of slaves cf. introduction to § 52.
[103] Since marriage between slave and freeman was impossible, slaves of both sexes, but especially women, were frequently liberated for the express purpose of marriage. Perhaps that is why Ales here purchases Helene's freedom.

Oxyrhynchus Papyrus No. 49 (= Mitteis, No. 359); A.D. 100

Theo and Theo to the *agoranomi*, greeting. Grant freedom to Horio, a slave being set free under Heaven, Earth, and Sun by his mistress, Sinthoös daughter of Pecysis (son of Zoilus) and Lucia (daughter of Longinus), of Oxyrhynchus, upon ransom of 600 drachmas and [transfer fee of] 10 drachmas in silver specie. Farewell. Year 4 of the Emperor Caesar Nerva TRAJAN Augustus Germanicus, month of New Augustus,[104] the 2d.

Under Roman law the situation involved in the following document could not exist, for if one of the owners of a jointly owned slave renounced his ownership, the manumitted share passed automatically to the remaining owners. Under the Hellenistic law of the eastern provinces, however, such part ownership was a salable commodity.

Oxyrhynchus Papyrus No. 716 (= Mitteis, No. 360); A.D. 186

To Asclepiades also known as Sarapio, gymnasiarch, greeting from Horio son of Panechotes (son of Doras) and Taous, from Apollonius son of Dorio (son of Heras) and Thaësis, and from Abascantus, freedman of Samus son of Heraclides, all three of Oxyrhynchus, guardians of the minor children of Theo also known as Dionysius, namely, Eudaemonis, whose mother is Sintheus, and Dionysius and Thaësis, the mother of both of whom is Tauris, all three of the same city. The said minors have inherited from their father and own, Eudaemonis one-sixth share, Dionysius and Thaësis one-half share, total two-thirds share, of a slave named Sarapio, about thirty years old, the remaining one-third share of whom, belonging to Diogenes their half-brother on their father's side, has been set free by him. We therefore present this petition, requesting that the indicated two-thirds share of the minors be sold at public auction and awarded to the highest bidder. Year 27 of the Emperor Caesar Marcus Aurelius COMMODUS Antoninus Pius Felix Augustus Armeniacus Medicus Parthicus Sarmaticus Germanicus Maximus Britannicus, Thoth. [The signatures of the three guardians follow, with Diogenes writing for the illiterate freedman.]

68. *The Condition of Slaves*

Despite the falling off in the number of war captives during the *Pax Romana*, the slave population of the Roman Empire remained quite large. "On one occasion a proposal was made by the senate," says Seneca (*On Clemency* I.

[104] Cf. Chapter II, Note 20.

xxiv. 1), "to distinguish slaves from freemen by their dress; it then became apparent how great would be the impending danger if our slaves began to count our number." The lot of many slaves was undoubtedly a life of toil under cruel masters, and the law was pitiless toward any who revolted or who fled and tried to pass themselves off as freemen. But the fact that more and more slaves were now home-bred rather than purchased foreigners (cf. Chapter III, Note 25), the influence upon the upper classes of Stoicism with its preachment of the brotherhood of man, and the general cosmopolitanism of the age were not without effect. Under such influences the attitude toward and the treatment of slaves, both in practice and in law, grew steadily more humane. We find slaves as well as freemen employed in many of the host of manual, clerical, and administrative posts in agriculture, private business, and government service. In the second century, if not earlier, slaves were admitted to membership in some of the lower-class burial societies along with freemen. But the gradual betterment of the slave's lot is reflected most strikingly, perhaps, in the law. Between Cato's literal application of Aristotle's definition of a slave as "a living tool" (Vol. I, §§ 94, 166) and the legislation of the Roman emperors, there lies a world of difference. The enactments of Augustus and his successors afforded slaves increasing protection against maltreatment. Thus, though the testimony of slaves could be taken only under torture, this practice was hedged about by a whole series of restrictions, including exemptions for women and children. Repeated legislation was directed also against various kinds of arbitrary abuse of slaves by their masters. A law of the first century provided that only judicially condemned slaves could be sent to fight (and die) in the arena. The Emperor Claudius deprived masters of the power to kill or discard sick slaves arbitrarily. Vespasian forbade selling a slave for use as a prostitute. Domitian forbade, under severe penalty, the castration of slaves for commercial purposes. Hadrian strengthened this and similar bans on abusing slaves' bodies, outlawed private prisons, banished a woman for five years for excessive cruelty to her slave girls, and forbade the killing of a slave without judicial sentence. Antoninus Pius gave slaves further protection against cruelty and personal outrage and made the killer of a slave liable for homicide. Thus, toward the end of the second century the jurist Florentinus was able to write, "Slavery is an institution of the law common to all peoples (*ius gentium* [105]), by which, in violation of the law of nature, a person is subjected to the mastery of another" (Justinian *Digest* I. v. 4). And not many years later the great Ulpian—formulating what, in a sense, the Romans had been recognizing from time immemorial by "freeing" their slaves one day a year on the Saturnalia— penned the classic statement: "As far as Roman law (*ius civile*) is concerned, slaves are regarded as nothing, but not so in natural law as well: because as far as the law of nature is concerned, all men are equal" (Justinian *Digest* L. xvii. 32).

[105] On the meaning of this term and of *ius civile*, mentioned a few lines below, see Vol. I, pp. 35–36.

SLAVES TURN ON THEIR MASTERS

Tacitus *Annals* XIV. xlii–xlv (abridged)

One of his own slaves murdured the prefect of the city [Rome], Pedanius Secundus,[106] either because he had been refused his freedom after the price had been agreed upon, or because in the passion of an infatuation for a catamite he was unable to brook his master's rivalry. In any case, according to ancient custom the whole slave household which had dwelt under the same roof was to be led to execution, but a sudden massing of the populace, which was bent on protecting so many innocent lives, brought matters to the point of insurrection, and the senate was besieged. In the senate itself there was a strong feeling on the part of some who were averse to excessive severity, but most held that no change should be made. One of these, Gaius Cassius, in stating his view, argued to the following effect:

". . . An ex-consul has been murdered in his own home by a slave's treachery which no one reported. . . . Certainly, decree impunity! But whom will rank shield, when it did not avail the prefect of the city? Whom will a large number of slaves keep safe, when four hundred did not protect Pedanius Secundus? . . . Many clues precede a crime; if our slaves report these, we may live singly amid numbers, safe amid an insecure throng, and, if perish we must, not unavenged, at least, upon the guilty. To our ancestors the temper of their slaves was always suspect, even when they were born on the same farm or under the same roof, and acquired an affection for their masters forthwith. But now that we have in our households foreigners with customs different from our own, with alien religions or none at all, you will not restrain such a motley rabble except by fear. But, it will be said, innocent lives will be lost. Well, when every tenth man of a routed army is felled by the club,[107] the lot falls on the brave also. In every wholesale punishment there is some injustice to individuals, which is compensated by the advantage to the state."

While no one member dared to oppose Cassius' view, a din of voices rose in reply from those who pitied the number, age, or sex of the victims, and the undoubted innocence of the great majority. Nevertheless, the side which was for decreeing their execution prevailed. But the decision could not be complied with, because a dense crowd had gathered, threatening to use stones and firebrands. Then the emperor reprimanded the people by edict, and when the condemned were being led to punishment he had the whole route lined with detachments of soldiers.

[106] This occurred in A.D. 61.
[107] The ancient Roman custom of decimation is described in Vol. I, p. 438.

Pliny *Letters* Book III, No. 14

Gaius Plinius to his dear Acilius, greeting.

Here is the terrible story, deserving of much more than a letter, of how Larcius Macedo, a man of praetorian rank, was treated by his slaves. To be sure, he was a haughty and cruel master, who remembered too little—or rather, only too well—that his own father was once a slave.

He was bathing at his villa near Formiae. Suddenly slaves surrounded him, one seized him by the throat, another struck him in the face, another pommeled him on the chest, the stomach, and even, shocking to relate, on the private parts; and when they thought he was lifeless they threw him onto the hot floor, to see if he was alive. He, either unconscious or pretending to be, lay stretched out and motionless, giving the impression that death was complete. Then, finally, they carried him out as if he had fainted with the heat. Faithful slaves received him, and his concubines rushed up, wailing and shrieking. So, aroused by their noise and refreshed by the cool air, he opened his eyes and moved his body to show, since it was now safe, that he was alive. Slaves fled in all directions, but most of them were apprehended, and search is going on for the rest. He himself was with difficulty kept alive a few days, and did not die without the consolation of revenge. [The rest of the letter is here omitted.]

FROM SLAVE BOY TO ADOPTED SON

CIL, Vol. III, No. 14,206 (21) (= Dessau, No. 7,479)

[Found near Philippi, Macedonia]

Here lies Vitalis, slave of Gaius Lavius Faustus and also his son, a slave born in his home. He lived sixteen years, [was] a clerk at the Aprian shop[?], popular with the public, but snatched away by the gods. I beg your pardon, wayfarers, if I ever gave short measure to make more profit for my father. I beg you by the gods above and below to take good care of my father and mother. And farewell.

THE STOIC INFLUENCE

Seneca *Moral Epistles* xlvii (abridged)
Adapted from LCL

I am glad to learn, through those who come from you, that you live on friendly terms with your slaves. This befits a sensible and well educated man like yourself. "They are slaves," people declare. Nay, rather they are men. "Slaves!" No, companions. "Slaves!" No, they are unpretentious friends. . . .

As a result of [their] high-handed treatment the proverb is current: "As many enemies as you have slaves." They are not enemies when we acquire them; we make them enemies. I shall pass over the other cruel and inhuman conduct toward them; for we maltreat them, not as if they were men, but as if they were beasts of burden. When we recline at a banquet, one slave mops up the disgorged food, another crouches beneath the table and gathers up the leftovers of the tipsy guests. Another carves the priceless game birds; with unerring strokes and skilled hand he cuts choice morsels along the breast and rump. . . . Another, who serves the wine, must dress like a woman and wrestle with his advancing years; he cannot get away from his boyhood, but is dragged back to it; and though he has already acquired a soldier's figure, he is kept beardless by having his hair smoothed away or plucked out by the roots, and he must remain awake throughout the night, dividing his time between his master's drunkenness and his lust—in the bedchamber he must be a man, at the feast a boy. Another, whose duty it is to put a valuation on the guests, must stick to his task, poor fellow, and watch to see whose flattery and whose immodesty, whether of appetite or of language, is to get them an invitation for tomorrow. . . .

Kindly remember that he whom you call your slave sprang from the same stock, is smiled upon by the same skies, and like yourself breathes, lives, and dies. It is just as possible for you to see in him a freeborn man as for him to see in you a slave. As a result of the massacres of Marius' day,[108] many a man of most distinguished birth who was taking the first steps of the senatorial career by service in the army was humbled by fortune, one becoming a shepherd, another a caretaker of a country cottage. Despise, then, if you dare, the man to whose estate you may possibly descend even while you are despising him. I do not wish to involve myself in too large a question and discuss the treatment of slaves, toward whom we Romans are excessively haughty, cruel, and insulting. But this is my advice in a nutshell: Treat those below you as you would be treated by those above you.[109] And as often as you reflect how much power you have over a slave, remember that your master has just as much power over you. "But I have no master," you say. You are still young, perhaps you will have one. . . .

"He is a slave." His soul, however, may be that of a freeman. "He is a slave." But is that an objection? Show me a man who is not a slave—

---

[108] That is, in the civil war between Marius and Sulla, in the first century B.C.
[109] This Stoic formulation of the Golden Rule by a Roman contemporary of Jesus, Peter, and Paul is noteworthy.

one is a slave to lust, another to greed, another to ambition, and all men are slaves to fear. I will name you an ex-consul who is a slave to an old hag, a millionaire who is a slave to a little slave girl. I will show you youths of noblest birth the slaves of mimes. No servitude is more disgraceful than that which is self-imposed.

You should therefore not be deterred by these finicky persons from showing yourself to your slave as an affable person and not proudly superior to them. They ought to respect you rather than fear you. Because I say slaves ought to respect their masters rather than fear them some may maintain that I am now offering the liberty cap [110] to slaves in general and toppling down masters from their high estate: "This is what he plainly means—slaves are to pay respect as if they were clients, or early-morning callers!" Anyone who says this forgets that what is enough for a god cannot be too little for a master. He who respects also loves, and love and fear do not mix.

LEGISLATION AGAINST THE ABUSE OF SLAVES

Justinian *Digest* XLVIII. viii. 11. 2

Since the passage of the Petronian Law [111] and the decrees of the senate relating thereto, masters have been deprived of the power of turning over slaves at their own discretion to fight with wild beasts. If, however, a slave has been brought before a judge and the complaint of the master should prove to be valid, then such penalty may be imposed.

Suetonius *Life of Claudius* xxv. 2

When certain men were abandoning their sick and worn-out slaves on the Island of Aesculapius [112] because of the trouble of treating them, Claudius decreed that all slaves thus abandoned, if they recovered, would be free and would not revert to the power of their masters.[113] And if anyone chose to kill such a slave instead of abandoning him, he would be liable to the charge of homicide.

Justinian *Digest* XXXVII. xiv. 7

The deified Vespasian decreed that a female slave would become free if she were made a prostitute after being sold on condition that she

[110] Cf. Chapter I, Note 154.
[111] Since this law is mentioned in an inscription from Pompeii, it must antedate the destruction of that town by the eruption of Vesuvius in A.D. 79. There is some possibility that it dates from A.D. 19.
[112] The island in the Tiber river in Rome, where there was a famous sanctuary of Aesculapius, the healer-god.
[113] Slaves thus freed received Latin status (see introduction to § 12).

should not be made a prostitute; and that if she were later sold to some-one else by the purchaser without such stipulation, she would become free by virtue of such sale and would become the freedwoman of the former seller.

"Historia Augusta" *Life of Hadrian* xviii. 7–11

Hadrian forbade masters to kill their slaves, ordering that any who deserved such punishment must be sentenced by the courts. He forbade anyone to sell a slave or slave girl to a procurer or trainer of gladiators without furnishing a reason. . . . He abolished private prisons for slaves and free. . . . He ordained that if a slave owner were murdered in his home not all the slaves should be subjected to questioning but only those who could have been near enough to notice anything.

Justinian *Digest* xlviii. xviii. 1. 1

A rescript of the deified Hadrian to Sennius Sabinus . . . reads as follows: "Recourse to torturing of slaves should be had only when there is a suspect under indictment and other evidence brings the proof so close that only the confession of slaves appears necessary [to complete it]."

Gaius *Institutes* i. liii

At the present time neither Roman citizens nor any other persons who are under the rule of the Roman people are permitted to treat their slaves with excessive and baseless cruelty. For, by enactment of the Emperor Antoninus, a man who kills his own slave without cause is ordered to be held just as liable as one who kills another's slave.[114] And even excessive severity of masters is restrained by enactment of the same emperor. For, when consulted by certain governors of provinces about those slaves who seek asylum in temples of the gods or at statues of the emperors, he ordained that if the cruelty of the masters is found to be intolerable they are to be compelled to sell their slaves.

Justinian *Digest* i. vi. 2 (= *Institutes* i. viii. 2)

A rescript of the deified [Antoninus] Pius to Aelius Marcianus, proconsul of Baetica . . . follows: "The power of masters over their slaves ought to remain unimpaired, nor should any man be deprived of his lawful rights; but it is to the masters' interest that relief against cruelty, hunger, or intolerable wrong should not be denied those who

[114] Further details on this are given by Gaius in iii. ccxiii: "The owner of a slave who has been killed has the free choice of prosecuting the killer on a capital charge [cf. Chapter VIII, Note 28] or suing him . . . for damages."

seek it with just cause. Investigate,[115] therefore, the complaints of those of Julius Sabinus' slave household who have fled for protection to [my] statue, and if you find that they have been treated more harshly than is just, or subjected to indecent acts, order them to be sold with the stipulation that they may not revert to Sabinus' power. And if the said Sabinus seeks to evade my ordinance, he will learn that I will deal more severely with his offense."

69. *Restrictions on Associations*

Restrictions on freedom of association, introduced during the political turmoils of the dying Republic (cf. Vol. I, p. 288), were revived and reinforced by Augustus and his successors. The main lines of imperial policy were laid down by Augustus' Julian Law on Associations (A.D. c.7), which required all societies to be authorized by the emperor or senate. Throughout the period of the Empire, no association (*collegium*) could legally exist without specific governmental permission, and no organization was authorized which might conceivably serve as a focus of political agitation. Associations which served imperial purposes were actually fostered by the emperors; cf. §§ 57, 74, 122. Others were tolerated, mainly burial societies and purely religious societies. These were permitted to hold meetings not more than once a month for religious observances or payment of dues. For the "by-laws" of such a *collegium*, see § 70, first selection, and for the bearing of the legislation concerning associations on the persecution of the Christians, see §§ 172, 174, 177.

Justinian *Digest* XLVII. XXII. 1–3

Governors of provinces are directed by imperial mandates not to permit political associations to exist and not to allow soldiers to form societies in camp. The lower classes are, however, permitted to make monthly contributions [to a society], provided, however, they meet only once a month, so that no illegal association may assemble under a pretext of this kind. The deified Severus also stated in a rescript that these provisions applied not only in the city [of Rome] but in Italy and the provinces as well. But they are not forbidden to assemble for religious purposes, provided however that nothing is thereby done contrary to the senate's decree by which illegal associations are enjoined.[116] A person may not, moreover, be a member of more than one legal association, as was ordained by the deified brothers [Marcus Aurelius and Lucius Verus]. If a man is a member of two, it was stated in this rescript,

---

115 At Rome, slaves' pleas for protection against cruel masters came before the prefect of the city; see § 5.
116 Part of this decree is quoted in § 70, first selection.

he is to choose the one in which he prefers to remain and is to receive from the association from which he resigns what is due him as his share of the common fund.

Anyone who maintains an illegal society is liable to the same penalty as persons who have been condemned for occupying public places or temples with armed men.[117]

All illegal societies are dissolved by imperial mandates and enactments and by decrees of the senate; but upon their dissolution the members are permitted to divide any common fund they may have and share the money among themselves. In sum, then, unless an association or any such body assembles under the authorization of a decree of the senate or of the emperor, it meets contrary to the decree of the senate and imperial mandates and enactments. Slaves, too, may be admitted into societies of the lower classes with the consent of their masters. Officers of these bodies should therefore be aware of this and not admit [a slave] into a lower-class association without the consent or knowledge of the master, and they should know that in the future they will be liable to a fine of 100 gold pieces [= 10,000 *denarii*] for each person [so admitted].

Pliny *Letters* Book x, Nos. 33–34

[Pliny to the Emperor Trajan]

While I was making a tour of another part of the province, an enormous fire at Nicomedia [118] destroyed many private dwellings and two public structures—the old men's shelter and the temple of Isis—though they stood on opposite sides of the street. It spread so far firstly owing to the force of the wind, and secondly to the inactivity of the people, who, it is clear, stood idle and motionless spectators of such a terrible calamity; and in any case the city possessed not a single pump or fire bucket or any equipment at all for fighting fires. These will, however, be procured, as I have already ordered. Do you, my lord, consider whether you think it well to organize an association of firemen, not to exceed 150 members. I will see to it that none but firemen are admitted into it, and that the privileges granted shall not be abused for any other purpose; and since they would be so few, it would not be difficult to keep them under surveillance.

[Trajan to Pliny]

You are of course thinking of the examples of a number of other places in suggesting that an association of firemen might be organized in Nicomedia. But we must remember that the peace of your province,

[117] That is, for the crime of treason (see § 7).   [118] Cf. Chapter III, Note 71.

and particularly of those cities, has been repeatedly disturbed by organizations of this kind. Whatever name we give them, and for whatever purpose, men who have gathered together will all the same become a political association before long. It is therefore better to provide equipment which can be helpful for controlling fires, advise property owners to use these themselves, and, if the situation warrants it, call on the populace for assistance.

Pliny Letters Book x, Nos. 92–93

[Pliny to the Emperor Trajan]

The free allied city [119] of Amisus enjoys, by benefit of your indulgence, the use of its own laws. A petition having been presented to me there concerning mutual-benefit societies, I append it to this letter, that you may consider, my lord, whether and to what extent these are either to be permitted or prohibited.

[Trajan to Pliny]

As to Amisus, whose petition you appended to your letter, if they are permitted by their laws, which they enjoy by virtue of their treaty, to maintain a mutual-benefit society, we cannot prevent them from having one, especially if the contributions are employed not for the purposes of rioting and illicit gatherings but for the support of the indigent. In other cities, however, which are subject to our laws, organizations of this nature are to be prohibited.

70. *Benevolent Societies*

Burial societies constituted the most common type of association sanctioned under the Empire. Organized in the name of a patron divinity, these societies met once a month and on their special holidays for collection of dues, religious ceremonies, and festal dinners. Though frequently composed of people engaged in the same trade or occupation, these societies were in no sense comparable to guilds or trade unions; they were organized neither to establish the standards of the trade nor to bargain for higher wages or improved working conditions. They served, rather, the function of a kind of social club, in which considerable numbers of humble folk, slave as well as free, found companionship in life and the assurance of decent burial.

[119] Cf. Vol. I, §§ 132–34.

BY-LAWS OF A SOCIETY

CIL, Vol. XIV, No. 2,112 (= Dessau, No. 7,212 = *FIRA*, Vol. III, No. 35)
[Lanuvium, Italy, A.D. 136]

In the consulship of Lucius Ceionius Commodus and Sextus Vettulenus Civica Pompeianus, May 28.

At Lanuvium in the temple of Antinoüs,[120] in which Lucius Caesennius Rufus, patron of the municipality had directed that a meeting be called through Lucius Pompeius . . . us, *quinquennalis* [121] of the worshippers of Diana and Antinoüs, he promised that he would give them . . . out of his generosity the interest on 15,000 sesterces, to wit 400 sesterces, on the birthday of Diana, August 13, and 400 sesterces on the birthday of Antinoüs, November 27; and he instructed the by-laws established by them to be inscribed on the inner side below the tetrastyle [of the temple] of Antinoüs as recorded below.

In the consulship of Marcus Antonius Hiberus and Publius Mummius Sisenna,[122] January 1, the Benevolent Society of Diana . . . and Antinoüs was founded, Lucius Caesennius Rufus son of Lucius, of the Quirine tribe, being for the third time sole magistrate and likewise patron.

Clause from the Decree of the Senate of the Roman People

These are permitted to assemble, convene, and maintain a society: those who desire to make monthly contributions for funerals may assemble in such a society, but they may not assemble in the name of such society except once a month for the sake of making contributions to provide burial for the dead.

May this be propitious, happy and salutary to the Emperor Caesar Trajanus HADRIAN Augustus and to the entire imperial house, to us, to ours, and to our society, and may we have made proper and careful arrangements for providing decent obsequies at the departure of the dead! Therefore we must all agree to contribute faithfully, so that our society may be able to continue in existence a long time. You, who desire to enter this society as a new member, first read the by-laws carefully before entering, so as not to find cause for complaint later or bequeath a lawsuit to your heir.

[120] Favorite of the Emperor Hadrian, accorded divine honors after death (A.D. 130).
[121] The chief officer of the society, who held office for a five-year period.
[122] A.D. 133.

By-laws of the Society

It was voted unanimously that whoever desires to enter this society shall pay an initiation fee of 100 sesterces and an amphora of good wine, and shall pay monthly dues of 5 *asses*. It was voted further that if anyone has not paid his dues for six consecutive months and the common lot of mankind befalls him, his claim to burial shall not be considered, even if he has provided for it in his will.[123] It was voted further that upon the decease of a paid-up member of our body there will be due him from the treasury 300 sesterces, from which sum will be deducted a funeral fee of 50 sesterces to be distributed at the pyre [among those attending]; the obsequies, furthermore, will be performed on foot.

It was voted further that if a member dies farther than twenty miles from town and the society is notified, three men chosen from our body will be required to go there to arrange for his funeral; they will be required to render an accounting in good faith to the membership, and if they are found guilty of any fraud they shall pay a quadruple fine; they will be given money for the funeral expenses, and in addition a round-trip travel allowance of 20 sesterces each. But if a member dies farther than twenty miles from town and notification is impossible, then his funeral expenses, less emoluments and funeral fee, may be claimed from this society, in accordance with the by-laws of the society, by the man who buries him, if he so attests by an affidavit signed with the seals of seven Roman citizens, and the matter is approved, and he gives security against anyone's claiming any further sum. Let no malice aforethought attend! And let no patron or patroness, master or mistress, or creditor have any right of claim against this society unless he has been named heir in a will. If a member dies intestate, the details of his burial will be decided by the *quinquennalis* and the membership.[124]

It was voted further that if a slave member of this society dies, and his master or mistress unreasonably refuses to relinquish his body for burial, and he has not left written instructions,[125] a token funeral ceremony will be held.

It was voted further that if any member takes his own life for any reason whatever, his claim to burial [by the society] shall not be considered.

[123] That is, even if he has provided for the payment of the arrears.
[124] People often specified in their wills whether they wished to be cremated or interred, and how much money from their estate was to be used for funeral expenses. Thus, for example, we read in Berlin Papyrus No. 1,695 (A.D. 157): "I desire that I be interred, and that 200 imperial *denarii* be spent on my body. Let no malice aforethought attend this last will and testament!"
[125] A slave could not legally make a will.

It was voted further that if any slave member of this society becomes free, he is required to donate an amphora of good wine.

It was voted further that if any master, in the year when it is his turn in the membership list to provide dinner, fails to comply and provide a dinner, he shall pay 30 sesterces into the treasury; the man following him on the list shall be required to give the dinner, and he [the delinquent] shall be required to reciprocate when it is the latter's turn.

Calendar of dinners: March 8, birthday of Caesennius . . . his [126] father; November 27, birthday of Antinoüs; August 13, birthday of Diana and of the society; August 20, birthday of Caesennius Silvanus, his brother; . . . birthday of Cornelia Procula, his mother; December 14, birthday of Caesennius Rufus, patron of the municipality.

Masters of the dinners in the order of the membership list, appointed four at a time in turn, shall be required to provide an amphora of good wine each, and for as many members as the society has a bread costing 2 *asses*, sardines to the number of four, a setting, and warm water with service.

It was voted further that any member who becomes *quinquennalis* in this society shall be exempt from such obligations[?] for the term when he is *quinquennalis*, and that he shall receive a double share in all distributions. It was voted further that the secretary and the messenger [127] shall be exempt from such obligations[?] and shall receive a share and a half in every distribution.

It was voted further that any member who has administered the office of *quinquennalis* honestly shall [thereafter] receive a share and a half of everything as a mark of honor, so that other *quinquennales* will also hope for the same by properly discharging their duties.

It was voted further that if any member desires to make any complaint or bring up any business, he is to bring it up at a business meeting, so that we may banquet in peace and good cheer on festive days.

It was voted further that any member who moves from one place to another so as to cause a disturbance shall be fined 4 sesterces. Any member, moreover, who speaks abusively of another or causes an uproar shall be fined 12 sesterces. Any member who uses any abusive or insolent language to a *quinquennalis* at a banquet shall be fined 20 sesterces.

It was voted further that on the festive days of his term of office each *quinquennalis* is to conduct worship with incense and wine and is to perform his other functions clothed in white, and that on the birthdays of Diana and Antinoüs he is to provide oil for the society in the public bath before they banquet.

[126] That is, of Caesennius Rufus, the patron.
[127] An attendant of the presiding officer.

ELECTION OF A PATRON

CIL, Vol. XI, No. 970 (= Dessau, No. 7,216 = *FIRA*, Vol. III, No. 39)
[Reggio Emilia, Italy, A.D. 190]

In the consulship of the Emperor Caesar Marcus Aurelius Commodus Antoninus Augustus Pius Felix (for the sixth time) and of Marcus Petronius Septimianus, March 23, in the temple of the Society of
Laborers and Rag Dealers [128] of Regium.

Whereas on the proposal of the treasurers, Publius Saenius Marcellinus and Gaius Aufidius Dialogus, it was stated that Tutilius Julianus,
a generous gentleman distinguished for his manner of life, his unas-
suming nature, and his innate modesty, ought to be adopted by our
society as its patron, so that the evidence of our decision might serve as
an example to other [prospective benefactors];

As to what we were pleased to see done concerning this matter it
was resolved as follows: We feel one and all that this very honorable
proposal has been made by the treasurers and masters of our society with
salutary counsel; that therefore apologies should certainly be made to
the honorable gentleman Julianus for the unavoidableness of this belated
consideration of ours; that he should be besought to undertake, if he
please, the function of patron of our society; and that a bronze tablet
inscribed with this resolution should be placed in his house.

Adopted.[129]

DISSOLUTION OF A SOCIETY

CIL, Vol. III, pp. 924–27, No. I (= Dessau, No. 7,215a = *FIRA*, Vol. III, No. 41)
[Alburnus Major, Dacia, A.D. 167]

Certified copy made from a notice which was posted at Alburnus
Major near the office of Resculum and in which was written the following:

Artemidorus son of Apollonius, master of the Society of Jupiter
Cernenus, and Valerius son of Nico and Offas son of Menofilus, treasurers of the said society, by depositing this notice publicly attest that of
the fifty-four members that used to constitute the above-mentioned
society there now remain at Alburnus no more than seventeen; that even

---

[128] Such societies of laborers and rag dealers (usually two separate associations)
were also mobilized to fight fires in numerous Roman communities.
[129] It is interesting to note that these societies, in the transaction of their humble
business, used the language and forms of the Roman and municipal administrations;
in this case the motion is presented in the traditional formulary of a decree of the
Roman senate (cf., e.g., Vol. I, pp. 267–69, Vol. II, § 50).

Julius son of Julius, his co-master, has not come to Alburnus or to [a meeting of] the society since the day he took office; that he rendered an accounting to those who were present of what he had of theirs and was returning or had spent on funerals and that he recovered the security he had posted for these sums; that now, moreover, there was not enough for burial expenses and he did not have a single coffin, and no one in all this period has been willing to come to meetings on the days required by the by-laws or to contribute burial money or services; and that they therefore publicly attest by this notice that no member is to think that if he dies he has a burial society, or that any request for burial will be entertained by them.

Posted at Alburnus Major, February 9, in the consulship of the Emperor Lucius Aurelius Verus (for the third time) and Quadratus. Done at Alburnus Major.

[The names and seals of seven witnesses—the usual number (cf. Note 138)—follow.]

71. *Roman Wills*

Roman citizens throughout the Empire had to draw their wills in Latin to conform to Roman law. In the third century, after Caracalla's grant had made practically all the inhabitants of the Empire Roman citizens (see § 113), the people of the provinces were given the right to draw Roman wills in Greek.

CIL, Vol. XIII, No. 5,708 (= Dessau, No. 8,379 = *FIRA*, Vol. III, No. 49)
[Langres, France, early second century]

. . . the chapel which I built to my memory I desire to be completed according to the plan I left, as follows: there is to be an exedra in this place, in which my statue, not less than five feet high and in a sitting position, is to be erected of the finest imported marble or of the best tablet-quality bronze. At the foot of the exedra a couch and a bench on either side are to be made of imported stone. The covering to be spread there on those days on which the chapel to my memory is opened is to consist of two counterpanes and two pairs of pillows such as are used at banquets, as well as two woolen robes and a tunic. Before this building an altar is to be erected of the finest Luna stone [130] with the finest possible sculptured decoration, and in it my bones are to repose. And this building is to be closed with Luna stone, in such a way that it can be easily opened and shut again.

[130] White Carrara marble quarried at Luna in northern Etruria, Italy.

This building and the [aforementioned] orchards and ponds are to be cared for under the supervision of my freedmen Philadelphus and Verus, and money shall be provided for rebuilding and repairing if any of these becomes spoiled or destroyed; they are to be cared for by three landscape gardeners and their apprentices, and if one or more of them die or are removed, another or others are to be substituted in their place; each of the three is to receive sixty *modii* of wheat annually and thirty *denarii* for clothing. Furthermore, my nephew Aquila and his heirs must singly and collectively provide these things.

And there shall be inscribed on the outside of the building the names of the magistrates in whose term of office this building was begun, and how many years I lived. If ever any other man or woman is cremated, entombed, buried[?], interred, or deposited[?] in these orchards . . . or closer to these orchards than 1,000[?] feet, or if anyone does anything contrary to what is written above, my heir and his heirs . . . shall be bound to see to it that all this is so done and not otherwise. Further, this regulation is established for this burial place in perpetuity, and no one after me is to have title or right to these burial places except to take proper care, or to plant or complete. Those who come to this building . . . to care for it shall have right of access on foot, by vehicle, or by litter[?]. . . . If anyone is cremated or buried[?], or if a monument is erected, or if bones are brought in . . . in these orchards and burial places and their enclosures as I have written above, then Sextus Julius Aquila son of Sextus Julius Aquilinus, and his heir or heirs, mentioned above, shall—if it is within their power to prevent it from being done or to take opposing action, or if they do not see to it that everything is kept by their heir or heirs as above stipulated—be condemned to pay 100,000 sesterces to the public treasury[?] of the Lingones. This penalty is to apply to all owners of this property in perpetuity.

Further, all my freedmen and freedwomen, both those whom I manumitted while still alive and those whom I manumit by this testament, are to make an annual contribution of . . . each, and my nephew Aquila and his heirs are to provide annually the sum of . . . with which they are to prepare food and drink to be offered in sacrifice below, in front of the chapel, to my memory at Litavicrar; [131] and they are to consume it there and to remain there until they use up the whole sum. For this ceremony they shall name from among themselves, by turns, caretakers who will hold this ceremony each year and who will have the right to demand the said sum of money. I entrust the care of this to Priscus, Phoebus, Philadelphus, and Verus. . . . The caretakers thus

131 The name is uncertain.

named shall perform the sacrifice at the above-mentioned altar annually on the first day of April, May, June, July, August, and October.

Further, I entrust the care of my funeral and obsequies and of all my property, buildings, and monuments to my nephew Sextus Julius Aquila and to Macrinus son of Reginus and to Sabinus son of Dumnedorix [132] and to Priscus my freedman and bailiff, and I request them to take care of all these things, and to pass upon the proper performance of the things I ordered done after my death.

Further, I desire all the equipment which I acquired for hunting and fowling to be cremated with me [133] including lances, swords, hunting knives, nets, snares, toils, lime twigs, tents, scarecrows, bathing utensils, litters, sedan chair, and all medicines and equipment of that science, and the rush-work Liburnian boat—nothing of these is to be omitted; also whatever damasks and embroideries I leave behind, and all the stars from the elk horns. . . . [The rest is lost.]

Etudes de Papyrologie, VI (1940), 1–20 (= *FIRA*, Vol. III, No. 47)
[Alexandria, Egypt, A.D. 142]

Antonius Silvanus, cavalryman of the First Mauretanian Company of Thracians, prefect's orderly, of the squadron of Valerius, made this last will and testament.

My son, Marcus Antonius Satrianus[?], shall be the sole heir of all my military and household possessions, and all other persons are hereby disinherited. He shall formally enter upon the inheritance within the first hundred days; if he does not so enter, he shall be disinherited. Then in second place my brother . . . Antonius R . . . shall be my heir, and he shall formally enter upon the inheritance within the next sixty days; if he does not become my heir, I give and bequeath to him 750 silver *denarii*.

I name Hierax son of Behex, *duplicarius*,[134] of the same company, of the squadron of Aebutius, trustee of my military estate to collect and deliver my property to Antonia Thermutha, mother of my heir above-named,[135] so that she may conserve it until my son and heir has come of age and can then receive it from her. To Hierax I give and bequeath 50

---

[132] Macrinus and Sabinus, despite these Romanized names, were apparently Gauls who had not yet attained Roman citizenship.
[133] Cf. Caesar's description of the customs of the Gauls in Vol. I, p. 210.
[134] Cf. Chapter VII, Note 59.
[135] Thermutha cannot be styled his wife, since soldiers on active duty could not contract legal marriages; since the time of Trajan and Hadrian, however, they could make legally valid wills, and their sons had the right to inherit from them (see § 154).

silver *denarii*. To Antonia Thermutha, mother of my heir above-named, I give and bequeath 500 silver *denarii*. To my prefect I give and bequeath 50 silver *denarii*. As for my slave Cronio, after my death, if he has performed all his duties properly and has turned over everything to my heir above-named or to my trustee, then I desire him to be free, and I desire the five-percent manumission tax to be paid for him out of my estate.

Let no malice aforethought attend this last will and testament! For the purpose of making this will, Nemonius, *duplicarius*, of the squadron of Marius, purchased the household and chattels; Marcus Julius Tiberinus, *sesquiplicarius*,[136] of the squadron of Valerius, acted as scales-holder; and Turbinius, standard-bearer of the squadron of Proculus, acted as witness.[137]

Last will and testament made at Alexandria on the coast of Egypt, in the imperial winter camp of Legion II Trajana Fortis and the Mauretanian Company, March 27 in the consulship of Rufinus and Quadratus.

I, the aforesaid Antonius Silvanus, verified the foregoing last will and testament of mine, and it was read aloud and I am satisfied with it as it stands.[138]

[Witnesses] I, Nemonius . . . , *duplicarius*, of the squadron of Marius, have affixed my seal.
> [Seal of] Julius Tiberinus, *sesquiplicarius*, of the squadron of Valerius.
> [Seal of] Turbinius, cavalryman and standard-bearer of the squadron of Proculus.
> [Seal of] Valerius . . . Rufus, cavalryman and standard-bearer of the squadron of. . . .
> I, Maximus, *duplicarius* . . . have affixed my seal.
> [One signature illegible.]
> I, Antonius Sianus, have affixed my seal.

[136] Cf. Chapter VII, Note 59.
[137] This paragraph, a survival from the property conveyance of very early times (cf. Vol. I, p. 105, Note 40), remained even under the Principate the regular legal formula for testamentary disposition. The testator, through a symbolical sale in the presence of witnesses, conveyed his whole estate to a friend for the price of a piece of bronze (hence one of the witnesses is termed the "scales-holder"). "In olden days," says Gaius, writing in the second century A.D. (*Institutes* II. ciii), "the purchaser of the household . . . held the position of heir, and that is why the testator instructed him on what he wanted to be given to each person after his death. But nowadays one person is instituted as heir by the will and charged with the payment of the legacies, and another person is used as purchaser of the household merely as a matter of form, in imitation of the ancient law."
[138] The text of this is written in Latin on a "book" of five waxed tablets. The testator and two of the witnesses following signed in Greek (cf. § 67, first selection). Seven was the standard number of witnesses for Roman legal documents.

Berlin Papyrus No. 326 (= *Select Papyri*, Vol. I, No. 85 = *FIRA*,
Vol. III, No. 50)

Adapted from LCL

[Caranis, Egypt, A.D. 191] [139]

[Greek] translation of will. Gaius Longinus Castor, veteran honorably discharged from the praetorian fleet of Misenum, made this will. I
direct that my slave Marcella, over thirty years of age, and my slave
Cleopatra, over thirty years of age,[140] shall be freed, and they shall each
in equal portion be my heirs. All others shall be disinherited. They shall
enter upon the inheritance, each on her own portion, as soon as each
thinks proper to attest that she is my heir, and it shall not be lawful to
sell or mortgage it. But if the aforesaid Marcella suffers the lot of human
kind, then I wish her portion of the inheritance to go to Sarapio and
Socrates and Longus. Similarly, in the case of Cleopatra, I wish her
portion to go to Nilus. Whoever becomes my heir shall be obligated to
give, perform, and provide all that is written in this my will, and I entrust
to him the faithful execution thereof. My slave Sarapias, daughter of my
freedwoman Cleopatra, shall be freed, and I give and bequeath to her five
arouras of grain land which I own in the vicinity of the village of Caranis
in a locality called Ostrich, likewise one and one quarter arouras of a
ravine, likewise one third portion of my house and the third portion of
the same which I bought formerly from Prapetheus mother of Thaseus,
likewise one third portion of a palm grove which I own close to the canal
called the Old Canal. I wish my body to be carried out and dressed for
burial through the care and piety of my heirs. If I leave any later provision written by my hand in any manner whatsoever, I wish it to be
valid. Let no malice aforethought attend this will!

On the making of this will Julius Petronianus purchased the household and chattels for 1 sesterce; Gaius Lucretius Saturnilus acted as
scales-holder (acknowledged); and Marcus Sempronius Heraclianus
acted as witness (acknowledged).[141]

This will was made in the village of Caranis in the Arsinoite nome on
November 17 in the consulship of the two Silani, in the thirtieth year of
the Emperor Caesar Marcus Aurelius COMMODUS Antoninus Pius Felix
Augustus Armeniacus Medicus Parthicus Sarmaticus Germanicus, Ha-

[139] This is the date of the original will; the date of a later codicil is not given. The
will was opened when the testator died, as we learn near the end of the document,
in 194.
[140] Slaves under the age of thirty manumitted by will did not acquire full citizenship (cf. § 12, third selection); hence this specification.
[141] Cf. Note 137 above.

thyr 21. If I leave any further document written by my hand, I wish it to be valid.

Opened and read in the Arsinoite metropolis in the Augustan Forum in the office of the five-percent tax on inheritances and manumissions on February 21 in the consulship of the present consuls, in the second year of the Emperor Caesar Lucius SEPTIMIUS SEVERUS Pertinax Augustus, Mecheir 27 [A.D. 194]. The remaining sealers:[142] Gaius Longinus Acylas (acknowledged); Julius Bolyssius; Marcus Antistius Petronianus; Julius Gemellus, veteran.

Translation of the codicillary tablets. I, Gaius Longinus Castor, veteran honorably discharged from the praetorian fleet of Misenum, have made a codicil. I have appointed Marcus Sempronius Heraclianus, my respected friend, trustee to act on his own good faith. To my kinsman Julius Serenus I give and bequeath 4,000 sesterces. Written in my own hand on February 7. Sealed by Longinus Acylas and Valerius Priscus. Sealers: Gaius Longinus Acylas (acknowledged); Julius Philoxenus; Gaius Lucretius Saturnilus (acknowledged); Gaius Longinus Castor; Julius Gemellus, veteran. Opened and read on the same day on which the will was unsealed.

I, Gaius Lucius Geminianus, expert in Roman law, translated the foregoing copy, and it agrees with the original will.

72. Sepulchral Inscriptions

Both inhumation and cremation were practiced in the Roman Empire. Burials and funerary monuments were protected by law against disturbance. As we have already seen in §§ 70–71, testators frequently included in their wills specific provisions for their funerals and for the upkeep of their tombs. The stipulations most commonly encountered in connection with sepulchres are (1) the property—tomb and site—is retained in the family in perpetuity by a permanent prohibition against alienation; (2) all persons are forbidden to damage the monument; (3) all persons are forbidden to violate the sepulture or place therein the remains of a stranger; (4) specified persons are allowed or forbidden access to the tomb. Tombstones and other memorials of the dead constitute the most numerous category of extant inscriptions, having been found by the thousands in all parts of the Mediterranean world. They tell their mournful story in an infinite variety of ways, some in trite, conventional phrases and some in genuine personal outpourings of love and grief, ranging in length from "the short and simple annals of the poor" to the long and often very flowery memorials of the well-to-do. A few samples follow;

[142] That is, four in addition to the three witnesses mentioned above, thus making the requisite seven witnesses (cf. Note 138 above).

these should be read in association with the funerary inscriptions included in §§ 30–31, 66, and 68.

Dessau, No. 7,663

[Pompeii, Italy]

Laturnia Januaria, lime burner, lived 45 years.

CIL, Vol. IX, No. 1,721 (= Dessau, No. 7,668)

[Beneventum, Italy]

Publius Marcius Philodamus, freedman of Publius, plasterer, [built this] for himself and his family. Jucunda, his darling, is buried [here].

CIL, Vol. VI, No. 11,602 (= Dessau, No. 8,402)

[Rome]

Here lies Amymone, wife of Marcus, most good and most beautiful, wool spinner, dutiful, modest, careful, chaste, stay-at-home.

CIL, Vol. XIV, No. 4,827

[Ostia, Italy]

To the spirits of the departed. Gaius Calpenius Hermes built this for himself and his family, and for his freedmen and freedwomen and their descendants, and for Antistia Coetonis, his wife. This place of burial shall not pass to an heir belonging to another family. He built a chamber on the right of the entrance; [placed] sarcophagi on the pavement outside; and opposite [the entrance] and to the left, in two walls, made niches with [funerary] urns and sarcophagi.

CIL, Vol. VI, No. 36,467 (= Dessau, No. 8,184)

[Rome]

To the spirits of the departed. Gaius Tullius Hesper built [this] tomb for himself, where his bones are to be placed. If anyone does violence to them or removes them hence, I wish for him that he may live a long time in bodily pain, and that when he dies the gods below may not receive him.

CIL, Vol. V, No. 952 (= Dessau, No. 8,239)

[Aquileia, Italy]

Marcus Vocusius Crescens, freedman of Marcus, built this in his lifetime for himself and Vocusia Veneria, his very good wife, and Petronius Vocusianus, his son, soldier of the Third Praetorian Cohort, aged 18 years, 3 months, 18 days. If anyone tries to sell, buy, or break open this repository, then he shall pay a penalty of 20,000 sesterces to the municipality of Aquileia, and the informer shall receive one fourth.

CIL, Vol. XI, No. 137 (= Dessau, No. 1,980)

[Ravenna, Italy]

Gaius Julius Mygdonius, a Parthian by origin, born a freeman, captured when a youth and sold into slavery in Roman territory. When I became a citizen with fate's kind help, I got together a nest egg against the day when I reached fifty. Ever since youth I sought to attain my old age; now receive me gladly, O stone; with you I shall be freed from care.

AE, 1947, No. 187, and 1948, p. 90 (= L. Robert, *Hellenica*, III
[Paris, 1946], 119)

[Nicomedia, Bithynia]

You see me a corpse, passers-by. My civilian name [143] was Apollonis, my native town Apamea, but now in[?] the soil of Nicomedia the thread of destiny spun by the Fates holds me fast to the ground. Eight times he won in athletic games, but in the ninth boxing match he met his fated end. Play, laugh, passer-by, knowing that you too must die. His wife Alexandria erected this memorial out of his money as a remembrance. If anyone dares to disturb this monument, he shall pay a fine of 2,500 *denarii* to the fisc.

CIL, Vol. VI, No. 35,887 (= Dessau, No. 8,168)

[Rome]

I lived dear to my family, I gave up my life yet a maiden.
Here I lie dead and I am ashes, and these ashes are earth.
But if the earth is a goddess, I am a goddess, I am not dead.
I beg you, stranger, do not desecrate my bones.
Mus, lived thirteen years.

CIL, Vol. VI, No. 14,672 (= Dessau, No. 8,156), abridged

[Rome]

To the spirits of the departed. To Cerellia Fortunata, dearest wife, with whom he lived forty years without the slightest cause for complaint,[144] Marcus Antonius Encolpus [145] built this. . . .

[143] As opposed to his professional name or nickname.
[144] This is a stock phrase in Latin sepulchral inscriptions (cf. also the following text), so much so that it is frequently reduced to its initials, *s.u.q.* (*sine ulla querela*).
[145] Interestingly enough, both Encolpus and Fortunata are the names of characters in Petronius' *Satyricon*.

Do not pass by this epitaph, wayfarer,
But stop, listen, and learn, then go.
There is no boat in Hades, no ferryman Charon,
No caretaker Aeacus, no Cerberus dog.
All we dead below
Have become bones and ashes, nothing more.
I have spoken you true; go now, wayfarer,
Lest even though dead I seem to you garrulous. . . .

CIL, Vol. XIII, No. 1,983 (= Dessau, No. 8,158)

[Lyons, France]

To the spirits of the departed. To the eternal memory of Blandinia Martiola, most blameless girl, who lived 18 years, 9 months, 5 days, Pompeius Catussa, Sequanian, plasterer, to his wife incomparable and most kind to him, who lived with me 5 years, 6 months, 18 days without any kind of fault, erected this in his lifetime for himself and his wife, and consecrated it while under construction.[146] You who read this, go bathe in the baths of Apollo, as I used to do with my wife—I wish I still could.

CIL, Vol. VI, No. 9,663 (= Dessau, No. 7,518)

[Rome]

To the spirits of the departed. In this tomb lies a lifeless body, whose spirit was received among the gods, for thus he deserved, Lucius Statius Onesimus, merchant of the Appian Way for many years, a man most trustworthy above all men, whose reputation is recorded forever, who lived sixty-eight years, more or less, without blemish. Statia Crescentina, his wife, built this for her well-deserving husband most worthy and deserving, with whom she lived in good accord without dissension.[147]

CIL, Vol. VI, No. 9,792 (= Dessau, No. 7,674)

[Rome]

To the spirits of the departed. You wanted to precede me, most sainted wife, and you have left me behind in tears. If there is anything good in the regions below—as for me, I lead a worthless life without you—be happy there too, sweetest Thalassia, nurse of a *vir clarissimus* and married to me for forty years. Paprius Vitalis, of the painters' craft, her husband, built this for his incomparable wife, himself, and their family.

[146] That is, in order to acquire for it, even while still empty, the religious and legal protection afforded tombs.
[147] Literally, "without hurting one another's feelings," "without getting on each other's nerves."

CIL, Vol. VI, No. 7,579 (= Dessau, No. 8,190)

[Rome]

To the departed spirit of Mevia Sophe. Gaius Maenius Cimber to his most sainted wife and protectress, my heart's desire, who lived with me 18 years, 3 months, 13 days, which I lived with her without cause for complaint. But now I complain to her spirit and demand her back of Dis,[148] or else, [ye gods], give me back to my wife, who lived with me so harmoniously to her dying day. Mevia Sophe, bring it to pass, if the spirits of the departed have any influence, that I need not suffer such a criminal separation any longer. Stranger, so may the earth rest lightly upon you after death as you do no damage here; or if anyone does damage, may the gods above not approve of him and the gods below not receive him, and may the earth rest heavily upon him.

CIL, Vol. VI, No. 18,817 (= Dessau, No. 8,006)

[Rome]

[Tomb of] a sainted cherished soul, sacred to the spirits of the departed. Furia Spes, freedwoman, to Sempronius Firmus, husband most dear to me. As boy and girl we were bound by mutual love at first sight. I lived with him but a very short time, and during the time we should have lived [together] we were separated by an evil hand. I beg of you, most holy spirit of the departed, take good care of my dear one, and please be most kind to him in the hours of the night, so that I may see him and he may wish me too to persuade fate to let me come and be with him tenderly and speedily.

CIL, Vol. VI, No. 18,131 (= Dessau, No. 8,155*a*)

[Rome]

To the spirits of the departed. Titus Flavius Martialis lies here. What I ate and drank is with me here; what I left behind is gone forever.

CIL, Vol. VIII, No. 3,463 (= Dessau, No. 8,162)

[Lambaesis, Africa]

Sacred to the spirits of the departed. To Aurelia Vercella, my wife most sweet, who lived seventeen years, more or less. I was not, I was, I am not, I have no more desires. Anthimus, her husband.

[148] The Roman god of the underworld, counterpart of the Greek Pluto.

73. *Education: The Curriculum*

Though the Roman Empire witnessed a great increase in the number of schools, there was nothing resembling a system of free public education. Formal education was available only to the children of the well-to-do. The initiative for the creation of lower schools was left in the hands of localities and parents able to pay. Institutions of higher learning flourished in leading urban centers, with Athens retaining its traditional place as the "university city" *par excellence*. But the emperors early adopted the royal rôle of patrons of learning and education, granting material privileges and sometimes even stipends to practitioners of the learned professions. The first such salaried professorship was the chair of literature and rhetoric to which Vespasian appointed Quintilian, the greatest of Roman rhetoricians, among whose pupils were the younger Pliny and probably Tacitus; other such chairs—at Rome, Athens, and elsewhere—were endowed by subsequent emperors. With the passage of time this patronage led the emperors to intervene increasingly in educational matters, and by the end of the third century practically all the schools of the Empire were under imperial control.

The curriculum of the Roman schools continued its traditional emphasis on grammar, rhetoric, literature, and philosophy, with oratory, "the mistress of all the arts," as the capstone (cf. Vol. I, §§ 186–187). But since the importance of political oratory in Roman public life ended with the fall of the Republic, leaving the law courts as almost the only practical outlet for oratorical skill, the training in the schools degenerated into rhetorical exercises divorced from reality. Attention was now fixed on style instead of content, the goal being artificial, superficial, epigrammatic brilliance developed through classroom recitations of several kinds. The most common of these were *declamationes,* or set pieces; *suasoriae,* speeches of deliberation, or self-persuasion, on imaginary, often fantastic, themes; and *controversiae,* debates in fictitious and frequently bizarrely contrived lawsuits. Roman education, it may be noted finally, continued to be bilingual until the end of the third century, when Greek began to disappear from the schools in the West.

INTELLECTUAL CAPACITY THE NATURAL BIRTHRIGHT
OF MEN

Quintilian *Institutes of Oratory* i. i. 1–3
From LCL

I would, therefore, have a father conceive the highest hopes of his son from the moment of his birth. If he does so, he will be more careful about the groundwork of his education. For there is absolutely no foundation for the complaint that but few men have the power to take in the knowledge that is imparted to them, and that the majority are so slow of understanding that education is a waste of time and labor. On the contrary, you will find that most are quick to reason and ready to learn. . . . Those who are dull and unteachable are as abnormal as prodigious births and monstrosities and are but few in number. A proof of what I say is to be found in the fact that boys commonly show promise of many accomplishments, and when such promise dies away as they grow up, this is plainly due not to the failure of natural gifts but to lack of requisite attention. But, it will be urged, there are differing degrees of intellectual ability. Undoubtedly, I reply, and there will be a corresponding variation in actual accomplishment; but that there are any who gain nothing from education, I absolutely deny.

EARLY TRAINING

Quintilian *Institutes of Oratory* I. i. 4–11
Adapted from LCL

Above all, see that the child's nurse speaks correctly. . . . No doubt the most important point is that they should be of good character; but they should speak correctly as well. It is the nurse that the child first hears, and her words that he will first attempt to imitate. And we are by nature most tenacious of childhood impressions. . . . Do not therefore allow the boy to become accustomed even in infancy to a style of speech that will have to be unlearned.

As regards parents, I should like to see them as highly educated as possible, and I do not restrict this remark to fathers alone. . . . And even those who have not had the fortune to receive a good education should not devote less care to their children's education but should for that very reason show all the greater diligence in other matters where they can help.

As regards the boys in whose company our budding orator is to be brought up, I would repeat what I have said about nurses. As regards his *paedagogi*,[149] I would urge in addition that they should have had a thorough education. . . . Still, if it should prove impossible to secure the ideal nurse, the ideal companions, or the ideal *paedagogus*, I would insist that there should be one person at any rate attached to the boy who has some knowledge of speaking and who will, if any incorrect expression is used by nurse or *paedagogus* in the presence of their charge, at once correct the error and prevent its becoming a habit.[150]

[149] A *paedagogus* was a slave who had charge of children at home and accompanied them to and from school.
[150] Tacitus comments on how careless of these precepts most parents were (*Dialogue on Oratory* xxix): "Nowadays we entrust the infant to any little Greek

BILINGUAL EDUCATION

Quintilian *Institutes of Oratory* I. i. 12–14
From LCL

I prefer that a boy should begin with Greek, because Latin, being in general use, will be picked up by him whether we will or no; while the fact that Latin learning is derived from Greek is a further reason for his being first instructed in the latter. I do not, however, desire that this principle should be so rigidly observed that he should for long speak and learn only Greek, as is generally done. Such a course gives rise to many faults of language and accent; the latter tends to acquire a foreign intonation, while the former through force of habit becomes impregnated with Greek idioms, which persist with extreme obstinacy even when we are speaking another tongue. The study of Latin ought therefore to follow at no great distance and in a short time proceed side by side with Greek. The result will be that, as soon as we begin to give equal attention to both languages, neither will prove a hindrance to the other.

LITERARY STUDIES

Quintilian *Institutes of Oratory* I. iv. 1–5
Adapted from LCL

As soon as the boy has learned to read and write without difficulty, it is the turn of the teacher of language and literature. My words apply equally to Greek and Latin teachers, though my preference is to start with a Greek; in either case the method is the same. This subject may be most briefly considered under two heads, the art of speaking correctly and the interpretation of the poets; but there is more beneath the surface than meets the eye. For the art of writing is connected with that of speaking, and faultless reading precedes interpretation, and in all of these criticism has its work to perform. . . . Nor is it sufficient to have read the poets only; every kind of writer must be carefully studied, not merely for the subject matter but for the vocabulary, for words often acquire authority from their use by a particular author. Nor can literary study be regarded as complete if it stops short of music, since meter and rhythm have to be taken up. Nor, if astronomy is omitted, can the poets be understood, since they, to mention nothing else, so frequently use

slave girl, with one or another of the male slaves to help her—usually the most worthless of the whole household, utterly unfit for any serious service. Tender and impressionable minds are filled from the very start with these slaves' stories and prejudices, and no one in the whole house cares a whit what he says or does in the presence of his infant master."

the rising and setting of the constellations to indicate time. Omission of philosophy, too, is a drawback, since there are numerous passages in almost every poem based on the most intricate questions of natural science, and Empedocles among the Greeks and Varro and Lucretius among the Latin authors actually expounded philosophical doctrines in verse. No small powers of eloquence also are required to enable the teacher to speak appropriately and fluently on each and every one of the various subjects just mentioned. For this reason those who criticize this branch of teaching as trivial and jejune deserve less consideration.[151] Unless the foundations of the orator-to-be are well and truly laid by this study of literature, the superstructure will collapse. This study is a necessity for boys and the delight of old age, the sweet companion of our privacy and the sole branch of study which has more solid substance than display.

DECLAMATION

Quintilian *Institutes of Oratory* II. x. 1–4
Adapted from LCL

These elementary stages are in themselves no small undertaking, but they are merely members and portions of the greater whole; when therefore the pupil has been thoroughly instructed and exercised in these departments, the time will as a rule have come for him to attempt deliberative and forensic themes.[152] But before I begin to discuss these, I must say a few words on the theory of declamation, which is at once the newest and most useful of rhetorical exercises, for it includes practically all the exercises of which we have been speaking and affords a close imitation of reality. As a result it has acquired such a vogue that many think that it is the sole training necessary to shape oratorical ability, since there is no virtue of ordinary speech which is not also to be found in this type of rhetorical exercise. But the actual practice of declamation has degenerated to such an extent through the fault of its teachers that it has come to be one of the chief causes of the corruption of modern oratory, such is the extravagance and ignorance of our declaimers. But it is possible to make sound use of anything that is naturally sound. The subjects chosen for themes should, therefore, be as true to life as possible,

---

[151] These criticisms, however, were directed not so much at the study as at the approach and methods used. Seneca, for example, writes (*Moral Epistles* cvi. 12): "It is clearly more useful to employ literature for the improvement of the mind, but we . . . waste our efforts on the inane. . . . We are educated not for life, but for the schoolroom."

[152] That is, *suasoriae* and *controversiae*: cf. introduction.

and the declamation should, to the greatest degree possible, be modeled on actual pleadings, as a training for which it was devised.

THE RHETORICIANS' SCHOOLS

Tacitus *Dialogue on Oratory* xxxv
'   *Adapted from LCL*

But nowadays our boys are escorted to the schools of those rhetoricians, as we call them—persons who came on the scene just before the time of Cicero but failed to find favor with our forefathers, as is obvious from the fact that the censors Crassus and Domitius ordered them to shut down what Cicero calls their "school of shamelessness." [153] They are escorted, as I was saying, to these schools, of which it would be hard to say what is most prejudicial to their intellectual growth, the place itself, or their fellow students, or the studies they pursue. The place has nothing about it that commands respect—no one enters it who is not as ignorant as the rest; there is no profit in the company of the students, since they are all boys or young men together, who are equally devoid of any feeling of responsibility whether they take the floor or make up the audience; and the exercises in which they engage largely defeat their purpose. You are of course aware that there are two kinds of subject matter handled in the rhetoricians' schools, the suasory and the controversial. Now, while the former is entrusted to mere boys, as being obviously of less importance and not making such demands of judgment, the more mature scholars are asked to deal with the latter—but, good heavens! what poor quality is shown in their themes, and how unnaturally they are made up! Then, in addition to a subject matter so remote from real life, there is the bombastic style in which it is presented. And so it comes about that themes such as "The Reward of the Tyrannicide," or "The Ravished Maid's Alternatives," or "A Remedy for the Plague," or "The Incestuous Mother," and all the other topics that are encountered every day in the school but seldom or never in actual legal practice, are set forth in magniloquent phraseology.

CLASSROOM EXERCISES

Seneca the Elder *Suasories* ii–vii

Each of the speeches in Seneca's handbook of rhetorical exercises is preceded by a brief statement of the subject. A selection from these captions is given here.

[153] Crassus and Domitius were censors in 92 B.C.; for their decree expelling rhetoricians from Rome, see Vol. I, p. 492.

Three hundred Spartans sent against Xerxes, when the contingents of three hundred sent from all [the rest of] Greece had fled, deliberate whether they too should flee.

Agamemnon deliberates whether he should sacrifice Iphigenia when Calchas avers that it is sinful to sail otherwise.

Alexander the Great deliberates whether he should enter Babylon after he has been warned of danger by a soothsayer's reply.

The Athenians deliberate whether they should remove their trophies of victory over Persia when Xerxes threatens to return unless they do.

Cicero deliberates whether he should beg Antony for mercy.

Cicero deliberates whether he should burn his writings since Antony promises he will be unharmed if he does.

Seneca the Elder *Controversies* i. ii, vi; ii. vii; iii. i; v. i

A priestess must be supremely chaste and pure. A maiden was captured by pirates and sold. She was bought by a procurer and made a prostitute. But she prevailed upon those who came to her to pay her her fee [without intercourse]. When she could not prevail upon a soldier who had come to her, and he struggled with her and attacked her, she killed him. She was indicted, acquitted, and returned to her people. She seeks to become a priestess. The petition is opposed.

.   .   .   .

A man was captured by pirates and wrote to his father for ransom; he was not ransomed. The daughter of the pirate chief made him swear that he would marry her if he were released, and he swore it. She left her father and eloped with the young man. He returned to his father and married her. A rich widow crosses their path. The father orders him to divorce the daughter of the pirate chief and marry the widow. He refuses and is disinherited.

.   .   .   .

A man who had a beautiful wife went abroad. A foreign merchant settled in the neighborhood of the woman. Three times he offered her money to commit adultery, and she refused. The merchant died, and in his will left the beautiful woman heir to all his property, adding the following words of praise: "I found her chaste." She accepted the inheritance. The husband returns and accuses her of adultery on suspicion.

.   .   .   .

A blind man is entitled to receive 1,000 *denarii* from the public treasury. Ten young men, when they had dissipated their fortunes, drew lots under an agreement that the one whose name was drawn would be blinded and thus get 1,000 *denarii*. The lot of one was drawn, and he was blinded. He applies for the 1,000 *denarii*. The application is denied.

.   .   .   .   .

Injury of known origin is actionable. A man whose life was wrecked, his three children and wife lost when his house burned, hanged himself. A passer-by cut down the noose. He is prosecuted by the released man for injury.

THE DECLINE OF ORATORY

Quintilian *Institutes of Oratory* VIII. Preface. 22–26
From LCL

The usual result of overattention to the niceties of style is the deterioration of our eloquence. . . . In our passion for words we paraphrase what might be said in plain language, repeat what we have already said at sufficient length, pile up a number of words where one would suffice, and regard allusion as better than directness of speech. So, too, all directness of speech is at a discount, and we think no phrase eloquent that another could conceivably have used. We borrow figures and metaphors from the most decadent poets and regard it as a real sign of genius that it should require a genius to understand our meaning. And yet Cicero long since laid down this rule in the clearest of language, that the worst fault in speaking is to adopt a style inconsistent with the idiom of ordinary speech and contrary to the common feeling of mankind. But nowadays our rhetoricians regard Cicero as lacking both polish and learning; we are far superior, for we look down upon everything that is dictated by nature as beneath our notice and seek not for the true ornaments of speech but for meretricious finery, as though there were any real virtue in words save in their power to represent facts. And if we have to spend our lives in a laborious effort to discover words which will at once be appropriate, lucid, and brilliant, and to arrange them with exact precision, we lose all the fruit of our studies.

Tacitus *Dialogue on Oratory* xxx–xxxii (abridged)

Only he is an orator who can speak on any topic with beauty and elegance and in a manner that carries conviction, in keeping with the importance of the subject, appropriately to the circumstances, with pleasure to the audience. The men of earlier days were convinced of this. They understood that to accomplish this required, not declaiming in rhetoricians' schools, not exercising merely the tongue and the voice in fictitious debates without any sort of approach to reality, but imbuing the mind with those disciplines that deal with good and evil, honor and dishonor, right and wrong; for this is the orator's subject matter. . . . The accomplished speakers of modern times are so completely unconcerned about this that you can detect in their pleadings the unseemly and shameful defects of modern colloquial speech. And also, they know nothing of legislation, have no grasp of the decrees of the senate, actually scoff at the civil law, and have a positive horror of the study of philosophy and the teachings of the sages. They have banished oratory, as it were, from her rightful realm and reduce her to a handful of commonplace and narrow platitudes, so that she who was once mistress of all the arts and imbued our minds with her noble retinue is now clipped and docked, without state, without esteem, I almost said without her free birthright, and is learned like one of the meanest handicrafts. This, then, is in my opinion the prime and principal reason why we have degenerated to such an extent from the eloquence of the orators of old.

74. Education: Imperial Patronage of the Learned Professions

The opposition of the Roman senatorial conservatives to Greek learning and its teachers died with the Republic. The Roman emperors adopted the practice of granting to members of the learned, artistic, and athletic professions subsidies, stipends, and certain legal privileges and exemptions (from taxation, from billeting of soldiers, from compulsory public services).

IMPERIAL SUBVENTION TO A PHILOSOPHER

Pliny *Letters* Book x, No. 58. 5

Letter of Domitian to Terentius Maximus [154]

Flavius Archippus the philosopher petitioned me to order an estate to be purchased for him for 100,000 sesterces [155] in the vicinity of Prusias, his native city, from the income of which he could support his family. I desire to grant him this. You will charge the sum expended to my "Personal Gifts" account.

[154] Apparently a procurator of imperial estates in Bithynia.
[155] This is the same amount as the salaries paid the holders of imperial professorships. Vespasian, Suetonius tells us in his biography (xvii–xviii), "greatly encouraged literary talent and the arts. He was the first to establish annual salaries of 100,000 sesterces from the fisc for Latin and Greek professors of rhetoric."

EXEMPTION PRIVILEGES

AE, 1936, No. 128 (= *FIRA*, Vol. I, Nos. 73 and 77)

[Pergamum, A.D. 74 and 93/94]

The Emperor Caesar VESPASIAN Augustus, *pontifex maximus*, holding the tribunician power for the sixth year, acclaimed *imperator* fourteen times, father of his country, consul five times and designate for a sixth, censor, declares:

Whereas professions befitting free men are deemed publicly and privately useful to cities and sacred to the gods, to wit, that of the grammarians and rhetoricians, who, under the aegis of Hermes and the Muses, train the minds of the youth to gentility and civic virtue, and that of the physicians and other practitioners, under the aegis of Apollo and Aesculapius, since the care of bodies has been entrusted solely to them[?];

Because these men are thus regarded as[?] sacred and godlike, I order that there is to be no billeting in their homes, nor are taxes to be exacted from them in any manner. And if any of those living under my rule shall dare to wrong, or demand security from, or bring an action against[?], any physician, teacher, or other practitioner, the offenders shall pay a fine of . . . drachmas to Jupiter Capitolinus; whoever cannot pay this sum shall have his property sold, and the fine imposed by the official in charge of this shall be consecrated to the god forthwith; likewise, if he hides and they find him, they may bring him before any tribunal they choose, without hindrance by anyone. And they are to have the undisturbed right to maintain societies in sacred precincts, sanctuaries, and temples, wherever they choose; if anyone shall eject them by force, he shall be brought to trial by the Roman people for sacrilege to the imperial house.

I, the Emperor Caesar Vespasian, have signed and ordered this to be posted in public.

Posted, year 6 . . . December 27.

.   .   .   .

The Emperor Caesar Domitian, holding the tribunician power for the thirteenth year, acclaimed *imperator* twenty-two times, censor for life, father of his country, to Aulus Licinius Mucianus and Gavius Priscus.

I have decided that the greed of physicians and teachers—who, not for the sake of culture but for the sake of increasing their gain, are most outrageously selling [instruction in] their art, which ought to be transmitted only to some freeborn youths, to many domestic[?] slaves sent to them for training—must be rigorously curbed. Therefore, whosoever of them takes a fee for teaching slaves is to be deprived of the privileges granted by my deified father. . . . [The rest is fragmentary.]

Justinian *Digest* xxvii. i. 6. 8–12

In the enactments of the Emperor Commodus there is cited a section of a rescript of Antoninus Pius in which it is made clear that philosophers, too, enjoy exemption from being appointed guardians. The exact wording is as follows: "Likewise my deified father,[156] immediately upon his accession, confirmed the existing privileges and immunities for all these by an edict declaring that philosophers, rhetoricians, grammarians, and physicians were exempt from the obligation to serve as gymnasiarchs, overseers of markets, or priests, or to provide billets, grain, or oil, and were not to serve on juries or on embassies or be conscripted into the army against their will or be forced into any other provincial or other service."

But this too must be understood, that only a man teaching or practicing in his home town enjoys this exemption. If a Comanite lectures on rhetoric or practices medicine or teaches in Neocaesarea, he does not enjoy exemption in Comana. This was ordained by the deified Severus and Antoninus.[157] [The jurist] Paulus, to be sure, stating that the deified Antoninus Pius had thus ordered, writes that learned men, both those above the approved number and those practicing in an alien city, are exempt. It was ordained by the deified Severus and Antoninus that a man lecturing on rhetoric in Rome either with or without salary enjoys release just as if he were teaching in his home town. For this enactment the following reasoning may be adduced: Since the imperial city is the common fatherland and is so regarded, then it is logical that such person should enjoy exemption as being one who makes himself useful in his native place. Teachers of law teaching in a province do not enjoy release, but those teaching in Rome are released.

THE EPICUREAN SCHOOL

This inscription of A.D. 121 records an exchange of correspondence between Plotina, Trajan's widow, and the Emperor Hadrian, her son by imperial adoption, concerning the succession to the headship of the Epicurean philosophical school in Athens. It not only illustrates Hadrian's philhellenism but reveals that even before his reign imperial intervention and control in educational matters had reached the point where the head of the school of Epicurus had to be a Roman citizen.

[156] That is, Hadrian.   [157] That is, Caracalla.

CIL, Vol. III, No. 12,283, lines 2–16 (= Dessau, No. 7,784 = FIRA, Vol. I, No. 79)

In the consulship of Marcus Annius Verus (for the second time) and Gnaeus Arrius Augur

Aula Plotina Augusta

How greatly I favor the school of Epicurus you know full well, my lord. The succession therein needs your help, for since none but a Roman citizen may be elected head of the school the choice is narrowly limited. I pray therefore on behalf of Popillius Theotimus, who is now the head at Athens, that you will allow him to provide by will in Greek [158] concerning that part of his instructions which pertains to the regulation of the headship, and to name a successor to himself of non-citizen status if he is so persuaded by the attainments of the person; and that future heads of the school may hereafter exercise with the same right the privilege you grant to Theotimus, all the more so because the practice is that whenever the testator errs concerning the choice of a head the best candidate is, by common consent, selected by the students of the school, and this will be easier if he can be chosen from a larger number.

The Emperor Caesar Trajanus HADRIAN Augustus to Popillius Theotimus. I permit him to draw his will in Greek in the matters pertaining to the headship of the Epicurean school. And since he will also choose a successor more easily if he has the privilege of naming even a noncitizen, I grant this also to him and to the others who hold the headship hereafter: this right may be transferred either to a noncitizen or to a Roman citizen.

Science and Pseudo Science in the Roman Empire

"Despite the stimulus that followed the contact with Alexandrian thought, Rome produced no great creative scientist. It is in the distribution and dissemination of the Greek wisdom rather than its development that we see the rôle of Rome" (C. Singer, "Science," in Cyril Bailey, ed., *The Legacy of Rome* [Oxford, 1923] 265). In the best of the Romans' scientific and technical knowledge, and in their underlying consideration of science as ancillary to ethics, the debt to Greece is everywhere apparent. Pliny (*Natural History* XXVII. i) boasts that the exchange of knowledge was "ensured to us by the immense majesty of the Roman peace," but he is fully aware of the stagna-

[158] Cf. introduction to § 71.

tion of theoretical and technical progress. The same author relates (XXXVI. lxvi. 195)—the story may of course be apocryphal—that, "in the reign of Tiberius . . . when a way of preparing glass was invented to make it flexible, the workshop of the artisan was completely destroyed to prevent the value of bronze, silver, and gold from depreciating." (In the version of Petronius *Satyricon* li, the inventor was put to death by the emperor's order.) The characteristic emphasis placed by the Romans on the practical application of scientific knowledge (especially in engineering and military installations), their suspicion of and contempt for theoretical science, their conviction, fostered by the determinism of Stoicism, of the worthlessness of research, and the basic economic parasitism of the Roman landed ruling class brought scientific advance to a standstill by the end of the second century. The last great scientific minds of antiquity were the mathematician, astronomer, and geographer Ptolemy and the physician and medical writer Galen, both Greeks. With the victory of astrology, irrationalism, and the Eastern mystery religions over the minds of men in the crisis of the third century, the eclipse of ancient science was complete.

75. *The Paucity of Research*

Pliny *Natural History* ii. xlv. 117–18
From LCL

More than twenty Greek authors of the past have published observations about these subjects. This makes me all the more surprised that, although when the world was at variance and split up into kingdoms, that is, sundered limb from limb, so many people devoted themselves to these abstruse researches, especially when wars surrounded them and hosts were untrustworthy, and also when pirates, the foes of all mankind, were holding up the transmission of information—so that nowadays a person may learn some facts about his own region from the notebooks of people who have never been there more truly than from the knowledge of the natives—yet now in these glad times of peace, under an emperor who so delights in the advancement of letters and science,[159] no addition whatever is being made to knowledge by means of original research, and in fact even the discoveries of our predecessors are not being thoroughly studied. The rewards were not greater when those ample successes were being contributed by many students, and in fact the majority of these made the discoveries in question with no other reward at all save the consciousness of benefiting posterity. Age has overtaken the character of mankind, not their revenues, and now that every sea has been opened up and every coast affords a hospitable land-

[159] For Vespasian's patronage of the learned professions, see § 74, first and second selections.

ing, an immense multitude goes on voyages—but their object is profit not knowledge; and in their blind engrossment with avarice they do not reflect that knowledge is a more reliable means even of making profit.

76. Farmers' Almanacs

Columella *On Agriculture* XI. ii (selections)

JANUARY

13. Windy weather; unsettled conditions.
15. Unsettled weather.
16. Sun enters Aquarius; Leo begins to set in the morning; southwest wind, sometimes south wind with rain.
17. Cancer finishes setting; cold.
18. Aquarius begins to rise; southwest wind forecasts storm.
22. Lyra sets in the evening; rainy day.
24. Setting of Cetus forecasts storm; sometimes actual storms.
27. The bright star on the breast of Leo sets, sometimes forecasts winter half over.
28. South or southwest wind; cold, rainy day.
30. Delphinus begins to set; Lyra also sets.
31. Setting of the above-mentioned constellations brings storm, sometimes only forecasts storm.

[There follow instructions, here omitted, on the farm operations to be performed in the above half month.]

FEBRUARY

1. Lyra begins to set; east wind, sometimes south wind with hail.
3. Lyra sets completely, Leo half; northwest or north wind, sometimes west wind.
5. Half of Aquarius rises; windy weather.
7. The constellation Callisto sets; west winds begin to blow.
8. Windy weather.
11. East wind.
[There follow the farming operations, here omitted.]
13. Sagittarius sets in the evening; severe cold.
14. Crater rises in the evening; change of wind.
15. Sun enters Pisces; sometimes windy weather.
17, 18. West or south wind, with hail and rain storms.
20. Leo finishes setting; the north winds called the "bird winds" generally blow for thirty days; then the swallow returns.

21. Arcturus rises at dusk; chill day with north or northwest wind, sometimes rainy.

22. Sagittarius begins to rise at twilight; variable weather; [period] called "halcyon days"—great calm observed in Atlantic Ocean.

23. Windy weather; swallows are sighted.
    [Agricultural instructions, here omitted.]

•   •   •   •

JUNE

13. Hot weather begins.

19. Sun enters Cancer; forecasts storm.

21. Serpentarius, called Ophiuchus by the Greeks, sets in the morning; forecasts storm.

24, 25, 26. Solstice; west wind and heat.

29. Windy weather.
    [Agricultural instructions, here omitted.]

•   •   •   •

SEPTEMBER

13. Cetus sometimes forecasts storm.

17. Arcturus rises; west or southwest wind, sometimes the east wind that some call Vulturnus.

18. The brightest star of Virgo rises; west or northwest wind.

19. Sun enters Libra; Crater appears in the morning.

21. Pisces sets in the morning; likewise Aries begins to set; west or northwest wind, sometimes south wind with rain squalls.

22. The constellation Argo sets; forecasts storm, sometimes rain.

23. Centaurus begins to rise in the morning; forecasts storm, sometimes rain.

24, 25, 26. Autumnal equinox forecasts rain.

27. Capricornus rises; west wind, sometimes south wind with rain.

28. Virgo finishes rising; forecasts storm.

[Agricultural instructions, here omitted.]

CIL, Vol. VI, No. 2,305 (= Dessau, No. 8,745)

Month of January. 31 days. The Nones fall on the fifth day. The day has 9¾ hours. The night has 14¼ hours. The sun is in the sign of Capricorn. The month is under the protection of Juno. Stakes are sharpened. Willow and reeds are cut. Sacrifices to the household gods.

Month of February. 28 days. The Nones fall on the fifth day. The day has 10¾ hours. The night has 13¼ hours. The sun is in the sign of Aquarius. The month is under the protection of Neptune. The grain fields are weeded. The part of the vines above ground is tended. Reeds are burned. Parentalia, Lupercalia, Dear Relatives' Day, Terminalia.[160]

Month of March. 31 days. The Nones fall on the seventh day. The day has 12 hours. The night has 12 hours. The equinox falls on the twenty-fifth day. The sun is in the sign of Pisces. The month is under the protection of Minerva. The vines are propped up in trenched ground and pruned. Three-month wheat is sown. The bark of Isis.[161] Sacrifices to Mamurius. Liberalia, Quinquatria, Bathing.[162]

Month of April. 30 days. The Nones fall on the fifth day. The day has 13½ hours. The night has 10½ hours. The sun is in the sign of Aries. The month is under the protection of Venus. The lustration of the sheep is made. Sacrifices to the Isis of Pharus.[163] Also festival of Sarapis.

Month of May. 31 days. The Nones fall on the seventh day. The day has 14½ hours. The night has 9½ hours. The sun is in the sign of Taurus. The month is under the protection of Apollo. The grain fields are cleared of weeds. The sheep are shorn. The wool is washed. Young steers are put under the yoke. The vetch for fodder is cut. The lustration of the grain fields is made. Sacrifices to Mercury and Flora.

Month of June. 30 days. The Nones fall on the fifth day. The day has 15 hours. The night has 9 hours. The solstice falls on the twenty-fourth day. The sun is in the sign of Gemini. The month is under the protection of Mercury. The hay is mown. The vines are cultivated. Sacrifice to Hercules and Fors Fortuna.

Month of July. 31 days. The Nones fall on the seventh day. The day has 14¼ hours. The night has 9¾ hours. The sun is in the sign of Cancer. The month is under the protection of Jupiter. Barley and beans are harvested. Apollinaria, Neptunalia.

Month of August. 31 days. The Nones fall on the fifth day. The day has 13 hours. The night has 11 hours. The sun is in the sign of Leo. The month is under the protection of Ceres. The stakes are prepared. Cereals are harvested, likewise the wheat. The stubble is burned. Sacrifices to Hope, Safety, and Diana. Volcanalia.

Month of September. 30 days. The Nones fall on the fifth day. The day has 12 hours. The night has 12 hours. The equinox falls on the twenty-fourth day. The sun is in the sign of Virgo. The month is under the protection of Vulcan. The casks are smeared with pitch. Fruits are gathered. The earth around the trees is dug up. Feast of Minerva.

[160] For some of the traditional Roman festivals mentioned here and below, see Vol. I, §§ 9 and 180.
[161] For this ceremony see § 171, third selection. It is interesting to note in this calendar the fusion of Roman religion with the worship of the Egyptian gods Isis and Osiris.
[162] A purification ceremony characteristic of mystery cults; cf. § 171.
[163] Pharus was the famous lighthouse in the harbor of Alexandria, Egypt.

Month of October. 31 days. The Nones fall on the seventh day. The day has 10¾ hours. The night has 13¼ hours. The sun is in the sign of Libra. The month is under the protection of Mars. Grape gathering. Sacrifices to Bacchus.

Month of November. 30 days. The Nones fall on the fifth day. The day has 9½ hours. The night has 14½ hours. The sun is in the sign of Scorpion. The month is under the protection of Diana. Sowing of wheat and barley. Digging of trenches for trees. Feast of Jupiter. Discovery.[164]

Month of December. 31 days. The Nones fall on the fifth day. The day has 9 hours. The night has 15 hours. The sun is in the sign of Sagittarius. The month is under the protection of Vesta. Beginning of winter, or winter solstice. The vines are manured. Beans are sown. Wood is cut. Olives are gathered and also sold. Saturnalia.

77. Architecture and Engineering

THE TRAINING OF THE ARCHITECT

Vitruvius *Architecture* i. i. 1–11 (abridged)
*Adapted in part from M. H. Morgan's translation (Cambridge, 1914),
in part from LCL*

The architect should be equipped with knowledge of many branches of study and varied kinds of learning, for it is by his judgment that all work done by the other arts is put to the test. This service of his is the child of practice and theory. Practice is the continuous and regular exercise of employment where manual work is done with any necessary material according to the design of the drawing. Theory, on the other hand, is the ability to demonstrate and explain things wrought in accordance with technical skill and method. It follows, therefore, that architects who have aimed at acquiring manual skill without theory have not been able to reach a position of authority to correspond to their pains, while those who relied only on theories and learning were obviously hunting the shadow, not the substance. . . .

He should be a man of letters, a skillful draftsman, instructed in geometry, versed in history, and a diligent student of philosophy; he should understand music, have some knowledge of medicine, know the opinions of the jurists, and be acquainted with astronomy and the theory of the heavens. The reasons for all this are as follows. An architect ought to be a man of letters so as to leave a lasting record in his treatises. Sec-

[164] A festival of Osiris.

ondly, he must have skill in draftsmanship so that he can readily make sketches to show the appearance of the work which he proposes. Geometry, also, is of much assistance in architecture, and in particular it teaches us the use of the rule and compasses, and this facilitates the planning of buildings on their sites, and the truing of them by the use of the square, the level, and the plummet. By means of optics, again, light in buildings can be properly drawn from definite quarters of the sky. It is true that by arithmetic the total cost of buildings is calculated, and measurements are computed, but difficult questions involving symmetry are solved by means of geometrical theories and methods.

A wide knowledge of history is requisite because, among the ornamental parts of an architect's design for a work, there are many the underlying idea of whose employment he should be able to explain to inquirers. . . . As for philosophy, it makes an architect high-minded, so that he may not be self-assuming but rather urbane, just, loyal, and without avariciousness. This is very important, for no work can be rightly done without honesty and incorruptibility. . . . Furthermore, philosophy treats of physics (in Greek, *physiologia*), where a rather careful knowledge is required because the problems which come under this head are numerous and varied; as, for example, in the case of water supply. . . . Music, also, the architect ought to know so that he may have knowledge of canonical and mathematical theory, and besides be able to adjust properly ballistas, catapults, and scorpions. For to the right and left in the beams are the holes of the "half tones" [165] through which ropes of twisted thongs are stretched by means of windlasses and levers, and these ropes must not be clamped and made fast until they make clear and equal sounds in the ear of the skilled workman. . . . If they are not of equal tone, they will prevent the course of the projectiles from being straight. . . . Water engines, too, and the other instruments which resemble them cannot be made by one who is without the principles of music.

The architect should also have a knowledge of the study of medicine on account of questions of climate . . . air, the healthiness and unhealthiness of sites, and water supply. For without these considerations, the healthiness of a dwelling cannot be assured. And as for laws, he should know those which are necessary in the case of buildings having party walls, those with reference to water dripping from the eaves, and also those about drains and windows. The water supply, also, and other things of this sort should be known to architects, so that before they begin building they may be careful not to leave disputes to the proprietors after the work is completed, and so that in drawing up specifications

[165] Or possibly, "equal tones."

the interests of both employer and contractor may be wisely safe-guarded. For if specifications are skillfully drawn, each may obtain a release from the other without captious objections. By astronomy, also, we find the east, west, south, and north, as well as the theory of the heavens, the equinox, solstice, and courses of the stars. If one has no knowledge of these matters he will not be able to have any comprehension of the theory of sundials.

WATER SUPPLY

Vitruvius *Architecture* viii. vi

*Adapted in part from M. H. Morgan's translation (Cambridge, 1914),
in part from LCL*

The supply of water is made by three methods: by channels through walled conduits, or by lead pipes, or by earthenware pipes. And they are arranged as follows. In the case of conduits, the structure must be very solid; the bed of the channel must be leveled with a fall of not less than half a foot in 100 feet. The walled conduits are to be arched over so that the minimum amount of sun may strike the water. When it comes to the city walls, a reservoir is to be made. To this reservoir a triple distribution tank is to be joined to receive the water; and three pipes of equal size are to be placed in the reservoir, leading to the adjoining tanks, so that when there is an overflow from the two outer tanks, it may deliver into the middle tank. From the middle tank pipes will be laid to all basins and fountains; from the second tank to the baths, in order to furnish an annual revenue to the treasury; to avoid a deficiency in the public supply, private houses are to be supplied from the third, for private persons will not be able to divert the water, since they have their own limited supply from the distribution sources. Another reason why I have made these divisions is that those who take private supplies into their houses may by their taxes paid through tax farmers contribute to the maintenance of the water supply.

If, however, there are hills between the city and the source, we must proceed as follows: underground channels are to be dug and leveled to the fall mentioned above. If the bed is of tufa or stone, the channel may be cut in it; but if it is of soil or sand, the bed of the channel and the walls with the vaulting must be constructed, and the water should be thus conducted. Air shafts are to be so constructed that they are 120 feet apart.

But if the supply is to be by lead pipes, first of all a reservoir is to be built at the source. Then the opening of the pipe is to be determined in accordance with the amount of water, and these pipes are to be laid from the source reservoir to a reservoir which is inside the city. The pipes are to be cast in lengths of not less than ten feet. If the lead pipes are *hundreds*, they should weigh 1,200 lbs. each; if *eighties*, 960 lbs.; if *fifties*, 600 lbs.; if *forties*, 480 lbs.; if *thirties*, 360 lbs.; if *twenties*, 240 lbs.; if *fifteens*, 180 lbs.; if *tens*, 120 lbs.; if *eights*, 100 lbs.; if *fives*, 60 lbs. The pipes receive their size names from the width in inches of the sheets of lead before they are rolled into pipes; for when a pipe is made of a sheet of lead 50 inches wide, it is called a *fifty*, and similarly the rest.

When an aqueduct is to be made with lead pipes it is to have the following arrangement. If there is a fall from the source to the city and the intervening hills are not high enough to interrupt the supply, then if there are valleys, we must build substructures to bring it up to a level, as in the case of channels and conduits. If the way round the valley is not long, a circuit should be used; but if the valleys are expansive, the course will be directed down the hill, and when it reaches the bottom it is carried on a low substructure so that the level there may continue as far as possible. This will form a "belly," which the Greeks call *koilia*. When the "belly" comes to the hill opposite, and the long distance of the "belly" makes the water slow in welling up, the water is to be forced to the height of the top of the hill. . . .

Again, it is not without advantage to put reservoirs at intervals of 24,000 feet, so that if a break occurs anywhere neither the whole load of water nor the whole structure need be disturbed, and the place where it has occurred may be more easily found. But these reservoirs are to be neither in the descent nor on the level portion of the "belly," nor at risings, nor anywhere in a valley, but on unbroken level ground.

But if we wish to employ a less expensive method, we must proceed as follows. Earthenware pipes are to be made not less than two inches thick, but these pipes should be so tongued at one end that they can fit into and join one another. The joints are to be coated with quicklime mixed with oil. . . . Everything also is to be fixed as for lead pipes. Further, when the water is first let in from the source, ashes are to be put in beforehand, so that if any joints are not sufficiently coated they may be lined with the ashes.

Water supply by earthenware pipes has these advantages. First, in the construction: if a break occurs, anybody can repair it. Again, water is much more wholesome from earthenware pipes than from lead pipes. For it seems to be made injurious by lead, because white lead is produced by it; and this is said to be harmful to the human body. So if what is produced by anything is injurious, there is no doubt that the thing itself is not wholesome. We can take an example from the workers in lead who have complexions affected by pallor. For when lead is smelted in casting, the fumes from it settle on the members of the body and, burning them, rob the limbs of the virtues of the blood. Therefore it seems that water should by no means be brought in lead pipes if we desire to have it wholesome. Everyday life can be used to show that the flavor from earthenware pipes is better, because everybody (even those who load their tables with silver vessels) uses earthenware to preserve the purity of water.

But if we are to create springs from which the water supplies come, we must dig wells. In digging wells we must not make light of science. The methods of nature must be considered closely in the light of intelligence and experience, because the soil contains an abundance of various elements. For, like everything else, it is composed of the four elements. First, it is itself earthy; and of the moist element, it has springs of water; likewise, it has heat, from which sulphur, alum, and bitumen arise; and mighty currents of air. When these currents are heavy and come through the porous intervals of soil to the wells which are being dug, they affect the excavators in that the nature of the exhalation chokes the animal spirits in their nostrils. Hence those who fail to escape quickly die there. The precautions against this are to be carried out as follows. Let a lighted lamp be lowered. If it remains alight the descent will be accomplished without danger. If, however, the light is extinguished by the power of the exhalation, then air shafts are to be dug right and left adjoining the well. In this way the bad vapors will be dissipated, as the air is through the nostrils. When this has been arranged and we come to the water, then let it be enclosed by walling without blocking up the veins.

But if the soil is hard, or if the veins of water lie too deep, then supplies of water are to be collected from the roofs or higher ground in concrete cisterns. . . . If the cisterns are made double or triple, so that they can be changed by percolation, they will make the supply of water much more wholesome. For when the sediment has a place to settle in, the water will be more limpid and will keep its taste without any smell. If not, salt must be added to purify it.

78. Geography

Great advances were made during the Empire in the practical exploration and mapping of the known world. In the field of geography, as in other branches of learning, most of the theoretical work was done by Greeks.

THE LIMITS OF THE KNOWN WORLD

Pliny *Natural History* ii. lxvii
From LCL

Today the whole of the west is navigated from Gades and the Pillars of Hercules [166] all around Spain and Gaul. But the larger part of the Northern Ocean was explored under the patronage of the deified Augustus, when a fleet sailed round Germany to the promontory of the Cimbrians,[167] and thence, seeing a vast sea in front of them or learning of it by report, reached the region of Scythia and localities numb with excessive moisture. On this account it is extremely improbable that there is no sea in those parts, as there is a superabundance of the moist element there. But next, on the eastward side, the whole quarter under the same star stretching from the Indian Ocean to the Caspian Sea was navigated throughout by the Macedonian forces in the reigns of Seleucus and Antiochus.[168] . . . And around the Caspian many coasts of the ocean have been explored, and very nearly the whole of the north has been completely navigated from one side to the other, so that similarly there is now overwhelming proof, leaving no room for conjecture, of the existence of the Maeotic Marsh, whether it be a gulf of that ocean, as I notice many have believed, or an overflow from it from which it is separated by a narrow space. On the other side of Gades, from the same western point, a great part of the Southern Gulf is navigated today in the circuit of Mauretania. Indeed, the greater part of it Alexander the Great's eastern conquests also explored as far as the Arabian Gulf; in which, when Augustus' son Gaius Caesar was operating there, it is said that figureheads of ships from Spanish wrecks were identified. Also, when the power of Carthage flourished, Hanno sailed round from Gades to the extremity of Arabia [169] and published a memoir of his voyage, as did Himilco when despatched at the same date to explore the outer coasts of Europe. Moreover, we have it on the authority of Cornelius Nepos that a certain contemporary of his named Eudoxus when fleeing from King Lathyrus [170] emerged from the Arabian Gulf and sailed right around to Gades; [171] and much before him Coelius Antipater states that

[166] That is, Cádiz and the Strait of Gibraltar.   [167] Cape Skagen, Jutland.
[168] The Caspian Sea was believed to have a narrow outlet into an outer ocean.
[169] This is untrue. Hanno was a Carthaginian explorer of the end of the sixth century B.C. who sailed down the west coast of Africa starting from Gades, but disappeared on the voyage.
[170] Ptolemy IX Lathyrus, King of Egypt 116–81 B.C.
[171] This is untrue. The Greek navigator Eudoxus, after exploring the east coast of Africa, attempted to circumnavigate Africa starting from Gades, but disappeared on the voyage.

he had seen someone who had gone on a trading voyage from Spain to Ethiopia.[172] Nepos also records as to the northern circuit that Quintus Metellus Celer, colleague of Afranius in the consulship but at the time proconsul of Gaul,[173] received from the king of the Suebians a present of some Indians, who on a trading voyage had been carried off their course by storms to Germany. Thus there are seas encircling the globe on every side and dividing it in two, so robbing us of half the world, since there is no region affording a passage from there to here or from here to there.[174]

THE SPHERICITY OF THE EARTH

Strabo *Geography* I. i. 20 (abridged)
From LCL

Most of all, it seems to me, we need . . . geometry and astronomy for a subject like geography. . . . Just as these sciences prove for us in other treatises all that has to do with the measurement of the earth as a whole, and as I must in this treatise take for granted and accept the propositions proved there, so I must take for granted that the universe is spheroidal, and also that the earth's surface is spheroidal . . .[175] and I need only indicate, in a brief and summary way, whether a proposition comes—if it really does—within the range of sense perception or of intuitive knowledge. Take, for example, the proposition that the earth is spheroidal. Whereas the suggestion of this proposition comes to us mediately from the law that bodies tend toward the center and that each body inclines toward its own center of gravity, the suggestion comes immediately from the phenomena observed at sea and in the heavens; for our sense perception and also our intuition can bear testimony in the latter case. For instance, it is obviously the curvature of the sea that prevents sailors from seeing distant lights that are placed on a level with their eyes. At any rate, if the lights are elevated above the level of the eyes they become visible, even though they be at a greater distance from the eyes; and similarly if the eyes themselves are elevated, they see what

---

[172] That is, around the southern tip of Africa. There is, however, no reliable evidence that the continent of Africa was ever circumnavigated in ancient times.

[173] That is, 62 B.C.

[174] This ancient theory involved the existence of another land mass in the antipodes, now the Americas. Cf. Note 175.

[175] Strabo (*Geography* I. iv. I) also commends the deduction of the Hellenistic geographer Eratosthenes "that if the earth is spheroidal, just as the universe is, it is inhabited all the way round." The polymath Posidonius (cf. Vol. I, p. 13, Note 10) "conjectures that the length of the inhabited world, about 70,000 stades, is half of the whole circle on which it has been taken, so that, he says, by sailing straight from the west the same distance one would come to India" (Strabo II. iii. 6).

was before invisible. . . . So also, when sailors are approaching land, the different parts of the shore become revealed progressively, more and more, and what at first appeared to be low-lying land gradually grows higher and higher.

ON MAP MAKING

"Drawing a map on a sphere," writes Ptolemy [176] (*Geography* I. xx), "gives the likeness of the shape of the earth . . . but it is not easy to make it large enough to provide room for the many details that will need to be indicated, and it is impossible to fix one's sight on the whole shape at one time. . . . Making the map on a plane surface is altogether free from these inconveniences, but requires a certain adjustment to correspond to the spherical form, in order to make the distances . . . on the unfolded surface commensurate with the real distances." He proceeds in the two following chapters to give instructions for making the two types of map.

Ptolemy *Geography* I. xxi–xxii
From M. R. Cohen and I. E. Drabkin, A Source Book in Greek Science
(New York, 1948)

PRECAUTIONS TO BE TAKEN IN THE CASE OF A
MAP DRAWN ON A PLANE

For the aforesaid reasons it would be well to keep the lines which represent meridians straight, and to make those which represent parallels of latitude arcs of circles drawn about one and the same center. Now, from this center, taken at the north pole, the straight meridian lines will have to be drawn in such a way that above all the resemblance, both as to form and appearance, to a spherical surface may be preserved. For the meridian lines cut the parallels of latitude here, too, at right angles and at the same time meet at the same common pole.

Now since it is impossible to preserve the spherical proportions through all the parallels of latitude, it would be sufficient to do so for the parallel through Thule [177] and for the equator. In this way the boundaries which encompass our latitudes may be accurately proportioned, and the parallel through Rhodes on which the most numerous measurements of longitudinal distance have been made may be divided in accordance with the ratio it bears to the meridian circle, that is, in

---

[176] Claudius Ptolemy (A.D. c.90–168), who worked at Alexandria, was the greatest geographer of antiquity. His celebrated work on astronomy is preserved only in Arabic translation and is known accordingly by its Arabic title *Almagest;* his equally famous *Geography* is the most scientific ancient work on the subject and the foundation of all modern cartography.

[177] The name used in antiquity to designate the northernmost point of the known world. Ptolemy, for example, held this to be the Shetland Islands.

accordance with the ratio of approximately 4 to 5 measured along equal arcs. This is Marinus's method.[178] Thus the length of the better-known part of the inhabited earth would be in proper relation to its breadth. The method of doing this we shall make clear after we have set forth how a map may be made on a sphere.

HOW THE INHABITED EARTH MAY BE REPRESENTED ON A SPHERE

The decision as to the size of the sphere will depend on the number of details the mapmaker wishes to include. And this, in turn, will depend on his skill and ambition, for as the sphere is increased the amount of detail and the accuracy of the map will likewise be increased. But whatever the size of the sphere is to be, we determine its poles and then carefully attach to it through the poles a semicircle raised just enough from the spherical surface to keep it from rubbing against the sphere as it rotates. This semicircle should be narrow so that it may not cover up many places. One of its edges should extend exactly between the points which mark the poles so that we may draw the meridian lines with that edge. We shall divide the latter into 180 parts and mark the numbers beginning with the midpoint of the semicircle where it will intersect the equator. Now similarly we shall draw the equator, and divide one of the semicircles comprising it into 180 parts, again setting the numbers opposite these parts, beginning with the boundary through which we are to draw the westernmost meridian line.

Now we shall make our map on the basis of the tables of degrees of longitude and latitude for each of the places to be represented, using the divisions on the semicircles, viz., the equator and the movable meridian. We turn the latter to the degree of longitude indicated, that is, to the division of the equator corresponding to that number, and we measure the latitudinal distance from the equator according to the divisions on the meridian. We place a mark corresponding to the indicated number of degrees just as we make a star map on a solid sphere.

Similarly, it will be possible to draw meridians at intervals of as many degrees of longitude as we wish, using as a ruler the aforesaid divided edge of the semicircular ring. It will also be possible to draw parallels of latitude at as great intervals as we wish, by placing the marker next to that number on the edge which indicates the latitude desired, and turning the marker and the semicircular ring as far as the meridians that indicate the limits of the known portion of the earth.

[178] Marinus of Tyre, the leading geographer of the generation preceding Ptolemy's, and the latter's principal source. He made the first attempt to draw a map of the world on the principle now known as projection.

79. *Medicine*

The status of the medical profession rose greatly during the Empire, the same
privileges and immunities being granted to doctors, who were almost exclusively Greeks, slaves, and freedmen, as to members of other learned professions (see § 74). There was no state certification or supervision of medical
practice, and widespread charlatanry and reliance on superstition and the
irrational prevailed. Nevertheless, there were advances in empirical knowledge, and great strides were made in the organization of military medicine
and in the development of a hospital system.

THE ART OF MEDICINE

Celsus [179] *On Medicine* 1. Preface. 1–5, 12, 74–75
From LCL

Just as agriculture promises nourishment to healthy bodies, so does
the art of medicine promise health to the sick. Nowhere is this art lacking, for the most uncivilized nations have knowledge of herbs, and other
things to hand for the aiding of wounds and diseases. This art, however,
has been cultivated among the Greeks much more than in other nations—
not, however, even among them from their first beginnings but only for
a few generations before ours. . . . Diseases were [in olden times]
ascribed to the anger of the immortal gods, and from them help used to
be sought; and it is probable that with no aids against bad health, nonetheless health was generally good because of good habits, which neither
indolence nor luxury had vitiated; since it is these two which have
afflicted the bodies of men, first in Greece and later amongst us. . . .

Of the different divisions of the art of medicine, the one which heals
diseases, as it is the most difficult, is also the most famous; hence we must
speak about it first. . . . There is a primary difference of opinion, some
holding that the sole knowledge necessary is derived from experience,
others propounding that practice is not sufficient except after acquiring
a reasoned knowledge of human bodies and of nature. . . .

[Celsus then presents the leading arguments of the theorists (or dogma-
tists) and of the empiricists.]

I am of the opinion that the art of medicine ought to be rational
but should also draw instruction from evident causes, all obscure ones

[179] Aulus Cornelius Celsus (early first century A.D.) was the author of an encyclopedia treating of medicine, agriculture, warfare, rhetoric, philosophy, and juris-
prudence. Only the section on medicine is extant. Whether he was a practicing
physician is much disputed.

being rejected from the practice of the art, although not from the practitioner's study. But to dissect the bodies of men while still alive is as cruel as it is needless; [180] that of the dead is a necessity for learners, who should know positions and relations, which the dead body exhibits better than does a living and wounded man. As for the remainder, which can only be learned from the living, actual practice will demonstrate it in the course of treating the wounded in a somewhat slower yet much milder way.

CLINICAL OBSERVATION THROUGH VIVISECTION

Galen [181] *On the Natural Faculties* III. iv. 155–57
From LCL

Suppose you should fill any animal whatsoever with liquid food—an experiment I have often carried out in pigs, to whom I give a sort of mess of wheaten flour and water, thereafter cutting them open after three or four hours; if you will do this yourself, you will find the food still in the stomach. For it is not chylification [182] which determines the length of its stay here—since this can also be effected outside the stomach; the determining factor is digestion, which is a different thing from chylification, as are blood production and nutrition. For just as . . . these two processes depend upon a change of qualities, similarly also the digestion of food in the stomach involves a transmutation of it into the quality proper to that which is receiving nourishment. Then, when it is completely digested, the lower outlet opens and the food is quickly ejected through it, even if there should be amongst it abundance of stones, bones, grape pips, or other things which cannot be reduced to chyle. And you may observe this yourself in an animal, if you will try to hit upon the time at which the descent of food from the stomach takes place. But even if you should fail to discover the time and nothing was yet passing down and the food was still undergoing digestion in the stomach, still even then you would find dissection not without its uses. You will observe, as we have just said, that the pylorus is accurately

180 Vivisection was practiced on criminals supplied to Hellenistic researchers by the Ptolemaic rulers of Egypt, according to Celsus I. Preface. 23.

181 The Greek physician Claudius Galen (A.D. c.130–c.200), a native of Pergamum, was the most important ancient writer on medicine. He attained a brilliant reputation throughout the Roman world, and was for some years consulting physician to the Emperor Marcus Aurelius. His great contribution in his prolific writings consists in the systematization of much of Greek medical theory. In particular, he gave definitive form to the theory of the four humors, which remained the basis of medical practice until the eighteenth century.

182 That is, the mere mechanical breakdown of food, as opposed to the distinctive altering action of digestion.

closed, and that the whole stomach is in a state of contraction upon the food very much as the womb contracts upon the foetus. . . .

Now, I have personally, on countless occasions, divided the peritoneum of a still living animal and have always found all the intestines contracting peristaltically upon their contents. The condition of the stomach, however, is found less simple; as regards the substances freshly swallowed, it had grasped these accurately both above and below, in fact at every point, and was as devoid of movement as though it had grown round and become united with the food. At the same time I found the pylorus persistently closed and accurately shut, like the os uteri on the foetus. In the cases, however, where digestion had been completed the pylorus had opened, and the stomach was undergoing peristaltic movements, similar to those of the intestines.

THE FOUR HUMORS

Galen *On the Natural Faculties* ii. viii. 116–18
From LCL

Aristotle stated and demonstrated [that] our bodies [are] compounded out of the Warm, the Cold, the Dry, and the Moist, that among these qualities the Warm is the most active, and that those animals which are by nature warmest have abundance of blood, whilst those that are colder are entirely lacking in blood, and consequently in winter lie idle and motionless, lurking in holes like corpses. . . . Now I, for my part, as I have already said, did not set before myself the task of stating what has been so well demonstrated by the ancients, since I cannot surpass these men either in my views or in my method of giving them expression. Doctrines, however, which they either stated without demonstration, as being self-evident . . . or else which they omitted to mention at all— these I propose to discover and prove.

Now in reference to the genesis of the humors, I do not know that anyone could add anything wiser than what has been said by Hippocrates, Aristotle, Praxagoras, Philotimus,[183] and many others among the ancients. These men demonstrated that when the nutriment becomes altered in the veins by the innate heat, blood is produced when it is in moderation, and the other humors [184] when it is not in proper proportion. And all the observed facts agree with this argument. . . . How could it be otherwise? For, seeing that every part functions in its own special way because of the manner in which the four qualities are compounded,

[183] Praxagoras and Philotimus were successive leaders of the Hippocratic school in the fourth century B.C.
[184] That is, bile, black bile, and phlegm.

it is absolutely necessary that the function [activity] should be either completely destroyed, or at least hampered, by any damage to the qualities, and that thus the animal should fall ill, either as a whole or in certain of its parts. Also the diseases which are primary and most generic are four in number, and differ from each other in warmth, cold, dryness, and moisture.

MEDICINE AND QUACKERY

Pliny *Natural History* xxix. viii. 17-25 (abridged)

Medicine is the only one of the arts of Greece that serious Romans have not yet begun to practice. Even though it is lucrative, very few Roman citizens have touched it; and those who do at once become deserters to the Greeks. Nay, even more than this, if they treat of it in any other language than Greek, they lose authority even with laymen . . . [who] have less confidence in matters which concern their lives if it is intelligible to them.

And so it happens that this is the only one of all the arts, by heaven, in which trust is at once put in any man who declares himself a doctor, whereas there is no form of deception that entails greater danger. To this, however, we pay no attention, so seductive is the hope [of a cure] which every patient entertains.

Besides, there is no law to punish this ignorance, no instance of capital punishment. It is at the expense of our perils that they learn, and by conducting experiments they put us to death; a physician is the only man that can kill a man with sovereign impunity. . . . I shall not even attempt to denounce their avarice, the rapacious haggling while their patients' fate hangs in the balance, the fees for our ailments, the deposits for our death, and their secret doctrines. . . . Not shame but competition keeps the fees down. It is well-known that Charmis . . . for 200 sesterces turned over a patient who was a provincial to the surgeon Alco, and that the Emperor Claudius removed the patient from him and condemned him to pay a fine of 100,000 sesterces; but the same doctor while in exile in Gaul—and later, when recalled—acquired an equally large sum within a few years.

These are faults, however, of individuals. I shall not expatiate on the dregs of the profession, and the ignorance of this crew, and their lack of restraint. . . . Which of the gods, pray, instructed them in this? Human subtlety could not achieve such heights, so apparent is their vain ostentation of skill and their monstrous display of knowledge.

MATERIA MEDICA

In Books xx–xxxII Pliny records hundreds of "remedies" for all sorts of ailments, mental as well as physical. Garlic, for example, figures in sixty-one remedies for a wide range of complaints including dropsy, leprosy, erysipelas, snake and animal bites, running ulcers, toothache, headache, epilepsy, and insanity (xx. xxiii). Medical practice was much given to the use of specifics and panaceas, in the concoction of which superstition and magic frequently played a larger part than empirical knowledge. Thus, although he several times in his work digresses to excoriate magicians and deprecate their popularity, Pliny does not scruple to record their "cures." The examples given here are selected from Pliny's lists of remedies using animal products; he has separate lists of those employing vegetable matter and waters.

Pliny *Natural History* XXVIII. vii. 35, lxiv. 227–lxvii. 230

[Spittle]

But we have shown that the most effective protection against snakes is the spittle of a fasting person; and actual daily experience confirms other effective uses of it. We spit against illnesses like epilepsy, that is, we repel contagion; in similar manner we repel witchcraft and the danger in meeting a person lame in the right leg. We also ask pardon of the gods by spitting in the bosom for entertaining some too presumptuous hope. On the same principle it is the custom in all cases where medicine is employed to spit three times in deprecation, so as to assist its efficacy.

[Remedies for broken bones]

For broken bones a quick remedy is the ashes of the jawbone of a boar or swine; likewise boiled lard, tied round the broken bone, knits it with marvellous rapidity. For fractures of the ribs, goat's dung applied in old wine is especially extolled; it has aperient, extractive, and healing properties.

[Remedies for fevers]

Deer's flesh . . . is a febrifuge. Recurrent fevers are cured, if we are to believe the magicians, by wearing the right eye of a wolf, salted and attached. There is a type of fever called quotidian; one can be cured of this, they say, if the patient takes three drops of blood from the vein of an ass's ear and swallows them in a pint of water. For quartan fever the magicians recommend cat's dung together with the toe of an owl to be attached to the body, and, to prevent a relapse, not to be removed until the seventh spasm. . . . More moderate ones recommend for quartan fever the liver of a cat killed during the waning moon, preserved in salt, to be taken in wine just before the attacks. The magicians also recommend that the toes of the patient should be smeared with the ashes of cow dung sprinkled with boy's urine, and that a hare's heart should be attached to the hands; they give hare's rennet to drink before attacks. Fresh goat's milk cheese is also given with honey, the whey being carefully extracted.

[Remedies for melancholy, lethargy, and phthisis]

For patients afflicted with melancholy, calf's dung boiled in wine is a remedy. Lethargic persons are aroused by applying to the nostrils the calluses from an ass's legs steeped in vinegar, or the fumes of goat's horns or hair, or wild boar's liver. This is also given to drowsy persons.

The cure of phthisis is effected by a wolf's liver taken in thin wine, the lard of a sow that has been fed upon grass, or the flesh of a she-ass taken with broth—this last type is used to cure this illness especially in Achaea. They say, too, that the smoke of dried cow dung inhaled through a reed . . . is good for phthisis.

80. *Curiosities of Nature*

In contrast to the heights of rationalism reached by the finest products of Greek genius, the Roman mind, in high places and in low, and the uneducated masses throughout the Empire, were increasingly responsive to the irrational. Symptomatic of this tendency is the collection of marvels by Phlegon, a freedman of the Emperor Hadrian, which catered to the popular taste in such matters.

Phlegon *Amazing Stories* x–xxviii (selections)

There was born in Rome a hermaphrodite, in the year when Jason was archon at Athens and Marcus Plautius Hypsaeus and Marcus Fulvius Flaccus were consuls at Rome.[185] On this account the senate bade the pontiffs consult the Sibylline Oracles, and they interpreted the oracular responses.

.   .   .   .

Not a few cities of Sicily and the area about Regium suffered from the earthquake, and not a few of the peoples in Pontus were also shaken. In the fissures in the earth were revealed bodies of quite large size. The natives were astounded and shrank from moving them, but they sent a tooth of one to Rome as a sample. The tooth was not just a foot long but actually exceeded that size. The envoys showed it to [the Emperor] Tiberius and asked whether he wanted the heroic figure brought to him.

[185] 125 B.C.

The emperor made a wise decision about this, by which he both did not deprive himself of learning its size and at the same time avoided the impiety of stealing corpses. He summoned a renowned geometer, Pulcher by name, whom he prized for his skill, and bade him reconstruct the face in scale to the size of the tooth. Pulcher calculated what the proportions of the whole body and the face would be by the size of the tooth, and quickly fashioned it and brought it to the emperor. The latter declared that he was satisfied with this viewing of it, and sent the tooth back whence it had been brought. . . . One should not mistrust these stories, reflecting that in early times nature in its prime bred everything close to the gods, but that as time wasted away the size of creatures wasted with it.

·   ·   ·   ·

There was brought to Nero a child having four heads and its other members corresponding, in the year when Thrasyllus was archon at Athens and Publius Petronius Turpilianus and Lucius Caesennius Paetus were consuls at Rome.[186] And another child was born with its head growing out of its left shoulder.

·   ·   ·   ·

There happened an incredible wonder in Rome, in the year when Demophilus was archon at Athens and Quintus Veranius and Gaius Pompeius Gallus were consuls at Rome.[187] One of the most esteemed serving women of the wife of Raecius Taurus, a man of praetorian rank, gave birth to an ape.

·   ·   ·   ·

Antigonus tells that in Alexandria one woman bore twenty offspring in four births, and that most of them survived.

81. *The Races of Man: Climate and Culture*

Vitruvius *Architecture* VI. i. 9–11
Adapted from LCL

Southern peoples, owing to the rarity of the atmosphere, with their minds rendered acute by the heat, are more readily and swiftly inclined to resourcefulness in planning; but northern peoples, steeped in a thick climate amid reluctant air, are chilled by the damp and have sluggish minds. We can observe this in the case of snakes: they move quickest when the heat has drawn away the damp with its chilling effect; but in

[186] A.D. 61.   [187] A.D. 49.

the cold and wintry seasons they are chilled by the change of climate, and are sluggish and motionless. Hence we need not wonder if warm air renders the human mind more acute, and a cool air impedes.

Now, while the southern peoples are of acute intelligence and infinite resource in planning, they give way when courage is demanded, because their strength is drained away by the sun; but those who are born in colder regions, by their fearless courage are better equipped for the clash of arms, yet by their slowness of mind they rush on without reflection, and through lack of tactics are balked of their purpose. Since, therefore the disposition of the world is such by nature, and all other peoples differ by their unbalanced temperament, it is in the true mean within the space of all the world and the regions of the earth that the Roman people holds its territories. For in Italy the inhabitants are exactly tempered in either direction, both in the structure of the body and by strength of mind corresponding to their courage. For just as the planet Jupiter is tempered by running in the middle between the heat of Mars and the cold of Saturn, in the same manner Italy presents laudable qualities which are tempered by admixture from either side both north and south, and are consequently unsurpassed. And so by its policy it shatters the courage of the barbarians and by its strong hand the plans of the southerners. Thus the divine mind placed the state of the Roman people in an excellent and temperate region in order that it might obtain dominion over the whole world.

CHAPTER V

THE ROMAN PEACE (A.D. 14–192):
LIFE IN THE MUNICIPALITIES
AND PROVINCES [1]

82. *Limited Local Autonomy*

Plutarch *Precepts of Statecraft* x, xvii, xix, xxxii (abridged)
From LCL

Nowadays, then, when the affairs of the cities no longer include leadership in wars, nor the overthrowing of tyrannies, nor acts of alliances, what opening for a conspicuous and brilliant public career could one find? There remain the public lawsuits and embassies to the emperor, which demand a man of ardent temperament and one who possesses both courage and intellect. But there are many excellent lines of endeavor that are neglected in our cities, which a man may take up, and also many practices resulting from evil custom that have insinuated themselves to the shame or injury of the city, which a man may remove, and thus turn them to account for himself. . . .

You who hold office are a subject, ruling a state controlled by proconsuls and by the procurators of the emperor. . . . Do not have great pride or confidence in your crown [of office], for you see soldiers' boots just above your head. . . .

Officials in the cities, when they foolishly urge the people to imitate the deeds, ideal, and actions of their ancestors,[2] however unsuitable they may be in the present times and conditions, stir up the common folk, and, though what they do is laughable, what is done to them is no laughing matter, except when they are treated with utter contempt. . . .

And not only should the statesman show himself and his native state blameless toward our rulers, but he should always have, as a firm bulwark, so to speak, of his administration, a friend among the men of

[1] The unusual proportion of Egyptian material in this chapter is the result of the fact that papyri provide unique documentation for many facets of provincial life, especially those concerning the agricultural masses in their private and governmental relations. While Egypt occupied an exceptional position in the Roman provincial system and some of the details revealed by the papyri have only local pertinence, much of the material can be taken as illustrative of Roman provincial life in general. A few of the documents included in this chapter are dated somewhat later than A.D. 192, but they are equally applicable to the earlier imperial period.
[2] Plutarch is referring to the autonomous city-states of the heyday of Greek civilization.

high station who have the greatest power; for the Romans themselves are most eager to promote the political interests of their friends. . . .

However, the statesman, while making his native state readily obedient to its sovereigns, must not further humble it; nor, when the leg has been fettered, go on and subject the neck to the yoke, as some do who, by referring everything great or small to the emperors, bring the reproach of slavery upon their country, or rather wholly destroy its constitutional government, making it dazed, timid, and powerless in everything. . . . Those who invite the emperor's decision on every decree, meeting of a council, granting of a privilege, or administrative measure, force their emperors to be their masters more than they desire. And the cause of this is chiefly the greed and contentiousness of the foremost citizens; for either, in cases in which they are injuring their inferiors, they force them into exile from the state, or, in matters concerning which they differ among themselves, since they are unwilling to occupy an inferior position among their fellow citizens, they call in those who are mightier; and, as a result, council, popular assembly, courts, and the entire local government lose their authority. . . .[3]

Then he [the statesman] will instruct his people both individually and collectively and will call attention to the weak condition of Greek affairs, in which it is best for wise men to accept one advantage—a life of harmony and quiet—since fortune has left us no prize open for competition. For what dominion, what glory is there for those who are victorious? What sort of power is it when a small edict of a proconsul may annul or transfer it to another man and which, even if it last, has nothing in it seriously worth while?

83. *Municipal Charters*

At its height, the Empire presented the appearance of an aggregate of cities and towns (see § 33), enjoying varying degrees of self-government according to the status granted by the central government. In increasing numbers during the Principate urbanized centers were raised to the status of Roman municipalities; some were granted the more privileged rank of colony. The bronze fragments of the charters of the Spanish towns of Salpensa (Municipium Flavium Salpensanum) and Malaca (Municipium Flavium Malacitanum), found near Málaga in 1851, provide valuable evidence for the spread of traditional Roman municipal institutions (see Vol. I, § 162) and their adaptation to changing conditions within the Empire. By edict of Vespasian, confirmed by Titus, these towns, like most Spanish urban communities, were granted *Latinitas* (Latin rights), a half-way station between alien status and

[3] Cf. § 88.

full Roman citizenship. The formal charters, patterned on Italian municipal constitutions, were promulgated by Domitian in A.D. 81/84. Noteworthy features are the strong local autonomy, the concentration of power in the hands of the local aristocracy, and the access to full Roman citizenship provided for the aristocracy through the holding of a magistracy. In the second century this latter privilege was granted to all members of municipal councils.

THE CHARTER OF SALPENSA

CIL, Vol. II, No. 1,963 and p. 876 (= Dessau, No. 6,088 = Abbott-Johnson, No. 64)

Adapted from E. G. Hardy, Three Spanish Charters

R.[4] *Magistrates to Obtain Roman Citizenship*

XXI. . . . All persons who become duovirs, aediles, or quaestors in accordance with this charter shall be Roman citizens on laying down the magistracy at the end of the year, together with their parents and wives, and children born in lawful wedlock and subject to the father's power,[5] and in like manner grandsons and granddaughters on the male side subject to the father's power, provided that no more shall be Roman citizens than the number of magistrates who are to be elected in accordance with this charter.[6]

R. *Persons Obtaining Roman Citizenship to Remain under the Legal Dominion, Marital Control, or Parental Power of the Same Persons*

XXII. All persons, male or female, obtaining Roman citizenship in accordance with this charter or in accordance with an edict of the Emperor Caesar Augustus VESPASIAN or the Emperor TITUS Caesar Augustus or the Emperor Caesar Augustus DOMITIAN, father of his country, shall be under the parental power or marital control or legal dominion of that person who becomes a Roman citizen by this charter and under whose control they would properly belong if the change to Roman citizenship had not taken place; and the said persons shall have the same right of choosing a legal guardian that they would have had if they had been born of a Roman citizen and had not changed their citizenship.

R. *Persons Obtaining Roman Citizenship to Retain Rights over Freedmen*

XXIII. All persons, male or female, obtaining Roman citizenship

[4] R(*ubrica*): "title"—so called because it was usually colored red.
[5] See Vol. I, § 8; Vol. II, §§ 157, 163.
[6] This proviso is intended to prevent more rapid extension of the citizenship through subterfuges.

in accordance with this charter or in accordance with an edict of the Emperor Caesar VESPASIAN Augustus or the Emperor TITUS Caesar Vespasianus Augustus or the Emperor Caesar DOMITIAN Augustus, shall have the same rights and status in respect to freedmen and freedwomen, whether their own or their fathers' (such freedmen and freedwomen not having come into Roman citizenship), and also in respect to the property of these persons and to the services imposed as a consideration for their freedom [7] as would have existed if the said persons had not changed their citizenship.[8]

XXIV. [On the powers of a prefect chosen to act in place of the emperor if the latter is elected honorary duovir.]

XXV. [On the powers and privileges of a prefect who acts as chief magistrate of the town when both of the duovirs are away for more than a day.]

R. Concerning the Oath of the Duovirs, Aediles, and Quaestors

XXVI. The incumbent douvirs with judicial power in this municipality, likewise the aediles and quaestors now holding office in this municipality, each of them within the five days next following the promulgation of this charter, and likewise the duovirs, aediles, or quaestors who shall henceforth be elected in accordance with this charter, each of them within the five days next following their entrance upon the office of duovir, aedile, or quaestor, and before a meeting of the decurions or *conscripti* is held, shall in a public meeting take oath by Jupiter, by the deified Augustus, by the deified Claudius, by the deified Vespasian Augustus, by the deified Titus Augustus, by the *genius* [9] of Domitian Augustus, and by the [municipal] tutelary gods, that they will properly perform whatsoever they believe to be in accordance with this charter and in the public interest of the citizens of the municipality Flavia Salpensa, and that they will not knowingly and with malice aforethought act contrary to this charter or the public interest of the citizens of the said municipality, and that they will as far as they can prevent others from so doing; and that they will neither hold nor allow any meeting of the decurions [10] nor express any opinion except such as in their judgment is consistent with this charter and the public interest of the citizens of the said municipality. Any person who fails to take such oath shall be condemned to pay to the citizens of the said municipality 10,000 sesterces, and may be sued or prosecuted for that amount at will

[7] Patrons retained certain rights over the property and labor of their freedmen (see introduction to § 66).

[8] That is, if they had not advanced from Latin rights to full Roman citizenship.

[9] See § 14.

[10] This specific clause refers only to duovirs, who alone could convoke the municipal council.

by any citizen of the said municipality who has the legal right to do so in accordance with this charter.[11]

XXVII. [On the veto power of magistrates.]
XXVIII. [On the manumission of slaves before a duovir.]
XXIX. [On the assignment of a legal guardian.]

THE CHARTER OF MALACA

CIL, Vol. II, No. 1,964 and pp. 876–77 (= Dessau, No. 6,089 =
Abbott-Johnson, No. 65)
Adapted from E. G. Hardy, Three Spanish Charters

R. On the Nomination of Candidates

LI. If, up to the day when declaration of intention [to be a candidate] must be made, declaration is made either in the name of no one or of fewer persons than the number which must be elected, or if, out of those persons in whose name a declaration of intention has been made, those who may properly stand for election in accordance with this charter are fewer than the number which must be elected, then the person responsible for conducting the elections [12] shall post, in a place where they may be plainly read from level ground, the names of as many persons, qualified by this charter to stand for the said offices, as are required to make up the number which must be elected by this charter. Each of those whose names are so posted shall, if he so desires, go before the magistrate who is to conduct the said elections, and nominate one [additional] person of his own status; in like manner each of the persons so nominated by the aforesaid shall, if he so desires, go before the same magistrate and nominate one [additional] person of his own status. And the said magistrate, before whom such nomination is made, shall post the names of all the aforesaid persons in a place where they may be plainly read from level ground and shall likewise conduct the elections in respect to all the said persons exactly as though, in accordance with the clause in this charter *On Candidature for Office*,[13] declaration of intention had been made in their names within the prescribed time, and as though they had of their own accord in the first instance stood for the said offices and had not withheld their candidacy.[14]

[11] On such oaths of office cf. Vol. I, p. 424.
[12] Usually the duovir who was senior in age.
[13] This clause is not extant.
[14] This clause involving compulsory nomination of candidates is one of the earliest pieces of evidence we have on the burdensome character of and the tendency to avoid municipal offices. Cf. further § 85.

LII. [On the mechanics of conducting the elections.]

LIII. [On the privilege of voting granted to resident aliens who are Roman or Latin citizens.]

R. On Those Whose Candidature May Properly Be Considered at the Elections

LIV. The person responsible for conducting the elections shall first see to the election of duovirs with judicial power from that category of freeborn persons already specified and set forth in this charter; then in succession he shall see to the election of aediles and likewise of quaestors from that category of freeborn persons already specified and set forth in this charter, provided that, in the case of candidates for the duovirate, he does not allow any person to stand for election who is less than twenty-five years of age or has held that office within five years; [15] likewise, in the case of candidates for the aedileship or the quaestorship, he shall not allow consideration of any person who is less than twenty-five years of age or who is subject to any impediments whereby, if he were a Roman citizen, he could not lawfully become a member of the decurions or *conscripti*.[16]

R. On the Casting of Votes

LV. The person conducting the elections in accordance with this charter shall summon the citizens to cast their votes by *curiae*,[17] issuing a single call to vote to all the *curiae*,[18] in such manner that the said *curiae*, each in a separate voting booth, may severally cast their votes by means of tablets. He shall likewise see to it that three citizens of the said municipality are placed at the ballot box of each *curia* who do not themselves belong to that *curia*, to guard and count the ballots; and that before performing such duty each of them shall take oath that he will handle the counting of the ballots and make report thereon in good faith. Furthermore, he shall not hinder candidates for an office from placing one watcher each at every ballot box. And the said watchers, both those placed by the person conducting the elections and those placed by candidates for office, shall each cast his vote in that *curia* at whose ballot box he is placed as a watcher, and the votes of the said watchers shall be just as lawful and valid as if each had cast his vote in his own *curia*.

---

[15] There were similar restrictions at Rome during the Republic (cf. Vol. I, p. 271). The decurions were recruited from the ex-aediles and ex-quaestors.

[16] Cf. the similar provisions in the "Julian Municipal Law," Vol. I, pp. 417–19.

[17] Voting units (wards) similar to the tribes at Rome.

[18] The *curiae* voted simultaneously, as did the tribes in the Comitia Tributa at Rome (cf. Vol. I, p. 34).

R. On the Course to be Taken in the Case of Those Who Have an Equal Number of Votes

LVI. The person conducting the said elections, according as any candidate has more votes in each *curia* than the others, shall declare the person who is ahead of the rest as chosen and elected with reference to that *curia*, until the number to be elected is made up. If in any *curia* two or more candidates have the same number of votes, he shall prefer a married man or one with the rights of a married man to an unmarried man without children or without the rights of married men, a man with children to a man without children, and a man with more children to a man with fewer children, and shall declare the former [elected]. In such matter, two children lost after the ceremony of naming or one boy lost after puberty or one girl of marriageable age lost shall be counted as equivalent to one surviving child.[19] If two or more candidates have the same number of votes and are of the same qualifications, he shall submit their names to choice by lot and shall declare the person whose name is drawn by lot to be ahead of the rest.

LVII–LVIII. [On announcement of candidates elected, and on the fine for obstructing the holding of elections.]

LIX. [On the oath to be taken by successful candidates.] [20]

LX. [On security to be given by candidates for the duovirate or quaestorship for public moneys which may be entrusted to their care.] [21]

LXI. [On the adoption of a patron of the municipality.] [22]

R. No Person to Destroy Buildings Except with a View to Restoration

LXII. No person shall unroof or destroy or cause to be demolished any building in the town of the municipality Flavia Malaca or any buildings in the environs of the said municipality except by resolution of the decurions or *conscripti*, passed when a majority of the same is present, unless he intends to restore the said building within the year. Any person acting in contravention of this shall be condemned to pay to the citizens of the municipality Flavia Malaca a sum of money equivalent to the value of the said property and may be sued or prosecuted for that amount at will by any citizen of the said municipality who has the legal right to do so in accordance with this charter.[23]

---

[19] These provisions are patterned after the Augustan Papian-Poppaean Laws (see § 11).

[20] Cf. the Charter of Salpensa above, clause XXVI.

[21] Cf. the Charter of Tarentum, Vol. I, p. 415.

[22] For patrons of municipalities see § 91.

[23] Cf. the Charter of Tarentum, Vol. I, p. 416; the Charter of Urso, Vol. I, p. 423; and Vol. II, § 50, first selection, and § 88, last selection.

LXIII. [On the recording and publication of public contracts by duovirs.]

LXIV–LXV. [On legal obligations of sureties to the municipality, and on penalties for false declaration of securities posted.]

LXVI. [On the imposition of fines by magistrates.]

LXVII. [On the rendering of account within thirty days to the municipality of corporate moneys belonging to it.] [24]

LXVIII–LXIX. [On the election of a commission of three to investigate accounts due the municipality, and on the assignment of a court to try cases involving corporate moneys.]

84. *Election Notices*

Hundreds of campaign notices, painted in red on white-washed walls of buildings in Pompeii, testify to the spirited political life of Roman municipalities in the first century of the Empire.

CIL, Vol. IV, Nos. 202, 710, 429, 113, 787, 635, 3,775, 3,294, 768, 6,626, 3,702, 581, 576, 1,147 (= Dessau, Nos. 6,411*a*, 6,419*e*, 6,412*e*, 6,412*a*, 6,420*b*, 6,436, 6,409, 6,414, 6,438*d*, 6,422*b*, 6,405, 6,418*d*, 6,418*f*, 6,431*d*), and *CIL*, Vol. IV, No. 1,904

i

The fruit dealers together with Helvius Vestalis unanimously urge the election of Marcus Holconius Priscus as duovir with judicial power.

ii

The goldsmiths unanimously urge the election of Gaius Cuspius Pansa as aedile.

iii

I ask you to elect Gaius Julius Polybius aedile. He gets good bread.

iv

The muleteers urge the election of Gaius Julius Polybius as duovir.

v

The worshippers of Isis unanimously urge the election of Gnaeus Helvius Sabinus as aedile.

vi

Proculus, make Sabinus aedile and he will do as much for you.

vii

His neighbors urge you to elect Lucius Statius Receptus duovir with

[24] In the Charter of Urso 150 days were allowed (Vol. I, p. 424).

judicial power; he is worthy. Aemilius Celer, a neighbor, wrote this. May you take sick if you maliciously erase this!

viii

Satia and Petronia support and ask you to elect Marcus Casellius and Lucius Albucius aediles. May we always have such citizens in our colony!

ix

I ask you to elect Epidius Sabinus duovir with judicial power. He is worthy, a defender of the colony, and in the opinion of the respected judge Suedius Clemens and by agreement of the council, because of his services and uprightness, worthy of the municipality. Elect him!

x

If upright living is considered any recommendation, Lucretius Fronto is well worthy of the office.

xi

Genialis urges the election of Bruttius Balbus as duovir. He will protect the treasury.

xii

I ask you to elect Marcus Cerrinius Vatia to the aedileship. All the late drinkers support him. Florus and Fructus wrote this.

xiii

The petty thieves support Vatia for the aedileship.

xiv

I ask you to elect Aulus Vettius Firmus aedile. He is worthy of the municipality. I ask you to elect him, ballplayers. Elect him!

xv

I wonder, O wall, that you have not fallen in ruins from supporting the stupidities of so many scribblers.[25]

85. *Selection of Municipal Councilmen*

The expense of office holding and the increasing financial responsibilities of local magistrates and councilmen during the growing economic crisis of the second century made the local rich increasingly reluctant to assume public

[25] Unlike the others above, this inscription is a *graffito*, scratched on the wall.

office. Since the municipalities served as the instrumentality of the central
government in the collection of the imperial revenues, and since the personal
contributions of the officeholders constituted the mainstay of municipal
finances (cf., e.g., §§ 86, 90, 92), the shortage of candidates threatened severe
administrative and financial dislocations, causing increasing imperial intervention in local affairs, which in turn further sapped the vitality of local self-
rule. On orders from the central government compulsion was resorted to increasingly to fill municipal posts, and by the end of the second century even
the formality of popular elections had been dispensed with and the choice
of municipal officers left to the local senates. Thus, as at Rome where the
elections had long since been transferred from people to senate (cf. Chapter
II, Note 43), the participation of the people was eliminated in the interest
of administrative efficiency, and the councils, whose members held office for
life, became the central organ of municipal administration. For further developments in the third and fourth centuries, see §§121, 134.

REQUEST FOR ELECTION TO THE CITY COUNCIL

Dittenberger, No. 838 (= Abbott-Johnson, No. 85)

[Ephesus, Asia, A.D. 129]

The Emperor Caesar Trajanus HADRIAN Augustus, son of the deified
Trajan Parthicus, grandson of the deified Nerva, *pontifex maximus*,
holding the tribunician power for the thirteenth year, three times consul, father of his country, to the chief magistrates and council of Ephesus,
greeting. Lucius Erastus states that he is a fellow citizen of yours, that
he has many times sailed the sea, making himself as useful as he could
thereby to his native city,[26] and that he has always transported the
governors of the province. He has already sailed with me twice, first
when I was traveling to Rhodes from Ephesus, and now on my journey
from Eleusis to you. He desires to become a member of your council. I
leave the scrutiny of his qualifications in your hands, and if nothing
stands in the way and he is judged worthy of the honor, I shall pay on
behalf of his election whatever sum of money the councillors pay.[27]

THE GROWTH OF COMPULSION

Pliny *Letters* Book x, Nos. 112–13

[Pliny to the Emperor Trajan]

The Pompeian Law,[28] my lord, which Bithynia and Pontus observe,

[26] Doubtless by bringing in supplies of food: see § 87.
[27] That is, the *honorarium* (office money) customarily paid into the local treasury by newly elected magistrates and councilmen on taking office.
[28] The law by which the province of Bithynia was organized by Pompey the
Great.

does not provide for those who are named to a city council by the [local] censors to pay any money. But those whom certain cities are permitted by your indulgence to admit beyond the legal number have contributed 1,000 and 2,000 *denarii* each. Then the proconsul Anicius Maximus ordered also those who are named by the censors, in a few cities at any rate, to contribute a sum varying from place to place. It remains, therefore, for you yourself to consider whether in all cities all who henceforth are chosen councilmen should not be required to pay for their admission. For it is appropriate that what is to endure forever should be established by you, whose every deed and word deserve immortality.

[Trajan to Pliny]

I can establish no general ruling as to whether all who become decurions in every city of Bithynia should be required to pay an entrance fee for the decurionate or not. I think therefore that—as is always the most prudent course—each city should conform to its own law. But as against those who are made decurions against their will. . . .[29]

86. *Municipal Revenues*

The following selections illustrate the major sources of municipal revenues other than the contributions of the local officials (see § 85), namely, local taxes and tolls, and leases of municipal property and concessions.

THE TARIFF OF PALMYRA

The caravan city of Palmyra (Tadmor), which lay in a fertile oasis astride the much-traveled caravan route between Damascus and the Euphrates river, derived its prosperity chiefly from the tolls it levied on the traffic plying the route. Although striving to maintain a nominal independence of both the Parthian and Roman empires, it was gradually absorbed under Roman control, receiving some form of supervision from the imperial legate in Syria, until it was captured and ruined in A.D. 273 after Queen Zenobia's ambitious and ill-starred attempt to renounce Roman overlordship. Though Palmyra occupied an exceptional position among the cities under Roman suzerainty, its customs regulation, published in Greek and Aramaic in A.D. 137, is characteristic of the municipal *octrois* which numerous communities of the Empire were permitted to levy. (For imperial customs dues and transit tolls, see § 35.)

[29] For the conclusion of this sentence, the text of which is hopelessly corrupt, various conjectures have been made. It suffices to note that the necessity of drafting some members to fill the municipal councils is here treated as a matter of course.

OGIS, No. 629 (= *IGRR*, Vol. III, No. 1,056)

In the reign of the Emperor Caesar Trajanus HADRIAN Augustus, son of the deified Trajan Parthicus, grandson of the deified Nerva, *pontifex maximus*, holding the tribunician power for the twenty-first year, twice acclaimed *imperator*, three times consul, father of his country; in the consulship of Lucius Aelius Caesar (for the second time) and Publius Coelius Balbinus.

Year 448, 18th day of the month Xandicus.[30] Decree of the council. Under the presidency of Bonnes son of Bonnes and grandson of Haeranus, with Alexander son of Alexander and grandson of Philopator serving as secretary of the council and people, in the magistracy of Malichus son of Olaeës and of Zebides son of Nesas, in a legal meeting of the council the following was voted.

Whereas in past times very many of the dues have not been listed in the customs regulation but have been exacted only according to custom, it being written into the contract that the tax farmer should collect taxes in accordance with the regulation and with custom; and whereas it frequently happened that controversies arose concerning this between the merchants and the tax farmers, it was decreed that the incumbent magistrates and the ten leading men [31] should determine the dues not listed in the regulation and should write them into the next contract and should stipulate for each type of goods the customary dues; and after they have been confirmed by the tax farmer they should inscribe them together with the earlier regulation on the stone stele opposite the temple called Rabaseire. And the magistrates, the ten leading men, and the syndics [32] in office at the time should see to it that the tax farmer does not exact anything more. . . .

The Customs Regulations of the Customs District of Hadriana Palmyra and of the Wells of Caesar

From those who import slaves into Palmyra or within its borders the tax farmer is to exact 22 *denarii* per head . . .; for a slave [who is sold in the town and is not to be?] exported, 12 *denarii*; for a slave of more than one year's service who is for sale, 10 *denarii*; for exported . . . slaves, 12 *denarii* per head.

Furthermore, in the case of a camel-load of dried products, the tax farmer shall exact 3 *denarii* for each camel-load imported, 3 *denarii* for

[30] This date is by the Seleucid era. In the Aramaic version the month is Nisan.
[31] Cf. introduction to § 121.
[32] Public advocates who represented Palmyra in its relations with the emperor or the governor of Syria.

one camel-load exported, 2 *denarii* for one donkey-load imported or exported.

In the case of purple wool he shall exact 8 *asses* for each fleece imported and also for each exported.

For each camel-load of myrrh imported in alabaster vessels he shall exact 25 *denarii;* for each load of myrrh[?] exported, 13 *denarii.* For each camel-load of myrrh imported in goatskins he shall exact 13 *denarii;* and for each load exported 7 *denarii.* For each donkey-load of myrrh imported in alabaster vessels he shall exact 13 *denarii,* and for each load exported 7 *denarii.* For each donkey-load of myrrh imported in goatskins he shall exact 7 *denarii,* and for each load exported 4 *denarii.*

For each camel-load of olive oil imported in four goatskins, [he shall exact] 13 *denarii,* and for each load exported 13 *denarii.* For each camel-load of olive oil imported in two goatskins he shall exact 7 *denarii,* and for each load exported 7 *denarii.* For each donkey-load of olive oil imported he shall exact 7 *denarii,* and for each load exported 7 *denarii.* . . .

Furthermore, the tax farmer shall exact on each woman who receives 1 *denarius* or more 1 *denarius* per woman, and on each woman who receives 8 *asses,* he shall exact 8 *asses,* and on each woman who receives 6 *asses,* he shall exact 6 *asses.*[33]

Furthermore, the tax farmer shall exact from the workshops as follows: from the leather shops . . . according to custom, 1 *denarius* per month per shop; from the importers and merchants of hides he shall take 2 *asses* per hide. Similarly, the clothing merchants and retailers who sell in the city shall pay the tax farmer the appropriate sum.

For the use of the two springs of the town, 800 *denarii* per annum.

The tax farmer shall exact 1 *denarius* for every load of grain, wine, fodder, and all similar commodities, that is, for each camel-load each trip.

For each camel brought in without a load he shall exact 1 *denarius,* as was exacted by Cilix, imperial freedman. . . .[34]

[The next sections, which are fragmentary, deal with customs dues on salt, and also with the salt monopoly, the tax farmer's right to take and dispose of security for claims, and an arbitration decision of the governor of Syria.]

. . . The butcher tax must be computed in *denarii,* as Germanicus Caesar [35] made clear in the letter to Statilius stating that the dues must be computed in Italian *asses;* the tax farmer shall exact sums below a

[33] This tax on prostitutes was probably exacted every month.
[34] Either a former tax farmer at Palmyra or an agent at the nearest imperial customs station.
[35] For Germanicus' activities as vice-regent in the eastern provinces see §§ 106, 168.

denarius in small [local] coin according to custom. With respect to animals discarded owing to death no tax is due.

I [36] decree that [the tax farmer] shall exact 1 *denarius* for a load of foodstuffs according to the regulation for import from outside the frontier or export; but those who transport produce to and from the villages [of the territory of Palmyra] are to be exempt in accordance with the concession made to them. With respect to pine cones and similar products which are imported for the market, it is decreed that the duty shall be assessed as for dried products, as is done in the other cities.

With respect to camels, whether they are brought in from outside the frontiers without loads or loaded, 1 *denarius* is due for each according to the regulation, as also Corbulo,[37] *vir clarissimus*, sanctioned in the letter to Barbarus. As concerns camel skins, no duty is to be exacted, and in the case of vegetable fodder . . . it is decided that it is subject to duty because it is salable. [The rest is here omitted.]

A MUNICIPAL TAX COLLECTOR

In a chest unearthed at Pompeii in 1875 were found 153 waxed diptychs and triptychs (cf. § 51) containing business records of one Lucius Caecilius Jucundus. Many of the tablets were charred or crumbled beyond legibility in the eruption of Vesuvius that buried the town. Most of those that can be read are receipts issued to Jucundus either when he paid the proceeds of sale to persons for whom he had auctioned off property (at a commission of two percent or more), or when he paid over to the municipality tax moneys which he had contracted to collect for a four-year period.

CIL, Vol. IV, No. 3,340, xxv and cxli (= *FIRA*, Vol. III, Nos. 129*a* and 131*b*); A.D. 56 and 58

i

11,039 sesterces, which sum, after commission, was realized by Lucius Caecilius Jucundus from Umbricia Januaria's auction: Umbricia Januaria declared that she had been paid in full by Lucius Caecilius Jucundus.

Done at Pompeii on December 12 in the consulship of Lucius Duvius and Publius Clodius.

[Signatures of witnesses] [38] [Seals of] Quintus Appuleius Severus, Marcus Lucretius Lerus, Tiberius Julius Abscantus, Marcus Julius Crescens, Publius Terentius Primus, Marcus Epidius Hymenaeus, Quin-

---

[36] It is not clear whether this is the drafter of the earlier customs regulation or the governor of Syria, whose arbitration is recorded in the tariff.

[37] Gnaeus Domitius Corbulo, generalissimo of the campaigns against the Parthians under Nero.

[38] Cf. Chapter IV, Note 138.

tus Granius Lesbus, Titus Vesonius Le . . . , Decimus Volcius Thallus.

In the consulship of Lucius Duvius Avitus and Publius Clodius Thrasea, December 12. I, Decimus Volcius Thallus, wrote at the request of Umbricia Januaria, after examination of the witnessed tablets,[39] that she had received from Lucius Caecilius Jucundus 11,039 sesterces as the proceeds of her auction less commission. . . . Done at Pompeii.

ii

Holograph [acknowledgment] of Privatus, public slave of the colony of Veneria Cornelia,[40] on receipt of 1,652 sesterces for the fullers' tax of the first year.[41]

Sextus Pompeius Proculus and Gaius Cornelius Macer being the duovirs with judicial power for the year, February 19. I, Privatus, slave of the colony, hereby declare in writing that I received from Lucius Caecilius Jucundus 1,652 sesterces for the fullers' tax from the balance of the first year.

Done at Pompeii in the consulship of Nero Augustus (for the third time) and Marcus Messalla.

A MUNICIPAL WATER ACCOUNT

This unique document contains an accounting of income and expenditures by the water commissioners of the town of Arsinoë, capital of the Arsinoite nome of Egypt. More than half the operating costs were defrayed by monthly contributions from various municipal magistrates.

British Museum Papyrus No. 1,177, abridged (= Wilcken, No. 193 = *Select Papyri*, No. 406); A.D. 113

To Demetrius, ex-gymnasiarch, auditor, from Crispus, also known as Sarapio; Mysthes, also known as Ptolemaeus, son of Ptolemaeus; Mysthes son of Didymus, acting through his father; and Sotas son of Zoilus—all four superintendents of the water supply for the reservoirs and fountains of the metropolis. Account of receipts and of expenses incurred for the water supply from Pachon of the past sixteenth year of the lord Trajan Caesar to Phaophi 30 of the current seventeenth year.

Receipts

From Pappus and Theo, gymnasiarchs of the sixteenth year of the lord Trajan Caesar, 420 drachmas per month: Pachon, dr. 420; Payni,

[39] That is, the preceding formal attestation, which is written on the first two tablets of the triptych; the additional personal acknowledgment of receipt is added on the third tablet.
[40] The full official name of Pompeii was Colonia Veneria Cornelia Pompeianorum.
[41] That is, of Jucundus' four-year contract: see introduction.

dr. 420; Epeiph, dr. 400; Mesore, dr. 400; and dr. 40 for Epeiph and Mesore, balance. Total, dr. 1,680.

From Asclepiades, *cosmetes*, 1,000 drachmas per month: Pachon, dr. 1,000; Payni, dr. 1,000; Caesareus,[42] dr. 2,000. Total, dr. 4,000. . . .

For supplying water to the baths of Severianus at 18 obols per day: Pachon, dr. 72 ob. 18; Payni, dr. 72 ob. 18; Epeiph, dr. 72 ob. 18. . . . Total, dr. 424 ob. 93. For the Colonnade[?] fountain, at ob. 9 per day: Pachon, dr. 36 ob. 9; Payni dr. 36 ob. 9; Epeiph, 27 days, the proportional dr. 33 ob. 4; Mesore, dr. 36 ob. 9; the five intercalary days, ob. 45. Total, dr. 141 ob. 76. . . . For the fountain in the Cleopatreum [43] quarter, likewise at ob. 9 per day: Pachon, dr. 36 ob. 9; Payni, dr. 36 ob. 9; . . . four intercalary days, dr. 5; Year 17, Thoth, 29 days, dr. 36 (because none supplied one day). . . . Total, dr. 205 ob. 36. For the brewery in the Serapeum quarter, at ob. 13 per day: Pachon, dr. 52 ob. 13. . . . Total, dr. 313 ob. 70. From the officers of the synagogue of the Theban Jews, at dr. 128 per month: Pachon, dr. 128; Payni, dr. 128. . . . Total dr. 768. For the house of prayer, likewise: Pachon, dr. 128. . . . Total, dr. 768.

Total receipts from Pachon 10 to Phaophi 30 [of the seventeenth year] of the lord Trajan Caesar: 1 talent 5,900 drachmas 6 obols.

Expenditures

For the reservoir at the Grove with its sixteen *shadufs*,[44] at a man and a half [45] drawing water from morning till evening, Year 16 of the lord Trajan Caesar: Pachon—to Aphrodisius, foreman of the pumpers, wages for himself for Pachon, dr. 40, and for payment to the pumpers from the 1st to the 30th, 797 men at the reservoir and the outlet[?], and likewise 306 night workmen, total 1,103 men at a wage of dr. 40 per 30,[46] dr. 1,470; for payment to the men working the Archimedean screws,[47] 200 men at ob. 10 each, ob. 2,000, equals dr. 276; cost of oil burned in lamps for the night workmen, dr. 12 ob. 2; cost of earthenware buckets, dr. 1. Total for the month, dr. 1,799 ob. 2. . . .

Wages of ox drivers at the reservoir at the Grove with its two

---

[42] That is, Mesore: cf. Chapter III, Note 132.

[43] A temple to a deified queen Cleopatra of the Ptolemaic dynasty.

[44] A water lifting device consisting of two uprights supporting a horizontal cross-bar, on which is balanced a long pole with a bucket at one end and a weight at the other. *Shaduf* is the modern Arabic name for this primitive machine, still in use in Egypt today.

[45] Here and in the remainder of this paragraph "men" corresponds to what we today should call "man-days."

[46] For these workmen employed by the month this averages slightly less than the 10 obols per day recorded in the following entry as the wage of day workers.

[47] Cf. Chapter III, Note 61.

sakiehs [48] and six ox drivers: Pachon—to Peteeus son of Patynis, ox-herd, dr. 32; to six ox drivers likewise for Pachon, three at dr. 16, dr. 48; two others at dr. 14, dr. 28; the remaining one, dr. 24. Equals for the month dr. 132.

[The remainder of the account includes expenditures for "water pots for the *sakiehs*," "light twine for fastening pots at the *sakiehs*," and miscellaneous other articles.]

A MUNICIPAL FERRY MONOPOLY

OGIS, No. 572 (= Abbott-Johnson, No. 128)

[Myra, Lycia, second or third century]

May good fortune attend! It was decreed by the council and the people, on motion of the chief magistrates: Since as a result of our inability to obtain an acceptable bid for the ferry rights on the river Limyra the revenues are decreased, no one else [49] is permitted to en-gage in any ferrying either from the Thicket or from the mouth of the harbor or from Andriace, or he will have to pay to the municipality 1,300 *denarii* for each trip, and the [ferry] concessionaire shall have the right to register an attachment[?] against his boat and gear. Only the registered boats and those to which the concessionaire grants per-mission shall make the crossing, and he shall receive one fourth of every fare and cargo. And if anyone carries a fare on his own, he shall declare it and pay one fourth of every fare, or he will be liable to the aforemen-tioned fine.

LEASE OF MUNICIPAL PROPERTY

Oxyrhynchus Papyrus No. 2,109 (= *Select Papyri*, No. 356); A.D. 261
Adapted from LCL

[Notice by] Aurelius Dioscurides, also known as Sabinus, ex-gymnasiarch, councilman, and, however I am styled, incumbent chief magistrate of the city of Oxyrhynchus, also director of municipal finances. Of the offer made by the person specified therein for a loca-tion belonging to the city in the Capitol [50] below the East Colonnade with a view to opening a tavern, a copy is publicly displayed [below],

[48] This is the modern Arabic name for the ox-driven wooden water wheels, which, like the *shadufs* (see Note 44 above), are still in common use in the Egyptian coun-tryside.
[49] That is, other than those who purchase the right from the city.
[50] The municipalities, in imitation of Rome, established precincts of the Capitoline Triad (cf. Vol. I, p. 55, Note 23).

in order that all may know and those who wish to make better offers may come forward, without prejudice to any kind of right of the city in the matter. Signed by me. Year 1 of our lords Macrianus and Quietus, Augusti, Tybi 30.

To Aurelius Dioscurides, also known as Sabinus, ex-gymnasiarch, incumbent chief magistrate of the city of Oxyrhynchus, also director of municipal finances, from Aurelius Horio son of Colluthus and Tereus, of Oxyrhynchus. I voluntarily engage to lease the shop in the city Capitol below the East Colonnade, with a view to opening a tavern, for one year from the first day of the coming month Mecheir of the current first year at a monthly rent of 8 drachmas. If my tender is confirmed, I am to use the shop with its entrance and exit for the term without hindrance, and I will pay the rent monthly on the 30th without delay, and at the end of the term I will surrender the location free from filth and all uncleanness, and any doors and keys which I received, or will forfeit the true value of whatever I fail to surrender, right of execution duly subsisting. This engagement is valid, and in answer to the formal question concerning it I gave my consent.[51] But if my offer is not accepted, I shall not be bound by this promise. Year 1 of the Emperors Caesars Titus Fulvius Junius MACRIANUS Pius Felix Augustus and Titus Fulvius Junius QUIETUS Pius Felix Augustus, Tybi 28.

[Signed] I, Aurelius Horio son of Colluthus, have submitted this tender to lease, and I will pay the rent as aforesaid. I, Aurelius Didymus, wrote for him as he is illiterate.

87. The Food Problem

The specter of hunger and famine hovered like a permanent incubus over the cities and towns of the ancient world. In an attempt to cope with the food problem, the cities of the Hellenistic world had instituted a regular magistracy expressly charged with procuring grain and regulating its local sale. The population centers of the Roman Empire continued to feel from time to time the pinch of scarcity and high prices. Sometimes in such crises wealthy townsmen provided money to feed the starving. But often some seized the opportunity for profiteering, cornering and hoarding food supplies, and holding out for famine prices. Food riots frequently ensued, necessitating governmental intervention.

One of the prime causes of the recurrent famines was the earmarking of vast quantities of grain to feed the city of Rome and the armies, while throughout the Empire large areas continued to be diverted from the cultivation of cereals to the more profitable production of wine and olive oil—so much so that

[51] Cf. Chapter III, Note 135.

before the end of the first century the emperors were taking steps to encourage the production of grains in the provinces (cf. §§ 41–42). A contributory cause was the difficulty of overland transport, so that inland towns frequently suffered dearth while grain was available a relatively short distance away.

PERMISSION TO ESTABLISH A MARKET

To operate a market, or fair, individuals and communities needed the sanction of the Roman senate or the emperor. We are told that the Emperor Claudius held markets on his estates (Suetonius *Life of Claudius* xii. 4). Pliny mentions in one of his *Letters* (Book v, No. 4. 1) that "Sollers, a man of praetorian rank, petitioned the senate to be allowed to establish a market on his estate. His petition was opposed by envoys from Vicetia"—no doubt because there was a market in that town which stood to lose from Sollers' competition.

CIL, Vol. VIII, Nos. 11,451 and 23,246 (= Abbott-Johnson, No. 96 = FIRA, Vol. I, No. 47)

[Casae, Africa, A.D. 138]

Decree of the senate concerning the market of the Beguensian estate in the territory of Casae. Certified copy from the record of motions made in the senate in the consulship of Canius Junius Niger and Gaius Pomponius Camerinus, in which were recorded the rights of Africanus and what follows.

October 15, at a meeting in the Julian Senate House. Present at the writing were [seven names follow]. Present in the senate were 250[plus] members. The decree of the senate was passed by a division of the house.[52]

Whereas Publius Cassius Secundus and Publius Delphius Peregrinus Alfius Alennius Maximus Curtius Valerianus Proculus Marcus Nonius Mucianus,[53] the consuls, spoke concerning the petition of the friends of Lucilius Africanus, *vir clarissimus*, requesting that he be permitted to establish and maintain market days at Casae in the province of Africa, Beguensian district, territory of the Musulamians, on November 2 and 20 and every month thereafter on the fourth day before the Nones and the twelfth day before the Kalends, [and the consuls asked the senate] what it was pleased to see done;

Concerning this matter the senate decreed as follows: That Lucilius Africanus, *vir clarissimus*, be permitted to establish and maintain a market at Casae in the province of Africa, Beguensian district, territory of

[52] Cf. Vol. I, § 156. It is interesting to note that the senate still adhered to its traditional forms of parliamentary procedure.
[53] Cf. Chapter II, Note 108.

the Musulamians, on November 2 and 20 and every month thereafter
on the fourth day before the Nones and the twelfth day before the
Kalends, and that people from the neighborhood and from outside the
district be permitted to gather and assemble there for the purpose of
attending market only,[54] without harm or inconvenience to anyone.

Done on October 15 in the consulship of Publius Cassius Secundus
and Marcus Nonius Mucianus. [The rest is here omitted.]

A BREAD RIOT

The riot described here may be compared with Dio Chrysostom's account (in
his *Discourse* xlvi) of how he and another rich landowner of Prusa (in
Bithynia) were nearly lynched by a mob which suspected them of manipu-
lating the grain market to raise prices.

Philostratus *Life of Apollonius of Tyana*[55] I. xv (abridged)
Adapted from LCL

When he came to Aspendus in Pamphylia . . . he found nothing
but vetch on sale in the market, and the citizens were feeding upon
this and on anything else they could get; for the rich men had locked up
all the grain and were holding it for export from the country. Consequently an excited crowd of all ages had set upon the chief magistrate
and was lighting a fire to burn him alive even though he was clinging to
the statues of the emperor, which were at that time more dreaded and
a more inviolable sanctuary than that of Zeus in Olympia.[56] . . . Apollonius turned to the bystanders and beckoned to them that they must
listen; and they not only held their tongues from wonderment at him,
but they placed their fire on the altars that were there. The chief magistrate then plucked up courage and said, "So-and-so and So-and-so,"
naming several, "are to blame for the famine which has arisen, for they
have taken away the grain and are keeping it in different parts of the
country." A hue and cry thereupon arose among the Aspendians to
make for these men's estates, but Apollonius shook his head to tell them
not to do that but rather to summon those who were to blame and obtain the grain from them with their consent. And when they arrived,
he very nearly broke out in speech against them, so affected was he by
the tears of the crowd—for the children and women had all flocked
together, and the old men were groaning as if they were on the point of

---

[54] Similar restrictions on assembly of frontier peoples were enforced along the Danube: cf. § 28.
[55] For Philostratus see below, Note 82. Apollonius was a first-century Pythagorean
ascetic, who carried out a five-year vow of silence and became famous as a holy man.
[56] Cf. § 68, last selection.

dying of hunger. However, he respected his vow of silence and wrote his indictment on a writing board, and handed it to the chief magistrate to read aloud; and his indictment ran as follows: "Apollonius to the grain dealers of Aspendus. The earth is the mother of us all, for she is just; but you, because you are unjust, have made her the mother of yourselves alone, and if you do not stop I will not permit you to remain upon her." They were so terrified by these words that they filled the market place with grain, and the city revived.

EMERGENCY MEASURES

In the first of the following edicts the governor of the province of Galatia orders the sale of surplus grain in a famine area and fixes a ceiling price. In the second, the proconsul of Asia steps in to end a bakers' strike with which the city authorities were unable to cope after, apparently, provoking it by their exacting demands. To assure the steady production of "the staff of life" some towns operated municipal bakeries.

AE, 1925, No. 162*b* (= Abbott-Johnson, No. 65*a*)

[Antioch, Pisidia, A.D. c.93]

Lucius Antistius Rusticus, legate with rank of praetor of the Emperor Caesar DOMITIAN Augustus Germanicus, declares:

Whereas the duovirs and decurions of the most illustrious colony of Antioch have written to me that on account of the severity of the winter the price of grain has soared, and they have petitioned that the populace be given an opportunity to buy;

Therefore—may good fortune attend!—all who are either citizens or residents of the colony of Antioch shall declare before the duovirs of the colony of Antioch, within thirty days after this edict of mine is posted in public, how much grain each has and in what place, and how much he deducts for seed or for the year's supply of food for his household; and he shall make all the remaining grain available to purchasers of the colony of Antioch. Furthermore, I fix next August 1 as the date of the sale. And if anyone fails to comply, let him know that I shall claim for confiscation whatever is withheld contrary to my edict, reserving a one-eighth share as a reward for informers.

Whereas, furthermore, I am assured that before this prolonged severe winter a *modius* of grain in the colony cost eight or nine *asses*, and it is most unjust for anyone to profiteer from the hunger of his fellow citizens, I forbid the price of grain to exceed one *denarius* per *modius*.[57]

[57] At that, the governor is permitting a maximum price of about twice the pre-famine normal price. It is probable that there is a reference to this famine in the New

SEG, Vol. IV, No. 512 (= Abbott-Johnson, No. 124)

[Ephesus, Asia, second century]

. . . Thus it happens at times that the populace is plunged into disorder and riots by the inexcusable audacity[?] of the bakers' agitation in the market place. Under these circumstances they should by now have been haled into court and have paid the penalty. But since it is necessary to prefer the welfare of the city to the punishment of these individuals, I thought it best to bring them to their senses by an edict. Wherefore, I forbid the bakers to assemble in association [58] and their officers to make inflammatory speeches, and I order them to give complete obedience to those in charge of the community's welfare and to provide the city fully with the necessary production of bread. If any of them is caught from this time on either meeting contrary to my orders or leading any riot or agitation, he shall be haled into court and suffer the appropriate punishment; and if anyone dares to hide and continue disrupting the city, he shall in addition be branded on the foot with the word *decuria*,[59] and anyone who harbors any such person shall thereby become liable to the same punishment. [The rest is here omitted.]

A LOCAL BENEFACTOR

CIL, Vol. III, No. 6,998 (= Dessau, No. 7,196)

[Nacolea, Asia, second century]

Section of the will of Publius Aelius Onesimus, imperial freedman. To the town of Nacolea, my beloved native town, although I owe it very much, I desire, in proportion to the moderate size of my property, that 200,000 sesterces be given on the following condition, that at the discretion of Cornelius . . . and Cornelius Hesycius this sum be let out at interest and the interest produced in the next three years be allocated to a grain fund, so that grain may be bought with it annually. And after the expiry of the three-year period I desire that the interest on this entire sum be divided annually among my fellow citizens, after a census is taken, on the most fortunate birthday of our lord Trajanus HADRIAN. I desire, moreover, that one half of this interest be allocated for gifts in such manner that one half is distributed on the holiday called. . . . [The rest is lost.]

Testament (*Revelation* 6:6): "And I heard a voice, as it were, in the midst of the four animals saying, 'A *choenix* of grain for a *denarius*, and three *choenices* of barley for a *denarius;* and cheat not on the oil and wine.'"

[58] The governor by this act suspends the right of association which the bakers had apparently enjoyed (cf. §§ 69–70).

[59] "City council," indicating presumably that he was branded by its order.

88. *Imperial Intervention*

Dependent in considerable part on the contributions of the wealthy and on other unstable sources of income, and freely disbursed by municipal administrations on nonproductive public works and services such as theaters, baths, festivals, and banquets, many civic treasuries were in a state of chronic insolvency by the second century. To overcome the chaotic effect of such conditions upon the imperial revenues, the central government took, increasingly, a direct hand in local affairs. This development was, it may be noted, in keeping with the growing centralization of administration in general in the hands of the emperors. Beginning with Nerva or Trajan, the emperors frequently appointed their own representatives (*correctores* or *curatores*) to direct the finances of municipalities in difficulties. One of the principal tasks with which Pliny the Younger was charged when sent to govern Bithynia was a systematic reorganization of municipal finances. Three of his letters on this subject are given in the second selection below. Among the others, one reported to the emperor that the town of Apamea refused to open its books for his inspection on the ground that it was guaranteed local autonomy in its treaty of alliance with Rome (cf. Vol. I, §§ 132, 134), but Trajan ordered the investigation to be made "at my personal wish without prejudice to their privileges." In another letter, Pliny suggested a plan whereby members of the municipal council would be compelled to pledge their own property as a means of solving the town's financial problem; though the emperor disapproved this proposal as "inconsistent with the justice of our times," it is in fact entirely in keeping with the already established principle and conditions of compulsory public services and a harbinger of the more widespread compulsion of the third and fourth centuries. It is one of the ironies of Roman history that the municipal status within the Roman body politic, for which Rome's "allies" once fought a war in order to gain citizenship and independence (cf. Vol. I, § 103), ended by placing the cities in even more complete subjection to the authority of Rome.

VESPASIAN'S GRANT TO SABORA

CIL, Vol. II, No. 1,423 (= Dessau, No. 6,092 = *FIRA*, Vol. I, No. 74)

[Sabora, Spain, A.D. 78]

The Emperor Caesar VESPASIAN Augustus, *pontifex maximus*, holding the tribunician power for the ninth year, acclaimed *imperator* eighteen times, eight times consul, father of his country, sends greetings to the *quattuorviri* [60] and decurions of Sabora. Since you inform me that you are impoverished and beset by many difficulties, I permit you to

[60] Cf. Vol. I, p. 415, Note 53.

build the town under my name in the plain, as you wish. The revenues which you say you were granted by the deified Augustus I reaffirm; if you desire to add any new ones, you must apply to the proconsul therefor, since I can make no decision if there is no appeal. I received your decree on July 25 and dismissed your envoys on the 29th of the same.[61] Farewell.

The duovirs, Gaius Cornelius Severus and Marcus Septimius Severus, had this inscribed on bronze at public expense.

PLINY IN BITHYNIA

Pliny *Letters* Book x, Nos. 17a, 37, 43

[Pliny to the Emperor Trajan]

. . . I am at present examining the expenditures, income, and outstanding debts of the municipality of Prusa, and the more I investigate the more necessary I perceive the examination to be. Many sums of money are detained in private hands for a variety of reasons, and in addition some are disbursed for quite illegitimate expenditures. This, my lord, I write to you immediately upon my arrival.

.   .   .   .

The town of Nicomedia, my lord, has expended 3,329,000 sesterces on an aqueduct, which has been abandoned still unfinished and has even been torn down. Again they disbursed 200,000 sesterces for another aqueduct, but this, too, has been abandoned. So now, after throwing away all that money, they must make a new expenditure in order to have water. I have personally visited a very pure spring from which in my opinion the water ought to be brought on arches, as was tried in the first place, so that it will reach not alone the level and low parts of the city. A very few arches are still standing, and some can also be erected with the hewn stone which has been torn down from the previous structure; some part, I think, will have to be carried out in brick, since that is easier and cheaper. But first of all it is necessary for you to send here an inspector of aqueducts or an engineer, so that what happened may not occur again. This one thing I am certain of, that the usefulness and beauty of the structure will be entirely worthy of your age.

[Trajan in reply approves completing the aqueduct, but wants Pliny to determine and report to him "whose fault it is that Nicomedia has squandered so much money up to now."]

.   .   .   .

[61] This sentence is added to impress the provincials with the promptness with which their petitions are answered by the emperor.

On looking into the very great expenditures which the municipality of Byzantium has made, I discovered, my lord, that an envoy is sent to you every year with a decree of greetings, and 12,000 sesterces are allocated for him. Therefore, mindful of your purpose,[62] I judged it proper that the decree should be sent but the envoy kept at home, so that the expense would be lightened and the public duty would at the same time be fulfilled. The same city is charged with 3,000 sesterces as the annual travel allowance for an envoy to go and bring official greetings to the governor of Moesia.[63] This expense, too, I deemed it right to eliminate in the future. I beg you, my lord, to write in reply what you think and deign either to confirm my counsel or correct my error.

[Trajan's reply is a terse approval of Pliny's actions.]

HADRIAN'S GRANT TO STRATONICEA

Dittenberger, No. 837 (= Abbott-Johnson, No. 83 = *FIRA*, Vol. I, No. 80)

[Stratonicea, Asia, A.D. 127]

The Emperor Caesar Trajanus HADRIAN Augustus, son of the deified Trajan Parthicus, grandson of the deified Nerva, *pontifex maximus*, holding the tribunician power for the eleventh year, three times consul, to the chief magistrates, council, and people of Stratonicea-Hadrianopolis, greeting. You appear to me to be requesting what is just and necessary for your recently constituted city.[64] Therefore, I grant you the revenues derived from your territory; and as for the house of Tiberius Claudius Socrates which is in the city, Socrates shall either repair it or give it up to one of the inhabitants, so that it may not become dilapidated through age and neglect.[65] I have sent these orders also to the proconsul Stertinius Quartus, *vir clarissimus*, and to my procurator Pompeius Severus. Claudius Candidus came [to me] as [your] envoy, and he is to be paid his travel allowance, unless he undertook it at his own expense. Farewell. March 1, from Rome. I, Claudius Candidus, delivered this letter to Lollius Rusticus, the chief magistrate, on May 14 in the assembly.

[62] To force municipalities to retrench unessential expenditures.
[63] Probably because of the trade of Byzantium with the towns and armies in Moesia and as a token of gratitude for protection.
[64] The city of Stratonicea was amalgamated with its surrounding territory by Hadrian. This emperor pursued an active policy of urbanization, evidenced by numerous city foundations, especially in the already highly urbanized eastern provinces. Donations of public works, enlargement of city territories, and grants of revenue rights were some of the methods by which he attempted to resuscitate municipal treasuries and stem the fiscal deterioration of towns.
[65] Cf. § 50, first selection.

89. *The Imperial Child-Assistance System* (*Alimenta*) [66]

In keeping with Augustus' policy of fostering the survival of the Italian stock (cf. introductions to §§ 11, 12), the Emperor Nerva in his short reign devised a scheme "for girls and boys born of needy parents to be supported at public expense throughout the towns of Italy" (Aurelius Victor [67] *Epitome* xii. 4). Implemented by Trajan and extended by succeeding emperors (eventually even to the provinces), this program of child assistance continued in existence for nearly two hundred years, though increasingly impaired by the economic crisis and monetary inflation of the third century. With the establishment of the Dominate the program was terminated, but it was later revived under Church auspices.

The imperial *alimenta* system operated as follows. In each town participating in the program the emperor's privy purse (the fisc) made loans to farm owners, which, to avoid the creation of an excessive burden of debt, were limited to very small fractions of the value of the farms registered as security. The interest on these loans, at 5 percent, was then paid into a special municipal fund earmarked for the support of a predetermined number of poor children. Thus working capital was made available to farmers at less than the normal interest rate, the payment of the interest was virtually assured by the low ratio of the loan to the value of the security, and the income from the loans provided a steady source of funds to help poor farmers raise their families and assure the necessary agricultural labor force. Though it is not specifically stated in the extant sources, these subsidies were presumably paid until boys came of age, at fifteen; for girls the payments may have ceased two years earlier (cf. p. 352). The program entailed a huge outlay of fiscal funds for the loans and for administrative expenses, but there is no evidence that it had more than a palliative effect.

Two extant inscriptions, both on large bronze tablets, contain the records of the loans making up the *alimenta* programs of the town of Veleia (near Parma) in northern Italy and an area near Beneventum in southern Italy.[68] Portions of both of these documents are given below. In the first, that of Veleia, the amount of the loan is uniformly about one twelfth, or 8 percent, of the stated value of the land offered as security; in the second the ratio of loan to valuation varies, but does not exceed approximately 12 percent. Apart from the *alimenta*, these inscriptions provide rare and vivid evidence

---

[66] See also § 90.

[67] Sextus Aurelius Victor wrote, about the middle of the fourth century, a short history of the emperors from Augustus to Constantine. A slightly later work purporting to be an epitome of his *Caesars* actually derives from it only slightly.

[68] A group of happy parents and *alimenta*-supported children is depicted in one of the reliefs decorating a triumphal arch of Trajan erected in A.D. 114 and still standing at Benevento.

of how small and medium-sized farms, though they had by no means disappeared completely in these parts of Italy, were here too being combined or incorporated into larger estates; in the Veleia register, for example, the names of more than three hundred different farms occur, but they belong to only forty-eight owners (one of them the town of Lucca).

CIL, Vol. XI, No. 1,147 (= Dessau, No. 6,675 = *FIRA*, Vol. III, No. 116)

[Veleia, A.D. 109/12]

Liens on properties to the amount of 1,044,000 sesterces, so that through the indulgence of the best and greatest *princeps*, the Emperor Caesar Nerva TRAJAN Augustus Germanicus Dacicus, boys and girls may receive support [as follows]: legitimate boys, 245 in number, at 16 sesterces each [per month], equals 47,040 sesterces; legitimate girls, 34 in number, at 12 sesterces each [per month], equals 4,896 sesterces; illegitimate boy, 1, 144 sesterces [per year]; illegitimate girl, 1, 120 sesterces [per year]; total, 52,200 sesterces, which equals 5 percent interest on the aforementioned principal.

Gaius Volumnius Memor and Volumnia Alce, through Volumnius Diadumenus their freedman, registered the Quintiac-Aurelian farm and Muletas Hill with its woods, which is in the territory of Veleia, Ambitrebian district, bounded by Marcus Mommeius Persicus, Satrius Severus, and the community,[69] worth 108,000 sesterces; he is to receive 8,692 sesterces and put up the aforementioned farm as security.

Marcus Virius Nepos registered country properties worth 310,545 sesterces, deducting rentals.[70] He is to receive 25,353 sesterces and to put up as security the Planian farm, which is in the territory of Veleia, Junonian district, bounded by Priscus Palamenus, Velleius Severus, and the community, and which he registered at 14,000 sesterces; the Suigian farm with three cabins, aforementioned district, bounded by Gaius Calidius, Velleius Proculus, and the community, which he registered at 20,000 sesterces; the Petronian farm, district and boundaries aforementioned, which he registered at 4,000 sesterces; [there follow the names of many more farms, to make up the total valuation of 310,545 sesterces]. . . .

Gaius Coelius Verus, through Onesimus his slave, registered country properties in the territories of Placentia, Veleia, and Libarna worth 843,879 sesterces, deducting rentals and the properties which Cornelius Gallicanus and Pomponius Bassus [71] placed under lien. He is to receive

[69] This is generally interpreted as meaning a public road.
[70] That is, lands held on lease are registered, for *alimenta*-loan purposes, at their valuation less the annual rental.
[71] These were agents of the emperor in the establishment of smaller child-assistance funds some years earlier; see the next paragraph.

67,850 sesterces and put up as security one half of the Collacteran farm . . . [the names of many other farms follow] . . . also one third of the Bitinian-Albitemian estate,[72] which is in the territory of Veleia and Luca, Albensian, Minervian, and Statiellian districts, bounded by the town of Luca, the Annius brothers, and the community, and which he registered at 350,000 sesterces for [a loan of] 30,000 sesterces; [and many more farms]. . . .

Likewise the liens on properties taken by Cornelius Gallicanus to the amount of 72,000 sesterces, so that through the indulgence of the best and greatest *princeps*, the Emperor Caesar Nerva TRAJAN Augustus Germanicus,[73] boys and girls may receive support [as follows]: legitimate boys, 18 in number, at 16 sesterces [per month], equals 3,456 sesterces; legitimate girl, 12 sesterces [per month]; total of both, 3,600 sesterces, which equals 5 percent interest on the aforementioned amount.

[There follows a list of properties like the preceding, but much shorter, in keeping with the much smaller sum of money involved.]

CIL, Vol. IX, No. 1,455 (= Dessau, No. 6,509 = FIRA, Vol. III, No. 117)

[Vicinity of Benevento, A.D. 101]

In the consulship of the Emperor Caesar Nerva TRAJAN Augustus Germanicus (for the fourth time) and Quintus Articuleius Paetus . . . in accordance with the ordinance of the best and greatest *princeps*, the following[?] Baebian Ligurians [74] offered properties as security . . . so that through his indulgence boys and girls may receive support. . . .

By Crispia Restituta: the Pomponian farms, in the territory assigned to Beneventum, Aequan district in the Ligurian area, adjoining Nasidius Vitalis, valued at 50,000 sesterces for [a loan of] 3,520 sesterces   88 sesterces [75]

By Lucius Naeratius Diadumenus: the Rubrian farms, in the Beneventan territory, Ligurian district, valued at 34,000 sesterces for [a loan of] 1,000 sesterces   25 sesterces

. . . . .

By Neratius Corellius: the Paccian farms and cabins of Aurelianus,

[72] The Latin word here is *saltus*, which is the term used to designate the imperial estates of North Africa (see § 42). However, it may be that the word is used here in its earlier meaning of "pasture land."
[73] Since Trajan's epithet Dacicus is here omitted, the date of this smaller *alimenta* undertaking must be earlier than A.D. 102.
[74] In 180 B.C. the Apuan Ligurians on the Riviera were subjugated by the consuls Publius Cornelius and Marcus Baebius, and 40,000 of them were deported to Samnium, where they were known thereafter as Cornelian or Baebian Ligurians.
[75] The figure placed alongside each entry, being 2½ percent of the amount of the loan, is presumably the interest for a half year (cf. the introduction to this section).

adjoining Julius Saturninus, valued at 22,000 sesterces for [a loan of]
2,000 sesterces   50 sesterces

· · · ·

By Gnaeus Marcius Rufinus: the Marcian and Satrian farms,
valued at 130,000 sesterces; also the Julian farms, valued at
14,000 sesterces; also the Avillian farms, valued at 42,000 sesterces;
also the Vitellian, Nasennian, and Marcellian farms, adjoining Suellius
Flaccus, valued at 120,000 sesterces for [a loan of] 10,000 sesterces; also
the Curian and Satrian farms, Herculanean district, adjoining Tettius
Etruscus, valued at 35,000 sesterces for [a loan of] 3,000 sesterces; also
the Albian farms with cabins, Meflan district, adjoining Nonius Restitutus, valued at 110,000 sesterces for [a loan of] 10,000 sesterces; also—
put up as security for the ninth time—the Caesian farms, in the Beneventan territory, Tucian district, adjoining Messius Aper, valued at
50,000 sesterces for [a loan of] 3,000 sesterces. Equals 466,000 sesterces [76]
for [a loan of] 42,440 sesterces   1,061 sesterces

By Lucius Tettius Etruscianus: the Albian, Amarantian, Surian, and
Annian farms, in the Beneventan territory, Saeculan district, adjoining
Marius Restitutus, valued at 150,000 sesterces for [a loan of] 12,000
sesterces   300 sesterces

By Publius Titius Ajax: the Veiaean farms, in the Beneventan territory, Roman district in the Ligurian area, adjoining our emperor,
valued at 14,000 sesterces for [a loan of] 1,000 sesterces

25 sesterces

· · · ·

By Clodius Conveniens: the Primigenian, Albian, Sutorian, and
Suellian farms, Salutarian district, adjoining Suellius Flaccus and Rufus,
purchased at 109,000 sesterces for [a loan of] 9,000 sesterces

225 sesterces

[The remaining entries follow the same pattern.]

90. *Private Philanthropy*

In addition to the expenses which they incurred on the assumption and in the
discharge of municipal offices and priesthoods, the wealthy frequently regaled
their fellow townspeople with banquets, entertainments, and largess to celebrate festive occasions such as births, weddings, and holidays, and they even
left bequests for such celebrations to be held annually in memory of themselves. Very common too, under imperial encouragement and example, were

[76] The total should be 501,000 sesterces; obviously the item of 35,000 sesterces was
overlooked in the addition.

donations or bequests to native towns or other places with which the donor had ties of property, family, or sentiment, for public works and embellishments. In the second century many of these local philanthropists followed the emperors' lead and established *alimenta* foundations for the support of poor children in their home towns. These public benefactors were frequently honored with the title of "patron" of the community. Inscribed plaques and bases of statues erected to them by the towns have been found by the hundreds throughout the Roman Empire. See further §§ 91–92.

CIL, Vol. II, No. 3,270

[Cazlona (Castulo), Spain, first century (?)]

To Quintus Toreus Culleo son of Quintus, imperial procurator of the province of Baetica—because he at his own expense repaired the town walls dilapidated through old age; gave a plot of ground to build baths; paved the road leading through the mountain passes of Castulo to Sisapo,[77] which had been washed out by incessant rains; erected statues of Venus Genetrix [78] and Cupid at the theater; remitted the sum of 10,000,000 sesterces which was owed him by the municipality and even gave a banquet to the public in addition—the municipality of Castulo held circus games for two days and dedicated this in gratitude.

CIL, Vol. II, No. 4,514 (= Dessau, No. 6,957)

[Barcelona (Barcino), Spain, second century]

Lucius Caecilius Optatus son of Lucius, of the Papirian tribe, centurion of Legion VII Gemina Felix and centurion of Legion XV Apollinaris, honorably discharged by the Emperors MARCUS AURELIUS Antoninus [Augustus] and [LUCIUS] Aurelius VERUS Augustus, included by the town of Barcino among those exempted from public charges, attained the offices of aedile, duovir three times, flamen of Rome and the deified emperors. He left a legacy to the municipality of Barcino as follows: I give, bequeath, and desire to have given 7,500 *denarii*, with the six-percent interest on which I desire a boxing contest to be held each year on June 10 at a cost of up to 250 *denarii*, and on the same day 200 *denarii* worth of oil to be supplied to the public in the public baths. I desire these bequests to be carried out on condition that my freedmen, and also the freedmen of my freedmen and freedwomen, who attain the honor of the board of six [79] be excused from all the obligations of the office. But if any of them is assigned such burdens, then I

---

[77] Modern Almadén. The road was important for the transportation of mine products (see § 40).

[78] "Venus the Procreatress" of the Julian imperial line.

[79] These were the Augustales, on whom see introduction to § 66. Their number in most municipalities was six.

order the said 7,500 *denarii* to be transferred to the municipality of
Tarraco,[80] with the same program of shows as aforementioned to be
held at Tarraco.

Pliny *Letters* Book VI, No. 34

Gaius Plinius to his dear Maximus, greeting.

You were right to promise a combat of gladiators to our good
friends the people of Verona, by whom you have so long been loved,
admired, and honored. It was from there, too, that you took your wife
most dear and lovely, to whose memory some public monument or
show was due, preferably this exhibition, which is especially appropriate for commemorating the dead. Besides, you were so unanimously
pressed to do so, that to refuse would have seemed not constancy but
obstinacy. It was a distinguished gesture, too, that you were so ready,
so generous in providing them; for these, too, are the marks of a noble
spirit. I am sorry the many African panthers you had purchased did
not arrive in time; but even though they were delayed by bad weather
and failed to appear, it was nevertheless understood, as you deserved,
that it was not your fault that you did not exhibit them. Farewell.

Dittenberger, No. 850 (= Abbott-Johnson, No. 101)

[Ephesus, Asia, A.D. 145]

The Emperor Caesar Titus Aelius Hadrianus Antoninus Augustus, son of the deified Hadrian, grandson of the deified Trajan Parthicus,
descendant of the deified Nerva, *pontifex maximus*, holding the tribunician power for the eighth year, twice acclaimed *imperator*, four times
consul, father of his country, to the chief magistrates, council, and people of Ephesus, greeting. The munificence which Vedius Antoninus
lavishes upon you I learned of not so much from your letter as from
his own. For, desiring to obtain assistance from me for the embellishment of the public works which he offered you, he made known to
me how many and what great buildings he is adding to the city,[81] but
you do not properly appreciate him. I granted him all he requested, and
I welcomed the fact that he prefers, not the usual method of those participating in public affairs, who for the sake of immediate popularity
expend their munificence on shows and doles and prizes for games, but
means whereby he hopes to make the city more stately in the future.
Documents transmitted by Claudius Julianus, *vir clarissimus*, proconsul.
Farewell.

[80] Modern Tarragona.
[81] Among these buildings was an Odeum (music hall), in the ruins of which this inscription was found.

PHILANTHROPY IN THE GRAND MANNER

One of the most noted philanthropists of all time was the fabulously wealthy Athenian, Herodes Atticus, who lived under the "Good Emperors" of the second century, held the consulship twice, and was a competent sophist in addition. The munificence of this man and his family extended to numerous Greek cities besides their native Athens, notably the famous sanctuaries at Delphi, Eleusis, and Olympia, where several of their statue bases have been found.

Philostratus [82] *Lives of the Sophists* ii. i (abridged)
Adapted from LCL

No man used his wealth to better purpose. . . . The sources of his wealth were many and derived from several families, but the greatest were the fortunes that came from his father [Atticus] and his mother. . . . This Atticus, [the father], was also distinguished for his lordly spirit. As an instance, at a time when his son Herodes was overseer of the free cities of Asia,[83] he observed that Troy was ill supplied with baths and that the inhabitants drew muddy water from their wells and had to dig cisterns to catch rain water. Accordingly, he wrote to the Emperor Hadrian to ask him not to allow an ancient city, conveniently near the sea, to perish from lack of water, but to bestow 3,000,000 drachmas upon them for a water supply, since he had already bestowed on mere villages many times that sum. The emperor approved of his advice in the letter as being in accordance with his own disposition and appointed Herodes himself to take charge of the water project. But when the outlay had reached the sum of 7,000,000 drachmas and the officials who governed Asia kept writing to the emperor that it was a scandal that the tribute of five hundred cities should be spent on the fountain of one city, the emperor expressed his disapproval of this to Atticus; whereupon Atticus replied in the most lordly fashion in the world, "Do not, O Emperor, allow yourself to be irritated over such trifles. The amount spent in excess of 3,000,000 I am presenting to my son, and my son will present it to the city." His will, moreover, in which he bequeathed to the people of Athens 100 drachmas annually for every citizen, proclaims the man's magnanimity, which he exer-

---

[82] Flavius Philostratus (A.D. c.170–c.250), one of a family of sophists and a favorite of the Empress Julia Domna (wife of Septimius Severus), wrote several works, the most important of which are the *Life of Apollonius of Tyana* and the *Lives of the* [Second-Century] *Sophists*.

[83] This office, to which he was appointed by the emperor, is an example of the increasing imperial supervision of municipal affairs (cf. § 88).

cised also in other ways. He would often sacrifice a hundred oxen to the goddess [Athena] in a single day and entertain at the sacrificial feast the whole population of Athens by tribes and families. And whenever the festival of Dionysus came around . . . he would furnish wine to drink for citizens and strangers alike as they lay in the Ceramicus on couches of ivy leaves. . . .

Herodes held the office of eponymous archon [84] at Athens, and the charge of the Panhellenic festival; and when he was offered the crowning honor of the charge of the Panathenaic festival he made this announcement: "I shall welcome you, O Athenians, and those Hellenes that shall attend, and the athletes that are to compete, in a stadium of pure white marble." In accordance with this promise he completed within four years the stadium on the other side of the Ilissus, a monument beyond all other marvels, for there is no theater that can rival it. . . . Herodes also erected for the Athenians the theater in memory of Regilla,[85] roofing it with cedar, though this wood is considered costly even for making statues. These two monuments, then, are at Athens, and they are such as exist nowhere else in the Roman Empire. Worthy of mention also are the roofed theater which he built for the Corinthians, far inferior indeed to the one at Athens but still among the few noteworthy ones anywhere, and the statues at the Isthmus—the colossus of the Isthmian god, that of Amphitrite, and the others—with which he filled the sanctuary; nor must I pass over the dolphin sacred to Melicertes. He also dedicated the stadium at Delphi to the Pythian god, and the aqueduct at Olympia to Zeus, and, for the Thessalians and Greeks around the Maliac Gulf, the swimming pools at Thermopylae that heal the sick. Further, he colonized Oricum in Epirus, which by this time had fallen into decay, and also Canusium in Italy, which he made habitable by giving it a much-needed water supply. And he benefited the cities of Euboea and the Peloponnesus and Boeotia in various ways.

IG, Vol. XIV, No. 1,392 (= Dittenberger, No. 858)

[Rome, after A.D. 161]

. . . Herodes erected this also to be a memorial of his misfortune and of his wife's virtue. But it is not her tomb. Her body is in Greece and now with her husband. His son by her was proposed to the senate by the Emperor Antoninus, called Pius by his fatherland and by all, and by decree of the senate was enrolled in Rome among the patricians.

[84] The chief archon, by whose name the year was designated at Athens.
[85] His wife. The theater was the Odeum (music hall), considerable remains of which still may be seen in Athens.

CHILD ASSISTANCE FUNDS (ALIMENTA)

Alimenta funds established by private philanthropy are attested in inscriptions from several places in Italy and from Spain and North Africa. Representative examples of these will be found under this and the following caption. An interesting forerunner of these child-assistance foundations is the grant of Helvius Basila to his native town of Atina in Latium, recorded in the inscription immediately following.

CIL, Vol. X, No. 5,056 (= Dessau, No. 977)

[Atina, Italy, middle of first century]

To Titus Helvius Basila son of Titus, aedile, praetor, proconsul, imperial legate, who bequeathed to the people of Atina 400,000 sesterces; out of the income from this bequest their children are to be given grain until they reach maturity, and thereafter 1,000 sesterces each. Procula, his daughter, set this up.

CIL, Vol. X, No. 6,328

[Tarracina, Italy, second century]

Caelia Macrina daughter of Gaius left 300,000 sesterces in her will for the construction of this monument, and . . . thousand sesterces for its decoration and upkeep. She also left 1,000,000 sesterces to the town of Tarracina in memory of her son Macer, so that out of the income from this money child-assistance subsidies might be paid to one hundred boys and one hundred girls—to each citizen boy 5 *denarii* each month, to each citizen girl 3 *denarii* each month, the boys up to sixteen years, the girls up to fourteen years—in such a way that the payments should always be received by groups of a hundred boys and a hundred girls.[86]

CIL, Vol. VIII, No. 1,641 (= Dessau, No. 6,818)

[Sicca, Numidia, A.D. 169/80]

To Publius Licinius Papirianus son of Marcus, of the Quirine tribe, imperial procurator of revenues of the Emperors Caesar MARCUS

---

[86] In this inscription and the next, interest at 5 percent on the principal of the fund exceeds the total of the *alimenta* payments stipulated by roughly one sixth. This difference, which some scholars have sought to explain and others to eliminate by emendation of the text, was perhaps intended to allow for the cost of administering the program and provide some leeway in case the fund did not produce the full amount of anticipated income in any given year. It is interesting to note, too, that in both inscriptions the payments to the girls terminate two years sooner than the payments to the boys.

Aurelius Antoninus Augustus Germanicus Sarmaticus Maximus, father of his country, and of the deified [Lucius] Verus, to whom the most illustrious senate of Sicca because of his services. . . .

"To my fellow townsmen of Cirta Sicca, most dear to me, I desire to give 1,300,000 sesterces. I commit this to your trust, my dearest fellow townsmen, so that out of the five-percent interest on this sum three hundred boys and two hundred girls may be supported each year, the boys from the age of three to the age of fifteen, each boy to receive 2½ *denarii* per month, the girls from the age of three to the age of thirteen, 2 *denarii*. Moreover, residents as well as townspeople are to be chosen, provided they are residents who remain domiciled within the confines of our colony. It will be best, if you approve, for them to be chosen by the duovirs of each year; and care should be taken to fill the place of each grown-up or deceased child promptly, so that the full number may always be supported.

THE YOUNGER PLINY'S PHILANTHROPIES

CIL, Vol. V, No. 5,262 (= Dessau, No. 2,927)

[Como, Italy, early second century]

This inscription reciting Pliny's career and philanthropies was placed by his home town of Como on the baths built with Pliny's bequest.

Gaius Plinius Caecilius Secundus [87] son of Lucius, of the Oufentine tribe; consul; augur; legate with rank of praetor in the province of Pontus and Bithynia sent to that province with consular power in accordance with a decree of the senate by the Emperor Caesar Nerva Trajan Augustus Germanicus Dacicus, father of his country; commissioner of the bed and banks of the Tiber and of the sewers of the city; prefect of the treasury of Saturn; prefect of the soldiers' bonus fund; praetor; tribune of the plebs; quaestor of the emperor; member of the board of six of the Roman *equites;* military tribune of Legion III Gallica; member of the board of fifteen for judging lawsuits. He left . . . sesterces in his will for the construction of baths, with an additional 300,000[plus?] sesterces for decoration, and in addition to that 200,000 sesterces for upkeep; and for the support of his freedmen, a hundred persons, he likewise bequeathed to the municipality 1,866,666 sesterces, the income from which he desired to have applied thereafter [88] to an annual banquet for the public. In his lifetime he also gave 500,000

[87] He was born Publius Caecilius Secundus but was adopted by his uncle, the Elder Pliny.
[88] That is, after the freedmen to be supported from the fund have died.

sesterces for the support of the boys and girls of the lower class,[89] and also a library and 100,000 sesterces for the upkeep of the library.

Pliny Letters Book IV, No. 13 (abridged)

Gaius Plinius to his dear Cornelius Tacitus, greeting. . . .

When I was in my native town recently, a young lad, the son of one of my fellow townsmen, came to pay his respects to me. "Do you go to school?" I asked. "Certainly," he replied. "Where?" "At Milan." [90] "Why not here?" "Because," rejoined his father, who was with him and had in fact brought the boy, "we have no teachers here." "Why no teachers?" I asked. "Surely it would be tremendously to the interest of you who are fathers" (and quite opportunely several fathers were listening) "that your sons should by all means have their schooling here. For where could they live more happily than in their native town, or be kept under better control than under the eyes of their parents, or at less expense than at home? It is no greater task, certainly, to collect the money to hire teachers, and you can apply toward their salaries what you now spend for [the boys'] lodgings, travel, and the things that have to be paid for when one is away from home (and away from home everything costs money). Indeed I, who do not yet have children, am ready to give for the benefit of the municipality, as if for a daughter or parent, one third of any sum it will please you to assemble. I would even promise the whole if I were not afraid that such an endowment might one day be tampered with through political corruption, as I see happen in many places where teachers are hired by the municipality. This danger can be met by only one remedy, namely, if the right of hiring is left to the parents alone and scrupulous care for choosing is instilled in them by the necessity of contributing. . . . Then agree among yourselves, unite, and draw increased spirit from mine, for I am desirous that what I shall have to contribute shall be as large as possible. . . ."

I thought it necessary to repeat all this in detail and from the very beginning, as it were, so that you might the better understand how glad I should be if you would undertake what I request. Now then, I

---

[89] Pliny tells in one of his Letters (Book VII, No. 18) how he set up this alimenta fund: "In lieu of 500,000 sesterces, which I had promised for the support of freeborn boys and girls, I deeded some land of mine worth far more to the public administrator and took it back on a rental basis to pay 30,000 sesterces a year. By this means the municipality's principal is secure and the income assured, and the land itself, inasmuch as [the income it produces] far exceeds the rent, will always find a master to work it." In this way Pliny retained the use of his land during his lifetime and Como received annually the equivalent of six-percent interest on 500,000 sesterces.

[90] About eighty miles away.

request, and in keeping with the importance of the matter I beg, that you look around among the great number of students who come to you out of admiration of your genius for teachers whom we can solicit —on this condition, however, that I do not make a binding contract with anyone, for I leave complete freedom of choice to the parents. They shall judge, they shall select. For myself I claim only the trouble and the expense.

Pliny *Letters* Book IV, No. 1 (abridged)

Gaius Plinius to Fabatus, his dear grandfather-in-law, greeting.

There is a town near my estate called Tifernum-on-Tiber,[91] which, with more good will than good sense, chose me as its patron when I was still practically a boy. They celebrate my arrivals, express sadness at my departures, rejoice in my honors. To express my thanks—for nothing is more shameful than to be outdone in affection—I have built a temple in this place at my own expense; and since it is completed, it is really irreligious to delay the dedication of it any longer. We shall therefore be there on the day of the dedication, which I have decided to celebrate with a public banquet.

91. *Patrons of Municipalities*

From the beginning of the Empire it was very common for local councils to adopt prominent personages as patrons to protect the interests of the municipality. It was possible for such an individual to be patron of several municipalities and for a community to have a number of patrons. Numerous bronze patronage tablets, presented to patrons in recognition of their acceptance of the relationship, have survived.

CIL, Vol. V, No. 4,919 (= Dessau, No. 6,100)

[Vicinity of Brescia, Italy, A.D. 27]

In the consulship of Marcus Crassus Frugi and Lucius Calpurnius Piso, February 11, the municipality of Themetra in Africa contracted a patronage relationship with Gaius Silius Aviola son of Gaius, of the Fabian tribe, and chose him, his children, and their descendants as patrons for themselves, their children, and descendants. Gaius Silius Aviola son of Gaius, of the Fabian tribe, accepted the people of the municipality of Themetra, their children, and descendants for himself, his children, and their descendants under his protection and patronage.

[91] Cf. § 41, fifth selection.

Done by Banno son of Himilo, *sufes*,[92] and by Azdrubal son of Baisillex and Iddibal son of Bosthar, envoys.

CIL, Vol. VIII, No. 8,837 (= Dessau, No. 6,103)

[North Africa, A.D. 55]

In the consulship of NERO Claudius Caesar Augustus Germanicus and Lucius Antistius Vetus, August 1, Quintus Julius Secundus son of Quintus, of the Quirine tribe, legate with rank of praetor, contracted a patronage relationship with the decurions and citizens of the colony Julia Augusta Tupusuctu, [composed of veterans] of Legion VII, and received them under his protection and patronage for himself, his children, and their descendants. Done by the envoys Quintus Caecilius Firmanus son of Quintus, of the Palatine tribe, and Marcus Pomponius Vindex son of Marcus, of the Quirine tribe.

CIL, Vol. XI, No. 4,815 (= Dessau, No. 6,638)

[Spoleto, Italy]

Gaius Torasius Severus son of Gaius, of the Horatian tribe, *quattuorvir* with judicial power,[93] augur, built this [94] in his own name and in the name of his son, Publius Meclonius Proculus Torasianus, pontiff, on his own land and at his own expense. He likewise gave to the community for celebrating the birthday of his son 250,000 sesterces, out of the income from which on August 30 annually the decurions are to hold a public banquet and the townspeople who are present receive eight sesterces apiece. Likewise he gave to the board of six priests of Augustus and the priests of the Lares of Augustus and the block captains [95] 120,000 sesterces, so that out of the income from this sum they might have a public repast on the same day. Because of his services to the municipality the council of decurions adopted him as patron of the municipality.

[92] It is interesting to note the survival of the Punic title for the chief magistrate, as well as of Punic personal names.
[93] Cf. Vol. I, p. 415, Note 53.   [94] Probably the public baths.
[95] All these were freedmen associated with the cult of the emperors; cf. introduction to § 66 and § 141.

92. *The Municipal Aristocracy*

See Introduction to § 90.

CIL, Vol. XIV, No. 3,014 (= Dessau, No. 6,252)

[Praeneste, Italy]

To Gnaeus Voesius Aper son of Gnaeus, quaestor, aedile, duovir, flamen of the deified Augustus, member of the board of six priests of Augustus, commissioner of the grain supply for three years in succession, commissioner of the public gladiatorial exhibition three times —because during the time of his public offices and commissionerships he made very great contributions with fullest zeal and munificence to the enjoyment and welfare of the people and also presented a public gladiatorial exhibition and a *spoliarium* [96] constructed on land purchased at his own expense. Because of his services, at the request of the people it was decreed to erect a statue to him at public expense. By decree of the decurions.

CIL, Vol. VIII, No. 22,737 (= Dessau, No. 6,780)

[Gigthis, North Africa]

To Marcus Servilius Draco Albucianus son of Publius, of the Quirine tribe, duovir, lifetime flamen—because, in addition to his many services to the town and his most generous acts of munificence, he undertook at his own expense two embassies to Rome to secure the greater Latin rights and finally brought back favorable news—the council decreed that [this statue] be erected with public funds. And when he, content with the honor, turned the money back to the town, the people erected it at their own expense.

IGRR, Vol. III, No. 739, col. 10, lines 1–45, and col. 11, lines 1–32 [97]

[Rhodiapolis, Lycia, A.D. 124/53]

Decreed by the league of the people of Lycia at a legal meeting. Whereas Opramoas son of Apollonius (son and grandson of Calliades), president of the league, scion of the leading families in the province, in addition to his other kindnesses to the people and the improvements

[96] A place in an amphitheater where the bodies of slain gladiators were stripped of clothing and equipment.
[97] From an enormous inscription, in twenty columns of writing, covering the walls of the mausoleum of Opramoas, president of the league of Greek cities of Lycia. The inscription contains over 150 honorary decrees passed by the league assembly and by towns in Lycia testifying to his benefactions.

he made during the offices he held, singularly displayed his magnanimity in all things by giving an additional 55,000 *denarii* [98]—may good fortune attend!—it was decreed to honor him now also in the present year, as the people voted, and to record this decree.

Cornelius Proculus, imperial legate with rank of praetor, to Julius Capitolinus[?], secretary of the city of Myra, greeting. As for the terms in which the council and people honored Opramoas, son of Apollonius (son and grandson of Calliades), I permit and authorize him to be so addressed, unless this is contrary to either your laws or your customs.[99] I bid you farewell. Recorded in the high-priesthood of Polycharmus. . . .

The Emperor Caesar Titus Aelius Hadrianus ANTONINUS Augustus, son of the deified Hadrian, grandson of the deified Trajan Parthicus, great-grandson of the deified Nerva, *pontifex maximus*, holding the tribunician power for the seventh year, hailed *imperator* twice, three times consul, father of his country, to the league of the Lycians. If Opramoas son of Apollonius had been so exceedingly zealous toward one city, he naturally would have obtained testimonials from that city. But since many cities, as you write, have received some contribution for the restoration of the places which suffered from the earthquake,[100] it was proper for the [entire] province to bear testimonial to him. Eupolemus son of Eupolemus was the envoy. Farewell. September 22, from Rome.

93. *The Humble Townspeople: From the Walls of Pompeii*

The house walls of Pompeii facing the streets were usurped not only for election appeals (see Vol. I, p. 430; Vol II, § 84) but for messages and jottings of every kind, from notices of entertainments, market days, properties to let, boldly painted in bright red, to the scribblings and scratchings (*graffiti*) of shoppers, drunkards, lovelorn swains—in short, a kaleidoscope as varied as the pulsating life of the community itself. A few examples are given here to illustrate this vast body of material.

[98] In honor of his election to the presidency of the Lycian League.
[99] The more important acts of municipal legislation were subject to approval by the governor of the province or by the emperor: cf. § 82, and § 95, first selection.
[100] Cf. Chapter II, Note 44.

CIL, Vol. IV, Nos. 3,884, 5,380, 1,679, 64, 1,824, 1,928, 5,372 (= E. Diehl,
Pompeianische Wandinschriften [Bonn, 1910], Nos. 242, 390, 34, 432,
27, 1, 463), and H. Geist, *Pompeianische Wandinschriften*
(Munich, 1936), pp. 98, 58, 74

i

Twenty pairs of gladiators [101] of Decimus Lucretius Satrius Valens,
lifetime *flamen* of Nero son of Caesar Augustus, and ten pairs of gladiators of Decimus Lucretius Valens, his son, will fight at Pompeii on
April 8, 9, 10, 11, 12. There will be a full card of wild beast combats, and
awnings [for the spectators]. Aemilius Celer [painted this sign], all alone
in the moonlight.

ii

Market days: Saturday in Pompeii, Sunday in Nuceria, Monday in
Atella, Tuesday in Nola, Wednesday in Cumae, Thursday in Puteoli,
Friday in Rome.[102]

iii

6th: cheese 1, bread 8, oil 3, wine 3 [103]
7th: bread 8, oil 5, onions 5, bowl 1, bread for the slave[?] 2, wine 2
8th: bread 8, bread for the slave[?] 4, grits 3
9th: wine for the winner 1 *denarius*, bread 8, wine 2, cheese 2
10th: . . . 1 *denarius*, bread 2, for women 8, wheat 1 *denarius*, cu-
cumber 1, dates 1, incense 1, cheese 2, sausage 1, soft cheese 4, oil 7

iv

Pleasure says: "You can get a drink here for an *as*, a better drink for
two, Falernian [104] for four.

v

A copper pot is missing from this shop. 65 sesterces reward if anybody brings it back, 20 sesterces if he reveals the thief so we can get our
property back.

vi

The weaver Successus loves the inkeeper's slave girl, Iris by name.

---

[101] Another similar notice speaks of "twenty pairs of gladiators and their replacements."
[102] In Latin the days of the week are called those of Saturn, Sun, Moon, Mars,
Mercury, Jupiter, Venus; cf. their names in the Romance languages.
[103] The initial number is the day of the month, the numbers following the items
of food indicate expenditures in *asses*, except where *denarii* are specified.
[104] One of the prized wines of the Italian countryside (named after a district in
Campania), best known from the poems of Horace which sing its praises.

She doesn't care for him, but he begs her to take pity on him. Written by his rival. So long.

[Answer by the rival:] Just because you're bursting with envy, don't pick on a handsomer man, a lady-killer and a gallant.

[Answer by the first writer:] There's nothing more to say or write. You love Iris, who doesn't care for you.

vii

Take your lewd looks and flirting eyes off another man's wife, and show some decency on your face!

viii

Anybody in love, come here. I want to break Venus' ribs with a club and cripple the goddess' loins. If she can pierce my tender breast, why can't I break her head with a club?

ix

I write at Love's dictation and Cupid's instruction;
But damn it! I don't want to be a god without you.

x

[A prostitute's sign:] I am yours for 2 *asses* cash.

94. *Provincial Administration*

TECHNIQUES OF ROMAN RULE

Tacitus *Agricola* xix–xxi

Agricola fully understood the temperament of the province [Britain], and he was aware from the experience of others that little is gained by conquest if it is followed by injustices. He therefore determined to root out the causes of war. Starting with himself and his retinue, he kept his household in check—a thing as difficult for many as governing a province. He transacted no official business through his freedmen or slaves. No personal feelings, no recommendations, no pleas induced him to take centurions or soldiers on his staff; in each case he regarded the best man as the most reliable. . . .

He made the exaction of grain and tribute less onerous by removing inequities in these obligations, eradicating schemes for profit which were more intolerable than the tribute itself. Previously the people used to be compelled to go through the farce of waiting around [with their grain] while the granaries were kept closed, and of actually buying grain and thus quitting themselves of their obligations in money.[105] In addition, devious routes and remote districts used to be assigned, so that some tribes, with an army camp nearby, had to carry their grain to remote and inaccessible places. . . .

By suppressing these abuses in the very first year [106] of his administration, Agricola restored the popularity of peace, whereas under his predecessors—thanks to their indifference or arrogance—peace had been dreaded no less than war. Furthermore, when summer came, the army was assembled, and he took an active part in maneuvers, praising good discipline and checking stragglers. He would personally choose the site of the camp and personally explore the estuaries and forests. Meanwhile, he allowed the enemy no rest, making sudden raids and devastating their lands. And when he had sufficiently cowed them, he would in turn by his clemency hold out to them the attractions of peace. In consequence, many tribes which up to that time had lived in independence gave hostages and abandoned their hostility, and they were so skillfully and carefully ringed with garrisons and forts that they were annexed with less incident than any part of Britain had previously been.

The following winter was employed in salutary measures. For, in order that people who were scattered, uncivilized, and hence prone to war might be accustomed to peace and quiet through comforts, Agricola gave personal encouragement and public assistance to the building of temples, forums, and houses. By praising the energetic and reproving the indolent, he replaced compulsion with competition for honor. He likewise provided a liberal education for the sons of the chiefs, and, preferring the native ability of the Britons to the industriousness of the Gauls, he so encouraged them that though they had lately disdained the Roman language they now eagerly aspired to rhetoric.[107] Hence, too, our style of dress came to be esteemed, and the toga became fashionable. Step by step they turned aside to alluring vices, porticoes, baths, elegant banquets. This in their inexperience they called "culture," whereas it was but an aspect of their enslavement.

[105] That is, they were forced to pay the officials money in lieu of grain to meet their tax assessments. This and the other corrupt practices mentioned just below are suspiciously reminiscent of the operations of Verres, the rapacious governor of Sicily in the last century of the Republic (see Vol. I, § 144), and are probably typical Tacitean rhetorical embellishments.

[106] A.D. 78.

[107] Cf. Juvenal *Satires* xv. 112: "Even Thule speaks of hiring a professor of oratory."

THE SPANISH PROVINCES

Strabo *Geography* III. iv. 20
Adapted from LCL

At the present time, now that some of the provinces have been declared the property of the people and senate and the others that of the emperor,[108] Baetica belongs to the people; and to govern it they send a praetor, who has under him both a quaestor and a legate. . . . But all the rest [of Iberia] is Caesar's; and he sends thither two legates, a praetorian and a consular—the praetorian legate, who has with him a legate of his own, being sent to administer justice to those of the Lusitanians whose country is situated alongside Baetica and extends as far as the Douro river and its outlets. . . . The remainder of Caesar's territory (and this is most of Iberia) is under the consular governor, who has under him not only a noteworthy army of three legions but also three legates. One of the three, with two legions, guards the frontier of the whole country beyond the Douro to the north. . . . The part beyond, along the mountains as far as the Pyrenees, is guarded by the second of the three legates and the other legion. The third legate oversees the interior and also protects the interests of the peoples who are already called "toga'd" (which is to say, "peaceably inclined"), and have become transformed, clad in their togas, to their present gentleness of disposition and their Italian mode of life; these latter are the Celtiberians and the peoples that live near them on both sides of the Ebro as far as the regions next to the sea. As for the governor himself, he passes his winters administering justice in the regions by the sea, and especially in New Carthage and Tarragona, while in the summertime he goes the rounds of his province, always making an inspection of some of the things that require rectification. There are also imperial procurators there, of equestrian rank, who distribute among the soldiers the things that are necessary for the maintenance of their lives.

THE ADMINISTRATION OF EGYPT

The province of Egypt possessed an exceptional status and a correspondingly unique administrative system. The existing Hellenistic administrative apparatus was preserved by Augustus and adapted to the function assigned to Egypt by him—to serve as a granary of Rome and as a copious source of a multiplicity of revenues for the imperial fisc. As the personal domain of the emperor, it was autocratically ruled under a virtual viceroy assisted by an elaborate bureaucracy, was deliberately kept unurbanized (except for a few

[108] Cf. § 8.

existing cities such as Alexandria), and was systematically exploited and drained of its wealth.

Strabo *Geography* XVII. i. 12

Adapted from LCL

Egypt is now a province. It pays considerable tribute and is governed by prudent men, the different prefects sent there. This official has the rank of the [former] king; and subordinate to him is the administrator of justice, who has authority over most of the lawsuits; [109] and another is the official called the *idiologus*, who inquires into all properties that are without owners and that ought to fall to Caesar; [110] and these [officials] are attended by imperial freedmen and also by procurators who are entrusted with affairs of greater or lesser importance. There are also three legions of soldiers,[111] one of which is stationed in the city [of Alexandria] and the others in the country; and apart from these there are nine Roman cohorts, three in the city, three on the borders of Ethiopia in Syene, as a guard for that region, and three in the rest of the country. And there are also three cavalry units, which are likewise assigned to the various critical points. Of the native officials in the city, one is the *exegetes*, who is clad in purple, has hereditary prerogatives, and has charge of the interests of the city; another is the recorder; another the chief judge; [112] and a fourth the commander of the night watch.

CONTROL OF MOVEMENT IN EGYPT

As the successor of three millennia of absolute monarchs in Egypt, the Roman emperor was the lord of the land and of all it contained, and the movement of goods and persons into and out of this private imperial preserve was rigidly controlled (cf. Chapter I, Note 106, and § 99, clauses 64–66).

Strabo *Geography* II. iii. 5

[In Ptolemaic times it was] not permitted to sail from Alexandria without a pass. . . . Nor could one have sailed out secretly, since the harbor and other exits were kept closed by as strong a guard as I (who have lived in Alexandria a long time) personally know still exists at this time,[113] though now, under Roman possession, it is much relaxed.

---

[109] The *juridicus*, an equestrian official who served as vice-prefect and to whom some of the prefect's judicial powers were delegated.
[110] Cf. pp. 52 and 378 and § 99.
[111] Reduced to two legions by Tiberius, and to one by Trajan.
[112] Despite his high-sounding title this local official had jurisdiction over only minor civil suits: he was, in other words, the chief judge of the local, as opposed to the imperial, administration.
[113] The first decades of the first century.

Oxyrhynchus Papyrus No. 1,271 (= *Select Papyri*, No. 304); A.D. 246

To Valerius Firmus, prefect of Egypt, from Aurelia Maeciana of Side.[114] I wish, my lord, to sail out via Pharus; [115] I request you to write to the procurator of Pharus to grant me clearance according to the usual practice. Pachon 1. Farewell.

THE ASSIZES OF THE PREFECT

The Roman governors periodically went on circuit through their provinces, holding assizes at major stops. This papyrus preserves part of the itinerary of a prefect of Egypt on such a tour some time in the first century.

Oxyrhynchus Papyrus No. 709 (= Wilcken, No. 32)

. . . the prefect on his journey will stop first at Pelusium, where he will hold the assizes for the Tanite, Sethroite, Arabian, and Avian nomes; then at Memphis similarly for the Thebaid, the Heptanomia, and the Arsinoite nome; and for the remaining nomes of the Lower Country . . . in Alexandria. . . . [The rest is fragmentary.]

PREPARATIONS FOR A PREFECT'S VISIT

An impending visit by the governor, even if only for an overnight halt, was a busy time for the inhabitants of the locality, who were required to provide lodgings, food, and often transport for the governor and his retinue (cf. Vol. I, p. 367).

British Museum Papyrus No. 1,159 (= Wilcken, No. 415); A.D. 145/47

From the village scribes. In accordance with your [116] request for a list of persons to provide the necessities being made ready for the beneficent visit of Valerius Proculus, most glorious prefect, we submit, omitting those excused in accordance with official memoranda, [a list of persons] in place of those transferred to other public services and of those deceased.[117]

[There follows a long list of names of individuals who will be responsible for the different provisions; among the latter are listed bread (pure), lamb, wine, vinegar, hay, chaff, barley, wood, charcoal, torches, lamps, geese, oil, relishes, cheeses, vegetables, fish, and pack asses.]

114 A town in Pamphylia, Asia Minor.
115 The island in the harbor of Alexandria, on which stood the famous lighthouse of the same name.
116 Probably the *strategus* of the nome.
117 Since the last such visit. The list of provisioners was obviously in the official files, and the present report was intended to bring it up to date.

95. *Arbitration of Inter-City Disputes*

Under the Empire inter-city disputes in the provinces were usually handled by the governor of the province, who might, in continuation of republican practices (cf. Vol. I, § 133), assign a neutral arbiter. The emperor was, of course, the final arbiter to whom a dispute might be referred by or appealed from a governor. But most of the time the governor's word was law; thus, in one such decision, the governor of Sardinia warned the losers "to keep the peace and abide by judgment rendered . . . but if they persist in their contumacy he would take severe measures against the instigators of sedition" (*CIL,* Vol X, No. 7,852 = Abbott-Johnson, No. 58; A.D. 69).

IG, Vol. XI, Part 2, No. 261, lines 7–16 (= Abbott-Johnson, No. 46)

[Cierium, Thessaly, A.D. 15/35]

To Gaius Poppaeus Sabinus,[118] legate of Tiberius Caesar, from . . . secretary of the assembly,[119] many greetings. You wrote us about the dispute which Cierium and Metropolis had about boundaries, requesting the assembly to arbitrate it, as you also indicated to me in person in Aedepsus. Please be informed that as soon as I returned home I placed the arbitration on the calendar of the current assembly of the Thessalian League meeting at Larissa in the month of Thyus. Both parties appeared at the arbitration and presented their cases, and the ballots were cast in secret under oath, 298 for Cierium, 31 for Metropolis, 5 invalid. We deemed it fitting to write you this. Farewell.

[There follows a letter from the *strategus* of the league, also reporting the vote and adding, "so that the decision may receive your confirmation."]

CIL, Vol. IX, No. 5,420, lines 1–28 (= Abbott-Johnson, No. 63 = *FIRA,* Vol. I, No. 75)

[Falerio, Italy, A.D. 82]

The Emperor Caesar DOMITIAN Augustus, son of the deified Vespasian, holder of the tribunician power, twice acclaimed *imperator,* eight times consul and designated for a ninth time, father of his country, sends greetings to the *quattuorviri* [120] and decurions of Falerio in Picenum. I have ordered appended to this letter, for your information, what I have decided concerning the unsurveyed land [121] after investigating the

---

[118] He was governor of Moesia, A.D. 11–35. In A.D. 15 the provinces of Achaea and Macedonia were added to his jurisdiction.
[119] That is, of the league of cities of Thessaly.
[120] Cf. Vol. I, § 162.
[121] Cf. Chapter III, Note 38.

dispute between you and the town of Firmium. In the consulship of Publius Valerius Patruinus and Domitian, July 19.

I, the Emperor Caesar DOMITIAN Augustus, son of the deified Vespasian, investigated the dispute between Falerio and Firmium in consultation with distinguished men of both orders [122] and decided what is written below. I am strongly influenced both by the antiquity of the suit which has been revived after so many years by Firmium against Falerio, since even fewer years can be sufficient for the security of the possessors,[123] and also by the letter of the deified Augustus, emperor most attentive and beneficent toward the soldiers of his Fourth Legion,[124] in which he advised them to gather together and sell all their unsurveyed land, and I doubt not that they obeyed such salutary advice. For these reasons I confirm the rights of the possessors. Farewell.

96. *Letter of Claudius to the Alexandrians*

On the accession of Claudius in A.D. 41 an embassy was sent by the Alexandrians to the new emperor to bestow various honors on him and to request favors and the solution of a number of problems. Among the latter was the explosive relationship between Greeks and Jews, which had erupted into riots and massacres at the news of the death of Caligula, whose aggressive claim to divine worship the Jews had resisted. One of the principal causes of the friction was the jealously guarded Alexandrian citizenship, which the Jews, who were juridically and politically inferior to the Greeks, were desirous of obtaining because of its political and economic advantages and because it provided an avenue to Roman citizenship.

British Museum Papyrus No. 1,912 (= *Select Papyri*, No. 212)

Adapted from LCL

Lucius Aemilius Rectus [prefect of Egypt] declares: Since the whole of the city, owing to its numbers, was unable to be present at the reading of the most sacred and most beneficent letter to the city, I have deemed it necessary to display the letter publicly in order that reading it individually you may admire the majesty of our god Caesar and feel gratitude for his good will toward the city. Year 2 of the Emperor Tiberius CLAUDIUS Caesar Augustus Germanicus, 14th of New Augustus.[125]

The Emperor Tiberius CLAUDIUS Caesar Augustus Germanicus,

---

[122] It is noteworthy that the emperor's *consilium* (see Chapter I, Note 13) at this time included men of equestrian as well as of senatorial rank.
[123] Cf. § 123, first selection.
[124] Cf. Vol. I, §§ 114, 117.   [125] Cf. Chapter II, Note 20.

pontifex maximus, holder of the tribunician power, consul designate, to the city of Alexandria, greeting. Tiberius Claudius Barbillus, Apollonius son of Artemidorus, Chaeremo son of Leonidas, Marcus Julius Asclepiades, Gaius Julius Dionysius, Tiberius Claudius Phanias, Pasio son of Potamo, Dionysius son of Sabbio, Tiberius Claudius Archibius, Apollonius son of Aristo, Gaius Julius Apollonius, Hermaiscus son of Apollonius, your envoys, delivered your decree to me and discoursed at length concerning the city, directing my attention to your good will toward us, which from long ago, you may be sure, had been stored up to your advantage in my memory; for you are by nature reverent toward the emperors, as I have come to know well from many things, and in particular you have taken a warm interest—warmly reciprocated—in my house, of which fact (to mention the latest instance, passing over the others) the supreme witness is my brother Germanicus Caesar when he addressed you in franker tones [by word of mouth].[126]

Wherefore I gladly accepted the honors given to me by you, though I am not partial to such things. And first I permit you to keep my birthday as an Augustan day [127] in the manner you have yourselves proposed, and I agree to the erection by you in their several places of the statues of myself and my family; for I see that you were zealous to establish on every side memorials of your reverence for my house. Of the two golden statues, the one made to represent the Claudian Augustan Peace, as my most honored Barbillus suggested and persisted in when I wished to refuse for fear of being thought too offensive, shall be erected at Rome, and the other according to your request shall be carried in procession on my name days in your city; and it shall be accompanied in the procession by a throne, adorned with whatever trappings you wish. It would perhaps be foolish, while accepting such great honors, to refuse the institution of a Claudian tribe and the establishment of sacred groves after the manner of Egypt; wherefore I grant you these requests as well, and if you wish you may also erect the equestrian statues given by Vitrasius Pollio my procurator. As for the erection of the statues in four-horse chariots which you wish to set up to me at the entrances to the country, I consent to let one be placed at the town called Taposiris, in Libya, another at Pharus in Alexandria, and a third at Pelusium in Egypt. But I deprecate the appointment of a high priest for me and the building of temples, for I do not wish to be offensive to my contemporaries, and my opinion is that temples and the like have by all ages been granted as special honors to the gods alone.[128]

[126] On Germanicus' visit to Egypt, see §§ 106, 168.
[127] See Note 143 below.
[128] On the policies of the emperors toward emperor worship, see §§ 14, 168.

Concerning the requests which you have been eager to obtain from me, I decide as follows. All those who have become ephebes [129] up to the time of my principate I confirm and maintain in possession of the Alexandrian citizenship with all the privileges and indulgences enjoyed by the city, excepting those who by fraud have contrived to become ephebes though born of slaves. And it is equally my will that all the other privileges shall be confirmed which were granted to you by the emperors before me, and by the kings and by the prefects, as the deified Augustus also confirmed them. It is my will that the overseers of the temples of the deified Augustus in Alexandria shall be chosen by lot in the same way as those of the same deified Augustus in Canopus are chosen by lot. With regard to the municipal magistracies being made triennial, your proposal seems to me to be very good; for through fear of being called to account for any misrule your magistrates will behave with greater circumspection during their term of office. Concerning the city council, what your custom may have been under the ancient kings I have no means of saying, but that you had no council under the former emperors you are well aware. As this is the first broaching of a novel project, whose utility to the city and to my interests is not evident, I have written to Aemilius Rectus to hold an inquiry and inform me whether in the first place it is right that the body should be constituted, and, if it should be right to create one, in what manner this is to be done.

As for which party was responsible for the riot and feud (or rather, if the truth must be told, the war) with the Jews, although your envoys, particularly Dionysius son of Theo, confronting [your opponents] put your case with great zeal, nevertheless I was unwilling to make a strict inquiry, though guarding within me a store of immutable indignation against any who renewed the conflict; and I tell you once for all that unless you put a stop to this ruinous and obstinate enmity against each other, I shall be driven to show what a benevolent emperor can be when turned to righteous indignation. Wherefore once again I conjure you that, on the one hand, the Alexandrians show themselves forbearing and kindly toward the Jews, who for many years have dwelt in the same city, and dishonor none of the rights observed by them in the worship of their god but allow them to observe their customs as in the time of the deified Augustus,[130] which customs I also, after hearing both sides, have confirmed. And, on the other hand, I explicitly order the Jews not to agitate for more privileges than they formerly possessed, and in the future not to send out a separate embassy as if they lived in a separate

---

[129] In Greek cities, youths of eighteen elegible for citizenship were termed ephebes. Formal enrollment in the list of ephebes constituted proof of citizenship.
[130] Cf. § 104, second selection.

city—a thing unprecedented—and not to force their way into gymnasi-
archic or cosmetic games,[131] while enjoying their own privileges and
sharing a great abundance of advantages in a city not their own, and not
to bring in or admit Jews from Syria or those who sail down from Egypt,
a proceeding which will compel me to conceive serious suspicions;
otherwise I will by all means proceed against them as fomenters of what
is a general plague of the whole world.[132] If, desisting from these courses,
you both consent to live with mutual forbearance and kindliness, I on
my side will exercise a solicitude of very long standing for the city, as
one bound to us by ancestral friendship. I bear witness to my friend
Barbillus of the solicitude which he has always shown for you in my
presence and of the extreme zeal with which he has now advocated your
cause, and likewise to my friend Tiberius Claudius Archibius. Farewell.

97. Growth of Compulsory Public Services

Conscription of manual labor for public works and services was a general
practice of the ancient Orient and the city-states of Greece. The assignment
of compulsory public offices (liturgies) to financially able citizens was especially developed among the Greeks. It was left for the Roman Empire to
organize such services into an elaborate system of municipal and provincial
administration. Our fullest and most detailed information on this subject
comes from Egypt, where the system doubtless attained its most extensive development. To guarantee the steady flow of local and imperial revenues the
emperors at first relied on a salaried bureaucracy and on the keen competition
for municipal offices, whose expenses were defrayed by the incumbents. But
increasing economic difficulties forced the abandonment of this policy. The
change is clearly apparent, though not yet fully developed, by the end of
the first century. Thereafter, the emperors found it increasingly necessary
to intervene, directly or through their provincial governors, in the local affairs
(especially financial) of the cities and towns, and it became increasingly
necessary to draft unwilling candidates to fill municipal offices (cf. §§ 83,
85). By the middle of the second century the liturgical system had been extended to embrace practically all local administrative functions, and the
principle of compulsory service in these functions was as firmly established
for all those who possessed certain minimum property qualifications as was
the assignment of imperial and public lands for compulsory cultivation when
no voluntary lessees appeared. Furthermore, municipal magistrates and

[131] That is, games presented under the supervision of the gymnasiarchs and the
cosmetae of Alexandria, who were in charge of the municipal gymnasia.
[132] Some commentators, remembering the similar expression of Tacitus (see p. 227),
have taken this phrase to be the earliest known allusion to Christianity. But it is
much more likely that it refers to the agitation for special privileges by the Jews
of the Diaspora, who had settled in many cities of the Empire: cf. § 110.

councilmen and all other liturgists were made collectively responsible for the expenses and revenues of their offices, so that any default by one automatically became an obligation of the remaining members of the group. "The main object of the system was to get public work done at private expense; in effect it was a heavy tax on the moneyed classes and eventually brought them to ruin" (*Select Papyri,* II, xx-xxi). Not infrequently, propertied liturgists— like penniless peasants—resorted to flight from home and to other measures of desperation in an attempt to escape from their crushing fiscal burdens. Only certain privileged groups and persons already performing essential services for the state or army in their regular capacities were exempted from liturgic service. Among these were soldiers and veterans, professional athletes, priests, members of learned professions, village secretaries, women, and men over sixty-five; and the exemptions of some of these even were occasionally canceled. See further §§ 121 and 134 for the continued spread and increasing rigor of the liturgic system in the third and fourth centuries.

TAX FARMERS BY COMPULSION

This papyrus of the latter part of the first century is particularly interesting in the light of the prefect's edict of A.D. 68 (§ 98) assailing the use of compulsion in the leasing of public contracts.

Oxyrhynchus Papyrus No. 44 (= Abbott-Johnson, No. 167 =
Select Papyri, No. 420)

Paniscus . . . *strategus* of the Oxyrhynchite nome, to Asclepiades, royal secretary of the same nome, greeting. At the last auction of tax contracts held by myself and you in the presence of the customary officials, since the farmers in charge of the tax on transfers of real property and of the *agoranomus* [133] office refused to bid on the ground that they were incurring substantial losses and may even withdraw, I wrote our opinion to His Excellency the Prefect concerning the matter. He replied to the effect that I should examine the former leases and as far as possible lighten the burden of the tax farmers, so as not to have persons engaged against their will become fugitives. I previously sent you a copy of the letter for your information and [told you] that in your absence, as the contracts had not been accepted by the tax farmers and no other persons were coming forward for them in spite of repeated announcements, I took affidavits from those in charge of the tax on sales of real property and the record office. . . .[134] [The rest is lost.]

[133] This tax on sales of real and certain other forms of property apparently remained fixed at ten percent under the Principate. On the function of the *agoranomus* see above, p. 262.

[134] Despite the implication in this letter that tax farmers were not to be compelled to renew their contracts, the practice continued. It is again deprecated in a rescript of the Emperor Hadrian (Justinian *Digest* XLIX. xiv. 3. 6): "It is a most inhuman

PERSONAL RESPONSIBILITY

The poll-tax collectors in this document have a fixed monthly quota to pay to the government, irrespective of the amount actually collected by them. Under the circumstances it is not surprising to find them employing an armed guard, no doubt both to provide them with physical protection and to help them enforce collections.

Tebtynis Papyrus No. 391; A.D. 100

Adapted from the translation of B. P. Grenfell, A. S. Hunt, and E. J. Goodspeed (London, 1907)

We, Heracles, Athenodorus, Hero, and Zoilus, all four collectors of the poll tax of the village of Tebtynis, agree voluntarily and of our own free will that we have made a division [of our duties], from the 15th of the month Hathyr, the receipts of which are credited to Phaophi, of the third year of the lord Trajan Caesar for the current third year only of the Emperor Caesar Nerva TRAJAN Augustus Germanicus; and that Athenodorus and Heracles have been allotted the inhabitants of and settlers in the village, while Hero and Zoilus have for their part been allotted all the inhabitants and settlers [of Tebtynis] at other villages or in the metropolis, with the stipulation that those who have been allotted the external district shall pay each month 1,100 silver drachmas, while those who have been allotted the village shall make up the balance of the monthly quota for the poll tax, the wages of the armed guard being chargeable to those who have been allotted the village. If any one of us four violates any of the aforesaid provisions, he shall pay to the party abiding by them 500 drachmas and to the public treasury an equal sum. This bond shall be valid, as if it had been publicly registered. The coming extra levy of the current third year shall be collected by each of them from persons allotted to him. Year 3 of the Emperor Caesar Nerva TRAJAN Augustus Germanicus, Hathyr. . . .

NOMINATION TO LITURGIC SERVICE

Berlin Papyrus No. 18 (= Wilcken, No. 398 = *Select Papyri*, No. 342); A.D. 169

Adapted from LCL

Copy of announcement. Serenus, royal secretary of the Arsinoite nome, division of Heraclides, and acting *strategus*. To be assessors of un-

---

practice to compel lessees of public revenues and lands to continue when the contracts cannot be let at the same price. Indeed, lessees will come forward even more readily if they can be sure that they will not be compelled to continue should they wish to withdraw when the five-year [contract] period is completed."

sold [state] lands—in place of Gaius Julius Ptollis, Amarantus son of Hestiaeus, Hero surnamed Eudaemo, and Diodorus son of Theogito, who have all four completed the prescribed period, and of Anubio son of Hero and Demetrius son of Suchammo, both stated to be deceased—the persons named below have been nominated by the city secretaries as well-to-do and suitable for compulsory public services. They are ordered to take up the task entrusted to them honestly and faithfully, so as not to incur blame in any respect. Signed. Year 9 of the lord [Marcus] Aurelius Antoninus Caesar Armeniacus Medicus Parthicus Maximus, Mesore 17. They are:

Gaius Julius Apollinaris, owning land at Caranis, having property worth 4,000 drachmas; Mysthes son of Cornelius, owning land at New Ptolemais, having property worth one talent; Antonius Heraclianus, owning land at the hamlet of Nestus, likewise 4,000 drachmas; Gaius Julius Saturnilus, owning land at Tanis, having property worth 4,000 drachmas; Ptolemaeus, or however he is styled, public secretary of Pharbaetha, worth 4,000 drachmas; Pasio son of Petermuthis (son of Petermuthis), of the Hellenium quarter [of Arsinoë], having property worth 4,000 drachmas.

Registered by me, Hero, special assistant, Mesore 20.

Museum Helveticum, II (1945), 54–62; first to second century

From the orders of Mettius Rufus [135] sent to the *strategi*. If any persons discharging compulsory public services appear to you to be unsuitable either because they do not have the requisite wealth or because of physical disability or because they seem unworthy for any other reason, you will send me three names in place of each one, after investigating that all are suitable not only in property but also in age [136] and in the conduct of life which those who are performing the emperor's business ought to have. Accordingly, you will add their wealth, their ages, whether they are literate, and what public offices they previously held. And be careful that the three are not from one household or from the same locality, that they have not previously been in the same offices or been found guilty of improper conduct in other offices, and that the officials for the same locality are not relatives.

. . . .

Year 15 of the deified Trajan, Phamenoth 25, in Naucratis. Dioscorus son of Dionysius appeared and said, "We are two brothers in compulsory public services, and I request that one of us be released in order

[135] Prefect of Egypt, A.D. 89–91 (cf. § 101).
[136] That is, under sixty-five: cf. introduction.

to have the time to attend to our farming." Sulpicius Similis [137] asked, "Have you a father [living]?" When he replied, "No," Sulpicius Similis ordered, "One is to be released."

EXEMPTION FROM LITURGIES

Petitions for release from compulsory public services were frequent. In the extant documents of this type the petitioners repeatedly plead illegal nomination, lack of means, and impoverishment caused by previous performance of liturgies. For further examples see § 121.

Philadelphia Papyrus No. 1, lines 18–34; early second century

Section from an edict of Vibius Maximus, prefect of Egypt.[138] Even among the categories listed below those will perform compulsory public service who own private land and whose wealth is established to exceed one talent, not by unofficial declaration but by their true value. As for priests, they will be compelled [to perform liturgies] only if they cultivate private land.

Those exempt from public services are: priests of important temples . . . cattle raisers . . . over-age and feeble, officially certified . . . physicians . . . merchants, potters[?], oil workers . . . fullers . . . carpenters . . . goldsmiths and . . . tax on trades. . . . [The rest is lost.]

Philadelphia Papyrus No. 10; A.D. 139

To Dio, *strategus* of the Arsinoite nome, division of Heraclides, from the weavers of the village of Philadelphia. There was recently sent us from the public treasury a sum of money with orders for us to make clothing for the state; [139] and our group of artisans, reduced as it is to a small number, considered it an answer to its prayer to be able to execute the orders received. But now four among us have been assigned to escort duty [on the grain boats]. They have been taken from us to perform compulsory public service and have departed for Alexandria; thus our number has been still further reduced. We are therefore compelled to appeal to you and to beg you, if you deem it proper, to give orders that we, who have hitherto been left to our trade, be left alone and undisturbed by other public service, so that we may make and deliver the clothing ordered (especially as we expect a further order to fill for the state), and so that we may thus be the beneficiaries of your benevolence.

[137] Prefect of Egypt, A.D. 107–12. The date of this hearing during his assizes at Naucratis is 112.
[138] In A.D. 103–7.
[139] No doubt intended for the army (cf. § 152).

We were twelve men in number, of whom four have been removed, so that we now remain only eight. Year 3 of the Emperor Caesar Titus Aelius Hadrianus ANTONINUS Augustus PIUS, month of Hadrianus, the 20th.

Fayum Papyrus No. 106, lines 6–25 (= Abbott-Johnson, No. 174 = *Select Papyri*, No. 283); A.D. c.140
From LCL

To Gaius Avidius Heliodorus, prefect of Egypt, from Marcus Valerius Gemellus, physician. Contrary to the prohibitions I have been impressed as a superintendent of confiscated property within the villages of Bacchias and Hephaestias in the Heraclides division of the Arsinoite nome, and through laboring on this task for the last four years I have become quite impoverished, my lord. Wherefore I entreat you, my preserver, to have pity on me and order me now to be released from my task, in order that I may be able to recover from the effects of my labors. I have at the same time appended precedents by which complete exemption from compulsory public services is granted to persons practicing the profession of medicine, especially to those who have been certified,[140] like myself, so that I may experience your benevolence. Farewell.

FLIGHT FROM LITURGY

Berlin Papyrus No. 372 (= Abbott-Johnson, No. 175 = Wilcken, No. 19); A.D. 154

Marcus Sempronius Liberalis, prefect of Egypt, declares: I learn that some persons have left their homes because of the recent disturbance [141] . . . and that others, who fled from certain liturgies because of the poverty about them at the time,[142] are still living away from home

140 Cf. Oxyrhynchus Papyrus No. 40 (= *Select Papyri*, No. 245); A.D. 141/42: "Copy of memorandum of Valerius Eudaemo, then prefect of Egypt. . . . Claim of Psasnis. Psasnis appeared and said, 'I am a physician by profession and I have treated these very persons who have nominated me for a compulsory public service.' Eudaemo said, 'Perhaps you have treated them unskilfully. If you are a state-salaried physician for mummification, tell me the solvent and you shall have exemption from compulsory public service.'"
141 In the preceding year there had been a revolt in Egypt in which the then prefect was killed by the rebels and which seems to have required the personal intervention of the emperor before it was suppressed.
142 Cf. § 105, second selection. Since the people could not pay their taxes, the collectors could not deliver to the government the tax quotas for which they were personally financially responsible; faced with ruin, they fled. Several other papyri give us further details on this desperate recourse to flight to avoid ruinous office-holding. One (British Museum Papyrus 342; A.D. 185) concerns two men who fled,

in fear of the proscriptions that were immediately declared. I therefore urge all to return to their own places of abode and reap the first and greatest fruit of prosperity and of the solicitude of our lord the emperor for all men, and not to wander abroad without hearth or home. That they may comply more readily and gladly, let them know that anyone . . . who is still held back for this reason will perceive the good will and kindness of our greatest emperor in his order that there shall be no judicial inquiry against them, or even against others proscribed by the *strategi* for any cause whatever. . . . [About one fourth of the text is lost here.]

. . . and they associate with fugitives who have chosen a life of criminals and brigands. That they may understand that I advise and do this not only for them but also for the others, let them know that their excellencies the *epistrategi*, the *strategi*, and the soldiers dispatched by me for the safety and security of the country districts have been given orders to nip incipient raids in the bud by provident and timely measures, to give immediate chase when raids are committed, and to call trouble-makers caught in the act to account as fully as those engaged in actual brigandage but not to annoy others of those once proscribed who are living quietly and attending to their farming at home. Let them return, therefore, without fear, and let their period of grace be three months from the time when this edict of mine is posted in each nome. But if any-one is found wandering abroad after such great benefaction of mine, such person shall be arrested and sent to me no longer as a suspected but as a confessed malefactor. Year 18 of the lord Antoninus, Thoth 1.

98. *Edict of the Prefect Tiberius Julius Alexander*

Considerable light on the internal administration of Egypt is afforded by this edict, issued in A.D. 68 by the prefect Tiberius Julius Alexander. The edict orders an end to a number of abuses which administrative personnel, es-pecially fiscal officials, had introduced during the reign of Nero, perhaps under pressure of increased exactions demanded by that emperor.

Evelyn White–Oliver, No. 4

Julius Demetrius, *strategus* of the Thebaid Oasis. I have subjoined for you a copy of the edict sent to me by the lord prefect, Tiberius Julius Alexander, so that you may be informed and may enjoy his bene-

---

fearing nomination to a liturgy. In another (Geneva Papyrus 37 [= Wilcken, No. 400]; A.D. 186) mention is made of four men who disappeared while their names were still on the list of possible nominees, even before the selection was made.

factions. Year 2 of the emperor Lucius Livius Sulpicius GALBA Augustus, Phaophi 1, Julian Augustan day.[143]

Tiberius Julius Alexander declares: Since I am exercising every solicitude for the city [of Alexandria] to maintain its proper political status in the enjoyment of the benefactions which it has from the emperors, and for Egypt to continue in prosperity and cheerfully contribute to the grain supply and to the very great felicity of the present times unoppressed by novel and unlawful exactions; and since practically from the moment I entered the city I have been assailed by clamors of petitioners, both in small groups and in throngs, both from the most respectable people here and from the country farmers, complaining about the recent abuses, I have lost no time in righting pressing matters to the extent of my authority. And that you may the more cheerfully expect everything for your salvation and happiness from our benefactor, the Emperor Galba Augustus, who has brought light to us for the salvation of the whole human race, and that you may know that I have been concerned with the matters relating to your relief, I have perforce set forth the decisions and actions that are in my power concerning each of the requests, and the weightier matters requiring the authority and majesty of the emperor I shall report to him in all truth, for the gods have preserved to this most sacred age the security of the inhabited world.

First of all, I recognize the complete reasonableness of your petition that persons not be forced against their will, contrary to the general practice of the provinces, into tax farming or other leases of imperial estate; no little harm has been done by the compulsion of many persons inexperienced in such duties, when [the collection of] the taxes was imposed upon them. Wherefore I myself have not forced and shall not force anyone into tax farming or lease, for I know that it is to the advantage of the imperial revenues, too, to have competent men administer these willingly and zealously. I am confident that in the future no [official] will force tax farmers or lessees against their will, but, observing the invariable practice of the former prefects instead of imitating someone's temporary wrongdoing, will lease to persons willing to come forward voluntarily.[144]

Whereas some [officials] have also had loans of others assigned to themselves under pretense of public obligations and have then proceeded to consign some persons to the debtor prison or to other jails which I

---

[143] September 28. The designation "Augustan" or "Julian Augustan" was applied to a number of days in the calendar to commemorate birthdays or other notable events in the life of the imperial family.

[144] By the beginning of the second century, however, practically all tax collectors in Egypt, at least on the local level, were assigned to their positions as compulsory public services (cf. § 97).

know have been abolished for this very reason, that loans may be executed out of the properties and not out of the persons [of the debtors]; in keeping with the wish of the deified Augustus I order that no one shall, under pretense of public obligations, have loans assigned from others which he did not originally make, and that no free persons shall ever be locked up in any jail whatsoever, except a criminal, or in the debtor prison, except those indebted to the fisc.

[The next section, here omitted, concerns prior liens of the state on the private property of persons who have entered into public contracts.]

I have also received petitions concerning tax exemptions and reductions . . . from persons requesting that these privileges be reaffirmed in accordance with the rescript of the deified Claudius to Postumus [145] granting such release. . . . Since, therefore, Balbillus and Vestinus granted these releases, I reaffirm the decisions of both prefects, especially as they are in accord with the grant of the deified Claudius; hence they have been released from the charges not yet exacted from them, and in the future certainly the tax exemption and reduction will remain in force for them.

[The next section, here omitted, guarantees purchasers of confiscated properties sold by the state against having to pay fiscal rents in addition to normal taxes.]

It is in keeping with the grants of the emperors that native Alexandrians residing in the country for business reasons are not to be forced into any rural compulsory public service. You have often requested this and I confirm it, so that no one of the native Alexandrians shall be forced into rural public services.

I shall take care of assigning appointees to the post of *strategus* for a term of three years after [my] assizes.

In general I order that whenever a prefect has already decided to dismiss a case brought before him, it is not to be brought again before the [prefect's] assizes. And if two prefects have been of the same mind, a state accountant who brings up the same matters before the assizes is also to be punished [in addition to having the case thrown out], seeing that he does nothing else than reserve for himself and the other civil officials a pretext for enrichment. Many persons, in fact, have decided rather to abandon their private possessions, because they had expended more than their value through the same matters being brought to judgment at each assize.

[145] Gaius Julius Postumus, prefect of Egypt A.D. 45–47. The prefects mentioned below and the known dates of their tenure of office are Tiberius Claudius Balbillus, 55–59, and Lucius Julius Vestinus, 59–62.

I also establish the same rule for matters brought up under the "Special Account," [146] so that if any matter has been judged and dismissed, or shall be dismissed, by the [procurator] appointed for the "Special Account," the [accuser] shall not again be permitted to submit [the same charge] to a prosecutor or to bring it to trial, or else the person so doing will be punished mercilessly; for there will be no end of vexatious denunciations if dismissed matters are brought up till someone decides to condemn. Since already the city has become practically uninhabitable because of the multitude of informers and every household is thrown into confusion, I perforce order that if any of the prosecutors attached to the "Special Account" introduces a suit as spokesman for another, he shall produce the real accuser in court, so that the latter, too, may not be free from risk;[147] and if he brings three suits on his own responsibility and does not prove them, he shall not again be permitted to prosecute, but half his estate shall be confiscated; for it is most unjust that a person who brings upon many the dangers of [loss of] property and penalty should himself be completely free from liability. In general I shall order that the code of regulations of the "Special Account" remain in force, since I have amended the innovations introduced contrary to the grants of the emperors. And I shall openly publicize how I have meted out condign punishment to convicted informers.

I am not unaware of the fact that you are very solicitous also for Egypt to continue in prosperity . . . I have righted whatever I could. For often the farmers throughout the whole country have petitioned me and revealed that they have been condemned to [pay] many unprecedented charges . . . through payments in kind and in money, although it is not open to any who like to introduce recklessly some general innovation. These and similar condemnations I have found extending not over the Thebaid alone or the far-off nomes of the Lower Country, but they have already seized upon the very suburbs of the city, the so-called country district of Alexandria and the Mareote nome. Wherefore I give orders to the nome *strategi* that, if farmers have been condemned in the last five years to any unprecedented charges not previously paid in all or most nomes or toparchies, they shall restore the previous status and discontinue the collection of such charges, and any such cases brought to the assizes I dismiss from court.

I have even before this checked also the excessive power of the state accountants, because everybody inveighed against them for entering numerous assessments on the basis of analogy—the result of which was

---

[146] See § 99.
[147] Informers whose denunciations proved to be false were penalized.

that they were getting rich and Egypt was becoming a wasteland. And I now issue orders to the said accountants to enter no assessment on the basis of analogy, nor anything else in general, without the decision of the prefect; I also order the *strategi* in turn to receive nothing of the sort from the state accountants without the instructions of the prefect. And the other civil officials, if they are found to have entered any false or improper assessment, shall repay to the individuals [concerned] whatever they have collected and shall pay a penalty of an equal amount to the fisc.

A malpractice of the same kind is the so-called collection [of taxes] according to estimate, based not on the actual rising of the Nile but on a comparison of certain risings of former times,[148] although nothing seems to be more just than the true facts. I desire men to live in confidence and cultivate with zeal, assured that the collection will be based on the true state of the actual rising and of the inundated land, and not on the trickery of those who enter assessments according to estimate. If anyone is convicted of falsifying it, he shall pay triple damages.

[The last two sections, here omitted, promise that the tax exemption of the territory about Alexandria will not be withdrawn and that other complaints of extortion against the officials will be referred to the emperor, "who alone has the power to put an end to such things completely, and whose constant benevolence and solicitude are the causes of the salvation of us all."]

Year 1 of the Emperor Lucius Livius Sulpicius GALBA Caesar Augustus, Epeiph 12.

99. *Rules for Administering the "Special Account" of Egypt*

This unique papyrus, "the most important document yet discovered in Roman Egypt" (*ESAR*, II, 711), contains a digest of the code of regulations which guided the administration of the *idiologus*. This high official—like the governor, he was of equestrian rank—had charge of the special account (*idios logos*) in which were collected the revenues of the imperial fisc from sources other than taxation, such as fines and confiscated or unclaimed property. The code, which has aptly been termed "a finished instrument of fiscal oppression," affords a striking illustration of the thoroughness and efficiency of the Roman exploitation of Egypt, revealing in particular detail the rigid class system maintained by the Roman rulers of that ancient land. A selection from the 115 clauses in this long document is given here.

[148] On the Nile flood in Egyptian agriculture see § 100.

Berlin Papyrus No. 1,210 (= *Select Papyri*, No. 206 = *FIRA*, Vol. I,
No. 99); A.D. 150/61
Adapted from LCL and ESAR

I [149] have appended for you a copy of the code of regulations which
the deified Augustus established for the administration of the Special
Account and of additions made to it from time to time either by the
emperors or the senate or the various prefects or *idiologi*, summarizing
the sections in current use, so that by applying your memory to the
condensed form of the exposition you may readily master the topics.

4. The estates of those who die intestate and who have no legal
heirs fall to the fisc.

5. Property bequeathed by Alexandrians to persons not qualified
is given to those who can legally inherit from them, if such there be and
if they claim it at law.

6. An Alexandrian may not bequeath to his wife, if he has no offspring by her, more than a fourth part of his estate; and if he has children
by her, he may not allot to his wife a larger share than what he bequeathes
to each of his sons.

7. All wills which are not in the form of public instruments are invalid.

8. If to a Roman will is added a clause saying, "Whatever bequests
I make in Greek codicils shall be valid," it is not admissible, for a Roman
is not permitted to write a Greek will.

16. All property which is bequeathed to freedmen of Romans with
the stipulation that it is to descend to their offspring is confiscated on the
decease of the recipients if it be proved that no offspring had yet been
born when the bequest was written.

17. Property left to provide sacrifices to the departed is confiscated
when there are no longer any persons to take charge of these.

18. Inheritances left in trust by Greeks to Romans or by Romans
to Greeks were confiscated by the divine Vespasian; nevertheless those
acknowledging their trust have received half.

19. Bequests made to freedmen who have not yet acquired legal
emancipation are confiscated. It is legal emancipation if the person freed
is over thirty years of age.[150]

20. Bequests made to one who as a slave was put in chains and
afterwards freed or who was freed when not yet thirty years old are
confiscated.

[149] Perhaps an *idiologus* who prepared this digest as a memorandum to his staff.
[150] This and the next clauses reveal the influence of the legislation of Augustus on
freedmen (see § 12).

22. The property of deceased Latins [151] is given to their patrons and to the sons and daughters and heirs of these; and bequests made by those who have not yet acquired legal Roman freedom are confiscated.

23. Romans are not permitted to marry their sisters or their aunts, but marriage with their brothers' daughters has been conceded. Pardalas,[152] indeed, when a brother married a sister, confiscated the property.

24. The dowry brought by a Roman woman over fifty years of age to a Roman husband under sixty years of age is after death confiscated by the fisc.[153]

25. That likewise is confiscated which is brought by a woman under fifty years of age to a husband over sixty.

27. Whatever property is inherited by a Roman sixty years old who has neither wife nor child is confiscated. If he has a wife but no children and declares his position, he is allowed to take half.

28. If a woman is fifty years old, she does not inherit; if she is younger and has three children, she inherits, but in the case of a freedwoman, if she has four children.

29. A freeborn Roman woman having a property of 20,000 sesterces pays 1 percent annually as long as she is unmarried, and a freedwoman possessing 20,000 sesterces pays the same until she marries.

30. Inheritances left to Roman women possessing 50,000 sesterces are confiscated if they are unmarried and childless.

31. A Roman woman is permitted to leave to her husband the tenth part of what she possesses; anything more is confiscated.

32. Romans possessing more than 100,000 sesterces, if unmarried and childless, do not inherit, but those who have less inherit.

34. Soldiers in service and after leaving service have been allowed to dispose of their property both by Roman and Greek wills and to use what words they choose; but in every case they must leave it to fellow nationals and to those to whom it is permitted.

35. Children and kinsmen of soldiers in active service who die intestate are permitted to inherit from them, if the claimants are of the same nationality.

36. The estates of persons convicted of murder or major crimes, and of those who go into voluntary exile on such charges are confiscated; but a tenth is allowed to their children, and the dowries consisting of

[151] That is, Junian Latins, on whom see introduction to § 12.
[152] An *idiologus*.
[153] This and the following clauses reveal the influence of the Papian-Poppaean legislation of Augustus (see § 11).

money are restored to their wives. The lord Antoninus Caesar allowed them a twelfth.

37. Those who acted in any way contrary to edicts of the kings or prefects were fined, some a fourth of their estates, some a half, and others their entire estates.

41. If an Egyptian rears a child exposed on a dung heap and adopts him, a fourth of his estate is confiscated at death.

42. Those who style themselves improperly [in public and private documents] and those who knowingly concur therein are fined a fourth of their estates.

43. A fourth of the estate has been confiscated in the case of any Egyptian who after the death of his father has declared him as a Roman.

49. Freedmen of Alexandrians may not marry Egyptian women.

52. Marriage between Romans and Egyptians is [not] [154] permitted.

53. Egyptian women married to discharged soldiers are, if they formally style themselves Romans, subject to the article on nonconformity of status.

56. Soldiers who have not received a legal discharge, if they style themselves Romans, are fined a fourth of their property.

58. Persons who do not register themselves and those whom they ought in the house-by-house census [155] are fined a fourth of their property, and if they are reported not to have registered on two occasions, they are sentenced to the same fine doubled.

60. Those who fail to register slaves suffer confiscation of the slaves only.

62. Soldiers in active service are not held responsible if unregistered, but their wives and children are called to account.

64. Cases of persons departing by sea without a pass are now under the jurisdiction of the prefect.[156]

66. Persons permitted to depart by sea who sail without a pass are fined a third of their property, and if they export slaves of their own without a pass they suffer confiscation of the whole.

70. Persons engaged in public services and members of their families are not permitted to engage in buying or moneylending in the districts in which they function, nor [acquire] land registered as unproductive or sold at public auction in the entire nome. Dummies put up for them are equally accountable, and such purchases were sometimes confiscated. The penalties are as follows: if a purchase from a private citizen, an amount equal to the purchase price; if a loan, an amount equal to the

---

[154] Scholars are divided as to whether the word "not" belongs here and was omitted from the text through error.

[155] See § 102.   [156] Cf. § 94, fourth and fifth selections.

principal; if a sale, the *bona fide* price received; and dummies the same, at the risk of their principals.

76. A priest wearing a woolen garment and long hair suffers a penalty of 1,000 drachmas.

92. A child who has been exposed on a dung heap may not become a priest.

100. Notaries are allowed sixty days to register documents from the Thebaid in the city [of Alexandria]; from other districts, thirty days; from the city itself, fifteen days. The penalty for nonregistration is 100 drachmas; . . . to register before the fifth of the following month.

101. A fine of fifty drachmas is assessed on anyone writing a contract of mortgage or sale without registry thereof.

104. It is forbidden to sell crops before harvest, nor may anyone export[?] a crop that has not been registered.

105. If money is loaned at more than 1 drachma [per mina per month],[157] half the estate is confiscated, and a fourth of the estate of the borrowers.

106. It is not permitted to exchange money at more than the value [fixed by law].

108. Members of [unauthorized] associations were fined 500 drachmas; sometimes only the presiding officers have been fined.[158]

109. *Caesariani*[159] are not permitted to purchase [confiscated] property sold at public auction.

110. *Vicarii* are forbidden to acquire ownership of property or to marry freedwomen.

111. Soldiers on active duty were forbidden to acquire property in the province wherein they were stationed.

100. *Egyptian Agriculture*

Egypt, the "gift of the Nile," was the agricultural country par excellence of the Empire, one of the principal granaries of Rome and Italy. The annual rise of the Nile, with its fertilizing silt, and the proper irrigation of the land were of paramount importance for Egypt's agricultural economy. On the island of Elephantine, near where the Nile enters Egypt, and at Memphis, where the delta begins, there were stone flood gauges called Nilometers (the former of these is *in situ* in good condition today). By taking the reading of each year's flood crest the administration was able, on the basis of experience

---

[157] Cf. introduction to § 51.
[158] On restrictions on association see § 69.
[159] *Caesariani* and *vicarii* (in the next clause) were minor functionaries in charge of confiscated property.

going back to Pharaonic times, to calculate accurately the expected crop and to impose taxes accordingly (cf. § 98). To keep the country's elaborate network of irrigation canals and dykes in repair, every male native, either in person or through a substitute, was required to perform five days of dyke corvée each year, and received a certificate attesting his performance of this compulsory service. When this work was neglected during crises, the canals became choked with silt, embankments collapsed, and the country faced economic catastrophe. Twice after such deterioration Roman emperors— Augustus in 30 B.C. and Probus in A.D. 275—put their armies to work cleaning out the canals. Most of the land of Egypt was imperial or state domain, leased out to tenant farmers, the backbone of the economy of Egypt.

THE NILOMETERS

Pliny *Natural History* v. x. 58

A rise of sixteen cubits [at Memphis] is just right. Smaller rises of water do not irrigate all places; larger ones delay operations by receding too slowly. In the latter case the time for sowing is used up, because the soil is soaked; in the former case no time for sowing is afforded, because the soil is parched. The province is concerned over either extreme. In a rise of twelve cubits it senses famine; in a rise of thirteen cubits it still feels hungry; but fourteen cubits brings rejoicing, sixteen security, and eighteen luxury.

Strabo *Geography* XVII. i. 48

The Nilometer [at Elephantine] is a well on the bank of the Nile constructed of ashlar masonry on which are indicated the greatest, least, and mean rises of the Nile; for the water in the well rises and drops with the river. Accordingly, there are marks on the wall of the well, measures of the full rises and of the others. Now, watchers inspect these and give out word to the rest of the people for their information; for long beforehand they know from such signs and the dates what the coming rise will be, and they predict it. This is useful both to the farmers with regard to water control, embankments, canals, and other such matters, and also to the prefects with regard to the revenues; for the greater rises mean also greater revenues.

IGRR, Vol. I, No. 1,290, col. D

The following is a portion of the record inscribed on the walls of the Nilometer at Elephantine.

      Year 14 of Trajan Caesar . . . 25 cubits . . .
      Year . . . of Tiberius Caesar, 24 cubits, 3 palms . . .

Year . . . of the lord . . . Caesar, 24 cubits, 5 palms, 2 digits
Year . . . of . . . Caesar, 24 cubits, 5 palms . . .
Year 7 of Nero Caesar . . .
Year 10 of Domitian Caesar, 24 cubits, 4 palms . . .
Year 25 of Augustus Caesar, 24 cubits, 4 palms, 1 digit
Year 13 of Nero Caesar, 24 cubits, 6 palms, 1 digit

CERTIFICATE FOR DYKE CORVÉE

Rylands Papyrus No. 210 (= *Select Papyri*, No. 389); A.D. 131

Year 16 of the Emperor Caesar Trajanus HADRIAN Augustus. Has worked on embankment operations of the said year 16 from Phaophi 4 through 8 at the canal of Patsontis in Bacchias: Zoilus son of Petesuchus (son of Elites), his mother being Taorsenuphis. I, Dioscorus signed [this certificate].

DECLARATION OF UNINUNDATED LAND

Michigan Papyrus No. 368; A.D. 170

To Sarapio, *strategus*, and to Serenus, royal secretary of the Arsinoite nome, division of Heraclides, and to the village secretary of Perseae, from Harpocratio son of Heracle . . . of the metropolis. I declare [160] the five and five-eighths arouras of catoecic land [161] belonging to me near the village of Perseae, entered for taxation in the name of Suchas son of Mysthes,[162] as unwatered for the current tenth year. I therefore present this declaration.[163]

[Signed] I, Phaseis, village secretary, have received a copy for verification. Phamenoth 1.

101. *Taxation: Property Records*

Upon the acquisition of taxable property, movable or immovable, owners were required to make a report thereof to the record office.

[160] This is usually preceded in such declarations of uninundated land by the phrase "in accordance with the orders issued by the prefect"; cf. § 101, second selection.
[161] Cf. p. 387, Note 167.
[162] Presumably Suchas was farming the land on lease from Harpocratio; such arrangements were quite common (cf. § 41).
[163] That is, with a view to tax abatement, since the productivity of this land would be subnormal because the fecundating Nile waters had not reached it during the annual flood. Cf. further § 98 and § 104, third selection.

EDICT OF THE PREFECT OF EGYPT

Oxyrhynchus Papyrus No. 237, col. 8, lines 27–43 (= *Select Papyri*,
No. 219); A.D. 89

From LCL

Marcus Mettius Rufus, prefect of Egypt, declares: Claudius Arius
the *strategus* of the Oxyrhynchite nome has informed me that neither
private nor public business is receiving proper treatment owing to the
fact that for many years the abstracts in the property record office have
not been kept in the manner required, although the prefects before me
have often ordered that they should undergo the necessary revision,
which is not really practicable unless copies are made from the beginning. Therefore I command all owners to register their property at the
property record office within six months, and all lenders the mortgages
which they hold, and all other persons the claims which they possess. In
making the return they shall declare the source from which in each case
the possession of the property devolved upon them. Wives also, if on
the strength of some native law they have a lien on the property, shall
add an annotation to the property statements of their husbands, and
likewise children to those of their parents, if the enjoyment of the property has been secured to the latter by public instruments and the possession of it after their death has been settled on their children, in order
that those who make agreements with them may not be defrauded
through ignorance. I also command the scribes and recorders of contracts to execute no deed without an authorization of the record office,
being warned that such a transaction has no validity and that they themselves will suffer the due penalty for disregarding orders. If the record
office contains any property returns of earlier date, let them be preserved with the utmost care, and likewise the abstracts [164] of them, in
order that if afterwards an inquiry should be held concerning persons
who have made false returns they may be convicted therefrom. In order,
then, that the use of the abstracts may become secure and permanent, so
that another [general] registration shall not be required, I command the
keepers of the record office to revise the abstracts every five years, transferring to the new lists the most recent property statement of each
person, arranged under villages and kinds. Year 9 of Domitian, Domi-
tianus [165] the 4th.

[164] Brief summaries of the real estate transactions reported in the returns were drawn
in the property office and kept in a continuous file.
[165] The month of Phaophi (September 28–October 27), so renamed in honor of
the reigning emperor.

PROPERTY DECLARATIONS

Oxyrhynchus Papyrus No. 715 (= Mitteis, No. 212); A.D. 131

To Heras and Origenes, ex-gymnasiarchs, keepers of property records of the Heracleopolite nome, from Gorgias and Galestus, both sons of Polemo (son of Gorgias) and Dionysia (daughter of Galestus), of the village of Toëmisis. In accordance with orders we register at our own risk [166] jointly and equally for the current fifteenth year of the lord Hadrian Caesar the property which has come to us from that belonging to our deceased father Polemo son of Gorgias and Tapontos of the said Toëmisis, namely: his one-third share of a house in the said Toëmisis, and his share of a bare plot of ground, and—previously the property of his sister Helene daughter of Gorgias and the said Tapontos, in accordance with a will opened in the twelfth year of the lord Hadrian Caesar—near the village of Ibio Pachnubis one and seven-eighths arouras of catoecic land [167] from the allotment of Zoilus and Numenius, and near Pselmach. . . one-fourth aroura of catoecic land from the allotment of Menippus and Artemidorus. And we swear by the fortune of the Emperor Caesar Trajanus HADRIAN Augustus and by our ancestral gods that we have submitted the foregoing return honestly and truthfully and have made no false statement, or else may we be liable under the oath.[168] Year 15 of the Emperor Caesar Trajanus HADRIAN Augustus, month of Caesareus,[169] the 5th.

[Signatures] I, Gorgias the aforementioned, have submitted this. I, Heras, ex-gymnasiarch, through Hippod . . . my appointed secretary, have entered it in the records at the joint risk of the registrants without injury to any public or private interest. Intercalary day 5.

Oxyrhynchus Papyrus No. 246 (= Wilcken, No. 247); A.D. 66

To Papiscus, ex-*cosmetes* of the city and *strategus* of the Oxyrhynchite nome, Ptolemaeus, royal secretary, and the nome secretaries, from Harmiusis son of Petosiris (son of Petosiris) and Didyme (daughter of

---

[166] That is, for fraudulent or erroneous statement.

[167] Land originally granted by the Ptolemies to Greek and Macedonian military settlers (*catoeci*). It is interesting to observe that these lands continued for hundreds of years embracing a change of régime (from Ptolemaic to Roman) to be designated not only as "catoecic" but even by the names of the original grantees.

[168] This oath by the reigning emperor or his fortune appears in some but not all property and census declarations. There does not seem to have been a fixed prescription in the matter, but the penalties of fraud applied whether the oath was written out or not.

[169] Cf. Chapter III, Note 132.

Diogenes), of the village of Phthochis in the eastern toparchy. I registered in the current twelfth year of the Emperor Nero Claudius Caesar Augustus Germanicus twelve lambs born from the sheep which I have near the said Phthochis, and I now register in this second return seven additional lambs born from the same sheep (= seven lambs). And I swear by the Emperor Nero Claudius Caesar Augustus Germanicus that I have kept nothing back. Farewell.

[Signatures] I, Apollonius, clerk of Papiscus, *strategus*, have recorded seven lambs. Year 12 of the lord Nero, Epeiph 30. I, Horio, clerk of Ptolemaeus, royal secretary, have recorded seven lambs. Year 12 of the lord Nero Caesar, Epeiph 30. I, Zeno, clerk of the nome secretaries, have recorded seven lambs. Year 12 of the lord Nero Caesar, Epeiph 30.

102. *Taxation: Census and Poll Tax*

The assessment of provincial taxes and tribute, which in some provinces at least included a head tax on the subject population, was based on census as well as property records. The periodicity and procedures of the census varied with the historical background of the province. Here again the papyri provide uniquely detailed information. In Egypt the census was instituted by Augustus in 10/9 B.C. and taken at fourteen-year intervals thereafter. For each census all heads of households had to submit in their *idia,* or place of origin, declarations registering themselves and all those living with them. The poll tax rolls were compiled on the basis of these declarations and the personal appearance at the registration office of the persons named therein. Except for Roman citizens and perhaps Alexandrians, who were exempt, all male inhabitants of Egypt between the ages of fourteen and (at different times) sixty or sixty-five were subject to the poll tax. The rate of the tax varied—townspeople, for example, paying less than villagers. Slaves were included in the declarations and paid for by their owners at the same rate as they paid for themselves.

THE CENSUS IN JUDAEA

Gospel according to Luke 2: 1–5

It happened that in those days an edict went forth from Caesar Augustus for the whole world to register in the census. This first census was taken when Quirinius was governor of Syria.[170] And all journeyed forth to register, each to his own [native] town. And Joseph too went

---

[170] Publius Sulpicius Quirinius conducted the first Roman assessment of Judaea while governor of Syria in A.D. 6. Efforts to assign another date for his governorship in order to reconcile it with the Gospels have proved unsuccessful.

up from Galilee from the town of Nazareth to Judaea to the city of David which is called Bethlehem, since he was of the house and family of David, to register with Mary his betrothed, who was with child.

EDICT OF THE PREFECT OF EGYPT

British Museum Papyrus No. 904, lines 18–38 (= Abbott-Johnson, No. 168 = Select Papyri, No. 220) and Aegyptus, XXXI (1951), 153; A.D. 104

Gaius Vibius Maximus, prefect of Egypt, declares: The house-by-house census having begun, it is essential that all persons who for any reason at all are absent from their nomes be notified to return to their own hearths in order that they may fulfill the customary procedure of registration and apply themselves to the farming incumbent upon them.[171] Knowing, however, that our city [172] has need of some of the people from the country, I desire all who think they have a satisfactory reason for remaining here to register their reasons with Bul . . . Festus, squadron prefect, whom I have appointed for this purpose. Those showing their presence to be necessary will receive signed permits from him in accordance with this edict before the 30th of the present month of Epeiph, and all others shall return home within . . . days. Anyone found without a permit thereafter[?] will be severely punished; for I know well. . . . [The rest of this final sentence is mutilated.]

A CENSUS DECLARATION

Michigan Papyrus No. 176; A.D. 91

To Horus son of Haryotes, census officer of Bacchias, and Apunchis son of Onnophris and the other elders [of the village], from Peteuris son of Horus, of the village of Bacchias. There belongs to me in the village one fourth of a house in which I dwell, and I register both myself and those of my household for the census of the past ninth year of the Emperor Caesar DOMITIAN Augustus Germanicus: myself, Peteuris son of Horus (son of Horus) and Herieus (daughter of Menches), cultivator of state land, about thirty years old, without identifying marks,[173] also my wife Tapeine daughter of Apkois, twenty-five years old, and my

---

[171] The prefect here profits by the occasion of the census to order fugitive peasants back to their land; cf. § 105 and § 97, last selection.
[172] Alexandria.
[173] Identifying scars, moles, etc., though not always specified in these returns, were carefully recorded in the census rolls when the registrants made their personal appearance at the census office.

full [174] brothers Horus, about twenty years old, and Horio, about seven years old. And my brothers also own one fourth of the aforementioned house and courtyard in which we live.

[Signatures] I, the aforementioned Peteuris, have submitted this, and I swear by the Emperor Caesar DOMITIAN Augustus Germanicus that the foregoing is true and that I have made no false statement.[175] Aphrodisius, village secretary, wrote for him since he is illiterate. Year 10 of the Emperor Caesar DOMITIAN Augustus Germanicus, Pachon 15.

103. *Taxation: Receipts and Reports*

In addition to the poll tax the inhabitants of Egypt paid a fantastic number and variety of taxes on agriculture, on trades and business activities, and for the maintenance of administrative and public services; lists of these taxes are given in *ESAR,* Vol II, Chapter IV, and in S. L. Wallace, *Taxation in Egypt*. Except for the basic agricultural tribute and army supplies, which were delivered in kind, most levies were paid in money. In the collection, tax farmers were gradually replaced by liturgic local officials (cf. § 97). Collectors sent reports of receipts to the *strategus* of the nome every five days and every month, and in some if not all cases they had to file annual reports as well. Since the taxpayer had to furnish the material on which the tax receipt was written, *ostraca* (potsherds) became a favorite material for the purpose, since a ready supply of sherds could always be had in any household, whereas papyrus had to be purchased; this fact also helps to explain why, when papyrus was used, a whole series of tax payments was often recorded on a single piece. The following is a brief selection from the hundreds of extant receipts for taxes of all kinds.

MISCELLANEOUS TAX RECEIPTS

Michigan Papyrus No. 393

[Caranis, A.D. 158]

Year 21 of the Emperor Caesar Titus Aelius Hadrianus ANTONINUS Augustus PIUS, Mesore 16. We, Ptolemaeus son of Teus and associate collectors of grain taxes of the village of Philopator, or Theogenes, have received at the granary of the aforesaid village from the produce of the same year by level public wheat measure for rent of state land in Allotment 63 [176] of Caranis to the account of Amatius Marcianus three artabs of wheat.

---

[174] Literally, "born of the same father and of the same mother."
[175] Cf. Note 168.   [176] Cf. Note 167.

I, Sarapio[?], grain collector, have received the aforesaid three artabs.

Strasbourg Ostracon No. 198

[Thebes, A.D. 117]

Copy of receipt. Chesphmoïs, collector of money taxes of the metropolis, to Peme son of Peme. I have received for the land-survey tax of Year 2 in debased coinage [177] six drachmas two and one half obols (debased dr. 6 ob. 2½), and in the name of Onnophris son of Psenmes[?] in debased coinage two drachmas two obols two *chalci* (dr. 2 ob. 2¼). Year 2 of the lord Hadrian, Hathyr 27.

Michigan Papyrus No. 383 (abridged)

[Caranis, A.D. 106–9]

Tenth year of the Emperor Caesar Nerva TRAJAN Augustus Germanicus Dacicus, Hathyr 30: paid to the collector Ptolemaeus[?] by Petheus son of Phaësis (son of Sarapio) and Taseus, for poll tax of the tenth year in Caranis, sixteen drachmas one half obol two *chalci* (dr. 16 ob. ¾); for police tax, dr. 1 ob. 2½. Tybi 23: eight drachmas (dr. 8). Pharmuthi 30: twelve drachmas (dr. 12) for half the bath tax, and for other taxes ob. 7, and for poll tax four drachmas (dr. 4). And in Year 11, month of Augustus: [178] for head tax[?] and prison-guard tax, two drachmas four obols (dr. 2 ob. 4). . . .

Twelfth year of the Emperor Caesar Nerva TRAJAN Augustus Germanicus Dacicus, Pachon 23: to the account of the eleventh year, paid to Socr . . . , collector's clerk[?], by Petheus son of Phaësis, for the one-sixth on gardens for the eleventh year in Psenarpsenesis, two drachmas four obols (dr. 2 ob. 4); for oil-delivery tax, ob. 2 *chal.* 2; for *naubium*,[179] ob. 1½ *chal.* 2; supplement, ob. 4; aroura tax, dr. 1 ob. 4½ *chal.* 2; supplement, ob. 1; for exchange,[180] ob. ½ *chal.* 2; fee for issuing receipt . . . for land survey tax, six drachmas four obols (dr. 6 ob. 4); supplement, ob. 2½; fee for issuing receipt. . . .

Eleventh year of the Emperor Caesar Nerva TRAJAN Augustus Germanicus Dacicus, Tybi 4: paid by Petheus son of Phaësis for per-capita beer tax of the current year 11 in Caranis, four drachmas (dr. 4). Pachon 6: further payment of three drachmas four obols (dr. 3 ob. 4).

---

[177] Presumably copper drachmas or small coins, which were handled at a discount.
[178] Cf. Chapter III, Note 50.
[179] The *naubium*, a cubic measure, was used as the unit of labor of the dyke corvée (cf. § 100). Landholders frequently paid a tax in money in lieu of digging the required number of *naubia*.
[180] Of copper money to silver. The supplementary charges mentioned in this receipt are also connected with the discount on copper coinage (cf. Note 177).

Wilbour Ostracon No. 30

[Elephantine, A.D. 78]

Pachumaras has received on account from Patrasnuphis for the tax on trades of Year 11 of the lord Vespasian, Choiak. . . .[181] I, Verris Philumenus, wrote this because he is illiterate.

Strasbourg Ostracon No. 54

[Thebes, A.D. 15]

Paid into the public bank at Diospolis Magna by Maieuris son of Horus, for the tax on builders for the second year, twenty-two drachmas (dr. 22), and supplement at the rate of ob. 1½ on the *stater*.[182] Year 2 of TIBERIUS Caesar Augustus, the Augustan day of New Augustus.[183]

Wilbour Ostracon No. 33

[Elephantine, A.D. 188]

Antonius Julius, farmer of the monthly tax on trades and the tax on prostitutes. Papremithes son of Pachnubis, weaver[?], has paid for Thoth and Phaophi of the current twenty-ninth year four drachmas (dr. 4). Year 29, Hathyr 10.

Wilbour Ostracon No. 14

[Thebes, A.D. 33]

Psenmonthes son of Phaëris has paid for the dyke tax [184] of the nineteenth year six drachmas four obols, and for the bath tax ob. 4½; total dr. 7 ob. 2½, and supplement at the rate of ob. 1½.[185] Year 20 of TIBERIUS Caesar Augustus, month of Augustus,[186] the 30th. [Signed] Petemenophis son of Picos.

Grenfell Papyrus, Vol. II, No. 50c (= *Select Papyri*, No. 382); A.D. 147

Paid at the toll house of Philadelphia, the desert-guard tax by Diogenes outward bound with one donkey-load of fresh dates and one donkey-load of wheat. Eleventh year of the lord Antoninus Caesar, Thoth eighteenth (18).

---

[181] The day of the month and the amount paid are lost in the lacuna.
[182] A *stater* was a four-drachma piece. The rate of the supplementary payment (cf. Note 180) is thus ⅟₁₆, or 6¼ percent.
[183] Cf. Chapter II, Note 20, and Note 143 above.
[184] This per-capita money tax for the maintenance of the irrigation canals was apparently paid in addition to, not in lieu of, the five days' corvée on the dykes, for which see § 100.
[185] Cf. Note 182.   [186] Cf. Chapter III, Note 50.

Rylands Papyrus No. 197*a* (= *Select Papyri*, No. 383); A.D. 162

Paid at the toll house of Socnopaei Nesus, the one-percent and one-half-percent taxes [187] by Sarapio outward bound with six artabs of vegetable seed, paying five drachmas, on one camel (1), and twelve artabs of wheat, paying three drachmas, on one camel and two donkeys. Third year of the lords [MARCUS AURELIUS] Antoninus and [LUCIUS] VERUS, Hathyr 4.

Wilcken Ostracon No. 579

[Thebes, A.D. 137]

Asclas and Soter, collectors of money taxes, to Picos son of Pamonthes (son of Picos) and Tasemis. We have received for the fugitives tax [188] of the Charax district of Year 21 in debased coinage [189] four drachmas (debased dr. 4), and for the hunting-spears tax [190] of the Charax district of Year 21 in debased coinage [four] drachmas four obols (debased dr. 4 ob. 4). Year 22 of the lord Hadrian, Thoth 28. I, Decius, have recorded dr. 4 ob. 4.

TAX COLLECTORS' REPORTS

Oslo Papyrus No. 90; A.D. 138

To Aelius Numisianus, *strategus* of the Arsinoite nome divisions of Themistes and Polemo, from Ptolemaeus son of Eudaemo, Gaius Longus son of Dioscorus, Didymus son of Didymus, Sarapio son of Patermuthis, Didymus son of Heraclides, and associate superintendents of the pastures and marshes of Theadelphia and Polydeucia. The account of revenues from fishing from the 26th to the 30th of the month of Phaophi of the current second year of the lord Antoninus Caesar: 26th, dr. 48 ob. 5; 27th, dr. 36 ob. 3; 28th, dr. 44 ob. 11; 29th, dr. 48 ob. 24; 30th, dr. 32 ob. 1; total, dr. 215. Submitted by Ptolemaeus son of Diodorus. Year 2 of the lord Antoninus Caesar, Hathyr 1. [Signed] I, Apollonius, keeper of records, have received a copy of this.

Berlin Papyrus No. 25 (= Wilcken, No. 270); A.D. 200

To Demetrius, *strategus* of the Arsinoite nome division of Heraclides, from Harpalus and associate collectors of money taxes of the

---

[187] The local toll and the import-export tax, respectively (cf. introduction to § 35).
[188] A tax levied per capita on the inhabitants of a village or town district to make up the tax loss resulting from the flight of residents who could not meet their taxes or compulsory-service obligations.
[189] Cf. Note 177.
[190] The revenues from this tax probably went to equip the corps that combatted the hippopotamuses and perhaps also crocodiles in the Nile.

village of Socnopaei Nesus. We paid into the public bank to the account of the month of Payni of the current eighth year for the tax on altars[?] four hundred drachmas (dr. 400). Year 8 of Lucius SEPTIMIUS SEVERUS Pius Pertinax Augustus and Marcus Aurelius Antoninus Augustus [CARACALLA], Epeiph 1.

Likewise, [Epeiph ?] 4, for the tax on art wares one hundred drachmas (dr. 100). Total, 500 dr.

104. *Taxation: Privileges and Abatements*

The emperors frequently granted temporary or permanent tax privileges and exemptions from liturgies to favored groups. A few examples follow; for others see §§ 46, 57, 74, 97, 156.

NERO "LIBERATES" GREECE

In A.D. 66–67 Nero toured Greece, competing in lyric and dramatic contests and chariot races in all the famous Greek games. "To make this possible, he gave orders that even those games which were widely separated in time should be brought together in a single year, so that some had to be given twice" (Suetonius *Life of Nero* xxiii. 1). Everywhere he went he was greeted with flattering enthusiasm, and of course he was awarded every prize for which he competed. This did not stop him from plundering the art treasures of Athens, like Sulla and Caligula before him. But "on his departure he presented the entire province with freedom and gave the judges [of the contests] Roman citizenship and a large sum of money" (*ibid.*, xxiv. 2). At a special convocation of the Isthmian Games, where in 196 B.C. Flamininus had proclaimed through a herald the liberation of Greece (cf. Vol. I, §§ 68, 122), Nero in person proclaimed a second liberation and granted all Greece exemption from tribute. The privilege of autonomy was withdrawn soon after by Vespasian, but most of the cities of Greece continued to enjoy freedom from imperial taxation. An inscription erected by the little town of Acraephiae (modern Karditza) in Boeotia preserves the text of Nero's edict summoning the Greeks to the Isthmus and of his "liberation" speech.

IG, Vol. VII, No. 2,713　(= Dessau, No. 8,794 = Dittenberger, No. 814); A.D. 67

The Emperor Caesar declares: Desiring to reward most noble Hellas for its good will and loyalty to me, I bid as many as possible from this province to assemble at Corinth on November 28.

When the crowds had gathered in assembly, he proclaimed the following: "It is an unexpected gift, Hellenes—though there is nothing that may not be hoped for from my magnanimity—which I grant you, one so great that you were incapable of requesting it. All Hellenes who inhabit Achaea and the land until now called [191] the Peloponnesus receive liberty and exemption from tribute, which not even in your most fortunate days did you all enjoy, for you were subjects either of foreigners or of one another. Would that I were making this gift while Hellas was still at its height, so that more people might enjoy this boon; for this, indeed, I have a grudge against time, for squandering in advance the fullness of my boon. Yet even now it is not out of pity but out of good will that I bestow this benefaction upon you, requiting your gods, whose care for me both on land and on sea I have never found to fail, for affording me an opportunity to bestow so great a benefaction; for to cities other rulers too have granted freedom, but Nero alone to an entire province."

[There follows a decree of the town of Acraephiae, here omitted, which repeats with adulatory embellishment some of Nero's language concerning "the restoration of our ancient state of autonomy and liberty," and orders the town's gratitude to be shown by the dedication of an altar inscribed "To Zeus the Liberator Nero forever" next to that of Zeus the Savior, and the dedication of "statues of Nero Zeus Liberator and the goddess Augusta Messalina alongside our ancestral gods in the sanctuary of Apollo."]

PRIVILEGES OF THE JEWS

Julius Caesar and the Roman emperors after him down to Claudius continued the privileges granted to the Jews of the Diaspora, because of their religious obligations, by earlier Persian and Seleucid kings. After the Jewish rebellion of A.D. 66–70, however, Vespasian canceled the tax privileges of the Jews throughout the Empire and established a special "Jewish Account" of the imperial fisc, in which the annual contribution of two drachmas per capita previously made, with the emperors' permission, to the Temple at Jerusalem was henceforth collected for the benefit of the Temple of Jupiter on the Capitoline Hill in Rome. In his *Jewish Antiquities* Josephus has recorded numerous documents emanating from Roman emperors and officials, reaffirming and extending the rights and privileges of the Jews in the Roman Empire. These documents, of which a typical example is given here, have provoked considerable discussion by modern scholars, with some questioning their authenticity because of the many patent inaccuracies which they contain. The consensus today holds, however, that the documents are authentic but carelessly quoted by Josephus.

[191] This suggests that Nero planned to change its name to Neronesus. Cf. Suetonius *Life of Nero* lv: "He had an unreasoning passion for perpetuating his name forever, and so he removed the old names from many things and places and assigned them new ones after his own name, and also he renamed the month of April Neroneus; he had even intended to call Rome Neropolis."

Josephus *Jewish Antiquities* XVI. vi. 2. 162–64

Caesar AUGUSTUS, *pontifex maximus*, holder of the tribunician power,[192] declares:

Whereas the Jewish people have proved themselves grateful toward the Roman people not only at the present time but also in the past— particularly under their high priest Hyrcanus in the time of my father, the dictator Caesar—I and my council [193] have decided . . . that the Jews [be allowed to] practice their own customs according to their ancestral law, just as they used to under Hyrcanus, high priest of the highest god, that their sacred moneys be inviolable and be sent to Jerusalem [194] and delivered to the custodians at Jerusalem, and that they not [be compelled to] post bail on the sabbath or on the day of preparation [195] for it from the ninth hour. If anyone is caught stealing their sacred scrolls or their sacred money whether from a synagogue or from an ark of the Law, he shall be guilty of sacrilege and his property confiscated to the public treasury of the Romans.

A TAX MORATORIUM

In addition to the general cancellations of tax arrears in the second century (see § 37), the emperors on occasion granted remissions or moratoria to distressed areas. In the following edict Hadrian proclaims such a moratorium in Egypt, which had suffered a series of low Niles and sharply reduced crops.

Oslo Papyrus No. 78 (= *FIRA*, Vol. I, No. 81); A.D. 135/36

The Emperor Caesar Trajanus HADRIAN Augustus, son of the deified Trajan Parthicus, grandson of the deified Nerva, *pontifex maximus*, holding the tribunician power for the twentieth year, twice acclaimed *imperator*, three times consul, father of his country, declares:

Since I have been informed that this year again, just as it did last year, the Nile has risen rather insufficiently and incompletely—even considering the fact that during the preceding years it produced successive rises that were not only full but even almost higher than at any time before, and that, flooding the entire country, it caused the produc-

---

[192] An instance of Josephus' carelessness in quoting documents: his omission of the number of years of Augustus' tribunician power deprives us of the date of this edict.

[193] Cf. Chapter I, Note 13. The sixth-century Latin translation of Josephus has here, "myself and the senate" (cf. pp. 37, 39).

[194] The Latin translation of Josephus reads here, "that their holy places remain inviolable and the moneys sent by them to Jerusalem be paid to the custodians of moneys."

[195] This word for "preparation" (*paraskeue*) became and still is the Greek name for Friday.

tion of most abundant and beautiful crops—nevertheless I have deemed it necessary to bestow a benefaction on the farmers, although I hope— may this be said with divine favor!—that any present deficiencies will be restored in the coming years by the Nile itself and the earth; [for such is (?)] the nature of things, changing from productivity and abundance to scarcity, and from scarcity to plenty.

May good fortune attend! Know that the money tax due for this year shall be distributed, as concerns inhabitants of the Thebaid, who have probably been most heavily injured by the scarcity, over five annual payments; as concerns those in the Heptanomia [196] over four, and those in the Delta over three. The mode of paying semi-annually is allowed those wishing to do so, the time limits granted remaining for those in the Thebaid five years, those in the Heptanomia four years, those in the Delta three years. Issued at Alexandria in the twenty-first year, Payni 16.

105. *Flight from Fiscal Oppression*

In a list of standard questions addressed to oracles (see § 109, last selection), along with inquiries concerning other personal fortunes and misfortunes, appears, "Shall I become a fugitive?" When the regular and irregular demands of the imperial régime and its implacable representatives became intolerable, the last resort of the peasant or the liturgist was to take to flight (cf. § 97). The fugitive Egyptian might make for Alexandria or one of the other cities, hoping to be swallowed up amid the motley population, or he might hide in the desert and live, with others like himself, by brigandage. When a man left home in this way "for parts unknown," his family was required to notify the authorities. In the second century the "Good Emperors" imposed a compensating tax which distributed the tax defaults of these fugitives per capita upon the remaining population of a village or district.

NOTICE OF FLIGHT

Oxyrhynchus Papyrus No. 252 (= Wilcken, No. 215); A.D. 19/20

To Theo and Eutychides, local and village secretaries, from Thoönis daughter of Ammonius. My brother Ammonius son of Ammonius, weaver, registered [197] in the part of a house formerly belonging to him in Teumenuthis Street . . . fled abroad possessed of no other taxable estate. I therefore submit this memorandum, requesting that he be entered in the list of fugitive paupers from the current sixth year of TIBERIUS Caesar Augustus. [The signature and date are fragmentary.]

[196] Cf. Chapter II, Note 22.   [197] Cf. § 102.

FROM A PETITION TO THE PREFECT OF EGYPT

Graux Papyrus No. 2, lines 1–13 (= *SB*, No. 7,462 = *Select Papyri*, No. 281); A.D. 55/59

To Tiberius Claudius Balbillus from . . . six collectors of poll tax of the aforesaid villages. . . . The formerly numerous inhabitants in the aforesaid villages have now been reduced to a few, some having fled in poverty, others having died without leaving heirs-at-law, and for this reason we are in danger, because of [the general] impoverishment, of having to abandon the collectorship.

OFFICIAL RECORD OF FUGITIVE PAUPERS

Rylands Papyrus No. 595; A.D. 57

[Report] from Nemesio, collector of poll tax of Philadelphia. Owed up to the month of New Augustus [198] of the fourth year of the Emperor NERO Claudius Caesar Augustus Germanicus for poll tax, pig tax, and dyke tax [199] of the said year:

Poll tax	dr. 4,728 ob. 3
Pig tax	dr. 121 ob. 1 [200]
Dyke tax	dr. 1,100

Breakdown. Fugitive paupers in the list from the first year: [There follow forty-three names with amounts owed.] [201]

Others who have fled since Payni of the aforesaid year to parts unknown: [Fifty-five names follow, with amounts owed.]

Defaulters in the . . . year, month of Augustus [202] . . . : [Seven names, with amounts, follow.] [203]

Others who have fled since Payni of the first year owing only the dyke tax, who have [returned], paid the poll tax, and thereafter been excused [from the dyke tax] by the royal secretary: [Forty-seven names follow, with the amount of the dyke tax.]

[198] Cf. Chapter II, Note 20.

[199] For the dyke tax see Note 184. The pig tax, anachronistically retaining its original name, was also levied by the Romans as a per-capita tax on the entire population of Egypt.

[200] This amount is crossed out on the papyrus, presumably an inaccurate total.

[201] A papyrus in the collection of Cornell University (No. 24) lists forty-four paupers missing from this village in July, A.D. 56. Of those forty-four, thirty-four are here recorded as still missing, fifteen months later; the other ten presumably returned and paid their arrears, at least in part (cf. below).

[202] Cf. Chapter III, Note 50.

[203] The total of 105 missing persons is estimated by the editors of the papyrus to equal "10 per cent. or over of the male inhabitants of Philadelphia."

106. *Abusive Conduct of Officials and Soldiers*

One of the boons of the Principate to the provinces was its check upon the almost limitless orgy of corruption, brutality, and extortion into which Roman provincial administration in the last century of the Republic had degenerated (see Vol. I, §§ 141–146). Despite the good intentions of some of the emperors to regularize the financial and personal obligations of provincials—"to have my sheep shorn, not skinned alive," in the classic phrase of Tiberius (Suetonius *Life of Tiberius* xxxii. 2)—the vastness of the Empire and its bureaucracy made it impossible for the central government to protect the population from the venality and arrogance of local officials and soldiers. From these it was subjected to a whole series of abuses, harbingers of the Roman holiday of violence and looting during the anarchy of the third century and of the pervasive corruption on all levels of officialdom during the fourth and fifth centuries.

Wilcken, No. 413, lines 1–30 (= *Select Papyri*, No. 211); A.D. 19

The proconsul Germanicus Caesar, son of Augustus, grandson of the deified Augustus, declares: [204]

[Inasmuch as I have heard that in view of my visit] requisitions . . . of boats and animals are being made and that quarters for lodgings are being occupied by force and private persons intimidated, I have deemed it necessary to make known that I wish neither boat nor beast of burden to be seized nor quarters to be occupied by anyone except on the order of my friend and secretary Baebius. For if it is necessary Baebius himself will allot the quarters fairly and justly; and for requisitioned boats or animals I order that hire be paid in accordance with my schedule. Those who oppose [my orders] I desire to be brought before my secretary, who will either himself prevent private persons from being injured or will report the case to me. And I forbid any who meet beasts of burden passing through the city [of Alexandria] to appropriate them by force; for this is but an act of confessed robbery.

Philo *Special Laws* ii. xix. 92–94, iii. xxx. 159–62
From the translation of M. Rostovtzeff, Journal of Economic and
Business History, *I (1928/29)*, 353–55

The rulers of the cities must stop breaking the necks of the cities by continuous and heavy taxes and imposts. In doing so they fill their own treasuries, hoarding in them alongside the money the ignoble vices which defile their whole life. They choose on purpose the most merciless tax

[204] For other records of Germanicus' visit to Egypt, see § 168, third selection.

collectors full of inhumanity, giving them by this a starting point for illicit gain. These men add to their natural brutality the free hand granted to them by the orders of their masters, and since they have set their mind on doing everything which pleases their masters they indulge in the most wicked deeds, while justice and gentleness never appear to them even in their dreams. Consequently they throw all things into confusion and disorder in collecting the taxes, to the extent of levying not only on the property but also on the person, with outrages and violence, and the invention of new and unprecedented torture. . . .[205]

Recently a man was appointed tax collector among us. When some of those who were supposed to owe taxes fled because of poverty and in fear of unbearable punishment,[206] he carried off by force their wives, their children, their parents, and the rest of their families, striking them, and insulting them, and visiting all manner of outrages upon them in an effort to force them either to inform against the fugitive or else to make payment in his stead. But they could satisfy neither of these requirements, for they knew nothing of the whereabouts of the fugitive and they were themselves no less poverty-stricken than the man who had run away. Nevertheless the tax collector did not release them until he had tortured their bodies with racks and wheels and had killed them with newly invented devices of death. . . . [Others, fearing the same fate,] took their own lives by sword, or poison, or hanging, deeming it great good fortune, in view of their evil plight, to be able to die without torture. But those who did not hasten to kill themselves but were seized before they could do so were led away in a row, according to their nearness of kin, as in the case of actions for inheritance, the closest relatives first, then those next to them in succession, in the second or third place, till they came to the last. When there were no relatives left, the cruelty was visited upon the friends and neighbors of the fugitives. At times it was carried even into the cities and villages, which soon became desolate, being emptied of all their inhabitants, who left their homes and scattered to places where they hoped to escape detection.

British Museum Papyrus No. 1,171 (= Abbott-Johnson, No.
162 = Wilcken, No. 439); A.D. 42

Lucius Aemilius Rectus [prefect of Egypt] declares:
No one shall be permitted to requisition transportation facilities from the people in the country districts nor demand viatica or anything else gratis without a permit from me; and each of those possessing such

[205] Tax collectors were frequently accompanied on their rounds by armed guards or soldiers (cf. § 97, second selection), whom they needed for protection but whom they often used to intimidate and maltreat the taxpayers. Cf. also § 98 and Note 211.
[206] Cf. § 105.

permit may take sufficient supplies on payment of the price therefor. But if any of the soldiers or police or anyone at all among the aides in the public services is reported to have acted in violation of my edict or to have used force against anyone of the country people or to have exacted money, I shall visit the utmost penalty upon him.[207] Year 2 of the Emperor Tiberius CLAUDIUS Caesar Augustus, Germaniceus [208] the 4th.

Evelyn White-Oliver, No. 1 (= *SEG*, Vol. VIII, No. 794); A.D. 49

Posidonius, *strategus*. I have subjoined for you a copy of the letter sent to me by the lord prefect together with the appended edict, so that you may know and comply and do nothing contrary to the orders. In the ninth year of the Emperor Tiberius CLAUDIUS Caesar Augustus Germanicus, Mecheir 7.

Vergilius Capito to Posidonius, *strategus* of the Oasis, greeting. I have sent you a copy of the edict which I have posted in the city [of Alexandria]. I wish you to post it promptly in a conspicuous place in the metropolis of the nome and at every village in clear and conspicuous characters, and to see to it that these [orders] of mine are enforced.

Gnaeus Vergilius Capito declares: Even before this I kept hearing that certain unlawful expenditures and frauds were being perpetrated by persons greedily and impudently abusing their powers; and now, too, I have noted particularly in the law suit of the Libyans that persons in the public services are brazenly peculating by making certain disbursements in the guise of allowances—which do not and ought not exist—for their expenses and accommodations, and likewise under the title of transportation requisitions. Wherefore I command that those passing through the nomes—soldiers, cavalrymen, orderlies, centurions, military tribunes, and all others—shall take nothing and make no transportation requisitions, excepting any who have my permits, and that even those travelers shall be provided with shelter only and no one shall draw any allowance beyond those fixed by Maximus.[209] But if anyone pays out or reports a sum as paid out and charges it to public expense, I will make him pay back ten times the amount which he obtained from the nome, and to the informer I will give a fourfold share from the property of the person convicted. The royal secretaries, the village secretaries, and the district secretaries in a nome shall record all sums expended from nome funds

[207] Cf. "Historia Augusta" *Life of Avidius Cassius* (see Chapter II, Note 55) iv. 2: "Soldiers who had forcibly carried off anything from provincials he crucified in the very places in which they had transgressed."
[208] The Egyptian month Pachon (April 26–May 25), so renamed probably in honor of the Emperor Claudius.
[209] Marcus Magius Maximus, a prefect of Egypt under Augustus.

for any purpose, or obtained fraudulently or otherwise; they shall deliver [these records] every sixty days (the secretaries in the Thebaid every four months) to the audit offices; and they shall send them to Basilides—the imperial freedman in charge of the audit bureau—and the state accountants, so that if anything has been illegally collected or obtained I will remedy the matter. I wish likewise to make clear . . . grain or money as the price of protection. . . . [The rest is mutilated.]

Italian Society Papyrus No. 446 (= *Select Papyri*, No. 221); A.D. 133/37
Adapted from LCL

Marcus Petronius Mamertinus, prefect of Egypt, declares:

I am informed that without having a permit many of the soldiers when traveling through the country requisition boats and animals and persons improperly, in some cases seizing them by force, in others obtaining them from the *strategi* through favor or obsequiousness, the result of which is that private persons are subjected to insults and abuses and the army is reproached for greed and injustice. I therefore command the *strategi* and the royal secretaries in any case not to furnish to any person whatsoever, whether traveling by river or by land, any contribution for the journey without a permit, understanding that I will vigorously punish anyone who after this edict is discovered receiving or giving any of the aforesaid things. Year . . . of the lord Hadrian Caesar, Thoth 8.

Revue de Philologie, XVII (1943), 111–19; A.D. c.140?

[Private account of payments]

To the *stationarius* [210]	2 drachmas 1 obol
Gift	240 drachmas
Suckling pig	24 drachmas
To the guard	20 drachmas
For extortion [211]	2,200 drachmas
To the two police agents	100 drachmas
To Hermias, police agent	100 drachmas
To the . . .	2,574 drachmas 3 obols

[210] On the *stationarii* (military police) see Chapter III, Note 55.
[211] The Greek term here is exactly translated by our American slang expression "shakedown." The artlessness with which this item is entered in the account is indicative of how completely matter-of-course the natives had come to regard such recurrent "shakedowns." This account, with its frequent payments to soldiers, is an apt footnote to the *Gospel according to Luke* 3:12–14: "And even tax farmers came to be baptized; and they said to him, 'Master, what shall we do?' He said to them, 'Exact no more than what has been assigned to you.' And even soldiers would ask him, 'And what shall we do?' He said to them, 'Do not extort money by intimidation, or make false accusations against anyone, but be content with your pay.'" Cf. also § 111, last selection, and introduction to § 114.

Second half-year: Phamenoth[?] . . .

To the soldier at his demand	500 drachmas
Currency exchange	12 drachmas
8 jars of wine at 10	
drachmas ⅛ obol	. . .
To the chief of police	. . .
Dyke tax	1 drachma
Cattle tax[?]	1 drachma
To the soldier at his demand	400 drachmas
Currency exchange	15 drachmas

OGIS, No. 609 (= Abbott-Johnson, No. 113); A.D. c.185

Julius Saturninus [governor of Syria] to Phaenae, chief village of the district of Tracho, greeting. If anyone billets himself by force in your houses, whether soldier or civilian, send word to me and you will receive satisfaction. For neither do you owe any contribution to visitors, nor, since you have a public hospice, can you be compelled to receive visitors in your homes. Post this letter of mine in a conspicuous place of your chief village, so that no one may plead ignorance.

IG, Vol. XII, Part 5, No. 132 (= Abbott-Johnson, No. 132)

[Island of Paros, A.D. 204]

Imperial letter.[212] You appear to us to be unaware of the decree of the senate, but if you consult persons who are informed you will learn that a senator of the Roman people is not required to receive guests in his house against his will. Issued on May 31, at Rome, in the consulship of Fabius Cilo (for the second time) and Annius Libo.

107. *Exposure of Children*

Among the Greeks and Romans unwanted infants were commonly cast out to die or to be picked up by a chance passer-by. By the Hellenistic tradition of the eastern provinces such children could be raised slave or free, at the option of the finder. In Roman law, however, the status of a child was determined by its parentage, so that foundlings who were freeborn could not be reduced to slavery. Trajan's extension of the Roman practice to the East, which made it possible for freeborn children reared as slaves to reclaim their freedom without the obligation of reimbursing the rearer for the expenses of upbringing, must have served as a deterrent to the rearing of exposed children

[212] This text, written in Greek and Latin, was posted on the wall of the house whose exemption it confirmed. A bronze tablet of the second century (*SB*, No. 4,226) reads: "Immunity from taxation and from requisitions for the estate of Agrippina and Rutilia, now belonging to our lord the emperor."

of uncertain parentage. The practice of exposure was condemned by Jews and Christians, and it was perhaps under such influence as well as because of the sharp rise in exposure produced by critical economic conditions that the first Christian emperor, Constantine, instituted various measures to alleviate the situation (see § 137), including public assistance to all needy and legalization throughout the Empire of the Hellenistic principle of finder's option. It was not until A.D. 374 that exposure was ruled a capital offense, and finally Justinian, in A.D. 529, reversing Constantine, enacted that exposure *per se* was to be regarded as evidence of freeborn status.

Oxyrhynchus Papyrus No. 744 (= Select Papyri, No. 105); 1 B.C.

Hilario to Alis, his sister,[213] many greetings, and to my lady Berous and Apollonarion. Know that we are still in Alexandria. Do not worry if they really go home and I remain in Alexandria. I ask and entreat you to take care of the child, and as soon as we receive our pay I will send it up to you. If you chance to bear a child and it is a boy, let it be; if it is a girl, expose it. You have said to Aphrodisias that I should not forget you. How can I forget you? I ask you, then, not to worry. Year 29 of [Augustus] Caesar, Payni 23.

Pliny Letters Book x, Nos. 65–66

[Pliny to the Emperor Trajan]

There is an important question, one that affects the whole province, namely, concerning the status and maintenance of those whom they call foundlings. I have had read to me the enactments of the emperors on this matter, but since I found nothing either specific or general referring to the Bithynians I thought it necessary to consult you as to what you desire to be observed. For I did not think that I could be content with precedent in a matter that demands your authoritative decision. A purported edict of the deified Augustus was read to me concerning Asia; also a letter of the deified Vespasian to Sparta, and another of Titus to the same . . . and others of Domitian to the proconsuls Avidius Nigrinus and Armenius Brocchus, and likewise to Sparta. The reason I have not transmitted them to you is that they seem poorly copied and some are of doubtful authenticity, and that I suppose genuine and perfect versions are in your archives.

[Trajan to Pliny]

The question relating to freeborn persons who have been exposed and subsequently picked up by certain persons and reared in slavery has often been treated. But no enactment for all the provinces is found in

---

[213] The word "sister" may be here merely a term of endearment, but it is just as possible that Hilario married his sister, a common practice in ancient Egypt.

the records of the emperors who preceded me. It is true that there are letters of Domitian to Avidius Nigrinus and Armenius Brocchus which ought perhaps to be observed, but only in those provinces concerning which he wrote; and Bithynia is not among these. My view therefore is that those who desire to be emancipated for such reason should not be denied the right to make a public declaration of their status, and they are not required to purchase their freedom by repaying the cost of their maintenance.

108. Complaints to the Police

The following two papyri are representative of numerous extant complaints of arson, assault and battery, theft, trespass, etc., addressed to police or judicial authorities.

Rylands Papyrus No. 125 (= *Select Papyri*, No. 278); A.D. 28
Adapted from LCL

To Serapio, chief of police, from Orsenuphis son of Harpaësis, notable of the village of Euhemeria in the division of Themistes. In the month of Mesore of the past fourteenth year of Tiberius Caesar Augustus I was having some old walls on my premises demolished by the builder Petesuchus son of Petesuchus, and while I was absent from home to gain my living, Petesuchus in the process of demolition discovered a hoard which had been secreted by my mother in a little box as long ago as the sixteenth year of [Augustus] Caesar, consisting of a pair of gold earrings weighing four quarters, a gold crescent weighing three quarters, a pair of silver armlets of the weight of twelve drachmas of uncoined metal, a necklace with silver ornaments worth eighty drachmas, and sixty silver drachmas. Diverting the attention of his assistants and my people, he had them conveyed to his own home by his unmarried daughter, and after emptying out the aforesaid objects he threw away the box empty in my house, and he even admitted finding the box, though he pretends that it was empty. Wherefore I request, if you approve, that the accused be brought before you for the due consequences. Farewell.

Orsenuphis, aged fifty, scar on left forearm.

Michigan Papyrus No. 423; A.D. 197
From the translation of H. C. Youtie and O. M. Pearl (Ann Arbor, 1944)

To Hierax also called Nemesio, *strategus* of the division of Heraclides of the Arsinoite nome, from Gemellus also called Horio, son of

Gaius Apolinarius, Antinoite. I appealed, my lord, by petition to the most illustrious prefect, Aemilius Saturninus, informing him of the attack upon me by a certain Sotas, who held me in contempt because of my weak vision and wished himself to get possession of my property with violence and arrogance, and I received his sacred subscription authorizing me to appeal to his excellency the *epistrategus*. Then Sotas died and his brother Julius, also acting with the violence characteristic of them, entered the fields that I had sown and carried away a substantial quantity of hay; not only that, but he also cut dried olive shoots and heath plants from my olive grove near the village of Cercesucha. When I came there at the time of the harvest, I learned that he had committed these transgressions. In addition, not content, he again trespassed with his wife and a certain Zenas, having with them an infant,[214] intending to hem in my cultivator with black magic so that he should abandon his labor after having harvested part of another allotment of mine, and they themselves gathered in the crops. When this happened, I went to Julius in the company of officials, in order that these matters might be witnessed. Again, in the same manner, they threw the same infant toward me, intending to hem me in also with black magic, in the presence of Petesuchus and Ptollas, elders of the village of Caranis who are exercising also the functions of the village secretary, and of Socras their assistant, and while the officials were there, Julius, after he had gathered in the remaining crops from the fields, took the infant away to his house. These acts I made matters of public record through the same officials and the collectors of grain taxes of the same village. Wherefore of necessity I submit this petition and request that it be kept on file so that I may retain the right to plead against them before his execllency the *epistrategus* concerning the outrages perpetrated by them and the public rents due to the imperial fisc from the fields, because they wrongfully did the harvesting.

Gemellus also called Horio, about twenty-six years of age, whose vision is impaired.

Year 5 of Lucius Septimius Severus Pius Pertinax Augustus. Pachon 27.

109. *Private Life in a Roman Province*

Thousands of inscriptions, papyri, and ostraca, of which the following documents are the merest sampling, reveal the multiform activities in the lives of the inhabitants of the Roman Empire from the cradle to the grave.

[214] Embryos and newborn infants (live as well as stillborn) were believed to have magical powers for evil.

MARRIAGE CONTRACT

Berlin Papyrus No. 1,052 (= *Select Papyri*, No. 3); 13 B.C.
From LCL

To Protarchus [215] from Thermion daughter of Apio, with her guardian Apollonius son of Chaereas, and from Apollonius son of Ptolemaeus. Thermion and Apollonius son of Ptolemaeus agree that they have come together to share a common life, and the said Apollonius son of Ptolemaeus acknowledges that he has received from Thermion by hand from the house a dowry of a pair of gold earrings weighing three quarters and . . . silver drachmas; and from now on Apollonius son of Ptolemaeus shall furnish to Thermion as his wedded wife all necessaries and clothing in proportion to his means and shall not ill-treat her nor cast her out nor insult her nor bring in another wife, or else he shall straightway forfeit the dowry increased by half, with right of execution both upon the person of Apollonius son of Ptolemaeus and upon all his property as if by legal decision; and Thermion shall fulfill her duties toward her husband and the common life and shall not absent herself from the house for a night or a day without the consent of Apollonius son of Ptolemaeus, nor dishonor nor injure their common home nor consort with another man, or she, if guilty of any of these actions, shall, after trial, be deprived of the dowry, and in addition the transgressing party shall be liable to the prescribed fine. Year 17 of [Augustus] Caesar, Pharmuthi 20.

DEED OF DIVORCE

Berlin Papyrus No. 1,103 (= *Select Papyri*, No. 6); 13 B.C.
From LCL

To Protarchus from Zois daughter of Heraclides, with her guardian —her brother Irenaeus son of Heraclides—and from Antipater son of Zeno. Zois and Antipater agree that they have separated from each other, severing the union which they had formed on the basis of an agreement made through the same tribunal in Hathyr of the current seventeenth year of [Augustus] Caesar, and Zois acknowledges that she has received from Antipater by hand from his house the material which he received for dowry, namely clothes to the value of 120 drachmas and a pair of gold earrings. The agreement of marriage shall henceforth be null, and neither Zois nor any other person acting for her shall take proceedings

[215] Chief of a tribunal at Alexandria, to whom contractual agreements had to be submitted for official validation.

against Antipater for restitution of the dowry, nor shall either party take proceedings against the other about cohabitation or any other matter whatsoever up to the present day, and hereafter it shall be lawful both for Zois to marry another man and for Antipater to marry another woman without either of them being answerable. In addition to this agreement being valid, the one who transgresses it shall moreover be liable both to damages and to the prescribed fine. Year 17 of [Augustus] Caesar, Pharmuthi 2.

INVITATION TO A FEAST

Fuad Papyrus No. 76; second century

Sarapous invites you to dine at his house on the occasion of the offering to our lady Isis, tomorrow, namely the 29th, beginning at the 9th hour.

ENGAGEMENT OF CASTANET DANCERS

Cornell Papyrus No. 9 (= *Select Papyri*, No. 20); A.D. 206
Adapted from LCL

To Isidora, castanet dancer, from Artemisia, of the village of Philadelphia. I wish to engage you with two other castanet dancers to perform at my house for six days from the 24th of the month of Payni according to the old reckoning; [216] you will receive among you for wages 36 drachmas for each day and for the whole six days four artabs of barley and twenty pairs of loaves; and whatever garments or gold ornaments you bring we will safely guard; and we will provide two donkeys for you when you come down and the same when you return. The fourteenth year of Lucius Septimius Severus Pius Pertinax Augustus and Marcus Aurelius Antoninus [Caracalla] Pius Augustus and Publius Septimius Geta Caesar Augustus, Payni 16.

DEATH IN CHILDBIRTH

Fuad Papyrus No. 75; A.D. 64

Thaubas to his father Pompeius, greeting. You will do well to come immediately upon receipt of my letter, because your unfortunate daughter Herennia, ever blessed, died on Phaophi 9 of premature childbirth. She gave birth to an eight-month child stillborn, lived for four days

---

[216] The old Egyptian year was still in common use despite the introduction of the Julian calendar.

after that, and then died and was given a fitting burial by us and her husband. She was taken to Alabanthis so that, if you come and wish to, you can see her. Alexander sends regards to you and the children. Farewell. Year 11 of the Emperor NERO Claudius Caesar Augustus Germanicus, Phaophi 18.

A PRODIGAL SON

Berlin Papyrus No. 846 (= *Select Papyri*, No. 120); second century
From LCL

Antonius Longus to Nilous his mother, very many greetings. I pray always for your health; every day I make supplication for you before the lord Serapis. I would have you know that I did not expect that you were going to the metropolis; for that reason I did not come to the city myself. I was ashamed to come to Caranis, because I go about in filth. I wrote to you that I am naked. I beg you, mother, be reconciled to me. Well, I know what I brought on myself. I have received a fitting lesson. I know that I have sinned. I heard from . . . who found you in the Arsinoite nome, and he has told you everything correctly. Do you not know that I would rather be maimed than feel that I still owe a man an obol? . . . [The rest is lost.]

HOROSCOPE

Oslo Papyrus No. 6 (= *Select Papyri*, No. 199); A.D. 150
From LCL

The birth of Philoë. Year 10 of the lord ANTONINUS Caesar, Phamenoth 15 to 16, first hour of the night. Sun in Pisces, Jupiter and Mercury in Aries, Saturn in Cancer, Mars in Leo, Venus and Moon in Aquarius, horoscope [217] Capricorn.

QUESTIONS TO ORACLES

Wilcken, No. 122; A.D. 6

To the most great, powerful god Socnopaeus from Asclepiades son of Areus. Is it not granted me that I marry Tapetheus daughter of Marrieus and that she not become the wife of another? Reveal it to me and fulfill this that I have written. Tapetheus was formerly the wife of Horio. Year 35 of [Augustus] Caesar, Pachon 1.

[217] That is, the point on the zodiac which was just rising above the horizon at the time of birth.

Oxyrhynchus Papyrus No. 1,477 (= *Select Papyri*, No. 195); A.D. C.300
From LCL

The following is a fragment of a list of standard questions addressed by visitors to an oracle.

72. Shall I receive the allowance? 73. Shall I remain where I am going? 74. Am I to be sold? 75. Am I to obtain benefit from my friend? 76. Has it been granted me to make a contract with another person? 77. Am I to be reconciled with my offspring[?]? 78. Am I to get a furlough? 79. Shall I get the money? 80. Is he who is away from home alive? 81. Am I to profit by the transaction? 82. Is my property to be put up at auction? 83. Shall I find a means of selling? 84. Am I able to carry off what I have in mind? 85. Am I to become a beggar[?]? 86. Shall I become a fugitive? 87. Shall I be an ambassador[?]? 88. Am I to become a senator? 89. Is my flight to be stopped? 90. Am I to be divorced from my wife? 91. Have I been poisoned? 92. Am I to get my own?

110. *Pro-Roman and Anti-Roman Sentiments*

The attitude of the subject peoples toward their Roman rulers under the Republic is described in Vol. I (see § 147). The masses hated their foreign conquerors and exploiters, the propertied minority in general acquiesced in and supported the foreign régime of "law and order" which protected their vested economic and political interests. This situation continued without essential change under the rule of the emperors, except for the increase in the size of the privileged classes throughout the Empire. The literature of the first two centuries, the imposing array of public works and philanthropies whose proud inscribed testimonials have come down to us—these, products of the upper strata of Roman and provincial society, echo faithfully the official imperial propaganda celebrating the enlightened, beneficent government of the Principate (cf. § 24). The major theme is that liberty has been exchanged for peace, protection, and prosperity; a secondary theme is that in any case revolt against the world-wide dominion and unprecedented might of Rome is futile. But underneath the surface calm of the *Pax Romana*, the hatred of the Roman régime and its visible symbols—the inexorable tax collector and the wealthy landholder or merchant, the arrogant government official and the bullying soldiery—smouldered among the masses and erupted in recurrent local riots and occasionally in sizable revolts.

THE BLESSINGS OF ROMAN IMPERIAL RULE

Tacitus *Histories* iv. lxxiv

The following is an excerpt from a speech put by Tacitus, in the conventional practice of ancient historiography, into the mouth of the Roman general Petilius Cerialis addressing the Gauls after suppressing their revolt of A.D. 70.

"Gaul always had its kingdoms and wars till you submitted to our authority. We, though so often provoked, have used the right of conquest to burden you only with the cost of maintaining peace. For the tranquillity of peoples cannot be had without armies, nor armies without pay, nor pay without tribute. All else is common between us. You often command our legions. You govern these and other provinces. There is no privilege, no exclusion. From praiseworthy emperors you derive equal advantage though you dwell far away, while the cruel ones are most formidable to those near them. Endure the extravagance and rapacity of your masters just as you bear barren seasons and excessive rains and other natural disasters. There will be vices as long as there are men. But they are not everlasting, and they are compensated by the intervals of better times. Perhaps you expect a milder rule under Tutor and Classicus,[218] and imagine that armies to repel the Germans and the Britons will be provided for less tribute than you now pay. Should the Romans be driven out—which the gods forbid!—what will result but wars among all these peoples? The good fortune and order of eight centuries has consolidated this mighty fabric of empire, and it cannot be pulled asunder without destroying those who sunder it. And yours will be the greatest peril, for you have gold and wealth, which are the chief causes of war. Therefore love and cherish peace and the city in which we enjoy an equal right, conquered and conquerors alike. Let the lessons of fortune in both its forms[219] warn you not to prefer contumacy and ruin to obedience and security."

Aelius Aristides[220] *To Rome* xxxvi–xxxix
Adapted from the translation of S. Levin (Glencoe, Illinois, 1950)

[The emperor] governs the whole world as if it were a single city. . . . Just as cases are appealed from a district court to a [provincial] jury, imperial officials have to answer to an appellate tribunal where they are no safer from an adverse verdict than the appellants. . . . Is not this better than any democracy? Under democracy, once a man's case is decided in his town, he cannot take it elsewhere or to other judges. . . .

[218] Leaders of the Trevirans in the unsuccessful revolt against Roman rule.
[219] That is, good and bad.   [220] Cf. Chapter II, Note 53.

Under the Roman Empire, neither the plaintiff nor the defendant need submit to an unjust decision.[221] Another great judge remains from whom justice is never hidden. At that bar there is profound and impressive equity between small and great, obscure and eminent, poor and rich, nobleman and commoner.

THE FUTILITY OF REVOLT

The following is part of a long, conventionally rhetorical harangue in which King Herod Agrippa of the Jews attempts, on the eve of the revolt of A.D. 66–70, to dissuade his people from taking up arms against Rome. See further the introduction to the following selection.

Josephus *The Jewish War* II. xvi. 4. 348–361 (abridged)

From LCL

"Now I know that there are many who wax eloquent on the insolence of the procurators and pronounce pompous panegyrics on liberty. . . . Granted that the Roman ministers are intolerably harsh, it does not follow that all Romans are unjust to you, and surely not Caesar; yet it is against them that you are going to war. It is not by their orders that an oppressive official comes from them to us. . . . How absurd it were because of one man to make war on a whole people, for trifling grievances to take arms against so mighty a power! . . .

"Will you, I say, defy the whole Roman Empire? Look at the Athenians, the men who, to maintain the liberty of Greece, once even consigned their city to flames. . . . Those men today are subjects of the Romans, and the city that was the queen of Greece is governed by order from Italy. Look at the Spartans . . . content to serve the same masters. Look at the Macedonians who . . . with Alexander scattered broadcast . . . the seeds of world empire; yet they submit to endure such a reversal of fate and bow before those to whom Fortune has transferred her favors. Myriads of other peoples, swelling with greater pride in the assertion of their liberty, have yielded. And will you alone disdain to submit to those to whom the whole world is subject?"

THE RAVAGES OF REVOLT

Among the most serious disturbances of the *Pax Romana* were the three Jewish revolts. Like the other peoples of the provinces, the Jews were divided by and large into pro-Roman rich and anti-Roman poor. There were additional stimulants to Jewish unrest, however, in their religious opposition to emperor

---

[221] This sentence is corrupt in the MSS. The translation gives the general sense, which seems clear.

worship and in other peoples' (especially Greeks') resentment of the privileges enjoyed by the Jews (§§ 96, 104). In fact, this anti-Semitism itself erupted at times in massacres of the Jews in cities, such as Alexandria and Cyrene, having sizable Jewish communities. The first revolt—of which Josephus has left us a long and detailed account in his *The Jewish War*—centered in Judaea and was put down after four years (A.D. 66–70), despite fanatic resistance. (Josephus' description of the triumph celebrated by Titus in Rome for this victory is given in § 22.) In reprisal, the Temple at Jerusalem was destroyed and the Jews' annual contributions for its upkeep were confiscated; this marked the end of Judaea as a Jewish religious and political center until recent times. The second revolt, kindled by reports that Trajan's armies were bogged down in Mesopotamia, erupted in A.D. 115 in a Greek-Jewish clash in Cyrene and spread swiftly all over the Levant, sowing destruction of lasting effect in many places; it was not completely suppressed until A.D. 117, after Trajan's death. The two inscriptions which follow attest to the damage wrought by this desperate struggle in Cyrene. The city, theretofore one of the most prosperous in the Mediterranean, and the province never recovered from these ravages. These inscriptions are followed by a brief selection on the outbreak and devastation of the final revolt (A.D. 132–35), led by Simon called *Bar Kochba* (Son of the Star) when Hadrian ordered a Roman colony founded on the site of Jerusalem.

AE, 1928, Nos. 1–2

[Cyrene, A.D. 119]

The Emperor Caesar Trajanus HADRIAN Augustus, son of the deified Trajan Parthicus, grandson of the deified Nerva, *pontifex maximus*, holding the tribunician power for the [third] time, three times consul, restored through the agency of Quintus . . . the road which had been ripped up and ruined in the Jewish revolt.

The Emperor Caesar Trajanus HADRIAN Augustus, son of the deified Trajan Parthicus, grandson of the deified Nerva, *pontifex maximus*, holding the tribunician power for the third time, three times consul, ordered the restoration for the city of Cyrene of the baths together with their porticoes and ball courts and other appurtenances, which had been torn down and burned in the Jewish revolt.

Dio Cassius *Roman History* LXIX. XII. 1–xiv. 1
From LCL

At Jerusalem Hadrian founded a city in place of the one which had been razed to the ground, naming it Aelia Capitolina, and on the site of the temple of the god he raised a new temple to Jupiter. This brought on a war of no slight importance nor of brief duration, for the Jews deemed it intolerable that foreign peoples should be settled in their city and foreign rites planted there. . . .

At first the Romans took no account of them. Soon, however, all Judaea had been stirred up, and the Jews everywhere were showing signs of disturbance, were gathering together, and giving evidence of great hostility to the Romans, partly by secret and partly by overt acts; many outside peoples, too, were joining them through eagerness for gain, and the whole world, one might almost say, was being stirred up over the matter. Then, indeed, Hadrian sent his best generals against them. Foremost among these was Julius Severus, who was dispatched against the Jews from Britain, where he was governor. . . . He was able, rather slowly . . . but with comparatively little danger, to crush, exhaust, and exterminate them. Very few of them in fact survived. Fifty of their most important strongholds and 985 of their most famous villages were razed to the ground; 580,000 men were slain in the various raids and battles, and the number of those that perished by famine, disease, and fire was past finding out.[222]

HATRED OF ROME THE OPPRESSOR

Babylonian Talmud, *Sabbath* 33*b*
From the translation of M. Hadas, Philological Quarterly,
VIII (1929), 373

Why did they call [Rabbi Judah ben Ilia] the first of the speakers? For once Rabbi Judah and Rabbi Jose and Rabbi Simeon were sitting, and Judah son of proselytes was sitting with them. Rabbi Judah began and said: "How excellent are the deeds of this nation. They have instituted market places, they have instituted bridges, they have instituted baths." Rabbi Jose was silent. Rabbi Simeon ben Yohai answered and said: "All that they have instituted they have instituted only for their own needs. They have instituted market places to place harlots in them; baths, for their own pleasure; bridges, to collect toll." Judah son of proselytes went and reported their words and they were heard by the government. They said: "Judah who exalted shall be exalted; Jose who remained silent shall be banished to Sopphoris; Simeon who reproached shall be put to death." [223]

[222] These figures, even if exaggerated, are sufficiently indicative of vast destruction. According to Eusebius (*Ecclesiastical History* IV. vi. 5), "Since then, by decree and enactments of Hadrian, the entire people is strictly forbidden to set foot even upon the land around Jerusalem; it was his order that not even from afar should they view their ancestral soil."

[223] He is said to have escaped and to have spent the next fourteen years hiding in a cave. The episode here reported took place A.D. c.135, about the time of the third Jewish revolt (see the preceding selection).

Dio Cassius *Roman History* LXII. iii. 1–iv. 2 (abridged)
From LCL

The following is part of a rhetorical speech put into the mouth of Budicca (Boadicea), queen of East Anglia, addressing the Britons after the initial success of their revolt under her leadership (A.D. 61).

"You have learned by actual experience how different freedom is from slavery. Hence, even if anyone of you had previously, through ignorance of which was better, been deceived by the alluring promises of the Romans, yet now that you have tried both, you have learned how great a mistake you made in preferring an imported despotism to your ancestral mode of life, and you have come to realize how much better is poverty with no master than wealth with slavery. For what treatment is there of the most shameful or grievous sort that we have not suffered since these men made their appearance in Britain? Have we not been robbed entirely of most of our greatest possessions, while for those that remain we pay taxes? Besides pasturing and tilling for them all our other possessions, do we not pay a yearly tribute for our very bodies? How much better it would be to have been sold to masters once and for all than, possessing empty titles to freedom, to have to ransom ourselves every year! How much better to have been slain and to have perished than to go about with a tax on our heads! Yet why do I mention death? For even dying is not free of cost with them; nay, you know what fees we pay even for our dead. Among the rest of mankind death frees even those who are in slavery to others; only in the case of the Romans do the very dead remain alive for their profit. . . . We have . . . been despised and trampled underfoot by men who know nothing else than how to secure gain."

Tacitus, *Life of Agricola* xxix–xxx

The following is a speech put into the mouth of Calgacus, a Caledonian chieftain, during the attempt of Agricola, governor of the Roman province of Britain, to subdue Caledonia to the north (A.D. 83–84).

Taught at last that a common danger must be repelled by union, the Britons had, by embassies and treaties, called forth the forces of all their states. Already more than 30,000 armed men were to be seen, and still there poured in all the youth and those whose old age was yet hale and vigorous, men renowned in war, each the bearer of decorations of his own. Preeminent among the many chieftains in valor and in birth was one named Calgacus, who is reported to have addressed in the following vein the multitude gathered round him and clamoring for battle.

"Whenever I consider the causes of this war and our present straits, my heart beats high that this very day and this unity of yours will be the beginning of liberty for all Britain. . . . Now they have access to the farthest limits of Britain; there are no more tribes beyond, nothing but waves and rocks, and, more deadly than these, the Romans, whose oppression you have sought in vain to escape by obedience and submissiveness. Plunderers of the world, now that there are no more lands for their all-devastating hands, they search even into the sea. If the enemy is rich, they are rapacious, if poor, they lust for dominion. Not East, not West has sated them; alone of all mankind they covet riches and poverty with equal passion. They rob, butcher, plunder, and call it "empire"; and where they make a desolation, they call it "peace." [224]

APOCALYPTIC VISIONS OF VENGEANCE

Sibylline Oracles [225] VIII. 1–3, 31–42, 91–95, 121–29
From the translation of M. S. Terry (New York, 1890)

God's revelation of great wrath to come
In the last time upon a faithless world,
I make known, prophesying to all men.

.   .   .   .

They waste the poor, that they themselves more land
Procuring may enslave them by deceit.
And if the huge earth from the starry heaven
Held not her throne afar, even light to men
Had not been equal, but, being bought with gold,
Had by the rich been owned, and for the poor
God must have then prepared another world.
On thee some day shall come, O haughty Rome,
A fitting stroke from heaven, and thou the first
Shalt bend the neck, be leveled to the earth,
And fire shall utterly consume thee, bent
Upon thy pavements, thy wealth shall perish,
And on thy site shall wolves and foxes dwell.
And then shalt thou become all desolate
As though thou hadst not been.

.   .   .   .

Near at hand
Is the end of the world, and the last day

---

[224] This is one of the most famous quotations in all Latin literature.
[225] Cf. Vol. I, introduction to § 147. Book VIII, which dates from the end of the second century, is clearly of Judaeo-Christian origin.

And judgment of immortal God for such
As are both called and chosen. First of all
Inexorable wrath shall fall on Rome;
A time of blood and wretched life shall come.
Woe, woe to thee, O land of Italy,
Great, barbarous nation.

. . . . .

With images of gold and silver and stone
Be ready, that unto the bitter day
Ye may come, thy first punishment, O Rome,
Even a gnashing anguish to behold.
And no more under slavish yoke to thee
Will either Greek or Syrian put his neck,
Barbarian or any other nation,
Thou shalt be plundered and shalt be destroyed
For what thou didst, and wailing aloud in fear
Thou shalt give until thou shalt all repay.

The Revelation of John [226] 18:1-20
Adapted from the American Standard Version

After this I saw another angel coming down out of heaven, having great authority; and the earth was lighted up with his glory. And he cried out in a mighty voice, saying: "Fallen, fallen is Babylon the great, and is become a habitation of demons, and a hold of every unclean spirit and a hold of every foul and loathsome bird. For from the wine of the passion of her fornication [227] all the heathen are fallen, and the kings of the earth committed fornication with her, and the merchants of the earth waxed rich from the power of her wantonness. . . .

"How much soever she glorified herself and waxed wanton, so much give her of torment and mourning. . . . And the kings of the earth, who committed fornication and lived wantonly with her, shall weep and wail over her, when they look upon the smoke of her burning, standing afar off for fear of her torment, saying, 'Woe, woe, the great city, Babylon, the mighty city! for in one hour is thy judgment come.' And the merchants of the earth weep and mourn over her, for no man buyeth their cargoes any more—cargoes of gold, and silver, and precious stone, and pearls, and fine linen, and purple, and silk, and scarlet, and

[226] This work, in the tradition of Jewish apocalyptic literature, was written A.D. c.95 in the province of Asia to console Christians there for the persecutions of Domitian.
[227] In the Septuagint this word is used in the metaphorical sense of "idolatry," and some scholars take it in this sense in this passage.

all thyine wood, and every vessel of ivory, and every vessel made of most precious wood, and of bronze and iron and marble, and cinnamon, and spice, and incense, and ointment, and frankincense, and wine, and oil, and fine flour, and wheat, and cattle, and sheep, and horses, and carriages, and slaves, and souls of men.

"And the fruit of thy soul's desire is gone from thee, and all luxury and splendor are perished from thee, and men shall find them no more at all. The merchants of these things, who waxed rich from her, shall stand afar off for fear of her torment, weeping and mourning, saying, 'Woe, woe, the great city, she that was arrayed in fine linen and purple and scarlet, and decked with gold and precious stone and pearl! for in one hour such great wealth is made desolate.' And every steersman, and everyone that saileth anywhither, sailors and all seafaring men, stood afar off, and cried out as they looked upon the smoke of her burning, saying, 'What city was like the great city?' And they cast dust on their heads, and cried out, weeping and mourning, saying, 'Woe, woe, the great city, wherein all that had their ships in the sea waxed rich from her extravagance! for in one hour is she made desolate.' Rejoice over her, heaven, and ye saints and apostles and prophets, for God hath judged your judgment upon her."

CHAPTER VI

THE CRISIS OF THE THIRD CENTURY AND THE EMERGENCE OF THE BYZANTINE STATE, A.D. 193–337

"Our history," proclaims Dio Cassius (*Roman History* LXXI. xxxvi. 4) as he records the death of Marcus Aurelius, "now plunges from a kingdom of gold to one of iron and rust." With foreign peoples exerting steadily increasing pressures on the frontiers and internal economic troubles reaching the proportions of an empire-wide crisis (see §§ 116–118), the might of the indispensable legions stood clearly revealed as the underlying foundation of the Principate. Beginning with Septimius Severus the imperial power was openly based upon the armed forces, and this marked the start of the social revolution of the third century. The state was rapidly militarized, and the soldiery, enriched by legal emoluments and illegal extortions, became the new privileged class, supplanting the civilian, propertied ruling class. Henceforth, this former privileged class had to shoulder the costs of government in increasing measure (see §§ 114, 121), while the actual power of their governmental bodies—the local councils, the provincial assemblies, and even the Roman senate—declined. The senate, indeed, ceased after A.D. 282 to share in the formalization of the emperor's powers (cf. § 21), ceased to legislate (its last known decree is dated A.D. c.280), and emerged at the end of the century as little more than the city council of Rome. Soldiers from the ranks now rose in increasing numbers into the equestrian order, and members of this class, which had already begun to encroach upon the prerogatives of the senatorial career in the middle of the second century, now replaced men of senatorial rank as provincial governors, legionary commanders, and even emperors. Marcus Aurelius had once "refused his soldiers' demand for a donative, saying that anything they received above and beyond the established practice would have to be wrung from the blood of their parents and relatives." In sharp contrast, Severus "before he died is reported to have said to his sons . . . 'Live in harmony, enrich the soldiers, and scorn all others' " (Dio Cassius LXXI. iii. 3 and LXXVI. xv. 2); cf. also below p. 429.

Under these conditions there took place in the third century a rapid polarization of society into two classes, officially recognized in law (cf. §§ 165–166). Those in the upper stratum of society were known as *honestiores*, or *potentiores*; among them were men (usually of military background) who were able, in connivance with or in open defiance of government functionaries, to build up positions of great power and estates of vast extent—the forerunners of feudal barons on medieval manors. The rest of the population—the poor and the *déclassés*—were known as *humiliores*; and these, helpless under the grinding oppression of fiscal demands compounded by the illegal extortions of soldiery and officialdom, sought refuge by placing themselves, in increasing numbers, under the protection of the local great, the *potentiores*.

The changes are clearly reflected also in the language of the period. For example, as the Principate drifted toward absolutism, the ruling house took on the attributes and terminology of divine-right monarchy. In the West as well as in the East (cf. § 14) the imperial family became the "divine" house, and everything connected with it was spoken of as sacred. By the fourth century the political, social, and cultural pattern of the Middle Ages was already clearly emerging.

111. *The Military Monarchy*

THE POWER OF THE PRAETORIAN GUARD: AN EMPIRE FOR SALE

Dio Cassius *Roman History* LXXIV. xi. 2–6
From LCL

Didius Julianus, at once an insatiate money getter and a wanton spendthrift, who was always eager for revolution, and hence had been exiled by Commodus to his native city of Milan, now, when he heard of the death of Pertinax,[1] hastily made his way to the [Praetorian] camp and, standing at the gates of the enclosure, made bids to the soldiers for the rule over the Romans. Then ensued a most disgraceful business and one unworthy of Rome. For, just as if it had been in some market or auction room, both the city and its entire Empire were auctioned off. The sellers were the ones who had slain their emperor, and the would-be buyers were Sulpicianus [2] and Julianus, who vied to outbid each other, one from the inside, the other from outside. They gradually raised their bids up to 20,000 sesterces per soldier. Some of the soldiers would carry word to Julianus, "Sulpicianus offers so much; how much more do you bid?" And to Sulpicianus in turn, "Julianus promises so much; how much do you raise him?" Sulpicianus would have won the day, being inside and being prefect of the city and also the first to name the figure of 20,000, had not Julianus raised his bid no longer by a small amount but by 5,000 at one time, shouting it in a loud voice and also indicating the amount with his fingers. So the soldiers, captivated by this extravagant bid and at the same time fearing

[1] The successor of Commodus, whose reign lasted for only eighty-seven days. For a proclamation in Egypt of his accession, see § 20, last selection.
[2] The father-in-law of Pertinax and prefect of the city.

that Sulpicianus might avenge Pertinax (an idea Julianus put into their heads), received Julianus inside and declared him emperor.[8]

NEW PRIVILEGES TO SOLDIERS

Herodian *History* III. viii. 4–5

[In A.D. 197, after defeating the pretender Albinus at Lugdunum (Lyons), Septimius Severus returned to Rome.] After going up to the sanctuary of Jupiter and performing the rest of the religious ceremonies, Severus returned to the palace and in honor of his victories distributed very great largess to the populace. He bestowed large donatives on the soldiers, granted them many privileges which they did not previously have: he was the first to increase their grain ration, and permitted them to wear gold rings [4] and to live with their wives in wedlock—all of which used to be considered incompatible with military discipline and with preparedness and readiness for war. He was the first to undermine their famous vigor, the austerity of their mode of life, their acquiescence in hard work, and their well-disciplined respect for their officers, teaching them to covet money and turning them aside to luxurious living.[5]

PROVINCIALIZATION OF THE PRAETORIAN GUARD

Dio Cassius *Roman History* LXXV. ii. 3–6

From LCL

There were many things Severus did that were not to our liking: [6] he was blamed for making the city turbulent through the presence of so many troops and for burdening the state by his excessive expenditures of money and, most of all, for placing his hope of safety in the strength of his army rather than in the good will of his associates [in the government]. But some found fault with him particularly because he abolished the practice of selecting the bodyguard exclusively from Italy, Spain, Macedonia, and Noricum—a plan that furnished men of more respectable appearance and of simpler habits—and ordered that

---

[3] Shortly afterward (see second selection following), Septimius Severus dismissed this Praetorian Guard and, in accordance with his policy of democratizing the army, reconstituted it with non-Italian provincials from the frontier legions.

[4] Until this time the exclusive insignia of the equestrian order.

[5] This is an exaggeration by Herodian. There is no reliable evidence that the discipline and training of the army were relaxed by Severus. The increases in pay were probably necessary because of inflation.

[6] Dio Cassius was a member of the senatorial order.

any vacancies should be filled from all the legions alike. Now, he did this with the idea that he should thus have guards with a better knowledge of the soldier's duties, and should also be offering a kind of prize for those who proved brave in war; but, as a matter of fact, it became only too apparent that he had incidentally ruined the youth of Italy, who turned to brigandage [7] and gladiatorial fighting in place of their former service in the army, and had filled the city with a throng of motley soldiers most savage in appearance, most terrifying in speech, and most boorish in conversation.

INCREASING DEMANDS OF THE SOLDIERS

Dio Cassius *Roman History* LXXVIII. xxxvi. 1–3

Macrinus [8] wrote a letter also to Maximus, prefect of the city, in which, after mentioning various matters of a routine nature, he stated that the soldiers, and even the recruits, were insisting on receiving everything they had previously gotten, and that those who had not been deprived of anything were making common cause with them over what was not being granted them. And, to pass over, he said, all the other means devised by Severus and his son [Caracalla] for the destruction of military discipline, it was impossible to give them their pay in full in addition to the donatives they were receiving (for the increase in their pay granted by Caracalla amounted to 280,000,000 sesterces annually), and [equally] impossible not to give it.

"EVERYONE IS IN THE ARMY"

Berlin Papyrus No. 1,680 (= *Select Papyri*, No. 134); third century
From LCL

Isis to Thermuthion her mother, very many greetings. I make supplication for you every day before the lord Sarapis and his fellow gods. I wish you to know that I arrived in Alexandria safe and sound in four days. I send salutations to my sister and the children, and Eluath and his wife, and Dioscorous and her husband and children, and Tamalis and her husband and son, and Hero and Ammonarion and her children and husband, and Sanpat and her children. And if Aio wishes to join the army, let him come; for everyone is in the army. I pray for the health of all your household.

[7] On the spread of brigandage in the third century, see § 115.
[8] Marcus Opellius Macrinus, a native of Mauretania, who ruled for about a year (217–18), the first equestrian to become emperor without first attaining senatorial rank.

THE PROBLEM OF MILITARY DISCIPLINE

"Historia Augusta" Life of Aurelian vii
Adapted from LCL

Aurelian was so feared by the soldiers that, under him, after offenses had once been punished by him in the camp with the utmost severity, no one offended again. . . . There is a letter of his, truly that of a soldier, written to his deputy as follows: "If you wish to be a tribune, or rather if you wish to remain alive, restrain the hands of your soldiers. None shall steal another's fowl or touch his sheep. None shall carry off grapes, or thresh out grain, or exact oil, salt, or firewood, and each shall be content with his own allowance. Let them have these things from the booty taken from the enemy and not from the tears of the provincials. Their arms shall be kept burnished, their implements bright, their boots stout. Let old uniforms be replaced by new. Let them keep their pay in their belts and not spend it in public houses. Let them wear their collars, arm rings, and finger rings.[9] Let each man curry his own horse and baggage animal, let no one sell the fodder allowed him for his beast, and let them take care in common of the mule belonging to the century. Let one yield obedience to another as to a master, and no one as a slave, let them be attended by physicians without charge, let them give no fees to soothsayers, let them conduct themselves in their lodgings with propriety, and let anyone who begins a brawl be thrashed."[10]

112. *Anarchy: the Legions Become Emperor Makers*

The specious stability of the Empire under the Severan dynasty was shattered by the rebellion of Maximinus in A.D. 235, which touched off a half century of civil war and internal chaos, attended by devastating epidemics, depopulation, runaway inflation, invasions of northern barbarians, and incursions by the resurgent Persian Empire of the Sassanids in the East. Armies became a law unto themselves, terrorizing the population, elevating and liquidating emperors at will. From the assassination of Severus Alexander in 235 to the accession of Diocletian in 284, twenty-six soldier-emperors were proclaimed, all but one of whom died a violent death, usually at the hands of their own soldiers. A number of them exercised their ephemeral reigns only in that part of the Empire which their armies controlled; other pretenders "ruled" simultaneously elsewhere. Political separatism emerged as Gaul was temporarily

[9] Cf. Note 4.
[10] On the authenticity of documents quoted in the "Historia Augusta," see Vol. I, p. 31.

detached from the Empire. When political unity was finally restored, the death blow had been given not only to the Principate but to the foundations of Graeco-Roman culture.

Aurelius Victor [11] *Lives of the Emperors* xxiv–xxvii (abridged)

Aurelius Alexander . . . although only a young man, with an ability beyond his age made great preparations at once for the war against Xerxes [Ardashir], king of the Persians. After conquering and routing him, he came with great speed to Gaul, which the Germans were trying to invade. When he arrived there, he discharged with great firmness several mutinous legions. This act, which at the time won him great glory, was not long after the cause of his destruction: the soldiers, offended by such great severity (whence he had acquired the surname Severus),[12] killed him in Vicus Britannicus,[13] where he chanced to be staying with a small escort. . . . Although he had reigned only thirteen years, he left the state strengthened on every side. From Romulus to Septimius [Severus] the state rose steadily in power, but it came to a halt at its peak, as it were, because of Caracalla's designs. It was Alexander's accomplishment to retard its rapid decline. The emperors after him, more concerned with tyrannizing their subjects than subduing foreign peoples, and with warring among themselves, precipitated the Roman state into a steep decline. Then good men and bad, nobles and low-born, and even many barbarians,[14] were indiscriminately elevated to the purple. This is to be expected where all is everywhere in confusion and things get out of hand: everyone considers it proper, in a mob spirit, to usurp the offices of others, which he is incapable of discharging, and which he foully corrupts because of lack of knowledge of good practices. Thus does the power of fortune . . . direct mankind. For a long time she can be checked by virtue as by a wall; but after almost everyone has succumbed to corruption, she entrusts the state to men of inferior station and inadequate training. . . .

[11] Author of an epitome of imperial history in the form of biographies of the emperors, published A.D. c.360: cf. Chapter V, Note 67.

[12] Actually, Alexander, a cousin of Elagabalus, his predecessor, assumed the name Severus to associate himself with the founder of the dynasty. Officially he was styled the son of Caracalla and grandson of Septimius Severus.

[13] Bretzenheim near Mainz. It is more probable that Alexander Severus was killed because of his inadequacy as a soldier and because the armies on the Rhine objected to his efforts to secure a peace with the Germans through the payment of cash subsidies.

[14] An exaggeration. Many of the emperors of the third century were of provincial origin, hailing from such provinces as Africa, Syria, Illyria, Thrace, Arabia, Pannonia: cf. Note 56.

After annihilating the Persians,[15] Aurelian returned to Italy, the cities of which were being distressed by the Alemannians. At the same time he drove the Germans from Gaul and cut to pieces the legions of Tetricus.[16]. . . Likewise the band of workers at the mint [in Rome] was destroyed. These men, under the leadership of Felicissimus, procurator of the imperial treasury, after debasing the coinage, had taken up arms through fear of punishment, and their revolt had become so serious that they killed about 7,000 troops in a pitched battle on the Caelian Hill. After so many great successes Aurelian erected at Rome a magnificent temple to the Sun [17] and adorned it with sumptuous offerings. And in order to avoid a repetition of what had occurred through Gallienus' negligence,[18] he increased the *pomerium*[19] of Rome and surrounded it with very strong walls.[20] Likewise, yielding to the wish of the Roman populace, he provided, wisely and generously, for a distribution of pork. He also did away with fiscal denunciations and those of the "twenty-five percenters," [21] that had been a scourge on the city; he consigned to the flames their records, together with documents concerning affairs of this kind. He decreed an amnesty, in the manner of the Greeks. Moreover, he savagely prosecuted—contrary to the practice of the military, of whom he was one—avarice, embezzlement, and plunderers of the provinces. This was the cause of his death near Caenophrurium,[22] through the deception and treachery of an assistant whom he had made his secretary. This man, who had plunder and crime on his conscience, transmitted to the military tribunes, as if to show them his good will, a skillfully fabricated document ordering them to be put to death. Fear seized these officers, and they committed the crime. After the death of the emperor the legions at once sent envoys to Rome to invite the senate to elect an emperor of their own choice. The senate replied that that right belonged more to the legions than to itself, but the legions referred the matter again to the senate. And so there ensued a contest of reserve and modesty on both sides, virtues quite rare among

[15] Actually the principality of Palmyra (cf. p. 329), which had revolted from the Romans and received the assistance of the Persians.
[16] Governor of Aquitania, who reigned for four years (270–74) as head of a Romano-Gallic Empire.
[17] For the growth of sun worship in the third century, see introduction to § 171.
[18] The incursion of the barbarian Juthungians into Italy is meant.
[19] See Vol. I, § 6.
[20] The walling of cities is characteristic of this era. The famous Wall of Aurelian, built to protect Rome from surprise raids of barbarians, was begun in A.D. 271 and completed in 275, during the reign of Probus. Extensive remains of Aurelian's Wall, which was twelve miles in circuit and twenty feet in height, survive.
[21] Informers who received one quarter of the victim's estate.
[22] A fortress near Byzantium.

men, especially in such matters, and practically unknown to soldiers. . . .[23]

After a month or two of unstable rule, Florian was killed by his troops near Tarsus. After him they accepted Probus, who had been elevated in Illyria.[24] Probus was a man highly skilled in military science, and almost another Hannibal in the art of exercising troops in various ways and of hardening young men. Indeed, just as Hannibal had employed his soldiers in planting olive trees in several places in Africa, fearing that their idleness might be dangerous to the state and its leaders, so Probus filled Gaul, Pannonia, and the hills of Moesia with vineyards,[25] after he had worn down the barbarian tribes which had made incursions when our emperors had been slain through their crimes, and after he had killed Saturninus in the East and Bonosus with his army at Cologne. Both had attempted, employing the troops which they commanded as generals, to seize the imperial power. For this reason, when all territory had been recovered and pacified, he is reported to have said that in a short time there would be no need of soldiers. Provoked by this, the troops, when he compelled them to dig openings and ditches in order to drain the land which the winter rains turn into marshes in the vicinity of Sirmium, his native city, murdered him near that city in the sixth year of his reign.[26] Thenceforth the military power regained the ascendant, and the senate has remained until our time [27] deprived of the power and right of choosing the emperor. It is uncertain whether this took place through default, with the consent of the senate, or through fear, or dislike of discord. Yet it is certain that . . . military discipline could have been reestablished in consequence of the moderate conduct of the legions during Tacitus' reign; that Florian would then not have been so bold as to seize power; that, finally, if the members of an order so distinguished and important had spent their lives in military camps, the imperial power would not be bestowed on anyone, even a good man, by the decision of the soldiery. But, by giving themselves up to the delights of leisure and fearing for their riches, whose enjoyment and abundance they thought

[23] This situation lasted for six months. Such deference to the senate may have been due to the regret of the officers when they discovered that they had been tricked into murdering their beloved leader, whom the soldiers had nicknamed "Hand-on-Hilt."

[24] Florian was the half-brother of the Emperor Tacitus. Actually, Probus was proclaimed emperor in 276 by the armies in the East, where he was governor of Syria and Egypt.

[25] Probus employed his troops on many projects in Egypt, including the cleaning of the irrigation canals (cf. introduction to § 100). On the assignment of soldiers to nonmilitary labor as part of their normal routine, see introduction to § 149.

[26] A.D. 282.

[27] That is, A.D. c.360, when Aurelius Victor's work was published.

would last longer than eternity, they paved the way for the soldiery, and almost the barbarians, to dominate them and posterity.

113. *The Extension of Citizenship*

The centuries-long process of enfranchisement and Romanization (see §§ 32, 83) reached its culmination in A.D. 212, when inhabitants of the Empire were admitted to Roman citizenship *en masse* by a sweeping edict of the Emperor Caracalla, the famous *Constitutio Antoniniana*. "It is true that by approximating the Empire formally to the politico-philosophical ideal of a universal community of equal men the edict impressed the imagination of later ages, but even in the political sphere it merely marked the end of a process. In practice it made so small a change that it was not much noticed by contemporaries, and officially it was made so little of that it has left hardly any traces upon the coinage" [28] (*Cambridge Ancient History*, XII, 47). The immediate motives behind Caracalla's grant as well as its precise effects are still imperfectly understood. Dio Cassius' statement (§ 114, first selection), that its principal object was to effect an increase in imperial revenues is superficial and biased. It did, among its effects, sweep away many administrative anomalies, simplify financial and judicial administration, and equalize municipal obligations throughout the Empire, and it may have been to achieve this simplification that the military-minded emperor issued his edict.[29]

The prime piece of evidence on Caracalla's measure is a papyrus from Egypt, unfortunately much mutilated, containing a Greek version of the edict. Despite an enormous literature of frequently heated controversy over attempted restoration and interpretation since the papyrus was first published in 1910, it is still not entirely clear which categories of the population were included in, and which excluded from, the grant of citizenship. It is certain, however, that after the *Constitutio Antoniniana* there remained many noncitizens in the Roman Empire, despite the classic statement of Ulpian, presumably incompletely quoted in Justinian's *Digest* (I. v. 17), that "all living in the Roman world were made Roman citizens by a constitution of the Emperor Caracalla." The newly enfranchised citizens and their descendants bore the name of Aurelius, just as citizens earlier enfranchised had taken the names of the emperors from whom they had received their citizenship (cf. introduction to § 32).

Giessen Papyrus No. 40, col. 1 (= Abbott-Johnson, No. 192 = *FIRA*, Vol. I, No. 88); A.D. 212

The Emperor Caesar Marcus Aurelius Severus Antoninus Augustus [CARACALLA] declares: . . . I may show my gratitude to the immortal

[28] For coin legends as a medium of imperial propaganda, cf. introduction to § 37.
[29] Such was the general administrative tendency of the military emperors of the third and fourth centuries: cf. further §§ 121–122, 126–131, 134–136.

gods for preserving me in such. . . .[30] Therefore I consider that in this way I can . . . render proper service to their majesty . . . by bringing with me to the worship[?] of the gods all who enter into the number of my people. Accordingly, I grant Roman citizenship to all aliens [31] throughout the world, with no one remaining outside the citizen bodies [32] except the *dediticii*.[33] For it is proper that the multitude should not only help carry[?] all the burdens but should also now be included in my victory. This edict shall . . .[34] the majesty of the Roman people. . . . [The rest is fragmentary.]

114. *Increased Financial Burden on the Civilian Population*

The civil wars of the third century and the increased military budget, necessitated by the demands of imperial defense and the upkeep of the privileged armies, brought widespread misery and opened the door to all manner of abuses of authority by civil and military officials far exceeding those of the preceding centuries (cf. §§ 98, 106). The vast confiscations by Septimius Severus and by other emperors of the estates of their political enemies, the sharp increases in taxes, requisitions and special contributions, and widespread looting by the soldiery convulsed economic life and ultimately brought on mass impoverishment. "The chief evil, however, was the enormous number of government agents, mostly soldiers performing the duties of policemen— the *frumentarii, stationarii* and *colletiones*—who in their pursuit of political 'criminals' penetrated into all the cities and villages and searched private houses, and who were, of course, accessible to bribes. Still more serious were the exactions of these same agents in connexion with the frequent military expeditions of the emperor. In time of civil war no one cared a straw for the people" (M. Rostovtzeff, *Social and Economic History of the Roman Empire*, p. 363).

[30] The reference here is to the alleged plot against his life by his brother and co-ruler Geta, whom he put to death earlier that year.
[31] This word is supplied in a lacuna; it may of course have been another similar term, for example, "my subjects."
[32] This clause, so vital to the interpretation of the text, has to be restored. Other restorations which have found considerable favor among different scholars read: (1) "with no one being excluded from my grant"; (2) "with every kind of local citizenship remaining intact."
[33] There is uncertainty and controversy, too, on the category of persons designated by this term. The word means, literally, "people who surrendered [to the Romans]," but its meaning and scope underwent considerable evolution in the course of the first two centuries.
[34] The missing word is presumably something like "increase," "extend," "consolidate," or "show."

Dio Cassius *Roman History* LXXVII. ix–x (abridged)

Antonius [35] was prodigal toward the soldiers, whom he kept in great numbers about him, alleging one excuse after another and one war after another; but he took pains to strip, despoil, and grind down all the rest of mankind, and not the least the senators. In addition to the gold crowns he frequently demanded, on the constant pretext that he had conquered some enemy (and I am not speaking of the actual making of the crowns—for what does that amount to?—but of the large quantity of money customarily given under that name by the cities for the "crowning" of the emperors), [36] there were the provisions that were exacted of us in great quantities and from every side, sometimes without payment, sometimes at additional cost to ourselves—all of which he either bestowed upon the soldiers or sold at retail; and there were the gifts which he kept demanding from wealthy private persons and from communities; and the taxes, both the new ones he promulgated and the ten-percent tax that he instituted in place of the five-percent tax on manumissions and bequests and legacies left to anyone, for he abolished the right of succession and tax exemption which had been granted in such cases to those who were closely related to the deceased. For this reason also he declared all the people in his empire Roman citizens; nominally he was honoring them, but his real purpose was to increase his revenues thereby, inasmuch as aliens did not have to pay most of these taxes. [37] But apart from all these burdens, we were also compelled to build at our own expense all sorts of houses for him whenever he set out from Rome, and costly lodgings in the middle of even the very shortest journeys; yet he not only never lived in these but was not destined even to see some of them. In addition, we constructed amphitheaters and race courses wherever he spent the winter or expected to spend it, all without receiving any remuneration from him; and they were all promptly demolished, the sole reason for their construction being, apparently, that we might be ruined. . . .

Indeed, Caracalla often used to say, "Nobody in the world should have money but I, so that I may bestow it upon the soldiers." And once, when Julia [Domna, his mother] censured him for his great expenditures for them and said, "There is no longer any revenue, either just or unjust, left to us," he answered, exhibiting his sword, "Be of good cheer, mother, for as long as we have this, we shall not run short of money."

[35] That is, Caracalla: cf. Note 56.
[36] Cf. § 119, second selection.
[37] Cf. introduction to § 113.

Herodian *History* VII. iii. 1–iv. 6, ix. 10–11

What was the use of destroying the barbarians, when the killing in Rome itself and in the provinces subject to her was on a larger scale? What was the use of seizing booty from the enemy, only to be stripped naked oneself and see one's relatives deprived of their property? An invitation has been given to informers to do their dastardly work with complete license, including attempts to rake up matters concerning one's ancestors—matters which one knows nothing about and therefore cannot refute. Any person merely summoned to court by an informer was immediately found guilty, and went away from the proceedings stripped of his entire property. Every day one could see the very wealthy of yesterday reduced to beggary for the future—so great was the love of money of the tyrannical government [of Maximinus]. The pretext was the constant need of supplies for the soldiers. . . .

So long as these things happened to individuals . . . it did not make any difference at all to the peoples of the cities or the provinces. The masses were not interested in the misfortunes of those believed to be well-off or rich. Indeed, some of the malicious and common type, in their envy of the more powerful and the well-to-do, are even delighted by such occurrences. But then Maximinus, after reducing most of the notable houses to poverty, and finding the income obtained thereby small and insufficient for his purpose, began to lay hands on the public treasuries. He expropriated whatever public moneys there were—funds which had been collected for the grain supply or for distribution to the people, or ear-marked for shows or festivals. Dedications in temples, statues of gods, honors to heroes, and whatever embellishment there was of a public nature, or adornment of a city, or material out of which money could be made—he melted all of it. . . . In the cities and provinces the hearts of the masses were inflamed. Now that exactions were being made upon themselves, they resented the soldiers; and relatives and friends reproached them with hate in their hearts, believing that Maximinus was doing these things on behalf of the soldiers.

For these reasons, not unjustifiable ones, the masses were being inflamed to hatred and revolt. . . . After three years of his reign, for a small and insignificant reason—the usual stumbling block of tyranny—the Africans were the first to take up arms, and resolutely raised the standard of revolt.

[The insurrection was touched off when the procurator of Africa moved to collect heavy fines imposed on a number of wealthy landowners, who would have been compelled to sell their property to pay the fines.]

The young men, though outraged at this, promised to pay the money to him but requested a delay of three days. Forming a conspiracy, and winning over all those who they knew had been ill-treated or feared they would be, they ordered their tenants to come down from their fields and to arm themselves with staves and axes. And, in obedience to the orders of their masters, they assembled in the city before dawn, concealing under their clothes the weapons which they had brought for a hand-to-hand battle. Quite a large number gathered, for Africa with its large population has many persons farming the land. As soon as dawn came, the young men came forward and bade the band made up of their tenants to follow them as if they were part of the mass of people. And they ordered them to conceal the weapons they were carrying and to make a brave stand if any of the soldiers or the people should set upon them to avenge the deed they had planned. They themselves, grasping daggers concealed under their garments, approached the procurator as if to discuss the payment of the money. Then, falling upon him suddenly and unexpectedly, they struck and slew him. When the soldiers in his guard drew their swords to avenge the assassination, the men who had come down from the fields brought out their staves and axes, came to the defense of their masters, and easily routed their opponents. . . .[38]

[The proclamation of Gordian as emperor was the signal for a large-scale revolt in the province of Africa against Maximinus' supporters.]

When Capellianus [39] entered Carthage, he killed all the leading men who were still alive after the battle, and he plundered the temples and seized the money of private persons and the public funds. And he attacked all the other cities that had taken down the dedications to Maximinus, killing the gentry and exiling the common citizens. He also gave orders to the soldiers to put fields and villages to the torch and to loot. This he did on the pretext of exacting vengeance for the wrongs to Maximinus, but secretly he was courting the good will of the soldiers, hoping that if the affairs of Maximinus came a cropper, he himself, in possession of a well-disposed army, might lay claim to the imperial power.

[38] This is interesting evidence of the growing reliance of many humble folk in the Empire on rich and powerful landowners because of the rapacity and corruption of officialdom and their own inability to obtain justice through an appeal to the emperor; cf. § 123 and Note 76.
[39] Governor of Numidia, who remained faithful to Maximinus.

115. *The Rise of Brigandage*

Under the harsh conditions prevailing in the third century, robber bands appeared in many parts of the Empire. To these bands flocked ruined people, war refugees, army deserters, and many persons who had fled from the land and the cities to escape onerous fiscal demands and compulsory public services.

Dio Cassius *Roman History* LXXVI. X. 1–5
From LCL

At this period one Bulla, an Italian, got together a robber band of about six hundred men, and for two years [40] continued to plunder Italy under the very noses of the emperors and of a multitude of soldiers. For though he was pursued by many men, and though Severus eagerly followed his trail, he was never really seen when seen, never found when found, never caught when caught, thanks to his great bribes and his cleverness. For he learned about everybody that was setting out from Rome and everybody that was putting into port at Brundisium, and knew both who and how many there were, and what and how much they had with them. In the case of most persons he would take a part of what they had and let them go at once, but he detained artisans for a time and made use of their skill, then dismissed them with a present. Once when two of his robber band had been captured and were about to be given to wild beasts, he paid a visit to the prison keeper, pretending that he was a magistrate of his native district and needed some men of this kind, and in this way he secured and saved the men. And he approached the centurion who was trying to exterminate the band and accused himself, pretending to be someone else, and promised, if the centurion would accompany him, to deliver the robber to him. So, on the pretext that he was leading him to Felix (this was another name by which he was called), he led him into a defile beset with thickets, and easily seized him. Later, he assumed the dress of a magistrate, ascended the tribunal, and having summoned the centurion caused part of his head to be shaved, and then said, "Carry this message to your masters: 'Feed your slaves, so that they may not turn to brigandage.'" Bulla had with him, in fact, a very large number of imperial freedmen, some of whom had been poorly paid, while others had received absolutely no pay at all.

[40] A.D. 206–7.

Oxyrhynchus Papyrus No. 1,408, lines 11–21 (= *Select Papyri*,
No. 224); A.D. 210/214
Adapted from LCL

Baebius Juncinus [prefect of Egypt] to the *strategi* of the Heptanomia and the Arsinoite nome, greeting. I have already ordered you in a
previous letter to make careful search for the robbers, warning you of
peril if you neglect this, and now I wish to add weight to my resolve by
an edict, in order that all the inhabitants of Egypt may know that I am
not treating this duty as an affair of secondary importance, but I am
offering rewards to those of you who cooperate and threaten with peril
those who choose to disobey. This edict I desire to be publicly displayed
in both the metropolises and the most conspicuous places of the nomes,
penalties and peril awaiting you if in the future any evil-doer is able to
use violence without being detected. I wish you good health. Year . . . ,
Phaophi 28.[41]

116. *Barbarian Invasions*

Internal political, social, and economic chaos so loosened the imperial defenses
that hordes of barbarian peoples were enabled to pierce the laboriously erected
limites of the Empire (see introduction to § 25) at many points, and to devas-
tate parts of Gaul, the Danubian provinces, Macedonia, Greece, Asia Minor,
Egypt, Africa, Spain, and even Italy (where a German tribe advanced up to
the gates of Rome during the reign of Gallienus). The emperors of the third
century—as a glance at their honorific military titles shows—were almost
without interruption occupied in wars with various German, Dacian, and
Gothic tribes, and with Parthia and its successor, Sassanid Persia. One of the
results of the fluidity of the Danube frontier was that Dacia, having lost its
strategic importance, was permanently evacuated in A.D. 275 under Aurelian,
after 150 years of Roman rule. The destruction of wealth and the depopulation caused by the incursions was so great that the emperors were forced to
grant regular subsidies to peoples beyond the frontiers in return for pledges
of nonaggression—the final debasement of the diplomatic policy introduced
by earlier emperors of giving cash payments to client states (see § 26). Under

[41] A contemporary petition (*SB*, No. 4,284 = Abbott-Johnson, No. 190; A.D. 207)
reveals that the emperors, in an edict issued presumably in connection with the
census of A.D. 201/2, had also taken cognizance of the prevalence of brigandage:
"Our lords the most divine and invincible Emperors Severus and Antoninus, when
they appeared in their Egypt [A.D. 199–201] desired, among the very many boons
they bestowed, also that those living away from home should all return to their
own places of abode [cf. introduction to § 102], breaking with their violent and
lawless life; and in accordance with their sacred urgings we returned." Cf. also
the language of § 97, last selection.

Caracalla the amount of money thus paid to the barbarian peoples is said to have equaled the pay of the Roman armies, and in the East Macrinus paid the king of Parthia 200,000,000 sesterces to terminate hostilities. Even more important was the enormous extension of the earlier policy of settling barbarians inside the frontiers (see § 28). In the third century large numbers were granted lands near the borders and entrusted with defending them against barbarians beyond. In addition, sizable numbers of foreign troops were incorporated into the auxiliary corps of the Roman armies. This barbarization of the Roman army is one of the prime causes of the crumbling of the Roman Empire in the subsequent two centuries.

Dio Cassius Roman History LXXVII. xiv
From LCL

Caracalla waged war also against the Cennians, a German tribe. These warriors are said to have assailed the Romans with the utmost fierceness, even using their teeth to pull out from their flesh the missiles with which the Osroenians [42] wounded them, so that they might have their hands free for slaying without interruption. Nevertheless, even they accepted a defeat in name for a large sum of money and allowed Caracalla to make his escape back into the province of Germany. Some of their women who were captured by the Romans, upon being asked by Caracalla whether they wished to be sold or slain, chose the latter fate; then, upon being sold, they all killed themselves and some slew their children as well.

Many also of the people living close to the ocean itself near the mouths of the Elbe sent envoys to him asking for his friendship, although their real purpose was to get money. This was made clear by the fact that, when he had done as they desired, many attacked him, threatening to make war, and yet he came to terms with all of them. For even though the terms proposed were contrary to their wishes, yet when they saw the gold pieces they were captivated. The gold he gave them was of course genuine, whereas the silver and gold currency that he furnished to the Romans was debased; for he manufactured the one kind out of lead plated with silver and the other out of copper plated with gold. [43]

"Historia Augusta" Life of Severus Alexander lviii. 3-5
From LCL

The captives taken from the various peoples, if their childhood or youth permitted it, were given to the emperor's friends, but those who were of royal blood or noble rank were enrolled for warfare, though not for any of great importance. The lands taken from the enemy were

[42] A people from the Roman province of Osroëne in northwestern Mesopotamia.
[43] For the debasement of Roman coinage in the third century, see §§ 118, 129.

presented to the leaders and soldiers of the frontier armies, with the provision that they should continue to be theirs only if their heirs entered military service, and that they should never belong to civilians, for, he said, men serve with greater zeal if they are defending their own lands.[44] He added to these lands, indeed, both draft animals and slaves, in order that they might be able to till what they had received and that it might not come to pass that, through a lack of inhabitants or the old age of the owners, the lands bordering on the country of the barbarians should be left uninhabited; for this, he thought, would be most reprehensible.

"Historia Augusta" *Life of Probus* xiv. 7, xviii. 1–2
From LCL

He took 16,000 [German] recruits, all of whom he scattered through the various provinces, incorporating bodies of fifty or sixty in the detachments or among the soldiers along the frontier, for he said that the aid that the Romans received from barbarian auxiliaries must be felt but not seen. . . . Having made peace, then, with the Persians, he returned to Thrace, where he settled 100,000 Bastarnians on Roman soil, all of whom remained loyal. But when he had likewise brought over many from other tribes—that is, Gepedians, Greuthungians,[45] and Vandals—they all broke faith, and when Probus was busied with wars against the pretenders they roamed over well-nigh the entire world on foot or in ships and did no little damage to the glory of Rome.

NEGOTIATIONS WITH THE JUTHUNGIANS

Dexippus[46] *Fragment* 6 (abridged)

When Aurelian had inflicted a smashing defeat upon the Scythian Juthungians,[47] and had slaughtered many of them as they withdrew to

[44] During the Principate, military service tended to become an occupation in which sons followed fathers, and with the Severan dynasty the military became a veritable caste. This is, however, the earliest known case where military service was formally made hereditary (cf. introduction to § 155). With similar grants of border lands by subsequent emperors, the entire frontier defense by the end of the fourth century had been reorganized on this principle. Along the Empire's frontiers was strung a chain of fortresses (*castella*), around which these hereditary military settlers (*limitanei*) were concentrated.
[45] These two were Gothic tribes. With this selection may be compared Zosimus' report (*Recent History* i. lxviii. 3) that Probus, after defeating Burgundians and Vandals, "sent to Great Britain the prisoners he had taken in the war, and gave them lands in that island to inhabit. They were subsequently very serviceable to him whenever the older inhabitants of the island undertook to revolt."
[46] Publius Herennius Dexippus, an Athenian, one of the last important historians in antiquity, wrote in the second half of the third century three major works, including a history of Rome's Scythian wars, from which this fragment and the next come.
[47] A Suebian tribe settled on the Lower Danube, east of Dacia. Elements of this

their refuge across the Danube, the survivors sent an embassy to make a truce. But they gave the appearance of making their plea for peace without the extreme fear and panic of defeat, in an attempt to obtain also the restoration of the regular subsidy previously paid them by the Romans.

[Aurelian drew up his army in full battle array in order to overawe the Juthungian envoys. The latter, speaking through an interpreter, delivered a long, rhetorical address, which ended as follows:]

"It would be best for you to make peace and obtain the advantages accruing from harmony, and to come to a settlement with us over the issues of the war and thus, strengthened by our alliance, to have greater resources against your attackers. If you should decide to do this, it is just that we should get what we used to receive from you regularly in gifts of coined and uncoined gold and silver to guarantee friendship. If we are denied this, we will defend ourselves against you as enemies and fight with all our might."

To this the king of the Romans replied as follows: ". . . If you bring an honest offer of peace, what need is there to mention a demand of money? . . . If you think that signing a treaty will weaken your position with respect to the profit and gains derived from the war and you therefore come here, though defeated, to demand tribute from us, thinking that we are eager at any cost for the pleasures of indolence which peace affords—why, then, try an attack like your previous one. . . . Although treaty-bound, you launched hostilities against us without a declaration of war. . . . Your horde is far from strong either in body or in spirit. It has been cut off inside . . . our territory; it is afflicted with scarcity of food and other hardship; some sufferings are now upon it, and still others await it; and, worn out in constant hardship, it will become more demoralized, and we shall be able without fighting to do whatever we please with it. . . ."

At these words of the king the Juthungians were panic-stricken, and as none of the results they had hoped for was being achieved, faced completely as they were with despair about the truce, they returned to their people.

TREATY WITH THE VANDALS, A.D. 271

Dexippus [48] *Fragment* 7

In the reign of Aurelian the Vandals, after suffering a smashing defeat at the hands of the Romans, sent an embassy to the Romans to

---

people had advanced as far as Rome during the reign of Aurelian's predecessor, Gallienus.

[48] See Note 46.

negotiate an armistice and a treaty. . . . The Roman soldiers were . . . assembled, and were asked by the king what they thought the better course in the existing circumstances. Deciding wisely . . . to preserve their present good fortune, they all voted for an end to the war, indicating their desire with a shout. . . .

The kings and chieftains of the barbarians came and, as they had been ordered, gave hostages not inferior to themselves in rank or station (their kings each give their sons as hostages without hesitation). . . . Thus they came to an agreement, and the treaty was drawn up. Thereafter two thousand Vandal cavalrymen would serve with the Romans, part of them drafted from the ranks and enrolled in this allied force, the rest volunteers undertaking military service of their own accord. The rest of the Vandal horde would return home, and the Roman governor would provide them with a market hard by the Danube.

117. Depopulation of City and Countryside

CITIES RAVAGED BY CIVIL WAR: THE CASE OF
AQUILEIA

Herodian *History* VIII. ii. 3–iv. 8 (abridged)

Aquileia was even in earlier times a very big city with a large population of its own. Situated on the sea like an emporium of Italy and fronting all the Illyrian peoples, she provided the merchants sailing there with the products received from the interior by land or river, and she shipped into the hinterland the products from overseas needed by the inhabitants, which their land did not readily produce because of its cold climate; and also, as they did not cultivate the vine and her territory was especially productive of wine, she furnished them with an abundance of drink. Accordingly, a large population lived there, consisting not only of citizens but also of foreigners and merchants. At this time,[49] however, the population was even further increased by all the crowds streaming thither from the countryside, leaving the neighboring towns and villages to seek safety inside the great city and its surrounding wall. The ancient wall had for the most part been demolished earlier, since after the advent of Roman rule the cities of Italy no longer needed walls or weapons, for they enjoyed, in place of wars, profound peace and association in Roman citizenship. But now necessity drove them to restore the wall, rebuild its ruins, and raise towers and battlements. . . .

[49] A.D. 238.

When he came to a very big river sixteen miles distant from the city, Maximinus found the stream at its greatest depth and width. . . . There was no way for the army to cross, for the Aquileians had torn down and destroyed the bridge, a great and most beautiful structure built under the early emperors, of squared stone supported on piers increasing gradually in height [toward the center]. . . .[50] Setting up [a pontoon bridge laid on large wine casks], the army crossed over and marched upon the city. Finding the houses of the suburbs deserted, they cut down all the vines and trees, set some on fire, and made a shambles of the once-thriving countryside. . . . After destroying all this to the root, the army pressed on to the walls . . . and strove to demolish at least some part of the wall, so that they might break in and sack everything, razing the city and leaving the land a deserted pasturage.

THE "PURGING" OF ALEXANDRIA

In A.D. 215 Caracalla turned his soldiery loose on the population of Alexandria, which had demonstrated against him on his arrival. After the massacre he sent to the prefect of Egypt a letter, from which this papyrus preserves two extracts, instructing him to expel from the city all persons who had no business there. On the floating population of Alexandria, cf. §§ 102, 105.

Giessen Papyrus No. 40, col. 2, lines 16–29 (= Abbott-Johnson,
No. 193 = *Select Papyri*, No. 215); A.D. 215
Adapted from LCL

All Egyptians who are in Alexandria, and especially countryfolk who have fled from other parts and can easily be detected, are by all means to be expelled, with the exception, however, of pig dealers and riverboatmen and the men who bring down reeds for heating the baths. But expel all others, as by the numbers of their kind and their uselessness they are disturbing the city. I am informed that on the festival of Sarapis and on certain other festal days Egyptians are accustomed to bring down bulls and other animals for sacrifice, and even on other days; for this they are not to be stopped. The persons who ought to be stopped are those who flee from their places of origin [51] to escape rustic toil, not those, however, who congregate here with the object of viewing the glorious city of Alexandria or come down for the sake of enjoying a more civilized life or for incidental business.

And farther along [in the letter]: For true Egyptians can easily be recognized among the linen weavers by their speech, which proves them

---

[50] Cf. the similar fate a century earlier of Trajan's stone bridge across the Danube (§ 27, third selection).
[51] Cf. introduction to § 102. A.D. 215/16 was a census year.

to have assumed the appearance and dress of another class;[52] moreover, their mode of life, their far-from-civilized manners, reveal them to be Egyptian countryfolk.

THE PETITION OF SCAPTOPARA

In this petition to the emperor we encounter again a picture already familiar in the two preceding centuries (§§ 105, 106): villagers fleeing from their homes to escape the abuses of officials and soldiers. Further examples for the third century will be found in § 111, last selection; in §123; and in Note 41 above.

CIL, Vol. III, No. 12,336, col. 2 (= Dittenberger, No. 888 = Abbott-Johnson, No. 139)

[Scaptopara, Thrace, A.D. 238]

To the Emperor Caesar Marcus Antonius GORDIAN Pius Felix Augustus, petition from the villagers of Scaptopara and Gresa[?]. During the most fortunate and eternal time of your reign you have often stated in rescripts that the villages should be inhabited and improved instead of having the inhabitants driven from their homes. Such a policy is conducive to the security of your subjects and the advantage of your most sacred treasury. Wherefore we too convey a just supplication to your divinity, praying that you may graciously grant our petition to this effect.

We dwell in and are property owners in the afore-mentioned village, which is exposed to wanton damage because it possesses the advantage of hot springs and is situated between two of the army camps which are in your Thrace. And in the past, as long as the inhabitants remained undisturbed and unharmed, they paid their tribute and other levies unexceptionably. But when certain parties began at times to proceed to insolence and employ violence, then indeed the village began to decline. A famous festival is celebrated two miles from our village, and those who visit there for fifteen days for the festival do not remain at the site of the festival but leave it and descend upon our village, forcing us to provide them with hospitality and furnish many other things for their entertainment without payment. In addition to these, soldiers too, when sent elsewhere, leave their proper routes and come to us, and likewise compel us to provide them with hospitality and supplies and pay us no money. And the governors of the province and even your procurators for the most part visit here for the benefit of the waters. We are continually entertaining the authorities, as we needs must; but, unable to bear the burden of the others, we appealed repeatedly to the governors

[52] On the rigid class barriers in Roman Egypt and the severe penalties for passing one's self off as a member of a higher class, see § 99.

of Thrace, who in accordance with the divine [53] ordinances gave orders
that we be left undisturbed. For we pointed out that we could no longer
abide it, but actually had a mind to abandon even our ancestral hearths
on account of the violence of those who descend upon us—and in truth
we have declined from many home owners to a very few.

For some time the edicts of the governors prevailed, and no one
disturbed us with a demand either for hospitality or for provision of
supplies; but as time went on, the whole throng who are contemptuous
of our defenselessness again dared to foist themselves upon us. Since,
therefore, we can no longer endure the oppression, and since in truth
we, too, like the rest, are in danger of having to abandon the abode of
our forefathers, on this account we beg you, O invincible Augustus, that
by your sacred rescript you give orders that everyone proceed by his
proper route, and that they not leave the other villages to come to us
and force us to furnish them with supplies free of charge, or even to
provide hospitality to those to whom we are not obliged to—for the
governors have more than once issued orders that hospitality is not to
be provided for any but those sent by the governors and procurators on
government service. And if we are oppressed, we will flee from our
homes, and the treasury will be involved in very great loss. But pitied
through your divine foresight, we will remain in our places of origin
and be able to provide the sacred tribute and the other taxes.[54] And this
will come about for us in the most fortunate times of your reign, if you
give orders for your divine letter to be inscribed on a stele and set up
in public, so that we shall be able, if we obtain this, to acknowledge our
thanks to your fortune. . . .[55]

118. *Monetary Crisis*

Debasement of the Roman coinage had begun as early as the reign of Nero.
But in the third century, as a result of mounting inflation, widespread hoarding of specie, and sharply reduced revenues, the emperors resorted to reckless adulteration of the imperial coinage to meet their military and administrative costs. As a result, distrust of new currency was widely manifested, by
individuals as well as by banks. Ultimately the government refused to accept
its own coinage for many taxes and insisted on payment in kind (cf. § 128).

[53] See Note 69.
[54] The plea of this sentence and the preceding is encountered also in the papyri
from Egypt (cf. § 105).
[55] The final clause of this sentence is not clear and is here omitted.

BLACK MARKET IN MONEY

The city of Mylasa in Caria, which leased its exchange monopoly to a private
banker, was forced to take action to halt illegal exchange between local and
imperial currencies in order to protect the city's revenues and the interests
of the lessee. This local monetary problem was probably precipitated by a
debasement of the imperial silver coinage by Septimius Severus.

OGIS, No. 515, lines 15–53 (= Abbott-Johnson, No. 133); A.D. 209/11

It has been decreed by the council and the people: If anyone, in any
manner whatever, whether freeman or slave, other than the lessee and
operator of the bank, is caught exchanging or buying currency, such
person shall be brought to face the banker on information laid before the
council by any citizen who so desires. Upon conviction before the magistrates and council, if he did it without agio, the banker and the informer
who obtained his conviction shall have the right to recover the money,
with the banker having also the right of legal execution against him as
he has been guaranteed; but if at an agio, a freeman shall pay a penalty of
500 *denarii* to the most sacred fisc of our most divine lords the emperors,
250 *denarii* to the municipality, and 100 *denarii* to the informer who obtained his conviction, and the money discovered to be involved shall be
forfeit to the banker, and a slave convicted as afore-stated shall be handed
over by his master to the magistrates in the presence of the council, given
fifty[?] stripes, cast into prison, and assigned to confinement for six
months; if the master wishes the slave not to be so treated, he shall owe
the afore-stated fines to the most sacred fisc, the municipality, and the
informer who obtained his conviction. Informations of this character
shall be received by the secretary of the magistrates, and after an information is presented public notice shall be given for three successive days
in sacred and public places, the notice expressly stating that the council
is being convened for this purpose. If the magistrates or the secretary
neglect to do any of the things decreed, or if the councilmen fail to assemble, though able to do so and present in town, the magistrates and the
secretary shall each pay a fine to the most sacred fisc of the emperors at
the rate of 300 *denarii*, and the councilmen at the rate of. . . .

This decree shall be inscribed on a stele which is also to be erected
in the agora in the most conspicuous place, as a law to be established for
all time. In truth, the safety of the city is in dire straits as a result of the
evil-doing and wickedness of some few who raid and embezzle the
public moneys and by whose power a kind of currency exchange has in-
vaded the market place which prevents the city from having the necessities of life, since many are in need and the community is in want. And

for this reason the flow of the revenues to our lords the emperors is delayed. . . . [The rest is fragmentary.]

DISTRUST OF IMPERIAL COINAGE

Because of the ephemeral character of some reigns in this period, banks were understandably hesitant to accept the coinage issued by the usurpers, as is shown by this official letter ordering them to accept the coins bearing the imprint of Macrianus and Quietus.

Oxyrhynchus Papyrus No. 1,411 (= Abbott-Johnson, No. 199 = *Select Papyri*, No. 230); A.D. 260
Adapted from LCL

From Aurelius Ptolemaeus, also called Nemesianus, *strategus* of the Oxyrhynchite nome. Whereas the public officials have assembled and have accused the bankers of the exchange banks of having closed them because of their unwillingness to accept the divine coin of the emperors, it has become necessary to issue an order to all the owners of the banks to open them and to accept and exchange all coin except the absolutely spurious and counterfeit—and not alone to them but to those who engage in business transactions of any kind whatever—knowing full well that if they disobey this order they will experience the penalties already ordained for them in the past by His Highness the Prefect. Signed by me. Year 1, Hathyr 28.

119. *Remission of Taxes*

Faced with sharply curtailed revenues, the emperors of the third century—in the absence of the concept of a national debt in antiquity—resorted to increased demands for taxes and personal services from the reduced population of the Empire. At the same time, acutely aware of the unrest due to the inability of the population to pay, they occasionally afforded relief through sweeping remissions of taxes, as had the emperors of the second century under less critical conditions (see § 37).

CANCELLATION OF TAXES IN AFRICA

This edict was issued by Caracalla for the benefit of the African provinces in A.D. 216, when he was engaged in a military campaign in the East and needed men and supplies.

AE, 1948, No. 109

The Emperor Caesar Marcus Aurelius Antoninus Pius Augustus Parthicus Maximus Britannicus Maximus Germanicus Maximus Ponticus

Maximus, son of the deified Severus Pius Arabicus Adiabenicus Parthicus Maximus Britannicus Maximus, grandson of the deified Marcus Antoninus Germanicus Sarmaticus, great-grandson of the deified Antoninus Pius, great-great-grandson of the deified Hadrian, descendant of the deified Trajan Parthicus and the deified Nerva,[56] holding the tribunician power for the nineteenth year, acclaimed *imperator* three times, consul four times, father of his country, proconsul, declares:

In reward for your allegiance and fidelity, I remit to you all debts whatsoever owed to the fisc, whether of grain or of money, even if suits therefor are pending, but not in cases where judgment has been rendered and no appeal has followed. What is more, I do hereby declare that my benefaction extends also to those cases where an appeal is proved to have been interposed, even if it has not yet been accepted. I am sure that you will repay my dispensation by loyally placing at my disposition all the resources of your villages and provinces, which serve the state well not only with brave men eminently distinguished in every rank of military and civilian office [57] but also with the very forests teeming with animals of a celestial species.[58] I anticipate that in return for my benefaction you will henceforth pay your annual assessments, whether in grain or in money, all the more readily when you recall that I did not wait but offered you of my own accord, without your petitioning or even hoping for them, new measures of relief and my magnanimous remission.

Lucius Antoninus Sosibianus and Aulus Pompeius Cassianus, duovirs, saw to [setting this up].

REMISSION OF CROWN TAX

"Crown gold" (*aurum coronarium*) was for centuries an important source of revenue for the fisc. The custom of communities offering golden crowns to rulers was of Hellenistic origin; eventually it became a tax imposed by these monarchs. Roman generals of the Republic operating in the East were accus-

[56] The Severan dynasty, of Punic-Syrian stock, was legitimized by its founder Septimius Severus, who shortly after his accession adopted himself into the family of the Antonines. The biographers of the "Historia Augusta" recount with evident gusto details illustrative of their non-Roman origin. Septimius Severus' voice "was clear, but retained an African accent even to his old age"; and a visit from his sister made him blush, "since she could scarcely speak Latin." Severus Alexander spoke Greek better than Latin, which he did not care for. Similarly, Maximinus, who succeeded the Severan dynasty, is described as "half barbarian and scarcely yet master of the Latin tongue, speaking almost pure Thracian."

[57] Macrinus, the later emperor, whom Caracalla had recently appointed prefect of the Praetorian Guard, was a Moor (cf. Note 8).

[58] Elephants are meant. They are called "celestial" because of their association with Caracalla, whose chariot they drew in processions, or from contemporary religious symbolism and mythological associations.

tomed to receive such crowns from various communities. During the Empire
the payment of "crown gold" became a tax on all communities of the Empire,
imposed annually and on various special occasions (cf. above, p. 429).

Fayum Papyrus No. 20 (= *Select Papyri*, No. 216; rev. ed. in
Archiv für Papyrusforschung, XIV [1941], 44–59); A.D. 222

The Emperor Caesar Marcus Aurelius SEVERUS ALEXANDER Pius Felix
Augustus, son of the deified Magnus Antoninus Pius, grandson of the
deified Septimius Severus Pius, *pontifex maximus*, holder of the tribunician power, consul, father of his country, declares:

. . . lest through making a manifestation of their joy, which they
experience at my accession to rule, they be compelled to pay[?] more
than they are able. Wherefore I have formed this resolution, not wanting
in precedents, among which I sought to imitate my ancestors Trajan
and Marcus [Aurelius], emperors most assuredly worthy of admiration;
and, in order to emulate their policy, I make the present decision—indeed, if the fact of the poverty of the state in these times had not stood
in the way, I should have shown a much more conspicuous proof of my
magnanimity and should not have hesitated to remit also any arrears
still owing from the past for contributions of this sort and whatever sums
had previously been voted under the title of crowns for my proclamation
as Caesar [59] or might yet be voted by the cities for the same cause. These,
however, I do not believe [I can remit], for the reasons which I have
stated just above, but I have not overlooked the fact that these, as I see
from present circumstances, are all that the cities can put up.

Therefore, let all persons in all the cities, those in Italy and those
in the other provinces, know that, on the occasion of my rule as emperor, to which I have acceded to the wishes and prayers of all, in lieu
of the golden crowns it behooves me to remit to them the sums called
for; and that I do this not because of a surplus of wealth but because it
is my policy to strive[?], even though hard pressed, to retrieve the decline, not by searching for limits [60] but by economy, even though expenses all but reach the privy purse. For this will be my earnest endeavor,
to increase the Empire not by exaction of money but rather by liberality
and benefactions, so that my Fortune may counsel the governors and
the men dispatched by me to procuratorships, whom I tested and selected
by the most rigid standards before dispatching, to behave with the utmost moderation. For the governors of the provinces will learn more and

[59] That is, emperor designate: cf. Chapter II, Note 12.
[60] At this point some scholars have emended the Greek text to read "not by quests
for revenues," but this seems supererogatory; the phrase as it stands means "not
by trying to squeeze out the last ounce of revenue," and its indirection is entirely
in keeping with the high-flown language of the edict.

more how zealously it behooves them to care for and look to the provinces to which they have been appointed, when they can all see the emperor also conducting the business of the realm with such propriety, economy, and self-restraint.

The chief magistrates in each city shall make it their business to post copies of this decree of mine in public where they will be most clearly visible to readers. Year 1, Payni 30.

120. *Decline of Provincial Assemblies*

THE INSCRIPTION OF THORIGNY

The base of a statue erected to Titus Sennius Sollemnis in his native village is inscribed on the front with the record of his career; on one side with a letter from Claudius Paulinus, governor of Britain and previously governor of Lyonese Gaul, who heaps presents upon him for his "services and good will"; and on the other side with the text which follows and which shows by what kind of services to the Roman governors he had earned such rich rewards. The action of Sollemnis here recorded illustrates how, in the disorders of the third century, the assemblies of the provincial leagues lost what little power and initiative they had once been allowed and fell completely under the thumb of the governors of the provinces. The inscription was cut when the statue was erected, in A.D. 238, but the following letter was originally written in 223.

CIL, Vol. XIII, No. 3,162 (= Abbott-Johnson, No. 140)

[Araegenuae (Vieux), Gaul]

Copy of a letter of Aedinius Julianus, prefect of the Praetorian Guard, to Badius Comnianus, procurator and acting governor. Aedinius Julianus to Badius Comnianus, greeting. When I was acting governor in the province of Lugdunensis, I observed that most [of the assembly delegates] were good men, particularly this Sollemnis, a native of the municipality of the Viducassians and the priest,[61] to whom, on account of the worth of his principles and his upright conduct, I took a great liking. In addition to this, when an attempt was made in the Gallic Assembly, at the instigation of certain members who considered themselves slighted by him in view of their services, to draft an indictment, as if it were the unanimous sense of the province, against Claudius Paul-

---

[61] Of the cult of Rome and Augustus at the provincial altar erected at the confluence of the Rhone and Saône rivers at Lyons. The holder of this office, elected by the Gallic Assembly, was at once the chief priest of Gaul and the president of the assembly.

inus, my predecessor,[62] this good friend of mine, Sollemnis, blocked their intention by interposing a challenge to the effect that his native town, when it had made him among others a delegate, had given him no instructions concerning any legal action but had on the contrary praised [Paulinus]. The consequence of this argument was that all abandoned the indictment. And so my fondness and liking for him grew more and more. Confident of my regard for him, he has come to see me in the capital [Rome], and, being now about to depart, he asks me to commend him to you. You will be doing the right thing if you accede to his request, etc.[63]

121. *Compulsory Services of Municipal Officers*

The interference of the imperial government in municipal administration, on the increase since the time of Trajan (see § 88), was sharply stepped up in the third century. One of the solutions of the central government for the shrink-age of taxable resources was to impose a form of capital levy on the rich through the regimentation of the propertied classes into a hereditary caste obligated, as members of the municipal councils (*decuriones,* or *curiales*), to discharge various local offices. The most important of these—and by the time of Constantine practically the only important function of the *curiales*—was the collection of the imperial revenues, and personal liability for the collection was placed upon the *decaproti,* a committee of the municipal council con-sisting of the ten (sometimes twenty) wealthiest decurions. Caught between the hammer of inexorable governmental demands and the anvil of limited means, the *curiales* sought with increasing desperation, which frequently erupted in physical violence, to avoid these ruinous duties, only to have one loophole after another closed as the rules governing their compulsory services were systematized by the jurists of the third and fourth centuries, from whose works the first selection following is drawn.

Justinian *Digest* L. ii. 1 and 2.8, iv. 1.2, iv. 3.15–16, iv. 4

The governor of the province shall see to it that decurions who are proved to have left the area of the municipality to which they belong and to have moved to other places are recalled to their native soil and perform the appropriate public services. . . .

Persons over fifty-five are forbidden by imperial enactments to be called to the position of decurion against their will, but if they do consent to this they ought to perform the duties, although if they are over

[62] As governor of Lyonese Gaul (*Gallia Lugdunensis*).
[63] The "etc." indicates the omission of the stereotype close of letters of recom-mendation.

seventy they are not compelled to assume compulsory municipal services. . . .

Municipal duties of a personal character are: representation of a municipality, that is, becoming a public advocate; assignment to taking the census or registering property; secretaryships; camel transport; commissioner of food supply and the like, of public lands, of grain procurement, of water supply; horse races in the circus; paving of public streets; grain storehouse; heating of public baths; distribution of food supply; and other duties similar to these. From the above-mentioned, other duties can be deduced in accordance with the laws and long-established custom of each municipality. . . .

The governor of the province shall see to it that the compulsory public services and offices in the municipalities are imposed fairly and in rotation according to age and rank, in accordance with the gradation of public services and offices long ago established, so that the men and resources of municipalities are not inconsiderately ruined by frequent oppression of the same persons. If two sons are under parental power, the father is not compelled to support their public services at the same time. . . .

The care of constructing or rebuilding a public work in a municipality is a compulsory public service from which a father of five living children is excused; [64] and if this service is forcibly imposed, this fact does not deprive him of the exemption that he has from other public services. The excusing of those with insufficient resources who are nominated to public services or offices is not permanent but temporary. For if a hoped-for increase comes to one's property by honorable means, when his turn comes an evaluation is to be made to determine whether he is suitable for the services for which he was chosen. . . . A person who is responsible for public services to his municipality and submits his name for military service for the purpose of avoiding the municipal burden cannot make the condition of his community worse.[65]

Oxyrhynchus Papyrus No. 705, lines 54–79 (= Abbott-Johnson,
No. 195 = Wilcken, No. 407); A.D. 200

The Emperor Caesar Lucius SEPTIMIUS SEVERUS Pius Pertinax Augustus Arabicus Adiabenicus Parthicus Maximus and the Emperor Caesar Marcus Aurelius Antoninus Pius Augustus [CARACALLA] to Aurelius Horio, greeting. We commend you also for this endowment which you see fit to bestow upon the villages of the Oxyrhynchite nome by presenting the wherewithal for acquisition of property. The established

[64] For other benefits enjoyed by parents of large families, cf. §§ 11, 163.
[65] That is, he is obligated to fulfill his duties to the community.

rule shall be observed in this case also, so that your grant shall be expended as you desired and not be diverted to any other purpose.

The request is as follows: "To the most gracious emperors Severus and Antoninus, the saviors and benefactors of all mankind, Aurelius Horio, former *strategus* and former chief judge of the most illustrious city of Alexandria, greeting. Certain villages of the Oxyrhynchite nome, O most benevolent emperors, in which I and my sons possess lands, have been utterly exhausted by the burdens of the annual liturgies of the fisc and of policing their districts, and there is danger that they will be ruined as far as the fisc is concerned and that your land will be left uncultivated.[66] Accordingly, in an endeavor to be both philanthropic and useful, I desire in the interest of their recovery to make to each village some small endowment for the purchase of land, the revenue from which shall be earmarked for the maintenance and expenses of those who perform the annual liturgies for the. . . ." [The rest is lost.]

Oxyrhynchus Papyrus No. 1,406 (= Abbott-Johnson, No. 195 = *FIRA*, Vol. I, No. 89); A.D. 215/16

The Emperor Caesar Marcus Aurelius Severus Antoninus Parthicus Maximus Britannicus Maximus Germanicus Maximus Pius Augustus [CARACALLA] declares: If a councilman strikes or reviles the council president or a councilman, such councilman shall be removed from council membership and reduced to common rank.

Posted in . . . in the public colonnade, in the magistracy of Aurelius Alexander son of . . . of Heliopolis.[67]

Oxyrhynchus Papyrus No. 1,405 (= Abbott-Johnson, No. 185); A.D. 200

. . . you ceded [your property] [68] . . . it is perfectly clear that the cession was made not to our fisc but to the person who nominated you for the liturgy. He will take possession of your property, furnish the . . . and perform the liturgy; our fisc is not concerned with such cessions. Your citizenship, however, will be not at all impaired as a result of this, nor will you be subjected to physical violence. Posted in Alexandria, year 8, Pharmuthi.

[66] The propertied class was understandably concerned for the normal functioning of the economy, because wealthy persons assigned to tax collection were personally liable for revenues due the fisc: cf. §§ 97, 105.
[67] In contrast to the traditional absence of city councils in Egypt (see p. 368), Septimius Severus had established such bodies in Alexandria and in the nome capitals, partly in order to extend and unify the system of municipal liturgies.
[68] Persons nominated to municipal office were permitted to surrender their property in a form of voluntary bankruptcy rather than serve (cf. the following document).

To Aurelius Leonides, *strategus* of the Oxyrhynchite nome, from Aemilius Stephanus son of Hatres and Tasorapis, of the village of Sinkepha. This present day I learned that I have been nominated by Aurelius Amois son of Patas and Demetrous, of the same village, as a person of means and qualified to succeed him in the office of collector of the village money revenues of the said Sinkepha for the current third year. This is unreasonable and not in keeping with the principle of sharing the liturgy. I therefore resign my property to him in accordance with the divine [69] decree cited above, and I declare that I have property at. . . . [The rest is lost.]

Rainer Papyrus No. 20, col. 1 (= Abbott-Johnson, No. 198 = Wilcken, No. 402); A.D. 250

Aurelius Hermophilus son of Horio, former *cosmetes* of the great, ancient, illustrious, and most august city of Hermopolis, to the right honorable Aurelius Eudaemo, also known as Theodotus, former gymnasiarch, former high priest, councilman, acting council president of the said city, greeting. The other day I submitted to the most excellent council through you the answer of our most illustrious prefect, Appius Sabinus, contained in the letter of the nome *strategus*, Aurelius Hiero, sent to me by his clerk Aurelius Hermes, in reply to my petition to him to relinquish all that I own to those who nominated my son, Aurelius Horio, also known as Hermaeus, for *cosmetes* of the said city, since my means had been exhausted by my own recent discharge of that office in my own name.

The prefect in his reply ruled that the nominators bear the risk involved in proposing names,[70] and he ordered the nome *strategus* to prevent the use of force if it should arise [71] contrary to his benign orders, which were delivered on the 21st of the present month Epeiph, according to the receipt issued to me by the clerk in charge of this. Yesterday, namely Epeiph 22, there was sent to me through a council clerk a letter from you, Eudaemo, also known as Theodotus, in which you give your personal answer concerning the said office even after my [offer of] surrender of property, and you invidiously cite some passages from the laws . . . taken [out of context] to suit your need. Now I write to you

---

[69] That is, "imperial." Cf. p. 420.

[70] Local officials who nominated inhabitants for compulsory public office did so at the risk of having to take on the office themselves if they nominated someone financially or otherwise ineligible.

[71] That this fear was not groundless is confirmed by a letter in Column 2 of this papyrus, addressed by Hermophilus on the same day to the prefect, in which he reports: "I have been kept under arrest since the 20th by a council attendant and the council president's guard."

again, since a man surrendering his property and relinquishing his possessions is entitled in accordance with the laws and the divine [72] enactments to . . . protection against any violence, in keeping with which
the most illustrious and devoted prefect desired the *strategus* to prevent
the use of force, adding that the risk of nomination rested with the
nominators. If you are so minded, take all my property yourself, returning the customary one third; then you can discharge all the duties of
the office, and not impair [the smooth functioning of] either the city or
the most excellent council. Such a reply [from you] will satisfy me in
my principal claim. I, Aurelius Hermophilus son of Horio, ex-*cosmetes*,
bid you farewell, most dear sir. Year 1 of the Emperor Caesar Gaius Messius Quintus Trajanus Decius Pius Felix Augustus, Epeiph 23.

122. *Increasing Regimentation of Merchant and Artisan Guilds*

Paralleling its intensified constraints upon the decurial class, the military
monarchy relied more and more upon merchant and artisan guilds (*collegia,
corpora*) to assure the vital economic needs of the Empire and exerted ever-
tighter control over these associations, especially over those which helped
supply the city of Rome and the armies. To obtain their ready cooperation,
their previously granted privileges (cf. § 46) were generally maintained, and
even somewhat extended. In the end, however, these functions, too, became
obligatory and hereditary (cf. § 135).

"Historia Augusta" *Life of Severus Alexander* xxxiii. 2
From LCL

He also formed guilds of all the wine dealers, the greengrocers, the
bootmakers, and, in short, of all the trades, and he granted them advocates chosen from their own number and designated the judge to whose
jurisdiction each should belong.

THE SHIPOWNERS' ASSOCIATIONS OF ARLES

The river port of Arelate (Arles) in Narbonese Gaul was one of the principal
grain export centers of the West. Its shipowners' associations had a central
office at Ostia (cf. § 44, fourth selection), an office in Beirut for the provisioning of the army in Syria (as attested by the following inscription), and presumably also branch offices in other important ports of the Empire. This inscription, containing a letter from the prefect of the grain supply, illustrates
the close government supervision of their activity and shows that they, like

[72] See Note 69.

other elements of the population, had cause to complain of their treatment at the hands of corrupt government functionaries.

CIL, Vol. III, No. 14,165 (8) (= *ESAR*, III, 478)

[Berytus, Syria, A.D. 201]

Claudius Julianus to the marine shipowners of the five associations of Arles, greeting. I have ordered appended what, after reading your resolution, I have written to Gaius Valerius Severus, imperial procurator, *vir eminens*. I send you my best wishes for your prosperity and health.

Copy of the letter

I have appended a copy of the resolution of the marine shipowners of the five associations of Arles, together with the measures taken on my part. And since the same complaint is spreading more widely, with others also imploring the aid of justice and making it clear that they will bring their loyal services to a halt shortly if the injustice continues, I request that attention be given both to the payment of the account and to the security of the persons who are in the service of the *annona*. Give orders under your authority that the iron fastenings [of the cargoes] be stamped with a mark, and that escorts be attached to deliver in the city [of Rome] the weight which they have taken on board.[73]

123. *Conditions of the Tenant Farmers* (*Coloni*)

The turbulent conditions of the third century resulted in the devastation of large areas of land and wholesale abandonment of cultivation. To encourage settlers and revive production Septimius Severus and Caracalla issued a rescript reaffirming the established custom whereby occupants of untilled land received a prescriptive right against eviction (cf. § 42). Another development was the spread of the imperial estates, brought about by the sweeping confiscations of the period, and the continued growth of the estates which remained in private ownership. The conditions of tenant farmers (*coloni*) in the general upheaval of the times are vividly illuminated by a number of extant petitions against illegal exactions and oppression by imperial officials, soldiers, and local magnates. It is noteworthy, moreover, that despite these abuses large numbers of people fled to country estates to escape municipal obligations and the general insecurity of city life. Agricultural tenants still possessed freedom of movement, but we can see a first step in the direction of serfdom in an administrative order of A.D. 247 by which *coloni* who had fallen in arrears to the fisc were bound to their tenancies till they discharged their tax debts. This order was for many tantamount to binding them, and their

[73] On the sealing and military escort of *annona* cargoes, cf. § 34, sixth selection.

children who succeeded to their tenancies, to the soil forever. This *de facto* situation was eventually formalized by Constantine and by later emperors (see § 136).

"SQUATTER RIGHTS"

Berlin Papyrus No. 267 (= *Select Papyri*, No. 214 = *FIRA*, Vol. I, No. 84); A.D. 199

The Emperor Caesar Lucius SEPTIMIUS SEVERUS Pertinax Augustus Arabicus Adiabenicus Parthicus Maximus and the Emperor Marcus Aurelius Antoninus Augustus [CARACALLA] to Juliana daughter of Sosthenianus, through her husband Sosthenes. To those who had a legal ground[74] and who remained in undisputed possession, the prescriptive right of long possession is secured by the space of twenty years as against persons dwelling in another city and ten years as against persons in the same city. Posted in Alexandria, Year 8, Tybi 3.

GRIEVANCES OF IMPERIAL TENANTS

Abbott-Johnson, No. 142

[Lydia, A.D. c.205]

. . . that they might appear to have some defense for such impudence, they arrested nine, put them in bonds, and claimed that they were sending them on to your[75] honorable procurators, since the honorable Aelius Aglaus is also acting proconsul. One of the nine they released after exacting over 1,000 Attic drachmas as a ransom for his safety, but the rest they held in bonds, and we do not know, most divine among emperors, whether they will send them on alive to the honorable Aglaus or dispose of them, too, as they did of the previous ones. And so we did the only thing possible for unfortunates thus cruelly deprived of life and kin, the only thing possible for us: we informed your procurator in charge of the bureau, Aurelius Marcianus, and your honorable procurators in Asia. We are suppliants, most divine among emperors that have ever been, of your divine and transcendent kingship, since we have been hindered from attending to the labors of cultivation by the threats

---

[74] For entering into possession. The importance of the legal origin of a right is emphasized also in another rescript of Septimius Severus and Caracalla (*CIL*, Vol. III, No. 781 [= Abbott-Johnson, No. 130 = *FIRA*, Vol. I, No. 86], lines 9–12): "The city of Tyra does not show the origin of the privilege granted, and it is not easy for anything that was acquired by error or at will to be confirmed by the prescriptive right of time."

[75] The emperors, addressed in the plural throughout this petition, are presumably Septimius Severus and Caracalla.

of the police agents and their representatives to put us, too, who are left, in danger of our lives, and we cannot, because we are thus hindered from working the land, even meet the imperial payments and other obligations for the immediate future. We beg you to favor our petition and order the governor of the province and your honorable procurators to exact justice for this wrong, and to prevent access to the imperial estates and the resultant molestation to us by both the police agents and those who, under pretext of public offices and liturgies, molest and trouble your farmers, since everything we have from our forebears belongs by prior claim to the most sacred fisc by the law on cultivation. We have communicated the truth to your divinity. And unless some justice is exacted for these wrongs by your heavenly right hand and unless aid is brought for the future, we who are left, unable to endure the greed of the police agents and their representatives[?] under the pretexts aforesaid, must abandon our ancestral hearths and forefathers' tombs and move to private land in order to save ourselves—since those who live a life of wrongdoing are more likely to spare the dwellers there than to spare your farmers [76]—and thus become exiles from the imperial estates, on which we were begotten and reared and, continuing as farmers for generations, have been fulfilling our obligations to the imperial account.[77]

CIL, Vol. III, No. 14,191 (= Abbott-Johnson, No. 141 = *IGRR*, Vol. IV, No. 598)

[Aragua, Phrygia, A.D. 244/47]

May good fortune attend!

The Emperor Caesar Marcus Julius PHILIP Augustus and Marcus Julius Philip, most noble Caesar, to Marcus Aurelius Eclectus. . . . The proconsul, *vir clarissimus*, will look into the truth of the facts you allege and will make it his care that no injustice is perpetrated.[78]

[76] This parenthetical remark is particularly noteworthy for its overtones suggestive of the great land barons who in the fourth and subsequent centuries became powerful enough to overawe local officialdom and even to defy the central government and create autonomous manors to which the peasantry turned for protection: cf. p. 419 and Note 38. An example of this kind of situation, on a small scale to be sure, is afforded by a papyrus of A.D. 207 (*SB*, No. 4,284 = Abbott-Johnson, No. 190), in which twenty-five *coloni* of the village of Socnopaei Nesus complain to the nome *strategus* of five brothers who are attempting to drive them from their holdings: "they do not contribute their share of . . . the grain and money taxes . . . and they have never yet performed any liturgies, for they intimidate the successive village secretaries." There is a mention also in the next document of local *potentiores* who flout the law and oppress the peasantry with impunity.

[77] With this language cf. p. 184 and Note 54 above.

[78] This reply from the emperors and the sentence quoted below from a rescript are inscribed in Latin. The petition which follows is in Greek.

To the Emperor Caesar Marcus Julius PHILIP Pius Felix Augustus and to Marcus Julius Philip, most noble Caesar, petition from Aurelius Eclectus on behalf of the community of Aragua, your *coloni* and farmers. . . . While all men in your most blessed times, most pious and faultless among kings that have ever been, live calm and peaceful lives and all wrongdoing and extortion [79] have ceased, we alone suffer treatment alien to these most fortunate times and come to you with this supplication, secure in the justice of the petition herein. We who flee as suppliants to the refuge of your divinity are the entire population of your most sacred estate. We are suffering extortion and illegal exactions beyond all reason at the hands of those who ought to preserve the public welfare.[80] Although we happen to be inlanders and not . . . we are suffering treatment alien to your most blessed times. For those passing through the Appian region abandon the highways—military commanders[?], soldiers, and powerful and influential men in the city and your officials abandon the highways, swoop down upon us, take us away from our work, requisition our plow oxen, and illegally exact what is not due them. As a result we are suffering extraordinary injustice by this extortion. We wrote about all this to your majesty, Augustus, when you held the prefecture of the Praetorian Guard . . . and how your divinity was moved the rescript quoted herewith makes clear: "We have transmitted the content of your petition to the governor, who will see to it that there is no further cause for complaint." But inasmuch as this rescript has brought us no aid, it has resulted that we are still suffering throughout the countryside illegal exactions of what is not owing, as certain parties assault us and trample upon us unjustly, and we are still suffering extraordinary extortion at the hands of the officials, and our resources[?] have been exhausted and the estates deserted. . . . [The rest is lost.]

RESTRICTION ON FREEDOM OF MOVEMENT OF COLONI

Berlin Papyrus No. 7; A.D. 247

Septimius Ammonius, also called Dionysius, *strategus* of the Arsinoite nome divisions of Themistes and Polemo. Orders are issued [81] to all those definitely reported to me by the *decaproti* [82] as being cultivators of the section called Little Phrôu that they are unequivocally bound by

[79] Cf. Chapter V, Note 211.

[80] The last five words of this sentence are supplied to fill a lacuna. Another proposed restoration would read, "least to wrong their neighbors." In any case, the general sense is clear enough.

[81] No doubt by the prefect of Egypt, possibly acting on instructions from the emperors.

[82] Cf. introduction to § 121.

their tenancy, in order that what is owed the most sacred fisc may be discharged[?] without hindrance . . . in accordance with the requests in the petitions which they submitted to me. . . . Year 5 of the Emperors Caesars Marcus Julius PHILIP Pii Felices Augusti, Hathyr 29. [There follows a list of persons, with the size of the holding of each.]

124. *Rome's Thousandth Birthday*

In A.D. 248, in the midst of civil war, anarchy, and unprecedented economic crisis, the Secular Games and other spectacles were held in celebration of the thousandth anniversary of the founding of Rome. The following passage gives a glimpse of the prodigal expenditure that must have gone into the making of that Roman holiday.

"Historia Augusta" *Lives of the Three Gordians* xxxiii. 1–2

There were at Rome in the time of Gordian thirty-two elephants (of which Gordian himself had sent twelve and [Severus] Alexander ten), ten elk, ten tigers, sixty tame lions, thirty tame leopards, ten *belbi*, or hyenas, 1,000 pairs of gladiators belonging to the imperial fisc, six hippopotamuses, one rhinoceros, ten wild lions, ten giraffes, twenty wild asses, forty wild horses, and various other animals of this nature without number. All of these [the Emperor] Philip presented or slaughtered at the Secular Games. All these animals, wild, tame, and savage, Gordian intended for a Persian triumph; but his public vow [83] proved of no avail, for Philip exhibited them all at the Secular Games and at the gladiatorial and circus spectacles when he celebrated Rome's thousandth anniversary in his own and his son's consulship.

The Reforms of Diocletian

125. *The Emergence of Absolute Monarchy (Dominate)*

In the century from the death of Marcus Aurelius to the accession of Diocletian the régime established by Augustus completed its evolution from Principate to undisguised absolutism, complete with Oriental royal trappings and court ceremonial. It is true that premature and abortive attempts had been made in the first two centuries of the Empire by such rulers as Caligula, Domitian, and Commodus to introduce the concept of the emperor as a god on earth

[83] That is, to present the spectacle if victorious: cf. Vol. I, p. 148.

(cf. § 168). But with the Punic-Syrian Severan dynasty the practices of Oriental autocracy came more commonly into use. Obeisance in the presence of the emperor came into vogue, and the appellation *dominus noster* (our lord and master) replaced the concept of *primus inter pares* attached to the earlier emperors. In conformity with these absolutist tendencies the great jurist Ulpian in the early third century formulated the principle that "the emperor is above the laws" (Justinian *Digest* I. iii. 31). With the reign of Diocletian all these developments, including the rite of adoration of the emperor, were standardized and made official.

"Historia Augusta" *Lives of the Two Gallieni* xvi. 3–6

Gallienus always spread his tables with golden table cloths. He had jeweled vessels made, and likewise golden ones. He sprinkled gold dust on his hair. He often came into public with the radiate crown.[84] At Rome, where the emperors always used to appear in the toga, he appeared in a purple cloak with jeweled and golden clasps. He wore a man's sleeved tunic of purple and gold. He used a jeweled sword belt. . . . He invited matrons into his council, and to those of them who kissed his hand he gave four gold pieces bearing his name.

Aurelius Victor [85] *Lives of the Emperors* xxxix. 1–8 (abridged)

By decision of the generals and [military] tribunes, Valerius Diocletian, commander of the palace guards, was chosen emperor because of his wisdom. A mighty man he was, and the following were characteristics of his: he was the first to wear a cloak embroidered in gold and to covet shoes of silk and purple decorated with a great number of gems. Though this went beyond what befitted a citizen and was characteristic of an arrogant and lavish spirit, it was nevertheless of small consequence in comparison with the rest. Indeed, he was the first after Caligula and Domitian to allow himself to be publicly called "lord," and to be named "god," and to be rendered homage as such. . . . But Diocletian's faults were counterbalanced by good qualities; for even if he took the title of "lord," he did act [toward the Romans] as a father.

126. *Diocletian and the Tetrarchy*

To divide the administrative responsibilities of the vast Empire, prevent a recurrence of the military anarchy of the preceding half century, and guaran-

---

[84] The radiate crown had been the emblem of a deified emperor only, until the emperors of the third century began to adopt it as part of their insignia.
[85] See Chapter V, Note 67.

tee orderly succession to the throne, Diocletian in A.D. 293 established a four-man rule, the tetrarchy. In 305 Diocletian and Maximian, the two senior members, abdicated, but their provisions for the continuation of the system by a new tetrarchy proved short-lived (cf. introduction to § 131).

Aurelius Victor *Lives of the Emperors* xxxix. 17–48 (abridged)

Forthwith he proclaimed as coemperor Maximian,[86] a faithful friend, a semi-rustic with, however, great military talent and native ability. Afterward he acquired the surname Herculius, from the cult of Hercules, his favorite divinity, while Valerius [Diocletian] took the surname of Jovius; and these surnames were assigned to those military units which excelled the rest of the army. . . . [The rise of usurpers and foreign attacks decided the two emperors] to select as Caesars Julius Constantius and Galerius Maximianus, surnamed Armentarius, and to associate them with themselves in marriage. The former received Herculius' stepdaughter, the latter Diocletian's daughter, the previous marriage of each being dissolved, just as Augustus had once done in the case of Tiberius Nero and his daughter Julia. All these men were, indeed, natives of Illyria; but although little cultured, they were of great service to the state, because they were inured to the hardships of rural life and of war. . . . The harmony which prevailed among them proved above all that their native ability and their skill in military science, which they had acquired from Aurelian and Probus, almost sufficed to compensate for lack of high character. Finally, they looked up to Valerius [Diocletian] as to a father or as one would to a mighty god. . . .

As the burden of the wars mentioned above became heavier, a sort of division of the Empire was made: all the countries beyond the Gallic Alps were entrusted to Constantius; Herculius had Africa and Italy;[87] Galerius, Illyria as far as the Black Sea; and Diocletian retained all the rest. After this, part of Italy was subjected to the heavy burden of paying tribute. . . . A new law for regular tax payments was introduced. At that time it was still endurable, because not excessive, but it has grown in our age[88] into a scourge. . . .

With no less zeal [than in their military exploits] did the emperors take up the administration of civil affairs, in which connection their laws were eminently just. They suppressed the *frumentarii*, a group that was a veritable scourge and whom now the *agentes in rebus* closely resem-

---

[86] Diocletian became emperor in A.D. 285 and made Maximian coregent the following year. Constantius and Galerius were named Caesars (emperors designate: cf. Chapter II, Note 12) in 293.

[87] Maximian's domain included Spain.

[88] Middle of the fourth century. On Italy's being made tributary, cf. introduction to § 128.

ble.[89] These men, who appear to have been established to investigate and report possible seditious movements that might exist in the provinces, trumped up false accusations, and under the universal terror they inspired, especially in persons in very remote areas, they practiced shameful rapine everywhere. The emperors showed no less concern and solicitude for the provisioning of the city and the welfare of those who paid tribute. . . . The ancient cults were maintained in all their purity. Rome and other cities, especially Carthage, Milan, and Nicomedia, were extraordinarily embellished with new structures of great splendor. . . .[90]

Diocletian kept his eyes on threatening dangers, and when he saw that the Roman state, in the course of destiny, was going to become a prey to civil wars and was approaching its breakup, so to speak, he celebrated the twentieth anniversary of his reign and abdicated the government of the state, although he was in good health. Herculius, who had held power one year less, he induced to follow his example, though he did so with great reluctance. Although there exists a variety of explanations [for Diocletian's abdication], and the truth has been perverted, it is my view that it was out of the excellence of his character that, scorning ambition for power, he descended to the life of an ordinary citizen.

127. *Diocletian's Administrative Reorganization*

Diocletian, the reorganizer of the Empire after the military anarchy, completed and systematized the political, social, and economic changes brought about by the revolution of the third century. The pattern of society he established, brought to completion by Constantine, remained the basis of the regimented life of the people in the Roman Empire for centuries to come. The following evaluation by a Christian writer of Diocletian's reorganization is colored by the severe persecution of the Christians during his reign.

Lactantius *On the Deaths of the Persecutors* vii

While Diocletian, who was the inventor of wicked deeds and the contriver of evils, was ruining everything, he could not keep his hands even from God. This man, through both avarice and cowardice, over-

[89] *Frumentarii* were imperial secret-service agents who replaced the *speculatores* in that activity toward the end of the first century and quickly became notorious for abusing their positions for personal gain (cf. pp. 399, 428). By A.D. 319, and perhaps as early as Diocletian's reign, they were replaced with a more comprehensive organization of *agentes in rebus*, who ultimately achieved the same evil reputation.
[90] The most famous of these are the Baths of Diocletian at Rome, and his palace at Salonae (modern Split in Yugoslavia, the older part of which is contained within the palace walls).

turned the whole world. For he made three men sharers of his rule; the world was divided into four parts, and armies were multiplied, each of the rulers striving to have a far larger number of soldiers than former emperors had had when the state was ruled by single emperors.[91] The number of those receiving [pay from the state] was so much larger than the number of those paying [taxes] that, because of the enormous size of the assessments, the resources of the tenant farmers were exhausted, fields were abandoned, and cultivated areas were transformed into wilderness. And to fill everything with fear, the provinces also were cut into bits; [92] many governors and more minor offices lay like incubi over each region and almost on every municipality, likewise many procurators of revenues, administrators, and deputy prefects.[93] Very few civil cases came before all of these, but only condemnations and frequent confiscations, and there were not merely frequent but perpetual exactions of innumerable things, and in the process of exaction intolerable wrongs.

Whatever was imposed with a view to the maintenance of the soldiery might have been endured; but Diocletian, with insatiable avarice, would never permit the treasury to be diminished. He was constantly accumulating extraordinary resources and funds so as to preserve what he had stored away untouched and inviolate. Likewise, when by various iniquities he brought about enormously high prices, he attempted to legislate the prices of commodities.[94] Then much blood was spilled . . . nothing appeared on the market because of fear, and prices soared much higher. In the end, after many people had lost their lives, it became absolutely necessary to repeal the law.

In addition, he had a certain endless passion for building, and made no small exactions from the provinces for maintaining laborers and artisans and for supplying wagons and whatever else was necessary for the construction of public works. Here basilicas, there a circus, here a mint, there a shop for making weapons, here a house for his wife, there one for his daughter. Suddenly a great part of the city [of Nicomedia] was demolished. All went elsewhere with their wives and children, as from a city taken by enemies. And when those structures were completed, to the ruin of the provinces, he said, "They are not properly made; let them be done on another plan." Then they had to be pulled down, and remodeled, to undergo perhaps another demolition. By such constant folly did he endeavor to make Nicomedia the equal of Rome.

[91] Lactantius exaggerates the size of Diocletian's military establishment. It was increased from the long-established army of 300,000 to 400,000.
[92] For Diocletian's provincial reorganization, see § 130.
[93] The *vicarii*, deputies to the Praetorian prefects, were purely civil officials; there was one for each of the twelve new dioceses of the Empire: cf. § 130.
[94] For Diocletian's edict on maximum prices, see § 129.

I omit mentioning, indeed, how many perished on account of their possessions or wealth; for this was a common thing and became almost lawful as people grew accustomed to these evils. But this was peculiar to him, that wherever he saw a rather well-cultivated field, or an uncommonly elegant house, a false accusation and capital punishment were ready against the owner, so that it seemed as if he could not seize someone else's property without bloodshed.

PROLIFERATION OF BUREAUCRACY

Occasional attempts were made under Diocletian to curtail the growth of bureaucracy. But these attempts were foredoomed to failure since it was the governmental system itself which engendered the bureaucracy and rendered it powerful.

Oxyrhynchus Papyrus No. 58 (= *Select Papyri*, No. 226); A.D. 288
Adapted from LCL

Serbaeus Africanus to the *strategi* of the *epistrategia* of Heptanomia and the Arsinoite nome, greeting.[95] It is apparent from the accounts alone that many persons wishing to batten on the estates of the treasury have devised titles for themselves, such as administrators, secretaries, or superintendents, whereby they procure no advantage for the treasury but eat up the revenues. It has therefore become necessary to send you instructions to have one competent superintendent chosen for each estate on the responsibility of the municipal council concerned,[96] and to put an end to the other offices, although the superintendent chosen shall have the power to choose two or at most three others to assist him in the superintendence. In this way the wasteful expenses will stop, and the estates of the treasury will receive proper attention. You will, of course, make sure that only such persons are chosen to assist the superintendents as will be able to pass the test. Farewell. Year 5, also year 4,[97] Thoth 16.

128. *The New Taxation System*

After the establishment and consolidation of the Tetrarchy Diocletian turned his attention to economic reorganization, in order to stabilize and assure the vast revenues which the imperial government required. Just as he had ended the political anarchy, so he sought to end the profound economic crisis which had ravaged the Empire for a century through measures of regimentation

[95] The writer of this letter was probably the *epistrategus* of the district formed by the Heptanomia (cf. Chapter II, Note 22) and the Arsinoite nome.
[96] Cf. §§ 85, 121.   [97] Cf. Note 86.

characteristic of his military background. In A.D. 296 he wiped out the by then anarchic accretion of local practices that had characterized the Roman taxation system and, regularizing the special requisitions to which the government had had to resort increasingly in recent years, he decreed a new, unified system of land tax and poll tax for the whole Empire, including Italy, which thus lost, at least in part, its tax-free status. Land and manpower together constituted the foundation of the new tax structure. The unit on which the basic tax in kind (*annona*) was calculated was an area of cultivable land (*iugum*) that could in theory be worked by one man (*caput*) and provide him with the means of subsistence. Many details of this new system are still not clear, but the taxpayer was evidently required to pay according to the number of *iuga* and *capita* he was assessed. Reassessment took place at first every five years, but beginning with A.D. 312 every fifteen years. Areas equivalent to a *iugum* were established by fiat for several different classes of land according to location and productivity; the host of other local variations were simply ignored. Thus there was substituted for the previous system of quotas and revenues varying from year to year a system of fixed returns. But the fixed return could be guaranteed only if the manpower to produce it were guaranteed. It was thus but a logical corollary of the new system that occupations should be made hereditary and people tied to them with increasing rigidity. The final result was the well-known economic "sclerosis" of the Byzantine state.

PROMULGATION OF THE NEW TAX SYSTEM IN EGYPT

Etudes de Papyrologie, II (1933), 1–8 (= SB, No. 7,622); A.D. 297 [98]

Aristius Optatus, *vir perfectissimus*, prefect of Egypt, declares: Our most provident Emperors, the eternal[?] Diocletian and Maximian, Augusti, and Constantius and Maximian, most noble Caesars, having learned that the levies of the public taxes are being made haphazardly, so that some persons are let off lightly and others overburdened, have decided to root out this most evil and baneful practice for the benefit of their provincials and to issue a deliverance-bringing rule to which the taxes shall conform. Accordingly, the levy on each aroura [99] according to the classification of the land, and the levy on each head of the peasantry, and from which age to which, may be accurately[?] known to all from the [recently] issued divine [i.e., imperial] edict and the schedule annexed thereto, copies of which I have prefaced for promulgation with this edict of mine. Accordingly, seeing that in this, too, they have received the greatest benefaction, the provincials should make it their

[98] We are indebted to Professor H. C. Youtie, of the University of Michigan, for generous assistance in our presentation of this document. Our translation is based on his improved rereading of the Greek text and has benefited in several significant points from his acute criticism.

[99] "Aroura" is here probably a Greek rendering of *iugum*.

business in conformity with the divinely issued regulations to pay their taxes with all speed and by no means wait for the compulsion of the collector; for it is proper to fulfill most zealously and scrupulously all the loyal obligations, and if anyone should be revealed to have done otherwise after such bounty, he will risk punishment. The magistrates and council presidents of every city have been ordered to send out to every village and even locality a copy of the divine edict together with the schedule, and also of this [edict] as well, in the interest of having the munificence of our Emperors and Caesars come speedily to the knowledge of all. And also the collectors of each revenue are reminded to uphold [the regulations] with all their might; for if any should be revealed to have transgressed, he will risk the death penalty.

Year 13 and 12 and 5 of our lords Diocletian and Maximian, Augusti, and Constantius and Maximian, most noble Caesars, Phamenoth 20.[100]

INTRODUCTION OF THE IUGUM UNIT

"Syro-Roman Law Book"[101] cxxi

The *iugum* measure was decreed in the days of the Emperor Diocletian and made law. Five *iugera*, which equal 10 *plethra*, of vineyard were established as 1 *iugum*; 20 *iugera* of grain land, which equal 40 *plethra*, pay the tax in kind of 1 *iugum*; 220 *perticae* of mature olive grove pay the tax in kind of 1 *iugum*; 450 *perticae* in the mountains pay 1 *iugum*. So, too, land which is of poorer quality and is reckoned just like mountainous land: 40 *iugera*, which equal 80 *plethra*, pay 1 *iugum*; if, however, it is reckoned or assessed as third quality, 60 *iugera*, equaling 120 *plethra*, pay 1 *iugum*.

Mountainous land is assessed as follows. At the time of the assessment there were certain men who were given the authority by the government; they summoned other mountain dwellers from other regions and bade them assess how much land, by their estimate, produces a *modius* of wheat or barley in the mountains. In this way they also assessed unsown land, the pasture land for cattle, as to how much tax it should yield to the fisc. And for the pasture land the prescription was that it pay annually to the fisc one *denarius*; but there is also such land which pays two and three *denarii*.

---

[100] The years are those of the reigns of Diocletian, of Maximian, and of the two Caesars, respectively: cf. Note 86. The date Phamenoth 20, corresponding to March 16, shows that the new tax system was inaugurated in Egypt early in the year following its promulgation.

[101] A schoolbook of Roman civil law written originally in Greek in the late fifth century but now extant only in a Syriac and various other Oriental-language versions made some centuries later. Our translation is based on a modern version, in Latin, in *FIRA*, II, 791.

129. *Diocletian's Edict on Maximum Prices*

In A.D. 296, in conjunction with his revision of the taxation system, Diocletian introduced a new coinage to replace the wildly inflated and depreciated currency of the preceding decades (see § 118). But the huge governmental expenditures for war, for the maintenance of the increased army, court, and bureaucracy, and for building operations in large part nonproductive—further aggravated possibly by widespread distrust of the new coinage, understandable after a century of repeated currency devaluations—brought on a new wave of inflation. At last, in an attempt to curb runaway prices and stabilize the economy, especially in the interest of assuring the needs of the army and bureaucracy, Diocletian took the drastic step—unprecedented in Roman history—of decreeing fixed ceilings on prices and wages throughout the Empire. Death or exile were prescribed as punishment for charging or paying above-ceiling prices or for attempting to circumvent the regulation by hoarding. The edict on maximum prices was published early in A.D. 301, but because of business opposition and the difficulty of enforcement it was finally revoked. (For Lactantius' biased account see § 127.) Numerous fragments of the official Latin text and of Greek copies of the edict are extant, all but one, which was recently discovered in Italy, coming from the eastern provinces. Together they form the longest extant document in the economic history of the ancient world. Most of the preamble and a few selections from the extensive price lists are given below.

INFLATION

This text is eloquent testimony both of the monetary troubles of the Empire and of the prevalence and impunity of official skulduggery shortly before the issuance of the edict on maximum prices. The writer, a government official, is here seen taking advantage of his inside knowledge of a forthcoming currency devaluation to have his agent convert all his available cash into goods.

Rylands Papyrus No. 607; A.D. c.300

Dionysius to Apio, greeting. The divine fortune of our masters has given orders that the Italian coinage be reduced to half a *nummus*.[102] Make haste therefore to spend all the Italian money you have and purchase for me all kinds of goods at whatever price you find them. . . . But I tell you in advance that if you try any shenanigans [103] I won't let you get away with it. I pray you may continue long in health, my brother.[104]

[102] *Nummus* is a synonym for sesterce.
[103] Such as pretending he paid more for things than he did and pocketing the difference.
[104] This is still a form of polite salutation in the Near East.

THE EDICT ON MAXIMUM PRICES

CIL, Vol. III, pp. 801–41, 1055–58, 1909–53, 2208–11, 2328 (= *ESAR*, V, 307–421) and *Transactions of the American Philological Association*, LXXI (1940), 157–74

Adapted in part from the translation of E. Graser [105]

The Emperor Caesar Gaius Aurelius Valerius Diocletian Pius Felix Invictus Augustus, *pontifex maximus*, Germanicus Maximus for the sixth time, Sarmaticus Maximus for the fourth time, Persicus Maximus for the second time, Brittannicus Maximus, Carpicus Maximus, Armenicus Maximus, Medicus Maximus, Adiabenicus Maximus, holding the tribunician power for the eighteenth year, seven times consul, acclaimed *imperator* for the eighteenth time, father of his country, proconsul; and the Emperor Caesar Marcus Aurelius Valerius Maximian [corresponding titles]; and Flavius Valerius Constantius [corresponding titles], most noble Caesar; and Galerius Valerius Maximian [corresponding titles], most noble Caesar, declare:

As we recall the wars which we have successfully fought, we must be grateful to the fortune of our state, second only to the immortal gods, for a tranquil world that reclines in the embrace of the most profound calm, and for the blessings of a peace that was won with great effort. That this fortune of our state be stabilized and suitably adorned is demanded by the law-abiding public and by the dignity and majesty of Rome. Therefore we, who by the gracious favor of the gods previously stemmed the tide of the ravages of barbarian nations by destroying them, must surround the peace which we established for eternity with the necessary defenses of justice.

If the excesses perpetrated by persons of unlimited and frenzied avarice could be checked by some self-restraint—this avarice which rushes for gain and profit with no thought for mankind . . . ; or if the general welfare could endure without harm this riotous license by which, in its unfortunate state, it is being very seriously injured every day, the situation could perhaps be faced with dissembling and silence, with the hope that human forbearance might alleviate the cruel and pitiable situation. But the only desire of these uncontrolled madmen is to have no thought for the common need. Among the unscrupulous, the immoderate, and the avaricious it is considered almost a creed . . . to desist from plundering the wealth of all only when necessity compels them. Through their extreme need, moreover, some persons have become acutely aware

[105] In *ESAR* and *Transactions of the American Philological Association*, as cited above.

of their most unfortunate situation, and can no longer close their eyes to it. Therefore we, who are the protectors of the human race, are agreed, as we view the situation, that decisive legislation is necessary, so that the long-hoped-for solutions which mankind itself could not provide may, by the remedies provided by our foresight, be vouchsafed for the general betterment of all. . . .

We hasten, therefore, to apply the remedies long demanded by the situation, satisfied that no one can complain that our intervention with regulations is untimely or unnecessary, trivial or unimportant. These measures are directed against the unscrupulous, who have perceived in our silence of so many years a lesson in restraint but have been unwilling to imitate it. For who is so insensitive and so devoid of human feeling that he can be unaware or has not perceived that uncontrolled prices are widespread in the sales taking place in the markets and in the daily life of the cities? Nor is the uncurbed passion for profiteering lessened either by abundant supplies or by fruitful years. . . .

But now we must set forth in detail the causes which have pressed and driven us to cease our long-enduring forbearance and to take steps. . . . Who does not know that wherever the common safety requires our armies to be sent, the profiteers insolently and covertly attack the public welfare, not only in villages and towns, but on every road? They charge extortionate prices for merchandise, not just fourfold or eightfold, but on such a scale that human speech cannot find words to characterize their profit and their practices. Indeed, sometimes in a single retail sale a soldier is stripped of his donative and pay. Moreover, the contributions of the whole world for the support of the armies fall as profits into the hands of these plunderers, and our soldiers appear to bestow with their own hands the rewards of their military service and their veterans' bonuses upon the profiteers. The result is that the pillagers of the state itself seize day by day more than they know how to hold.

Aroused justly and rightfully by all the facts set forth above, and in response to the needs of mankind itself, which appears to be praying for release, we have decided that maximum prices of articles for sale must be established. We have not set down fixed prices, for we do not deem it just to do this, since many provinces occasionally enjoy the good fortune of welcome low prices and the privilege, as it were, of prosperity. Thus, when the pressure of high prices appears anywhere—may the gods avert such a calamity!—avarice . . . will be checked by the limits fixed in our statute and by the restraining curbs of the law.

It is our pleasure, therefore, that the prices listed in the subjoined schedule be held in observance in the whole of our Empire. And every person shall take note that the liberty to exceed them at will has been ended, but that the blessing of low prices has in no way been impaired in those places where supplies actually abound. . . . Moreover, this universal edict will serve as a necessary check upon buyers and sellers whose practice it is to visit ports and other provinces. For when they too know that in the pinch of scarcity there is no possibility of exceeding the prices fixed for commodities, they will take into account in their calculations at the time of sale the localities, the transportation costs, and all other factors. In this way they will make apparent the justice of our decision that those who transport merchandise may not sell at higher prices anywhere.

It is agreed that even in the time of our ancestors it was the practice in passing laws to restrain offenses by prescribing a penalty. For rarely is a situation beneficial to humanity accepted spontaneously; experience teaches that fear is the most effective regulator and guide for the performance of duty. Therefore it is our pleasure that anyone who resists the measures of this statute shall be subject to a capital penalty for daring to do so. And let no one consider the statute harsh, since there is at hand a ready protection from danger in the observance of moderation. . . . We therefore exhort the loyalty of all, so that a regulation instituted for the public good may be observed with willing obedience and due scruple, especially as it is seen that by a statute of this kind provision has been made, not for single municipalities and peoples and provinces but for the whole world. . . .

The prices for the sale of individual items which no one may exceed are listed below.

I.				
Wheat	1	army *modius* [106]	100	*denarii*
Barley	1	" "	60	"
Rye	1	" "	60	"
Millet, ground	1	" "	100	"
Millet, whole	1	" "	50	"
Panic grass	1	" "	50	"
Spelt, hulled	1	" "	100	"

. . . . .

Beans, crushed	1	" "	100	"
Beans, not ground	1	" "	60	"
Lentils	1	" "	100	"
Pulse	1	" "	80	"
Peas, split	1	" "	100	"
Peas, not split	1	" "	60	"

. . . . .

[106] *Castrensis modius*, literally "the *modius* of the army camps."

Rice, cleaned	1 army *modius*	200 *denarii*
Barley grits, cleaned	1 *modius*	100 "
Spelt grits, cleaned	1 *modius*	200 "
Sesame	1 army *modius*	200 "

. . . . .

II. Likewise, for wines:

Picene	1 Italian *sextarius*	30 "
Tiburtine	1 " "	30 "
Sabine	1 " "	30 "

. . . . .

Falernian	1 " "	30 "
Likewise, aged wine, first quality	1 " "	24 "
Aged wine, second quality	1 " "	16 "
Ordinary	1 " "	8 "
Beer, Gallic or Pannonian	1 " "	4 "
Beer, Egyptian	1 " "	2 "

. . . . .

III. Likewise, for oil:

From unripe olives	1 " "	40 "
Second quality	1 " "	24 "

. . . . .

Salt	1 army *modius*	100 "
Spiced salt	1 Italian *sextarius*	8 "
Honey, best quality	1 " "	40 "
Honey, second quality	1 " "	24 "

. . . . .

IV. Likewise, for meat:

Pork	1 Italian pound	12 "
Beef	1 " "	8 "

. . . . .

Leg of pork, Menapic or Cerritane, best	1 " "	20 "

. . . . .

Pork mincemeat	1 ounce	2 "
Beef mincemeat	1 Italian pound	10 "
Pheasant, fattened		250 "
Pheasant, wild		125 "

. . . . .

Chickens	1 brace	60 *denarii*
• • •		
Beccafico [107]	10	40 ”
Sparrows	10	16 ”
Dormice [108]	10	40 ”
• • •		
Venison	1 Italian pound	12 ”
• •		
Butter	1 ” ”	16 ”

V. Likewise, for fish:

Sea fish with rough scales	1 ” ”	24 ”
Fish, second quality	1 ” ”	16 ”
River fish, best quality	1 ” ”	12 ”
River fish, second quality	1 ” ”	8 ”
Salt fish	1 ” ”	6 ”
Oysters	100	100 ”

• • •

VII. For wages:

Farm laborer, with maintenance	daily	25 ”
• •		
Carpenter, as above	”	50 ”
• • •		
Wall painter, as above	”	75 ”
Picture painter, as above	”	150 ”
• •		
Baker, as above	”	50 ”
Shipwright working on a seagoing ship, as above	”	60 ”
Shipwright working on a river boat, as above	”	50 ”
• •		
Camel driver or ass and hinny driver, with maintenance	”	25 ”
Shepherd, with maintenance	”	20 ”

[107] Cf. Chapter IV, Note 84.
[108] Cf. Chapter IV, Note 81.

Muleteer, with maintenance	daily	25 *denarii*
Veterinary, for clipping and preparing hoofs	per animal	6 "
Veterinary, for bleeding and cleaning the head	per animal	20 "
Barber	per man	2 "

.   .   .   .   .   .

Sewer cleaner, working a full day, with maintenance	daily	25 "

.   .   .   .   .   .

Scribe, for the best writing	100 lines	25 "
Scribe, for second-quality writing	100 "	20 "
Notary, for writing a petition or legal document	100 "	10 "

.   .   .   .   .   .

Tailor, for cutting and finishing a hooded cloak of first quality		60 "

.   .   .   .   .   .

Tailor, for breeches		20 "
Tailor, for leggings		4 "

.   .   .   .   .   .

Elementary teacher,[109] per boy	monthly	50 "
Teacher of arithmetic, per boy	"	75 "
Teacher of shorthand, per boy	"	75 "

.   .   .   .   .   .

Teacher of Greek or
Latin language and literature, and teacher of

[109] On the teachers here listed in ascending order in the educational sequence, see § 73.

geometry, per pupil	monthly	200 *denarii*
Teacher of rhetoric or public speaking, per pupil	"	250 "
Advocate or jurist, fee for a complaint		250 "
Advocate or jurist, fee for pleading		1,000 "
Teacher of architecture, per boy	"	100 "
Check room attendant, per bather		2 "

· · · ·

XI. . . . For boots:

Muleteers' or farmworkers' boots, first quality, without hobnails, pair	120 "
Soldiers' boots, without hobnails	100 "
Shoes, patrician	150 "
Shoes, senatorial	100 "
Shoes, equestrian	70 "
Boots, women's, pair	60 "

· · · ·

XII. For timber:

Fir, 50 cubits long by 4 cubits square perimeter	50,000 "
45 cubits long by same perimeter	40,000 "

· · · ·

The same prices are fixed for pine timber.

· · · ·

XVII. For transportation charges:

Fare per man	per mile	2 "

· · ·

Freight for a 1,200-pound wagon load	"	"	20 "
Freight for a 600-pound camel load	"	"	8 "

Freight for an ass load	per mile	4 *denarii*

. . . .

XXIII. For the price of silks:

White silk	1 pound	12,000 "
For those unraveling silk,[110] with maintenance	1 ounce	64 "

XXIV. For purple:

Raw silk, dyed purple	1 pound	150,000 "
Wool[?], dyed purple	1 "	50,000 "

. . . .

XXV. Wool from Tarentum, washed	1 "	175 "
Wool from Laodicea, washed	1 "	150 "
Wool from Asturia, washed	1 "	100 "
Wool, best medium quality, washed	1 "	50 "

. . . .

XXX. For gold:

Gold, refined in bars or coins	1 "	50,000 "
Gold, drawn	1 "	12,000 "
For craftsmen working the metal	for 1 pound	5,000 "

. . . .

Freight charges between places and provinces which it is absolutely forbidden to exceed:

From Alexandria to Rome	for 1 army *modius*	16 *denarii*
From Alexandria to Nicomedia	"	12 "
From Alexandria to Byzantium	"	12 "
From Alexandria to Dalmatia	"	18 "

[110] "Clothing made wholly of silk was rare until Elagabalus set the example, the material normally being woven into linen or woolen fabrics after importation. Wholly silk cloth was perhaps pulled to pieces for this purpose" (E. H. Warmington, *The Commerce between the Roman Empire and India* [Cambridge, 1928], 175).

From Alexandria to Aquileia	for 1 army *modius*	24 *denarii*
From Alexandria to Africa	„	10 „
From Alexandria to Sicily	„	10 „
From Alexandria to Ephesus	„	8 „
From Alexandria to Thessalonica	„	12 „
From Alexandria to Pamphylia	„	6 „

. . . .

Likewise, from Asia to Rome	„	16 „
Likewise, from Asia to Africa	„	8 „
Likewise, from Asia to Dalmatia	„	12 „
Likewise, from Africa to Rome	„	. . .
Likewise, from Africa to Salona	„	18 „
Likewise, from Africa to Sicily	„	6 „
Likewise, from Africa to Spain	„	8 „
Likewise, from Africa to the Gauls	„	4 „
Likewise, from Africa to Achaea	„	12 „

. . . .

A DECLARATION OF PRICE CONFORMITY

When the edict on maximum prices was promulgated in Egypt, the artisan guilds were apparently ordered to file sworn schedules of the prices at which they sold their products, as proof that they did not exceed the ceilings fixed by the edict. It is possible that this procedure was followed in all provinces by imperial order.

Antinoöpolis Papyrus No. 38; April 13, A.D. 301

To the superintendent[?] of . . . of Antinoöpolis the most illus-trious . . . from the silversmiths' guild of the said city. . . . We swear by the fortune of our lords Diocletian and Maximian, Augusti, and Constantius [and Maximian, the most noble] Caesars, that we report for your information, in accordance with the governor's order, the price of a pound of worked silver to be 62 *denarii* and of a pound of cast silver, 31 *denarii;* and that we have made no false statement, or else may we be liable under the divine oath. In response to the formal question we gave our assent.[111]

Year 16 and year 15 of our lords Diocletian and Maximian, Augusti, and year 8 of our lords Constantius and Maximian, the most noble Caesars, Pharmuthi 17. I, Aurelius Sarapammo, councilman of Antinoöpolis, swore the oath as aforesaid. I, Aurelius Ammonis son of Besario, swore the oath as aforesaid. I, Aurelius Isidorus, swore the oath as aforesaid.

130. *The Provincial Reorganization*

In the latter years of his reign (A.D. 297–305), Diocletian effected a complete provincial reorganization, the first such since that of Augustus. The separation into imperial and senatorial provinces was ended, as was also the privileged treatment of Italy. The whole Empire was divided into twelve dioceses, six in the East and six in the West, and it is striking to observe how those of the West, at least, foreshadow national entities of modern Europe. To reduce the power concentrated in the hands of any governor, the dioceses were subdivided into a total of about a hundred provinces, and the civil and military administrations were divided and placed under separate chief officers. One result was, of course, a multiplication of the already swollen bureaucracy. Although some provinces were further subdivided by later emperors, and although some other organizational changes were made (for example, the city of Rome was made a separate diocese), Diocletian's scheme remained the fundamental administrative structure of the Empire for centuries to come. The roster of dioceses and provinces, with a few later interpolations but substantially as set up by Diocletian, is preserved in a seventh-century manuscript of an unknown fourth-century source. The "Verona List," as the manuscript is called, for the place where it was discovered, lists the provinces in a generally geographical sequence for the Eastern dioceses, and according to the rank of the governors for the Western.

Theodor Mommsen, *Gesammelte Schriften*, V (Berlin, 1908), 563–64
(= O. Seeck, *Notitia Dignitatum* [Berlin, 1876], pp. 247–51)

The Names of All the Provinces

The Diocese of the Orient has provinces to the number of eighteen: Libya Superior, Lybia Inferior, Thebais, Aegyptus Jovia, Aegyptus

[111] Cf. Chapter III, Note 135.

Herculia,[112] Arabia, Arabia Augusta Libanensis, Palaestina, Phoenice, Syria Coele, Augusta Euphratensis, Cilicia, Isauria, Cyprus, Mesopotamia, Osroena.[113]

The Diocese of Pontus has provinces to the number of seven: Bithynia, Cappadocia, Galatia, Paphlagonia . . . , Diospontus, Pontus Polemiacus, Armenia Minor. . . .

The Diocese of Asia has provinces to the number of nine: Pamphylia, Phrygia Prima, Phrygia Secunda, Asia, Lydia, Caria, The Islands, Pisidia, Hellespontus.

The Diocese of Thrace has provinces to the number of six: Europa, Rhodope, Thracia, Haemimontus, Scythia, Moesia Inferior.

The Diocese of the Moesias has provinces to the number of eleven: Dacia, Moesia Superior Margensis, Dardania, Macedonia, Thessalia, Achaea, Praevalentia, Epirus Nova, Epirus Vetus, Creta.

The Diocese of the Pannonias has provinces to the number of seven: Pannonia Inferior, Savensis, Dalmatia, Valeria, Pannonia Superior, Noricus Ripariensis, Noricus Mediterranea.

The Diocese of the Britains has provinces to the number of six: Britannia Prima, Britannia Secunda, Britannia Maxima Caesariensis, Britannia Flavia Caesariensis.

The Diocese of the Gauls has provinces to the number of eight: Belgica Prima, Belgica Secunda, Germania Prima, Germania Secunda, Sequania, Lugdunensis Prima, Lugdunensis Secunda, Alpes Graiae et Poeninae.

The Diocese of Vienne has provinces to the number of seven: Viennensis, Narbonensis Prima, Narbonensis Secunda, Nine Peoples, Aquitanica Prima, Aquitanica Secunda, Alpes Maritimae.

The Diocese of Italy has provinces to the number of sixteen: Venetia Histria, Flaminia, Picenum, Tuscia Umbrena, Apulia, Calabria, Lucania, Corsica, Alpes Cottiae, Raetia. . . .[114]

The Diocese of the Spains has provinces to the number of seven: Baetica, Lusitania, Carthaginiensis, Gallaecia, Tarraconensis, Mauretania Tingitania.

The Diocese of Africa has provinces to the number of seven: Proconsularis Zeugitana, Byzacena, Numidia Cirtensis, Numidia Militiana, Mauretania Caesariensis, Mauretania Zabia Insidiana.[115]

---

[112] On the epithets Jovia and Herculia cf. p. 457.

[113] The discrepancy between the stated total and the number of provinces actually listed in this and other dioceses presumably reflects to some extent the changes introduced between the provincial reorganization of Diocletian and the time when this roster was compiled, some decades later.

[114] There is a lacuna here. The other provinces of Italy at this time were perhaps Aemilia, Liguria, Samnium, Campania, Sicilia, Sardinia, Valeria.

[115] The text is corrupt here. At the time of Diocletian's reorganization this prov-

The Age of Constantine

131. *Constantine's Administrative and Military Reorganization*

The system of the tetrarchy established by Diocletian did not long survive his abdication in A.D. 305. Out of the rivalries among his successors there emerged in 313 two joint emperors, Licinius and Constantine, and in 324 the latter, after defeating his colleague, became sole ruler. Constantine brought to completion the imperial reorganization initiated by Diocletian. The essence of his administrative reforms was the fractioning of the power of his chief functionaries and the almost universal separation of civil and military functions. These remained the fundamental principles of the imperial administration for the next three centuries, during which the size and power of the Byzantine bureaucracy increased steadily. Constantine also transformed the Roman military system. Reducing the importance and strength of the frontier garrisons, which became local border militias (*limitanei, riparienses*) commanded by *duces* (dukes) and *comites* (counts), he based the imperial defenses primarily on mobile field armies (*comitatenses*), under the direct command of himself and his deputies. In a further break with tradition, Constantine made the cavalry, instead of the infantry, his basic military arm, thus introducing the type of military organization which prevailed throughout the Middle Ages.

Zosimus [116] *Recent History* II. xxxii–xxxv (abridged)

Constantine drastically reorganized the long-established offices. There had been two Praetorian prefects, who administered the office jointly and controlled by their supervision and power not only the Praetorian cohorts but also those which were entrusted with the guarding of the city and those which were stationed in the outskirts.[117] The

---

ince may have been called Mauretania Tripolitania; by A.D. 315 it was named Mauretania Sitifensis.

[116] Zosimus was a Greek historian of the first half of the fifth century. Little is known about him. His *Recent History*, in six books, covers the period from Diocletian to A.D. 410, preceded by a brief account of the emperors from Augustus. The theme of his work is that the decline of the Roman Empire began with the overthrow of the Republic and the subsequent increasing concentration of power in the hands of the emperor, and that the collapse set in with the abandonment of the ancestral religion. Hence his hostility to Constantine, whom he calls "the initiator of impiety."

[117] Septimius Severus, who abolished the privileged position of Italy in this respect, had stationed a legionary garrison at Albanum near Rome.

office of Praetorian prefect had been considered second to that of the emperor; he made the distributions of grain and redressed all offenses against military discipline by appropriate punishments. Constantine, altering this good institution, divided the single office into four. To one prefect he assigned all Egypt, together with the Pentapolis in Libya, and the East as far as Mesopotamia, and, in addition, Cilicia, Cappadocia, Armenia, the entire coast from Pamphylia to Trapezus, and the forts along the Phasis river; to the same person were entrusted Thrace, and Moesia as far as the Haemus and Rhodope mountains, and the territory of the town of Doberus, and likewise Cyprus and the Cyclades Islands except Lemnos, Imbros, and Samothrace. To another he assigned Macedonia, Thessaly, Crete, Greece together with the nearby islands, both Epiruses, and in addition the Illyrians, the Dacians, the Triballians, the Pannonians as far as Valeria, and Upper Moesia besides. To the third prefect he entrusted all Italy and Sicily with the neighboring islands, and also Sardinia and Corsica, and Africa from the Syrtes to Cyrene; to the fourth, the Transalpine Gauls and Iberia, and in addition the island of Britain. Having thus divided the office of these prefects, he strove to reduce their power in other ways. For though there were not only centurions and tribunes in command of the soldiers everywhere but also those called *duces*, who in each district held the rank of commanders, he established masters of the soldiers, some for the cavalry, some for the infantry, and by transferring to these the power of marshaling the soldiers and punishing offenders, he diminished in this respect the authority of the prefects. . . .

Constantine likewise took another measure, which gave the barbarians unhindered access into the lands subject to the Romans. For the Roman Empire was, by the foresight of Diocletian, everywhere protected on its frontiers . . . by towns and fortresses and towers, in which the entire army was stationed; it was thus impossible for the barbarians to cross over, there being everywhere a sufficient opposing force to repel their inroads. But Constantine destroyed that security by removing the greater part of the soldiers from the frontiers and stationing them in cities that did not require protection; thus he stripped those of protection who were harassed by the barbarians and brought ruin to peaceful cities at the hands of the soldiers, with the result that most have become deserted. He likewise softened the soldiers by exposing them to shows and luxuries. To speak plainly, he was the first to sow the seeds of the ruinous state of affairs that has lasted up to the present time.

132. *Legislation on Taxation*

Theodosian Code XI. vii. 3; A.D. 320 [118]

In connection with the payment of taxes due, no person shall fear that he will suffer, at the hands of perverse and enraged judges, imprisonment, lashes of leaded whips, weights, or any other tortures devised by the arrogance of judges.[119] Prisons are for criminals. . . . In accordance with this law, taxpayers shall proceed in security; or indeed, if a man is so alien to human feeling that he contumaciously abuses this indulgence, he shall be detained in the free and open military custody established for ordinary use. If he persists in his stubborn wickedness, his fellow citizens shall be given access to his property and all his substance, and with the ownership of his substance they shall undertake the performance of his obligations [to the state].[120] Since we grant such an opportunity, we believe that all men will be the more inclined to pay that which is demanded for the use of our army in behalf of the common safety.

Theodosian Code XI. xvi. 3; A.D. 324/25

Whenever it is necessary for a tax assessment to be made, the assessment of each municipality shall be made in accordance with the plans and direction of the governor, so that the mass of the lower classes may not be subjected to the wantonness and subordinated to the interests of the more powerful and thus suffer the infliction of grave and iniquitous outrages.

Theodosian Code XI. iii. 2; A.D. 327

Slaves assessed in the census rolls shall be sold within the boundaries of the province, and any persons who obtain ownership by purchase shall know that they must look into this. It is reasonable that the same rule should be observed also in the case of landholding . . . [where] the burdens and public payments shall pertain to the duty of those to whose ownership the said holdings have passed.

[118] Selections from the *Theodosian Code* (in Chapters VI, VII, and IX) are mostly based on or adapted from the translation of C. Pharr (Princeton, 1952). These laws are all in the form of imperial rescripts addressed to various high officials.
[119] Maltreatment of taxpayers by officials and collectors was a common and long-standing abuse of Roman rule: cf. Vol. I, §§ 140, 144, 146; Vol. II, §§ 106, 117, 123.
[120] Cf. § 121, fourth and fifth selections.

133. *Economic Distress: Remission of Taxes* [121]

Latin Panegyrics [122] v. v–xiv (abridged)

I have told, O Emperor [Constantine], how much the Aeduans deserved the aid you brought them; it follows that I should tell how serious was their distress. . . . Our community lay prostrate, not so much because of the destruction of our walls as from exhaustion of resources, ever since the severity of the new tax assessment had drained our very life. We could not, however, rightly complain, since we had the lands which had been assigned to us, and we were comprised in the common formula of the Gallic assessment, we who can be compared to none in our good fortune. Wherefore, O Emperor, all the more do we give thanks to your clemency for granting remedies of your own accord and making us appear to have obtained justly what we could not rightfully request. . . .

And yet anyone would deservedly forgive these tillers of the soil, who are grieved by labor that brings no return. Indeed a field which never meets expenses is of necessity deserted; likewise the poor country folk, staggering beneath debts, were not permitted to bring in water or cut down forests, so that whatever usable soil there was has been ruined by swamps and choked with briers. . . . Why should I speak of other districts of that community, over which you admitted that you yourself wept? For whereas throughout the fields of other cities you saw almost all parts under cultivation, cleared and flowering, and accessible roads, and rivers under navigation washing the very gates of the towns, here directly from the bend which leads the highway back toward Belgica, you saw everything waste, uncultivated, neglected, silent, shadowy—even military roads so broken . . . that scarcely half-filled, sometimes empty wagons cross them. As a result it often happens that our taxes are late, since our little produce is more difficult for us to transport than a great abundance for others. . . .

You gave us our whole life. . . . To relieve the tax assessment you restricted the total; to remit our arrears you asked how much we owed. . . . You remitted 7,000 *capita*,[123] more than a fifth of our assessment,

---

[121] Cf. §§ 104, 119.

[122] These are a collection of eleven anonymous orations from the late third and fourth centuries, preserved together with Pliny's *Panegyric* of Trajan (§ 24), on which they are patterned. When their fulsomeness is discounted, these works become valuable sources for the history of the Dominate. The panegyric from which the following selection is taken is numbered v in some editions, viii in others.

[123] Cf. § 128.

and yet you inquired often whether this would be enough for us. . . .
By your remission of 7,000 *capita* you gave strength to 25,000 [persons].
. . . You remitted our arrears for five years. . . . Therefore the immortal gods created you emperor for us especially; for each of us this
felicity was born when you began to rule. . . . How many, Emperor
Augustus, whom poverty had compelled to lie in hiding on the estates,
or even to go into exile, are coming forth to the light, returning to their
native land, as a result of this remission of arrears!

134. *Compulsory Public Services*

Under the fiscal system of the Dominate, compulsory public services became
an all-pervading institution of rigidly controlled, hereditary classes. Those
who suffered the heaviest economic burdens were the town decurions, who
were liable with their own property for imperial taxes due from the local
population. They constantly sought to evade their burdensome responsibilities
by flight into the army, bureaucracy, or clergy.

Theodosian Code XI. xvi. 4; A.D. 328

The assessment of extraordinary public services shall not be entrusted to chief decurions, and therefore governors of the provinces shall
be admonished to perform this assessment themselves and with their own
hand write out and in ink annex the names. The following general rule
shall be observed, namely, that the services to be given shall be rendered
first by the more powerful and then by those of middle and lowest station. A farmer urgently occupied in planting or in gathering his harvest
shall never be dragged off to extraordinary burdens, since it is a matter
of prudence to satisfy such necessities at the opportune season. The
neglect of these regulations affects the honorable status of your vicars,[124]
and shall entail capital punishment for the office staffs of governors.
Moreover, governors must write with their own hand what is needed
and in what obligation for each *caput* [125]—how much public post service
or how much personal service, or what and in what measure it must be
furnished. Thus they shall write that they have certified it, and the aforesaid order of exaction among the richer, the middling, and the lowest
shall be observed.

Theodosian Code XV. ii. 1; A.D. 330

It is our will that the landholders over whose lands the courses of
aqueducts pass shall be exempt from extraordinary burdens, so that by

[124] This constitution is addressed to a praetorian prefect; on vicars see Note 93.
[125] Cf. introduction to § 128.

their work the aqueducts may be cleansed when they are choked with dirt. The said landholders shall not be subject to any other burden of a superindiction,[126] lest they be occupied in other matters and not be present to clean the aqueducts. If they neglect this duty, they shall be punished by the forfeiture of their landholdings; for the fisc will take possession of the landed estate of any man whose negligence contributes to the damage of the aqueducts. Furthermore, persons through whose landed estates the aqueducts pass should know that they may have trees to the right and left at a distance of fifteen feet from the aqueducts, and your [127] office shall see to it that these trees are cut out if they grow too luxuriantly at any time, so that their roots may not injure the structure of the aqueduct.

BURDENS OF DECURIONS

Theodosian Code XII. i. 1; A.D. 313/26

No judge shall attempt to grant exemption from compulsory municipal services to any decurion, nor shall he free anyone from the municipal council at his own discretion. For if anyone is impoverished by a misfortune of such kind that he needs to be relieved, his name should be referred to our wisdom, so that an exemption from compulsory municipal services may be extended to him for a limited space of time.

Theodosian Code XII. i. 10; A.D. 325

Since we have granted to different persons the privilege of being assigned to the legions or cohorts or of being restored to the military service, if any person should produce a grant of this kind, inquiry shall be made as to whether he is of a family of decurions or whether he has been previously nominated to the municipal council, so that, if any such thing is proved, he may be returned to his own municipal council and municipality. It will be appropriate to observe this general rule with reference to all who have already been approved and are serving in military offices, or who have already been restored and are protected by the oath of military service, or who shall be approved hereafter by official decisions.

Theodosian Code XII. i. 11; A.D. 325

Since some men desert the municipal councils and flee for refuge to the protection of the military service, we command that all persons who

[126] That is, special tax levies.
[127] This rescript was addressed to the administrator of the water supply. On the care of aqueducts under the Principate, see § 15, third selection.

are found to be not yet under the authority of the chief centurion shall be discharged from the military service and shall be returned to the same municipal council. Only those persons shall remain in the military service who, in accordance with their position and rank, are already in the commissary service.

Theodosian Code XII. i. 12; A.D. 325

If anyone derives his origin from a greater or lesser municipality, and if in an effort to avoid [the duties of] the said origin he betakes himself to another municipality for the purpose of establishing residence there and attempts to submit a plea [to the emperor] about this or to depend on any fraud whatsoever in order to escape the origin of his own municipality, he shall sustain the burdens of the decurionate of both municipalities, in the one because of his personal desire, in the other because of his origin.

Theodosian Code XII. i. 13; A.D. 326

Since we have learned that the municipal councils are being left deserted by persons who, though subject to them through origin, are requesting military service for themselves through supplications [to the emperor] and are running away to the legions and the various government offices, we order all municipal councils to be advised that if they catch any persons in government service less than twenty years who have either fled from [the duties of] their origin or, rejecting nomination [to municipal office], have enrolled themselves in the military service, they shall drag such persons back to the municipal councils. . . .

Theodosian Code XVI. ii. 3; A.D. 320 or 329

An enactment was issued which directs that henceforth no decurion or descendant of a decurion or even any person provided with adequate resources and suitable for undertaking compulsory public services shall take refuge in the name and service of the clergy,[128] but that in the future only such persons shall be chosen in place of deceased clerics as have slender fortunes and are not held bound to such compulsory municipal services. But we have learned that those persons also are being disturbed who joined in the fellowship of the clergy before the promulgation of the law. We therefore command that such persons be freed from all annoyance, but that those who after the issuance of the law took refuge in the number of the clergy in evasion of public duties shall be completely separated from that body, shall be restored to their municipal councils and [social] orders, and shall perform their municipal duties.

[128] That is, of the Christian Church.

135. *Occupations Become Hereditary*

The crisis of the third century had led to steadily tighter imperial control over the numerous trade associations or "guilds" (*collegia, corpora, consortia*) of the Empire, especially those engaged in activities essential to the provisioning of urban centers and of the military or to the protection of life and property (cf. § 122). With the increase in taxes collected in kind under the Dominate, regimentation of persons concerned with the shipment, storage, and processing of such revenues was deemed essential by the state. Like the decurions, persons bound to such services sought to escape their obligations by entry into the army or civil service, or by becoming tenant farmers. By the time of Constantine many occupations (including military service: cf. Note 44 above) had been transformed into compulsory hereditary obligations to the state.

Theodosian Code VII. xxii. 1; A.D. 313 or 319

Of the veterans' sons who are fit for military service, some indolently object to the performance of their compulsory military duties and others are so cowardly that they desire to evade the necessity of military service by mutilation of their bodies. If they should be judged useless for military service because of amputated fingers, we order them to be assigned to the compulsory services and duties of decurions with no ambiguity.

Theodosian Code XIII. v. 1; A.D. 314

If any shipmaster by birth becomes captain of a lighter, he shall nonetheless continue right along to remain in the same group in which his parents appear to have been.

Theodosian Code XIII. v. 2; A.D. 314/15

Shipmasters nominated to the guild of city breadmakers but not subject to these breadmakers by any succession of inheritance must be released from this compulsory public service. But if they should chance to be bound to the breadmakers by hereditary right, they shall have the opportunity, if they perchance prefer, to relinquish the adventitious inheritance of breadmakers to the said guild or yield it to any next of kin of the deceased, in order to free themselves from the guild of breadmakers. But if they embrace the inheritance, it is necessary for them to undertake association in the compulsory public service of breadmaking by reason of the inheritance, and to sustain from their own resources the burdens of shipmasters. Evidently the prefect of the city, *vir clarissimus*, will make decisions concerning such matter.

136. *The Colonate: Tenant Farmers Bound to the Soil*

The crisis in Roman agriculture during the third and early fourth centuries was partly due to the decline in the rural population and to flight from the land because of heavy fiscal burdens. For some time, barbarians had been settled inside the Empire as state tenants bound to their tenancies (cf. § 116), and the *coloni* of imperial and private estates had tended all through the Principate to become hereditary tenants (see § 123). Now, in keeping with the tendency toward making all occupations hereditary, a long series of laws formally transformed the *coloni* into hereditary serfs permanently bound to the soil of the estates they tilled. The earliest datable enactment of this series is the following rescript of Constantine.

Theodosian Code v. xvii. 1; A.D. 332

Any person whatsoever in whose possession a *colonus* belonging to another is found not only shall restore the said *colonus* to his place of origin but shall also assume the capitation tax on him for the time [that he had him]. And as for *coloni* themselves, it will be proper for such as contemplate flight to be bound with chains to a servile status, so that by virtue of such condemnation to servitude they may be compelled to fulfill the duties that befit free men.

137. *Child Assistance*

Cf. the introduction to § 107.

Theodosian Code XI. xxvii. 1; A.D. 315 or 329

A law shall be written on bronze or waxed tablets or on linen cloth, and posted throughout all the municipalities of Italy, to restrain the hands of parents from infanticide and turn their hopes to the better. Your office shall administer this regulation, so that, if any parent should report that he has offspring which on account of poverty he is unable to rear, there shall be no delay in issuing food and clothing, since the rearing of a newborn infant can not tolerate delay. For this matter we order that both our fisc and our privy purse shall furnish their services without distinction.

Theodosian Code XI. xxvii. 2; A.D. 322

We have learned that provincials suffering from scarcity of food and lack of sustenance are selling or pledging their children. Therefore, if any such person is found who is sustained by no substance of family possessions and is supporting his children with hardship and difficulty, he shall be assisted through our fisc before he becomes a prey to calamity. The proconsuls, governors, and procurators of accounts throughout all Africa shall have the power and shall distribute the necessary support to all persons whom they observe to be placed in dire need, and they shall immediately assign adequate substance from the [state] storehouses. For it is repugnant to our customs to allow any person to be destroyed by hunger or rush forth to the commission of a shameful deed.

138. *Efforts to Suppress Official Corruption*

The ever present corruption practiced by the huge bureaucracy of the Empire during earlier centuries reached unprecedented proportions in the enlarged officialdom of the autocratic state. Constantine's fulminations against official corruption were followed by a long series of similar enactments by the emperors of succeeding centuries in a continuing but largely futile attempt to control the rapacity of their functionaries (cf. also § 132).

Theodosian Code I. xii. 2; A.D. 319

It is to the interest of public discipline, and it likewise befits the proconsular dignity, that you should bring under your power the administration and cognizance of public-revenue collection and all other matters. You shall not be content with the prepared reports and fraudulent statements of the functionaries, but you shall study the administration of the very judges and the statement of the prefect of the grain supply and of the procurators of accounts [to determine] whether the aforesaid prepared reports are trustworthy. For thus it will be possible to afford relief to the provincials against unjust exactions.

Theodosian Code I. xvi. 7; A.D. 331

The rapacious hands of the functionaries shall immediately stop, they shall stop, I say; for, if after due warning they do not stop, they shall be cut off with the sword. The curtain of the judge['s chamber] shall not be venal; [129] entrance shall not be purchased; his private chamber shall not be notorious for its bids; [130] the very sight of the governor shall not be at a price. The ears of the judge shall be open equally to the poorest as well as to the rich. The introduction of persons inside shall be free from depredation by the one who is called the office head; the as-

[129] A curtain shut off the private council chamber of the judge from the public. Court attendants demanded bribes to conduct litigants before the judge in chambers.
[130] By litigants who desired priority in having cases heard.

sistants of the said office heads shall employ no extortion on litigants; the intolerable onslaught of the centurions and other officials who demand small and large sums shall be crushed; and the unsated greed of those who deliver records to litigants shall be restrained. The ever-watchful diligence of the governor shall see that nothing is taken from a litigant by the aforesaid classes of men. And if they imagine they have to demand something in connection with civil cases, armed punishment will be at hand to cut off the heads and necks of the scoundrels, for all persons who have suffered extortion will be given an opportunity to provide information for an investigation by the governors. And if they dissemble, we open to all persons the right of complaint thereon before the *comites* [131] of the provinces—or before the Praetorian prefects, if they are closer at hand—so that we may be informed by their referrals and may produce punishments for such villainy.

Theodosian Code I. xxxii. 1; A.D. 333

Through the fault of the procurators of the privy purse, of dyeworks, and of weaving establishments, our private substance is being diminished, the products manufactured in the weaving establishments are being ruined, and in the dyeworks the fraudulent admixture of impure dye produces blemishes. Such procurators shall abstain from the patronage whereby they obtain the aforementioned administrative positions, or, if they contravene this order, they shall be removed from the number of Roman citizens and beheaded.

Theodosian Code x. iv. 1; A.D. 313 or 326

If any person is harassed by an agent or procurator of our privy purse, he shall not hesitate to lodge a complaint concerning his chicanery and depredations. When such charge is proved, we sanction that such person as dares to contrive anything against a provincial shall be publicly burned, since graver punishment should be fixed against those who are under our jurisdiction and ought to observe our mandates.

139. *Restrictions on Informers*

CIL, Vol. III, No. 12,043, lines 1–45 (= *FIRA*, Vol. I, No. 94);
A.D. 314/23

Copy of Sacred Edict

. . . It has been proved that many men are punished not only by loss of their property . . . and that in cases of this kind accused as well as

---

[131] Officers of the court ("counts"), created by Constantine as part of his administrative fragmentation (cf. § 130) and entrusted by him with a variety of functions in the central government and in the provinces.

witnesses experience very serious troubles. Wherefore, taking counsel for the security of our provinces, we have provided the following remedies.

An accuser shall not be completely denied access to court, but anyone who is confident that he can adduce proofs for his charges shall have ready opportunity of access to a judge and shall expose a defendant by clear evidence of the offense, so that suitable punishment in proportion to the nature of the acts may be inflicted upon the person convicted. But if he cannot at all prove his charges, he must know that he himself is to be subjected to a severe sentence. Indeed, if someone brings a charge of treason against another, since an accusation of this kind affords no one the slightest protection against rigorous examination [132] through privilege of rank, he must know that he, too, is to be subjected to torture if he is unable to prove his accusation by other clear evidence and proofs, since in the case of a person who is discovered to be of such temerity this also ought to be extracted by torture, namely, upon whose advice and instigation he appears to have resorted to the accusation, so that punishment can be meted out to all the accomplices of so great an offense.

In regard to [professional] informers, however, it is known to all to what extent opportunity of access to a judge has been denied by the statutes of our parents as well as by our own enactments, since a hearing must not be afforded to persons of this kind, inasmuch as it is fitting that they be subjected to punishment for daring so great a crime.

In the case also of slaves or freedmen who attempt to accuse or inform against their masters or patrons, we decree that the following regulation—according to a statute of the ancient law, too—is to be observed, namely, that the expression of such outrageous impudence shall be forthwith suppressed at the very beginning of the offense by sentence of the court, and [the accuser] denied a hearing and crucified for resorting to such villainy, thus providing an example to others, so that no one may display like impudence in the future.

Furthermore, that counsel may be taken in every direction for the security of innocent people, it is our pleasure also that libelous statements shall not be admitted. If anyone finds any such posted anonymously, he must at once pull them down and tear them up or destroy them by fire. In such cases, too, judges ought to observe the following practice: if perchance such a statement is brought to them, they shall instruct that it be

[132] From the time of Tiberius the torture of citizens to secure evidence was legal, though such inquisition had long been reserved for slaves (cf. § 68). Even after Marcus Aurelius and Lucius Verus exempted persons of higher social rank (*honestiores*) from torture in general, in cases of suspected treason no one was exempt.

consumed by fire, since writings of this kind ought to be entirely removed from the cognizance of judges; and an investigation shall continue against those daring to offer statements of this kind, so that when found they may be subjected to the punishments their temerity deserves.[133]

140. *Legislation on Slaves*

The institution of slavery survived for centuries after the triumph of Christianity. Under Christian influence, however, the growing tendency of the preceding centuries toward more humane treatment of slaves (cf. § 68) received fresh impetus. The following is a directive of Constantine on the subject.

Theodosian Code II. xxv. 1; A.D. 325 or 334

When . . . estates in Sardinia were recently distributed among the various present proprietors, the division of holdings ought to have been made in such a way that a whole family of slaves would remain with one individual landholder. For who could tolerate that children should be separated from parents, sisters from brothers, and wives from husbands? Therefore, any persons who have separated slaves and dragged them off to serve under different ownerships shall be forced to restore such to single ownership; and anyone who loses slaves through the reuniting of families shall be given slaves in exchange by the person who receives the aforesaid. And take pains that throughout the province no complaint shall hereafter persist over the separation of the loved ones of slaves.

141. *The Grandeur of Rome*

With the construction of the new imperial capital of the East, Constantinople, the New Rome, ceremonially inaugurated in A.D. 330 on the site of the ancient Greek city of Byzantium, old Rome receded in importance, except as the center of the Catholic Church. The following anonymous document, known by the titles *Curiosum Urbis Romae* or *Notitia*, was composed about the middle of the fourth century but is derived from earlier sources, probably official documents. The fourteen districts of the city—the administrative division instituted by Augustus—are treated in numerical order. The four districts given here indicate the pattern of the whole catalogue. Suspension points, except in the summary at the end, indicate our omission of unidentified or uncertain items.

[133] Cf. §§ 23, 172.

Catalogue of the Fourteen Districts of the City (abridged)

District II, Caelimontium, contains:

Temple of Claudius; great meat market; . . . Grotto of the Cyclops; Cohort V of the night patrol; . . . sacred tree; Peregrine Barracks; house of Philip; . . . training school for gladiators in the Morning Games . . . ; stripping room; [134] . . . wards—7; crossroad shrines—7; block captains—48; commissioners—2; blocks of tenements—4,600; private houses—127; storehouses—27; baths—85; fountains—65; bakeries [135] —15; area—12,200 feet.[136]

District III, Isis and Serapis, contains:

Mint; amphitheater, which has 87,000 *loca;* [137] great training school for gladiators; house of Bruttius Praesens; central theatrical storehouse; Shepherds' Fountain; . . . Baths of Titus and Trajan; Portico of Livia; camp of the sailors of the Misenum fleet; wards—12; crossroad shrines —12; block captains—48; commissioners—2; blocks of tenements— 2,757; private houses—60; storehouses—18; baths—80; fountains—65; bakeries—16; area—12,350 feet.

District VIII, Great Roman Forum, contains:

Three rostra; [shrine of the] Genius of the Roman People; Senate House; Atrium of Minerva; Forums of Caesar, of Augustus, of Nerva, of Trajan; Temple of Trajan, and the spiral column 128½ feet high, with 185 steps and 45 windows inside; [138] Cohort VI of the night patrol; bank basilica; Temples of Concord, of Saturn, of Vespasian and Titus; Capitolium; Golden Milestone;[139] Vicus Jugarius; [140] . . . Julian Basilica; Temple of Castor and Pollux; [Temple of] Vesta; storehouses of Agrippa; . . . Atrium of Cacus; Portico of the Pearl Dealers; [statue of

[134] Cf. Chapter V, Note 96. On the Morning Games see Chapter II, Note 111.
[135] Or "mills," where bakeries were frequently located.
[136] Probably in circuit.
[137] The Colosseum, whose seating capacity could not have exceeded 45,000. The term *loca* is now generally interpreted to mean running feet of sitting space; the number of spectators accommodated must be calculated here and in other places in this catalogue at slightly more than half the number of *loca.*
[138] This column was erected to commemorate Trajan's Dacian victory (see § 27, third selection). The height given here includes the pedestal. The actual number of "windows"—narrow slits lighting the spiral stair in the interior—is forty-three.
[139] A column of gilt bronze, erected under Augustus and regarded as the point of convergence of all the great roads radiating from the city. On it were engraved the names of the principal cities of the Empire and their distances from the gates of Rome.
[140] A main street leading from the Forum.

the] elephant eating grass[?]; wards—34; crossroad shrines—34; block captains—48; commissioners—2; blocks of tenements—3,480; private houses—130; storehouses—18; baths—86; fountains—120; bakeries—20; area—14,067 feet.

District IX, Circus Flaminius, contains:

Six stables of the four circus factions; Portico of Philip; the Minucian porticoes—the old one and the one for the grain dole; Grotto of Balbus; three theaters: Balbus', which has 11,510 *loca*, Pompey's, with 17,580 *loca*, Marcellus', with 20,000 *loca*; Odeum,[141] with 10,600 *loca*; Stadium, with 30,088 *loca*; Campus Martius; Trigarium;[142] Kneeling Storks [statue]; Pantheon; Basilicas of Neptune, of Matidia, of Marcianus; Temple of Antoninus and the spiral column 175½ feet high, with 203 steps and 56 windows inside;[143] Baths of Alexander and of Agrippa; Portico of the Argonauts and Meleager; [Temple of] Isis and Serapis; . . . [Temple of the] Deified Emperors; Felicles tenement;[144] wards—35; crossroad shrines—35; block captains—48; commissioners—2; blocks of tenements—2,777; private houses—140; storehouses—25; baths—63; fountains—120; bakeries—20; area—32,500 feet.

[Summary]

Libraries—28; obelisks—6: two in the Circus Maximus (the smaller 87½ feet high, the taller 122½), one on the Vatican (75 feet high), one in the Campus Martius (72½ feet high), two at the Mausoleum of Augustus (each 42½ feet high);[145] bridges—8 . . . ; hills—7 . . . ; fields—8 . . . ; forums—11 . . . ; basilicas—10 . . . ; baths—11[146] . . . ; aqueducts—19 . . . ; roads—29. . . .

---

[141] For musical performances.

[142] An open space for exercising horses.

[143] The temple of Marcus Aurelius and the column were erected to commemorate his victories over the Marcomannians and Sarmatians (see Chapter II, Note 87). The true height of the column is 106½ English feet (= c.116 Roman feet), the number of steps only 200.

[144] Famous for its height.

[145] More complete descriptions of these obelisks are given by Pliny (*Natural History* XXXVI. xiv–xv), who gives slightly different heights for some of them.

[146] Only the great public baths are included in this figure.

CHAPTER VII

THE ROMAN ARMY

142. *Disposition of the Armed Forces*

The "Roman Peace," which the Principate held forth as its gift to the peoples of the Empire, was assured by strong military concentrations guarding the frontiers and by smaller garrisons policing the interior. Throughout the Principate, this professional army remained, as established by Augustus, a force consisting of about thirty legions of Roman citizens (c.150,000 men) complemented by an equal number of conscripted provincial auxiliaries. Under the conditions of the first two centuries the army tended to become provincialized and transformed into a sedentary garrison army. These tendencies were formalized by Hadrian, who began the practice of recruiting the frontier garrisons from the provinces in which they were stationed, and by Septimius Severus, who completed this evolution by barbarizing and democratizing the Roman armies. The strategic disposition of the armed forces of the Empire underwent such occasional modifications as were necessitated by the annexation of additional provinces on the periphery and by increasing pressures on the northern and eastern frontiers.

Tacitus *Annals* IV. iv. 4–v. 6

[The Emperor Tiberius in a speech stated that] the number of army volunteers was inadequate,[1] and that even if there were a sufficient number, they did not conduct themselves with the traditional bravery and discipline, as it was principally the needy and the vagrants who adopted military service of their own choice. He rapidly reviewed the number of the legions and the provinces they had to protect. I think that I ought to do the same here, showing what forces Rome then had under arms, what client kings there were, and how much smaller our empire was.

Italy was guarded on both seas by two fleets, [based] at Misenum and at Ravenna; the nearby coast of Gaul was protected by warships captured in the victory at Actium and sent by Augustus, powerfully manned, to the town of Forum Julium.[2] But our chief strength was along the Rhine, serving as a defense against Germans and Gauls alike; this force numbered eight legions. The Spanish provinces, recently subjugated,[3] were held by three legions. Mauretania had been received by

---

[1] Voluntary enlistments usually sufficed to keep the military forces at maximum strength. It has been estimated that the legions required about 7,000 recruits annually.

[2] Present-day Fréjus, near Marseilles.

[3] Though Spain was annexed in the third century B.C., some parts of the Iberian

King Juba as a gift of the Roman people; the rest of Africa was garrisoned by two legions, and Egypt by the same number. Next, from the borders of Syria to the Euphrates river, all the territory that is encompassed in this vast sweep was controlled by four legions, flanked by the Iberian, Albanian, and other kings, who are protected by our greatness against foreign powers. Thrace was held by Rhoemetalces and the children of Cotys; the bank of the Danube, by two legions in Pannonia and two in Moesia. The same number were stationed in Dalmatia, where, because of the situation of the region, they served as a rear guard for the Danubian legions and could be summoned from a short distance should Italy suddenly require aid. But the capital was garrisoned by its own special soldiery, three urban and nine Praetorian cohorts, levied for the most part in Etruria and Umbria, or ancient Latium and the old Roman colonies. There were besides, in appropriate places in the provinces, allied fleets, cavalry forces, and auxiliary cohorts, whose strength was about the same [as that of the legions]. But it is difficult to recount them in detail since they moved from place to place as circumstances required, and they were sometimes increased in number and sometimes decreased.

THE ROSTER OF THE LEGIONS

This inscription, dating probably from the reign of Antoninus Pius, lists the legions in territorial order proceeding clockwise from Britain along the frontiers. It is known that at that time three of the legions were in Britain, four along the Rhine, eleven on the Danube, nine in the East, one each in Egypt, Numidia, and Spain, and the remainder directly north of Italy.

CIL, Vol. VI, No. 3,492 (= Dessau, No. 2,288)

Names of the Legions

II Augusta	I Parthica
VI Victrix	II Adjutrix
XX Victrix	IV Flavia
VIII Augusta	VI Claudia
XXXII Primigenia	I Italica
I Minervia	V Macedonica
XXX Ulpia	XI Claudia
I Adjutrix	XIII Gemina
X Gemina	XII Fulminata
XIV Gemina	XV Apollinaris

peninsula were not completely subjected to Roman rule until the campaigns of Agrippa in 19 B.C.

III Gallica	II Trajana
II Parthica	III Augusta
IV Scythica	VII Gemina
XVI Flavia	II Italica
VI Ferrata	III Italica
X Fretensis	III Parthica
III Cyrenaica	

143. *The Imperial Army*

Josephus *The Jewish War* III. v. 71–107
Adapted from LCL

If one goes on to study the organization of their army as a whole,[4]
it will be seen that this vast empire of theirs has come to them as the prize
of valor, and not as a gift of fortune. For they do not wait for the outbreak of war, nor do they sit with folded hands in peacetime only to
put them in motion in the hour of need. On the contrary, as though they
had been born with weapons in hand, they never have a truce from training, never wait for the emergencies to arise. Moreover, their peacetime
maneuvers are no less strenuous than veritable warfare; each soldier daily
throws all his energy into his drill, as though he were in action. Hence
that perfect ease with which they sustain the shock of battle. . . .

The Romans never lay themselves open to a surprise attack; for,
whatever hostile territory they may invade, they engage in no battle
until they have fortified their camp. [The traditional Roman encampment arrangements are next described in detail.] [5] Thus an improvised
city, as it were, springs up, with its market place, its artisan quarter, its
judgment seats, where officers [6] adjudicate any differences which may
arise. The outer wall and all the installations within are completed more
quickly than thought, so numerous and skilled are the workmen. . . .

Once entrenched, the soldiers take up their quarters in their tents
by companies, quietly and in good order. All their fatigue duties are
performed with the same discipline, the same regard for security: the
procuring of wood, of food supplies, and water, as required—each company having its allotted task. The hour for supper and breakfast is not
left to individual discretion; all take their meals together. The hours for
sleep, sentinel duty, and rising are announced by the sound of trumpets;

[4] On this subject cf. Polybius' description of the Roman army in the second century B.C. (Vol. I, § 164).
[5] For the structure of a Roman camp, see Vol. I, pp. 435–37.
[6] It is not clear which officers are meant.

nothing is done without a word of command. At daybreak the rank and file report to their respective centurions, the centurions go to salute the tribunes, the tribunes with all the officers then wait on the commander-in-chief, and he gives them according to custom the watchword and other orders to be communicated to the lower ranks. The same precision is maintained on the battlefield; the troops wheel smartly round in the requisite direction, and, whether advancing to the attack or retreating, all move as a unit.

When the camp is to be broken up, the trumpet sounds a first call; at that none remain idle; instantly, at this signal, they strike the tents and make all ready for departure. The trumpets sound a second call to prepare the march; at once they pile their baggage on the mules and other beasts of burden, and stand ready to start. . . . They then set fire to the encampment, both because they can easily construct another . . . and to prevent the enemy from ever making use of it. A third time the trumpets give a similar signal for departure, to hasten the movements of stragglers, whatever the reason for their delay, and to ensure that none is out of his place in the ranks. Then the herald, standing on the right of the commander, inquires in their native tongue whether they are ready for war. Three times they loudly and lustily shout in reply, "We are ready," some even anticipating the question; and worked up to a kind of martial frenzy, they raise their right arms in the air along with the shout. . . .

The infantry are armed with cuirasses and helmets and carry a sword on either side; that on the left is far the longer of the two, the dagger on the right being no longer than a span. The picked infantry, forming the general's guard, carry a spear and round shield, the regiments of the line a javelin and oblong shield; the equipment of the latter includes, further, a saw, a basket, a pick, and an axe, not to mention a strap, a bill-hook, a chain, and three days' rations, so that an infantry man is almost as heavily laden as a pack mule.

The cavalry carry a large sword on their right side, a long pike in the hand, a buckler resting obliquely on the horse's flank, and in a quiver slung beside them three or more darts with broad points and as long as spears; their helmets and cuirasses are the same as those worn by all the infantry. The select cavalry, forming the general's escort, are armed in precisely the same manner as the ordinary troopers. The legion which is to lead the column is always selected by lot. . . .

By their military exercises the Romans instill into their soldiers fortitude not only of body but also of soul; fear, too, plays its part in their training. For they have laws which punish with death not merely desertion but even a slight neglect of duty; and their generals are held in even greater awe than the laws. For the high honors with which they reward the brave prevent the offenders whom they punish from regarding themselves as treated cruelly.

This perfect discipline with regard to their generals makes the army an ornament of peacetime, and in battle welds the whole into a single body; so compact are their ranks, so alert their movements in wheeling, so quick their ears for orders, their eyes for signals, their hands for tasks. Prompt as they consequently ever are in action, none are slower than they in succumbing to suffering, and never have they been known in any predicament to be beaten by numbers, by ruses, by difficulties of terrain, or even by fortune; for victory is more certain for them than fortune. When counsel thus precedes active operation, where the leaders' plan of campaign is followed up by so efficient an army, no wonder that the Empire has extended its boundaries on the east to the Euphrates, on the west to the Ocean, on the south to the most fertile tracts of Africa, and on the north to the Danube and the Rhine.

THE ARMY ON THE MARCH

Josephus The Jewish War *III. VI. 115-126*
Adapted from LCL

But Vespasian, impatient to invade Galilee himself, now set out from Ptolemais, after drawing up his army for the march in the customary Roman order. The auxiliary light-armed troops and archers were sent in advance, to repel any sudden incursions of the enemy and to explore suspected woodland suited for the concealment of ambushes. Next came a contingent of heavy-armed Roman soldiers, infantry and cavalry. They were followed by a detachment composed of ten men from each century, carrying their own equipment and the instruments for marking out the camp; after these came the road makers to straighten the curves on the road, to level the rough places and to cut down obstructing woods, in order to spare the army the fatigues of a toilsome march. Behind these Vespasian posted his personal baggage and that of his legates, with a strong escort of cavalry to protect them. He himself rode behind with the pick of the infantry and cavalry and his guard of lancers. Then came the cavalry units of the legions; for to each legion are attached 120 horse. These were followed by the mules carrying the siege towers and the other machines. Then came the legates, the prefects of the cohorts, and the tribunes, with an escort of picked troops. Next the standards surrounding the eagle, which in the Roman army precedes every legion. . . . These sacred emblems were followed by the trumpeters, and behind them came the solid column, marching six

abreast. A centurion, according to custom, accompanied them to superintend the order of the ranks. Behind the infantry the servants attached
to each legion followed in a body, conducting the mules and other
beasts of burden which carried the soldiers' baggage. At the end of the
column came the crowd of mercenaries, and last of all for security a
rearguard composed of light and heavy infantry and a considerable body
of cavalry.

144. *Recruitment*

Oxyrhynchus Papyrus No. 39 (= Wilcken, No. 456); A.D. 52

Copy of release. Year 12 of the Emperor Tiberius CLAUDIUS Caesar
Augustus Germanicus, Pharmuthi 29, Augustan.[7] Released by Gnaeus
Vergilius Capito, prefect of both [Upper and Lower Egypt]: Trypho
son of Dionysius, weaver from the metropolis of Oxyrhynchus, suffering from cataract impairing vision. Examined and certified in Alexandria.

Chronique d'Egypte, XXIV (1949), 296–301; A.D. 92

Titus Flavius Longus, subaltern of Legion III Cyrenaica, of the century of Arellius[?], attested . . . and declared on oath[?] . . . that he
was freeborn and a Roman citizen, and had the right to serve in a legion.
Hereupon his guarantors[?] . . . declared on oath by Jupiter Best and
Greatest and by the *genius* [8] of the Emperor Caesar DOMITIAN Augustus
Germanicus . . . that the said Titus Flavius Longus was freeborn and
a Roman citizen, and had the right to serve in a legion.

Done in the Augustan camp in the winter quarters of Legion III.
[Month and day], year 17 of the Emperor Caesar DOMITIAN Augustus
Germanicus, consulship of Quintus Volusius Saturninus and Lucius
Venuleius Montanus Apronianus.

Pliny *Letters* Book x, Nos. 29–30

[Pliny to the Emperor Trajan]

Sempronius Caelianus, an outstanding young man, sent two slaves
to me who were discovered among the recruits. I have deferred punishing them so as to consult you, the founder and strengthener of military
discipline, on the proper penalty. For I am especially in doubt about
this, because though they have already taken the oath, yet they have
not yet been assigned to the ranks. I beg you therefore, my lord, to write
me what course I should follow, especially since precedent is involved.

[7] Cf. Chapter V, Note 143.   [8] Cf. § 14.

[Trajan to Pliny]

Sempronius Caelianus acted in accordance with my instructions in sending to you these persons, concerning whom an investigation will be necessary to determine whether they seem deserving of capital punishment. It is material whether they enlisted voluntarily, or were levied, or offered as proxies. If they were levied, the examination was at fault; if they were offered as proxies, the guilt lies with those who offered them; but if they themselves, although they were fully aware of their status, enlisted, then they are the ones to be punished. It does not make much difference that they have not yet been assigned to the ranks; for on the very day on which they were approved they were required to give a true statement of their birth status.

Oxyrhynchus Papyrus No. 1,022 (= Select Papyri, No. 421); A.D. 103

Gaius Minucius Italus [prefect of Egypt] to his Celsianus, greeting. Give instructions that the six recruits approved by me for the cohort you command be included in the rolls as of February 19. I append their names and descriptions to this letter. Farewell, dearest brother.

Gaius Veturius Gemellus, aged 21, without distinguishing mark
Gaius Longinus Priscus, aged 22, scar on left eyebrow
Gaius Julius Maximus, aged 25, without distinguishing mark
. . . Lucius Secundus, aged 20, without distinguishing mark
Gaius Julius Saturninus, aged 23, scar on left hand
Marcus Antonius Valens, aged 22, scar on right side of forehead

[Docket] Received February 24, year 6 of our Emperor Trajan, through Priscus, orderly. I, Avidius Arrianus, adjutant of the Third Cohort of Ituraeans,[9] hereby declare that the original letter is in the archives of the cohort.

Berlin Papyrus No. 423 (= Select Papyri, No. 112); second century
Adapted from LCL

Apio to Epimachus, his father and lord, very many greetings. Before all else I pray for your health and that you may always be well and prosperous, together with my sister and her daughter and my brother. I thank the lord Serapis that when I was in danger at sea he straightway saved me. On arriving at Misenum I received from Caesar three gold pieces for traveling expenses. And it is well with me. Now I ask you, my lord and father, write me a letter, telling me first of your welfare, secondly of my brother's and sister's, and enabling me thirdly to make

[9] See Note 28.

obeisance before your handwriting, because you educated me well and I hope thereby to have quick advancement, the gods willing. Give many salutations to Capito and my brother and sister and Serenilla and my friends. I have sent you by Euctemo a portrait of myself. My name is now Antonius Maximus, my century the Athenonica. I pray for your health.

[P.S.] Serenus son of Agathodaemo salutes you, as does . . . and Turbo son of Gallonius. . . .

[Address, on back] To Philadelphia, to Epimachus from Apio his son.

[Additional notation] Deliver at [the camp of] the First Cohort of Apamenians to Julianus, vice-secretary, this letter from Apio to be forwarded to his father Epimachus.

145. *Military Training*

Vegetius [10] *Military Science* I. i, ix, x, xix, xxvii; II. xxiii, xxv

In every battle victory is granted not by mere numbers and innate courage but by skill and training. For we see that the Roman people owed the conquest of the world to no other cause than military training, discipline in their camps, and practice in warfare. What chance would the small number of Romans have had against the multitude of Gauls? How could they have ventured, with their small stature, against the tall Germans? It is clear that the Spaniards excelled our men not only in numbers but also in physical strength. We have always been inferior to the Africans in the use of deception and in wealth. And no one doubts that we were surpassed by the Greeks in skills and intelligence. But against all these we prevailed by skillful selection of recruits, by teaching, as I have said, the principles of war, by hardening them in daily exercise, by acquainting them beforehand through field maneuvers with everything that can happen in the line of march and in battles, and by severe punishment for indolence. For knowledge of military science nourishes boldness in combat. No one fears to do what he is confident he has learned well. . . .

At the very beginning of their training, recruits should be taught

[10] Flavius Vegetius Renatus, a writer of the fourth to fifth centuries A.D. His manual on military affairs, in four books, based on secondary sources, describes the Roman military establishment of earlier centuries. This work has exerted great influence in modern times: from the Renaissance on, military men have regarded it as the classic handbook on military organization and have trained their armies according to its precepts.

the military step. For there is nothing to be maintained more, on the march and in the line, than the keeping of their ranks by all the soldiers. This cannot be attained in any other way than by learning through training to march quickly and together. For a separated and disorderly army exposes itself to the gravest danger at the hands of the enemy. Now, twenty miles with the military step should be done in five hours, in the summer only; with the full step, which is quicker, twenty-four miles should be completed in the same number of hours. . . .

The soldier is to be trained in leaping also, to enable him to leap across ditches or overcome some impeding height, so that when difficulties of this nature arise he can cross without effort. Moreover, in actual combat the soldier, advancing with running and leaping, dulls the eyesight of his adversary, strikes terror into his mind, and inflicts a blow before the latter makes definite preparations to avoid it or resist. . . .

Every recruit, without exception, should in the summer months learn to swim; for it is not always possible to cross rivers on bridges, but a retreating and pursuing army is frequently compelled to swim. Sudden rains or snowfalls often cause torrents to overflow their banks, and risk is increased by ignorance not only of the enemy but of water. The ancient Romans, therefore, perfected in every branch of military science by so many wars and perpetual dangers, chose the Field of Mars next to the Tiber in which the youth might wash off the sweat and dust after military exercise, and by swimming gain relaxation from their weariness in marching. It is opportune for not only the infantry but also the cavalry, the horses, and the sutlers, whom they call "helmeters," to be trained to swim, lest they be inexperienced when necessity arises and faces them. . . .

Recruits should be obliged frequently to carry burdens weighing up to sixty pounds, and to march with the military step. For on arduous expeditions they find themselves under the necessity of carrying their provisions as well as their arms. . . .

It was a survival of ancient custom, confirmed by enactments of the deified Augustus and Hadrian, to exercise both cavalry and infantry three times a month by marches. . . . The infantry was instructed to march ten miles with the military step, wearing armor and equipped with all weapons, and return to camp; and to take part of the journey at the quicker pace. The cavalry, likewise, separated in squadrons and similarly armed, performed the same march, practicing cavalry exercises, sometimes pursuing, sometimes retreating, and then returning to the attack. They did not make these marches in plains; rather, both branches were compelled to ascend and descend sloping and steep places. . . .

The younger soldiers and recruits used to be drilled morning and afternoon in every type of weapon; the older and experienced ones were drilled in weapons once a day. . . . For length of service or age alone does not bestow the science of war, but after any number of years of service an undisciplined soldier is always a recruit. . . . It is very desirable to drill them also at the post with wooden stakes, as they learn to attack the sides or feet or head both with the point and the edge [of the sword]. They should be accustomed also to leap and strike blows at the same time, to rise up with a bound and sink down again below the shield, now eagerly rushing forward with a leap, now leaping back to the rear. They must also practice throwing their javelins at the posts from a distance in order to increase their skill in aiming and the strength of the arm.

The archers and slingers set up twigs as marks, that is, bundles of shoots or straw, at a distance of 600 feet, and aim to hit the mark with arrows or stones hurled from the sling. . . . The slingers should be trained to whirl the sling only once about the head when letting loose a stone. But all soldiers used to be trained to throw stones of a pound weight with the bare hand. . . .

In the winter time, porticoes for the cavalry were covered with tiles or shingles, or if these were lacking, with reeds, rushes, or straw; and there were halls like basilicas for the infantry, in which the army during stormy or windy weather, when the sky was disturbed, were trained in arms under cover. But even on winter days, if the snow or rain stopped, they were obliged to drill in the field, lest the interrupted training weaken the spirit and bodies of the soldiers. They should very frequently cut trees, carry burdens, leap over ditches, swim in the sea or in rivers, march in the full step, and even run with their armor and baggage, so that, inured to daily labor in peace, they may not find this difficult in war. . . .

The legion in practice is victorious because of the number of soldiers and the type of machines. First of all, it is equipped with hurling machines which no cuirass, no shield can withstand. For the practice is to have a ballista mounted on a carriage for each century, to each of which are assigned mules and a detail of eleven men for loading and firing. The larger these are, the farther and more powerfully do they hurl missiles. Not only do they defend the camps, but they are placed in the field in the rear of the heavy-armed infantry. Before their fire power neither enemy cavalrymen with cuirasses nor infantry men with shields can hold their ground. It is customary to have fifty-five such mounted ballistas in each legion. Likewise, there are ten *onagri*,[11] one for each cohort; they are drawn ready-armed on carriages by oxen, so that in case of an

---

[11] Literally, "wild asses"; they were catapults for discharging stones.

enemy attack on the rampart the camp can be defended with arrows and stones.

The legion also carries with it small boats, each hollowed out of a single piece of timber, with very long cables and sometimes iron chains. When these "single plankers," as they are called, are joined together and covered with boards, rivers which cannot be forded are crossed without bridges by the infantry and cavalry without danger. The legion is provided with grappling hooks, called "wolves," and with iron scythes fixed to the ends of long poles; likewise mattocks, hoes, spades, shovels, buckets, and baskets to carry earth in ditch-digging operations; also hatchets, axes, and saws for hewing and sawing timber. Besides these, it has workmen equipped with all tools, who make various kinds of wooden sheds, battering rams, and movable towers for besieging cities. To avoid the enumeration of more of these, I shall add that the legion ought to carry with it everywhere everything which is believed necessary for every kind of warfare, so that whenever it pitches its camp it forms an armed city.[12]

146. *Military Operations*

The strategy and tactics of the imperial army remained for two centuries based on the principles developed by the great generals of the last century of the Republic, familiar to readers of Caesar's *Gallic War* and *Civil War*. During the third century, with the growing provincialization and barbarization of the army and the importance of a mobile army for wars of movement, native tactics came to the fore, and by the time of Constantine the famous legionary tactics, encampment, and weapons had become virtually obsolete (cf. introduction to § 131).

THE TESTUDO

Dio Cassius *Roman History* XLIX. XXX
From LCL

This *testudo* ("tortoise shell") and the way in which it is formed are as follows. The baggage animals, the light-armed troops, and the cav-

---

[12] In II. xi Vegetius gives the following details about the corps of engineers: "The legion has, moreover, carpenters, masons, wagon makers, smiths, painters, and other artisans on hand for the construction of the barracks and the winter quarters, for making or repairing damaged machines, wooden towers, and other equipment with which cities of the enemy are besieged or our own defended, also arms, carriages, and various kinds of shooting instruments. They had also workshops for shields, cuirasses, and bows, in which arrows, missiles, nets, and all types of weapons were made. For it was their special concern that whatever seemed necessary for an army should never be lacking in camp. . . . The officer in charge of these was the prefect of the workmen."

alry are placed in the center of the army. The heavy-armed troops who use the oblong, curved, and cylindrical shields are drawn up around the outside, making a rectangular figure; and, facing outward and holding their arms at the ready, they enclose the rest. The others, who have flat shields, form a compact body in the center and raise their shields over their own heads and the heads of all the others, so that nothing but shields can be seen in every part of the phalanx alike, and all the men by the density of the formation are under shelter from missiles. Indeed, it is so marvelously strong that men can walk upon it, and whenever they come to a narrow ravine, even horses and vehicles can be driven over it. Such is the plan of this formation, and for this reason it has received the name *testudo*, with reference both to its strength and to the excellent shelter it affords. They use it in two ways: either they approach some fort to assault it, often even enabling men to scale the very walls, or sometimes, when they are surrounded by archers, they all crouch together—even the horses being taught to kneel or lie down—and thereby cause the foe to think that they are exhausted; then, when the enemy draws near, they suddenly rise and throw him into consternation.[13]

A BRIDGE ON PILES

Caesar *Gallic War* iv. xvii. 1–xviii. 1

Caesar . . . had resolved to cross the Rhine. But to cross by boat he neither deemed to be sufficiently safe nor considered in keeping with his own prestige or that of the Roman people. Therefore, although he was faced with the greatest difficulty in building a bridge on account of the breadth, the swift current, and the depth of the river, he nevertheless considered that he should make the attempt, and that otherwise his army ought not to be brought across. Accordingly, he adopted the following plan for his bridge. He joined together sets of two piles placed two feet apart, each pile a foot and a half thick, sharpened a little at the lower end and proportioned in length to the depth of the river. By mechanical means he sank these in the river and fixed them at the bottom; and with pile drivers he drove them in, not quite perpendicularly, like stakes, but leaning forward and sloping with the river current. Then he likewise placed sets of two piles forty feet downstream facing these, fastened together in the same manner but directed against the force and current of the river. The sets in these two rows were kept firmly apart from each other by beams two feet thick (exactly the distance between their piles) laid in at the upper ends with a brace on either side of each set of piles;

---

[13] The effectiveness of this formation impressed all the peoples with whom the Romans fought in combat. Knowledge of it penetrated, it seems, indirectly to China: cf. H. H. Dubs, *American Journal of Philology*, LXII (1941), 322–30.

and because these were kept apart and fastened back on opposite sides, the firmness of the structure was so great and the character of the structure such that the greater the force of the water that dashed against the bridge, the closer were its parts held fastened together. The beams were joined together by timbers laid horizontally across them, and these were then covered over with long poles and wickerwork. Even so, piles were driven into the water obliquely on the downstream side of the bridge, and these, joined to every part of the structure, were applied to serve as buttresses to help sustain the force of the river; other piles were placed a short distance upstream, so that if trunks of trees or vessels were floated down the river by the barbarians for the purpose of destroying the structure, the force of such objects might be lessened by these defenses and might not injure the bridge.

Within ten days after the timber began to be collected the whole structure was completed and the army led across.

A PONTOON BRIDGE

Dio Cassius *Roman History* LXXI. iii. 1
Adapted from LCL

River channels are bridged by the Romans with very great ease, since the soldiers are always practicing this operation, like any other military exercise, on the Danube, the Rhine, and the Euphrates. Now the method, which is not familiar to everybody, is as follows. The boats by means of which the river is to be bridged are flat bottomed, and these are anchored a little way upstream from the spot where the bridge is to be constructed. When the signal is given, they first let one ship drift downstream close to the bank that they are holding; and when it has come opposite to the spot that is to be bridged, they throw into the stream a wicker basket filled with stones and fastened by a cable, which serves as an anchor. Made fast in this way, the ship remains in position near the bank, and by means of plank and clamps, which the vessel carries in large quantity, a floor is at once laid to the landing place. Then they send down another ship at a little distance from the first, and another one beyond that, until they have extended the bridge to the opposite bank. The ship that is nearest the enemy's bank carries towers upon it and a gate and archers and catapults.

THE SIEGE

"There is nothing of which barbarians are so ignorant," writes Tacitus (*Annals* XII. xlv. 4), "as military engines and skill in siege operations, while that is a branch of military science in which we are especially skilled." Construction details and measurements of the principal siege mechanisms and of machines for defense against sieges (many of Greek origin) are given in Vitruvius *Architecture* x. xiii–xvi. Among other features of Roman siege operations was the use of carrier birds to transmit messages across siege lines (Frontinus *Strategems* III. xiii. 8). A typical Roman siege operation, described below, is the famous investment and storming of Marseilles by Caesar's army in 49 B.C.

Caesar *Civil War* II. i–ii, viii–xi (abridged)
In part adapted from LCL

Gaius Trebonius, Caesar's lieutenant, who had been left for the siege of Marseilles, began to build a mound, breaching huts, and towers near the city. . . . To complete these works Trebonius called for a great number of draught animals and men from the entire province; he ordered twigs and lumber to be gathered. When these were procured, he constructed a mound eighty feet high. But there was so much war equipment of all kinds in the town from older times, and such a quantity of hurling engines, that none of the huts woven with twigs could stand up against their power. For poles twelve feet long with pointed ends, shot from enormous ballistas, pierced four layers of wickerwork and lodged in the earth. Consequently, galleries were covered over by joining one-foot-thick beams, and thereby the mound was carried forward by a hand-to-hand operation. In advance of this was a sixty-foot shed for leveling the area, constructed likewise of very strong beams and enveloped in everything that could protect it against the firebrands and stones being hurled. But the size of the works, the height of the wall and towers, and the mass of engines slowed up the whole operation. . . .

In consequence of the frequent sorties of the enemy, the legionaries who were conducting operations on the right noticed that they could provide a great protection to themselves if they constructed there a tower of brick hard by the wall, to serve as a stronghold and a place of retreat. This they constructed at first of low elevation and small size to meet sudden sallies. To this they used to retire; from this shelter they fought if a strong assault pressed them; from this they issued forth to repel and pursue the foe. Its dimensions were thirty feet each way, and the thickness of the walls was five feet. But afterwards, as experience is the guide in all human conduct, by applying their wits they discovered that this tower could be of greater service to them if it were raised in height. This was accomplished in the following manner.

[Under complete protection, the soldiers laboriously raised the tower to a height of six stories.]

When they were sure that from the tower they could protect all the surrounding works, they set about making out of timber two feet square a shed sixty feet long, to be carried from the brick tower to the enemy's tower and wall. . . . They completed this construction, entirely protected by breaching huts, up to the tower itself, and suddenly, when the enemy was off guard, they put rollers under it . . . and pushed it forward to the enemy's tower, so as to join it onto that structure.

Dismayed at this sudden calamity, the townsmen brought forward with cranes the largest possible stones, and rolled them headlong from the wall onto the shed. The strength of the timber bore the blow, and everything that fell on it slipped off owing to the sloping roof of the shed. Observing this, they changed their plan and set on fire barrels filled with pine wood and pitch, and rolled them down from the wall onto the shed. When, however, they had rolled onto it they slipped off and, having fallen from the tiles, were removed from the work with poles and forks. Meanwhile some soldiers under the shed pried out with crowbars the lowest stones of the enemy's tower which served to hold the foundations together. The shed was defended by our men on the brick tower with missiles and catapults; the enemy were dislodged from their wall and towers; and no easy opportunity of defending their wall was allowed them. When now a number of stones had been withdrawn from the tower next to the shed, a part of it suddenly collapsed and fell. The rest was beginning to follow it and fall forward, when the enemy, terrified at [the prospect of] the sacking of their city, flung themselves, without their arms and wearing fillets, in a mass outside the gate and stretched out their hands as suppliants to the lieutenants and the army.

147. *Mutiny in the Ranks*

"The principal glory and the mainstay of the Roman Empire, maintained with salutary perseverance sound and unimpaired to the present time, is the unrelaxing bond of military discipline, in the embrace and protection of which reposes our serene and tranquil state of blessed peace," wrote Valerius Maximus (*Memorable Deeds and Sayings* II. vii. Introd.). Nevertheless, the conditions of the *Pax Romana* tended to relax the traditional rigors of Roman military discipline (cf. § 150), and the history of the Principate was marked by a number of serious military mutinies. The first of these, a harbinger of the evolution that was ultimately to raise the military to the ruling class in the third century (see §§111–112), was the rebellion of the legions in Pannonia and on the Rhine that greeted the news of the death of Augustus in A.D. 14.

Tacitus *Annals* 1. xvii, xxxi, xxxv

[A leader of the mutineers in Pannonia harangues the soldiers.]

Why should they obey like slaves a few centurions and fewer tribunes? When would they dare to claim redress if they did not approach with petitions or weapons the new and still unstable emperor? Mistakes enough had been made in all the years by inaction, when old men, and many who had lost limbs from wounds, were serving thirty and forty years. Even after discharge their service was not over; but in the reserve they endured the same labors under another name.[14] And suppose that a man survived this multitude of hazards: he was dragged again to the ends of the earth to receive under the name of a "farm" some swampy morass or a barren mountain side. In fact, military service itself was burdensome and profitless. Ten *asses* a day was the value set on body and soul; with that they had to buy clothes, weapons and tents, bribe the cruel centurion, and purchase exemptions from duties. But lashings and wounds, hard winters and severe summers, terrible war or barren peace —these, by heaven, were everlasting. There would be no relief until military service was entered under precise regulations—the pay to be a *denarius* a day, the sixteenth year to end the term of service, no further detention in the reserve to be required, but the bonus to be paid in cash right in the camp. Did the Praetorian cohorts, who received two *denarii* a day—and who were restored to their homes after sixteen years—face more dangers? They did not disparage sentinel duty at Rome; still, they were among savage clans, with the enemy visible from their very tents. . . .

On almost the same days and for the same reasons the legions of Germany mutinied, with more violence because of their greater numbers and with high hopes that Germanicus Caesar would be unable to endure the sovereignty of [Tiberius] and would offer himself to the legions, whose force could carry everything before it. There were two armies along the bank of the Rhine. The upper army was under the legate Gaius Silius, and Aulus Caecina was in charge of the lower one. The supreme command was in the hands of Germanicus, then occupied with taking the census of the Gallic provinces. . . . The soldiery of the lower army flared up in a frenzy, beginning with the twenty-first and fifth legions. Then the first and twentieth legions also were dragged into it; for they were quartered in the same summer camp in the territory of the Ubians, idle or on light duties. Thus, when they heard of the death of Augustus, the multitude of city-bred men from the recent levy held at Rome, ac-

[14] Veterans remained in camp in this period for five additional years as a privileged élite corps, technically exempt from onerous camp duties. Cf. also p. 29.

customed to license, chafing at hardships, filled the simple minds of the rest [with talk such as this]: The time had come for veterans to demand timely discharge, for the younger men to ask for higher pay, and for all to obtain a limit to their suffering and to take vengeance for the cruelty of the centurions. . . . The Roman state lay in their hands; by their victories the state was extended. . . .

When Germanicus [in a speech to the army] touched on the sedition, asking where their military restraint was, where their famous former discipline, where they had driven the tribunes, where the centurions, all bared their bodies, complaining of the scars from wounds and marks of lashes. Next, in a confusion of voices they complained of the fees for exemption from duties, the smallness of the pay, the strenuousness of the work, mentioning specifically the rampart, trenches, the gathering of fodder, timber, and firewood, and the other duties which were imposed by necessity or devised to prevent idleness in camp. The fiercest outcry arose from the veterans, who, enumerating their thirty or more years of service, begged him to give relief to weary men and not leave them to die in the same labors, but to fix a limit for such trying service and not abandon them to a poverty-stricken retirement. There were some also who demanded of him the money bequeathed by the deified Augustus. They suggested favorable omens for Germanicus—if he wished the imperial power, they showed that they were ready. Then indeed, as if defiled by their crime, he leaped straight from the tribunal. They opposed his withdrawal with their weapons and threatened him unless he returned. But, shouting that he would rather die than break his oath, he drew the sword from his side, raised it and would have plunged it into his side had not those nearby seized his arm and forceably restrained it. . . . But a soldier by the name of Calusidius drew his own sword and offered it to him, adding that it was sharper.

148. *Hadrian's Tour of Inspection*

After abandoning most of Trajan's conquests because the economic resources and manpower of the Empire could not support the strain of further territorial expansion, Hadrian reconstituted the Roman military establishment as a garrison army. For about half of his twenty-one-year reign he toured the provinces of the Empire, principally to inspect its military forces and installations. His efforts were concentrated on strengthening frontier fortifications and reforming military discipline to raise it to the highest level of efficiency.

Dio Cassius *Roman History* LXIX. ix. 1–5
From LCL

Hadrian traveled through one province after another, visiting the various regions and cities and inspecting all the garrisons and forts. Some of these he removed to more desirable places, some he abolished, and he also established new ones. He personally viewed and investigated absolutely everything, not merely the usual installations of the camps, such as weapons, engines, trenches, ramparts, and palisades, but also the private affairs of everyone, both of the men serving in the ranks and of the officers themselves—their lives, their quarters and their habits—and he reformed and corrected in many cases practices and arrangements for living that had become too luxurious. He drilled the men for every kind of battle, honoring some and reproving others, and he taught them all what should be done. And in order that they should be benefited by observing him, he everywhere led a rigorous life and either walked or rode on horseback on all occasions, never once at this period setting foot in either a chariot or a four-wheeled vehicle. He covered his head neither in hot weather nor in cold, but alike amid German snows and under scorching Egyptian suns he went about with his head bare. In short, both by his example and by his precepts he so trained and disciplined the whole military force throughout the entire Empire that even today the regulations then introduced by him are the code of the army. This best explains why he lived for the most part at peace with foreign nations; for as they saw his state of preparation and were themselves not only free from [Roman] aggression but received money besides,[15] they made no uprising.

HADRIAN REVIEWS THE GARRISON OF AFRICA

In A.D. 128 Hadrian inspected the frontier defenses of North Africa and reviewed the garrison army of the province of Numidia, the Legion III Augusta and its auxiliary contingents, at its headquarters at Lambaesis (modern Lambèse, the site of the best-preserved Roman fortified camp). To commemorate the emperor's review, the garrison set up a column on the base of which were inscribed excerpts from his five addresses to the troops following maneuvers.

CIL, Vol. VIII, Nos. 2,532 and 18,042 (= Dessau, Nos. 2,487
and, 9,133–35)

The Emperor Caesar Trajanus HADRIAN Augustus addressed his Legion III Augusta after inspecting their exercises, as recorded below, in the consulship of Torquatus (for the second time) and of Libo, July 1.

[15] For cash subsidies paid to foreign peoples, see §§ 26, 116.

To the Chief Centurions

. . . [Your commander] himself has on your behalf told me in detail the circumstances which should excuse you in my eyes, to wit: that one cohort is absent, because one is detailed annually in rotation to the service of the proconsul; that two years ago you gave up a cohort and four men from each of the centuries as reinforcements for your comrades of the Third Legion; [16] that many widely scattered posts keep you separated. In my own recollection you have not only changed camp twice, but actually built new ones. For these reasons I would have excused you if the legion had been remiss in its exercise for any length of time. But you were not at all remiss. . . . The chief centurions and the other centurions were quick and brave as usual.

To the Cavalry of the Legion

Military exercises have, I may say, their own rules, and if anything is added to or taken away from these rules, the exercise becomes either of little value or too difficult. The more elaborateness is added, the poorer a show it makes. But you performed the most difficult of all exercises, namely, javelin throwing, clad in cuirass. . . . In addition, I congratulate you on your spirit. . . .

[To a cavalry cohort]

. . . Entrenchments which others take several days to construct you have completed in a single day. You have built a wall entailing long labor, such as is customarily made for permanent winter quarters, in a time not much longer than that required to build one of sod. In this kind the turf is cut to standard size and is easy to carry and to handle, and the laying is not troublesome, as the turf is naturally soft and level. But yours was built of large heavy stones of all sizes; and no one can carry or lift or lay these without their irregularities making themselves felt. You have cut a trench straight through hard coarse gravel and have made it even by smoothing it. When this task was approved, you entered the camp speedily, got your rations and your arms, following the cavalry that had been sent out, and with a loud shout as it returned. . . .

I compliment [my legate] for having introduced this maneuver among you, which assumed the appearance of real combat; and it trains you [so well that] I am able to praise you. Cornelianus too, your prefect, has handled his duties satisfactorily. . . . The cavalryman should ride out from cover and use caution in pursuit. For unless he sees where he

[16] That is, Legion III Gallica or III Cyrenaica, both of which were stationed in the East.

is going and is able to check his horse whenever he wants to, he will surely be exposed to pitfalls. . . .

On July . . . to the First Company of Pannonians

You did everything in orderly fashion. You filled the field with maneuvers. Your javelin hurling was not without grace, although you used javelins which are short and stiff. Several of you hurled your lances equally well. And your mounting was smart just now and lively yesterday. If there were anything lacking I should notice it; if there were anything conspicuously bad, I should point it out. But you pleased me uniformly throughout the whole exercise. My legate Catullinus,[17] *vir clarissimus*, devotes equal care to all the branches he commands. . . . Your prefect evidently looks after you carefully. I bestow upon you a largess. . . .

To the Cavalry of the Sixth Cohort of Commagenians

It is difficult for the cavalry of the cohorts to make a good impression even by themselves, and still harder for them not to give dissatisfaction after the exercise of the auxiliary cavalry. They have a larger ground coverage, a larger number of men throwing javelins; their right wheeling is in close array, their Cantabrian maneuver closely knit; the beauty of their horses and the elegance of their equipment is in keeping with their level of pay. Nevertheless, and despite the heat, you avoided being tedious by doing promptly what had to be done. In addition you hurled stones from slings and fought with missiles. Your mounting was everywhere brisk. That the care taken by my legate Catullinus, *vir clarissimus*, has been outstanding is apparent from the fact that such men as you under his command. . . . [The rest is lost.]

149. *Duties and Occupations of the Garrison Army*

The Roman armies were an important factor in the administrative and economic life of the provinces where they were stationed. In addition to their prime function of guarding the frontiers, the soldiers were regularly detailed to police and patrol duties, especially in connection with the grain supply and the exploitation of natural resources. Moreover, the labor of the army was frequently employed for the construction and maintenance of public works, such as roads, bridges, canals, and temples and other public buildings.

[17] Quintus Fabius Catullinus, who was rewarded with the consulship in A.D. 130.

TOURS OF DUTY

Geneva Latin Papyrus No. 1, col. 3

[From the records of a legion stationed near Alexandria, Egypt, A.D. c.80–90]

MARCUS PAPIRIUS RUFUS C. . . .

Assigned to granary at Neapolis [18] as secretary[?] . . . to Titus Suedius Clemens, prefect of the camp, year 3 of the Emperor Titus. . . . Returned, same year, January 21. Assigned to granary at Mercurium, year 1 of the Emperor Domitian. . . . Returned, same year, July 13. Assigned with . . . year 4 of Domitian, April 21. Returned, same year. . . . Assigned to granary at Neapolis, year. . . . Returned, same year, July 7.

TITUS FLAVIUS SATURNINUS

Assigned to harbor dredging, year . . . January 14. Returned, same year. . . . Assigned with Timinius, prefect[?] . . . Returned, same year, November 28. Assigned with Maximus Liberalis. . . .

TITUS FLAVIUS VALENS

Assigned to papyrus manufacture, year . . . January 15. Returned, same year. . . . Assigned to mint, year. . . . Returned, same year, January 17. Assigned to . . . year . . . of the Emperor Domitian, A[pril?] 13. . . . Assigned to granary at Mercurium. . . . Returned, same year, July 14. Assigned to . . . year 7 of Domitian, September 19. . . .

TITUS FLAVIUS CELER

Assigned to granary at Neapolis, year . . . February 11. Returned, same year. . . . Assigned with river patrol boat. . . . Returned, same year, May 24. . . . [The rest is fragmentary.]

LIFE OF A GUARD DETAIL

The following are from a group of several dozen Latin and Greek ostraca found at the site of an ancient quarry and gold mine on the desert road from Coptus to the Red Sea (cf. § 47, third selection). These ostraca, which date from the late first to the middle of the second century, show that a military garrison was stationed there in that period for the double purpose, no doubt, of guarding both the trade route and the diggings: cf. § 151, last selection.

Bulletin de l'Institut français d'archéologie orientale, XL (1941),
141–96, Nos. 1 and 13

i

Rustius Barbarus to his brother Pompeius, greeting. How come you haven't answered me if you received the loaves of bread? I sent you

[18] Neapolis and Mercurium were the names of districts of the city of Alexandria.

fifteen loaves by Popillius and Dutuporis, then fifteen more and a vase [?] by the carter Draco; you've used up four *matia* [19] of wheat. I sent you six loaves by the cavalryman Thiadices, who said he could take them with him. Please, brother, have some . . . made for my personal use, as beautiful as possible, and write me so that in payment for them I can make you bread or send you money, whichever you wish. I want you to know, now, that I'm getting married. As soon as I have, I'll write you at once to come. Goodbye. Regards to . . . lius.

ii

. . . to Terentius and . . . and Atticus, his . . . , heartiest greeting. First of all I pray that you are in good health; my dearest wish . . . is for you and the children to stay well.[20] I received from Ca . . . the bunch of radishes [?] that you sent. You are getting [from me] gourds and citron; divide it with your brothers as you yourselves wish. Regards to the soldiers. Isidorus sends regards. I pray that you are well.

150. *Relaxation of Discipline*

The natural tendency toward relaxation of strict discipline in a garrison army was aggravated by Hadrian's reform of military recruitment, whereby soldiers were assigned to service in units stationed in their native provinces (cf. § 142). The purpose of this measure was undoubtedly to make the professional military career more attractive to provincials and to make the soldiers the defenders of their own homes, but it also had the adverse effect of fostering a centrifugal provincial consciousness as well as a breakdown in discipline. The selections below reveal the unmilitary behavior of the army in Syria about the middle of the second century. For the third century see § 111.

Fronto *Letter to Lucius Verus* xix

From LCL

The army you took over was demoralized by luxury and immorality and prolonged idleness. The soldiers at Antioch were wont to spend their time applauding actors and were more often found in the nearest tavern garden than in the ranks. Horses shaggy from neglect, but every hair plucked from their riders; a rare sight was a soldier with arm or leg hairy. Withal the men were better clothed than armed, so much so that Pontius Laelianus, a man of character and a disciplinarian of the old

---

[19] Four *matia* = ⅓ artab.

[20] Even in this remote military outpost many of the soldiers lived with their "wives" and children (cf. § 154).

school, in some cases ripped up their cuirasses with his finger tips; he found horses saddled with cushions, and by his orders the little pommels on them were slit open and the down plucked from the saddles of the cavalry as from geese. Few of the soldiers could vault upon their steeds, the rest scrambled clumsily up by dint of heel or knee or ham; not many could make their spears hurtle, most tossed them like toy lances without verve and vigor. Gambling was rife in camp, sleep night-long, or, if a watch was kept, it was over the wine cups.

Fronto *Elements of History* xi–xii

From LCL

So by long unfamiliarity with fighting the Roman soldier was reduced to a cowardly condition. For as to all the arts of life, so especially to the business of war is sloth fatal. It is of the greatest importance also for soldiers to experience the ups and downs of fortune, and to take strenuous exercise in the open.

The most demoralized of all, however, were the Syrian soldiers, mutinous, disobedient, seldom with their units, straying in front of their prescribed posts, roving about like scouts, tipsy from one noon to the next, unused even to carrying their arms, and, as one man after another from dislike of toil laid them aside, like skirmishers and slingers half naked. Apart from scandals of this kind, they had been so cowed by unsuccessful battles as to turn their backs at the first sight of the Parthians and to listen for the trumpet as the signal for flight.

151. *Military Pay and Expenses*

The pay of the rank-and-file legionnaire, which had been one third of a *denarius* a day (minus deductions) in the second century B.C. (cf. Vol. I, p. 438), was fixed by Augustus at 225 *denarii* annually (minus deductions for equipment and maintenance). Legionary soldiers' pay rose, with inflation and increased privileges to the army, to 300 *denarii* under Domitian, to 500 under Septimius Severus, and to 750 under Caracalla. It has been estimated that a soldier could live fairly comfortably on about five sevenths of his pay.

COMPULSORY SOLDIERS' DEPOSITS

Vegetius *Military Science* II. xx

It was indeed an admirable institution of the ancients that one half of the donatives which the soldiers obtained was sequestered in the soldiers' depository and kept there for the soldiers, lest it be squandered by them in luxuries and the purchase of useless things. For very many men, particularly poorer ones, spend whatever they can get. This laying aside of money, moreover, is, in the first place, evidently for the welfare of the soldiers themselves; since they are maintained at the public expense, their personal camp funds increase proportionately with every donative. Secondly, the soldier who knows that his money is kept in the soldiers' depository entertains no thoughts of desertion, cherishes the standards more, and fights for them in the line with greater bravery. . . . One bag was placed in each of the ten cohorts, and in it these funds were kept. There was, in addition, an eleventh bag in which the entire legion made a small contribution for a burial fund, so that if any of the soldiers died, the expenses for his burial were taken from this eleventh bag; this fund was kept in a basket in the custody of the standard bearers. . . . And therefore standard bearers are chosen not only for their integrity but also for their education, so that they will know how to protect the deposits and render accounts to each man.

MILITARY PAYROLL ACCOUNT

Geneva Latin Papyrus No. 1, col. 1 (abridged)

[Account for A.D. 81 of a cavalryman of a legion stationed outside Alexandria]

Year 3 of the Emperor Titus Vespasianus Augustus, consulship of Lucius Flavius and Lucius Asinius.

QUINTUS JULIUS PROCULUS, FROM DAMASCUS

	drachmas
Received first salary payment for our lord's third year	248
Deductions	
Hay	10
Toward rations	80
Boots, leggings	12
Camp Saturnalia	20
Toward clothing	60
[Total] expenses	182
Remainder deposited to his account	66
Previous balance	136
Total balance	202

	drachmas
Received second salary payment for same year	248
Deductions	
Hay	10
Toward rations	80
Boots, leggings	12
To "the standards" [21]	4
[Total] expenses	106
Remainder deposited to his account	142
Previous balance	202
Total balance	344
Received third salary payment for same year	248
Deductions	
Hay	10
Toward rations	80
Boots, leggings	12
Toward clothing	146
[Total] expenses	248
On deposit to his account	344

[Verified by] Rennius Innocens

AN ADVANCE OF RATIONS AND PAY

This receipt is written on an ostracon found at the site of one of the quarries between the Nile and the Red Sea, where a military garrison guarded the convict labor, the road, and the vital water store (cf. § 149, last selection). Archaeological excavation has revealed the characteristic rectangular enclosure of the Roman military camp (cf. Vol. I, pp. 435–37), wells, water conduits, baths, houses, and a temple.

Chronique d'Egypte, XXVI (1951), 354–63; A.D. 136/37[?]

Ptolemaeus son of Irenaeus to Adrastus, commissary officer, greeting. I acknowledge that I have been advanced my ration and one *denarius*[?] of my allowance for clothing and beans for the month of Choiak, which I will repay to Gaio, imperial agent[?]. Year 21[?] of the lord Hadrian[?] Caesar.

[Signed] I have received in accordance with the above-written. Ptolemaeus son of Irenaeus.

[21] This was probably an assessment for a burial fund for deceased soldiers; such military funds were kept by the standard bearers: see the preceding selection.

152. *Provisions for the Army*

Food and equipment were supplied to the armies from the production of provincial agriculture and industry. Considerable quantities of most supplies
were delivered from provincial tribute; additional requirements were supplied by purchase or requisition from farmers and artisans in the regions
where the units were stationed. For large-scale military operations, requisitions were made upon other provinces as well.

PROCUREMENT OF GARMENTS AND BLANKETS

Berlin Papyrus No. 1,564; A.D. 138

Copy of authorization. Ammonius son of Polydeuces and Syrio son
of Heras and Heraclides son of Heraclides, all three collectors of [req-
uisitioned] clothing, and Hermas, ex-*agoranomus*,[22] to the banker Heraclides, greeting. Pay out to Heraclides son of Horigas, to Hero, freedman of Publius Mevius, and to Dioscorus, freedman of the great god
Sarapis,[23] weavers of the village of Philadelphia, for themselves and all[?]
the other weavers of the same village, on their mutual responsibility,
[the following sums] as advance payment for the price of the clothing
which the prefect [of Egypt], Avidius Heliodorus, *vir egregius*, ordered
manufactured for the requirements of the armies in Cappadocia: for
one belted tunic, white, length 3½ cubits, width 3 cubits 4 digits,
weight 3¾ minas—24 drachmas on account; and for four Syrian cloaks,
white, length 6 cubits each, width 4 cubits, weight 3¾ minas—24 drachmas each on account, equals 96 drachmas; total, 120 drachmas; and for
the requirements of the infirmary in the imperial camp,[24] for one blanket,
plain white, length 6 cubits, width 4 cubits, weight 4 minas—28 drachmas
on account, making a total for this authorization of 148 drachmas of
silver, less 6½ percent deducted for the imperial fisc from the 28 drachmas advanced for the blanket; on condition that they will use for the
clothing only fine, soft, pure white wool, free of all dirt, and will produce
the clothing well-woven, firm-textured, with finished hems, meeting
specifications, flawless, and full value for the advance payment made
them for these items. If at [the time of] delivery any of these items is
missing or is appraised as inferior, they shall, on their mutual responsibility, pay the price of the missing items (together with dues and expenses)

[22] On the office of *agoranomus*, see introduction to § 67, second selection.
[23] On the survival of Greek sacral manumission, see § 67.
[24] It is uncertain whether this means the camp of the emperor himself, or merely
the camp of imperial troops.

and the difference on the inferior items, delivering these promptly in the aforesaid sizes and weights and entirely apart from other public clothing requisitions which they owe. Year 2 of the Emperor Caesar Titus Aelius Hadrianus Antoninus Pius, Thoth 12.

DELIVERY OF GRAIN

Amherst Papyrus No. 107 (= Wilcken, No. 417); A.D. 185

To Damario, *strategus* of the Hermopolite nome, from Antonius Justinus, *duplicarius*,[25] dispatched by Valerius Frontinus, prefect of the Heraclian Company stationed at Coptus. Of the 20,000 artabs of barley ordered by the prefect [of Egypt], Longaeus Rufus, *vir clarissimus*, to be purchased from the harvest of the past twenty-fourth year for the requirements of the aforesaid company, I have received, in accordance with the assessment made by the nome officials, from the elders of the village of Terton Epa in the Upper Patemite district the quota imposed upon their village, viz., one hundred artabs of barley (100 art. barley) by the public receiving measure for the stipulated delivery. I have issued this receipt in quadruplicate. Year 25 of the Emperor Caesar Marcus Aurelius Commodus Antoninus Augustus Pius Armeniacus Medicus Parthicus Sarmaticus Germanicus Britannicus Maximus, Payni. . . .

[Signed] I, Antonius Justinus, *duplicarius*, have received the one hundred artabs (100 art.) of barley, as stated above.

ACKNOWLEDGMENT OF PURCHASE FOR THE ARMY

This waxed tablet, found in Frisia (northern Netherlands), records the purchase of a cow from a German farmer by a Roman, probably an army provisioner. The document is unique, and the text at points extremely abbreviated; the translation must therefore be based in part on conjecture. Especially noteworthy is the waiver of Roman legal formalities such as might lead to needless controversy or litigation.

FIRA, Vol. III, No. 137; A.D. 29 or 116

I, Gargilius Secundus, duly and in lawful manner purchased a cow for 115 pieces [26] from Stelus son of Reperius, Beosian, of the estate of Lopetius, with Cesdius, first[?] centurion of Legion V, and Mutus Admetus, first[?] centurion of Legion I, as witnesses. Right to cancel[?] and formalities of Roman civil law are waived. Bought in the consulship of Gaius Fufius and Gnaeus Minicius, September 9. Proper delivery vouched for by Lilus Duerretus, veteran.

[25] See Note 59.   [26] Probably *denarii*.

[Witnesses] Titus Cesdius son of Titus, of Legion V; Numerius Junnius son of Marcus; Tiberius Lieuus Erepus son of Numerius, of Legion V; Gaius Seceduus son of Tiberius. [Seal] of the seller himself.

153. *Personnel Record of a Cohort*

Berlin Papyrus No. 696, col. 1 (= *Select Papyri*, No. 401 = *American Journal of Philology*, LXIII [1942], 61–71, and LXXIII [1952], 75–78); A.D. 156

Register of the month of August [27] in the consulship of Silvanus and Augurinus of the First Augustan Praetorian Mounted Cohort of Lusitanians,[28] which has been encamped opposite Apollinopolis Major in the Thebaid since July 8 in the consulship of Pontianus and Rufinus.[29]

Prefect: Marcus Julius Silvanus son of Marcus, of the Quirine tribe, native of Thubursicum,[30] began his duties on April 23 in the consulship of Commodus and Lateranus,[31] replacing Allius Pudentillus.

August 31.

Total number of men on January 1	505
Includes 6 centurions, 3 decurions, 114 cavalry, 19 dromedary riders, 363 infantry.	
Added since January 1	
Appointed from civilian [32] by Sempronius Liberalis, prefect of Egypt: Sextus Sempronius Candidus (of the consulship of Silvanus and Augurinus),[33] April 27	
Transferred back from the First Mauretanian Company of Thracians to office in the cohort: Aulus Flavius Vespasianus (of the consulship of Vibius and Varus),[34] March 2	1 centurion 1 decurion
Recruits, voluntary, approved by Sempronius Liberalis, prefect of Egypt, including 1 cavalryman, 1 dromedary rider:	9

[27] The year in the Egyptian calendar ended in late August.
[28] Units of the auxiliaries were named for the region where they were first recruited, and they retained their original names even after Hadrian instituted the policy of recruiting replacements in the regions where the units were stationed. Thus in this Lusitanian Cohort stationed in Egypt the new recruits mentioned below are clearly Egyptians, as may be seen from their names.
[29] A.D. 131.   [30] In Numidia.   [31] A.D. 154.
[32] An appointment to officer rank directly from civilian status was rare, and was usually awarded to persons with "connections."
[33] This is the year of enlistment, a necessary part of every soldier's identification.
[34] A.D. 134.

In the century of Herculanus, Philo Isiog-
nis[?] (of the consulship of Silvanus and
Augurinus), May 2[?] . . .
In the century of Marcus, Anubas Ammo
(same consulship), May 2[?]
In the century of Gaianus, Gaius Sigillius
Valens (same consulship) . . .
In the century of Sempronianus, Ammo-
nius . . . (same consulship). . . .

154. *The Families of Soldiers*

All classes of soldiers through the grade of centurion were forbidden to marry
while in military service, and even legal marriages contracted before admission to the army were dissolved by entry into service. Despite the official ban,
most soldiers did "marry" and beget children during their period of military
service (cf. Note 20). The practice was so common that by the second century
the emperors, without altering the illegitimate status of such "wives" (legally,
concubines) and children, allowed a soldier the privilege of drawing a will
to provide for his family in the event of his death during military service
(cf. § 71 and p. 381). The ban on soldier marriages was lifted in A.D. 197 by
Septimius Severus.

RULINGS OF PREFECTS

Mitteis, No. 372 (in part); A.D. 114–42

Year 20 of the deified Trajan, Tybi 10.[35] Lucia Macrina, represented
by the advocate Fannius, stated that she claimed a deposit from the property of the deceased soldier Antonius Germanus. Lupus [36] declared: "We
assume that such deposits are dowries. I do not grant a trial for such
causes, since a soldier is not permitted to marry; and if you claim a dowry
and I do grant a trial, I shall give the appearance of believing that the
marriage is legal." . . .

Year 18 of Trajan, Phaophi 27.[37] Longinus Hy . . . declared that
he, a Roman citizen, had served in the First Cohort of Thebans under
Severus and had during military service cohabited with a Roman woman
by whom he had begotten Longinus Apollinarius and Longinus Pomponius, and he requested that these sons be certified [as Roman citizens].

[35] January 5, A.D. 117.
[36] Marcus Rutilius Lupus, prefect of Egypt A.D. 113–17.
[37] October 24, A.D. 114.

Lupus discussed it with his legal experts and declared: "The children will be so certified, as being born of a Roman woman. You desire also to make them [legitimate on the basis of this certification?], but I cannot make you their legal father."

Year 18 of Trajan, Payni 10.[38] Chrotis, represented by the advocate Philoxenus, stated that she, an Alexandrian, had married Isidorus, an Alexandrian; that thereafter, while he was serving in a cohort, she bore him a son, Theodorus, concerning whom she now petitioned, requesting that his inheritance tax be remitted if it had been neglected; and that it was clear from the will he had drawn that this was his son since he had made him heir to his property. The will of Julius Martialius,[39] soldier of the First Cohort of Thebans, was read. Lupus then discussed it with his advisers and declared: "Martialius could not while in military service have a legal son, but he made him his heir legally."

INHERITANCE RIGHTS OF SOLDIERS' CHILDREN

Berlin Papyrus No. 140 (= *Select Papyri*, No. 213 = *FIRA*,. Vol. I, No. 78); A.D. 119

Copy of a letter, translated from the Latin, of the Emperor Trajanus HADRIAN Augustus, posted, in the consulship of Publius Aelius [40] (for the third time) and Rusticus, in . . . at the headquarters of the winter camp of Legion III Cyrenaica and Legion XXII Deioteriana on August 4, which equals Mesore 11:

I am aware, my dear Rammius,[41] that those whom their parents acknowledged as their offspring during their period of military service have been debarred from succession to their paternal property, and this was not considered harsh, since the parents had acted contrary to military discipline. But for my own part I am very glad to introduce a precedent for interpreting more liberally the quite stern rule established by the emperors before me. Therefore, whereas offspring acknowledged during the period of military service are not legal heirs of their fathers, nevertheless I rule that they, too, can claim possession of property in accordance with that part of the edict by which this right is given also to blood relatives. This grant of mine it will be your duty to make clearly known to both my soldiers and my veterans, not for the sake of seeming

---

[38] June 4, A.D. 115.

[39] The Roman name acquired by Isidorus on entering the cohort.

[40] The Emperor Hadrian. The text of this prescript is given according to the revision in A. Stein, *Die Präfekten von Ägypten* (Bern, 1950), p. 207, Note 212.

[41] Quintus Rammius Martialis, prefect of Egypt A.D. 117–19.

to exalt me to them, but in order that they may avail themselves of this privilege if they are unaware of it.

DECLARATIONS OF BIRTH OF SOLDIERS' CHILDREN

By the Aelian-Sentian and Papian-Poppaean laws of Augustus (see §§ 11–12), for every child born of lawful wedlock of two Roman citizens, the father (or his representative) was required to file a declaration with the appropriate official within thirty days after the birth. These declarations were recorded in a public register, and official notices were posted in a central place in Rome or in the provincial capitals, from which families might have certified copies made. Illegitimate children were until the reign of Marcus Aurelius excluded from the public register. Therefore, parents of children born during the father's military service frequently drew up unofficial attestations of birth, signed by witnesses, to provide *prima facie* evidence for establishing the child's civic status after the father's discharge and enfranchisement.

AE, 1937, No. 112; A.D. 127

Marcus Lucretius Clemens, cavalryman in the squadron of Silvanus in the First Cohort of Thracians, called the undersigned to witness and swore by Jupiter Best and Greatest and by the divinity of the deified emperors and by the *genius* [42] of the Emperor Caesar Trajanus Hadrian Augustus that while in military service he had become the father, by Octavia Tamustha, of a natural son, named Serenus, on April 25 in the year 11 of the Emperor Caesar Trajanus Hadrian Augustus; and he stated that he made this attestation on account of the restriction imposed by military service, so as to be able to have proof at his certification of [citizen] status after his honorable discharge that he [Serenus] is his natural son.

Done in the winter camp of the First Cohort of Thracians opposite Apollinopolis Magna in the Thebaid, on May 1 in the year above-stated.

[Witnesses] Gaius Antonius Maximus, keeper of arms in the squadron[?] of Lucius Farsuleius; Marrius Antoninus, of the squadron of Rufus; Gaius Barga, soldier in the squadron[?] of Lucius Farsuleius; Gaius Julius Marcellus, adjutant in . . . ; Titus Marsias Bammogalis[?] . . . ; Numerius Alexa son of Longus; Marcus Lucretius Clemens. . . .

Michigan Papyrus No. 169 (= *FIRA*, Vol. III, No. 4); A.D. 145

Sempronia Gemella, acting with the approval of her guardian,[43] Gaius Julius Saturninus, called the undersigned to witness that on March 21 last she had borne twin sons of uncertain father, and that these are

---

[42] Cf. § 14.   [43] See § 163.

named Marcus Sempronius Sarapio and Marcus Sempronius Socratio, sons of Spurius;[44] and she stated that she interposed this attestation for the reason that the Aelian-Sentian and Papian-Poppaean Laws forbid illegitimate sons and daughters to be entered in the public register. . . .

Done at Alexandria on the coast of Egypt on April 29 in the consulship of the Emperor Caesar Titus Aelius Hadrianus ANTONINUS Augustus PIUS (for the fourth time) and MARCUS AURELIUS Caesar (for the second time), in year 8 of the Emperor Caesar Titus Aelius Hadrianus ANTONINUS Augustus PIUS, on the 4th day of the month Pachon.

I, Sempronia Gemella, with my guardian Gaius Julius Satornilus, called witnesses to attest that twin sons had been born of uncertain father and that these have been named Marcus Sempronius Sarapio and Marcus Sempronius Socratio, sons of Spurius, as stated above. I, Gaius Julius Satornilus, was designated her guardian, and I wrote for her since she is illiterate.[45]

[Witnesses] Marcus Vibius Pollio; Marcus Octavius Serenus; Lucius Aemilius Maximus; Lucius Caponius Saturninus; Gaius Aebutius Saturninus; Gaius Vibievius Crassus; Marcus Holconius Ampissus.

155. *Privileges of Veterans: Citizenship and Legal Marriage*

The length of military service was fixed by Augustus at twenty years in the legions. Before the end of his reign, veterans were kept in service an additional five years as active reservists assigned to light duties (cf. Note 14). By the second century, the enlistment period was uniformly twenty-five years for all branches (including legions and infantry and cavalry auxiliaries), except for the fleets, where the term was one year longer, and the Praetorian and urban cohorts, who served sixteen years. The legions and élite Praetorian and urban cohorts were composed exclusively of Roman citizens. The provincials who served in the cavalry and infantry auxiliaries and in the fleets were granted Roman citizenship upon discharge. But in the second and third centuries the distinction in status between legions and auxiliaries tended to disappear. All classes of soldiers received upon discharge the right to contract a legal Roman marriage (*conubium*), forbidden during military service; for many, however, this grant meant the legitimization of a long-established conjugal relation and the enfranchisement of offspring begotten during service. The grant of citizenship to veteran auxiliaries was until A.D. 140 uniformly

[44] That is, "father unknown."
[45] This summary paragraph is written in Greek, the *lingua franca* of the eastern part of the Roman Empire; the rest of the document is in Latin, the official language used in military circles.

made to the veteran, his children, and descendants; by then provincials were being admitted to the legions, and the grant was made thereafter to the veteran alone, and children born during military service did not receive the franchise until they enlisted in the legions—a regulation which gave new impetus to the tendency for military service to become a hereditary profession (cf. Chapter VI, Note 44).

Grants of honorable discharge were made by the emperor or, in the frontier provinces, by the provincial governor acting on orders from the emperor. These were not issued to each veteran as he completed his period of service, but from time to time to all eligibles in a military unit; as a result many veterans were obliged to remain in service beyond their time. The emperor's edict granting official discharge and citizen status was inscribed on bronze and posted in Rome; the veteran received a small bronze diptych, inscribed in his name and containing a copy of the emperor's edict, to serve him in civilian life as proof of his privileges. About two hundred of these military "diplomas" have been found in various parts of the Empire, especially in the frontier provinces. A perusal of this body of documents reads like a cross section of the peoples of the Empire and reveals how widely the manpower of the Empire was recruited to guard the frontiers.

CERTIFICATE OF DISCHARGE

A wooden tablet containing temporary certification of discharge to serve the veteran until the official bronze "diploma" became available.

Wilcken, No. 457 (= Dessau, No. 9,060); A.D. 122

Consulship of Marcus Acilius Aviola and Pansa, January 4. Titus Haterius Nepos, prefect of Egypt, granted honorable discharge to Lucius Valerius Noster, cavalryman in the Gavian Squadron of the Vocontian Company, who had completed his service.

[Signature of prefect] I perused the foregoing statement and granted the honorable discharge. [January] 4.

MILITARY DIPLOMAS

CIL, Vol. XVI, No. 12; A.D. 71

The Emperor Caesar VESPASIAN Augustus, *pontifex maximus*, holding the tribunician power for the second year, acclaimed *imperator* six times, father of his country, three times consul, has granted to the veterans whose names appear below, who served in the fleet of Misenum under Sextus Lucilius Bassus, completing twenty-six or more years, and who have been settled in a colony at Paestum,[46] to themselves, their chil-

[46] Such specific mention in diplomas of settlement in a veterans' colony is found only in a group issued to men discharged from the fleets in A.D. 71. The veterans of the Misenum fleet were settled in that year at Paestum in southern Italy, those of the Ravenna fleet in Pannonia. Since this diploma was found in Thrace, it is evident

dren and descendants, citizenship and right of marriage with the wives
they had when citizenship was granted them, or, if any were single, with
those they might later take, limited to one wife for each man.

Done on February 9 in the consulship of the Emperor Caesar
VESPASIAN Augustus (for the third time) and Marcus Cocceius Nerva.

CENTURION HEZBENUS SON OF DULAZENUS, SAPPAEAN,[47] AND HIS SON DOLES[48]

Certified copy taken from bronze tablet posted at Rome in the
Capitol at the altar of the Julian family, on the outer side at the foot,
Tablet I.

[Witnesses] Decimus Liburnius Rufus, from Philippi; Gaius Sallustius Crescens, soldier in the century of Augurinus [?] in the Fourth
Praetorian Cohort, from Philippi; Publius Popillius Rufus, from Philippi;
Lucius Betuedius Valens, from Philippi; Lucius Betuedius Primigenius,
from Philippi; Gnaeus Cornelius Florus, from Philippi; Gaius Heren-
nuleius Chryseros, from Philippi.

CIL, Vol. XVI, No. 21 (= Dessau, 1,993); A.D. 76

The Emperor Caesar VESPASIAN Augustus, *pontifex maximus*, holding the tribunician power for the eighth year, acclaimed *imperator* for
the eighteenth time, father of his country, censor, seven times consul,
consul designate for an eighth time. I have appended the names of the
members of my personal bodyguard who have served in my Praetorian
guard, likewise of the soldiers who have served in the nine Praetorian
cohorts and the four urban cohorts. To these, who have bravely and dutifully completed their service, I grant the right of marriage, with one
woman only and with first wives, so that even if they join to themselves
in matrimony women of foreign legal status they may raise up children
just as if they were born of two Roman citizens.

December 2 in the consulship of Galeo Tettienus Petronianus and
Marcus Fulvius Gillo.

SIXTH PRAETORIAN COHORT: LUCIUS ENNIUS FEROX SON OF LUCIUS, OF THE TROMENTINE TRIBE, OF AQUAE STATELLAE[49]

Certified copy taken from bronze tablet posted at Rome in the
Capitol on the base of the statue of the African Jupiter.

---

that Hezbenus returned to his native land (cf. Note 47). Cf. Tacitus *Annals* XIV.
xxvii (A.D. 60): "A further enrollment of veterans in Tarentum and Antium did but
little to arrest the depopulation of these places, for most scattered themselves in the
provinces where they had completed their military service."
[47] The Sappaeans were a Thracian people.
[48] Inclusion of wife or children by name is rare in these documents.
[49] In Liguria, northern Italy, modern Acqui. His diploma, however, was found near
Constanta, Rumania: cf. Note 46.

CIL, Vol. XVI, No. 35; A.D. 88

The Emperor Caesar DOMITIAN Augustus Germanicus, son of the deified Vespasian, *pontifex maximus*, holding the tribunician power for the eighth year, acclaimed *imperator* seventeen times, fourteen times consul, censor for life, father of his country, has granted to the cavalrymen and infantrymen whose names appear below, who completed twenty-five or more years of service in three companies and seventeen cohorts stationed in Syria under Publius Valerius Patruinus—namely, the Second Pannonian, the Third Thracian Augustan, and the Veteran Gallic [Companies], and the First Flavian composed of Roman citizens, the First Thousand-Man, the First Lucan, the First Ascalonian, the First Sebastene, the First Ituraean, the First Numidian, the Second Italic composed of Roman citizens, the Second Thracian composed of Roman citizens, the Second Marine, the Third Thracian Augustan, the Third Thracian Syrian, the Fourth Bracaraugustan, the Fourth Syrian, the Fourth Galician Lucan, the Pannonian Augustan, and the Musulamian [Cohorts] [50]— to themselves, their children and descendants, citizenship and right of marriage with the wives they had when citizenship was granted them, or, if any were single, with those they might later take, limited to one wife for each man.

November 7 in the consulship of Marcus Otacilius Catulus and Sextus Julius Sparsus.

TO INFANTRYMAN BITHUS SON OF SEUTHUS, BESSIAN,[51] OF THE
MUSULAMIAN COHORT, WHOSE COMMANDING OFFICER IS
MARCUS CAECILIUS SEPTEMBER

Certified copy taken from bronze tablet posted at Rome in the Capitol on the left side of the Public Archives.

[Witnesses] Quintus Mucius Augustalis; Marcus Calpurnius Justus; Gaius Lucretius Modestus; Gaius Claudius Sementivus; Gaius Pompeius Eutrapelus; Gaius Julius Helenus; Lucius Pullius Verecundus.

GRANT OF CITIZENSHIP BEFORE DISCHARGE

Soldiers were sometimes discharged and granted citizenship before the completion of the regular term of service for bravery or physical disability.

[50] The places or peoples after which these cohorts were named (cf. Note 28) are as follows (only less familiar ones are listed): Lucan—probably Dalmatia (or Galicia); Ascalonian–southern Palestine; Sebastene—Samaria in Palestine[?]; Ituraean—Lebanon; Bracaraugustan—Tarragonese Spain; Galician—Spain-Portugal; Musulamian —Tripolitania.

[51] The Bessians were a Thracian people; since his diploma was found in Thrace, Bithus obviously returned to his native land after his discharge: cf. Note 46.

AE, 1944, No. 57; A.D. 106

The Emperor Caesar Nerva TRAJAN Augustus Germanicus Dacicus, son of the deified Nerva, *pontifex maximus*, holding the tribunician power for the fourteenth year,[52] acclaimed *imperator* six times, five times consul, father of his country, has granted Roman citizenship before completion of military service to the infantrymen and cavalrymen whose names appear below, serving in the First British Thousand-Man Ulpian Decorated Loyal Fortunate Cohort composed of Roman citizens, which is on duty in Dacia under Decimus Terentius Scaurianus, for having dutifully and faithfully discharged the Dacian campaign.

August 11, at Darnithithium[?], in the consulship of Lucius Minicius Natalis and Quintus Silvanus Granianus.

TO INFANTRYMAN MARCUS ULPIUS NOVANTICO SON OF ADCOBROVATUS,
RATAEAN [53]

Certified copy taken from bronze tablet posted at Rome on the wall behind the temple of the deified Augustus, near [the statue of] Minerva.

[Witnesses] Publius Cornelius Alexander; Lucius Pullius Verecundus; Publius Atinius Amerimus; Gaius Tuticanius Saturninus; Lucius Pullius Trophimus; Gaius Julius Paratus; Marcus Junius Eutychus.

REQUEST FOR DISCHARGE CERTIFICATES

Italian Society Papyrus No. 1,026; A.D. 150

Certified copy taken from a petition posted together with others in the portico of Junia . . . containing the text which follows:

To Villius Cadus, legate of the emperor with rank of praetor, from twenty-two veterans of Legion X Fretensis who began their military service in the consulship of Glabrio and Torquatus or of Paulinus and Aquilinus,[54] and whose names are subjoined. Since we served, my lord, in the Praetorian Fleet of Misenum and, after transfer to the Fretensis Legion through the indulgence of the deified Hadrian, we maintained an unbroken record as good soldiers for over twenty years, now we have in most auspicious times been released from our military oaths and seek to go home to Alexandria on the coast of Egypt, and we ask that you deign to confirm in writing that we have been discharged by you, so that it may be plain from your confirmation that we have been discharged [from the said legion], not from the fleet, so that your subscript

[52] This is an error for "tenth."
[53] That is, from Ratae in Brittany; but the diploma was found in Dacia (Rumania), where the veteran presumably settled: cf. Note 49.
[54] A.D. 125 and 126.

may be able to serve us as credentials in case of necessity and we may render thanks forever to your kindness.

[There follow the names of the twenty-two veterans, each with indication of the century in which he had served.]

I, Lucius Petronius Saturninus, submitted this petition on behalf of myself and my fellow veterans. I, Pomponius, wrote it.

Subscript: It is not customary for veterans from the legions to receive a written document, but you want the prefect of Egypt to be informed that you have been released from your military oaths by me under orders from our emperor. I shall give you such a document in addition to your bonus.[55] Post [this]. Done at the First Flavian Augustan Colony of Caesarea,[56] January 22 in the counsulship of Squilla Gallicanus and Carminius Vetus.

CERTIFICATION OF STATUS OF VETERAN

Hamburg Papyrus No. 31; A.D. 103

Extract from the register of certifications of status by the then prefect, Vibius Maximus, headed "Certifications of status by Vibius Maximus, with the tribune . . . son of Proclus [as adjutant], in year 7 of the deified Trajan, month Hathyr."

Reference—Page 27: Lucius Cornelius Antas, desiring to make his home in the Arsinoite nome with his wife and children, Heraclides aged   , Crispina aged   , and Ammonarion aged   .[57] The aforesaid Antas exhibited a bronze tablet (copy herewith), showing that he has been enrolled as a citizen together with his children and wife, viz.: "Lucius Cornelius Antas son of Heraclides, soldier "born in camp" [58] and *duplicarius* [59] of the Augustan Company, whose prefect is Messius Junianus, his wife Antonia daughter of Crispus, his son Heraclides, his daughter Crispina, his daughter Ammonarion." He has produced also a copy from the archives [in the temple] of Castor and Pollux containing the statement that he has served in the armed forces twenty-six years and has been honorably discharged; and he furnished three witnesses of

[55] Since soldiers in the legions were normally Roman citizens, they needed no discharge document to attest that fact. The case of these veterans was, however, slightly anomalous because they had begun their service as noncitizens in the fleet before being transferred to a legion. On the soldiers' bonus, see § 6.

[56] In Palestine.

[57] The blank spaces left for the ages of the children were never filled in.

[58] That is, born while his father was in military service. Sons of ex-soldiers formed a specially privileged group in the legions.

[59] A soldier receiving double pay as a reward for bravery. A soldier who received pay and a half was known as a *sesquiplicarius*.

his identity, Claudius . . . , Ignatius Niger, and Julius . . . . [The rest is lost.]

156. *Privileges of Veterans: Immunities and Exemptions*

In addition to Roman citizenship and legal wedlock (see § 155), honorably discharged veterans enjoyed various legal and economic privileges, including exemption from taxes, billeting, and other compulsory public services. During the second century, probably because of the growing economic crisis, their economic privileges were reduced; they were required to pay various taxes, and —in Egypt, at least—their general exemption from public services seems to have been limited to the first five years after discharge. Under the military monarchy of the third and fourth centuries these privileges were again increased.

EDICT OF DOMITIAN ON PRIVILEGES OF VETERANS

With this document should be compared the similar edict of Octavian (Vol. I, § 153).

Wilcken, No. 463, col. 2, lines 10–20 (= Dessau, No. 9,059 = *FIRA*, Vol. I, No. 76); A.D. 88/89

The Emperor Caesar DOMITIAN Augustus Germanicus, son of the deified Vespasian, *pontifex maximus*, holding the tribunician power for the eighth year, acclaimed *imperator* sixteen times, censor for life, father of his country, declares: It has seemed appropriate to me to make known by edict that veteran soldiers among all of you are to be freed and exempt from all state taxes and customs tolls; that they, their wives, children, and parents . . . are to be Roman citizens with fullest legal right; that they are freed and released with total exemption, and their above-mentioned parents and children have total exemption by the same right and condition; and that the lands, homes, and shops of honorably discharged[?] veterans are not to be entered against their will. . . .[60] [The rest is lost.]

COMPLAINT OF A VETERAN

Berlin Papyrus No. 180 (= *Select Papyri*, No. 285); A.D. 172

To . . . from Gaius Julius Apollinarius, a veteran owning land in the village of Caranis. It has been decreed, my lord, that veterans are to

[60] The last clause is garbled and mutilated. Our translation gives an approximation of the sense.

have a five-year period of respite after their discharge. Yet despite this regulation I was molested two years after my discharge and was arbitrarily nominated for a compulsory public service, and from then until now I have been on duty without a break. Since there is a rigid ban on treating the natives in such a way, it ought much more to be observed in the case of myself who have served such a long time in the army. Wherefore I have been compelled to have recourse to you with a righteous request, and I ask you to secure for me an equivalent period of respite, in accordance with the decree on this subject, in order that I may be able to tend to my own property, now that I am elderly and alone, and may be forever grateful to your fortune. Farewell.

I, Gaius Julius Apollinarius, have submitted [this petition]. Year 12, Mecheir 29.

[Subscript] Submit your case to the *strategus*, and he will take suitable action.

PRIVILEGES GRANTED SOLDIERS BY CONSTANTINE

This bronze tablet, discovered in Hungary in 1930 on the site of the camp of the Legion I Adjutrix at Brigetio on the Danube, contains a letter from the Emperors Constantine and Licinius to the military commander in Illyricum decreeing improved tax privileges and discharge procedures for soldiers. The purpose of this ordinance was obviously to win and consolidate the loyal support of the troops after the recent civil wars by reaffirming and extending existing privileges.

AE, 1937, No. 232 (= *FIRA*, Vol. I, No. 93); A.D. 311

The Emperor Caesar Flavius Valerius CONSTANTINE Pius Felix Invictus Augustus, *pontifex maximus*, holding the tribunician power for the seventh year, acclaimed *imperator* six times, consul, father of his country, proconsul, and the Emperor Caesar Valerius Licinianus LICINIUS Pius Felix Invictus Augustus, *pontifex maximus*, holding the tribunician power for the fourth year, acclaimed *imperator* three times, consul, father of his country, proconsul.[61]

Copy of Sacred [62] Letter

Greeting, our dearest Dalmatius. Since we are ever desirous that due provision be made in all matters for the welfare and advantages of

---

[61] The date of this prescript is about ten years later than the date placed at the end of the letter. Actually, the prescript was, it seems, omitted through inadvertence when the letter was inscribed on the tablet and was added in the upper margin years later.

[62] That is, "imperial"; cf. p. 420.

our soldiers in keeping with their devotion and labors, so also in this matter, dearest Dalmatius, we believe that provision must be made for our
said soldiers through the foresight of our arrangements. Wherefore, observing the labors which our said soldiers in their incessant movements
undergo for the stability and welfare of the state, we believe that provision and arrangement should be made so that during the period of their
military service they may happily enjoy as a result of our foresight the
pleasant fruits of their labors, and that after their military service they
may obtain peaceful retirement and fitting security. Accordingly, we
believe Your Devotion [63] should be notified that our said soldiers even
in the period of their military service are to enjoy in consequence of our
decision an exemption of five *capita* [64] on property rating and on the
customary deliveries of taxes in kind, and that they are to have the same
privileges also when they obtain honorable discharge after completing
the legal period of service; [65] those, however, who have likewise obtained
honorable discharge although after only twenty years of service are to
enjoy an exemption from taxes in kind of two *capita*, that is both their
own and their wives'; anyone who happens to become disabled as a result
of a battle wound, even if he obtains release from his duties for that reason before twenty years of service, is to share in the benefaction of this
same indulgence of ours so as to enjoy an exemption of his own and his
wife's *capita;* so that the said soldiers may rejoice that thanks to our
foresight provision has been made in every way both for the security of
their retirement and also for their welfare. It has hitherto been the custom
that a large number of men were issued their honorable discharge simultaneously by the general, with each man receiving a copy for himself
while the original of the discharge document remained in the adjutant's
office; we, however, desire that when soldiers obtain a discharge, either
honorable or for disability as stated above, each shall receive from the
general a separate discharge addressed to him in person, so that with this
authentic and reliable proof in their own possession they may enjoy undisturbed and lasting security. Of course, Your Consecration [66] realizes
that those who are discharged for offense cannot share in the benefaction
of this same law, since both things ought to be taken into account—the
habits of a commendable life and honorable discharge. Moreover, since
it is only right that they should know the fitting rewards decreed by us
for meritorious military service, so that the said soldiers may enjoy forever the perpetual benefaction of the said indulgence of ours and that

[63] This is one of the many honorific abstractions used, with the advent of the Dominate, in addressing officials.
[64] Cf. introduction to § 128.   [65] Probably twenty-four years at this time.
[66] Cf. Note 63.

the everlasting foresight of our arrangement may acquire force, we desire the content of this indulgence of ours to be transcribed onto a bronze tablet and dedicated amid the military standards [67] in each and every camp, so that alike the legionary soldiers of Illyricum and also the cavalrymen there organized in detachments may enjoy equal benefits from our foresight, even as they undergo equal labors in military service.

Added in the divine [68] hand: Farewell, dearest Dalmatius.

In the consulship of the deified Maximianus, consul for the eighth time, and of our lord Maximinus Augustus, consul for the second time, June 10, at Serdica.[69]

Theodosian Code VII. xx. 2; A.D. 320 or 326

When he had entered the army headquarters and had been saluted by the prefects and tribunes and most eminent men, the acclamation arose, "Augustus Constantine! May the gods preserve you for us! Your salvation is our salvation. In truth we speak, on our oath we speak."

The assembled veterans cried out, "Constantine Augustus! To what purpose have we been made veterans if we have no special privilege?"

Constantine Augustus said, "I should more and more increase rather than diminish the happiness of my fellow veterans."

Victorinus, a veteran, said, "Do not allow us to be liable for compulsory public services and burdens in all places."

Constantine Augustus said, "Indicate more plainly. Which in particular are the compulsory public services that insistently oppress you?"

All the veterans said, "Surely, you yourself understand."

Constantine Augustus said, "Now be it manifest that this has been granted to all veterans by my munificence: that no one of them shall be liable for any compulsory municipal service, any public works, or any contribution. . . . In whatsoever public markets they participate, they shall not have to pay any imposts; the tax collectors also, as they are accustomed to collect more than is due . . . shall keep away from such veterans. After their labors the veterans shall forever enjoy tranquillity. By this same letter we have also prohibited our fisc from disturbing any one at all of these [veterans], but they shall be allowed to buy and sell [freely], so that they may enjoy their benefits unimpaired under the repose and peace of our era, and their old age may enjoy tranquillity after labors. . . ."

Theodosian Code VII. xx. 3; A.D. 320 or 326

Pursuant to our order, veterans shall receive vacant lands, and they shall hold them tax-free in perpetuity. They shall receive 25,000 *folles*

---

[67] That is, posted in the camp sanctuary, where the military standards were kept.
[68] Cf. Note 62.   [69] Modern Sofia.

in cash for the purchase of equipment necessary for farm life and also a pair of oxen and 100 *modii* of assorted grains. If, however, any veteran desires to engage in business, we permit him to have the sum of 100 *folles* tax-free. Except those veterans, therefore, who are established in homesteads or in businesses, all you who are unemployed and are engaged in no occupation should have recourse to this relief that you may not suffer want.

CHAPTER VIII

ROMAN LAW

This chapter illustrates some of the general principles and basic concepts of the Roman legal system, whose continuing influence is apparent from the striking resemblance to legal principles and practices of the present day. Because of limitations of space no attempt has been made to sample the minutiae of cases and actions that constitute the bulk of the voluminous source materials for Roman law.

The jurists of the Republic and the Principate were concerned essentially with the meaning and application of legal rules; related matters, whether incidental (for example, procedural, formulaic) or causal they disregarded almost completely. "The politico-economic conditions underlying the establishment of a legal rule are nowhere described or even mentioned," [1] yet they are everywhere apparent to the modern reader. The growing and repeated insistence, for example, that the spirit or intent should prevail over the letter or wording of a statute or document, the increasing emphasis on the claim of equity, on the benevolent interpretation, on the benefit of the doubt, are all evidences of the progressive humanization of the law under the influence of social forces.[2] The maxim, "Letter of law is height of injustice," was already trite in Cicero's day.[3]

The Roman legal writers, however, showed a marked disinclination for abstract formulation of legal rules, preferring instead to make a point by citing one or more illustrative cases. Cicero, impressed by Greek systematization, complained that "jurisconsults split up into endless cases what can be stated in a single formulation." [4] In addition, the Roman jurists distinguished public law very carefully from private law, concentrating on the latter. In the provinces, where it was carried by Roman citizens and armies, the law of Rome was influenced by contact with native legal institutions, especially those of the Hellenistic law in the eastern provinces. Caracalla's Empire-wide grant of citizenship (see § 113) accelerated the interaction of these and other forces, under whose influence the law of the city of Rome developed ultimately into the ecumenical legal system of Justinian's codification.

On the legal sources included in this chapter, see Vol. I, pp. 34–40. The specific topics and texts of §§ 159–165 should be compared with the relevant parts of §§ 157–158.

[1] F. Schulz, *Principles of Roman Law* (Oxford, 1936), p. 24.
[2] Cf. § 68.
[3] Cicero *On Duties* I. x. 33.
[4] Cicero *Laws* II. xix. 47.

157. *Definitions and Divisions of the Law*

Gaius *Institutes* 1. i–xi, xlviii–xlix
From the translation of F. de Zulueta, The Institutes of Gaius
(*Oxford, 1946*)

Every people that is governed by statutes and customs observes partly its own peculiar law and partly the common law of all mankind. That law which a people establishes for itself is peculiar to it, and is called civil law (*ius civile*) as being the law peculiar to that particular state (*civitas*), while the law which natural reason establishes throughout all mankind is followed by all peoples alike and is called the law of nations (*ius gentium*), as being the law observed by all peoples (*gentes*). Thus the Roman people observes partly its own peculiar law and partly the common law of mankind. This distinction we shall apply in detail at the proper places.

The laws of the Roman people consist of statutes, plebiscites, decrees of the senate, imperial constitutions, edicts of those possessing the right to issue them, and responses of the learned. . . . An imperial constitution is what the emperor by decree, edict, or letter ordains; it has never been doubted that this has the force of statute, seeing that the emperor himself receives his *imperium* through a statute. The right of issuing edicts is possessed by magistrates of the Roman people. Very extensive law is contained in the edicts of the two praetors, the urban and the peregrine, whose jurisdiction is possessed in the provinces by the provincial governors; also in the edicts of the curule aediles, whose jurisdiction is possessed in the provinces of the Roman people by quaestors; no quaestors are sent to the provinces of Caesar, and consequently the aedilician edict is not published there. The responses of the learned are the decisions and opinions of those who are authorized to lay down the law. If the decisions of all of them agree, what they so hold has the force of statute, but if they disagree the judge is at liberty to follow whichever decision he pleases. This is declared by a rescript of the deified Hadrian.

The whole of the law observed by us relates either to persons or to things or to legal actions. Let us first consider persons.

The principal distinction in the law of persons is this, that all men are either free or slaves. Next, free men are either freeborn or freedmen. Freeborn are those born free, freedmen those manumitted from lawful slavery. . . .

Next comes another division in the law of persons. For some persons are independent and others are dependent upon another. Again, of dependent persons some are in the power of parents, others of husbands, and others of masters.

[There follow illustrative cases of each category. After the law of persons Gaius takes up the law of things (Books II–III), and then the law of legal actions (Book IV).]

Justinian Digest I. i, iii–iv [5]

Justice and Law

(Ulpian *Institutes* 1) [6] When a man means to give his attention to law, he ought first to know whence the term law (*ius*) is derived. Now it is so called from justice (*iustitia*). In fact, as Celsus neatly defines it, *ius* is the art of the good and the fair. Of this art we may deservedly be called the priests; we cherish justice and profess the knowledge of the good and the fair,[7] separating the fair from the unfair, discriminating between the permitted and the forbidden, desiring to make men good, not only by the fear of penalties, but also by the incentives of rewards, affecting, if I mistake not, a true and not a simulated philosophy.

This subject comprises two categories, public law and private law. Public law is that which regards the constitution of the Roman state, private law that which looks to the interest of individuals; for some things are beneficial from the point of view of the state, and some with reference to private persons. Public law is concerned with sacred rites, with priests, with public officers. Private law is tripartite, being derived from the rules of natural law, or of the law of nations, or of civil law. Natural law is that which all animals have been taught by nature; this law is not peculiar to the human race, but is common to all animals which are produced on land or sea, and to the birds as well. From it comes the union of male and female, which we call matrimony, and the procreation and rearing of children; we find in fact that animals in general, even the wild beasts, are marked by acquaintance with this law. The law of nations is that which the various peoples of mankind observe. It is easy to see that it falls short of natural law, because the latter is common to all living creatures, whereas the former is common only to human beings in their mutual relations—

(Pomponius *Manual*) for example, devotion to a god, obedience to parents and country;

---

[5] Part of Title ii, omitted here, appears in Vol. I, § 25.
[6] For illustrative purposes we include here and in § 158 the source citation (jurist and work) which precedes every *Digest* text. The names encountered in these references are those of eminent jurists from the late first to the mid-third or early fourth century.
[7] Cf. Note 14.

(Florentinus *Institutes* 1) or repelling violence and injury. It is by virtue of this law that whatever a man does for the protection of his own person he is deemed to have done lawfully; and since nature has established a certain kinship among us, it follows that it is sinful for man to waylay man.

(Ulpian *Institutes* 1) Manumissions are also comprised in the law of nations. Manumission is the dismissal from hand (*manus*), that is, the giving of freedom. For as long as anyone is in a state of slavery, he is subject to hand and control; when manumitted, he is freed from control. This had its origin in the law of nations, seeing that by natural law all were born free and manumission was not known since slavery was unknown; but after slavery made its appearance under the law of nations, the benefaction of manumission followed. And whereas we used to be called by the one natural name of men, under the law of nations there came to be three classes: freemen; in contradistinction to these, slaves; and a third class, freedmen, that is those who had ceased to be slaves.

(Hermogenianus *Epitomes of Law* 1) Under this same law of nations, wars were begun, peoples distinguished, kingdoms founded, ownerships marked off, boundary stones placed for fields, buildings erected, commercial relations, sale, hire, and obligations instituted, with the exception of a few which were introduced under civil law.

(Ulpian *Institutes* 1) Civil law is that which neither wholly departs from natural law or the law of nations nor is altogether subordinate thereto; thus, when we add to or subtract from universal law, we bring about our own peculiar law, that is, civil law. Now, this law of ours exists either in writing or without writing; as the Greeks say, "of the laws some are written and some are unwritten."

(Papinian *Definitions* 11) The civil law is that which is derived from statutes, plebiscites, decrees of the senate, enactments of the emperors, and the authority of the learned [in the law]. Praetorian law is that which was introduced by the praetors in order to clarify, supplement, or amend the civil law with a view to the public advantage. This is also called honorary law, so named after the public office (*honor*) of the praetors.

(Marcianus *Institutes* 1) Indeed, this very honorary law is the living voice of the civil law.

(Gaius *Institutes* 1) [Gaius' two opening sentences—see first selection, above—are quoted here.]

(Ulpian *Rules* 1) Justice is a constant, unfailing disposition to give everyone his legal due. The principles of law are these: to live uprightly, not to injure another man, to give every man his due. To be learned in the law (*jurisprudentia*) is the knowledge of things divine and human, the science of the just and the unjust. . . .

Statutes, Decrees of the Senate, and Long Usage

(Papinian *Definitions* I) A statute is a rule of general application, a decision of prudent men, a restraint upon offenses committed voluntarily or in ignorance, a general covenant of the state.

(Marcianus *Institutes* I) The orator Demosthenes defines it thus: "A law is that which all men ought properly to obey for many reasons, and chiefly because every law is an invention and gift of God,[8] a decision of prudent men, a means of correcting offenses intentional and unintentional, a general covenant of the city in accordance with which all in the city ought properly to live." And Chrysippus, the philosopher of the highest wisdom of the Stoics, begins his book *On Law* thus: "Law is the king of all things, both divine and human. It should be an indicator, ruler, and guide of both the good and the base, and accordingly a standard of just and unjust and of beings political by nature,[9] enjoining what ought to be done and forbidding what ought not to be done."

(Pomponius *On Sabinus* xxv) Laws ought to be laid down, as Theophrastus said, in matters which happen "for the most part," not which happen "against reasonable expectation." . . .

(Modestinus *Rules* I) The essence of a statute is this: to order, to forbid, to permit, to punish.

(Ulpian *On Sabinus* III) Laws are not laid down with reference to particular individuals but for general application.

(The same *On the Edict* xvi) There is no question that the senate can make law.

(Julianus *Digest* LIX, XC, XV) Neither statutes nor decrees of the senate can be drafted so as to comprehend every case that ever arises, but it is enough if they encompass such things as happen most of the time. Consequently, in matters for which rules are first laid down, more precise provision has to be made either by interpretation or by a constitution of the excellent emperor. It is impossible for every point to be individually comprehended in statutes or decrees of the senate; but when their sense in a given case is clear, the magistrate presiding over the jurisdiction ought to extend it to analogous situations and render judgment accordingly. . . .

(Paulus *On the Edict* LIV) But a rule that has obtained currency contrary to legal principle must not be extended to its logical consequences. . . .

(Celsus *Digest* XXVI, XXIX, XXXIII) To know the statutes means to grasp, not their wording, but their force and scope. Statutes ought to be interpreted rather liberally, so as to preserve their intent. Where a

---

[8] Demosthenes actually wrote, "of the gods."

[9] This phrase is the famous Aristotelian definition of man (*Politics* I. ii. 9).

term in a statute is ambiguous, that meaning ought to be adopted which is free of fault, especially since the intent of the statute, too, can be deduced thereby. . . .

(Ulpian *On the Edict* xxxv) When a statute excuses something for the past, it still forbids it for the future.

(Paulus *On Plautius* iv) Absolutely no change ought to be made in matters where a fixed interpretation has always prevailed.

(Celsus *Digest* ix) It is not civil practice to put forward some one portion of a statute and found a judgment or juristic opinion upon it without examining the whole statute.

(Modestinus *Responses* viii) It is inconsistent with all legal principle and liberality of equity for rules which are salutarily introduced for the benefit of men to be through harsher interpretation extended by us in the direction of severity to their disadvantage.

(Paulus *Questions* iv) It is not new for earlier statutes to be adduced for interpreting later ones. . . .

(Paulus *On the Cincian Law*) A man who does what a statute prohibits acts contrary to the statute, while one who circumvents the intent of a statute without disobeying the actual words evades it. . . .

(Ulpian *On the Julian-Papian Law* xiii) The emperor is not bound by statutes.[10] The empress to be sure is bound by statutes, but the [reigning] emperor grants her the same privileges that he himself enjoys.

(Julianus *Digest* lxxxiv) In cases where we have no written statutes to observe, that rule ought to be followed which has been established by custom and usage; and if such should be lacking in any matter, then that which is nearest and consequent thereto; and if even this cannot be found, then we ought to go by the law which is observed in the city of Rome. Long-standing usage is not unreasonably followed in place of a statute; and this is what is called the law established by custom. For, since statutes themselves are binding upon us for no other reason than that they have been accepted by the judgment of the people, all will properly be bound also by whatever the people approves without any writing; for what difference does it make whether the people declares its will by vote or by actual fact and deed? Wherefore this also is accepted, and very rightly so, that statutes are abrogated not only by the vote of the legislator, but also by falling out of use with the tacit consent of all.

(Ulpian *On the Office of Proconsul* i) It is the practice for usage of long standing to be observed in place of law and statute in such matters as do not come under a written rule. . . .

(Callistratus *Questions* i) In fact our Emperor Severus ruled in a

[10] On the emergence of this principle, see introduction to § 125.

rescript that in ambiguities proceeding from statutes, usage or the authority of matters constantly decided in similar manner ought to acquire the force of a statute.

(Celsus *Digest* XXIII) But a rule introduced not by legal principle but by initial error and subsequently maintained by usage does not obtain in other similar cases.

(Modestinus *Rules* I) Accordingly, all law was either made through consent or created by necessity or established by usage. . . .

Imperial Constitutions

(Ulpian *Institutes* I) What the emperor has determined has the force of a statute; seeing that by a royal law which was passed concerning his authority the people transfers to him and upon him the whole of its own authority and power. Accordingly, whatever the emperor has laid down by letter with his signature, or has decreed upon judicial investigation, or has pronounced extrajudicially, or ordained by edict, amounts beyond question to a statute. Clearly, some of these are of individual application and are not extended into a precedent; for whatever an emperor grants to anyone for his merits, or if he imposes any penalty or provides someone with unprecedented aid, it applies only to the individual.

(Ulpian *Trusts* IV) In establishing new ordinances there ought to be evident benefit in departing from the law which has long been regarded as fair.

(Javolenus *Epistles* XIII) A benefaction of the emperor, which naturally proceeds from his divine indulgence, ought to be interpreted by us in its fullest possible construction.

(Modestinus *Excuses* II) Later enactments have more force than those which precede them.

158. *General Rules of Law*

Justinian *Digest* L. xvii [11]

(Paulus *On Sabinus* VIII) [12] That which is faulty in the beginning cannot become valid with the passage of time.

(Ulpian *On Sabinus* XXXVI) Not cohabitation but consent makes a marriage.

(*Ibid.*, LI) No one who has the power to condemn lacks the power to acquit.

[11] This, the final title of the *Digest*, contains 211 entries; only a selection is given here.
[12] Cf. Note 6.

(Ulpian *On the Edict* xxvi) Anything not permitted the defendant ought not be allowed the plaintiff.

(*Ibid.*, xxx) Advice not fraudulent entails no obligation; but if calculated deceit is involved, an action for fraud is in order.

(Paulus *On the Edict* xxxix) He who has knowledge [of a crime] but is unable to prevent it is free of blame.

(Ulpian *On the Edict* xlvi) No one can transfer to another more legal right than he himself may possess.

(Gaius *On the Urban Edict, Concerning Legacies* iii) In cases of doubt, the more liberal interpretations should always be preferred.

(Papinian *Questions* vi) Whenever the principle of natural desire or doubt as to the law blocks equity, the matter should be tempered by just decisions.

(Paulus *Questions* xv) In all matters certainly, but especially in the case of law, equity should be given due regard.

(Scaevola *Responses* v) If a copyist commits an error in transcribing the text of a stipulation, it in no way impairs the liability of the debtor and the surety.

(Ulpian *Trusts* ii) Superfluous matter ordinarily does not vitiate a document.

(Maecianus *Trusts* xii) In ambiguous language the intention of the party who produced it should be given chief consideration.

(Paulus *On Judicial Investigations*) When a statute makes mention of two months, a party who appears on the sixty-first day should be heard; for thus the Emperor Antoninus together with his deified father ruled in a rescript.

(Paulus *On the Edict* i) No one may be forcibly removed from his own house.

(*Ibid.*, ii) Liberty is a possession on which no evaluation can be placed.

(*Ibid.*, ix) In cases of obscurity it is customary to consider what is more likely or what the general practice is.

(Ulpian *On the Edict* xi) Nothing is so contrary to consent . . . as force and fear, to approve which is contrary to morality.

(Gaius *On the Provincial Edict* v) Freedom is beloved above all things.

(Paulus *On the Edict* xix) In case of equal [conflicting] claims, the party in possession ought to be considered in the stronger position.

(*Ibid.*, xxvii) The gravity of a past offense never increases *ex post facto*.

(Ulpian *On the Edict* lxx) No one is compelled to defend a cause against his will.

(*Paulus On Plautius* II) He inflicts an injury who orders it to be inflicted; but no guilt attaches to him who is obliged to obey.

(*Ibid.*, III) An act of a judge which does not pertain to his office is not valid.

(*Ibid.*, VI) When judgment is rendered against persons to the extent of their ability, their entire possessions are not to be taken away, but consideration is to be shown them so that they are not reduced to want.

(*Ibid.*, XVI) When the intent of a person granting manumission is obscure, a decision should be rendered in favor of freedom.

(*Marcellus Digest* III) Although no change should be made lightly in legal formalities, still relief should be granted where equity clearly demands it.

(*Celsus Digest* VIII) An obligation to do the impossible is null and void.

(*Javolenus Epistles* VII) Whenever a judicial investigation cannot be made without injury, the course should be adopted which is productive of the least unfairness.

(*Pomponius From Various Texts* IX) It is right under natural law that no one should increase his wealth through harm or injury to another.

(*Ulpian On the Julian-Papian Law* I) An adjudicated matter is accepted as truth.[13]

(*Paulus On the Julian-Papian Law* III) He who never had cannot be considered to have ceased to have.

Justinian *Digest* XLVIII. xix. 18, 42

(*Ulpian On the Edict* III) No one suffers a penalty for what he thinks.

(*Hermogenianus Epitomes* I) By the interpretation of statutes penalties should be mitigated rather than increased in severity.

159. *Equity and Custom*

Cicero *Classification of Oratory* xxxvii. 130
Adapted from LCL

"Equity" has a twofold meaning, one of which rests on the straightforward principle of truth and justice—of the "fair and good," as the

[13] An interesting instance of the application of this principle of *res adjudicata* is preserved in *CIL*, Vol. VI, No. 266 (= *FIRA*, Vol. III, No. 165). This inscription concerns a lawsuit brought in A.D. 226 before the prefect of the night patrol (probably in his capacity as superintendent of public thoroughfares), and twice appealed to subsequent holders of that office, one of them being the celebrated jurist Herennius Modestinus. Both these later prefects dismissed the case as already adjudicated, Modestinus ruling, "Any matter which has been duly judged possesses its own authority."

phrase is [14]—while the other concerns requital, which in the case of a kindness is called gratitude and in the case of an injury retaliation. These things belong in common to nature and to law; but peculiar to law are the written and unwritten rules preserved by the law of nations or by ancestral custom. Of the written code, part is private and part public; the public code consists of laws, decrees of the senate, and treaties, while the private code includes compacts, covenants, and contracts. The unwritten rules are maintained either by custom or by the conventions and virtual consensus of men. And also—a point of primary importance —it is, in a way, prescribed by natural law that we shall preserve our own customs and laws.

Justinian *Code* viii. lii. 2

The Emperor Constantine to Proculus.[15] The authority of custom and long-continued usage should not be treated lightly, but it should not of its own weight prevail to the extent of overcoming either reason or statute.

160. *No Ex Post Facto Laws*

Cicero *Second Speech against Verres* [16] i. xli. 106–xlii. 109
Adapted from LCL

Read please [from Verres' praetorian edict]: "*Any man who, since the censorship of Aulus Postumius and Quintus Fulvius or any following year . . . has done or shall do so.*"

"Has done or shall do!" Did ever such an expression occur in an edict before? Did an edict ever before attach illegality, or liability to punishment, to an act that . . . there was no reason to avoid before it was issued? . . . It appears the Voconian Law enjoyed your approval. You might well have followed the example of Quintus Voconius himself, then. For his statute did not deprive any girl or woman of her position of heiress if she had it already; it merely enjoined that no one registered in the census after the year of the censors named should make a girl or woman his heiress in the future. In the Voconian Law we do not find "has done or shall do"; nor in any statute is a past action made subject to censure, except such as of their own nature are criminal and vile, so that they ought to have been avoided at all costs even if no statute forbade them. And even so we often find that a statute prohibiting such

---

[14] This traditional definition of law continued in use for centuries and was included in the first citation of Justinian's *Digest* (§ 157, second selection).
[15] The date of this imperial constitution is A.D. 319.
[16] For Cicero's prosecution of Verres, see Vol. I, §§ 143, 144, 158, 188. On the Voconian Law mentioned below, see Chapter I, Note 207.

actions precludes prosecution of those who have already committed
them. The Cornelian Laws on wills, for instance, and coinage, and a
number of others, set up no new legal principle for the community but
provide that what has always been in fact an immoral action shall become subject to criminal proceedings before the community after a fixed
date. Surely, then, where a man introduces some innovation in *civil* law,
he must allow all acts previously committed to be legally valid. Look at
the Atinian Law, the Furian, the Fusian, the Voconian Law itself, as I
have said, in fact all that are concerned with civil law: in all of them you
will find the same thing, law that is to be binding on the community
after the statute comes into force.

161. *The Spirit vs. the Letter of the Law*

Cicero *In Defense of Caecina* xviii. 51–53
Adapted from LCL

Can it indeed be doubted that neither our own language, which is
said to be deficient, nor even any other contains so large a store of words
to distinguish every matter by a definite and peculiar term; or indeed,
that words are superfluous when the matter is clear? . . . What statute,
what senatorial decree, what magisterial edict, what treaty or agreement,
or (to speak once more of our private concerns) what testament, what
rules of law or undertakings or formal pacts and agreements can not
be invalidated and nullified if we choose to sacrifice the meaning to the
words without taking into account the plan, the purpose, and the intention of the writer? Why, the familiar speech of every day will not have
a consistent meaning if we set verbal traps for one another. Even our
authority at home will cease to exist if we allow our slave boys to obey
our orders to the letter only, without paying any attention to the meaning implied in our words. And now I suppose I must produce examples
of all these points . . . to support my plea that law does not depend
on words, but that words are subservient to the purpose and intentions
of men. This opinion was supported by the great orator Lucius Crassus
. . . who proved to everyone, and with ease, that Manius Curius, who
was named heir "in the event of the death of a posthumous son," [17] was
entitled to be the heir although the son not only was not dead, but had
not even been born. Well, did the wording of the will provide adequately
for this situation? Far from it. Then what was the deciding consideration? Intent. And if this could be made clear without our speaking, we

[17] "Posthumous" here has the sense of one born after the father's will was drawn,
and not necessarily after his death.

should not use words at all; but because it cannot, words have been invented, not to conceal but to reveal intent.

Justinian Digest L. xvi. 6, 219

The expression "in accordance with statutes" is to be taken to mean in accordance with the spirit of the statutes as well as in accordance with the words.

It has been held that in agreements the intent of the contracting parties is to be taken into consideration rather than the words.

162. *Bona Fides*

Cicero On Duties III. xvii. 70–72
Adapted from LCL

It was Quintus Scaevola, the *pontifex maximus*, who used to attach the greatest importance to all questions of arbitration to which the formula "as good faith requires" was appended; and he held that the expression "good faith" had a very extensive application, for it was employed in guardianships and partnerships, in trusts and commissions, in buying and selling, in hiring and letting—in a word, in all the transactions on which the social relations of daily life depend; in these, he said, it required a judge of great ability to decide the extent of each individual's obligation to the other, especially as there were counterclaims in most cases. . . .

It is not only in the case of real-estate transactions that the civil law, based upon a natural feeling for the right, punishes trickery and deception; but also in the sale of slaves every form of deception on the vendor's part is disallowed. For by the aediles' edict, [the vendor], who ought to know if a slave is unhealthy, a runaway, or a thief, is responsible therefor.[18]

From this we come to realize that since nature is the source of right, it is in accord with nature that no one should so act as to profit by his neighbor's ignorance.

163. *Guardianship of Women and Minors*

Cicero In Defense of Murena xii. 27

Our ancestors established the rule that all women, because of their weakness of intellect, should be under the power of guardians.

[18] Cf. Chapter III, Note 141.

Ulpian *Rules* xi. 1, 18, 25, 27

Guardians are appointed for males as well as for females: for males only when under age, on account of their tender age; but for females, when under and of age, on account of the weakness of their sex and their ignorance of business matters.

The Atilian Law orders that, for women and for wards who have none, guardians be granted by the praetor and a majority of the tribunes of the plebs, and these we call Atilian guardians. But, because the Atilian Law is in force only at Rome, it is provided by the Julian-Titian Law that guardians of such persons be similarly granted in the provinces also by the governors.[19]

The guardians of male and female wards transact their business and give their authorization; the guardians of women merely give their authorization.

The authority of a guardian is necessary for women in the following transactions: if they take legal action in accordance with statute or judgment, if they undertake an obligataion, if they transact any civil business, if they permit a freedwoman of theirs to cohabit with the slave of another, if they alienate salable property.

APPOINTMENT OF GUARDIANS

Oxyrhynchus Papyrus No. 1,466; A.D. 245

To Valerius Firmus, prefect of Egypt, from Aurelia Arsinoë. I beg, my lord, that you assign Aurelius Herminus to me as guardian in accordance with the Julian and Titian Laws. Year 2, Pachon 26. Page 94, Volume I.[20]

Translation of the [preceding] Latin. To Valerius Firmus, prefect of Egypt, from Aurelia Arsinoë. I beg, my lord, that you assign Aurelius Herminus to me as guardian in accordance with the Julian and Titian Laws. Submitted on May 21 in the consulship of the Emperor Philip Augustus and Titianus. I, Aurelia Arsinoë, daughter of Sarapio, have submitted the petition requesting that Aurelius Herminus be appointed my guardian. I, Aurelius Timagenes[?] son of . . . wrote for her since she is illiterate. I, Aurelius Herminus son of Dionysius, consent to the petition. Year 2, Pachon 26.

[The prefect's subscription] Unless you are under the control of another guardian,[21] I grant you the guardian you request.

---

[19] The Atilian Law is known to have been in effect by 186 B.C.; how much earlier than that it was passed is unknown. The Julian and Titian Laws (they were probably separate though related measures) belong to the principate of Augustus.

[20] This notation gives the file number of the petition in the prefect's office.

[21] See Note 22.

FIRA, Vol. III, No. 25; A.D. 198

Quintus Aemilius Saturninus, prefect of Egypt, at the request of Gaius Terentius Sarapammo assigned to Mevia Dionysarion, in accordance with the Julian and Titian Laws and a decree of the senate, Marcus Julius Alexander as guardian, provided the guardianship is not thereby taken away from the legal guardian. . . .[22] Done at Alexandria on the coast of Egypt on September 23 in the consulship of Saturninus and Gallus, in the seventh year of the Emperors Caesars Lucius SEPTIMIUS SEVERUS Pius Pertinax Arabicus Adiabenicus Parthicus Maximus Augustus and Marcus Aurelius Antoninus Augustus [CARACALLA], month of Thoth, 26th day.

[Signed] I, Mevia Dionysarion, requested that Julius Alexander be assigned to me as guardian, as stated above. I, Gaius Julius Heraclas, wrote for her since she is illiterate.[23]

WOMEN INDEPENDENT OF GUARDIANSHIP: THE "THREE-CHILDREN PRIVILEGE"

See §§ 11, 64.

Gaius *Institutes* I. cxlv, cxciv

If anyone by will assigns a guardian to his son and daughter and both reach puberty, the son ceases to have a guardian but the daughter nonetheless remains under guardianship; for, in accordance with the Julian and Papian-Poppaean Laws, it is only by the right of children that women are freed from guardianship.

Moreover, freeborn women are freed from guardianship by the right of three children; freedwomen, if they are under the legal guardianship of their patron or of his children, by that of four.

REQUEST FOR RELEASE FROM GUARDIANSHIP

Oxyrhynchus Papyrus No. 1,467 (= *Select Papyri*, No. 305); A.D. 263

. . . [laws have been made], Most Eminent Prefect, which empower women who are honored with the right of three children to be independent and act without a guardian in whatever business they transact, especially those who know how to write.[24] Accordingly, as I have

[22] By this clause the grant is restricted to *bona fide* requests and is automatically invalidated if obtained through misrepresentation (that is, of who the legal guardian is).

[23] There follow the names of seven witnesses (the customary number: cf. Chapter IV, Note 138).

[24] Literacy was not a necessary condition for the "three-children privilege." This superfluous detail was doubtless added as another evidence of the petitioner's qualifications for independence.

been fortunate in being blessed with goodly offspring and am literate and able to write with a high degree of ease, it is with complete assurance that I address Your Highness through this petition of mine with the object of being empowered to accomplish without hindrance whatever business I henceforth transact. I beg you to place it without prejudice to my rights in Your Eminence's file, in order that I may obtain your aid and acknowledge my eternal appropriate[?] gratitude. Farewell.

[Signed] I, Aurelia Thaïsous, also called Lolliana, transmitted this for submission. Year 10, Epeiph 21.

[Subscription] Your petition shall be kept in the file.

164. *Funerary Law*

Paulus *Opinions* i. xxi (abridged)

It is not permissible to bring a corpse into a city, lest the sacred places of the city be polluted; and anyone who acts contrary to this is punished without delay. A corpse cannot be committed to burial or burned within the walls of a city.

Anyone who strips a body committed to permanent burial or temporarily deposited in some place, and exposes it to the rays of the sun, commits sacrilege; and therefore, if he is of superior rank he is generally deported to an island, if he is of inferior rank he is sent to the mines. Persons who violate a sepulcher or remove anything from a sepulcher are, according to the rank of the person, either sent to the mines or deported to an island. Anyone who breaks open or uncovers a sepulcher belonging to another and places therein his own or another's dead, is considered to have violated sepulture. . . . Anyone who erases an inscription on a tomb, or overturns a statue, or carries off anything therefrom, or removes a stone or a column, is considered to have violated sepulture. In a sarcophagus or vault where a body has already been deposited another body may not be placed, and he who does so can be prosecuted for violation of sepulture. . . .[25]

Parents and children over ten years of age are to be mourned for a year; minors up to the age of three years, one month for each year of their age at the time of their death;[26] a husband, ten months; and cognates closer than the sixth remove, eight months. Anyone who acts contrary

---

25 With this section on violation of sepulture cf. § 8, last selection.
26 This is the generally accepted emendation of the text, which reads simply, "minors, a month." For the beginnings of Roman regulation of mourning, see Vol. I, pp. 61, 108–9.

is visited with public disgrace.[27] Anyone who is in mourning ought to eschew banquets, ornaments, and purple and white clothing.

Anything expended for a funeral is deducted as the first claim among the debts [of the estate].

165. *Criminal Law*

CAPITAL PUNISHMENT
Justinian *Institutes* IV. xviii. 1–2

Public trials are so called because generally any citizen at all has the right to institute their prosecution. Of public prosecutions some are capital, some are not capital. We call those capital which inflict the supreme penalty, or interdiction from fire and water, or deportation, or condemnation to the mines;[28] the others, if they impose public disgrace[29] and money fine, are public also but not capital.

BENEFIT OF THE DOUBT; INTENT
Justinian *Digest* XLVIII. xix. 5

. . . The deified Trajan ruled in a rescript to Assidius Severus that no one was to be convicted on suspicion alone, saying that it was better for the crime of a guilty person to be left unpunished than for an innocent person to be condemned. . . . In the case of major offenses it makes a difference whether something is committed purposely or accidentally. And, indeed, in all crimes this distinction ought either to elicit a strict penalty or permit moderation.

INDIVIDUAL GUILT, NOT COLLECTIVE
Justinian *Digest* XLVIII. xix. 26; L. xviii. 111, 164

The guilt or punishment of a father can impose no stigma upon the son; for every individual is subjected to treatment in accordance with

---

[27] *Infamia*, or public disgrace, was visited upon Roman citizens for any of a variety of criminal or moral offenses, such as dishonorable discharge from the army, engaging in a dishonorable occupation (such as acting or procuring), conviction on a charge of violation of a trust, slander, theft, and the like.

[28] The "supreme penalty" means death; "interdiction from fire and water," exile. Deportation was usually to an island. A citizen's *caput* was either his head or, politically speaking, his civic status (cf. Vol. I, p. 361); hence those penalties which entailed the impairment of the *caput* in one sense or the other, were all forms of "capital" punishment.

[29] See Note 27.

his own action and no one is made the inheritor of the guilt of another, as the deified brothers stated in a rescript addressed to the city of Hierapolis.[30]

Legal actions which are penal as a result of such infractions as theft, damage, armed robbery, or injuries do not carry over to an heir.

Penal cases once accepted [by the court] can be carried over to heirs.

EXTENUATING CIRCUMSTANCES

Justinian *Digest* L. xvii. 108 and 155. 2

In inflicting penalties, the age and inexperience of the guilty party must be taken into account.

In penal cases the most benevolent construction should be adopted.

CAPITAL CRIMES

Paulus *Opinions* v. xxii–xxiv (abridged)

Concerning Seditious Persons [31]

Instigators of sedition and riot or rousers of the people are, according to the nature of their rank, either crucified, thrown to wild beasts, or deported to an island. As for those who dig up or plow up boundary stones or destroy boundary trees, if slaves do it of their own volition, they are condemned to the mines; if humble persons, to [labor on] public works; if of superior rank, they are deprived of one third of their property and relegated to an island or driven into exile. Roman citizens who permit themselves or their slaves to be circumcised under the Jewish rite are deprived of their property and relegated to an island for life; the physicians [who perform the operation] suffer capital punishment. . . .

On the Cornelian Law Concerning Assassins and Poisoners [32]

The Cornelian Law inflicts the penalty of deportation on a person who kills a man, or carries a weapon for that purpose or to commit robbery, or has in his possession, sells, or prepares poison for the purpose of killing a man, or gives false testimony so that some one may lose his life,

---

[30] "The deified brothers" refers to the Emperors Marcus Aurelius and Lucius Verus. The emperors, especially in the first century, did not always abide by this precept, as for example when Nero punished the children of the men involved in the conspiracy of Piso by banishment, death, or deprivation of livelihood (Suetonius *Life of Nero* xxxvi).

[31] Cf. also §§ 7, 23.

[32] A law passed c.81 B.C., in the dictatorship of Lucius Cornelius Sulla.

or causes a death. For all these crimes it has been decreed that capital punishment shall be meted out to persons of superior rank; humble persons, however, are either crucified or thrown to wild beasts.

One who kills a man is sometimes acquitted, and one who does not kill is condemned as a homicide, for an individual's purpose and not his act is punished. Therefore, one who intended to kill but was unable to accomplish the crime through some accidental circumstance is punished as a homicide, and a person who accidentally and inadvertently kills a man by throwing a weapon is acquitted. . . .

A judge who takes money [for a decision] against the life or property of a man is deprived of his property and deported to an island.

Instigators of murder are punished in the same way as homicides. . . .

Persons who administer abortion potions or love philtres—even if they do not do so with evil intent, nevertheless, as it is an evil practice— are, if humble, deported to the mines; if of superior rank, deprived of part of their property and relegated to an island. But if the man or the woman perishes as a result, they are visited with the supreme penalty.

Persons who perform, or cause to be performed, impious or nocturnal rites in order to enchant, bewitch, or bind, are crucified or thrown to wild beasts. . . . It has been decreed that persons who are privy to the art of magic shall be visited with the supreme penalty, that is, be thrown to wild beasts or crucified. The magicians themselves are burned alive. No one is permitted to have books on the art of magic in his possession; those in whose possession they are found (the books are burned in public) are deprived of their property and deported to an island if of superior rank, and suffer capital punishment if humble. Not only the profession but even the knowledge of this art is prohibited. . . .

On the Pompeian Law Concerning Parricides [33]

Persons who kill father or mother, grandfather or grandmother, brother or sister, patron or patroness, although formerly they were sewn up in a sack and hurled into the sea,[34] are nowadays burned alive or offered to wild beasts.

[33] This law was passed in one of the consulships of Pompey the Great (70, 55, or 52 B.C.).

[34] Cf. Justinian *Institutes* IV. xviii. 6: "The Pompeian Law on parricides provides that if anyone hastens the death of a parent or child or any relation comprehended in the term 'parricide' . . . he will be subjected neither to sword nor to fire nor to any other ordinary punishment, but he is to be sewn up in a sack with a dog, a cock, a snake, and an ape, and . . . cast into the nearby sea or river, so that he may begin while still alive to be deprived of all enjoyment of the elements and may be denied the light of heaven while living and the earth when dead."

166. *Rules of Evidence*

Acts of the Apostles 25: 16

It is not the Roman custom to condemn any man before the accused meets his accusers face to face and has an opportunity to defend himself against the charge.

Justinian *Digest* XXII. iii. 2

The burden of proof is upon the party affirming, not on the party denying.

Justinian *Digest* XXII. v. (abridged)

The credibility of witnesses should be carefully weighed. Therefore, in investigating their persons attention should be paid first of all to the rank of each, whether a man is a decurion or a plebeian; and whether his life is honorable and blameless or on the contrary he is a man branded with public disgrace [35] and is reprehensible; whether he is rich or poor, so that he may readily do something for the purpose of gain; [36] whether he is hostile to the party against whom he bears testimony, or friendly to the party for whom he gives testimony. For if his testimony is free from suspicion either in view of the person by whom it is borne (because he is honorable), or in view of his motives (because he is motivated neither by gain, nor by favor, nor by hostility), he is to be admitted. Therefore the deified Hadrian stated in a rescript to Vivius Varus, governor of the province of Cilicia, that the person sitting in judgment is better able to know how much credence should be placed in witnesses. The wording of the letter is as follows: "You are better able to know how much credence should be placed in the witnesses; who they are and of what rank and reputation; which among them have apparently spoken frankly; whether they have offered one and the same premeditated story or have without preparation made true-sounding answers to the questions you put to them."

There is extant also a rescript of the same emperor to Valerius Verus on ascertaining the credibility of witnesses, in the following terms: "No adequate ruling can be laid down with any fixed precision as to what manner of evidence is sufficient to constitute proof of a given matter. Though not always, yet often the truth of a given matter is discovered

---

[35] See Note 27.
[36] Juvenal in his famous Third Satire remarks bitterly on how the credibility of witnesses varied with their wealth: see above, p. 240.

without public records. In some cases, the number of the witnesses, in others their rank and authority, in still others, for example, their unanimous reputation, confirms the credibility of the matter under investigation. Therefore, I can write you only this in brief, that a judicial investigation certainly ought not to be confined exclusively to one kind of proof, but you have to determine what in your best judgment you are to believe or what you think has not been proved to your satisfaction." . . .

The Julian Law Concerning Violence [37] provides that the following are not permitted to give testimony under this statute against a defendant: a person who has obtained freedom from him or his father, or persons who are under age, or anyone who has been condemned in a public trial and has not been completely reinstated, or who is in chains or in a public prison, or who has hired himself out to fight with wild beasts, or any woman who is or has been a prostitute, or anyone who has been sentenced or convicted for having taken money for giving or withholding testimony. For some persons should not be admitted to credibility of testimony because of deference to persons, others because of the unreliability of their judgment, and still others because of the stigma and public disgrace of their lives.

Witnesses should not be summoned rashly from great distances, and much less should soldiers be called away from their units or duties for the purpose of presenting testimony, as the deified Hadrian ruled in a rescript. . . .

The deposition of a slave is to be believed when there is no other proof for getting at the truth.

A father is not a competent witness for a son, nor a son for a father.

It is understood that no one is a competent witness in his own case. . . .

If the circumstances of a case are such that we are compelled to admit a gladiator or similar person [38] as a witness, his testimony is not to be believed unless taken under torture. . . . If some of the witnesses contradict the others, even though they are a minority [they may] be believed . . . for it is not to numbers that one must look, but to the sincere credibility of the witnesses and to the testimony in which the light of truth most probably resides.

---

[37] Enacted probably in the principate of Augustus.
[38] That is, a slave: cf. introduction to § 68.

CHAPTER IX

THE CONFLICT OF RELIGIONS AND
THE TRIUMPH OF CHRISTIANITY

167. *Roman State Religion*

During the first two centuries of the Empire the official state religion was an amalgam of the traditional native ritual as rehabilitated by Augustus and of the ruler cult instituted by him. The formal ceremonials of the native religion were almost exclusively the domain of the senatorial aristocracy, who conservatively preserved its legalistic formulae and antiquated priesthoods. In its domestic counterpart the native cult survived longest among the country folk (*pagani*). But all through the Principate the older gods of the state cult —with the exception of the Capitoline Triad of Jupiter, Juno, and Minerva (cf. Vol. I, p. 55, Note 23)—declined steadily in importance and became, in fact, appanages of the increasingly dominant cult of the imperial house (§ 168).

RELIGIOUS FORMALISM

Pliny *Natural History* xxviii. iii. 10–12, iv. 18

To slaughter a sacrificial victim without a prayer does not seem to be of any avail or to constitute due consultation of the gods. In addition, there is one formula for obtaining favorable omens, another for averting evil, another for praising the gods. And we see that the highest magistrates employ definite formulae in their prayers, that not a single word may be omitted or said out of its proper place, that someone dictates from writing [the formula to the magistrate], and another is assigned as watcher to listen carefully, and a third is placed in charge of ordering that ceremonial silence be maintained, while a flutist plays to prevent any other words from being heard. There are memorable instances on record of the times when unlucky portents impeded and spoiled [the ceremony], and when there was a mistake in the prayer. . . . There still exists an outstanding example in the formula by which the Decii, father and son, devoted themselves; [1] there is also preserved the prayer which the Vestal Tuccia employed to ward off violation of chastity as she carried water in a sieve, in the 609th year of the city.[2] Indeed, even our own age has seen a Greek man and woman, or persons of some other people with whom we had difficulties at that time, buried alive in the cattle market.[3] If anyone should read the prayer used for this ritual,

[1] See Vol. I, p. 147.   [2] 145 B.C.   [3] Cf. Vol. I, p. 475.

which is customarily dictated by the master of the College of Fifteen,[4] he would assuredly admit the potency of the formulae, all of which are confirmed by the experience of 830 years. . . .[5] Verrius Flaccus[6] cites authors whom he considers reliable to show that in sieges it was the practice of the Roman priests before all else to summon forth the tutelary divinity of the town and to promise him the same or more splendid rites among the Romans,[7] and this ritual still exists in the discipline of the pontiffs.

THE REBUILDING OF THE CAPITOL

In A.D. 70, Vespasian restored the temple of Jupiter Best and Greatest on the Capitoline Hill, the center of the state cult, which had been razed by fire the previous year. After another fire in 80, it was rebuilt by Domitian, and survived until 455.

Tacitus *Histories* IV. liii

The supervision of the rebuilding of the Capitol was entrusted by Vespasian to Lucius Vestinus,[8] a man of the equestrian order, in influence and reputation on a par with the nobility. The soothsayers assembled by him directed that what was left of the old shrine should be carried away to the marshes, and a new temple should be erected on the original site, declaring that the gods were unwilling that the old plan be altered. On June 21, beneath a cloudless sky, the entire space devoted to the sacred precinct was encircled with fillets and garlands. Soldiers who had auspicious names entered with boughs of good-omened trees. Next, the Vestal Virgins, together with boys and girls both of whose parents were alive, sprinkled it with water drawn from springs and rivers. Then the praetor Helvidius Priscus, in terms dictated by the pontiff Plautius Aelianus, having first purified the area with pig-sheep-bull sacrifices and placed the entrails on an altar of turf, prayed to Jupiter, Juno, and Minerva, and to the tutelary gods of the Empire, to prosper the undertaking and by their divine help to raise up their abodes begun by human piety. He then touched the fillets which were wound around the foundation stone and entwined around the ropes. At the same time the other magistrates, the priests, senators, *equites*, and a great part of the people, uniting their efforts with zeal and joy, dragged the huge stone. Everywhere there were thrown into the foundations contributions of silver and gold, and of virgin metals never smelted in furnaces but in their natural state; the

---

[4] Cf. Vol. I, p. 140; Vol. II, pp. 57–61, 558–59.
[5] That is, from the traditional date of the founding of Rome, 753 B.C., to the time when Pliny was writing.
[6] A scholar and teacher of the Augustan period.
[7] See Vol. I, pp. 145–46.   [8] Cf. § 32, third selection.

soothsayers had previously declared that the work should not be defiled by stone or gold intended for any other purpose. The height of the temple was increased; this was the only variation which religious scruple permitted, and the one feature which had been thought wanting in the magnificence of the old temple.

RITUAL OF THE ARVAL PRIESTS

The Arval Brotherhood, devoted to the worship of the agricultural deity Dea Dia, had its origin in the time of the early Roman kingdom (see Vol. I, § 11, where the primitive hymn still sung in the third century is given). Reestablished by Augustus, this priestly college, which included the emperor, continued its traditional activities until the collapse of the native religion in the late third or early fourth century. It is noteworthy that the priesthood devoted most of its activity to expressions of loyalty to the ruling house. The twelve members of the college met in a sacred grove near Rome, where extensive remains of the inscribed record of their proceedings, dating from 21 B.C. to A.D. 241, have been found. Only selections from these lengthy archives of the Arval priests are given here.

CIL, Vol. VI, No. 2,041, lines 9–23, 35–56 (= Dessau, No. 229);
A.D. 58–59

In the same consulship, on October 13, Lucius Salvius Otho Titianus, master of the college, performed the following sacrifices in the name of the Arval Brethren in the Capitol in behalf of the rule of NERO Claudius Caesar Augustus Germanicus: to Jupiter, an ox; to Juno, a cow; to Minerva, a cow; to Public Felicity, a cow; to the *genius* of the emperor, a bull; to the deified Augustus, an ox; to the deified Augusta, a cow; to the deified Claudius, an ox. Present in the college: Lucius Salvius Otho Titianus, master of the college, Gaius Piso, Gaius Vipstanus Apronianus, Marcus Valerius Messalla Corvinus, Aulus Vitellius, Sulpicius Camerinus, Publius Memmius Regulus, Titus Sextius Africanus.

In the same consulship, on November 6, Lucius Salvius Otho Titianus, master of the college, in the name of the Arval Brethren performed the following sacrifices in the Capitol for the birthday of Agrippina, mother of the emperor: to Jupiter, an ox; to Juno, a cow; to Minerva, a cow; to Public Safety, a cow; to the Concord of the Emperor, a cow. Present in the college: [Three members are listed.]

In the same consulship, on December 4, Lucius Salvius Otho Titianus, master of the college, in the name of the Arval Brethren performed the following sacrifices in the Capitol for the tribunician power of NERO Claudius Caesar Augustus Germanicus: to Jupiter, an ox; to

Juno, a cow; to Minerva, a cow. Present in the college: [Six members are listed.]

In the consulship of Gaius Vipstanus Apronianus and Gaius Fonteius Capito, on January 3,[9] Lucius Piso son of Lucius, master of the college, in the name of the Arval Brethren pronounced vows for the safety of NERO Claudius Caesar Augustus Germanicus, son of the deified Claudius, grandson of Germanicus Caesar, great-grandson of Tiberius Caesar Augustus, great-great-grandson of the deified Augustus, *pontifex maximus*, holding the tribunician power for the fifth year, acclaimed *imperator* six times, three times consul, consul designate for a fourth time, and of his wife Octavia, sacrificing victims in the Capitol in fulfilment of the vows which the master of the preceding year had made, and he pronounced the vows for the next year, in terms dictated by the consul Gaius Vipstanus Apronianus, as recorded below: to Jupiter, two oxen; to Juno, two cows; to Minerva, two cows; to Public Safety, two cows; in the new temple to the deified Augustus, two oxen; to the deified Augusta, two cows; to the deified Claudius, two oxen. Present in the college: [Five members are listed.]

In the same year, on January 12, in the Pantheon, Lucius Calpurnius Piso son of Lucius, master, with Gaius Vipstanus Apronianus, consul, Lucius Salvius Otho Titianus, Marcus Aponius Saturninus, Marcus Valerius Messalla Corvinus, Sulpicius Camerinus, and Titus Sextius Africanus, Arval Brethren, being present, Lucius Calpurnius son of Lucius, master, proclaimed a sacrifice to Dea Dia, in terms dictated by Lucius Salvius Otho Titianus, on May 27 at his home, on May 29 in the grove and at his home, and on May 30 at his home. Present in the college: the same as recorded above.

CIL, Vol. VI, No. 2,059, lines 35–52 (= Dessau, No. 5,033); A.D. 81

In the consulship of Lucius Flavius Nonius Bassus and Asinius Pollio Verrucosus, on January 3, the master Gaius Junius Tadius Mefitanus, in the name of the college of Arval Brethren, proclaimed vows for the safety of the Emperor TITUS Caesar Vespasianus Augustus, son of the deified [Vespasian], *pontifex maximus*, holder of the tribunician power, eight times consul, and of Caesar Domitian, son of the deified [Vespasian], seven times consul, and of Julia Augusta and their children, and sacrificed victims in the Capitol in fulfilment of the vows which the master of the preceding year had made, as follows: to Jupiter Best and Greatest, two oxen; to Juno the Queen, two cows; to Minerva, two cows; to Public Safety, two cows. And he pronounced the vows for the follow-

[9] See introduction to § 20.

ing year, in terms dictated by Lucius Pompeius Vopiscus Gaius Arruntius Catellius Celer, in the words recorded below:

"O Jupiter Best and Greatest, if the Emperor Titus Caesar Vespasianus Augustus, *pontifex maximus*, holder of the tribunician power, father of his country, and Caesar Domitian, son of the deified [Vespasian], of whom we deem that we are speaking, should live and their house be safe on the next January 3 that comes to pass for the Roman people, the Quirites, and for the state of the Roman people, the Quirites, and you preserve that day and them safe from dangers (if there are or shall be any before that day), and if you have granted a felicitous issue in the manner that we deem that we are speaking of, and you have preserved them in their present condition or better—and may you so do these things!—then we vow that you shall have, in the name of the college of the Arval Brethren, two gilded oxen."

CIL, Vol. VI, No. 2,065, lines 15–40 (= Dessau, No. 5,037); A.D. 87

In the consulship of Gaius Bellicus Natalis Tebanianus and Gaius Ducenius Proculus, May 19, in the grove of Dea Dia, during the mastership of Gaius Julius Silanus, under the supervision of Gaius Nonius Bassus Salvius Liberalis, the Arval Brethren made a sacrifice to Dea Dia. Gaius Salvius Liberalis, acting master in place of Gaius Julius Silanus, before the grove sacrificed on the altar two expiatory sows for the pruning and the work done in the grove; [10] then he sacrificed a white honorary cow to Dea Dia. Gaius Salvius Liberalis Nonius Bassus, Lucius Maecius Postumus, Aulus Julius Quadratus, Publius Sallustius Blaesus, Quintus Tillius Sassius sat down in the tetrastyle and dined from the sacrifice, and assuming their purple-bordered robes and wreaths with ears of grain and fillets, they ascended the grove of Dea Dia to the retreat, and through Salvius Liberalis Nonius Bassus, acting master, and Quintus Tillius Sassius, acting flamen, they sacrificed a fat lamb to Dea Dia, and when they had completed the sacrifice they all offered incense and wine. Then, after the wreaths were brought in and the images were anointed, they made Quintus Tillius Sassius annual master from the coming Saturnalia to the next, likewise Tiberius Julius Celsus Marius Candidus flamen; then they descended to the tetrastyle and there, reclining on couches, they dined in honor of [?] the master Gaius Julius Silanus. After the banquet, veiled and wearing sandals and a wreath plaited with roses, he ascended to the retreat above the starting point and sent a signal to the charioteers and acrobats, who were supervised by Lucius Maecius Postumus; he honored the victors with palms and silver wreaths. On the same

[10] That is, to expiate the work done to keep the grove in good condition. Iron, for example, was forbidden to be brought into the grove.

day in Rome at the home of Gaius Julius Silanus the same persons dined as had dined in the grove.

CIL, Vol. VI, No. 2,068 (= Dessau, No. 5,036); A.D. 91

In the same consulship, on January 7, in the vestibule of the Temple of Concord, the Arval Brethren, under the mastership (for the second time) of Lucius Veratius Quadratus, proclaimed a sacrifice to Dea Dia. In the vestibule of the Temple of Concord Lucius Veratius Quadratus, master of the Arval Brethren, having washed his hands and veiled his head, under the sacred roof and facing east, proclaimed together with his colleagues a sacrifice to Dea Dia: "May it be good, auspicious, propitious, fortunate, and salutary for the Emperor Caesar DOMITIAN Augustus Germanicus, *pontifex maximus*, and for his wife Domitia Augusta, and for their whole house, and for the Roman people, the Quirites, and for the Arval Brethren and for me! There will be a sacrifice to Dea Dia this year on May 17 at my home, on May 19 at the grove and at my home, and on May 20 at my home." Present in the college: [Three members are listed.]

CIL, Vol. VI, No. 2,074, lines 22–33 (= Dessau, No. 5,035); A.D. 101

In the consulship of Quintus Articuleius Paetus and Sextus Attius Suburanus, on March 25, in the Capitol, the Arval Brethren proclaimed vows for the safety, return, and victory of the Emperor Caesar Nerva TRAJAN Augustus Germanicus, in the words recorded below:

"O Jupiter Best and Greatest, we pray, beseech, and supplicate that you will cause the Emperor Caesar Nerva TRAJAN Augustus Germanicus, son of the deified Nerva, our *princeps* and father, *pontifex maximus*, holding the tribunician power, father of his country, of whom we deem that we are speaking, prosperously and happily to return safe and victorious from those places and provinces to which he is going, and grant him a felicitous issue of those affairs which he is now conducting and will conduct, and preserve him in his present condition or better, and convey him back safe and victorious to the city of Rome at the earliest possible time—and may you so do these things!—then we vow that you shall have, in the name of the Arval Brethren, a gilded ox." [This is followed by similar vows to Juno the Queen, Minerva, Jupiter Victor, Public Safety, Father Mars, Mars Victor, Victory, Fortune the Homebringer, Mother Vesta, Father Neptune, Hercules Victor. The occasion of these vows was the opening of Trajan's first Dacian campaign.]

THE SECULAR GAMES

The 110-year cycle adopted by Augustus for the solemn Secular Games (see § 13) was followed by Domitian and by Septimius Severus and Caracalla, who celebrated the famous "centennial" event in A.D. 88 and 204. The Emperors Claudius, Antoninus Pius, and Philip the Arab, adhering to the tradition of the 100-year cycle, conducted the games in A.D. 47, 147, and 248, the last time the games were celebrated, on the occasion of Rome's thousandth birthday (see § 124).

> *CIL*, Vol. VI, No. 32,327 (= Dessau, No. 5,050a) and Accademia
> Nazionale dei Lincei, *Notizie degli Scavi*, 1931, pp. 322-45, lines
> 49-56 (= *AE*, 1932, No. 70); A.D. 204

. . . on April 15 . . . [the College of Fifteen] took action on a communication sent by the emperors, to wit: "The Emperor Caesar Lucius SEPTIMIUS SEVERUS Pius Augustus and the Emperor Caesar Marcus Aurelius Antoninus Pius Augustus [CARACALLA], members of the College of Fifteen, to their colleagues, greeting. If it meets with your approval, assemble on May 25 next on the Palatine in the Temple of Apollo for the purpose of choosing by lot the places in which the various members, seated on tribunals, are to distribute means of purification to the people. Farewell, our dearest colleagues." Pompeius Rusonianus, the master, read it. "The Emperor Caesar Lucius SEPTIMIUS SEVERUS Pius Augustus and the Emperor Caesar Marcus Aurelius Antoninus Pius Augustus [CARACALLA], members of the College of Fifteen, to their colleagues, greeting. If you reach a decision concerning the days and nights on which the Secular Games should be presented . . . likewise those on which the matrons should offer prayers and incense, we shall so decree. Farewell, our dearest colleagues." Pompeius Rusonianus, the master, read it. . . . May 25, on the Palatine, in the Temple of Apollo, the college convened to choose by lot the places in which the various members, seated on tribunals, were to distribute means of purification to the people. . . . Present: Emperor Caesar Lucius SEPTIMIUS SEVERUS Pius Pertinax Augustus Arabicus Adiabenicus Parthicus Maximus, Emperor Caesar Marcus Aurelius Antoninus Pius Augustus [CARACALLA], Nonius Mucianus[?] . . . Pollienus Auspex, Manilius Fuscus, Cocceius Vibianus, Atulenus Rufinus, Ajacius Modestus, Fabius Magnus . . . Pompeius Musonianus, master . . . Crescens Calpurnianus, Cassius Pius Marcellinus, quaestor designate, Ulpinus Soter, consul designate, Venidius Rufus, commissioner of the bed of the Tiber, Fulvius Granianus, quaestor of the emperors. After the lots were inspected and placed into an urn, a drawing was held: On the Palatine, on the tribunal of our emperors which is in the precinct of the Temple of Apollo . . . Salvius Fuscus; the tribunal attached to . . . which is near Roma Quadrata,[11] Nonius Mucianus, Ajacius Modestus, Atulenus Rufinus . . . Ofilius Macedo; before the temple . . . Fulvius Fuscus, Vetina Mamertinus; before the temple . . . Cocceius Vibianus. After the lots were drawn . . . on May 26 the Emperors Severus and Antoninus . . . on the Palatine in the precinct of the Temple of Apollo; when they had ascended . . . they distributed means of purification . . . to the equestrian order and the plebs and the Roman people. . . . [The list of games performed is here omitted.]

. . . [Geta Caesar] sacrificed to Mother Earth a pregnant sow as a whole burnt offering according to the Greek-Achaean rite, with the following prayer: "O Mother Earth! As it has been prescribed for thee in those books—and by virtue of this may every good fortune come to the Roman people, the Quirites—let sacrifice be made to thee with a perfect pregnant sow as a whole burnt offering. I beseech and pray thee, just as thou hast increased the empire and majesty of the Roman people, the Quirites, in war and in peace, so may the Latins ever be obedient," the rest as above. He followed the order of sacrifice in the same manner as on the first night to the Fates, and having completed the sacrifice, placed aside his fringed tunic . . . with the other members of the College of Fifteen, were present at the night games. Julia Augusta, mother of the camps,[12] and the 109 matrons held *sellisternia* for Juno and Diana.

On June 3 the Emperors Severus and Antoninus Augusti, together with Geta Caesar, the Praetorian prefects, and the other members of the College of Fifteen . . . proceeded to the Temple of Apollo on the Palatine garbed in the purple-bordered toga and wearing wreaths, and there Severus Augustus at the temporary wooden altar . . . in the precinct of Apollo before the tetrastyle . . . in terms dictated by his son Antoninus Augustus, assisted by Geta Caesar, the Praetorian prefects and the other members of the College of Fifteen, made it sacred with incense and honorary wine; then Severus Augustus made a sacrifice to Apollo and Diana of nine sacrificial cakes, nine *popana*, and nine *phthoes*, with the following prayer which he himself read: "O Apollo! As it has been prescribed for thee in those books—and by virtue of this may every good fortune come to the Roman people, the Quirites—let sacrifice be made to thee with nine sacrificial cakes, nine *popana*, and nine

---

[11] A small shrine on the Palatine Hill serving as a repository of sacred objects associated with the early history of the Palatine.

[12] Honorary title of Julia Domna, wife of Septimius Severus.

phthoes. I beseech and pray thee, just as thou hast increased the empire and majesty of the Roman people, the Quirites, in war and in peace, so may the Latins ever be obedient," the rest as above. . . .[13]

168. *The Imperial Cult*

Emperor worship in the first two centuries followed in the main the lines laid down by Augustus (see § 14)—divine honors to the *genius* of the living emperor and deification after death (the latter honor being often accorded to other members of the imperial family as well). Despite official deprecation, the worship of the living emperor was widely practiced throughout the Empire, especially in the eastern provinces. The attempts by Caligula and Domitian in the first century to institute such worship at Rome were premature aberrations. Cf. Dio Cassius *Roman History* LXVII. v. 7: "Domitian even insisted upon being considered a god and was exceedingly proud of being called 'master' (*dominus*) and 'god' (*deus*). These titles were used not merely orally but also in written documents." But with the passage of time the transition to divinization of the living emperor was not a difficult one. In the first place, the emperor was usually the natural or adoptive "son of a god," his deified predecessor. Further, with the increasing centralization of administration in the hands of the emperor, the Eastern concept of the divine ruler gradually spread to the West. By the third century the divine nature of the imperial house was firmly established, and in the reorganization of Diocletian the emperor assumed officially the character of a god-king.

TIBERIUS DEPRECATES DIVINE HONORS

The following inscriptions of A.D. 14/15 contain a decree of the Greek city of Gythium and the emperor's reply thereto.

AE, 1929, Nos. 99–100 (= Ehrenberg-Jones, No. 102)

i

. . . he [14] shall place . . . on the first [pedestal the statue] of the deified Augustus Caesar, his father; on the second, to the right, that of Julia Augusta; [15] and on the third, [to the left], that of the Emperor TIBERIUS Caesar Augustus, the city providing him with the statues. And a table shall be set out by him in the middle of the theater and a censer placed upon it, and the councilmen and all the magistrates shall offer

---

[13] On details of this text, cf. the Augustan Secular Games in § 13. The conservatism of the ritual and formulae is noteworthy.
[14] Probably a public official of Gythium.
[15] That is, Livia, wife of Augustus and mother of Tiberius. The term, "our rulers," below, refers to Tiberius and Livia.

sacrifice for the preservation of our rulers, but not before the performers enter. On the first day the performance shall honor the son of the deified [Julius] Caesar, the deified Augustus our savior and deliverer; on the second day, the Emperor TIBERIUS Caesar Augustus, father of his country; on the third day, Julia Augusta, the Good Fortune of our province and city; on the fourth, the Victory of Germanicus Caesar; on the fifth, the Venus of Drusus Caesar; and on the sixth, Titus Quinctius Flamininus; [16] and he shall see to the orderly behavior of the contestants. . . . And when the procession reaches the Temple of Caesar, the superintendents shall sacrifice a bull for the preservation of our rulers and for the deified ones and for the eternal duration of their rule. . . .

ii

TIBERIUS Caesar Augustus, son of Augustus, *pontifex maximus*, holding the tribunician power for the . . . year . . . to the superintendents and city of Gythium, greeting. Decimus Turranius Nicanor, the envoy sent by you to me and to my mother, transmitted to me your letter to which were appended the measures passed by you in reverence to my father and in my honor. I commend you for this, and consider it fitting that all men in general and your city in particular should reserve special honors befitting the gods in keeping with the greatness of my father's services to the whole world; but I myself am content with the more modest honors appropriate to men. My mother, however, will answer you herself when she learns from you your decision about honors to her.

Tacitus *Annals* IV. xxxvii–xxxviii

About the same time [17] Farther Spain through envoys sent to the senate requested permission to erect a shrine to Tiberius and his mother, following the example of Asia. On this occasion the emperor, vigorously scornful of honors in any case, and considering that an answer was due those who in their gossip charged him with having descended to vainglory, began a speech of the following tenor:

"I know, Conscript Fathers, that in the eyes of a good many I was lacking in consistency inasmuch as recently when the cities of Asia made this same request, I offered no opposition. I shall therefore disclose both a defense for my previous silence and what I have determined for the future. Since the deified Augustus had not forbidden the erection of a temple at Pergamum to himself and the city of Rome, [18] observing as I

[16] The conqueror of Philip V of Macedon and "liberator" of Greece: see Vol. I, § 68.

[17] A.D. 25.   [18] Cf. introduction to § 14.

do his every action and word as law, I followed the precedent already approved by him all the more readily as reverence for the senate was associated with worship of myself. To have accepted once is pardonable; but to be consecrated in the image of deity through all the provinces would be pretentious and arrogant, and the honor paid to Augustus will become empty if it is vulgarized by indiscriminate acts of flattery.

"As for myself, Conscript Fathers, that I am mortal, that my functions are those of human beings, and that I hold it enough if I occupy the foremost place—this I call upon you to witness, and I desire posterity to remember. For they will do justice, and more, to my memory if they believe me worthy of my ancestors, solicitous of your interests, firm in danger, not fearful of offense for the sake of the public welfare. These are my temples in your hearts, these my fairest and abiding statues. For those that are erected of stone, if the judgment of posterity should turn to hatred, are scorned as sepulchers. Accordingly, my prayers to allies, citizens, and the gods themselves are these: to the gods, that to the end of my life they may endow me with an unperturbed mind, gifted with understanding of human and divine law; and to the others that, whenever I depart, they may escort my deeds and fair name to the tomb with praise and kindly remembrances."

And henceforth, even in private conversations he persisted in spurning this worship of himself.[19]

EDICT OF GERMANICUS

Germanicus Caesar, nephew and adopted son of the Emperor Tiberius, while on a special mission to settle affairs in the eastern part of the Empire, journeyed to Alexandria in A.D. 19 to alleviate a food shortage there. His benefactions occasioned such enthusiastic public demonstrations that he judged it politic to issue the following edict.

Wilcken, No. 413, lines 31–45 (= Select Papyri, No. 211)

Germanicus Caesar, son of Augustus and grandson of the deified Augustus, proconsul, declares: Your good will, which you always display when you see me, I acknowledge, but your acclamations, which are odious to me and such as are accorded to the gods, I altogether deprecate. For they are appropriate only to him who is really the savior and

[19] Cf. Suetonius *Life of Tiberius* xxvi: "He forbade the decreeing of temples, flamens, and priests in his honor, and even the setting up of statues and busts without his permission; and these latter he permitted only on the following condition, that they were not to be placed among the statues of the gods but among the adornments of temples. He was opposed to an oath being taken in support of his acts, and to changing the name of the month of September to Tiberius and of October to Livius [in honor of his mother Livia]."

benefactor of the whole human race, my father, and to his mother, my grandmother. But my position is [but a reflection?] of their divinity, so that if you do not obey me, you will compel me not to show myself to you often.

HONORS DECREED AT ROME TO THE DEAD GERMANICUS

Accademia Nazionale dei Lincei, *Notizie degli Scavi*, 1947, pp. 49–68
(= Ehrenberg-Jones, No. 365 = *American Journal of Philology*,
LXXV [1954], 225–49)

[Heba, Italy, A.D. 19/20]

. . . And that in the portico which is near the Temple of Apollo, in which temple meetings of the senate are customarily held . . . busts of Germanicus Caesar, a man of distinguished ability, and of Drusus Germanicus, his natural father, brother of TIBERIUS Caesar Augustus, who was also a man of abundant ability, be placed on the capitals of the column which shelter the statue of Apollo.

And that the Salian priests insert in their litanies the name of Germanicus Caesar among the names of the deified ones, an honor which was accorded also to Gaius and Lucius Caesar, brothers of TIBERIUS Caesar Augustus.[20]

And that to the number of the centuries which customarily cast their votes for the election of consuls and praetors there shall be added five centuries, and since the ten previous ones are named after Gaius and Lucius Caesar, the next five shall be named after Germanicus Caesar; and in all these the senators and likewise the *equites* of all the decuries which have been or shall be established for public trials shall cast their votes. [There follow lengthy amendments, made necessary by the creation of these five new centuries, to a law of A.D. 5 on electoral procedures.]

And that at the games in honor of Augustus, when the seats of the priests of Augustus are placed in the theaters, curule chairs for Germanicus Caesar shall be placed among them, together with oak-leaf crowns in honor of that priesthood; and these chairs, when the Temple of the Deified Augustus has been completed, shall be brought forward from that temple; meanwhile, they shall be put back in the Temple of Mars the Avenger and be brought forward from that place, and whoever shall conduct the aforementioned games shall see to it that they are taken from the aforementioned temple and placed in the theaters, and that when they are to be replaced they are put back in that temple.

And that, when the bones and ashes of Germanicus Caesar are

[20] For honors accorded to Gaius and Lucius Caesar after death, see § 16.

brought to the tomb, the temples of the gods shall be closed, and those who are enrolled in the equestrian order and have private horses, who desire to perform their duty and are not impeded by health or by a death in their own family, shall come to the Campus Martius arrayed in the striped tunic, and those who have public horses shall come arrayed in the striped mantle.

And that annually on the day on which he died the temples of the immortal gods which are or shall be in the city of Rome or within a mile of the city of Rome shall be closed, and those who have contracts for the care of these temples shall see to it that this is done.

And that on that same day the annual masters of the college of priests of Augustus shall see to it that sacrifices to the dead are made before the tomb into which the bones of Germanicus Caesar have been brought; and if the masters, one or more, should not make this sacrifice, those of the priests who do so shall during the next year have the right to hold the office of master in place of those who did not perform this duty. . . . [The rest is lost.]

EXCESSES OF CALIGULA

Suetonius *Life of Caligula* xxii

Caligula came close to assuming the diadem at once and changing the semblance of a principate into the form of a monarchy. On being reminded once that he had surpassed the heights both of princes and of kings, he began from that time on to lay claim to divine majesty for himself. He made it his business to have statues of the gods which were famous for the reverence attached to them or for their artistic merit, including the Olympian Zeus,[21] brought from Greece, so as to remove their heads and replace them with his own. He extended a part of the palace as far as the Forum, and, transforming the Temple of Castor and Pollux into its vestibule, he often took his stand between the brother gods and exhibited himself in their midst to be worshiped by those who approached; and some hailed him as Jupiter of Latium. He also set up a separate temple to his own godhead, with priests and with sacrificial victims of the choicest kind. In this temple stood a golden life-size statue [of Caligula], and it was dressed each day in clothing such as he himself wore. Very rich persons obtained in turn the office of master of the priesthood through influence and by offering the highest bids. The sacrificial victims were flamingoes, peacocks, woodcocks, guinea hens, and pheasants, one kind being sacrificed each day.

[21] By the famous Greek sculptor Phidias.

IG, Vol. VII, No. 2,711, lines 21–43 (= Dessau, No. 8,792)

[Acraephiae, Greece, A.D. 37]

The Emperor Augustus Caesar [CALIGULA], great-grandson of the deified Augustus, grandson of Tiberius Caesar, *pontifex maximus*, holder of the tribunician power, consul, to the League of Achaeans, Boeotians, Locrians, Phocians, and Euboeans, greeting. I have read the decree given me by your envoys and perceive that you have omitted no extreme of zeal and reverence for me. You have offered sacrifice each individually and have held a common festival for my safety, and you have voted me the greatest honors you could. For all these I commend you, and I accept them, and mindful of the age-old fame of each of the Greek states, I permit you to convene your league. As for the statues you voted me, dispense with the greater part, if it be your pleasure, and confine yourselves to those to be set up at Olympia, Nemea, Delphi, and the Isthmus,[22] so as . . . not to burden yourselves more heavily with expenses. Your decree was transmitted to me by the envoys whose names are recorded below. Farewell.

[There follow, fragmentarily preserved, the names of some seventeen envoys.]

Done on August 19, at Rome.

APOTHEOSIS OF AN EMPEROR

Herodian *History* IV. ii

It is the custom among the Romans to deify those of their emperors who die with sons to succeed them.[23] This rite is called apotheosis. The whole city takes on the air of a religious festival mingled with mourning. They bury the body of the departed in the customary manner of mortals, giving it a sumptuous funeral, and they fashion a wax image like the deceased in every respect and let it lie in state on a huge ivory couch spread with coverlets interwoven with gold and raised up high at the entrance to the palace. . . . During most of the daytime a watch is kept on both sides of the couch: on the left by the entire senate wearing black garments, on the right by all the matrons on whom the rank of their husbands or fathers confers honored status; all the latter appear unadorned by gold or necklaces but, clothed in plain white garb, present the ap-

[22] The sites of the four great Panhellenic games.
[23] This is an error. In fact, emperors (for example, Pertinax) were sometimes deified even when their successor was not a son (natural or adopted).

pearance of mourners. This is done for seven days, during which physicians make daily visits; they approach the couch, actually examine the "invalid," and issue daily bulletins announcing that his condition is more serious. When he is reported to have died, the noblest of the equestrian order and chosen youths of the senatorial order raise up the couch and convey it along the Sacred Way and place it in state in the ancient Forum, where the Roman magistrates lay down their offices. On either side are some steps like a staircase, and on the one side stands a chorus of noble and patrician children, on the opposite a chorus of matrons of high reputation, singing both hymns and paeans to the departed, intoned in solemn, mournful measure.

After this they lift up the couch again and bear it out of the city to the so-called Field of Mars. There, at the widest part of the field a square structure has been erected, constructed exclusively of very large-sized logs, in the form of a chamber. The whole structure is filled inside with firewood and adorned on the outside with coverlets interwoven with gold, ivory statues, and colorful paintings. Above this is another chamber, similar in shape and decoration but smaller, with its little gates and doors open. A third and fourth, each smaller than the one below, lead to the last and narrowest. . . . They carry the couch up into the second chamber and place therein all the spices and incense that the earth produces, and they gather also any fruits, herbs, or juices that produce fragrance, and they bring it up and pour it out in profusion. There is no province, no city, no man of reputation or rank, that does not vie in sending these last gifts in honor of the emperor. When there is a huge mound of spices and the whole space is filled, there is a cavalry procession around this structure, and the entire equestrian order rides in a circle around it, in a regular order and wheeling movement, in the Pyrrhic course and rhythm.[24] Chariots are driven around in the same ordered array, bearing the officials in charge [of the ceremony], who are garbed in the purple-bordered toga and wear masks in the likenesses of all the outstanding Roman generals and emperors.

When this ritual has been completed, he who has succeeded to the throne takes a torch and applies it to the chamber. Then the others apply fire on all sides; with the mass of firewood and incense piled there, all is most readily and easily kindled by the fire. Then from the last and narrowest chamber, as from a battlement, an eagle is released to rise up into the upper air with the fire; the bird is believed by the Romans to carry the soul of the emperor from earth to heaven. And from then on the emperor is worshiped along with the other gods.[25]

[24] The Pyrrhic dance was a war dance of Greek origin.
[25] The tradition of consecrating the dead emperor survived even in the early Chris-

MILITARY CALENDAR OF RELIGIOUS FESTIVALS

This unique document is contained in a papyrus roll found in the 1931/32 excavation of the Roman town of Europus (Dura) on the Euphrates river. A calendar of the official religious holidays celebrated by the garrison stationed at that military base on the Empire's eastern frontier during the third century, it affords striking evidence of the focal role the worship of the imperial house played in the religion of the Empire.

Yale Classical Studies, VII (1940), 1–222; A.D. 224/35

January 1. . . .

January 3. Vows fulfilled and offered for the preservation of our lord Marcus Aurelius SEVERUS ALEXANDER Augustus and for the eternity of the Empire of the Roman people.[26] To Jupiter Best and Greatest, an ox; to Juno, a cow; to Minerva, a cow; to Jupiter Victor, an ox . . . to Father Mars, a bull; to Mars Victor, a bull; to Victory, a cow. . . .

January 7. Honorable discharge and enjoyment of privileges granted, and salary installment paid to soldiers. To Jupiter Best and Greatest, an ox; to Juno, a cow; to Minerva, a cow; to Safety, a cow; to Father Mars, a bull. . . .

January 11[?]. Birthday of Lucius Seius Caesar, father-in-law of the emperor. . . .

January 24. Birthday of the deified Hadrian. To the deified Hadrian, an ox.

January 28. The Arabian, Adiabenic and very great Parthian victories of the deified Severus, and accession of the deified Trajan. To the Parthian Victory, a cow; to the deified Trajan, an ox.

February 4. Accession of the deified Antoninus Magnus. . . .[27] To the deified Antoninus Magnus, an ox.

March 1. Birthday rites of Father Mars Victor. To Father Mars, a bull. . . .

March 6. Accession of the deified Marcus [Aurelius] Antoninus and the deified Lucius Verus. To the deified Marcus, an ox; to the deified Lucius, an ox. . . .

March 13. The Emperor Caesar Marcus Aurelius SEVERUS ALEXANDER acclaimed emperor. To Jupiter, an ox; to Juno, a cow . . . to Mars, an ox. Also, the Emperor Caesar Marcus Aurelius SEVERUS ALEXANDER Augustus first acclaimed *imperator* by the soldiers. Public prayer[?].

---

tian period. But the rites accorded to Constantine and a few of his successors could hardly have been more than a traditional honor.

[26] See introduction to § 20.   [27] That is, Caracalla.

March 14. Our Emperor Alexander acclaimed Augustus and Father of his Country and *pontifex maximus*. Public prayer. . . .

March 19. Day of the Quinquatria.[28] Public prayers continuing to the 23d. . . .

April 21. Birthday of the city of Eternal Rome. To the city of Eternal Rome, a cow.

April 26. Birthday of the deified Marcus [Aurelius] Antoninus. To the deified Marcus Antoninus, an ox.

May 7. Birthday of the deified Julia Maesa.[29] Public prayer to the deified Julia Maesa.

May 10. Crowning of the military standards.[30] Public prayer. . . .

May 24. Birthday of Germanicus Caesar. Public prayer to the memory of Germanicus Caesar. . . .

June 9. Vestalia. Public prayer to Mother Vesta. . . .

June 26. Our lord Marcus Aurelius SEVERUS ALEXANDER named Caesar and clad in the toga of manhood. To the *genius* of Alexander Augustus, a bull. . . .

July 12. Birthday of the deified Julius [Caesar]. To the deified Julius, an ox.

July 23. Day of the Neptunalia. Public prayer; sacrifice.

August 1. Birthday of the deified Claudius and the deified Pertinax. To the deified Claudius, an ox; to the deified Pertinax, an ox. . . .

September. . . . Birthday of the deified Faustina.[31] To the deified Faustina, public prayer.

September 23. Birthday of the deified Augustus. To the deified Augustus, an ox. . . .

December 17. [Day of the Saturnalia.] [32] Public prayers continuing to the 23d. . . . [The rest is lost.]

169. *The Spread of Irrationalism*

Under the societal conditions of the Roman Empire the rational spirit underwent a complete collapse (cf. p. 298), and in its place came widespread superstition and a conviction of fatalism in human affairs. In this milieu astrology attained its greatest vogue in history, dominating all levels of society,

[28] A festival of Minerva, originally in honor of Mars: cf. Vol. I, p. 63, Note 39.
[29] The sister-in-law of Septimius Severus and grandmother of the Emperors Elagabalus and Severus Alexander.
[30] In this ceremony the standards were grouped by the camp altar and decorated with crowns of roses.
[31] The wives of both Antoninus Pius and Marcus Aurelius bore this name.
[32] Cf. § 58.

even the best minds, with supreme authority. Side by side with the spread of Oriental mystery religions, magical practices penetrated the life of the Roman world; despite recurrent police action against practitioners of the occult, they maintained a flourishing existence throughout the Empire.

MAGIC CHARMS

This document, characteristic of the numerous magical texts in the papyri and inscriptions, contains a variety of spells which derive from traditional formulae.

British Museum Papyrus No. 46, col. 1, lines 1–52, col. 3, lines 172–201 and 293–303; fourth century

A Sarapian Divination

[To be wrought by the help] of a boy, with a lamp, a bowl, and a stand. I invoke thee, O Zeus, Helius, Mithra, Sarapis, unconquerable, possessor of honey, Melicertes, father of honey, abraalbabachambechi, baibeizoth, ebaibeboth, seriabeboth, amelchipsithiouthipithoio, pnoutenin, thereterou, iueueoo, aieia, eeoia, eeai, eueie, ooooo, eueoiao, ai, bakaxichuch, bosepseteth, phobe, biboth, the great, great Sarapis; samasphreth, odargazas, odarmagas, odaphar, ykiaboth, ephia, zelearthar, methomeo, lamarmera, optebi, ptebi, marianou, appear and give heed to him who has manifested before fire and snow, bainphooooch, for thou art he who didst manifest light and snow, terrible-eyed-thundering-and-lightning-swift-footed one, pintouche, etomthoout, opsianaeak, arourongoa, paphtha, enosade, iae, iaoai, aoiao, oeu. . . .

Tell what I inquire of thee. Say as follows: Let the throne of the god enter, zatera kyma, kyma, luageu, apsitadrus, ge moliandron, bonblilon, peuchre. Let the throne be brought in. Then, if it be borne by four men, inquire what they are crowned with and what precedes the throne. If he says, "They are crowned with olive, and a censer precedes," the boy speaks true. The dismissal: Depart, lord, to thine own world, and to thine own thrones, to thine own orbits, and guard me and this boy unhurt, in the name of the most high god Samasphreth. Perform [this divination] when the moon is in a firm sign of the zodiac in conjunction with beneficent stars, or when she is in favorable limits, not when she is at the full, for thus it is better, and thus is the divination performed in orderly fashion. But in other versions it has been recorded that it should be performed when the moon is full.

To Catch a Thief

I call thee, Hermes, immortal god, who cuttest a furrow down Olympus, and who [presidest over] the sacred boat, O light-bringer

Iao, the great ever-living, terrible to behold and terrible to hear, give up the thief whom I seek. Aberamentho oulerthe xenax sonelueothnemareba. This spell is to be said twice at the purification. The spell of bread and cheese. Come to me, lisson maternamau, erte, preptektioun, intiki, ous, olokotous, periklusai, bring to me that which is lost, and make the thief manifest on this very day. And I invoke Hermes, the discoverer of thieves, and the sun and the eye-pupils of the sun, the two bringers-to-light of unlawful deeds, and Justice, and Errinys, and Ammon, and Parammon, to seize the throat of the thief and to manifest him this very day, at the present hour. The ceremony: the same spell [as that] pronounced at the purification. Take a flush-green vessel and put water in it and myrrh, and the herb cynocephalium, and dipping in it a branch of laurel, sprinkling each person with the water, take a tripod and place it upon an altar of earth. . . . Offer myrrh and frankincense and a frog's tongue, and taking some unsalted winter wheat and goat's cheese, give these to each, pronouncing the spell at length. And write this name, and glue it beneath the tripod: "Lord Iao, light-bearer, give up the thief whom I seek." And if any of them does not swallow what was given him, that one is the thief.

CURSE BY ENCHANTMENT

On such "binding" curses, inscribed on thin lead tablets, see Vol. I, § 179. The following inscription was found in Rome.

IGRR, Vol. I, No. 117

I conjure you up, holy beings and holy names; join in aiding this spell, and bind, enchant, thwart, strike, overturn, conspire against, destroy, kill break Eucherius, the charioteer, and all his horses tomorrow in the circus at Rome. May he not leave the barriers well; may he not be quick in the contest; may he not outstrip anyone; may he not make the turns well; may he not win any prizes; and if he has pressed someone hard, may he not come off the victor; and if he follows someone from behind, may he not overtake him; but may he meet with an accident; may he be bound; may he be broken; may he be dragged along by your power, in the morning and afternoon races. Now! Now! Quickly! Quickly!

MIRACULOUS CURES

IGRR, Vol. I, No. 41
[Rome]

In these very days [Aesculapius] [33] gave a response to a certain Gaius, a blind person, to go to the sacred platform and make obeisance, then to go from right to left and place his five fingers on the platform and lift up his hand and place it on his own eyes; and he recovered his sight, in the presence of the populace, who rejoiced that the active divine powers manifested themselves during the reign of our Augustus, Antoninus. [34]

[Aesculapius] gave a response to Lucius, who was suffering from pleurisy and was given up in despair by everyone, to go and lift up the ashes from the altar and mix well with wine and apply it to his side; and he was saved, and he gave thanks to the god publicly, and the populace rejoiced with him.

[Aesculapius] gave a response to Julianus, who was spitting up blood and had been given up in despair by everyone, to go and lift up from the altar pine-cone seeds and eat them with honey for three days; and he was cured, and he came and gave thanks publicly before the populace.

The god gave a response to the blind soldier Valerius Aper that he should go and take blood from a white cock and mix an eye salve with honey, and smear it on his eyes for three days; and he recovered his sight, and he came and gave thanks publicly to the god.

170. *Greek Mystery Religions*

There is evidence that in the second century the Dionysiac mysteries enjoyed a renascence in Italy. Elsewhere the famous Hellenic mystery cults continued to attract adherents. The Greek inscription given below, found in Latium in the vicinity of Rome, is of especial importance not only because it is the first evidence for the complete structure of a Bacchic association but also because one of the priestesses of the organization was Pompeia Agrippinilla, wife of Gavius Squilla, consul in A.D. 150. When one recalls the vigorous police measures taken by the Roman senate in the second century B.C. to suppress the Bacchanalia in Italy (see Vol. I, § 176), the contrast with the new religious climate is striking. Of the several hundred names listed in this inscription, the greatest number are of Greek origin, and only a small minority are Roman. Most of the names reflect servile origin.

[33] The Graeco-Roman god of medicine (see Vol. I, § 53). With these cures cf. also those described in § 79 in the present volume.
[34] Apparently Caracalla.

American Journal of Archaeology, XXXVII (1933), 215-70
(= *AE*, 1933, No. 4)

The members of the association whose names are recorded below
[erected this statue] to Agrippinilla, their priestess.

Leader [followed by one masculine name]
Torch-bearer [35] [one feminine name]
Priests [seven masculine names]
Priestesses [three feminine names, including Agrippinilla]
Hierophant [36] [one masculine name]
God-bearer [37] [two masculine names]
Acolyte and beadle[?] [one masculine name]
Bearers of the mystic chest [three feminine names]
Chief neatherds [38] [three masculine names]
Holy neatherds [seven masculine names]
Leaders of Bacchants [two masculine names]
Acolytes [two masculine names]
Bearers of the winnowing fan [39] [three feminine names]
Bearer of the sacred phallus [one feminine name]
Fire-bearer [one masculine name]
Steward [one masculine name]
Youth-leaders [40] [one masculine name; space for two additional
    names]
Neatherds [eleven masculine names]
Leaders of female Bacchants [four feminine names]
Initiates [41] [eighty-nine masculine and feminine names]
Bacchant initiates [fifteen masculine names]
Female Bacchant initiates [three feminine names]
Holy Bacchants [over one hundred masculine names]
Wardens of the sacred cave [two masculine names]
Female Bacchants [over forty feminine names]
Novices [twenty-three masculine and feminine names]

[35] In connection with nocturnal feasts.
[36] Supervised initiations of priests and priestesses.
[37] Carried the statue of Dionysus.
[38] The neatherds were dancers clad in rustic garments.
[39] Believed to be the cradle of Dionysus; it was a symbol of fertility and purification.
[40] Instructors of adolescent members.
[41] The literal rendering of the Greek is "wearers of the fawn skin."

DIFFUSION OF ORIENTAL RELIGIONS

171. *Diffusion of Oriental Religions*

"The propagation of the Oriental religions, with the development of Neo-Platonism, is the leading fact in the moral history of the pagan empire" (F. Cumont, *Oriental Religions in Roman Paganism,* p. xv). Despite the efforts of various emperors to strengthen the Hellenized state religion and the native family cult (cf. Vol. I §§ 52–3), and despite the official policy of exclusion of Oriental gods from the Roman pantheon, the vitality of the ancestral religion steadily diminished. The West was with constantly mounting intensity penetrated by a variety of Oriental cults, especially mystery religions, of which Christianity was one. This religious ferment was facilitated by numerous factors: the tolerance by the Roman government of private religious activity entailing no political dangers or threats to law and order; the political unity of the Empire; the movement of merchants, slaves, and armies; the appeal of cosmopolitanism and individualism to the masses of the Empire; the breakdown of rationalism and the scientific spirit. By the third century, Oriental cults began to be adopted into the state religion, and for a time sun worship, tending toward solar monotheism, was a powerful rival (especially in military circles) of the traditional religion and of the mystery cults. The attempt of the Emperor Elagabalus to organize a solar religion by replacing Jupiter with El Gabal, the Syrian baal of Emesa whose name he bore, was abortive. Of greater importance was the organization by the Emperor Aurelian, in A.D. 274, of the Romanized cult of an Oriental baal under the title of *Sol Invictus* (Unconquered Sun) This religion, with its great temple of the sun god, its new college of pontiffs, and its great festival on December 25, the birthday celebration of the sun at the winter solstice, was thereafter the principal official imperial cult until the triumph of Christianity. But it was the eschatological mystery cults, among which Persian Mithraism (mostly known through monumental and a mass of brief inscriptional evidence) and Christianity were the most powerful rivals, that won the greatest number of adherents. Banded in private religious brotherhoods, the worshipers were attracted by the pageantry of the mysteries, the elaborate rituals often culminating in orgiastic frenzy (including initiation, often by baptism, and other purification rites), the esoteric doctrines, and above all by the intense emotional appeals and the promise of personal immortality. In the third century these developments brought about both a chaos of belief and a striving, through syncretism, for a unification of similar cults. The following selections are illustrative of the content of the mystery religions and of the religious tendencies of the third century.

INVASION OF ORIENTAL CULTS

Minucius Felix *Octavius* vi, xxiii. 1–4
From LCL

Hence it is that throughout wide empires, provinces, and towns, we see each people having its own individual rites and worshiping the local gods—the Eleusinians Ceres, the Phrygians the Great Mother, the Epidaurians Aesculapius, the Chaldaeans Baal, the Syrians Astarte, the Taurians Diana, the Gauls Mercury, the Romans one and all. Thus it is that their power and authority have embraced the circuit of the whole world, and have advanced the bounds of the Empire beyond the paths of the sun and the confines of ocean; while they practise in the field god-fearing valor, make strong their city with awe of sacred rites, with chaste virgins, with many a priestly dignity and title. . . . In captured fortresses, even in the first flush of victory, they reverence the conquered deities.[42] Everywhere they entertain the gods and adopt them as their own; they raise altars even to the unknown deities, and to the spirits of the dead. Thus is it that they adopt the sacred rites of all nations, and withal have earned dominion. . . .

Consider the sacred rites of the mysteries; you will find tragic deaths, dooms, funerals, mourning and lamentations of woebegone gods. Isis, with her Dog-head [43] and shaven priests, mourning, bewailing, and searching for her lost son; her miserable votaries beating their breasts and mimicking the sorrows of the unhappy mother; then, when the stripling is found, Isis rejoices, her priests jump for joy, the Dog-head glories in his discovery; and, year by year, they cease not to lose what they find or to find what they lose. Is it not absurd either to mourn your object of worship, or to worship your object of mourning? Yet these old Egyptian rites have now found their way to Rome, so that you may play the fool to the swallow and sistrum of Isis, the scattered limbs and the empty tomb of your Serapis or Osiris.

Ceres, with lighted torches, serpent-girt, with anxious, troubled footsteps follows the trail of her decoyed and ravished Proserpina—such are the Eleusinian mysteries. . . . Of Cybele and Dindyma it is a shame to speak: unable to satisfy the affections of her luckless paramour—for mothering of many gods had made her plain and old—she could not allure him to lust and castrated him, so as to make a god, no less, a eunuch; and in deference to this fable her *galli* priests worship her by inflicting the same mutilation on their own bodies. Such practices are not sacred rites but tortures.

[42] See Vol. I, pp. 145–46.   [43] The jackal-headed god Anubis.

Tertullian *Apology* vi. 7–10
From LCL

To come next to your gods themselves, the decrees which your fathers prudently enacted you, the most law-abiding of men, have repealed. Father Bacchus and his mysteries—the consuls with the approval of the senate turned him not only out of the city but out of the whole of Italy.[44] Serapis and Isis and Harpocrates [45] with his Dog-head were forbidden the Capitol—in other words, expelled from the assembly of the gods; and Piso and Gabinius [46]—consuls, not Christians, you know—actually overturned their altars and banished them, in the endeavor to restrain the vices that go with foul and idle superstition. You have restored them and bestowed on them supreme majesty. Where is the religious awe, where is the veneration owed by you to your ancestors? In dress, habit of life, furniture, feeling, yes! and speech, you have renounced your great-grandfathers! You are forever praising antiquity, and every day you improvise some new way of life. All of which goes to prove that while you abandon the good usages of your ancestors you keep and maintain the practices you should not have, and what you should have kept you have not maintained. In fact, as to that very point of ancestral tradition, which you think you most faithfully guard, which above all else you have used to mark down the Christians as lawbreakers —I mean the passion for worshiping the gods (and that is where antiquity made its worst mistake)—though you may have rebuilt his altars for Serapis Romanized, though you make an offering of your frenzy to Bacchus Italianate, I will show in its proper place that you despise, neglect, and destroy that tradition, straight against the authority of your ancestors.

WORSHIP OF ISIS

The Hellenized Egyptian cult of Isis and Serapis had reached Italy through the Greek cities in the south as early as the third century B.C. After a long period of official persecution, it was granted public recognition by Caligula. Thereafter it spread throughout the Empire, reaching its height in the third century. The following is a famous description of one of the festivals of the cult, the "Bark of Isis," symbolizing the spring opening of the navigation season.

[44] See Vol. I, § 176.
[45] That is, the Egyptian god Horus, son of Isis and Serapis.
[46] In 58 B.C.

Apuleius *The Golden Ass* (*Metamorphoses*) XI. ix–xi, xvi–xvii

Now the special procession of the savior goddess was moving by. Women resplendent in white garments, rejoicing in varied ornaments and wearing wreaths of spring flowers, strewed with blossoms from their bosoms the path along which the sacred procession was passing. Others turned shining mirrors, held behind their backs, toward the goddess as she came, to demonstrate their reverence on the way. Others, carrying ivory combs, with the gestures of their arms and the movements of their fingers went through the motions of combing and adorning the queenly hair. Others also sprinkled the streets with various ointments, including delightful balsam scattered drop by drop. In addition, there came a great number, of both sexes, with lamps, torches, wax tapers and other lights, propitiating with light the offspring of the celestial stars. Then pleasant harmonies sounded, pipes and flutes in the sweetest tones. These were followed by a delightful chorus of very select young men, re-splendent in white garments and festal array, repeating a charming song. . . . There came, too, the trumpeters devoted to great Serapis, who with slanting reeds stretched to the right ear repeated the familiar melody of the temple and god. And there were many who called for free room for the sacred rites. Then poured in masses of initiates in the divine rites, men and women of every rank and every age, who glistened in their pure white linen garb. The women had their hair anointed and decked with a bright covering, but the men, their hair completely shaven, had glisten-ing pates . . . and with timbrels of bronze, silver, aye and gold, they made a loud shrill jingling. But the principal priests, overseers of the sacred rites, who were appareled in surplices tightly girt round with white linen cloth and hanging down to the ground, carried the splendid trappings of the most powerful gods. . . .

Presently the gods came forth, deigning to walk on human feet. Here was Anubis, the awful messenger of the gods above and below, his face partly black and partly golden, lofty, raising up on high his dog's head, and bearing in his left hand his wand, and in his right hand shaking the green palm. Directly after followed, raised to an upright position, the image of the goddess, that is, the fruitful mother of all. . . . Another carried a spacious box of secrets concealing within the mys-teries of the glorious religion. Another bore in his happy bosom the ven-erable image of the highest godhead, not like any beast, bird, wild ani-mal or even human being, but made by a clever discovery, and therefore to be revered, an emblem ineffable of a somehow higher religion, one to be guarded with great silence. . . .

Meanwhile, amid the hubbub of the festive prayers, proceeding little by little we reached the sea. . . . There, after the images were duly arranged, we saw a boat skillfully wrought and variegated round about with the marvelous paintings of the Egyptians. This boat, most scrupulously purified, the high priest named after and dedicated to the goddess, intoning the most solemn prayers from his holy lips and purifying it with a glowing torch, an egg, and sulphur. The gleaming sail of this blessed bark bore the words of a vow woven into it; these words renewed the vow concerning the prosperous navigation of the new sailing season. The mast rose up high, made of pine, round and splendid, conspicuous for its remarkable masthead; the poop, fashioned in the shape of a goose's neck, gleamed with its covering of gold plate; and the whole ship, finished with bright citron wood, was magnificent. Then all the people, both priestly and lay, vied in heaping winnowing fans loaded with spices and such like offerings, and poured over the waves libations of these offerings mixed with milk, until the ship was filled with abundant devotions and propitious prayers; then it was loosened from its cables and given to the sea with a special serene breeze. And when we had lost sight of it because of the distance it had gone, each of them that bore the holy objects took up again and carried what he had brought, and eagerly took his way back to the shrine, maintaining the same order of procession.

When we came to the temple itself, the high priest, those who carried the divine images, and especially those who had long been initiated in the venerable secrets went into the chamber of the goddess and arranged in due fashion the lifelike images. Then one of these, whom all call the secretary, taking his place before the doors, summoned to a kind of meeting the company of the *pastophori*,[47] which is the name of the holy college. From a raised platform he read forth from a book, offering propitious vows for the great emperor, the senate, the *equites*, the entire Roman people, and for the sailors and ships under the control and sovereignty of our world. Then he pronounced in the Greek tongue and manner, "*Ploiaphesia*." [48] The ensuing shout of the people indicated that this word brings good luck to all. And then, gleaming with joy, the populace, carrying leafy boughs, twigs, and garlands, kissed the places on the steps where the silver statue of the goddess had rested, and departed to their homes.

[47] Literally "shrine bearers," priests of Isis.
[48] That is, "release of the ship."

RELIGIOUS SYNCRETISM

Apuleius *The Golden Ass* (*Metamorphoses*) XI. v

I am she that is the mother of the nature of things, mistress of all the elements, the initial progeny of the ages, highest of the divine powers, queen of the departed spirits, the first of the heavenly deities, the uniform manifestation of the gods and goddesses. The luminous summits of the sky, the wholesome breezes of the sea, and the lamented silences of the dead below I control at my will. My sole divine power is adored throughout all the world in manifold guise, with varied rites, and by varied names. Hence the Phrygians, first born of mankind, call me Mother of the Gods at Pessinus; the autochthonous Athenians, Cecropian Minerva; the Cyprians, sea-girt, Paphian Venus; the arrow-bearing Cretans, Dictynnian Diana; the trilingual Sicilians, Stygian Proserpina; the Eleusinians, their ancient goddess Ceres; some Juno, others Bellona, others Hecate, others Rhamnusia; and both types of Ethiopians, whose land is lighted by the first rays of the rising god of the sun, and the Egyptians, who are preeminent in ancient lore and worship me with special ceremonies, call me by my true name, Queen Isis.

ORGIASTIC FRENZY

Widespread over the Mediterranean was the worship of the Syrian fish-goddess of Hierapolis (Bambyce), Atargatis, and her spouse Hadad. The Syrian cults, though not as popular in the West as those of Asia Minor and Egypt, were spread by Syrian slaves, merchants, and soldiers, who also brought with them the worship of various local baals. The following passage describes the devotees of Atargatis; similar ritual orgies characterized several of the mystery cults.

Apuleius *The Golden Ass* (*Metamorphoses*) VIII. xxvii–xxviii

They appeared garbed in various colors, misshapen, their faces smeared with foul paint and their eyes painted with oil, wearing turbans, saffron-colored vestments, and garments of fine linen and silk; and some wore white tunics painted with purple stripes in all directions like little spears, girt with belts, their feet shod with yellow shoes. . . . Then with their arms naked up to their shoulders, holding up huge swords and axes, they shout and dance a frenzied dance, aroused by the sound of the pipe. After we had passed not a few cottages, we came to the villa of a certain rich property owner, where as soon as they entered they let forth with discordant howlings and darted about in a frenzied way. And for a long time they would bend their heads down, twist their necks with supple movements, and whirl their hanging hair in a circle. And sometimes they would take to biting their own flesh, and finally each one cut his arms with the two-edged sword he was carrying, while one of them, who was more frenzied, panting rapidly from the depths of his heart, as though he were filled with the divine spirit of deity, feigned he was smitten with madness. . . . He began to speak with a noisy prophecy, inventing a lie, assailing and accusing himself, alleging that he had perpetrated some wrong against the rules of the holy religion, and demanding just punishment at his own hands for the noxious crime. And finally, seizing a whip, a special accoutrement of these effeminate men . . . he scourged himself. . . . You might see the ground wet and defiled with the effeminate blood from the cutting of the swords and the blows of the scourges. . . . But when at length they were weary, or at least satisfied with lacerating themselves, they put a stop to this bloody business; and they received in the wide folds of their garments contributions of bronze coins—aye, silver too—many vying to offer these, and also a cask of wine, cheese, and some meal and winter-wheat.

THE WORSHIP OF CYBELE

For six centuries, from its importation in 205/4 B.C. (see Vol. I, § 177) to the triumph of Christianity, the cult of the Phrygian mother-goddess Cybele (*Magna Mater*) remained one of the important mystery religions of the Roman Empire. The center of the cult was Rome itself. Though it was kept under close surveillance until the end of the Republic, and though participation in its priesthoods and rituals was forbidden to Roman citizens, all such restrictions were rescinded by the Emperor Claudius, and the worship of Cybele and her lover Attis became part of the state religion. One of the important rites of this cult, later taken over into Mithraism, was the *taurobolium*, baptism with a shower of the blood of a freshly slain bull.

Lucretius [49] *On the Nature of Things* II. 600–28
From LCL

She it is of whom the ancient and learned poets of the Greeks have sung, [how that from her sanctuary she rides in state] on a chariot driving a pair of lions. . . . And they have surrounded the top of her head with a mural crown, because embattled in excellent positions she sustains cities; which emblem now adorns the divine mother's image as she is carried over the earth in awesome state. She it is whom different nations in their ancient ritual acclaim as the Idaean Mother, and give her troops of Phrygians to escort her, because men declare that first from that realm

[49] Titus Lucretius Carus (c.99–c.55 B.C.), author of the Latin poem *De rerum natura* (On the Nature of Things), which expounds aspects of Epicureanism.

came the wheat, which then spread over the world. They gave her eunuch priests, as wishing to indicate that those who have violated the majesty of the Mother, and have been found ungrateful to their parents, should be thought unworthy to bring living offspring into the regions of light. The taut tomtoms thunder under the open palm, the hollow cymbals sound around, horns with hoarse-echoing blare affright, hollow flutes prick up the spirits with their Phrygian cadences, martial arms show a front of violent fury, that they may amaze the ungrateful minds and impious hearts of the vulgar with fear of the goddess's majesty. Therefore as soon as she rides through mighty cities, silently blessing mankind with unspoken benediction, they bestrew the whole of her progress with silver and bronze, enriching it with bounteous largess, and snow down rose flowers in a shower, overshadowing the Mother and her escorting troops.

EDICT AGAINST MANICHAEISM

The ascetic Persian cult founded by the Babylonian prophet Mani in the middle of the third century began to penetrate the Roman Empire c. A.D. 270. This cult, which is regarded by some scholars as a Christian heresy, was persecuted by both the Persian and the Roman governments. It was destined, nevertheless, to become one of the great universal religions. The following edict against the Manichaeans was issued by Diocletian, probably in A.D. 296, as part of his policy of strengthening the traditional native cults.

Comparison of Mosaic and Roman Law [50] xv. 3

The Emperors Diocletian and Maximian, Augusti, and Constantius and Maximian, most noble Caesars, to Julianus, proconsul of Africa. Excessive idleness, my dear Julianus, sometimes drives people to join with others in devising certain superstitious doctrines of a most worthless and depraved kind. In so doing, they overstep the bounds imposed on humans. Moreover, they lure on many others to accept the authority of their erroneous doctrine.

But the immortal gods in their providence have deigned to dispose and arrange matters so that good and true principles should be approved and fixed by the wisdom and constant deliberation of many good, eminent, and very wise men. These principles it is not right to oppose or resist, nor ought the age-old religion be disparaged by a new one. For it is the height of criminality to reexamine doctrines once and for all settled and fixed by the ancients, doctrines which hold and possess their recog-

[50] Composed between A.D. 390 and 438 by an unknown Christian writer. The text appears in *FIRA*, II, 544–89; there is an edition with English translation by M. Hyamson (Oxford, 1913).

nized place and course. Wherefore it is our vigorous determination to punish the stubborn depraved minds of these most worthless people.

We take note that those men concerning whom Your Sagacity has reported to Our Serenity,[51] namely the Manichaeans, have set up new and unheard-of sects in opposition to the older creeds, with the intent of driving out to the benefit of their depraved doctrine what was formerly granted to us by divine favor. We have heard that these men have but recently sprung up and advanced, like strange and unexpected portents, from the Persian people, our enemy, to this part of the world, where they are perpetrating many outrages, disturbing the tranquillity of the peoples and also introducing the gravest harm to the communities. And it is to be feared that peradventure, as usually happens, they may try, with the accursed customs and perverse laws of the Persians, to infect men of a more innocent nature, namely the temperate and tranquil Roman people, as well as our entire Empire with what one might call their malevolent poisons. And since, as Your Sagacity has set forth in your report on their religion, all types of offenses against the statutes have very plainly been devised and falsehoods contrived, we have accordingly established for these people afflictions and deserving and condign penalties.

Now, therefore, we order that the founders and heads be subjected to severe punishment: together with their abominable writings they are to be burned in the flames. We instruct that their followers, and particularly the fanatics, shall suffer a capital penalty, and we ordain that their property be confiscated for our fisc. But if indeed any office holders or persons of any rank or distinction have gone over to a hitherto unheard-of, disgraceful, and wholly infamous sect, particularly to the creed of the Persians, you shall cause their estates to be added to our fisc, and the persons themselves to be sent to the Phaenensian or Proconnesian mines.[52]

In order, then, that this plague of iniquity may be extirpated by the roots from this most happy age of ours, Your Devotion shall carry out with despatch the orders and enactments of Our Tranquillity.

Given on March 31, at Alexandria.

172. *Imperial Policy toward the Christians*

This famous correspondence between Trajan and Pliny (governor of Bithynia-Pontus in A.D. c.111–113) is a prime source for the spread of Christianity

[51] For such appellations cf. Chapter VII, Note 63.
[52] Phaena is modern el-Musmieh, about 25 miles south of Damascus; Proconnesus is the large island (modern Marmora) in the Sea of Marmora.

in Asia Minor and for the official policy toward the Christians in the two centuries from Nero to Decius, in whose brief reign (A.D. 249–51) the organized imperial persecution of Christianity was begun. Before that the Roman state did not proscribe the religion *per se* but treated the Christians with a hostility based on political considerations. Christians were constantly exposed to prosecution for such overt acts as obstinate disobedience of imperial officials, violation of the statutes on illegal associations, disloyalty and treason (evidenced by their refusal to participate in the state religion and the imperial cult), and other specific offenses. In addition, there was persistent popular agitation against Christians locally, so that provincial governors often employed their police powers for summary repression of the growing religion in the interest of maintaining civil order.

Pliny *Letters* Book x, Nos. 96–97

[Pliny to the Emperor Trajan]

It is my practice, my lord, to refer to you all matters concerning which I am in doubt. For who can better give guidance to my hesitation or inform my ignorance? I have never participated in trials of Christians. I therefore do not know what offenses it is the practice to punish or investigate, and to what extent. And I have been not a little hesitant as to whether there should be any distinction on account of age or no difference between the very young and the more mature; whether pardon is to be granted for repentance, or, if a man has once been a Christian, it does him no good to have ceased to be one; whether the name itself, even without offenses, or only the offenses associated with the name are to be punished.

Meanwhile, in the case of those who were denounced to me as Christians, I have observed the following procedure: I interrogated these as to whether they were Christians; those who confessed I interrogated a second and a third time, threatening them with punishment; those who persisted I ordered executed. For I had no doubt that, whatever the nature of their creed, stubbornness and inflexible obstinacy surely deserve to be punished. There were others possessed of the same folly; but because they were Roman citizens, I signed an order for them to be transferred to Rome.

Soon accusations spread, as usually happens, because of the proceedings going on, and several incidents occurred. An anonymous document was published containing the names of many persons. Those who denied that they were or had been Christians, when they invoked the gods in words dictated by me, offered prayer with incense and wine to your image, which I had ordered to be brought for this purpose together with statues of the gods, and moreover cursed Christ—none of which those who are really Christians, it is said, can be forced to do—these I thought should be discharged. Others named by the informer declared that they were Christians, but then denied it, asserting that they had been but had ceased to be, some three years before, others many years, some as much as twenty-five years. They all worshiped your image and the statues of the gods, and cursed Christ.

They asserted, however, that the sum and substance of their fault or error had been that they were accustomed to meet on a fixed day before dawn and sing responsively a hymn to Christ as to a god, and to bind themselves by oath, not to some crime, but not to commit fraud, theft, or adultery, not to falsify their trust, nor to refuse to return a trust when called upon to do so.[53] When this was over, it was their custom to depart and to assemble again to partake of food—but ordinary and innocent food.[54] Even this, they affirmed, they had ceased to do after my edict by which, in accordance with your instructions, I had forbidden political associations. Accordingly, I judged it all the more necessary to find out what the truth was by torturing two female slaves who were called deaconesses. But I discovered nothing else but depraved, excessive superstition.

I therefore postponed the investigation and hastened to consult you. For the matter seemed to me to warrant consulting you, especially because of the number involved. For many persons of every age, every rank, and also of both sexes are and will be endangered. For the contagion of this superstition has spread not only to the cities but also to the villages and farms. But it seems possible to check and cure it. It is certainly quite clear that the temples, which had been almost deserted, have begun to be frequented, that the established religious rites, long neglected, are being resumed, and that from everywhere sacrificial animals are coming, for which until now very few purchasers could be found. Hence it is easy to imagine what a multitude of people can be reformed if an opportunity for repentance is afforded.

[Trajan to Pliny]

You observed proper procedure, my dear Pliny, in sifting the cases of those who had been denounced to you as Christians. For it is not possible to lay down any general rule to serve as a kind of fixed standard. They are not to be sought out; if they are denounced and proved guilty, they are to be punished, with this reservation, that whoever denies that he is a Christian and really proves it—that is, by worshiping our gods—even though he was under suspicion in the past, shall obtain pardon

---

[53] This is apparently a reference to the Ten Commandments.
[54] See § 173.

through repentance. But anonymously posted accusations ought to have no place in any prosecution. For this is both a dangerous kind of precedent and out of keeping with [the spirit of] our age.

173. *Propaganda against Christianity*

During the second and third centuries the spread of Christianity was rapid, especially among the lowest social strata in the urban centers of Asia and Africa. It gradually penetrated the highest circles of the provinces and of Italy, gaining adherents even in the senate, the court, and the imperial family. The contemporary Christian apologists are given to rhetorical overstatements of the extension of their religion (it has been estimated that by the time of Constantine's conversion in A.D. 312 about one tenth of the inhabitants of the Empire were Christians). As the new religion began to gain sizable strength, it was called upon to defend itself from fantastic charges, the most persistent of which were atheism, eating of babies, sexual orgies, and incest.

SPREAD OF CHRISTIANITY

Tertullian *Apology* xxxvii. 4

We are but of yesterday, and we have filled everything of yours— cities, islands, forts, towns, *conciliabula*,[55] even the camps, tribes, courts, palace, senate, Forum. We have left you only the temples.

CALUMNIES AGAINST THE CHRISTIANS

Minucius Felix *Octavius* viii. 3–xii. 6 (abridged)

Is it not deplorable that a faction . . . of abandoned, hopeless outlaws makes attacks against the gods? They gather together ignorant persons from the lowest dregs, and credulous women, easily deceived as their sex is, and organize a rabble of unholy conspirators, leagued together in nocturnal associations and by ritual fasts and barbarous foods, not for the purpose of some sacred rite but for the sake of sacrilege—a secret tribe that shuns the light, silent in public but talkative in secret places. They despise the temples as if they were tombs, they spit upon the gods, they ridicule our sacred rites. Pitiable themselves, they pity . . . our priests; half-naked themselves, they despise offices and official robes. What amazing folly! What incredible arrogance! They despise present tortures yet dread uncertain future ones; while they fear to die after death, they have no fear of it in the meantime; deceptive hope soothes away their terror with the solace of a life to come.

[55] See Vol. I, p. 417, Note 57.

Already . . . decay of morals spreads from day to day throughout the entire world, and the loathsome shrines of this impious conspiracy multiply. This plot must be completely rooted out and execrated. They recognize one another by secret signs and tokens; they love one another almost before they are acquainted. Everywhere a kind of religion of lust is also associated with them, and they call themselves promiscuously brothers and sisters, so that ordinary fornication, through the medium of a sacred name, becomes incest. And thus their vain and mad superstition glories in crimes. And for themselves, if there were not a basis of truth, knowing rumor would not tell of gross and unspeakable abominations. I hear that in some absurd conviction or other they consecrate and worship the head of an ass,[56] the most repulsive of beasts—a religion worthy of the morals that begot it. Others say that they reverence the private parts of their director and high priest, and adore them as if belonging to a parent. Whether this is false I know not, but suspicion naturally attaches to secret and nocturnal rites. To say that a man put to death for a crime and the lethal wooden cross are objects of their veneration is to assign altars suitable for abandoned and impious men, the kind of worship they deserve. What is told of the initiation of neophytes is as detestable as it is notorious. An infant covered with spelt to deceive the unsuspecting is set before the one to be initiated in the rites. The neophyte is induced to strike what seem to be harmless blows on the surface of the spelt, and this infant is killed by his random and unsuspecting blows. Its blood—oh, shocking!—they greedily lap up; the limbs they eagerly distribute; and by this victim they league themselves, and by this complicity in crime they pledge themselves to mutual silence. . . . Their form of banqueting is notorious; everywhere all talk of it. . . . On an appointed day they assemble at a feast with all their children, sisters, and mothers, people of both sexes and every age. There, after much feasting, when the banquet has become heated and intoxication has inflamed the drunken passions of incestuous lust, a dog which has been tied to a lamp is incited to rush and leap forward after a morsel thrown beyond the range of the cord by which it was tied. The telltale light is upset and extinguished, and in the shameless dark they exchange embraces indiscriminately, and all, if not actually, yet by complicity are equally involved in incest. . . .

Furthermore, they threaten the whole world and the universe itself and its stars with fire, and work for its destruction. . . .[57] Not content with this insane notion, they add to and weave old wives' tales: they say

---

[56] This was also said of the Jews (cf. Tacitus *Histories* v. iii. 4-iv. 3).
[57] This refers to early Christian belief in the imminent destruction of the world and the coming Day of Judgment.

that they are reborn after death from the cinders and ashes, and with unaccountable confidence believe in one another's lies. . . .

But you [Christians] meanwhile in anxious doubt abstain from wholesome pleasures; you do not attend the shows; you take no part in the processions; fight shy of public banquets; abhor the sacred games, meats from the sacrificial victims, drinks poured in libation on the altars.

Athenagoras [58] *Plea for the Christians* ii. 7, 9; iii. 12–13

It is not in accord with your justice that, when others are charged with crimes they are not punished till they are convicted, but in our case the name bears more weight than the evidence at the trial, at which the judges, instead of inquiring whether the accused has committed any wrong, insult the name, as if that were itself a crime. . . . Therefore what is conceded equally to all we claim for ourselves, that we shall not be hated and punished because we are called Christians (for what bearing has the name on evil-doing?), but shall be tried on any charges anyone may bring against us, and either be released on our disproving the charges, or punished if convicted of wickedness—not for the name (for no Christian is a bad man unless he falsely profess our doctrines) but for the wrong done. . . .

Three charges are alleged against us: atheism, cannibalistic banquets, incestuous unions. But if these charges are true, spare no class; proceed at once against the crimes; kill us root and branch, with our wives and children, if any Christian is found to live like the beasts. . . . But if these things are only gossip mongering and empty slanders . . . it is left for you to make inquiry concerning our life, our beliefs, our loyalty and obedience to you,[59] your house, and the monarchy, and thus at length to accord to us nothing more than to those who persecute us.

Tertullian *Apology* x. 1, xxviii. 2–3, xxxv. 1, xl. 1–2
From LCL

"You do not," say you, "worship the gods; you do not offer sacrifice for the emperors." It follows by parity of reasoning that we do not sacrifice for others because we do not for ourselves—it follows from our not worshiping the gods. So we are accused of sacrilege and treason at once. That is the chief of the case against us—the whole of it, in fact. . . .

So now we have come to the second charge, the charge of treason against a majesty more august. For it is with greater fear and shrewder timidity that you watch Caesar than the Olympian Jove himself. . . .

[58] An Athenian convert, whose pamphlet in defense of Christianity was written c.177.
[59] That is, the Emperor Marcus Aurelius.

So that in this too you will be found irreligious to those gods of yours, when you show more fear for the rule of a man. In fact, among you perjury by all the gods together comes quicker than by the *genius* of a single Caesar. . . .

So that is why Christians are public enemies—because they will not give the emperors vain, false, and rash honors; because, being men of a true religion, they celebrate the emperors' festivals more in heart than in frolic. . . .

On the contrary, the name faction may properly be given to those who join to hate the good and honest, who shout for the blood of the innocent, who use as a pretext to defend their hatred the absurdity that they take the Christians to be the cause of every disaster to the state, of every misfortune of the people. If the Tiber reaches the walls, if the Nile does not rise to water the fields, if the sky does not move [60] or the earth does, if there is famine, if there is plague, the cry at once arises: "The Christians to the lions!" [61]

174. *Defense of the Christian Way of Life*

The calumnies and attacks against Christians led to the production of a body of Christian apologetic literature during the second and third centuries. The Christian apologists, such as Aristides of Athens, Justin Martyr, Athenagoras, Minucius Felix, and Tertullian, give us an idealized picture of the early Christian community, generally glossing over the numerous defections under the stress of the persecutions and the fierce internal schisms.

Tertullian *Apology* xxx. 1, 4, xxxviii–xxxix, xlii (abridged)
Adapted from LCL

For we invoke the eternal God, the true God, the living God for the safety of the emperors. . . . Looking up to heaven, the Christians—

---

[60] That is, if there is no rain.
[61] Except in the Christian writers (see § 174), praise of the Christian way of life is practically unknown in extant ancient sources. There is evidence, however, that some independent and rational minds were not swept away by the popular anti-Christian hysteria. For example, the Greek scientist Galen (A.D. 130–c.200; cf. p. 312) wrote in his summary of Plato's *Republic* (the work is lost except for some fragments preserved in an Arabic translation): "Now we see the people called Christians . . . acting in the same way [as those who philosophize]. For their contempt of death [and of its sequel] is patent to us every day, and likewise their restraint in cohabitation. For they include not only men but also women who refrain from cohabiting all through their lives; and they also number individuals who, in self-discipline and self-control in matters of food and drink, and in their keen pursuit of justice, have attained a pitch not inferior to that of genuine philosophers" (R. Walzer, *Galen on Jews and Christians* [Oxford, 1949], p. 15).

with hands outspread, because innocent, with head bare because we do not blush, yes! and without a prompter [62] because we pray from the heart—are ever praying for all the emperors. We pray for a fortunate life for them, a secure rule, a safe house, brave armies, a faithful senate, a virtuous people, a peaceful world. . . .

Should not this sect have been classed among the legal associations, when it commits no such actions as are commonly feared from unlawful associations? For unless I am mistaken, the reason for prohibiting associations clearly lay in forethought for public order—to save the state from being torn into parties, a thing very likely to disturb election assemblies, public gatherings, local senates, meetings, even the public games, with the clashing and rivalry of partisans. . . .[63] We, however, whom all the passion for glory and rank leave cold, have no need to combine; nothing is more foreign to us than the state. One state we recognize for all—the universe.

Your public games, too, we renounce, as heartily as we do their origins; we know these origins lie in superstition. . . . We have nothing to do, in speech, sight, or hearing, with the madness of the circus, the shamelessness of the theater, the savagery of the arena, the vanity of the gymnasium. Why should we offend you if we assume the existence of other pleasures? . . .

I will now show you the proceedings with which the Christian association occupies itself. I have proved they are not wrong; so now I will make you see they are good. We are a society with a common religious feeling, unity of discipline, a common bond of hope. We meet in gathering and congregation to approach God in prayer, massing our forces to surround Him. This violence that we do Him pleases God. We pray also for the emperors, for their ministers and those in authority, for the security of the world, for peace on earth, for postponement of the end. We meet to read the divine Scriptures. . . . Our presidents are elders of proved character, men who have reached this office not for a price [64] but by character; for nothing that is God's goes for a price.

Even if there is a treasury of a sort, it is not made up of money paid in initiation fees, as if religion were a matter of contract. Every man once a month brings some modest contribution—or whenever he wishes, and only if he does wish, and if he can; for nobody is compelled; it is a voluntary offering. You might call them the trust funds of piety. For they are not spent upon banquets [65] or drinking parties or thankless eating

---

[62] Cf. § 167, first selection.

[63] On the Roman government's policy toward associations, see § 69.

[64] Tertullian refers to the purchase of priesthoods among the Greeks and Romans.

[65] Formal banquets were one of the principal activities of associations among the Romans (cf. § 70, first selection).

houses; but to feed the poor and to bury them, for boys and girls who lack property and parents, and then for slaves grown old and for shipwrecked mariners; and any who may be in mines, islands, or prisons, provided that it is for the sake of God's sect, become the pensioners of their confession. . . .

So we, who are united in mind and soul, have no hesitation about sharing property. All is common among us—except our wives. At that point we dissolve our partnership. . . .

Our dinner shows its idea in its name; it is called by the Greek name for love. . . .[66] Since it turns on the duty of religion, it allows nothing vile, nothing immodest.[67] We do not take our places at table until we have first partaken of prayer to God. Only so much is eaten as satisfies hunger, only so much drunk as meets the needs of the modest. . . . After water for the hands come the lights; and then each, from what he knows of the Holy Scriptures, or from his own heart, is called before the rest to sing to God. . . . Prayer in like manner ends the banquet. . . .

This gathering of Christians may properly be called illegal, if it is like illegal gatherings; may properly be condemned, if any complaint can be made against it such as are made against factions. To whose hurt have we ever met? We are when assembled just what we are when apart; taken together the same as singly; we injure none; we grieve none. When decent people, when good men gather, when the pious and when the chaste assemble, that is not to be called a faction. . . .

But there is another charge of wrong-doing made against us. We are said to be useless in business. How so, when we are human beings and live alongside of you—men with the same ways, the same dress and furniture, the same necessities of life? . . . So not without a *forum*, not without a meat market, not without baths, shops, workshops, stalls, and market days, and the other aspects of business, we live with you—in this world. We sail ships together with you, we serve in the army, go to the country, to market with you. Our skills and yours work together; our labor is openly at your service.

EARLY CHRISTIAN WORSHIP

Justin Martyr *First Apology* lxi, lxv–lxvii

All who are convinced and believe that what is taught and said by us is true, and promise that they are able to live accordingly, are taught to pray and with fasting to ask forgiveness of God for their former sins; and we pray and fast with them. Then they are brought by us to where

[66] That is, *agape*.
[67] For the popular charges against the Christians, see § 173.

there is water, and they are reborn in the same manner as we ourselves were reborn.[68] For in the name of God, the Father and Lord of the universe, and of our Savior Jesus Christ, and of the Holy Ghost, they then are washed in the water. . . .

After thus washing the one who has been convinced and has given his assent, we conduct him to the place where those who are called the brethren are assembled, to offer earnest prayers in common for ourselves, for him who has been enlightened, and for all others everywhere, so that we, now that we have learned the truth, may by our works also be deemed worthy of being found to be good practitioners and keepers of the commandments, and thus be saved with eternal salvation. When we end our prayers we greet each other with a kiss. Then bread and a chalice of wine mixed with water are brought to the one who presides over the brethren; and he takes it, and offers up praise and glory to the Father of the universe, through the name of the Son and the Holy Ghost; and he gives thanks at length for our being deemed worthy of these things by Him. When he has finished the prayers and thanksgiving, all the people present express their assent, saying "Amen." . . . And when he who presides has celebrated the eucharist [thanksgiving], and all the people have expressed their assent, those called among us deacons allow each one of those present to partake of the bread and wine and water for which thanks have been given, and they bring it also to those not present. And this food is called among us the eucharist. . . .

And on the day called Sunday there is a gathering in one place of all who dwell in the cities or in the country places, and the memoirs of the Apostles or the writings of the prophets are read as long as time allows. Then when the reader has finished, he who presides gives oral admonition and exhortation to imitate these excellent examples. Then we all rise together, and offer prayers; and, as stated before, when we have ended our praying, bread and wine and water are brought. And he who presides similarly offers up prayers and thanksgiving, as far as lies in his power, and the people express their approval by saying "Amen." And each receives a share and partakes of the food for which thanks have been given,[69] and through the deacons some is sent to those not present. The prosperous, if they so desire, each contribute what they wish, according to their own judgment, and the collection is entrusted to the one who presides. And he assists orphans and widows, and those who are in need because of illness or any other reason, and those who are in prison, and strangers sojourning with us; in short, all those in need are his care.

[68] The rite of baptism.
[69] Justin refers to the *agape* ("love feast"); cf. Note 66.

175. *Atrocities against Christians*

In the reign of Marcus Aurelius, the "philosopher on the throne," occurred the only large-scale persecution of the Christians during the second century. Mass hysteria generated by serious internal and frontier troubles led to violent anti-Christian outbreaks in various provinces. The cruel torture and execution of forty-eight Christians, with the approval of the emperor, at Lyons and Vienne in A.D. 177, is a gruesome commentary on the brutality of the age.

Eusebius *Ecclesiastical History* v. i (abridged)
From LCL

First they endured nobly all that was heaped upon them by the mob, howls and stripes and dragging about, and rapine and stoning and imprisonment, and all things that are wont to happen at the hands of an infuriated populace against its supposed enemies and foes. Then they were dragged into the market place by the tribune and by the chief authorities of the city, were indicted and confessed, and at last they were shut up until the coming of the governor. Then they were brought before the governor, and when he used all his cruelty against them, then intervened Vettius Epagathus, one of the brethren. . . . His character forbade him to endure the unreasonable judgment given against us, and, overcome with indignation, he asked to be heard himself in defense of the brethren to the effect that there was nothing atheistic or impious among us. He was howled down by those around the judgment seat—he was a man of position—and the governor would not tolerate the just requests which he had put forward but merely asked if he were a Christian himself. He then confessed in clear tones and was himself taken into the ranks of the martyrs. . . .

There were also arrested certain heathen slaves of our members, since the governor had publicly commanded that we should all be prosecuted, and these by the snare of Satan, fearing the tortures which they saw the saints suffering, when the soldiers urged them, falsely accused us of cannibalistic feasts and incestuous intercourse,[70] and things which it is not right for us either to speak of or to think of or even to believe that such things could ever happen among men. When this rumor spread, all men turned like beasts against us, so that even if any had formerly been lenient for friendship's sake, they then became furious and raged against us. . . . All the fury of the mob and of the governor and of the soldiers was raised beyond measure against Sanctus, the deacon from Vienne,

[70] Cf. § 173.

and against Maturus, who was a neophyte but a noble contender, and against Attalus, a Pergamene by origin, who had always been a pillar and support of the Christians there, and against Blandina. . . . The blessed woman, like a noble athlete, kept gaining in vigor in her confession, and found comfort and rest and freedom from pain from what was done to her by saying, "I am a Christian woman and nothing wicked happens among us." . . .

But when the tyrant's torments had been brought to naught by Christ through the endurance of the blessed saints, the devil thought of other devices, imprisonment in jail in darkness and in the most horrible place, and stretching their feet in the stocks, separated to the fifth hole, and the other outrages which angry warders filled with the devil were accustomed to inflict on the prisoners. Thus most of them were strangled in prison. . . .

Maturus, Sanctus, Blandina, and Attalus were led forth to the wild beasts, to the public, and to the common exhibition of the inhumanity of the heathen, for the day of fighting with beasts was specially appointed for the Christians. Maturus and Sanctus passed again through all torture in the amphitheater. . . . Blandina was hung on a stake and offered as a prey to the wild beasts that were let in. . . . Then, when none of the beasts would touch her, she was taken down from the stake and brought back into the jail. . . .

But Attalus was himself loudly called for by the crowd, for he was well known. He went in, a ready combatant, for his conscience was clear, and he had been nobly trained in Christian discipline and had ever been a witness for truth among us. He was led round the amphitheater and a placard was carried before him on which was written in Latin, "This is Attalus, the Christian." The people were very bitter against him, but when the governor learned that he was a Roman [citizen], he commanded him to be put back with the rest, who were in the jail, about whom he had written to the emperor and was awaiting a reply. . . .

Caesar wrote that they should be tortured to death, but that if any should recant they should be let go, and at the beginning of the local feast (and this is widely attended by the concourse of all the heathen to it) the governor led them to the judgment seat, making a show and spectacle of the blessed men to the mob. He accordingly interrogated them again, beheaded all who appeared to possess Roman citizenship, and sent the rest to the beasts. . . .

Those who had been strangled in the jail they threw to the dogs, and watched carefully night and day that none should be cared for by us. Then they threw out the remains left by the beasts and by the fire, torn and charred, and for many days watched with a military guard the heads of the rest, together with their trunks, all unburied. And some raged and gnashed their teeth at the remains seeking some further vengeance from them, others laughed and jeered glorifying their idols and ascribing to them the punishment of the Christians. . . . Thus the bodies of the martyrs, after having been exposed and insulted in every way for six days, and afterwards burned and turned to ashes, were swept by the wicked into the river Rhone, which flows near by, that not even a relic of them might still appear upon the earth.

176. *Interrogation of Christians*

From the middle of the second century there began to be disseminated in Christian circles descriptions of the manner in which those who perished for their faith endured martyrdom. A number of the early Acts of the Martyrs—the first of which is the martyrdom of Polycarp, bishop of Smyrna, in A.D. 155/56, recorded by Eusebius *Ecclesiastical History* IV. xv. 1–24—are contemporary literary testimonials based on official records of the legal proceedings before Roman authorities (cf. § 172).

THE SCILLITAN MARTYRS

The following is an account of the interrogation of six Christians from Scillium, in the province of Africa, by the proconsul Vigellius Saturninus at Carthage in A.D. 180.

R. Knopf, *Ausgewählte Märtyrerakten*, 3d ed. (Tübingen, 1929), No. 6

In the consulship of Praesens (for the second time) and Claudianus, on July 17, Speratus, Nartzalus, Cittinus, Donata, Secunda, and Vestia were put on trial in the [governor's] council chamber at Carthage. The proconsul Saturninus said, "You can secure the indulgence of our lord the emperor if you return to your senses."

Speratus said, "We have never done any wrong; we have lent ourselves to no injustice; we have never spoken ill of anyone; but when we have been ill-treated, we have given thanks, because we honor our emperor."

The proconsul Saturninus said, "We, also, are religious, and our religion is simple; and we swear by the *genius* of our lord the emperor, and pray for his welfare, as you too ought to do."

Speratus said, "If you grant me your undivided attention, I will tell you the mystery of simplicity."

Saturninus said, "I shall not grant you a hearing, if you begin to speak evil about our sacred rites; but swear rather by the *genius* of our lord the emperor."

Speratus said, "The empire of this world I do not recognize; but rather I serve that God whom no man has seen nor can see with human eyes. I have not committed theft; if I buy anything, I pay the tax, because I recognize my Lord, the King of kings and Emperor of all peoples."

The proconsul Saturninus said to the others, "Cease to be of this persuasion."

Speratus said, "It is an evil persuasion to commit murder, or to bear false witness."

The proconsul Saturninus said, "Do not participate in this madness."

Cittinus said, "We have none other to fear except only our Lord God who is in heaven."

Donata said, "Honor to Caesar as to Caesar, but fear to God."

Vestia said, "I am a Christian."

Secunda said, "What I am, that I wish to be."

The proconsul Saturninus said to Speratus, "Do you persist in being a Christian?"

Speratus said, "I am a Christian." And they all concurred with him.

The proconsul Saturninus said, "Do you desire some time to reconsider?"

Speratus said, "In a matter so just there is no reconsidering."

The proconsul Saturninus said, "What are the things in your box?"

Speratus said, "The Books, and the letters of Paul, a just man."

The proconsul Saturninus said, "Take a postponement of thirty days and reconsider."

Speratus said again, "I am a Christian." And they all concurred with him.

The proconsul Saturninus read out the decree from the tablet: "Since Speratus, Nartzalus, Cittinus, Donata, Vestia, Secunda, and the rest who have confessed that they live according to the rite of the Christians have obstinately persevered when an opportunity was offered them to return to the practice of the Romans, it is my decision that they be punished with the sword."

Speratus said, "We give thanks to God."

Nartzalus said, "Today we are martyrs in heaven; thanks to God!"

The proconsul Saturninus ordered the herald to proclaim: "I have ordered the execution of Speratus, Nartzalus, Cittinus, Veturius, Felix, Aquilinus, Laetantius, Januaria, Generosa, Vestia, Donata, and Secunda."

They all said, "Thanks be to God!"

And so they were crowned with martyrdom all together: and they reign with the Father and the Son and the Holy Ghost forever and ever. Amen.

THE MARTYRDOM OF MARCELLUS

Though there were numerous Christians in the Roman armies, some were driven by conscience or religious fervor to renounce military service.

R. Knopf, *Ausgewählte Märtyrerakten*, 3d ed. (Tübingen, 1929), No. 20. iii–v

In the consulship of Faustus and Gallus, on October 30, at Tingis,[71] Marcellus, a centurion from the municipality of Asta, was brought into court, and it was officially stated: "Marcellus, a centurion, has been referred to your authority [72] by the governor Fortunatus. There is at hand a letter dealing with his case, which at your command I shall read."

Agricolanus said, "Read it."

The official report was read, as follows: "To you, my lord, from Fortunatus, etc."

When this was read, Agricolanus said, "Did you say what appears in the official records of the governor?"

Marcellus answered, "I did."

Agricolanus said, "Were you in service with the rank of centurion first class?"

Marcellus answered, "I was."

Agricolanus said, "What madness possessed you to renounce your oath of allegiance and to speak as you did?"

Marcellus answered, "There is no madness in those who fear God."

Agricolanus said, "Did you say each of the things contained in the official records of the governor?"

Marcellus answered, "I did."

Agricolanus said, "Did you throw away your arms?"

Marcellus answered, "I did. For a Christian, who is in the service of the Lord Christ, ought not to serve the cares of this world."

Agricolanus said, "The acts of Marcellus are such that they must receive disciplinary punishment. Accordingly, Marcellus, who was in service with the rank of centurion first class, having declared that he has degraded himself by publicly renouncing his oath of allegiance, and having, moreover, put on record insane statements, it is my pleasure that he be put to death by the sword."

[71] Tingis (modern Tangier) was an important town and military base in Mauretania. The date is A.D. 298.
[72] That is, to the jurisdiction of Aurelius Agricolanus, the deputy prefect (cf. Chapter VI, Note 93).

When he was being led to execution, Marcellus said, "Agricolanus, may God be kind to you!"

And after he said these words he was killed by the sword, and obtained the glory of martyrdom he desired.

177. *Organized Persecution of Christianity*

The statement of Orosius (*History against the Pagans* VII. xxvi. 9), that "the Church of Christ suffered ten persecutions from Nero [see § 55] to Maximian," is unfounded. Before the middle of the third century, action against Christians was sporadic and local, undertaken as police measures in a climate of popular anti-Christian agitation and violence. But in the great crisis of the Empire, by which time the sect had developed into a powerful organization—virtually a "state within a state"—systematic Empire-wide efforts to suppress the religion as a challenge to the state were organized by imperial order.

THE PERSECUTION UNDER DECIUS: THE LOYALTY TEST

The first systematic persecution was that conducted by the Emperor Decius in A.D. 249–51. In the course of the persecution, Decius, in an ineffective attempt to expose all Christians, issued an edict apparently requiring all inhabitants of the Empire to take a "loyalty oath" to the state cult. Local commissions were set up in all communities of the Empire to administer the loyalty test. Each individual, even priests and priestesses of pagan gods, was required to give formal evidence of religious loyalty, which was certified in writing by the commissioners. About fifty such certificates, all from Egypt, are extant. There were many defections at this time; but considerable numbers of Christians managed to obtain certificates of loyalty (*libelli*) through influence or bribery or by performing pagan sacrifice with mental reservations. The question of readmitting such *libellatici* (certificate holders), after the persecution was over, roused vigorous discussion among Church authorities.

Michigan Papyrus No. 158; A.D. 250

To those superintending the sacrifices of the village of Theadelphia, from Aurelia Bellias, daughter of Peteres, and her daughter Capinis. We have sacrificed to the gods all along, and now in your presence according to orders I poured a libation and sacrificed and tasted of the sacred offerings, and I request you to subscribe this for us. Farewell.

[Signatures] We, Aurelius Serenus and Aurelius Hermas, saw you sacrificing. Signed by me, Hermas.

Year 1 of the Emperor Caesar Gaius Messius Quintus Trajanus
DECIUS Pius Felix Augustus, Payni 27.

THE PERSECUTION UNDER VALERIAN

After disastrous military defeats in A.D. 257, the Emperor Valerian organized
a general persecution of the Christians, seeking to destroy the Church as an
organization by depriving it of its leaders and by confiscating its economic
resources. Cyprian, bishop of Carthage, the author of the following letter,
perished in this persecution, which lasted until 270.

Cyprian *Letters* lxxx

Cyprian to Successus, his brother, greeting.

The reason I did not write to you at once, dearest brother, is the
fact that all the clergy have been placed under stress of peril and are unable to leave here at all: all are prepared, by virtue of the devotion of
their minds, for divine and heavenly glory. You should know, however,
that those have come whom I sent to the city [of Rome] for the purpose
of investigating and bringing back to us the truth concerning whatsoever
had been decreed concerning us. For many, various, and indefinite reports are rumored about. But the truth about them is as follows: Valerian
has sent an address to the senate, to the effect that bishops, presbyters,
and deacons should be immediately punished; [73] but that senators, distinguished men, and Roman *equites* should lose their rank and be deprived of their property also; and if, when their goods have been taken
away, they should persist in being Christians, that they should then also
be punished capitally; but that matrons should be deprived of their property and relegated to exile. Moreover, persons of the imperial household
who had either previously confessed or should now confess, should be
expropriated and put in chains and assigned to Caesar's estates. The Emperor Valerian also appended to his address a copy of the letters he prepared for the governors of the provinces concerning us. We are daily
expecting these letters to come, and we are, according to the firmness
of our faith, awaiting the endurance of suffering and expecting from the
help and mercy of the Lord the crown of eternal life. But know that
Sixtus [74] was executed in the cemetery on August 6, and four deacons with him. The prefects of the city, furthermore, are daily pressing
this persecution; so that any who are brought before them are punished
and their property assigned to the fisc.

[73] Here begins the second edict of Valerian, issued in A.D. 258. The first, in 257,
ordered bishops and priests who refused to sacrifice to the state gods to be exiled
and forbade Christians to assemble or to enter their cemeteries.
[74] The bishop of Rome.

I beg that these things be made known through you to our other colleagues, so that everywhere by their exhortations the brotherhood may be able to be strengthened and prepared for the spiritual struggle, that each one of our people may not be more concerned about death than about immortality, and, dedicated to the Lord with full faith and complete courage, they may rejoice rather than be afraid in this confession, in which they know that the soldiers of God and Christ are not slain but crowned. I bid you, dearest brother, ever farewell in the Lord.

THE PERSECUTION UNDER DIOCLETIAN

The persecution carried out by Diocletian and his colleagues was the last to which Christians were subjected on an Empire-wide basis, but it was also the severest and most sustained, lasting from 303 to 311.

Lactantius *On the Deaths of the Persecutors* xii–xiv

A suitable and auspicious day was sought for accomplishing this business, and the Terminalia,[75] which takes place on February 23, was especially chosen to put an end, as it were, to this religion. . . . When that day dawned, in the eighth and seventh consulships of the two emperors [Diocletian and Maximian], suddenly, while it was hardly light, the prefect, together with the military commanders, tribunes, and treasury officers, came to the church,[76] and when the doors had been broken down they sought for an image of God. Scriptures were found and burnt; spoil was given to all. Rapine, confusion, and tumult reigned. The emperors, watching from a vantage point (for the church, situated on an elevation, was visible from the palace), disputed for a long time with one another whether it should be set on fire. The opinion of Diocletian prevailed, for he feared that if such a great fire should be started some part of the city might be burned; for many large dwellings surrounded the church on all sides. Accordingly, the Praetorian Guard poured in from all sides in battle array, with axes and other iron implements, and in a few hours leveled that very lofty shrine to the ground.

On the following day an edict was published providing that men of that religion should be deprived of all honors and rank; that they should be subjected to torture, from whatever rank and station they might come; that every legal action should be pressed against them, but they themselves were not to have the right to sue for any wrong or for adultery or theft; and finally, that they should be accorded no freedom and no voice. A certain person, although it was wrong, yet with great courage ripped down this edict and tore it up, saying in derision, "These are the victories of Goths and Sarmatians." Brought to judgment at once,

---

[75] Cf. Vol. I, pp. 480–81.   [76] In Nicomedia.

he was not only tortured but was burned in the legal manner, and displaying admirable endurance was finally consumed by the flames.

But Galerius was not satisfied with the terms of the edict and sought another way to influence Diocletian. For to drive him to a determination to employ an excess of cruelty in persecution, he employed private agents to set the palace on fire; and when some part of it had gone up in flames, the Christians were accused as public enemies, and tremendous prejudice flared up against the very name of Christian as the palace burned. It was said that the Christians had plotted in concert with the eunuchs to destroy the princes, and that the two emperors had almost been burned alive in their own palace. But Diocletian, who always wanted to appear shrewd and intelligent, suspected nothing of the deception; inflamed with anger, he began immediately to torture all his domestics.[77]

Eusebius Ecclesiastical History VIII. ii, vi (abridged)
From LCL

We saw with our very eyes the houses of prayer cast down to their foundations from top to bottom, and the inspired and sacred Scriptures committed to the flames in the midst of the market places, and the pastors of the churches, some shamefully hiding themselves here and there, others ignominiously captured and made a mockery by their enemies. . . .

It was the nineteenth year of the reign of Diocletian,[78] and the month Dystrus, or March as the Romans would call it, in which, as the festival of the Savior's Passion was coming on, an imperial letter was everywhere promulgated, ordering the razing of the churches to the ground and the destruction of the Scriptures by fire, and proclaiming that those who held high positions would lose all civil rights, while those attached to households, if they persisted in their profession of Christianity, would be deprived of their liberty. Such was the first document against us. But not long afterwards we were further visited with other letters, and in them the order was given that the bishops of the churches should all, in every place, be first committed to prison, and then afterwards compelled by every kind of device to sacrifice. . . .

We shall mention the kind of death that one of them met, and leave our readers to gather from that instance what happened to the others. A certain man was publicly brought forward in the city of which we have spoken above,[79] under the rulers we have mentioned.[80] He was ordered

---

[77] Not only servants in the imperial household but even Diocletian's own wife and daughter had by this time embraced Christianity.

[78] A.D. 303/4.   [79] That is, Nicomedia.

[80] Diocletian and Galerius, who ruled the eastern half of the Empire under the Tetrarchy.

to sacrifice; and, as he refused, the command was given that he should be raised on high naked and have his whole body torn with scourges until he should give in and even against his will do what was bidden him. But when he remained unmoved even under these sufferings, they proceeded to mix vinegar and salt together and pour them into the mangled parts of his body, where the bones were already showing. And as he despised these pains also, a gridiron and fire were then produced, and the remnants of his body, just as if it were flesh for eating, were consumed by the fire, not all at once, in case he might find immediate release, but little by little; nor were those who placed him on the pyre allowed to desist until, after such sufferings, he should signify his assent to what was commanded. But he clung fixedly to his purpose, and triumphantly gave up the ghost in the midst of his tortures. . . .

Such were the things that were done in Nicomedia at the beginning of the persecution. But not long afterwards, when some in the district known as Melitene [81] and again on the other hand when others in Syria had attempted to revolt against the government, an imperial command went forth that the bishops of the churches everywhere should be thrown into prison and bonds. And the spectacle of what followed surpasses all description; for in every place a countless number were shut up, and everywhere the prisons, that long ago had been prepared for murderers and grave robbers, were then filled with bishops and presbyters and deacons, readers and exorcists, so that there was no longer any room left for those condemned for wrongdoing.

Moreover, the first letter was followed by others, wherein the order had been given that those in prison should be allowed to go in liberty if they sacrificed, but if they refused should be mutilated by countless tortures. And then, once more, how could one here number the multitude of the martyrs in each province?

THE PERSECUTION UNDER MAXIMINUS

Despite the promulgation of the Edict of Toleration and the "Edict of Milan" (see § 178), persecution continued in various parts of the empire until A.D. 324, especially in the East. The following inscription from Asia Minor is connected with renewed persecution by Maximinus Daia.

OGIS, No. 569

[Arycanda, A.D. 311/12]

To the saviors of the entire human race, the divine Augustus Caesar Galerius Valerius MAXIMINUS, the divine Augustus Caesar Flavius Va-

---

[81] In the province of Armenia Minor.

lerius Constantine, and the divine Augustus Caesar Valerius Licinianus Licinius. Supplication and petition from the loyal province of Lycia and Pamphylia.

Whereas the gods, of the same family as you, have ever by deeds displayed benevolence to all, O Most Illustrious Emperors who have been seriously concerned with the divine worship on behalf of the eternal safety of yourselves, our lords, conquerors of all, we have decided that it would be well to seek refuge in your immortal majesty, and to request that the Christians, who of old have been seditious and still persist in the same disease, should finally desist and not, by introducing some new mischief, neglect the honor owed to the gods. This would easily be realized if by your divine and eternal will it were ordained to all that the wickedness of the hateful practice of the atheists be forbidden and prohibited, and if injunctions were given for all to devote themselves steadfastly to the worship of the gods, of the same family as you, on behalf of your eternal and indestructible majesty, the extent of whose benefits to all your people is manifest.

178. The End of the Persecutions

THE EDICT OF TOLERATION

On April 30, A.D. 311, the Emperor Galerius, stricken with a serious illness from which he died shortly after, promulgated at Nicomedia the famous Edict of Toleration. This marked a turning point in the history of Christianity, which, by this enactment, became a fully legal religion, though sporadic persecutions continued for some time after.

Lactantius *On the Deaths of the Persecutors* xxxiv and Eusebius
Ecclesiastical History VIII. xvii. 6–10

Among other measures which we are constantly formulating for the advantage and benefit of the state, we had formerly desired to set all things right in accordance with the ancient laws and public order of the Romans, and to provide that the Christians, too, who had abandoned the doctrines of their own fathers, should return to a sound mind. For somehow such obstinacy had taken possession of the said Christians and such folly had seized them that, abandoning the institutions of the ancients, which their own fathers perhaps had previously established, they made laws for themselves to observe at their own will and as it pleased the said persons, and assembled various persons in sundry places. Accordingly, when our command had gone forth to the effect that they should return to the institutions of the ancients, many indeed were subjected to danger, and many also were struck down. But since very many persevered in their determination, and we saw that the said persons were neither paying worship and reverence to the gods nor worshiping the god of the Christians, in view of our most gentle clemency and considering our consistent practice whereby we are wont to grant pardon to all men, we have thought fit in this case, too, to extend immediate indulgence, to wit: that they may be Christians once more and that they may reconstitute their places of assembly, on condition that they do nothing contrary to public order. In another letter, moreover, we shall indicate to governors of provinces what rules they are to observe. Wherefore, in accordance with this indulgence of ours, they are bound to implore their own god for our safety, for that of the state, and for their own, so that on every side the state may be rendered secure and they may be able to live tranquilly in their own homes.

THE "EDICT OF MILAN"

Early in A.D. 313 Constantine and Licinius at a conference at Milan agreed upon an Empire-wide religious policy. As a compromise between Licinius' pagan position and Constantine's pro-Christian views, the Roman state adopted a position of neutrality and enunciated a policy of complete religious freedom. No general edict was issued at Milan, but in all probability detailed instructions were drawn up for provincial governors to implement the new policy, already in force in the West under Constantine's rule. The famous "Edict of Milan" was probably a directive of Licinius despatched several months later from Nicomedia to governors of the Eastern provinces.

Lactantius *On the Deaths of the Persecutors* xlviii and Eusebius
Ecclesiastical History x. v. 2–14

Observing that freedom of worship should not be denied, but that each one should be given the right in accordance with his conviction and will to adhere to the religion that suits his preference, we had already long since given orders that both to the Christians [82] . . . to maintain the faith of their own sect and worship. But since many and various sects seem clearly to have been appended to that rescript in which such right was granted to the said persons, it may be perchance that some of them after a short time were driven away from such observance.

When I, Constantine Augustus, and I, Licinius Augustus, met under happy auspices in Milan and had under discussion all matters that concerned the public advantage and security, among other measures that

[82] There is a lacuna in the text. Perhaps the text read: "and to all others freedom should be given."

we saw would benefit most men we considered that first of all regulations should be drawn up to secure respect for divinity, to wit: to grant both to the Christians and to all men unrestricted right to follow the form of worship each desired, to the end that whatever divinity there be on the heavenly seat may be favorably disposed and propitious to us and all those placed under our authority. Accordingly, with salutary and most upright reasoning, we resolved on adopting this policy, namely that we should consider that no one whatsoever should be denied freedom to devote himself either to the cult of the Christians or to such religion as he deems best suited for himself, so that the highest divinity, to whose worship we pay allegiance with free minds, may grant us in all things his wonted favor and benevolence. Wherefore, it is fitting that Your Devotion should know that it is our will that the conditions which were contained in our previous letter sent to your office with respect to the Christians be entirely removed, and that now each one of those who possess the same desire, namely to observe the form of worship of the Christians, should proceed freely to observe the same freely and unconditionally, without any interference or molestation to himself. These matters we decided to explain very fully to Your Solicitude, so that you may know that we have granted to the said Christians free and absolute power to observe their religion. And while you perceive that this indulgence has been granted to the said persons by us, Your Devotion will understand that free and untrammeled freedom in their religion or cult has similarly been granted to others also, in keeping with the peace of our times, so that each person may have unrestricted freedom to practice the cult he has chosen. This has been done by us so that we should not appear to have detracted anything from any form of worship or religion.

And, moreover, with special regard to the Christians we have decided that the following regulation should be set down: That, as for the said places in which they were wont to assemble previously, concerning which a definite regulation was previously contained also in the letter sent to your office, if any person should appear to have purchased them in prior times either from our fisc or from any other source, they shall restore the said places to the Christians without payment or any demand for compensation, setting aside all fraud and ambiguity; and if any persons have obtained them as gifts, they shall similarly restore the same as quickly as possible to the said Christians; and in addition, if either those who have purchased the said places or those who have obtained them as gifts make some request of our benevolence, let them make the demands of the deputy prefect,[83] so that we may take thought for them too through our clemency. All these things must be transferred to the or-

83 Cf. Chapter VI, Note 93.

ganization of the Christians by your intervention at once and without delay.

And since the said Christians not only possessed those places in which they were wont to assemble but are also known to have had others belonging not to individual men but to their corporate body, that is the churches, all these, under the provisions of the law we have set forth above, you will give orders to have restored without any uncertainty at all or controversy to the said Christians, that is to the organization and to their places of assembly, observing, of course, the aforesaid regulation, that those persons who restore the same without compensation, as we have stated, may look for compensation from our benevolence.

In all these matters you shall employ your most effective intervention for the aforesaid organization of the Christians, that this directive of ours may be fulfilled with all speed, so that in this also thought may be taken for the public peace through our clemency. To this extent it will come about, as set forth above, that the divine favor toward us, which we have already enjoyed in many matters, will continue for all time with good fortune for our successes together with the public happiness. And that, moreover, the form which this decree and benevolence of ours takes may be brought to the knowledge of all, it will be proper for you to issue your proclamation and publish this document everywhere and bring it to the knowledge of all, to the end that the decreeing of this benevolence of ours may not remain unknown.

179. *The Triumph of Christianity*

Before his conversion to Christianity in A.D. 312, Constantine had been an adherent of the syncretic solar cult. Constantine's Christianity, whether genuine or inspired by political expediency, was expressed by a series of administrative and legal acts in favor of the Christian Church. As a Christian emperor ruling a predominantly pagan world, he was compelled to move slowly; until 324, when he became sole emperor after the defeat of Licinius, he strove by his legislation to give Christianity the same privileges which the pagan cults enjoyed, thus maintaining a balance between Christianity and paganism (cf. § 178). But after 324 his negative attitude toward paganism took sharper form, though there is no trustworthy evidence that he took measures for the general abolition of pagan worship and the destruction of pagan temples. This final step was taken by the Emperor Theodosius in 395.

PRIVILEGES GRANTED THE CHURCH BY CONSTANTINE

Eusebius *Ecclesiastical History* x. vii

Greeting, our most esteemed Anulinus.[84] Since it appears from many things that the setting at naught of divine worship, through which the highest reverence for the most holy power of heaven is preserved, has brought great dangers to the state, and that the lawful restoration and maintenance of this have bestowed good fortune on the Roman name and extraordinary prosperity on all the affairs of mankind (for it is divine Providence which bestows these blessings), it is our decision that those men who, with due holiness and devotion to this ordinance, offer their services in the performance of divine worship, should receive rewards for their labors, most esteemed Anulinus. Wherefore it is my will that those persons in the Catholic Church presided over by Caecilianus in the province entrusted to you who devote their service to this holy worship—those who are customarily named clerics—shall once and for all be kept completely exempt from all compulsory public services. They shall not be dragged away from the worship due the Divinity through any mistake or irreverent error, nor shall they be disturbed in any way from devoting themselves completely to serving their own law. For when they render supreme service to the Deity, it seems that they confer the greatest possible benefits upon the state. Farewell, our most esteemed and dearest Anulinus.

Eusebius *Ecclesiastical History* x. vi

Constantine Augustus to Caecilianus, bishop of Carthage.[85] Whereas we have resolved that throughout all provinces, namely the African, Numidian, and Mauretanian, some additional assistance be given to certain specified ministers of the lawful and most holy Catholic religion for expenses, I have sent a letter to Ursus, the most eminent procurator of Africa, and have notified him to see to the payment of 3,000 *folles* to Your Steadfastness. Accordingly, when you obtain delivery of the aforesaid sum of money, give orders that this money be distributed among all the aforementioned persons in accordance with the schedule sent to you by Hosius. But if, nevertheless, you should find that the sum is insufficient for the fulfillment of this purpose of mine with respect to all of them, you should request without hesitation whatever you find to be necessary from Heraclides, the procurator of our estate. For indeed I gave him instructions in person that if Your Steadfastness should request

---

[84] Proconsul of Africa in A.D. 313.
[85] The date of this letter is also A.D. 313.

any money from him, he should see to the payment of it without any hesitation. And since I have learned that certain men of unstable conviction are desirous of turning aside the laity of the most Holy and Catholic Church by some miserable seduction, know that I have personally given orders to Anulinus, the proconsul, and moreover to Patricius, prefect's deputy,[86] to the effect that they should give due attention to all other matters and especially to this, and not permit such an occurrence to be overlooked. Therefore if you observe any such persons continuing in this madness, do not hesitate to go to the aforementioned governors and bring this said matter before them, so that they, as I personally ordered them, may bring these persons back to the right path. May the divinity of the great God preserve you for many years.

Theodosian Code VIII. xvi. 1; A.D. 320

Those persons who were considered celibates under the old law shall be freed from the threatening terrors of the statutes [87] and shall live just as if supported by the bond of matrimony in the number of married men, and all men shall have equal status with respect to accepting what each is entitled to.[88] Nor indeed shall any person be considered childless, and the disabilities attached to that term shall not harm him. We apply this provision also with respect to women, and we release all of them indiscriminately from the legal compulsions imposed like yokes on their necks.

Theodosian Code II. viii. 1; A.D. 321

Just as it appeared most unseemly for the day of the Sun,[89] solemn in its veneration, to be occupied with the altercations of the law courts and the noxious controversies of contending parties, so it is gratifying and pleasing for those acts which are especially longed for to be accomplished on that day. Therefore all men shall have freedom to emancipate and manumit on a festive day, and the legal formalities concerning such matters shall not be forbidden.

Theodosian Code IV. vii. 1; A.D. 321

Any persons who with pious intention grant deserved freedom to their favorite slaves in the bosom of the Church shall be deemed to have bestowed it with the same legality as Roman citizenship has been customarily conferred under the usual formalities. But it is our pleasure that

[86] Cf. Chapter VI, Note 93.
[87] The Papian-Poppaean laws of Augustus (see § 11). The present enactment of Constantine was not a general repealer but affected only the clergy.
[88] That is, legacies and gifts, which unmarried and childless persons were permitted under the Augustan legislation to receive only in limited amount.
[89] That is, Sunday.

this indulgence be allowed only to persons who make such grant in the presence of the bishops. To clerics, moreover, we further grant that when they bestow freedom on their own slaves, not only shall they be said to have granted full enjoyment of such freedom [when they manumit] in the presence of the Church and the religious congregation, but also when they confer freedom in a last will or give instructions in any words whatsoever that it be conferred. Accordingly, such grant of freedom takes immediate effect on the day of the publication of the expressed intent without any witness or intermediary required by law.[90]

Theodosian Code XVI. ii. 5; A.D. 323

Since we have learned that certain ecclesiastics and others who serve the Catholic sect are compelled by men of different religions to perform lustral sacrifices,[91] we ordain by this sanction that if any person believes that those who serve the most holy law are to be compelled to [perform] the ritual of an alien superstition, he shall be publicly beaten with clubs if his legal status so permits;[92] or, if the consideration of honorable rank protects him from such outrage, he shall sustain the penalty of a very heavy fine, which shall be claimed by the municipalities.

Theodosian Code XVI. V. 1; A.D. 326

The privileges which have been granted in consideration of religion must benefit only the adherents of the Catholic faith. It is our will, moreover, that heretics and schismatics shall not only be excluded from these privileges but shall also be bound and subjected to the various compulsory public services.

CONSTANTINE'S OFFICIAL POSITION TOWARD PAGANISM

Theodosian Code IX. xvi. 2; A.D. 319

We forbid soothsayers and priests and persons accustomed to serve that rite to approach a private home or under pretext of friendship to cross the threshold of another; and punishment will threaten them if they disregard the statute. You, however, who think this profits you, go to the public altars and shrines and celebrate the ceremonies of your custom; for we do not forbid the services of a bygone usage to be conducted in open view.

Theodosian Code XVI. X. 1; A.D. 320/21

If it is established that any part of our palace or of other public works has been touched by lightning, the custom of the ancient religion shall be maintained: inquiry shall be made of the soothsayers as to the

[90] For the usual procedures employed in manumitting slaves, see § 67.
[91] Cf. Vol. 1, § 56.   [92] Cf. § 165.

portent thereof, and the written record thereof shall be very carefully collected and referred to our wisdom. Others are also to be granted freedom to practice this custom, provided they abstain from domestic sacrifices, which are specifically prohibited.

CONSTANTINE AND EMPEROR WORSHIP

As a Christian, Constantine prohibited all forms of worship of himself. He did not, however, take measures to suppress the imperial cult as an institution, for it was by this time largely secularized and offered, moreover, distinct social and political advantages. A striking illustration of what has been called "his half-Christian, half-pagan state of mind" is afforded by the following reply to a petition from the town of Hispellum, in Umbria.

CIL, Vol. XI, No. 5,265 (= Dessau, No. 705 = Abbott-Johnson, No. 155); A.D. 333/37

Copy of Sacred Rescript

The Emperor Caesar Flavius CONSTANTINE Maximus Germanicus Sarmaticus Gothicus, victorious, triumphant Augustus, and Flavius CONSTANTINE, and Flavius Julius CONSTANTIUS, and Flavius CONSTANS.[93] All things which protect human society we embrace in the deliberation of our ever-watchful administration; but it is especially incumbent upon our providential care to see to it that all cities, which are distinguished among the ornaments of all the provinces and regions for their splendor and beauty, should not only retain their former distinction but should also be elevated to a better state by virtue of our beneficence.

You declare that you [Umbrians] are administratively joined to Tuscia, and that by an established ancient custom you and the aforesaid [Tuscians] in alternate years appoint the priests who present theatrical shows and gladiatorial games at Vulsinii, a municipality of Tuscia. But because the journey lies over steep and wooded mountains you earnestly request that relief be granted to your priest, so that it will not be necessary for him to proceed to Vulsinii to celebrate the spectacles. Your request is that to the municipality which is now called Hispellum and which, you state, adjoins and connects with the Flaminian Way, we grant a name from our family name; that a temple of the Flavian family may be constructed there in magnificent style truly in keeping with the splendor of the name; and that the priest whom Umbria has provided every other year may there present an exhibition of both theatrical shows and gladiatorial games—the said custom to continue in Tuscia, where a

[93] Constantine, Constantius, and Constans, the sons of Constantine the Great, held the rank of Caesar under their father and divided the Empire among them after his death.

priest chosen from that region shall celebrate the aforementioned exhibitions at Vulsinii as in the past.

To your petition and desire we have acceded with ready assent. For to the municipality of Hispellum we have granted an eternal title and revered name from our appellation, so that in the future the aforesaid city shall be called Flavia Constans; and in its midst, as you wish, we desire a temple of the Flavian family, that is, our family, to be constructed in magnificent style, with this restriction, that a temple dedicated to our name be not defiled by the evils of any contagious superstition. Accordingly, we have also given you permission to exhibit spectacles in the aforementioned city, with the understanding that, as has been stated, the periodic celebration of the spectacles shall not cease at Vulsinii, where the aforementioned celebration is to be conducted by priests to be chosen from Tuscia. Thus not very much will seem to have been detracted from old institutions, and you, who for the aforesaid reasons have appeared as suppliants before us, will rejoice to have obtained what you earnestly requested.

180. *The Council of Nicaea, A.D. 325*

"Constantine sitting amongst the Christian bishops at the oecumenical council of Nicaea is in his own person the beginning of Europe's Middle Age" (*Cambridge Ancient History*, XII, 699).

Eusebius *Life of Constantine* III. vi–x (abridged)

Constantine summoned a general synod, inviting the bishops in all parts with honorary letters to be present as soon as possible. . . . At that time there were to be seen congregated in one place persons widely different from one another not only in spirit but also in physical appearance, and in the regions, places, and provinces from which they came. . . . From all the churches which had filled all Europe, Africa, and Asia, those who held the chief place among the servants of God assembled at the same time; and one sacred hall, extended as it were by the will of God, embraced in its compass Cilicians, Phoenicians, Arabs, Palestinians, Egyptians, Thebans, Libyans, and some coming from Mesopotamia. A bishop from Persia also participated in the synod, nor was Scythia absent from this body. Pontus, likewise Galatia, Pamphylia, and Cappadocia, Asia, too, and Phrygia provided their most carefully chosen persons. Thracians also, Macedonians, Achaeans, and Epirotes, and those who are situated at a very long distance beyond these were nonetheless present. . . . Present among the body were more than 250 bishops. . . .

But on the day fixed for the council which was to put an end to the controversies, when the various persons who composed the synod were at hand, in the very middle of the hall of the palace which seemed to surpass all the rest in size, there were many seats arranged in rows on both sides; and all who had been summoned entered and each sat down in his place. After the entire synod had seated itself with seeming modesty, all at first fell silent, awaiting the coming of the emperor. Soon one of those closest to the emperor, then a second and a third entered. Others, too, preceded—not, as customary, from among the soldiers and bodyguard, but only those of his advisers who professed the faith of Christ. And when the signal was given which announced the entry of the emperor, all rose, and finally he himself approached proceeding down the center . . . dazzling the eyes of all with the splendor of his purple robe and sparkling with fiery rays, as it were, adorned for the occasion as he was with an extraordinary splendor of gold and jewels. . . . As for his soul, it was sufficiently apparent that he was adorned with the fear of God and religion.

EPILOGUE

The optimism of the Gallo-Roman poet Rutilius Namatianus, as he wrote what has since been called "the swan song of Rome" in A.D. 416 (six years after the capture of Rome by the Goths under Alaric), stands in sharp contrast to the prophecy of doom written centuries earlier by Seneca, who, as a Stoic, held to a cyclical theory of history developed by Greek historians and philosophers.

Rutilius Namatianus *On his Return* I. 46–66, 133–38
Adapted from LCL

Listen, O fairest queen of thy world, Rome, welcomed amid the starry skies, listen thou mother of men and mother of gods, thanks to thy temples we are not far from heaven. Thee do we chant, and shall, while destiny allows, forever chant. None can be safe if forgetful of thee. Sooner shall guilty oblivion overwhelm the sun than the honor due thee quit my heart; for thy benefits extend as far as the sun's rays, where are the waves of the circling Ocean-flood. For thee the very Sun-god who embraceth all doth revolve; his steeds that rise in thy domains he putteth in thy domains to rest. Thee Africa hath not stayed with scorching sands, nor hath the Bear, armed with native cold, repulsed thee. As far as habitable nature hath stretched toward the poles, so far hath earth opened a path for thy valor. For nations far apart thou hast made a single fatherland; under thy dominion conquest hath meant profit for those who knew not justice; and by offering to the vanquished a share in thine own law, thou hast made a city of what was erstwhile a world. . . . Spread forth the laws that are to last throughout the ages of Rome; thou alone needst not dread the distaffs of the Fates. . . . The span which doth remain is subject to no bounds, so long as earth shall stand and heaven uphold the stars!

Seneca *Moral Epistles* lxxi. 15

The entire human race, both present and future, is condemned to death. All the cities that have ever held dominion or have been the splendid jewels of empires belonging to others—some day men will ask where they were. And they will be swept away by various kinds of destruction: some will be ruined by wars, others will be destroyed by idleness and a peace that ends in sloth, or by luxury, the bane of those of great wealth. All these fertile plains will be blotted out of sight by a sudden overflowing of the sea, or the subsiding of the land will sweep them away suddenly into the abyss.

GLOSSARY OF FREQUENT TERMS *

ACHAEA, the Roman province of Greece.

AMPHORA, a Greek and Roman liquid measure, 8 *congii*, or c. 6 gallons, 7 pints.

AROURA, a land measure in Graeco-Roman Egypt, slightly more than ½ acre.

ARTAB, an Egyptian dry measure, varying from three to six *modii* in capacity.

AS, plur. ASSES, the smallest Roman copper coin (about 2 cents); for its history see Vol. I, p. 515.

ASIA, the Romans' designation of that part of Asia Minor constituting the Roman province of Asia.

CAPITAL OFFENSE, any crime for which a citizen paid with his *caput* ("head"), that is, his physical or civic existence: cf. Chapter VIII, Note 28.

CAPITOL, the temple of Jupiter Optimus Maximus (Jupiter Best and Greatest), center of the Roman civic religion, situated on the Capitoline Hill in Rome.

CENTURION, the principal professional Roman military officer, in charge of a century (100 men at maximum strength). Each Roman legion had 60 centurions.

CENTURY: see centurion.

CHOENIX, a dry measure, c. 1 quart.

CLERUCHY, "allotment," a numbered division of the land in Roman Egypt. The term derives from the allotment of lands to military settlers in Ptolemaic times.

COLLEGIUM, plur. COLLEGIA, an association of any kind, especially artisan "guilds" and benevolent or burial societies.

CONSCRIPT FATHERS (*Conscripti*), Roman senators; variant name of members of governing council of Roman municipalities (see DECURIO).

COSMETES, in Greek cities and towns the magistrate in charge of matters concerning the ephebes (see Chapter V, Note 129).

DECURIO, member of local senate of Roman municipalities, composed usually of 100 decurions.

DENARIUS, a Roman silver coin, equal to 4 sesterces; initially worth about 30 cents, it was reduced in the successive devaluations of the third century to a mere fraction of its original value.

DRACHMA, the basic silver coin of the Greek monetary system, which continued in use in the Greek-speaking Roman provinces. The drachma was equated with the Roman *denarius* (except in Egypt, where the equation was 4 drachmas = 1 *denarius*, 1 drachma = 1 *sestertius*).

DUOVIR, member of two-man board; most commonly, *duoviri iure dicundo*, "two-man board with judicial power," the two chief magistrates of Roman municipalities.

* Approximate modern equivalents are given for ancient weights, measures, and monetary units. The latter are equated on the basis of the current dollar rate (1 ounce of gold = $35). It should be noted, however, that these amounts of money would in antiquity have had many times their present purchasing power.

EPISTRATEGUS, head of one of the three administrative divisions in which the nomes of Egypt (each governed by a *strategus*) were grouped under Roman rule.

EQUES, plur. EQUITES, originally "cavalrymen," or "knights." The equestrian order was a social and economic class in Rome, Italy, and the provinces, second in status to the senatorial order. Members of this class, for which a minimum of 400,000 sesterces was required, served as army officers of intermediate rank and staffed important posts in the imperial civil service.

FASCES, a bundle of rods with an axe protruding from the upper part, carried by lictors in front of magistrates possessing *imperium* as symbols of the power of these magistrates to scourge (rods) or behead (axe) Roman citizens.

FATHERS, Roman senators.

FISC, the privy purse of the emperor, as distinct from the state treasury, which it at first outstripped in resources and eventually superseded.

FLAMEN, priest assigned to the cult of an individual god.

FOLLIS, plur. FOLLES, a copper coin introduced in Diocletian's currency reform of A.D. 296. No fully satisfactory determination of its value has yet been made.

FORUM, the Roman Forum, civic center in Rome (also in Roman municipalities), situated between the Capitoline and Palatine Hills; Rome possessed five additional fora for the transaction of public business, constructed under Julius Caesar, Augustus, Vespasian, Nerva, and Trajan.

GENIUS, a tutelary spirit which, according to Roman belief, each man was assigned at birth as his personal protecting deity and which he worshiped accordingly, especially on his birthday. Under the Empire, the worship of the *genius* of the emperor was an important aspect of the ruler cult.

GYMNASIARCH, in Greek cities and towns, the magistrate who superintended the functioning of the gymnasium.

IMPERATOR, commander-in-chief, a title bestowed on a victorious general by his soldiers. Under the Empire, it denoted the supreme power of the emperor and was, beginning with Vespasian's reign, regularly the first title in the imperial nomenclature. In addition, the emperor added after his name the number of times he was acclaimed *imperator* for military victories won by himself or his legates.

IMPERIUM, the right or power to command, supreme military and administrative power.

IUGERUM, a Roman land measure, 28,800 square Roman feet, or c. ⅝ acre.

LICTOR, an attendant who carried the *fasces* before a Roman magistrate invested with *imperium* and who served as his apparitor.

MILE, *Roman,* in Latin *mille passus* ("1,000 paces"), i.e., 5,000 Roman feet or c. 4,850 English feet, or c. 0.92 English mile.

MINA: see talent.

MODIUS, a Roman dry measure, 16 *sextarii,* or c. 1 peck.

NOME, an administrative division of Egypt, in charge of a *strategus*.

OBOL, a Greek coin, ⅙ of a drachma (c. 5 cents).

PONTIFEX MAXIMUS, "supreme pontiff," head of the college of pontiffs and of other priests in charge of the Roman state cult. This office was always held by the emperor.

PRINCEPS, "first citizen," unofficial title of the Roman emperors during the Principate.

PROCURATOR, title of a large variety of imperial officials, many being *equites* in rank. Most procurators held administrative posts connected with the far-flung imperial properties and revenues; a few were (especially in the third century) governors or acting governors of provinces.

PUBLICAN, tax farmer.

QUINQUENNALIS, "fifth-year official," title of chief magistrates of Roman municipalities who took the local census and possessed other censorial powers; honorary title of officers of *collegia*.

QUIRITES, Roman citizens.

SESTERTIUS, a Roman coin worth in imperial times 4 *asses,* or ¼ *denarius* (about 8 cents; for its devaluation see DENARIUS). The English plural is sesterces.

SEXTARIUS, a Roman liquid measure, ⅙ *congius,* or c. 1 pint; also a dry measure, ¹⁄₁₆ *modius*.

SITOLOGUS, in Egypt a collector of grain taxes at a local granary.

STADE or STADIUM, a Greek linear measure, 625 Roman feet, or ⅛ Roman mile.

STRATEGUS, (1) in Egypt, the governor of a nome; (2) in other Greek-speaking provinces, a high city official or head of a league of cities.

TALENT, a Greek weight (80 Roman lbs., or c. 57 lbs. avoirdupois) and monetary unit worth 60 minas or 6,000 drachmas (c. $1,800).

TRIBUNICIAN POWER, one of the constitutional bases of the Principate, granting the emperors supreme power over civil affairs in the capital. The emperors counted their regnal years from the date of the assumption of this power.

VIR CLARISSIMUS (literally, "most illustrious man"), an honorific appellation which became under the Empire the distinctive title of Roman senators.

VIR EGREGIUS (literally, "distinguished man"), honorary title of an *eques,* approximately equivalent in English to "the honorable."

VIR EMINENS or EMINENTISSIMUS (literally, "prominent" or "most prominent man"), the highest honorary appellation of public officials of equestrian rank. From the time of Hadrian this was the distinctive title of Praetorian prefects.

VIR ORNATISSIMUS (literally, "most honored man"), an honorific appellation, probably equivalent to *vir clarissimus*.

VIR PERFECTISSIMUS (literally, "most excellent man"), honorific appellation of high-ranking equestrian officials.

BIBLIOGRAPHY
(REVISED 1966)

General Bibliography

Included in this list are general histories of Rome during the period of the Empire and other books pertinent to all or most of that period. Books noted here are as a rule not repeated in the individual chapter bibliographies.

Abbott, F. F.   A History and Description of Roman Political Institutions. 3d ed. Boston, 1911.
————Roman Politics. Boston, 1923.
Adcock, F. E.   Roman Political Ideas and Practice. Ann Arbor, 1959.
Bailey, C., ed.   The Legacy of Rome. 7th ed. Oxford, 1947.
————The Mind of Rome. Oxford, 1926.
Barrow, R. H.   The Romans. Harmondsworth, 1949.
Bevan, E. R.   The World of Greece and Rome. London, 1937.
Boak, A. E. R.   A History of Rome to 565 A.D. 5th ed. New York, 1965.
Caldwell, W. E.   The Ancient World. Rev. ed. New York, 1949.
Cambridge Ancient History. Vols. X–XII and Vol. V of Plates. Cambridge, 1934–1939.
Cary, M.   The Geographic Background of Greek and Roman History. Oxford, 1949.
————A History of Rome down to the Reign of Constantine. New ed. London, 1954.
Cary, M., and T. J. Haarhoff.   Life and Thought in the Greek and Roman World. 6th ed. New York, 1959.
Chapot, V.   The Roman World. New York, 1928.
Croon, E.   The Encyclopedia of the Ancient World. New York, 1965.
Durant, W. J.   Caesar and Christ; a History of Roman Civilization and of Christianity from Their Beginnings to A.D. 325. New York, 1944.
Ferrero, G.   The Greatness and Decline of Rome. 5 vols. New York, 1907–1909.
Fowler, W. W.   Rome. 2d ed., rev. by M. P. Charlesworth. Oxford, 1947.
Frank, T.   Aspects of Social Behavior in Ancient Rome. Cambridge, Mass., 1932.
Geer, R. M.   Classical Civilization: Rome. 2d ed. New York, 1950.
Grant, M.   Ancient History. London, 1952.
————, ed.   The Birth of Western Civilization. Greece and Rome. New York, 1964.
Greene, W. C.   The Achievement of Rome: a Chapter in Civilization. Cambridge, Mass., 1933.
Grenier, A.   The Roman Spirit in Religion, Thought and Art. New York, 1926.
Grimal, P.   The Civilization of Rome. New York, 1963.
————Rome of the Caesars. London, 1956.

Heichelheim, F. M., and C. A. Yeo. A History of the Roman People. Englewood Cliffs, 1962.

Homo, L. Roman Political Institutions from City to State. New York, 1929.

Jones, H. S. Companion to Roman History. Oxford, 1912.

———The Roman Empire, B.C. 29–A.D. 476. 3d impression. London, 1916.

Leddy, J. F. "Toynbee and the History of Rome," Phoenix, XI (1957), 139–52.

Lemprière's Classical Dictionary of Proper Names Mentioned in Ancient Authors. New ed., rev. by F. A. Wright. New York, 1949.

MacKendrick, P. L. The Mute Stones Speak. The Story of Archaeology in Italy. London, 1962.

Mattingly, H. Man in the Roman Street. New York, 1947.

———Roman Imperial Civilization. London, 1959.

Moore, R. W. The Roman Commonwealth. London, 1942.

Nilsson, M. P. Imperial Rome. London, 1926.

Oxford Classical Dictionary. Oxford, 1949.

Parker, H. M. D. A History of the Roman World from A.D. 138 to 337. 2d ed. London, 1958.

Petrie, A. An Introduction to Roman History, Literature and Antiquities. 3d ed. New York, 1963.

Phillipson, C. The International Law and Custom of Ancient Greece and Rome. 2 vols. London, 1911.

Platner, S. B. The Topography and Monuments of Ancient Rome. 2d ed. Boston, 1911.

———and T. Ashby. A Topographical Dictionary of Ancient Rome. London, 1929.

Robinson, C. A., Jr. Ancient History from Prehistoric Times to the Death of Justinian. New York, 1951.

Rose, H. J. The Mediterranean in the Ancient World. Cambridge, 1933.

Rostovtzeff, M., and E. Bickerman. A History of the Ancient World. Rome. New York, 1961.

———The Social and Economic History of the Roman Empire. 2d ed. by P. M. Fraser. 2 vols. Oxford, 1956.

Salmon, E. T. A History of the Roman World from 30 B.C. to A.D. 138. 3d ed. London, 1957.

Sandys, J. E., ed. A Companion to Latin Studies. 3d ed. Cambridge, 1921.

Scramuzza, V. M., and P. L. MacKendrick. The Ancient World. New York, 1958.

Semple, E. C. Geography of the Mediterranean Region: its Relation to Ancient History. New York, 1931.

Showerman, G. Eternal Rome: the City and Its People from the Earliest Times to the Present Day. New Haven, 1924.

Smith, W., W. Wayte, and G. E. Marindin, eds. A Dictionary of Greek and Roman Antiquities. 3d ed. 2 vols. London, 1890–1891.

Starr, C. G., Jr. The Emergence of Rome as Ruler of the Western World. Ithaca, 1950.

———A History of the Ancient World. New York, 1965.

Stobart, J. C. The Grandeur that Was Rome: a Survey of Roman Culture and Civilization. 3d ed., rev. by F. N. Pryce. London, 1934.

Swain, J. W.   The Ancient World. Vol. II. New York, 1950.

Trever, A. A.   History of Ancient Civilization. Vol. II: The Roman World. New York, 1939.

Van Sickle, C. E.   A Political and Cultural History of the Ancient World from Prehistoric Times to the Dissolution of the Roman Empire in the West. Vol. II: The Hellenistic World and Rome to the Dissolution of the Western Empire. Boston, 1948.

Waddy, L. H.   Pax Romana and World Peace. New York, 1950.

Wylie, J. K.   Roman Constitutional History from Earliest Times to the Death of Justinian. Pasadena, 1948.

Bibliography for Chapter I

For works on the literary history and the religious developments of the Augustan Age, see also the bibliographies for Chapter IV and Chapter IX, respectively.

Allen, B. M.   Augustus Caesar. London, 1937.

Allison, J. E., and J. D. Cloud.   "The Lex Julia Maiestatis," *Latomus*, XXI (1962), 711–31.

Anderson, J. G. C.   "Augustan Edicts from Cyrene," *Journal of Roman Studies*, XVII (1927), 33–48.

Astin, A. E.   "Leges Aelia et Fufia," *Latomus*, XXIII (1964), 422–45.

Baker, G. P.   Augustus; the Golden Age of Rome. New York, 1937.

Bowersock, G. W.   Augustus and the Greek World. Oxford, 1965.

Charlesworth, M. P.   "The Refusal of Divine Honours, an Augustan Formula," *Papers of the British School at Rome*, XV (1939), 1–10.

Chilver, G. E. F.   "Augustus and the Roman Constitution 1939–50," *Historia*, I (1950), 408–35.

D'Alton, J. F.   Horace and his Age; a Study in Historical Background. London, 1917.

Duff, J. W.   The Literary History of Rome. Vol. I: From the Origins to the Close of the Golden Age. Rev. and ed. by A. M. Duff. New York, 1953.

Field, J. A., Jr.   "The Purpose of the Lex Julia et Papia Poppaea," *Classical Journal*, XL (1944/45), 398–416.

Firth, J. B.   Augustus Caesar and the Organisation of the Empire at Rome. New York, 1903.

Fowler, W. W.   Roman Ideas of Deity in the Last Century before the Christian Era. London, 1914.

————The Religious Experience of the Roman People. London, 1911.

Fraenkel, E.   Horace. Oxford, 1957.

Frank, T.   Catullus and Horace; Two Poets in their Environment. New York, 1928.

————Vergil, a Biography. New York, 1922.

Fränkel, H.   Ovid; a Poet between Two Worlds. Berkeley, 1945.

Glover, T. R.   Virgil. 5th ed. London, 1923.

Hammond, M.   City-state and World State in Greek and Roman Political Theory until Augustus. Cambridge, Mass., 1951.

————"Hellenistic Influences in the Structure of the Augustan Principate," *Memoirs of the American Academy in Rome*, XVII (1940), 1–25.

————The Augustan Principate in Theory and Practice during the Julio-Claudian Period. Cambridge, Mass., 1933.

Holmes, T. R.   The Architect of the Roman Empire. 2 vols. Oxford, 1928–31.

Jones, A. H. M.   "The Elections under Augustus," *Journal of Roman Studies*, XLV (1955), 9–21.

————"The Imperium of Augustus," *Journal of Roman Studies*, XLI (1951), 112–19.

Knight, W. F. J.   Roman Vergil. London, 1944.

Letters, F. J. H.   Virgil. New York, 1946.

McFayden, D.   The History of the Title *Imperator* under the Roman Empire. Chicago, 1920.

Marsh, F. B.   The Founding of the Roman Empire. 2d ed. London, 1927.

Otis, B.   Virgil, a Study in Civilized Poetry. Oxford, 1963.

Parker, H. M. D.   The Roman Legions. Rev. ed. Cambridge, 1958.

Pöschl, V.   The Art of Vergil. Ann Arbor, 1962.

Prescott, H. W.   The Development of Virgil's Art. Chicago, 1927.

Reinhold, M.   Marcus Agrippa: a Biography. Geneva, N.Y., 1933.

Reynolds, P. K. B.   The Vigiles of Imperial Rome. London, 1926.

Rowell, H. T.   Rome in the Augustan Age. Norman, 1962.

Salmon, E. T.   "The Evolution of the Augustan Principate," *Historia*, V (1956), 456–78.

Sedgwick, H. D.   Horace; a Biography. Cambridge, Mass., 1947.

Sellar, W. Y.   The Roman Poets of the Augustan Age. Horace and the Elegiac Poets. Oxford, 1892.

————The Roman Poets of the Augustan Age. Virgil. 3d ed. Oxford, 1897.

Shuckburgh, E. S.   Augustus; the Life and Times of the Founder of the Roman Empire (B.C. 63–A.D. 14). London, 1903.

Stevenson, G. H.   Roman Provincial Administration till the Age of the Antonines. 2d ed. Oxford, 1949.

Syme, R. "Livy and Augustus," *Harvard Studies in Classical Philology*, LXIV (1959), 27–87.

————The Roman Revolution. Oxford, 1939.

Walsh, P. G.   Livy, Historical Aims and Methods. Cambridge, 1961.

Wilkinson, L. P.   Horace and his Lyric Poetry. 2d ed. Cambridge, 1951.

Bibliography for Chapter II

Allen, W., Jr.   "The Political Atmosphere of the Reign of Tiberius," *Transactions of the American Philological Association*, LXXII (1941), 1–25.

Baker, G. P.   Tiberius Caesar. New York, 1928.

Balsdon, J. P. V. D.   The Emperor Gaius (Caligula). Oxford, 1934.

Beare, W.   "Tacitus on the Germans," *Greece and Rome*, XI (1964), 64–76.

Birley, E.   "The Equestrian Officers of the Roman Army," *Durham University Journal*, XI (1949), 8–19.

————"Senators in the Emperor's Service," *Proceedings of the British Academy*, XXXIX (1953), 197–214.

Bishop, J.   Nero: The Man and the Legend. London, 1964.

Bourne, F. C. The Public Works of the Julio-Claudians and Flavians. Princeton, 1946.

Brogan, O. "The Roman Limes of Germany," *Archaeological Journal*, XCII (1935), 1–41.

Broughton, T. R. S. The Romanization of Africa Proconsularis. Baltimore, 1929.

Brunt, P. A. "The Revolt of Vindex and the Fall of Nero," *Latomus*, XVIII (1959), 531–59.

Charlesworth, M. P. *"Pietas* and *Victoria:* the Emperor and the Citizen," *Journal of Roman Studies*, XXXIII (1943), 1–10.

———"The Virtues of a Roman Emperor: Propaganda and the Creation of Belief," *Proceedings of the British Academy*, XXIII (1937), 105–33.

Chilver, G. E. F. "The Army in Politics, A.D. 68–70," *Journal of Roman Studies*, XLVII (1957), 29–35.

———*"Princeps* and *Frumentationes,"* *American Journal of Philology*, LXX (1949), 7–21.

Collingwood, R. G. A Guide to the Roman Wall. 5th ed., by I. A. Richmond. Newcastle-upon-Tyne, 1948.

———"Hadrian's Wall: a History of the Problem," *Journal of Roman Studies*, XI (1921), 37–66.

Crook, J. A. Consilium Principis. Imperial Councils and Counsellors from Augustus to Diocletian. Cambridge, 1954.

DeWitt, N. J. Urbanization and the Franchise in Roman Gaul. Lancaster, 1940.

Dudley, D. R., and G. Webster. The Rebellion of Boudicca. New York, 1962.

Farquharson, A. S. L. Marcus Aurelius; his Life and his World. Oxford, 1951.

Franzero, C. M. The Life and Times of Nero. London, 1954.

Gordon, C. D. "Subsidies in Roman Imperial Defense," *Phoenix*, III (1949), 60–69.

Grant, M. "Pax Romana: an Early Imperial Definition," *University of Edinburgh Journal*, XIV (1946–1949), 229–40.

———"Roman Coins as Propaganda," *Archaeology*, V (1952), 79–85.

———Roman Imperial Money. Edinburgh, 1953.

Gregorovius, F. The Emperor Hadrian: a Picture of the Graeco-Roman World in his Time. London and New York, 1898.

Hammond, M. The Augustan Principate in Theory and Practice during the Julio-Claudian Period. Cambridge, Mass., 1933.

———"Composition of the Senate, A.D. 68–235," *Journal of Roman Studies*, XLVII (1957), 74–81.

———"The Transmission of the Powers of the Roman Emperor from the Death of Nero in A.D. 68 to that of Alexander Severus in A.D. 235," *Memoirs of the American Academy in Rome*, XXIV (1956), 61–133.

———The Antonine Monarchy. Rome, 1959.

Hardy, E. G. Studies in Roman History. Second Series. London, 1909.

———Three Spanish Charters and Other Documents. Oxford, 1912.

Harrer, G. A. Studies in the History of the Roman Province of Syria. Princeton, 1915.

Harrison, D. Along Hadrian's Wall. London, 1956.

Harry, B. F. Bithynia under Trajan: Roman and Greek Views of the Principate. Auckland, 1964.

Haverfield, F. The Romanization of Roman Britain. 4th ed., rev. by G. Macdonald. Oxford, 1923.

Hayward, F. H. Marcus Aurelius, a Saviour of Men. London, 1935.

Hellems, F. B. R. Lex de Imperio Vespasiani: a Consideration of Some of the Constitutional Aspects of the Principate at Rome. Chicago, 1902.

Henderson, B. W. Civil War and Rebellion in the Roman Empire A.D. 69–70. London, 1908.

———Five Roman Emperors; Vespasian, Titus, Domitian, Nerva, Trajan, A.D. 69–117. Cambridge, 1927.

———The Life and Principate of the Emperor Hadrian, A.D. 76–138. London, 1923.

Jones, A. H. M. "Imperial and Senatorial Jurisdiction in the Early Principate," Historia, III (1955), 464–88.

———"The Roman Civil Service (Clerical and Sub-Clerical Grades)," Journal of Roman Studies, XXXIX (1949), 38–55.

Jones, H. S. "The Historical Interpretation of the Reliefs of Trajan's Column," Papers of the British School at Rome, V (1910), 435–59.

Kuntz, O. Tiberius Caesar and the Roman Constitution. Seattle, 1924.

Lacey, R. H. The Equestrian Officials of Trajan and Hadrian. Princeton, 1917.

Lepper, F. A. Trajan's Parthian War. London, 1948.

Macdonald, G. "The Building of the Antonine Wall: a Fresh Study of the Inscriptions," Journal of Roman Studies, XI (1921), 1–24.

Marsh, F. B. The Reign of Tiberius. London, 1931.

Mason, E. Tiberius. New York, 1960.

Mattingly, H. The Imperial Civil Service of Rome. Cambridge, 1910.

———"The Imperial Vota," Proceedings of the British Academy, XXXVI (1950), 155–95.

McAlindon, D. "Senatorial Advancement in the Age of Claudius," Latomus, XVI (1957), 252–62.

Mendell, C. W. Tacitus: The Man and His Work. New Haven, 1957.

Millar, F. G. B. A Study of Cassius Dio. Oxford, 1964.

Miller, N. P. "The Claudian Tablet and Tacitus," Rheinisches Museum, XCIX (1956), 304–15.

Momigliano, A. Claudius, the Emperor, and his Achievement. Oxford, 1934.

Perowne, S. Hadrian. London, 1960.

Pringsheim, F. "The Legal Policy and Reforms of Hadrian," Journal of Roman Studies, XXIV (1934), 141–53.

Ramsay, A. M. "The Speed of the Roman Imperial Post," Journal of Roman Studies, XV (1925), 60–74.

Ramsay, H. G. "Government Relief during the Roman Empire," Classical Journal, XXXI (1935/36), 479–88.

Rogers, R. S. Criminal Trials and Criminal Legislation under Tiberius. Middletown, 1935.

———Studies in the Reign of Tiberius. Baltimore, 1943.

Salmon, E. T. "Trajan's Conquest of Dacia," Transactions of the American Philological Association, LXVII (1936), 83–104.

Schisas, P. M.   Offences against the State in Roman Law. London, 1926.

Sedgwick, H. D.   Marcus Aurelius: a Biography. New Haven, 1921.

Sherwin-White, A. N.   "Procurator Augusti," *Papers of the British School at Rome,* XV (1939), 11–26.

———The Roman Citizenship. Oxford, 1939.

Smith, R. E.   "The Law of Libel at Rome," *Classical Quarterly,* XLV (1951), 169–79.

Starr, C. G., Jr.   "The Perfect Democracy of the Roman Empire," *American Historical Review,* LVIII (1952/53), 1–16.

Sutherland, C. H. V.   Coinage in Roman Imperial Policy, 31 B.C.–A.D. 68. London, 1951.

Syme, R.   "The Imperial Finances under Domitian, Nerva, and Trajan," *Journal of Roman Studies,* XX (1930), 55–70.

———Tacitus. 2 vols. Oxford, 1955.

Walker, B.   The Annals of Tacitus. A Study in the Writing of History. 2nd ed. Manchester, 1960.

Walton, C. S.   "Oriental Senators in the Service of Rome: a Study of Imperial Policy down to the Death of Marcus Aurelius," *Journal of Roman Studies,* XIX (1929), 38–66.

Waters, K. H.   "The Character of Domitian," *Phoenix,* XVIII (1964), 49–77.

———"The Second Dynasty of Rome," *Phoenix,* XVII (1963), 198–218.

Weigall, A.   Nero the Singing Emperor of Rome. New York and London, 1930.

Welch, G. P.   Britannia: The Roman Conquest and Occupation of Britain. Middletown, 1963.

Wirszubski, C.   Libertas as a Political Idea at Rome during the Late Republic and Early Principate. Cambridge, 1950.

Bibliography for Chapter III

Bedford, O. H.   "The Silk Trade of China with the Roman Empire," *China Journal,* XXVIII (1938), 207–16.

Bolen, S.   State and Currency in the Roman Empire. Stockholm, 1958.

Brewster, E. H.   Roman Craftsmen and Tradesmen of the Early Roman Empire. Philadelphia, 1917.

Brogan, O.   "Trade between the Roman Empire and the Free Germans," *Journal of Roman Studies,* XXVI (1936), 195–222.

Broughton, T. R. S.   "Roman Landholding in Asia Minor," *Transactions of the American Philological Association,* LXV (1934), 207–39.

Casson, L.   "Speed under Sail of Ancient Ships," *Transactions of the American Philological Association,* LXXXII (1951), 136–48.

Charleston, R. J.   Roman Pottery. London, 1955.

Charlesworth, M. P.   Trade-Routes and Commerce of the Roman Empire. 2d ed., rev. Cambridge, 1926.

Coleman-Norton, P. R., ed.   Studies in Roman Economic and Social History in Honor of Allan Chester Johnson. Princeton, 1951.

Cummings, A. D., W. R. Chalmers, and H. B. Mattingly, "A Roman Mining Document," *Mine and Quarry Engineering*, 1956, 339–42.

Davies, O.   Roman Mines in Europe. Oxford, 1935.

Dubs, H. H.   A Roman City in Ancient China. London, 1957.

Finley, M. I., ed.   Slavery in Classical Antiquity. Cambridge, 1960.

Forbes, R. J.   Metallurgy in Antiquity. Leiden, 1950.

Forster, E. S.   "Columella and his Latin Treatise on Agriculture," *Greece and Rome*, XIX (1950), 123–28.

Frank, T.   An Economic History of Rome. 2d ed. Baltimore, 1927.

———, ed.   An Economic Survey of Ancient Rome. Vols. II–V. Baltimore, 1936–1940.

———"The Financial Crisis of 33 A.D.," *American Journal of Philology*, LVI (1935), 336–41.

Grant, M.   Roman Imperial Money. London, 1954.

Heitland, W. E.   Agricola. A Study of Agriculture and Rustic Life in the Greco-Roman World from the Point of View of Labour. Cambridge, 1921.

Jones, A. H. M.   "Inflation under the Roman Empire," *Economic History Review*, V (1953), 293–318.

———"The Roman Colonate." *Past and Present*, XIII (1958), 1–13.

Loane, H. J.   Industry and Commerce of the City of Rome (50 B.C.–200 A.D.). Baltimore, 1938.

Millar, F.   "The Fiscus in the First Two Centuries," *Journal of Roman Studies*, LIII (1963), 29–42.

Mooney, W. W.   Travel among the Ancient Romans. Boston, 1920.

Oates, D.   "The Tripolitanian Gebel. Settlement of the Roman Period around Gasr ed-Dauun," *Papers of the British School at Rome*, XXI (1951), 81–117.

Rickard, T. A.   "The Mining of the Romans in Spain," *Journal of Roman Studies*, XVIII (1928), 129–43.

Rostovtzeff, M. I.   Caravan Cities. Oxford, 1932.

de Sainte-Croix, G. E. M.   "Greek and Roman Accounting," *Studies in the History of Accounting* (London), 1956, 14–74.

Schoff, W. H.   The Periplus of the Erythraean Sea. New York, 1912.

Seligman, C. G.   "The Roman Orient and the Far East," *Smithsonian Institute Annual Report*, 1938, 547–68.

Toutain, J.   The Economic Life of the Ancient World. New York, 1930.

Van Nostrand, J. J.   The Imperial Domains of Africa Proconsularis: an Epigraphical Study. Berkeley, 1925. University of California Publications in History, XXIV, No. 1.

Warmington, E. H.   The Commerce between the Roman Empire and India. Cambridge, 1928.

West, L. C.   "Commercial Syria under the Roman Empire," *Transactions of the American Philological Association*, LV (1924), 159–89.

———Imperial Roman Spain. The Objects of Trade. Oxford, 1929.

———Roman Britain. The Objects of Trade. Oxford, 1931.

———Roman Gaul. The Objects of Trade. Oxford, 1935.

Westermann, W. L.   "On Inland Transportation and Communication in Antiquity," *Political Science Quarterly*, XLIII (1928), 364–87.

————The Slave Systems of Greek and Roman Antiquity. Philadelphia, 1955.

Wheeler, M. Rome beyond the Imperial Frontiers. London, 1954.

Wheeler, R. E. M., A. Ghosh, and K. Deva. "Arikamedu, an Indo-Roman Trading Station on the East Coast of India," *Ancient India*, 1946, 17–124.

————"Roman Contact with India, Pakistan, and Afghanistan," in Essays Presented to O. G. S. Crawford (London, 1951), 345–81.

Yeo, C. A. "The Economics of Roman and American Slavery," *Finanzarchiv*, XIII (1952), 445–85.

————"Land and Sea Transportation in Imperial Italy," *Transactions of the American Philological Association*, LXXVII (1946), 221–44.

————"The Overgrazing of Ranch Lands in Ancient Italy," *Transactions of the American Philological Association*, LXXIX (1948), 275–309.

Bibliography for Chapter IV

Abbott, F. F. The Common People of Ancient Rome. New York, 1911.

————Society and Politics in Ancient Rome. New York, 1909.

Allbutt, T. C. Greek Medicine in Rome. London, 1921.

Arnold, E. V. Roman Stoicism. Cambridge, 1911.

Ashby, T. The Aqueducts of Ancient Rome. Ed. by I. A. Richmond. Oxford, 1935.

Bagnani, G. "The House of Trimalchio," *American Journal of Philology*, LXXV (1954), 16–39.

Balsdon, J. P. V. D. Roman Women. Their History and Habits. London, 1962.

Barrow, R. H. Slavery in the Roman Empire. London, 1928.

Berenson, B. The Arch of Constantine and the Decline of Form. London, 1954.

Bernal, J. D. Science in Antiquity. London, 1954.

Boëthius, A. The Golden House of Nero and Some Aspects of Roman Architecture. Ann Arbor, 1961.

Bonner, S. F. Roman Declamation in the Late Republic and Early Empire. Liverpool, 1949.

Bréhier, E. The History of Philosophy: The Hellenistic and the Roman Age. Chicago, 1965.

Brooks, A. M. Architecture. Boston, 1924.

Brown, F. E. Roman Architecture. New York, 1961.

Carcopino, J. Daily Life in Ancient Rome; the People and the City at the Height of the Empire. New Haven, 1940.

Cary, M., and E. H. Warmington. The Ancient Explorers. New York, 1929.

Clark, D. L. Rhetoric in Greco-Roman Education. New York, 1954.

Clarke, M. L. Rhetoric at Rome. A Historical Survey. London, 1953.

————The Roman Mind: Studies in the History of Thought from Cicero to Marcus Aurelius. London, 1956.

Claggett, M. Greek Science in Antiquity. New York, 1956.

Cramer, F. H. Astrology in Roman Law and Politics. Philadelphia, 1954.

626 BIBLIOGRAPHY

Dampier, W. C. A History of Science and Its Relations with Philosophy and Religion. 4th ed. New York, 1949.

Davis, W. S. The Influence of Wealth in Imperial Rome. New York, 1910.

Dill, S. Roman Society from Nero to Marcus Aurelius. 2d ed. London, 1905.

Dobson, J. F. Ancient Education and its Meaning to Us. New York, 1932.

Duff, A. M. Freedmen in the Early Roman Empire. Oxford, 1928.

Duff, J. W. A Literary History of Rome in the Silver Age from Tiberius to Hadrian. Rev. and ed. by A. M. Duff. London, 1953.

Farrington, B. Greek Science, Its Meaning for Us. Vol. II. Harmondsworth, 1949.

————Science in Antiquity. London, 1936.

Forbes, R. J. Studies in Ancient Technology. 9 vols. Leiden, 1955–65.

Friedländer, L. Roman Life and Manners under the Early Empire. 4 vols. New York, 1908–1913.

Gest, A. P. Engineering. New York, 1930.

Gordon, M. L. "The Nationality of Slaves under the Early Roman Empire," *Journal of Roman Studies*, XIV (1924), 93–111.

Gossen, H. "The Legacy of Greece and Medical Thought in Ancient Rome," *Ciba Symposia*, I (1939), 2–32.

Grant, M. Roman Literature. London, 1958.

Gwynn, A. O. Roman Education from Cicero to Quintilian. Oxford, 1926.

Hadas, M. A History of Latin Literature. New York, 1952.

Halliday, W. R. Greek and Roman Folklore. New York, 1927.

Hamberg, P. G. Studies in Roman Imperial Art. Copenhagen, 1945.

Hamilton, E. The Roman Way. New York, 1932.

Hanfmann, G. M. A. Roman Art. A Modern Survey of the Art of Imperial Rome. Greenwich, 1964.

Harte, G. B. The Villas of Pliny. New York, 1928.

Hicks, R. D. Stoic and Epicurean. London, 1910.

Jennison, G. Animals for Show and Pleasure in Ancient Rome. Manchester, 1937.

Kenyon, F. G. Books and Readers in Ancient Greece and Rome. 2d ed. New York, 1951.

Koehler, H. The Art of Rome and Her Empire. New York, 1963.

Laidlaw, W. A. Latin Literature. New York, 1951.

La Piana, G. "Foreign Groups in Rome during the First Centuries of the Empire," *Harvard Theological Review*, XX (1927), 183–403.

McDaniel, W. W. Roman Private Life and its Survivals. 3d ed. New York, 1929.

MacKendrick, P. The Roman Mind at Work. Princeton, 1958.

Maiuri, A. Roman Painting. Geneva, 1955.

Marrou, H. I. A History of Education in Antiquity. Toronto, 1964.

Mohler, S. L. "Slave Education in the Roman Empire," *Transactions of the American Philological Association*, LXXI (1940), 262–80.

Neppi Modona, A. "Etruscan Metallurgy," *Scientific American*, CIII (1955), 90–98.

Neugebauer, O. The Exact Sciences in Antiquity. 2d ed. Providence, 1957 (Harper Torchbook edition, 1962).

Paoli, U. E. Rome: Its People, Life, and Customs. New York, 1964.

Parker, E. R.   "The Education of Heirs in the Julio-Claudian Dynasty,"
   American Journal of Philology, LXVII (1946), 29–50.
Parks, E. P.   The Roman Rhetorical Schools as a Preparation for the Courts
   under the Early Empire. Baltimore, 1945.
Pinner, H. L.   The World of Books in Classical Antiquity. Leiden, 1948.
Reymond, A.   History of the Sciences in Greco-Roman Antiquity. New
   York, 1927.
Rivoira, G. T.   Roman Architecture and its Principles of Construction
   under the Empire. Oxford, 1925.
Robathan, D. M.   The Monuments of Ancient Rome. Rome, 1950.
Robertson, D. S.   Handbook of Greek and Roman Architecture. Cam-
   bridge, 1929.
Rose, H. J.   A Handbook of Latin Literature from the Earliest Times to
   the Death of St. Augustine. 5th ed. London, 1962.
Sherwin-White, A. N.   Roman Society and Roman Law in the New
   Testament. New York, 1963.
Singer, C., *et al.*   History of Technology, Vol. I–II. Oxford, 1954–1958.
Smail, W. M.   Quintilian on Education. Oxford, 1938.
Smith, W. A.   Ancient Education. New York, 1955.
Stahl, W. H.   Roman Science. Madison, 1962.
Starr, C. G., Jr.   Civilization and the Caesars. Ithaca, 1954.
Strong, D. E.   Roman Imperial Sculpture. London, 1961.
Strong, E.   Art in Ancient Rome. 2d ed. 2 vols. London, 1930.
Swindler, M. H.   Ancient Painting. New Haven, 1929.
Tanzer, H. H.   The Villas of Pliny the Younger. New York, 1924.
Tomson, J. O.   History of Ancient Geography. 2d ed. Cambridge, 1948.
Toynbee, J. M. C.   Some Notes on Artists in the Roman World. Brussels,
   1951.
Tozer, H. F.   A History of Ancient Geography. 2d ed. by M. Cary. Cam-
   bridge, 1935.
Tucker, T. G.   Life in the Roman World of Nero and St. Paul. New York,
   1910.
Van Deman, E. B.   The Building of the Roman Aqueducts. Washington,
   1934.
Walters, H. B.   The Art of the Romans. New York, 1911.
Wheeler, M.   Roman Art and Architecture. New York, 1964.
Wright, F. A.   A History of Later Greek Literature. London, 1932.

Bibliography for Chapter V

Abbott, F. F., and A. C. Johnson.   Municipal Administration in the Roman
   Empire. Princeton, 1926.
Arnold, W. T.   The Roman System of Provincial Administration to the
   Accession of Constantine the Great. 3d ed., by E. S. Bouchier. Oxford,
   1914.
Bell, H. I.   "The Economic Crisis in Egypt under Nero," *Journal of Roman
   Studies*, XXVIII (1938), 1–8.

————Egypt from Alexander the Great to the Arab Conquest. Oxford, 1948.

————Jews and Christians in Egypt. London, 1924.

————"Roman Egypt from Augustus to Diocletian," *Chronique d'Égypte*, XIII (1938), 347–63.

Bouchier, E. S.   Life and Letters in Roman Africa. Oxford, 1913.

————Sardinia in Ancient Times. Oxford, 1917.

————Spain under the Roman Empire. Oxford, 1914.

————Syria as a Roman Province. Oxford, 1916.

Brogan, O.   Roman Gaul. London, 1953.

Broughton, T. R. S.   "Roman Landholding in Asia Minor," *Transactions of the American Philological Association*, LXV (1934), 207–39.

————The Romanization of Africa Proconsularis. Baltimore, 1929.

Buckler, W. H.   "Labour Disputes in the Province of Asia Minor," in Anatolian Studies Presented to Sir William Mitchell Ramsay. Manchester, 1923. Pages 27–50.

Burn, A. R.   Agricola and Roman Britain. New York, 1953.

Carrington, R. C.   Pompeii. Oxford, 1936.

Charlesworth, M. P.   The Lost Province, or, The Worth of Britain. Cardiff, 1949.

Chilver, G. E. F.   Cisalpine Gaul; Social and Economic History from 49 B.C. to the Death of Trajan. Oxford, 1941.

Collingwood, R. G.   Roman Britain. Rev. ed. Oxford, 1945.

Corti, E. C.   The Destruction and Resurrection of Pompeii and Herculaneum. London, 1951.

Cottrell, L.   Seeing Roman Britain. London, 1956.

Davis, S.   Race Relations in Ancient Egypt: Greek, Egyptian, Hebrew, Roman. New York, 1952.

Day, J.   "Agriculture in the Life of Pompeii," *Yale Classical Studies*, III (1932), 165–208.

————An Economic History of Athens under Roman Domination. New York, 1942.

Duncan-Jones, R.   "The Purpose and Organization of the Alimenta," *Papers of the British School at Rome*, XXXII (1964), 123–46.

————"Wealth and Munificence in Roman Africa," *Papers of the British School at Rome*, XXXI (1963), 159–77.

Duyvendak, N.   "Restraining Regulations for Roman Officials in the Roman Provinces," in Symbolae . . . Van Oven Dedicatae. Leiden, 1946. Pages 333–48.

Finlay, G.   Greece under the Romans. London and New York, 1907.

Graham, A.   Roman Africa. London, 1902.

Gwatkin, W. E., Jr.   Cappadocia as a Roman Procuratorial Province. Columbia, Missouri, 1930.

Hardy, E. G.   Three Spanish Charters and Other Documents. Oxford, 1912.

Harper, G. M., Jr.   "Village Administration in the Roman Province of Syria," *Yale Classical Studies*, I (1928), 105–68.

Harrer, G. A.   Studies in the History of the Roman Province of Syria. Princeton, 1915.

Haverfield, F. The Roman Occupation of Britain. Rev. ed., by G. Macdonald. Oxford, 1924.

———The Romanization of Roman Britain. 4th ed., rev. by G. Macdonald. Oxford, 1923.

Heitland, W. E. The Roman Fate: An Essay in Interpretation. Cambridge, 1922.

———Iterum: or, A Further Discussion of the Roman Fate. Cambridge, 1925.

———Last Words on the Roman Municipalities. Cambridge, 1928.

———Repetita: An Unwilling Restatement of Views on the Subject of Roman Municipalities. Cambridge, 1930.

Johnson, A. C. Egypt and the Roman Empire. Ann Arbor, 1951.

Jones, A. H. M. The Cities of the Eastern Roman Provinces. Oxford, 1937.

———The Greek City from Alexander to Justinian. Oxford, 1940.

Lewis, N. "On Official Corruption in Roman Egypt. The Edict of Vergilius Capito," *Proceedings of the American Philosophical Society*, XCVIII (1954), 153–58.

MacMullen, R. "Roman Imperial Buildings in the Provinces," *Harvard Studies in Classical Philology*, LXIV (1959), 207–35.

Magie, D. Roman Rule in Asia Minor. 2 vols. Princeton, 1950.

Mahaffy, J. P. The Greek World under Roman Sway. London and New York, 1890.

Maiuri, A. Herculaneum. Rome, 1937.

———Pompeii. Rome, 1929.

Marcus, R. "Antisemitism in the Hellenistic-Roman World," *Jewish Social Studies*, II (1942), 3–25.

Mau, A. Pompeii, Its Life and Art. Rev. ed. New York, 1904.

Meiggs, R. Roman Ostia. Oxford, 1960.

Milne, J. G. A History of Egypt under Roman Rule. 3d ed. London, 1924.

———"The Ruin of Egypt by Roman Mismanagement," *Journal of Roman Studies*, XVII (1927), 1–13.

Mommsen, T. The Provinces of the Roman Empire from Caesar to Diocletian. 2 vols. London, 1909.

Oliver, J. H. "The Ruling Power. A Study of the Roman Empire in the Second Century after Christ through the Roman Oration of Aelius Aristides," *Transactions of the American Philosophical Society*, XLIII (1953), 871–1003.

Parvan, V. Dacia. Cambridge, 1928.

Radin, M. The Jews among the Greeks and Romans. Philadelphia, 1915.

Ramsay, W. M. The Social Basis of Roman Power in Asia Minor. Aberdeen, 1941.

Reid, J. S. The Municipalities of the Roman Empire. Cambridge, 1913.

Reinmuth, O. W. "The Edict of Tiberius Julius Alexander," *Transactions of the American Philological Association*, LXV (1934), 248–59.

———The Prefect of Egypt from Augustus to Diocletian. Leipzig, 1935.

Richmond, I. Roman Britain. London, 1947.

Roberts, C. H. "Literature and Society in the Papyri," *Museum Helveticum*, X (1953), 264–79.

Rostovtzeff, M. "Pontus, Bithynia and the Bosporus," *Annual of the British School at Athens*, XXII (1916–18), 1–22.

———"Roman Exploitation of Egypt in the First Century A.D.," *Journal of Economic and Business History*, I (1928/29), 337–64.

Sanford, E. M. "Contrasting Views of the Roman Empire," *American Journal of Philology*, LVIII (1937), 437–56.

———"Political Campaigns in Roman Municipalities," *Classical Journal*, XXV (1929/30), 453–63.

Schulz, F. "Roman Registers of Births and Birth Certificates," *Journal of Roman Studies*, XXXII (1942), 78–91; XXXIII (1943), 55–64.

Stevenson, G. H. Roman Provincial Administration till the Age of the Antonines. 2d ed. Oxford, 1949.

Sutherland, C. H. V. The Romans in Spain, 217 B.C.–A.D. 117. London, 1939.

Tanzer, H. H. The Common People of Pompeii. A Study of the Graffiti. Baltimore, 1939.

Taubenschlag, R. The Law of Greco-Roman Egypt in the Light of the Papyri. 2d ed. Warsaw, 1955.

Wallace, S. L. Taxation in Egypt from Augustus to Diocletian. Princeton, 1938.

Wilson, F. H. "Studies in the Social and Economic History of Ostia," *Papers of the British School at Rome*, XIII (1935), 41–68; XIV (1938), 152–62.

Winter, J. G. Life and Letters in the Papyri. Ann Arbor, 1933.

Wiseman, F. J. Roman Spain. An Introduction to the Roman Antiquities of Spain and Portugal. London, 1956.

Youtie, H. C. "Publicans and Sinners," *Michigan Alumnus: Quarterly Number*, 1937, pp. 650–62.

Bibliography for Chapter VI

Arragon, R. F. The Transition from the Ancient to the Medieval World. New York, 1936.

Bell, H. I. "The Byzantine Servile State in Egypt," *Journal of Egyptian Archaeology*, IV (1917), 86–105.

———"The Constitutio Antoniniana and the Egyptian Poll-Tax," *Journal of Roman Studies*, XXXVII (1947), 17–23.

Bell, M. R. Roman Society from Commodus to Alexander Severus. Chicago, 1937.

Boak, A. E. R. Manpower Shortage and the Fall of the Roman Empire in the West. Ann Arbor, 1955.

Burckhardt, J. Constantine the Great. New York, 1949.

Bury, J. B. The Invasion of Europe by the Barbarians. London, 1928.

Cambridge Economic History of Europe. Vol. II. Cambridge, 1952.

Chambers, M., ed. The Fall of Rome: Can It Be Explained? New York, 1964.

Clausing, R. The Roman Colonate. New York, 1925.

Crees, J. H. E. The Reign of the Emperor Probus. London, 1911.

Crook, J. A. Consilium Principis. Imperial Councils and Counsellors from Augustus to Diocletian. Cambridge, 1954.

Graser, E. R. "The Significance of the Two New Fragments of the Edict of Diocletian," *Transactions of the American Philological Association*, LXXI (1940), 157–74.

Hammond, M. "Septimius Severus, Roman Bureaucrat," *Harvard Studies in Classical Philology*, LI (1940), 137–73.

Haywood, R. M. "The African Policy of Septimius Severus," *Transactions of the American Philological Association*, LXXI (1940), 175–85.

————The Myth of Rome's Fall. New York, 1958.

Heitland, W. E. The Roman Fate: An Essay in Interpretation. Cambridge, 1922.

————Iterum: or, A Further Discussion of the Roman Fate. Cambridge, 1925.

————Last Words on the Roman Municipalities. Cambridge, 1928.

————Repetita: An Unwilling Restatement of Views on the Subject of Roman Municipalities. Cambridge, 1930.

Holsapple, L. B. Constantine the Great. New York, 1942.

Hopkins, R. V. N. The Life of Alexander Severus. Cambridge, 1907.

Howe, L. L. The Praetorian Prefect from Commodus to Diocletian. Chicago, 1942.

Johnson, A. C. Egypt and the Roman Empire. Ann Arbor, 1951.

Jones, A. H. M. "Capitatio and Iugatio," *Journal of Roman Studies*, XLVII (1957), 88–94.

————"Census Records of the Later Roman Empire," *Journal of Roman Studies*, XLIII (1953), 49–64.

————Constantine and the Conversion of Europe. Rev. ed. New York, 1962.

————"The Decline and Fall of the Roman Empire," *History*, XL (1955), 209–26.

————The Later Roman Empire 284–602. 3 vols. Norman, 1964.

————"Over-Taxation and the Decline of the Roman Empire," *Antiquity*, XXXIII (1959), 39–49.

Kagan, D., ed. Decline and Fall of the Roman Empire: Why Did It Collapse? Boston, 1963.

Katz, S. The Decline of Rome and the Rise of Medieval Europe. Ithaca, 1955.

Lot, F. The End of the Ancient World and the Beginnings of the Middle Ages. New York, 1931.

Magie, D. Roman Rule in Asia Minor. 2 vols. Princeton, 1950.

Manley, I. J. "Effects of the Germanic Invasions on Gaul, 234–284 A.D.," *University of California Publications in History*, XVII (1934), 25–141.

Mattingly, H. "The Monetary Systems of the Roman Empire from Diocletian to Theodosius I," *Numismatic Chronicle*, 1946, pp. 111–20.

Metropolitan Museum of Art. Symposium: The Age of Diocletian. New York, 1953.

Olmstead, A. T. "The Mid-Third Century of the Christian Era," *Classical Philology*, XXXVII (1942), 241–62, 398–420.

Platnauer, M. The Life and Reign of the Emperor Lucius Septimius Severus. London, 1918.

Richmond, I. A. The City Wall of Imperial Rome. Oxford, 1930.

Rostovtzeff, M. "The Decay of the Ancient World and its Economic Explanations," *Economic History Review*, II (1929/30), 197–214.

————"The Problem of the Origin of Serfdom in the Roman Empire," *Journal of Land and Public Utility Economics*, II (1926), 193–207.

Sanders, J. J. "The Debate on the Fall of Rome," *History*, XLVIII (1963), 1–17.

Sherwin-White, A. N. The Roman Citizenship. Oxford, 1939.

Townsend, P. W. "The Revolution of A.D. 238," *Yale Classical Studies*, XIV (1955), 49–105.

Tsunoda, B. E. "The Problem of the Ending of the Ancient World," *Palaeologia*, IV (1955), 296–318.

Van Sickle, C. E. "Changing Bases of the Roman Imperial Power in the Third Century A.D.," *Antiquité Classique*, VIII (1939), 153–70.

————"Diocletian and the Decline of the Roman Municipalities," *Journal of Roman Studies*, XXVIII (1938), 9–18.

————"Particularism in the Roman Empire during the Military Anarchy," *American Journal of Philology*, LI (1930), 343–57.

Walbank, F. W. The Decline of the Roman Empire in the West. London, 1946.

Warmington, B. H. The North African Provinces from Diocletian to the Vandal Conquest. Cambridge, 1954.

Welles, C. B. "Another Look at P. Giss. 40," *Études de Papyrologie*, IX (1962), 1–20.

Bibliography for Chapter VII

Adcock, F. E. The Roman Art of War under the Republic. Cambridge, Mass., 1940.

Birley, E. Roman Britain and the Roman Army: Collected Papers. Kendal, 1953.

Brunt, P. A. "Pay and Superannuation in the Roman Army," *Papers of the British School at Rome*, XVIII (1950), 50–71.

Cheesman, G. L. The Auxilia of the Roman Imperial Army. Oxford, 1914.

Dean, L. R. A Study of the Cognomina of Soldiers in the Roman Legions. Princeton, 1916.

Forestier, A. The Roman Soldier. London, 1928.

Fuller, J. F. C. A Military History of the Western World. Vol. I. New York, 1954.

Gilliam, J. F. "The Roman Military Feriale," *Harvard Theological Review*, XLVII (1954), 183–96.

Ginsburg, M. "Roman Military Clubs and their Social Functions," *Transactions of the American Philological Association*, LXXI (1940), 149–56.

Hardy, E. G. Studies in Roman History. Second Series. London, 1909.

Lind, L. R. "Roman Military Exemption," in Classical Studies in Honor of W. A. Oldfather. Urbana, 1943. Pages 94–103.

McCartney, E. S. Warfare by Land and Sea. Boston, 1923.

Mann, J. C. "A Note on the Numeri," *Hermes*, LXXXII (1954), 501–6.

Nock, A. D. "The Roman Army and the Roman Religious Year," *Harvard Theological Review*, XLV (1952), 187–252.

Parker, H. M. D. The Roman Legions. Rev. ed. Cambridge, 1958.

Richmond, I. A. "Trajan's Army on Trajan's Column," *Papers of the British School at Rome*, XIII (1935), 1–40.

Rodgers, W. L. Greek and Roman Naval Warfare. Annapolis, 1937.

Rowell, H. T. "The *Honesta Missio* of the Roman Imperial Army," *Yale Classical Studies*, VI (1939), 71–108.

Starr, C. G., Jr. "Coastal Defence in the Roman World," *American Journal of Philology*, LXIV (1943), 56–70.

————The Roman Imperial Navy, 31 B.C.–A.D. 324. 2d ed. Cambridge, 1960.

Watson, G. R. "The Pay of the Roman Army," *Historia*, V (1956), 332–40.

Welles, C. B., R. O. Fink, and J. F. Gilliam. The Excavations at Dura-Europos: The Parchments and Papyri. New Haven, 1959.

Bibliography for Chapter VIII

A bibliography on legal sources and commentaries is given in Vol. I, pp. 522–24.

Berger, A. Encyclopedic Dictionary of Roman Law. Philadelphia, 1953. Transactions of the American Philosophical Society, XLIII, Part 2.

Blatt, F. "Written and Unwritten Law in Ancient Rome," *Classica et Medievalia*, III (1942), 137–58.

Bryce, J. The Ancient Roman Empire and the British Empire in India. London, 1914.

Buckland, W. W. The Main Institutions of Roman Private Law. Cambridge, 1931.

————and A. D. McNair. Roman Law and Common Law: A Comparison in Outline. Cambridge, 1936.

de Zulueta, F. The Institutes of Gaius. 2 vols. Oxford, 1946–1952.

Daube, D. Forms of Roman Legislation. Oxford, 1956.

Jolowicz, H. F. Roman Foundations of Modern Law. Oxford, 1957.

————Historical Introduction to the Study of Roman Law. 2d ed. Cambridge, 1961.

Leage, R. W. Roman Private Law. 3rd ed. London, 1961.

Lee, R. W. An Historical Conspectus of Roman Law, 753 B.C. to A.D. 1948. London, 1956.

Montgomery, H. C. "The Development of Humanitarianism in Roman Law," in Classical Studies in Honor of W. A. Oldfather. Urbana, 1943. Pages 104–21.

Pharr, C. "Roman Legal Education," *Classical Journal*, XXXIV (1938/39), 257–70.

————The Theodosian Code. Princeton, 1952.

Pringsheim, F. "The Legal Policy and Reforms of Hadrian," *Journal of Roman Studies*, XXIV (1934), 141–53.

Schiller, A. A. "Bureaucracy and the Roman Law," *Seminar*, VII (1949), 26–48.

Schulz, F. Classical Roman Law. Oxford, 1951.

Taubenschlag, R. The Law of Greco-Roman Egypt in the Light of the Papyri. 2d ed. Warsaw, 1955.

Turner, J. W. C.   Introduction to the Study of Roman Private Law. Cambridge, 1953.
Welles, C. B.   "Rhetoric and the Law," *Seminar*, XIII (1955–56), 1–16.
Wenger, L.   Institutes of the Roman Law of Civil Procedure. New York, 1939.
Wolff, H. J.   Roman Law. An Historical Introduction. Norman, 1951.

Bibliography for Chapter IX

Alföldi, A.   The Conversion of Constantine and Pagan Rome. New York, 1948.
Angus, S.   The Mystery Religions and Christianity. London, 1925.
————The Religious Quests of the Graeco-Roman World. London, 1929.
Bailey, C.   Phases in the Religion of Ancient Rome. Berkeley, 1932.
Baker, G. P.   Constantine the Great and the Christian Revolution. London and New York, 1930.
Barnes, E. W.   The Rise of Christianity. London and New York, 1948.
Baynes, N. H.   Constantine the Great and the Christian Church. London, 1929.
Bone, R. G.   Roman Persecution of Non-Christian Religions before 200 A.D. Urbana, 1937.
Burn, A. E.   The Council of Nicaea. London, 1925.
Carrington, P.   The Early Christian Church. 2 vols. Cambridge, 1957.
Charlesworth, M. P.   "Some Observations on Ruler-cult, Especially in Rome," *Harvard Theological Review*, XXVIII (1935), 5–44.
Cochrane, C. N.   Christianity and Classical Culture. A Study of Thought and Action from Augustus to Augustine. Oxford, 1940.
Crake, J. E. A.   "Early Christians and Roman Law," *Phoenix*, XIX (1965), 61–70.
Cumont, F.   After Life in Roman Paganism. New Haven, 1923.
————Astrology and Religion among the Greeks and Romans. New York and London, 1912.
————The Mysteries of Mithra. 2d ed. Chicago, 1910.
————Oriental Religions in Roman Paganism. Chicago, 1911.
Davies, J. G.   Daily Life in the Early Church: Studies in the Church Social History of the First Five Centuries. London, 1952.
Doerries, H.   Constantine and Religious Liberty. New Haven, 1961.
Foakes-Jackson, F. J.   History of the Christian Church from Earliest Times to A.D. 461. 7th ed. New York, 1924.
Glover, T. R.   The Conflict of Religions in the Early Roman Empire. 10th ed. London, 1923.
Goodenough, E. R.   The Church in the Roman Empire. New York, 1931.
Gough, M.   The Early Christians. New York, 1961.
Grant, F. C.   Ancient Roman Religion. New York, 1957.
Grant, R. M.   The Sword and the Cross. New York, 1955.
Halliday, W. R.   The Pagan Background of Early Christianity. Liverpool, 1925.

Hardy, E. G.   Christianity and the Roman Government: A Study in Imperial Administration. New York, 1925.

Harnack, A.   Mission and Expansion of Christianity in the First Three Centuries. New York, 1961 (Harper Torchbook).

Hoey, A. S.   "Official Policy towards Oriental Cults in the Roman Army," *Transactions of the American Philological Association*, LXX (1939), 456–81.

Hyde, W. W.   Paganism to Christianity in the Roman Empire. Philadelphia, 1946.

Jones, A. H. M.   Constantine and the Conversion of Europe. Rev. ed. New York, 1962.

Knipfing, J. R.   "The Libelli of the Decian Persecution," *Harvard Theological Review*, XVI (1923), 345–90.

Laing, G. J.   Survivals of Roman Religion. New York, 1931.

La Piana, G.   "Foreign Groups in Rome during the First Centuries of the Empire," *Harvard Theological Review*, XX (1927), 183–403.

Latourette, K. S.   A History of the Expansion of Christianity. Vol. I: The First Five Centuries. New York, 1937.

Lebreton, J., and J. Zeiller.   The History of the Primitive Church. 4 vols. London, 1949.

Legge, F.   Forerunners and Rivals of Christianity. 2 vols. Cambridge, 1915.

Leon, H. J.   The Jews of Ancient Rome. Philadelphia, 1960.

Lietzmann, H.   A History of the Early Church. 4 vols. New York, 1949–1960.

Mattingly, H.   "The Roman 'Virtues,'" *Harvard Theological Review*, XXX (1937), 103–17.

Momigliano, A., ed.   The Conflict Between Paganism and Christianity in the Fourth Century. Oxford, 1963.

Moore, C. H.   "The Distribution of Oriental Cults in the Gauls and the Germanies," *Transactions of the American Philological Association*, XXXVIII (1907), 109–50.

————Pagan Ideas of Immortality during the Early Roman Empire. Cambridge, Mass., 1918.

Morrison, K. F.   Rome and the City of God: An Essay on the Constitutional Relationships of Empire and Church in the Fourth Century. Philadelphia, 1963.

Nock, A. D.   Conversion: The Old and New in Religion from Alexander the Great to Augustine of Hippo. Oxford, 1933.

Patterson, L.   Mithraism and Christianity: A Study in Comparative Religion. Cambridge, 1921.

Riddle, D. W.   The Martyrs: A Study in Social Control. Chicago, 1931.

Robertson, A.   The Origins of Christianity. Rev. ed. New York, 1962.

Rose, H. J.   Ancient Roman Religion. London, 1948.

Rostovtzeff, M. I.   Mystic Italy. New York, 1927.

Scott, K.   The Imperial Cult under the Flavians. Stuttgart, 1936.

Sherwin-White, A. N.   "The Early Persecutions and Roman Law Again," *Journal of Theological Studies*, III (1952), 199–213.

Snyder, W. F.   "Public Anniversaries in the Roman Empire," *Yale Classical Studies*, VII (1940), 225–317.

Strong, E. S.   Apotheosis and After Life. London, 1915.

Taylor, L. R.   The Divinity of the Roman Emperor. Middletown, 1931.

————"New Light on the History of the Secular Games," *American Journal of Philology*, LV (1934), 101–20.

————"Tiberius' Refusal of Divine Honors," *Transactions of the American Philological Association*, LX (1929), 87–101.

Vermaseren, M. J.   Mithras, the Secret God. London, 1963.

Weiss, J.   The History of Primitive Christianity. 2 vols. New York, 1937 (Harper Torchbook edition, under the title Earliest Christianity, 1959).

Westbury-Jones, J.   Roman and Christian Imperialism. London, 1939.

INDEX

INDEX OF AUTHORS AND DOCUMENTS

GENERAL INDEX

harper ✦ torchbooks

American Studies: General

HENRY ADAMS Degradation of the Democratic Dogma. ‡ *Introduction by Charles Hirschfeld.* TB/1450

LOUIS D. BRANDEIS: Other People's Money, *and How the Bankers Use It. Ed. with Intro, by Richard M. Abrams* TB/3081

HENRY STEELE COMMAGER, Ed.: The Struggle for Racial Equality TB/1300

CARL N. DEGLER: Out of Our Past: *The Forces that Shaped Modern America* CN/2

CARL N. DEGLER, Ed.: Pivotal Interpretations of American History
Vol. I TB/1240; Vol. II TB/1241

A. S. EISENSTADT, Ed.: The Craft of American History: *Selected Essays*
Vol. I TB/1255; Vol. II TB/1256

LAWRENCE H. FUCHS, Ed.: American Ethnic Politics TB/1368

MARCUS LEE HANSEN: The Atlantic Migration: 1607-1860. *Edited by Arthur M. Schlesinger. Introduction by Oscar Handlin* TB/1052

MARCUS LEE HANSEN: The Immigrant in American History. *Edited with a Foreword by Arthur M. Schlesinger* TB/1120

ROBERT L. HEILBRONER: The Limits of American Capitalism TB/1305

JOHN HIGHAM, Ed.: The Reconstruction of American History TB/1068

ROBERT H. JACKSON: The Supreme Court in the American System of Government TB/1106

JOHN F. KENNEDY: A Nation of Immigrants. *Illus. Revised and Enlarged. Introduction by Robert F. Kennedy* TB/1118

LEONARD W. LEVY, Ed.: American Constitutional Law: *Historical Essays* TB/1285

LEONARD W. LEVY, Ed.: Judicial Review and the Supreme Court TB/1296

LEONARD W. LEVY: The Law of the Commonwealth and Chief Justice Shaw: *The Evolution of American Law, 1830-1860* TB/1309

GORDON K. LEWIS: Puerto Rico: *Freedom and Power in the Caribbean. Abridged edition* TB/1371

HENRY F. MAY: Protestant Churches and Industrial America TB/1334

RICHARD B. MORRIS: Fair Trial: *Fourteen Who Stood Accused, from Anne Hutchinson to Alger Hiss* TB/1335

GUNNAR MYRDAL: An American Dilemma: *The Negro Problem and Modern Democracy. Introduction by the Author.*
Vol. I TB/1443; Vol. II TB/1444

GILBERT OSOFSKY, Ed.: The Burden of Race: *A Documentary History of Negro-White Relations in America* TB/1405

CONYERS READ, Ed.: The Constitution Reconsidered. *Revised Edition. Preface by Richard B. Morris* TB/1384

ARNOLD ROSE: The Negro in America: *The Condensed Version of Gunnar Myrdal's* An American Dilemma. *Second Edition* TB/3048

JOHN E. SMITH: Themes in American Philosophy: *Purpose, Experience and Community* TB/1466

WILLIAM R. TAYLOR: Cavalier and Yankee: *The Old South and American National Character* TB/1474

American Studies: Colonial

BERNARD BAILYN: The New England Merchants in the Seventeenth Century TB/1149

ROBERT E. BROWN: Middle-Class Democracy and Revolution in Massachusetts, 1691–1780. *New Introduction by Author* TB/1413

JOSEPH CHARLES: The Origins of the American Party System TB/1049

HENRY STEELE COMMAGER & ELMO GIORDANETTI, Eds.: Was America a Mistake? *An Eighteenth Century Controversy* TB/1329

WESLEY FRANK CRAVEN: The Colonies in Transition: 1660-1712† TB/3084

CHARLES GIBSON: Spain in America † TB/3077

CHARLES GIBSON, Ed.: The Spanish Tradition in America + HR/1351

LAWRENCE HENRY GIPSON: The Coming of the Revolution: 1763-1775. † *Illus.* TB/3007

JACK P. GREENE, Ed.: Great Britain and the American Colonies: 1606-1763. + *Introduction by the Author* HR/1477

AUBREY C. LAND, Ed.: Bases of the Plantation Society + HR/1429

JOHN LANKFORD, Ed.: Captain John Smith's America: *Selections* from his Writings † TB/3078

LEONARD W. LEVY: Freedom of Speech and Press in Early American History: *Legacy of Suppression* TB/1109

2

ARNOLD M. PAUL: Conservative Crisis and the Rule of Law: *Attitudes of Bar and Bench, 1887-1895. New Introduction by Author*   TB/1415

JAMES S. PIKE: The Prostrate State: *South Carolina under Negro Government.* ‡ *Intro. by Robert F. Durden*   TB/3085

WHITELAW REID: After the War: *A Tour of the Southern States, 1865-1866.* ‡ *Edited by C. Vann Woodward*   TB/3066

FRED A. SHANNON: The Farmer's Last Frontier: *....Agriculture, 1860-1897*   TB/1348

VERNON LANE WHARTON: The Negro in Mississippi, 1865-1890   TB/1178

American Studies: The Twentieth Century

RICHARD M. ABRAMS, Ed.: The Issues of the Populist and Progressive Eras, 1892-1912 +   HR/1428

RAY STANNARD BAKER: Following the Color Line: *American Negro Citizenship in Progressive Era.* ‡ *Edited by Dewey W. Grantham, Jr. Illus.*   TB/3053

RANDOLPH S. BOURNE: War and the Intellectuals: *Collected Essays, 1915-1919.* ‡ *Edited by Carl Resek*   TB/3043

A. RUSSELL BUCHANAN: The United States and World War II. † *Illus.*
Vol. I TB/3044; Vol. II TB/3045

THOMAS C. COCHRAN: The American Business System: *A Historical Perspective, 1900-1955*   TB/1080

FOSTER RHEA DULLES: America's Rise to World Power: 1898-1954. † *Illus.*   TB/3021

JEAN-BAPTISTE DUROSELLE: From Wilson to Roosevelt: *Foreign Policy of the United States, 1913-1945. Trans. by Nancy Lyman Roelker*   TB/1370

HAROLD U. FAULKNER: The Decline of Laissez Faire, 1897-1917   TB/1397

JOHN D. HICKS: Republican Ascendancy: 1921-1933. † *Illus.*   TB/3041

ROBERT HUNTER: Poverty: *Social Conscience in the Progressive Era.* ‡ *Edited by Peter d'A. Jones*   TB/3065

WILLIAM E. LEUCHTENBURG: Franklin D. Roosevelt and the New Deal: 1932-1940. † *Illus.*   TB/3025

WILLIAM E. LEUCHTENBURG, Ed.: The New Deal: *A Documentary History* +   HR/1354

ARTHUR S. LINK: Woodrow Wilson and the Progressive Era: 1910-1917. † *Illus.* TB/3023

BROADUS MITCHELL: Depression Decade: *From New Era through New Deal, 1929-1941* ∧   TB/1439

GEORGE E. MOWRY: The Era of Theodore Roosevelt and the Birth of Modern America: 1900-1912. † *Illus.*   TB/3022

WILLIAM PRESTON, JR.: Aliens and Dissenters: *Federal Suppression of Radicals, 1903-1933*   TB/1287

WALTER RAUSCHENBUSCH: Christianity and the Social Crisis. ‡ *Edited by Robert D. Cross*   TB/3059

GEORGE SOULE: Prosperity Decade: *From War to Depression, 1917-1929* ∆   TB/1349

GEORGE B. TINDALL, Ed.: A Populist Reader: *Selections from the Works of American Populist Leaders*   TB/3069

TWELVE SOUTHERNERS: I'll Take My Stand: *The South and the Agrarian Tradition. Intro. by Louis D. Rubin, Jr.; Biographical Essays by Virginia Rock*   TB/1072

Art, Art History, Aesthetics

CREIGHTON GILBERT, Ed.: Renaissance Art **   *Illus.*   TB/1465

EMILE MALE: The Gothic Image: *Religious Art in France of the Thirteenth Century.* § *190 illus.*   TB/344

MILLARD MEISS: Painting in Florence and Siena After the Black Death: *The Arts, Religion and Society in the Mid-Fourteenth Century. 169 illus.*   TB/1148

ERWIN PANOFSKY: Renaissance and Renascences in Western Art. *Illus.*   TB/1447

ERWIN PANOFSKY: Studies in Iconology: *Humanistic Themes in the Art of the Renaissance. 180 illus.*   TB/1077

JEAN SEZNEC: The Survival of the Pagan Gods: *The Mythological Tradition and Its Place in Renaissance Humanism and Art. 108 illus.*   TB/2004

OTTO VON SIMSON: The Gothic Cathedral: *Origins of Gothic Architecture and the Medieval Concept of Order. 58 illus.*   TB/2018

HEINRICH ZIMMER: Myths and Symbols in Indian Art and Civilization. *70 illus.* TB/2005

Asian Studies

WOLFGANG FRANKE: China and the West: *The Cultural Encounter, 13th to 20th Centuries. Trans. by R. A. Wilson*   TB/1326

L. CARRINGTON GOODRICH: A Short History of the Chinese People. *Illus.*   TB/3015

DAN N. JACOBS, Ed.: The New Communist Manifesto and Related Documents. *3rd revised edn.*   TB/1078

DAN N. JACOBS & HANS H. BAERWALD, Eds.: Chinese Communism: *Selected Documents*   TB/3031

BENJAMIN I. SCHWARTZ: Chinese Communism and the Rise of Mao   TB/1308

BENJAMIN I. SCHWARTZ: In Search of Wealth and Power: *Yen Fu and the West*   TB/1422

Economics & Economic History

C. E. BLACK: The Dynamics of Modernization: *A Study in Comparative History*   TB/1321

STUART BRUCHEY: The Roots of American Economic Growth, 1607-1861: *An Essay in Social Causation. New Introduction by the Author.*   TB/1350

GILBERT BURCK & EDITORS OF *Fortune:* The Computer Age: *And its Potential for Management*   TB/1179

JOHN ELLIOTT CAIRNES: The Slave Power. ‡ *Edited with Introduction by Harold D. Woodman*   TB/1433

SHEPARD B. CLOUGH, THOMAS MOODIE & CAROL MOODIE, Eds.: Economic History of Europe: *Twentieth Century* #   HR/1388

THOMAS C. COCHRAN: The American Business System: *A Historical Perspective, 1900-1955*   TB/1180

ROBERT A. DAHL & CHARLES E. LINDBLOM: Politics, Economics, and Welfare: *Planning and Politico-Economic Systems Resolved into Basic Social Processes*   TB/3037

PETER F. DRUCKER: The New Society: *The Anatomy of Industrial Order*   TB/1082

HAROLD U. FAULKNER: The Decline of Laissez Faire, 1897-1917 ∆   TB/1397

PAUL W. GATES: The Farmer's Age: *Agriculture, 1815-1860* ∧   TB/1398

WILLIAM GREENLEAF, Ed.: American Economic Development Since 1860 +   HR/1353

J. L. & BARBARA HAMMOND: The Rise of Modern Industry. || *Introduction by R. M. Hartwell*   TB/1417

3

ROBERT L. HEILBRONER: The Future as History: *The Historic Currents of Our Time and the Direction in Which They Are Taking America* TB/1386

ROBERT L. HEILBRONER: The Great Ascent: *The Struggle for Economic Development in Our Time* TB/3030

FRANK H. KNIGHT: The Economic Organization TB/1214

DAVID S. LANDES: Bankers and Pashas: *International Finance and Economic Imperialism in Egypt. New Preface by the Author* TB/1412

ROBERT LATOUCHE: The Birth of Western Economy: *Economic Aspects of the Dark Ages* TB/1290

ABBA P. LERNER: Everybody's Business: *A Reexamination of Current Assumptions in Economics and Public Policy* TB/3051

W. ARTHUR LEWIS: Economic Survey, 1919-1939 TB/1446

W. ARTHUR LEWIS: The Principles of Economic Planning. *New Introduction by the Author°* TB/1436

ROBERT GREEN MC CLOSKEY: American Conservatism in the Age of Enterprise TB/1137

PAUL MANTOUX: The Industrial Revolution in the Eighteenth Century: *An Outline of the Beginnings of the Modern Factory System in England°* TB/1079

WILLIAM MILLER, Ed.: Men in Business: *Essays on the Historical Role of the Entrepreneur* TB/1081

GUNNAR MYRDAL: An International Economy. *New Introduction by the Author* TB/1445

HERBERT A. SIMON: The Shape of Automation: *For Men and Management* TB/1245

PERRIN STRYKER: The Character of the Executive: *Eleven Studies in Managerial Qualities* TB/1041

RICHARD S. WECKSTEIN, Ed.: Expansion of World Trade and the Growth of National Economies ** TB/1373

Education

JACQUES BARZUN: The House of Intellect TB/1051

RICHARD M. JONES, Ed.: Contemporary Educational Psychology: *Selected Readings ** TB/1292

CLARK KERR: The Uses of the University TB/1264

Historiography and History of Ideas

HERSCHEL BAKER: The Image of Man: *A Study of the Idea of Human Dignity in Classical Antiquity, the Middle Ages, and the Renaissance* TB/1047

J. BRONOWSKI & BRUCE MAZLISH: The Western Intellectual Tradition: *From Leonardo to Hegel* TB/3001

EDMUND BURKE: On Revolution. Ed. by Robert A. Smith TB/1401

WILHELM DILTHEY: Pattern and Meaning in History: *Thoughts on History and Society.° Edited with an Intro. by H. P. Rickman* TB/1075

ALEXANDER GRAY: The Socialist Tradition: *Moses to Lenin °* TB/1375

J. H. HEXTER: More's Utopia: *The Biography of an Idea. Epilogue by the Author* TB/1195

H. STUART HUGHES: History as Art and as Science: *Twin Vistas on the Past* TB/1207

ARTHUR O. LOVEJOY: The Great Chain of Being: *A Study of the History of an Idea* TB/1009

JOSE ORTEGA Y GASSET: The Modern Theme. *Introduction by Jose Ferrater Mora* TB/1038

RICHARD H. POPKIN: The History of Scepticism from Erasmus to Descartes. *Revised Edition* TB/1391

G. J. RENIER: History: *Its Purpose and Method* TB/1209

MASSIMO SALVADORI, Ed.: Modern Socialism # HR/1374

GEORG SIMMEL et al.: Essays on Sociology, Philosophy and Aesthetics. *Edited by Kurt H. Wolff* TB/1234

BRUNO SNELL: The Discovery of the Mind: *The Greek Origins of European Thought* TB/1018

W. WARREN WAGER, ed.: European Intellectual History Since Darwin and Marx TB/1297

W. H. WALSH: Philosophy of History: In Introduction TB/1020

History: General

HANS KOHN: The Age of Nationalism: *The First Era of Global History* TB/1380

BERNARD LEWIS: The Arabs in History TB/1029

BERNARD LEWIS: The Middle East and the West ° TB/1274

History: Ancient

A. ANDREWS: The Greek Tyrants TB/1103

ERNST LUDWIG EHRLICH: A Concise History of Israel: *From the Earliest Times to the Destruction of the Temple in A.D. 70 °* TB/128

ADOLF ERMAN, Ed.: The Ancient Egyptians: *A Sourcebook of their Writings. New Introduction by William Kelly Simpson* TB/1233

THEODOR H. GASTER: Thespis: *Ritual Myth and Drama in the Ancient Near East* TB/1281

MICHAEL GRANT: Ancient History ° TB/1190

A. H. M. JONES, Ed.: A History of Rome through the Fifgth Century # *Vol. I: The Republic* HR/1364
Vol. II The Empire: HR/1460

SAMUEL NOAH KRAMER: Sumerian Mythology TB/1055

NAPHTALI LEWIS & MEYER REINHOLD, Eds.: Roman Civilization *Vol. I: The Republic* TB/1231

Vol. II: The Empire TB/1232

History: Medieval

MARSHALL W. BALDWIN, Ed.: Christianity Through the 13th Century # HR/1468

MARC BLOCH: Land and Work in Medieval Europe. *Translated by J. E. Anderson* TB/1452

HELEN CAM: England Before Elizabeth TB/1026

NORMAN COHN: The Pursuit of the Millennium: *Revolutionary Messianism in Medieval and Reformation Europe* TB/1037

G. G. COULTON: Medieval Village, Manor, and Monastery HR/1022

HEINRICH FICHTENAU: The Carolingian Empire: *The Age of Charlemagne. Translated with an Introduction by Peter Munz* TB/1142

GALBERT OF BRUGES: The Murder of Charles the Good: *A Contemporary Record of Revolutionary Change in 12th Century Flanders. Translated with an Introduction by James Bruce Ross* TB/1311

F. L. GANSHOF: Feudalism TB/1058

F. L. GANSHOF: The Middle Ages: *A History of International Relations. Translated by Rémy Hall* TB/1411

W. O. HASSALL, Ed.: Medieval England: *As Viewed by Contemporaries* TB/1205

DENYS HAY: The Medieval Centuries ° TB/1192

DAVID HERLIHY, Ed.: Medieval Culture and Society # HR/1340

J. M. HUSSEY: The Byzantine World   TB/1057
ROBERT LATOUCHE: The Birth of Western Economy: *Economic Aspects of the Dark Ages* °
TB/1290
HENRY CHARLES LEA: The Inquisition of the Middle Ages. || *Introduction by Walter Ullmann*   TB/1456
FERDINAND LOT: The End of the Ancient World and the Beginnings of the Middle Ages. *Introduction by Glanville Downey*   TB/1044
H. R. LOYN: The Norman Conquest   TB/1457
ACHILLE LUCHAIRE: Social France at the time of Philip Augustus. *Intro. by John W. Baldwin*
TB/1314
GUIBERT DE NOGENT: Self and Society in Medieval France: *The Memoirs of Guibert de Nogent.* || *Edited by John F. Benton* TB/1471
MARSILIUS OF PADUA: The Defender of Peace. *The Defensor Pacis. Translated with an Introduction by Alan Gewirth*   TB/1310
CHARLES PETET-DUTAILLIS: The Feudal Monarchy in France and England: *From the Tenth to the Thirteenth Century* °   TB/1165
STEVEN RUNCIMAN: A History of the Crusades Vol. I: *The First Crusade and the Foundation of the Kingdom of Jerusalem. Illus.*
TB/1143
Vol. II: *The Kingdom of Jerusalem and the Frankish East 1100-1187. Illus.*   TB/1243
Vol. III: *The Kingdom of Acre and the Later Crusades. Illus.*   TB/1298
J. M. WALLACE-HADRILL: The Barbarian West: *The Early Middle Ages, A.D. 400-1000*
TB/1061

History: Renaissance & Reformation

JACOB BURCKHARDT: The Civilization of the Renaissance in Italy. *Introduction by Benjamin Nelson and Charles Trinkaus. Illus.*
Vol. I TB/40; Vol. II TB/41
JOHN CALVIN & JACOPO SADOLETO: A Reformation Debate. *Edited by John C. Olin*   TB/1239
FEDERICO CHABOD: Machiavelli and the Renaissance   TB/1193
THOMAS CROMWELL: Thomas Cromwell on Church and Commonwealth,: *Selected Letters 1523-1540.* ¶ *Ed. with an Intro. by Arthur J. Slavin*   TB/1462
R. TREVOR DAVIES: The Golden Century of Spain, 1501-1621 °   TB/1194
J. H. ELLIOTT: Europe Divided, 1559-1598 *a* °
TB/1414
G. R. ELTON: Reformation Europe, 1517-1559 ° *a*
TB/1270
DESIDERIUS ERASMUS: Christian Humanism and the Reformation: *Selected Writings. Edited and Translated by John C. Olin* TB/1166
DESIDERIUS ERASMUS: Erasmus and His Age: *Selected Letters. Edited with an Introduction by Hans J. Hillerbrand. Translated by Marcus A. Haworth*   TB/1461
WALLACE K. FERGUSON et al.: Facets of the Renaissance   TB/1098
WALLACE K. FERGUSON et al.: The Renaissance: *Six Essays. Illus.*   TB/1084
FRANCESCO GUICCIARDINI: History of Florence. *Translated with an Introduction and Notes by Mario Domandi*   TB/1470
WERNER L. GUNDERSHEIMER, Ed.: French Humanism, 1470-1600. * *Illus.*   TB/1473
MARIE BOAS HALL, Ed.: Nature and Nature's Laws: *Documents of the Scientific Revolution* #   HR/1420
HANS J. HILLERBRAND, Ed., The Protestant Reformation #   HR/1342
JOHAN HUIZINGA: Erasmus and the Age of Reformation. *Illus.*   TB/19

JOEL HURSTFIELD: The Elizabethan Nation
TB/1312
JOEL HURSTFIELD, Ed.: The Reformation Crisis   TB/1267
PAUL OSKAR KRISTELLER: Renaissance Thought: *The Classic, Scholastic, and Humanist Strains*
TB/1048
PAUL OSKAR KRISTELLER: Renaissance Thought II: *Papers on Humanism and the Arts*
TB/1163
PAUL O. KRISTELLER & PHILIP P. WIENER, Eds.: Renaissance Essays   TB/1392
DAVID LITTLE: Religion, Order and Law: *A Study in Pre-Revolutionary England.* § *Preface by R. Bellah*   TB/1418
NICCOLO MACHIAVELLI: History of Florence and of the Affairs of Italy: *From the Earliest Times to the Death of Lorenzo the Magnificent. Introduction by Felix Gilbert* TB/1027
ALFRED VON MARTIN: Sociology of the Renaissance. ° *Introduction by W. K. Ferguson*
TB/1099
GARRETT MATTINGLY et al.: Renaissance Profiles. *Edited by J. H. Plumb*   TB/1162
J. E. NEALE: The Age of Catherine de Medici °
TB/1085
J. H. PARRY: The Establishment of the European Hegemony: 1415-1715: *Trade and Exploration in the Age of the Renaissance* TB/1045
J. H. PARRY, Ed.: The European Reconnaissance: *Selected Documents* #   HR/1345
BUONACCORSO PITTI & GREGORIO DATI: Two Memoirs of Renaissance Florence: *The Diaries of Buonaccorso Pitti and Gregorio Dati. Edited with Intro. by Gene Brucker. Trans. by Julia Martines*   TB/1333
J. H. PLUMB: The Italian Renaissance: *A Concise Survey of Its History and Culture*
TB/1161
A. F. POLLARD: Henry VIII. *Introduction by A. G. Dickens.* °   TB/1249
RICHARD H. POPKIN: The History of Scepticism from Erasmus to Descartes   TB/139
PAOLO ROSSI: Philosophy, Technology, and the Arts, in the Early Modern Era 1400-1700. || *Edited by Benjamin Nelson. Translated by Salvator Attanasio*   TB/1458
FERDINAND SCHEVILL: The Medici. *Illus.* TB/1010
FERDINAND SCHEVILL: Medieval and Renaissance Florence. *Illus.* Vol. I: *Medieval Florence*
TB/1090
Vol. II: *The Coming of Humanism and the Age of the Medici*   TB/1091
R. H. TAWNEY: The Agrarian Problem in the Sixteenth Century. *Intro. by Lawrence Stone*
TB/1315
H. R. TREVOR-ROPER: The European Witch-craze of the Sixteenth and Seventeenth Centuries and Other Essays °   TB/1416
VESPASIANO: Rennaissance Princes, Popes, and XVth Century: *The Vespasiano Memoirs. Introduction by Myron P. Gilmore. Illus.*
TB/1111

History: Modern European

RENE ALBRECHT-CARRIE, Ed.: The Concert of Europe #   HR/1341
MAX BELOFF: The Age of Absolutism, 1660-1815
TB/1062
OTTO VON BISMARCK: Reflections and Reminiscences. *Ed. with Intro. by Theodore S. Hamerow* ¶   TB/1357
EUGENE C. BLACK, Ed.: British Politics in the Nineteenth Century #   HR/1427

Literature & Literary Criticism

W. J. BATE: From Classic to Romantic: *Premises of Taste in Eighteenth Century England* TB/1036

VAN WYCK BROOKS: Van Wyck Brooks: The Early Years: *A Selection from his Works, 1908-1921* Ed. with Intro. by Claire Sprague TB/3082

ERNST R. CURTIUS: European Literature and the Latin Middle Ages. *Trans. by Willard Trask* TB/2015

RICHMOND LATTIMORE, Translator: The Odyssey of Homer TB/1389

JOHN STUART MILL: On Bentham and Coleridge. *Introduction by F. R. Leavis* TB/1070

SAMUEL PEPYS: The Diary of Samual Pepys. ° *Edited by O. F. Morshead. 60 illus. by Ernest Shepard* TB/1007

ROBERT PREYER, Ed.: Victorian Literature ** TB/1302

ALBION W. TOURGEE: A Fool's Errand: *A Novel of the South during Reconstruction. Intro. by George Fredrickson* TB/3074

BASIL WILEY: Nineteenth Century Studies: *Coleridge to Matthew Arnold* ° TB/1261

RAYMOND WILLIAMS: Culture and Society, 1780-1950 ° TB/1252

Philosophy

HENRI BERGSON: Time and Free Will: *An Essay on the Immediate Data of Consciousness* ° TB/1021

LUDWIG BINSWANGER: Being-in-the-World: *Selected Papers. Trans. with Intro. by Jacob Needleman* TB/1365

H. J. BLACKHAM: Six Existentialist Thinkers: *Kierkegaard, Nietzsche, Jaspers, Marcel, Heidegger, Sartre* ° TB/1002

J. M. BOCHENSKI: The Methods of Contemporary Thought. *Trans. by Peter Caws* TB/1377

CRANE BRINTON: Nietzsche. *Preface, Bibliography, and Epilogue by the Author* TB/1197

ERNST CASSIRER: Rousseau, Kant and Goethe. *Intro. by Peter Gay* TB/1092

FREDERICK COPLESTON, S. J.: Medieval Philosophy TB/376

F. M. CORNFORD: From Religion to Philosophy: *A Study in the Origins of Western Speculation* § TB/20

WILFRID DESAN: The Tragic Finale: *An Essay on the Philosophy of Jean-Paul Sartre* TB/1030

MARVIN FARBER: The Aims of Phenomenology: *The Motives, Methods, and Impact of Husserl's Thought* TB/1291

MARVIN FARBER: Basic Issues of Philosophy: *Experience, Reality, and Human Values* TB/1344

MARVIN FARBER: Phenomenology and Existence: *Towards a Philosophy within Nature* TB/1295

PAUL FRIEDLANDER: Plato: *An Introduction* TB/2017

MICHAEL GELVEN: A Commentary on Heidegger's "Being and Time" TB/1464

J. GLENN GRAY: Hegel and Greek Thought TB/1409

W. K. C. GUTHRIE: The Greek Philosophers: *From Thales to Aristotle* ° TB/1008

G. W. F. HEGEL: On Art, Religion Philosophy: *Introductory Lectures to the Realm of Absolute Spirit.* || *Edited with an Introduction by J. Glenn Gray* TB/1463

G. W. F. HEGEL: Phenomenology of Mind. ° || *Introduction by George Lichtheim* TB/1303

MARTIN HEIDEGGER: Discourse on Thinking. *Translated with a Preface by John M. Anderson and E. Hans Freund. Introduction by John M. Anderson* TB/1459

F. H. HEINEMANN: Existentialism and the Modern Predicament TB/28

WERER HEISENBERG: Physics and Philosophy: *The Revolution in Modern Science. Intro. by F. S. C. Northrop* TB/549

EDMUND HUSSERL: Phenomenology and the Crisis of Philosophy. § *Translated with an Introduction by Quentin Lauer* TB/1170

IMMANUEL KANT: Groundwork of the Metaphysic of Morals. *Translated and Analyzed by H. J. Paton* TB/1159

IMMANUEL KANT: Lectures on Ethics. § *Introduction by Lewis White Beck* TB/105

WALTER KAUFMANN, Ed.: Religion From Tolstoy to Camus: *Basic Writings on Religious Truth and Morals* TB/123

QUENTIN LAUER: Phenomenology: *Its Genesis and Prospect. Preface by Aron Gurwitsch* TB/1169

MAURICE MANDELBAUM: The Problem of Historical Knowledge: *An Answer to Relativism* TB/1338

GEORGE A. MORGAN: What Nietzsche Means TB/1198

H. J. PATON: The Categorical Imperative: *A Study in Kant's Moral Philosophy* TB/1325

MICHAEL POLANYI: Personal Knowledge: *Towards a Post-Critical Philosophy* TB/1158

KARL R. POPPER: Conjectures and Refutations: *The Growth of Scientific Knowledge* TB/1376

WILLARD VAN ORMAN QUINE: Elementary Logic *Revised Edition* TB/577

WILLARD VAN ORMAN QUINE: From a Logical Point of View: *Logico-Philosophical Essays* TB/566

JOHN E. SMITH: Themes in American Philosophy: *Purpose, Experience and Community* TB/1466

MORTON WHITE: Foundations of Historical Knowledge TB/1440

WILHELM WINDELBAND: A History of Philosophy *Vol. I: Greek, Roman, Medieval* TB/38 *Vol. II: Renaissance, Enlightenment, Modern* TB/39

LUDWIG WITTGENSTEIN: The Blue and Brown Books ° TB/1211

LUDWIG WITTGENSTEIN: Notebooks, 1914-1916 TB/1441

Political Science & Government

C. E. BLACK: The Dynamics of Modernization: *A Study in Comparative History* TB/1321

KENNETH E. BOULDING: Conflict and Defense: *A General Theory of Action* TB/3024

DENIS W. BROGAN: Politics in America. *New Introduction by the Author* TB/1469

CRANE BRINTON: English Political Thought in the Nineteenth Century TB/1071

ROBERT CONQUEST: Power and Policy in the USSR: *The Study of Soviet Dynastics* ° TB/1307

ROBERT A. DAHL & CHARLES E. LINDBLOM: Politics, Economics, and Welfare: *Planning and Politico-Economic Systems Resolved into Basic Social Processes* TB/1277

HANS KOHN: Political Ideologies of the 20th Century TB/1277

ROY C. MACRIDIS, Ed.: Political Parties: *Contemporary Trends and Ideas* ** TB/1322

ROBERT GREEN MC CLOSKEY: American Conservatism in the Age of Enterprise, 1865-1910 TB/1137

MARSILIUS OF PADUA: The Defender of Peace. *The Defensor Pacis. Translated with an Introduction by Alan Gewirth* TB/1310

KINGSLEY MARTIN: French Liberal Thought in the Eighteenth Century: *A Study of Political Ideas from Bayle to Condorcet* TB/1114

BARRINGTON MOORE, JR.: Political Power and Social Theory: *Seven Studies* || TB/1221
BARRINGTON MOORE, JR.: Soviet Politics—The Dilemma of Power: *The Role of Ideas in Social Change* || TB/1222
BARRINGTON MOORE, JR.: Terror and Progress— USSR: *Some Sources of Change and Stability*
JOHN B. MORRALL: Political Thought in Medieval Times TB/1076
KARL R. POPPER: The Open Society and Its Enemies *Vol. I: The Spell of Plato* TB/1101 *Vol. II: The High Tide of Prophecy: Hegel, Marx, and the Aftermath* TB/1102
CONYERS READ, Ed.: The Constitution Reconsidered. *Revised Edition, Preface by Richard B. Morris* TB/1384
JOHN P. ROCHE, Ed.: Origins of American Political Thought: *Selected Readings* TB/1301
JOHN P. ROCHE, Ed.: American Political Thought: *From Jefferson to Progressivism* TB/1332
HENRI DE SAINT-SIMON: Social Organization, The Science of Man, and Other Writings. || *Edited and Translated with an Introduction by Felix Markham* TB/1152
CHARLES SCHOTTLAND, Ed.: The Welfare State ** TB/1323
JOSEPH A. SCHUMPETER: Capitalism, Socialism and Democracy TB/3008
PETER WOLL, Ed.: Public Administration and Policy: *Selected Essays* TB/1284

Psychology

ALFRED ADLER: The Individual Psychology of Alfred Adler: *A Systematic Presentation in Selections from His Writings. Edited by Heinz L. & Rowena R. Ansbacher* TB/1154
ALFRED ADLER: Problems of Neurosis: *A Book of Case Histories. Introduction by Heinz L. Ansbacher* TB/1145
LUDWIG BINSWANGER: Being-in-the-World: *Selected Papers. || Trans. with Intro. by Jacob Needleman* TB/1365
ARTHUR BURTON & ROBERT E. HARRIS: Clinical Studies of Personality Vol. I TB/3075 Vol. II TB/3076
HADLEY CANTRIL: The Invasion from Mars: *A Study in the Psychology of Panic* || TB/1282
MIRCEA ELIADE: Cosmos and History: *The Myth of the Eternal Return* § TB/2050
MIRCEA ELIADE: Myth and Reality TB/1369
MIRCEA ELIADE: Myths, Dreams and Mysteries: *The Encounter Between Contemporary Faiths and Archaic Realities* § TB/1320
MIRCEA ELIADE: Rites and Symbols of Initiation: *The Mysteries of Birth and Rebirth* § TB/1236
HERBERT FINGARETTE: The Self in Transformation: *Psychoanalysis, Philosophy and the Life of the Spirit* || TB/1177
SIGMUND FREUD: On Creativity and the Unconscious: *Papers on the Psychology of Art, Literature, Love, Religion.* § *Intro. by Benjamin Nelson* TB/45
J. GLENN GRAY: The Warriors: *Reflections on Men in Battle. Introduction by Hannah Arendt* TB/1294
WILLIAM JAMES: Psychology: *The Briefer Course. Edited with an Intro. by Gordon Allport* TB/1034
C. G. JUNG: Psychological Reflections. *Ed. by J. Jacobi* TB/2001
KARL MENNINGER, M.D.: Theory of Psychoanalytic Technique TB/1144
JOHN H. SCHAAR: Escape from Authority: *The Perspectives of Erich Fromm* TB/1155

MUZAFER SHERIF: The Psychology of Social Norms. *Introduction by Gardner Murphy* TB/3072
HELLMUT WILHELM: Change: *Eight Lectures on the I Ching* TB/2019

Religion: Ancient and Classical, Biblical and Judaic Traditions

W. F. ALBRIGHT: The Biblical Period from Abraham to Ezra TB/102
SALO W. BARON: Modern Nationalism and Religion TB/818
C. K. BARRETT, Ed.: The New Testament Background: *Selected Documents* TB/86
MARTIN BUBER: Eclipse of God: *Studies in the Relation Between Religion and Philosophy* TB/12
MARTIN BUBER: Hasidism and Modern Man. *Edited and Translated by Maurice Friedman* TB/839
MARTIN BUBER: The Knowledge of Man. *Edited with an Introduction by Maurice Friedman. Translated by Maurice Friedman and Ronald Gregor Smith* TB/135
MARTIN BUBER: Moses. *The Revelation and the Covenant* TB/837
MARTIN BUBER: The Origin and Meaning of Hasidism. *Edited and Translated by Maurice Friedman* TB/835
MARTIN BUBER: The Prophetic Faith TB/73
MARTIN BUBER: Two Types of Faith: *Interpenetration of Judaism and Christianity* ° TB/75
MALCOLM L. DIAMOND: Martin Buber: *Jewish Existentialist* TB/840
M. S. ENSLIN: Christian Beginnings TB/5
M. S. ENSLIN: The Literature of the Christian Movement TB/6
ERNST LUDWIG EHRLICH: A Concise History of Israel: *From the Earliest Times to the Destruction of the Temple in A.D. 70* ° TB/128
HENRI FRANKFORT: Ancient Egyptian Religion: *An Interpretation* TB/77
MAURICE S. FRIEDMAN: Martin Buber: *The Life of Dialogue* TB/64
ABRAHAM HESCHEL: The Earth Is the Lord's & The Sabbath. *Two Essays* TB/828
ABRAHAM HESCHEL: God in Search of Man: *A Philosophy of Judaism* TB/807
ABRAHAM HESCHEL: Man Is not Alone: *A Philosophy of Religion* TB/838
ABRAHAM HESCHEL: The Prophets: *An Introduction* TB/1421
T. J. MEEK: Hebrew Origins TB/69
JAMES MUILENBURG: The Way of Israel: *Biblical Faith and Ethics* TB/133
H. J. ROSE: Religion in Greece and Rome TB/55
H. H. ROWLEY: The Growth of the Old Testament TB/107
D. WINTON THOMAS, Ed.: Documents from Old Testament Times TB/85

Religion: General Christianity

ROLAND H. BAINTON: Christendom: *A Short History of Christianity and Its Impact on Western Civilization. Illus.* Vol. I TB/131; Vol. II TB/132
JOHN T. MCNEILL: Modern Christian Movements. *Revised Edition* TB/1402
ERNST TROELTSCH: The Social Teaching of the Christian Churches. *Intro. by H. Richard Niebuhr* Vol. I TB/71; Vol. II TB/72

Religion: Early Christianity Through Reformation

ANSELM OF CANTERBURY: Truth, Freedom, and Evil: *Three Philosophical Dialogues.* Edited and Translated by Jasper Hopkins and Herbert Richardson TB/317
MARSHALL W. BALDWIN, Ed.: Christianity through the 13th Century # HR/1468
W. D. DAVIES: Paul and Rabbinic Judaism: *Some Rabbinic Elements in Pauline Theology. Revised Edition* ° TB/146
ADOLF DEISSMAN: Paul: *A Study in Social and Religious History* TB/15
JOHANNES ECKHART: Meister Eckhart: *A Modern Translation by R. Blakney* TB/8
EDGAR J. GOODSPEED: A Life of Jesus TB/1
ROBERT M. GRANT: Gnosticism and Early Christianity TB/136
WILLIAM HALLER: The Rise of Puritanism TB/22
GERHART B. LADNER: The Idea of Reform: *Its Impact on the Christian Thought and Action in the Age of the Fathers* TB/149
ARTHUR DARBY NOCK: Early Gentile Christianity and Its Hellenistic Background TB/111
ARTHUR DARBY NOCK: St. Paul ° TR/104
ORIGEN: On First Principles. *Edited by G. W. Butterworth. Introduction by Henri de Lubac* TB/311
GORDON RUPP: Luther's Progress to the Diet of Worms ° TB/120

Religion: The Protestant Tradition

KARL BARTH: Church Dogmatics: *A Selection. Intro. by H. Gollwitzer. Ed. by G. W. Bromiley* TB/95
KARL BARTH: Dogmatics in Outline TB/56
KARL BARTH: The Word of God and the Word of Man TB/13
HERBERT BRAUN, et al.: God and Christ: *Existence and Province. Volume 5 of Journal for Theology and the Church, edited by Robert W. Funk and Gerhard Ebeling* TB/255
WHITNEY R. CROSS: The Burned-Over District: *The Social and Intellectual History of Enthusiastic Religion in Western New York, 1800-1850* TB/1242
NELS F. S. FERRE: Swedish Contributions to Modern Theology. *New Chapter by William A. Johnson* TB/147
WILLIAM R. HUTCHISON, Ed.: American Protestant Thought: *The Liberal Era* ‡ TB/1385
ERNST KASEMANN, et al.: Distinctive Protestant and Catholic Themes Reconsidered. *Volume 3 of Journal for Theology and the Church, edited by Robert W. Funk and Gerhard Ebeling* TB/253
SOREN KIERKEGAARD: On Authority and Revelation: *The Book on Adler, or a Cycle of Ethico-Religious Essays. Introduction by F. Sontag* TB/139
SOREN KIERKEGAARD: Crisis in the Life of an Actress, *and Other Essays on Drama. Translated with an Introduction by Stephen Crites* TB/145
SOREN KIERKEGAARD: Edifying Discourses. *Edited with an Intro. by Paul Holmer* TB/32
SOREN KIERKEGAARD: The Journals of Kierkegaard. ° *Edited with an Intro. by Alexander Dru* TB/52
SOREN KIERKEGAARD: The Point of View for My Work as an Author: *A Report to History.* § *Preface by Benjamin Nelson* TB/88

SOREN KIERKEGAARD: The Present Age. § *Translated and edited by Alexander Dru. Introduction by Walter Kaufmann* TB/94
SOREN KIERKEGAARD: Purity of Heart. *Trans. by Douglas Steere* TB/4
SOREN KIERKEGAARD: Repetition: *An Essay in Experimental Psychology* § TB/117
SOREN KIERKEGAARD: Works of Love: *Some Christian Reflections in the Form of Discourses* TB/122
WILLIAM G. MCLOUGHLIN, Ed.: The American Evangelicals: 1800-1900: *An Anthology* TB/1382
WOLFHART PANNENBERG, et al.: History and Hermeneutic. *Volume 4 of Journal for Theology and the Church, edited by Robert W. Funk and Gerhard Ebeling* TB/254
JAMES M. ROBINSON, et al.: The Bultmann School of Biblical Interpretation: New Directions? *Volume 1 of Journal for Theology and the Church, edited by Robert W. Funk and Gerhard Ebeling* TB/251
F. SCHLEIERMACHER: The Christian Faith. *Introduction by Richard R. Niebuhr.*
Vol. I TB/108; Vol. II TB/109
F. SCHLEIERMACHER: On Religion: *Speeches to Its Cultured Despisers. Intro. by Rudolf Otto* TB/36
TIMOTHY L. SMITH: Revivalism and Social Reform: *American Protestantism on the Eve of the Civil War* TB/1229
PAUL TILLICH: Dynamics of Faith TB/42
PAUL TILLICH: Morality and Beyond TB/142
EVELYN UNDERHILL: Worship TB/10

Religion: The Roman & Eastern Christian Traditions

A. ROBERT CAPONIGRI, Ed.: Modern Catholic Thinkers II: *The Church and the Political Order* TB/307
G. P. FEDOTOV: The Russian Religious Mind: *Kievan Christianity, the tenth to the thirteenth Centuries* TB/370
GABRIEL MARCEL: Being and Having: *An Existential Diary. Introduction by James Collins* TB/310
GABRIEL MARCEL: Homo Viator: *Introduction to a Metaphysic of Hope* TB/397

Religion: Oriental Religions

TOR ANDRAE: Mohammed: *The Man and His Faith* § TB/62
EDWARD CONZE: Buddhism: *Its Essence and Development.* ° *Foreword by Arthur Waley* TB/58
EDWARD CONZE: Buddhist Meditation TB/1442
EDWARD CONZE et al, Editors: Buddhist Texts through the Ages TB/113
ANANDA COOMARASWAMY: Buddha and the Gospel of Buddhism TB/119
H. G. CREEL: Confucius and the Chinese Way TB/63
FRANKLIN EDGERTON, Trans. & Ed.: The Bhagavad Gita TB/115
SWAMI NIKHILANANDA, Trans. & Ed.: The Upanishads TB/114
D. T. SUZUKI: On Indian Mahayana Buddhism. ° *Ed. with Intro. by Edward Conze.* TB/1403

Religion: Philosophy, Culture, and Society

NICOLAS BERDYAEV: The Destiny of Man TB/61
RUDOLF BULTMANN: History and Eschatology: *The Presence of Eternity* ° TB/91
RUDOLF BULTMANN AND FIVE CRITICS: Kerygma and Myth: *A Theological Debate* TB/80

9

RUDOLF BULTMANN and KARL KUNDSIN: Form Criticism: *Two Essays on New Testament Research. Trans. by F. C. Grant* TB/96
WILLIAM A. CLEBSCH & CHARLES R. JAEKLE: Pastoral Care in Historical Perspective: *An Essay with Exhibits* TB/148
FREDERICK FERRE: Language, Logic and God. *New Preface by the Author* TB/1407
LUDWIG FEUERBACH: The Essence of Christianity. § *Introduction by Karl Barth. Foreword by H. Richard Niebuhr* TB/11
C. C. GILLISPIE: Genesis and Geology: *The Decades before Darwin* § TB/51
ADOLF HARNACK: What Is Christianity? § *Introduction by Rudolf Bultmann* TB/17
KYLE HASELDEN: The Racial Problem in Christian Perspective TB/116
MARTIN HEIDEGGER: Discourse on Thinking. *Translated with a Preface by John M. Anderson and E. Hans Freund. Introduction by John M. Anderson* TB/1459
IMMANUEL KANT: Religion Within the Limits of Reason Alone. § *Introduction by Theodore M. Greene and John Silber* TB/FG
WALTER KAUFMANN, Ed.: Religion from Tolstoy to Camus: *Basic Writings on Religious Truth and Morals. Enlarged Edition* TB/123
JOHN MACQUARRIE: An Existentialist Theology: *A Comparison of Heidegger and Bultmann.* ° *Foreword by Rudolf Bultmann* TB/125
H. RICHARD NIEBUHR: Christ and Culture TB/3
H. RICHARD NIEBUHR: The Kingdom of God in America TB/49
ANDERS NYGREN: Agape and Eros. *Translated by Philip S. Watson* ° TB/1430
JOHN H. RANDALL, JR.: The Meaning of Religion for Man. *Revised with New Intro. by the Author* TB/1379
WALTER RAUSCHENBUSCHS Christianity and the Social Crisis. ‡ *Edited by Robert D. Cross* TB/3059
JOACHIM WACH: Understanding and Believing. *Ed. with Intro. by Joseph M. Kitagawa* TB/1399

Science and Mathematics

JOHN TYLER BONNER: The Ideas of Biology. Σ *Illus.* TB/570
W. E. LE GROS CLARK: The Antecedents of Man: *An Introduction to the Evolution of the Primates.* ° *Illus.* TB/559
ROBERT E. COKER: Streams, Lakes, Ponds. *Illus.* TB/586
ROBERT E. COKER: This Great and Wide Sea: *An Introduction to Oceanography and Marine Biology. Illus.* TB/551
W. H. DOWDESWELL: Animal Ecology. *61 illus.* TB/543
C. V. DURELL: Readable Relativity. *Foreword by Freeman J. Dyson* TB/530
GEORGE GAMOW: Biography of Physics. Σ *Illus.* TB/567
F. K. HARE: The Restless Atmosphere TB/560
S. KORNER: The Philosophy of Mathematics: *An Introduction* TB/547
J. R. PIERCE: Symbols, Signals and Noise: *The Nature and Process of Communication* Σ TB/574
WILLARD VAN ORMAN QUINE: Mathematical Logic TB/558

Science: History

MARIE BOAS: The Scientific Renaissance, 1450-1630 ° TB/583
W. DAMPIER, Ed.: Readings in the Literature of Science. *Illus.* TB/512

STEPHEN TOULMIN & JUNE GOODFIELD: The Architecture of Matter: *The Physics, Chemistry and Physiology of Matter, Both Animate and Inanimate, as it has Evolved since the Beginnings of Science* TB/58
STEPHEN TOULMIN & JUNE GOODFIELD: The Discovery of Time TB/58
STEPHEN TOULMIN & JUNE GOODFIELD: The Fabric of the Heavens: *The Development of Astronomy and Dynamics* TB/57

Science: Philosophy

J. M. BOCHENSKI: The Methods of Contemporary Thought. *Tr. by Peter Caws* TB/137
J. BRONOWSKI: Science and Human Values. *Revised and Enlarged. Illus.* TB/50
WERNER HEISENBERG: Physics and Philosophy: *The Revolution in Modern Science. Introduction by F. S. C. Northrop* TB/54
KARL R. POPPER: Conjectures and Refutations: *The Growth of Scientific Knowledge* TB/137
KARL R. POPPER: The Logic of Scientific Discovery TB/5'
STEPHEN TOULMIN: Foresight and Understanding: *An Enquiry into the Aims of Science. Foreword by Jacques Barzun* TB/56
STEPHEN TOULMIN: The Philosophy of Science: *An Introduction* TB/5'

Sociology and Anthropology

REINHARD BENDIX: Work and Authority in Industry: *Ideologies of Management in the Course of Industrialization* TB/30
BERNARD BERELSON, Ed., The Behavioral Sciences Today TB/11
JOSEPH B. CASAGRANDE, Ed.: In the Company of Man: *Twenty Portraits of Anthropological Informants. Illus.* TB/30
KENNETH B. CLARK: Dark Ghetto: *Dilemmas of Social Power. Foreword by Gunnar Myrdal* TB/13
KENNETH CLARK & JEANNETTE HOPKINS: A Relevant War Against Poverty: *A Study of Community Action Programs and Observable Social Change* TB/14
W. E. LE GROS CLARK: The Antecedents of Man: *An Introduction to the Evolution of the Primates.* ° *Illus.* TB/5
LEWIS COSER, Ed.: Political Sociology TB/12
ROSE L. COSER, Ed.: Life Cycle and Achievement in America ** TB/14
ALLISON DAVIS & JOHN DOLLARD: Children of Bondage: *The Personality Development of Negro Youth in the Urban South* ‖ TB/30
ST. CLAIR DRAKE & HORACE R. CAYTON: Black Metropolis: *A Study of Negro Life in a Northern City. Introduction by Everett C. Hughes. Tables, maps, charts, and graphs.* Vol. I TB/1086; Vol. II TB/10
PETER E. DRUCKER: The New Society: *The Anatomy of Industrial Order* TB/1
CORA DU BOIS: The People of Alor. *With a Preface by the Author* Vol. I Illus. TB/1042; Vol. II TB/10
EMILE DURKHEIM et al.: Essays on Sociology and Philosophy: *with Appraisals of Durkheim's Life and Thought.* ‖ *Edited by Kurt H. Wolff* TB/1
LEON FESTINGER, HENRY W. RIECKEN, STANLEY SCHACHTER: When Prophecy Fails: *A Social and Psychological Study of a Modern Group that Predicted the Destruction of the World* TB/1

CHARLES Y. GLOCK & RODNEY STARK: Christian Beliefs and Anti-Semitism. *Introduction by the Authors* TB/1454

ALVIN W. GOULDNER: The Hellenic World TB/1479

ALVIN W. GOULDNER: Wildcat Strike: *A Study in Worker-Management Relationships* || TB/1176

CESAR GRANA: Modernity and Its Discontents: *French Society and the French Man of Letters in the Nineteenth Century* TB/1318

L. S. B. LEAKEY: Adam's Ancestors: *The Evolution of Man and His Culture. Illus.* TB/1019

KURT LEWIN: Field Theory in Social Science: *Selected Theoretical Papers.* || *Edited by Dorwin Cartwright* TB/1135

RITCHIE P. LOWRY: Who's Running This Town? *Community Leadership and Social Change* TB/1383

R. M. MACIVER: Social Causation TB/1153

GARY T. MARX: Protest and Prejudice: *A Study of Belief in the Black Community* TB/1435

ROBERT K. MERTON, LEONARD BROOM, LEONARD S. COTTRELL, JR., Editors: Sociology Today: *Problems and Prospects* || Vol. I TB/1173; Vol. II TB/1174

GILBERT OSOFSKY, Ed.: The Burden of Race: *A Documentary History of Negro-White Relations in America* TB/1405

GILBERT OSOFSKY: Harlem: The Making of a Ghetto: *Negro New York 1890-1930* TB/1381

TALCOTT PARSONS & EDWARD A. SHILS, Editors: Toward a General Theory of Action: *Theoretical Foundations for the Social Sciences* TB/1083

PHILIP RIEFF: The Triumph of the Therapeutic: *Uses of Faith After Freud* TB/1360

JOHN H. ROHRER & MUNRO S. EDMONSON, Eds.: The Eighth Generation Grows Up: *Cultures and Personalities of New Orleans Negroes* || TB/3050

ARNOLD ROSE: The Negro in America: *The Condensed Version of Gunnar Myrdal's* An American Dilemma. *Second Edition* TB/3048

GEORGE ROSEN: Madness in Society: *Chapters in the Historical Sociology of Mental Illness.* || *Preface by Benjamin Nelson* TB/1337

PHILIP SELZNICK: TVA and the Grass Roots: *A Study in the Sociology of Formal Organization* TB/1230

PITIRIM A. SOROKIN: Contemporary Sociological Theories: *Through the First Quarter of the Twentieth Century* TB/3046

MAURICE R. STEIN: The Eclipse of Community: *An Interpretation of American Studies* TB/1128

WILLIAM I. THOMAS: The Unadjusted Girl: *With Cases and Standpoint for Behavior Analysis. Intro. by Michael Parenti* TB/1319

EDWARD A. TIRYAKIAN, Ed.: Sociological Theory, Values and Sociocultural Change: *Essays in Honor of Pitirim A. Sorokin* ° TB/1316

FERDINAND TONNIES: Community and Society: *Gemeinschaft und Gesellschaft. Translated and Edited by Charles P. Loomis* TB/1116

SAMUEL E. WALLACE: Skid Row as a Way of Life TB/1367

W. LLOYD WARNER and Associates: Democracy in Jonesville: *A Study in Quality and Inequality* || TB/1129

W. LLOYD WARNER: Social Class in America: *The Evaluation of Status* TB/1013

FLORIAN ZNANIECKI: The Social Role of the Man of Knowledge. *Introduction by Lewis A. Coser* TB/1372